MASS MEDIA ISSUES

COMPILED & EDITED BY

GEORGE RODMAN

FOURTH EDITION

KENDALL/HUNT PUBLISHING COMPANY
2460 Kerper Boulevard P.O. Box 539 Dubuque, Iowa 52004-0539

Formerly entitled *Mass Media Issues, Analysis and Debate*

Library of Congress Catalog Card Number: 92–81871

ISBN 0–8403–6757–0

Printed in the United States of America
10 9 8 7 6 5 4 3 2 1

Contents

Part II The Print Media

Part III The Sight and Sound Media

Alternate Contents

Ownership

Sex, Sexism and Gender Roles

Technology (In which we look at the effects of what humankind has wrought)

Introduction

The goals of this edition of *Mass Media Issues* remain the same as in previous editions. First and foremost, I have tried to expand on controversial media issues in such a way that students will be motivated to discuss them, either in class or on their own. As in the first three editions, articles were chosen on the basis of being well-written, provocative and substantive.

Another objective is to introduce the student to a set of authors who represent a wide sweep of the political and intellectual spectrum. Thus they will find here articles by Victor Navasky and Irving Kristol, George Will and Ben Bagdikian, Allan Bloom and Frank Zappa.

Another objective is to introduce the student to as wide a range of magazine and journal articles as possible. Thus they will find here items from *Newsweek* as well as *Critical Studies in Mass Communication, Vogue* as well as *Columbia Journalism Review.*

Although the goals of this edition remain the same, there are many changes. Users of previous editions asked for more articles from academic journals, more articles on America's cultural influence worldwide, and on media's effect on our own culture. They also asked me to return some of the historical pieces from earlier editions.

Other changes were made necessary by political changes in the country at large. For example, there have been more threats to the First Amendment, and those threats have come from higher circles of government, so a chapter on that topic leads off the book. The behavior of both our press and our government during the recent Persian Gulf conflict also necessitated a chapter on that topic.

There are some new pedagogical touches, also. The introduction for each article includes a "reading difficulty level," a device we'll explain more in the introduction to students. There's also an instructor's manual for this edition, expertly prepared by Denis Mercier of Glassboro State College. The I.M. is available from Kendall/Hunt.

I've retained the original citation style for each article, to stay true to each author's style. For the Suggestions for Further Reading and the occasional footnote of my own, I've used an adaptation of MLA style in which, rather than giving the range of page numbers for an article I give, in parentheses, the total number of pages, along the lines of what you'll find in the Academic Index.

Forty-six of these sixty readings are new to this edition. Many of the issues have remained the same, however, and we can trace some important themes over the course of these four editions. We still continue to debate the legitimacy of the power of the agents who control the media, including corporations, governments, and even consumers. We still debate the quality of the media, and whether they perform their information, entertainment and public opinion functions as well as they can. And we continue to debate the power of the media, especially in terms of the effects of their messages on society.

I'd like to thank the reviewers of this edition, Marsha Jeffer of Cypress College and Robert Dardenne of the University South Florida, for their helpful suggestions. A special thanks goes to Denis Mercier of Glassboro State College, who once again contributed several of the articles that made the final cut, as well as writing the instructor's manual.

My friend Bruce Cotler, *New York Post* photographer, was a big help once again.

I'd also like to thank the reviewers of previous editions, including Mary V. Crowley (Kingsboro Community College), Mark Edelstein (Palomar College), Howard Finklestein (Brookdale Community College), Gilbert Len Fowler, Jr. (Arkansas State University), Harry H. Griggs (University of Florida), Peter Longini (formerly of Brooklyn College), John B. Haney (Queens College), Russell Hulet (Fort Steilacom Community College), Thomas Jacobson (SUNY Buffalo), Mark Kozaki (University of Maryland), Robert G. Main (California State University, Chico), James Mattimore (Suffolk Community College), Sheri Parks (University of Maryland), Don Pember (University of Washington), Rosilind Routt (Laramie County Community College), Harold Shaver (Bethany College), Donald E. Smith (Elizabethtown College), Michael Torreano (University of Colorado), Kamil Winter (Southern Illinois University) and Morris M. Womack (Pepperdine University).

I hope students and teachers alike will enjoy this new edition. If you have any suggestions, feel free to contact me.

To the Student

All of the articles in this edition of *Mass Media Issues* were chosen at least partially because they are well-written. Unfortunately, "well written" does not always mean "easily read." Because of this, I have designed this book to enhance your reading experience as much as possible. Introductions position the articles within the context of the course and point the way to main points, while the marginal display lines and headings will enable you to leaf through a reading and get the main ideas before you start an in-depth reading. (I have tried to place the display lines as close as possible to where those ideas appear in the text.) Also, in the introduction to each piece I will mention a Reading Difficulty Level, as a sort of reader's advisory. These are not meant to scare you off; rather, they are intended as a guide to the kind of time and environment you will need to get the most out of that particular reading.

The Reading Difficulty Levels range from 10 (most difficult) to 1 (easiest). They are *not* based on the kind of readability formula that you will read about in Chapter 7 (p. 172) of this book; those are mechanical formulae, dealing with such things as sentence length and level of vocabulary. Whereas I have taken those things into consideration, I have also taken into consideration such variables as meaning, importance, style, human interest and depth of main points. For example, sometimes the "think pieces" might contain ideas that are, at least initially, a little difficult to accept. This slows down the reading process and increases the reading difficulty level.

As a general guide, a level 10 reading requires a sufficient amount of time (probably around 10 minutes a page for the average reader), a quiet, distraction-free atmosphere, note-taking, a good college-level dictionary and perhaps the use of other reference works. A quiet corner of your college library might be the best place for a level 10 reading. For a level 5 reading you'll need five minutes a page and you can highlight the reading in the book. At level 1, you can knock off the reading with a cup of coffee in the cafeteria on your way to class.

Let me offer two final hints on getting the most out of your reading: First, no matter what the level of the reading, make sure that you have actually "read" each paragraph before you move on. When you finish a paragraph, stop momentarily to think about it. If you realize you can't remember anything that was said in that passage, you have to go back and read it again. Your mind was wandering—the words didn't register.

Secondly, no matter what level, the fewer distractions, the better. It's better to stand up in a well-lit, quiet closet than to be perfectly comfy in your favorite chair, if that favorite chair happens to be in front of a blaring TV set or stereo, with friends or family interrupting every 5 seconds with small talk.

Good luck, and feel free to write me if you feel like commenting on anything about this book.

George Rodman
Department of Television and Radio
Brooklyn College of CUNY
Brooklyn, N.Y. 11210

Mass Media Issues

Fourth Edition

Part I

THE BIG QUESTIONS

The First Amendment

These are dangerous times, and the First Amendment is under assault from many sides. One survey showed that if there was a nationwide referendum on the First Amendment, the American public would vote to rescind it.[1] The battles surrounding the First Amendment are the linchpins of several—perhaps all—of the issues discussed in the rest of this book.

The First Amendment to the U.S. Constitution reads as follows:

> Congress shall make no law respecting an establishment of religion, or prohibiting the free exercise thereof; or abridging the freedom of speech, or of the press; or the right of the people peaceably to assemble, and to petition the Government for a redress of grievances.

It is important to recognize what the First Amendment means for the media in America. Congress is prohibited from making laws that curtail freedom of the press, but there remains the problem of defining such terms as "curtailment" and "free speech." Over the years, the Supreme Court has ruled that laws restricting obscenity, libel, invasions of privacy, and speech that threatens national security are *not* considered a curtailment of free speech.

Also, it is important to realize that the First Amendment restricts government only; it doesn't stop publishers, corporations, individuals or universities from restricting speech in their own domains.

With all this in mind, however, you should keep in mind that the First Amendment is more than a law; it is an attitude—the spirit, if you will—that defines the type of democracy we enjoy in the United States. It is also the spirit of our faith in that democracy.

The readings in this chapter look at some of the intricacies of our First Amendment. In the first reading, Juliet Dee examines the ramifications of the way free speech sometimes leads to people getting hurt. In the second reading Franklyn Haiman, one of the best-known experts on freedom of speech, analyzes some of the threats facing the First Amendment today.

---

1. George Garneau, "Press Freedom in Deep Trouble," *Editor and Publisher,* April 20, 1991, p. 11 (2).

Heavy Metal, Hit Men, Dial-a-Porn, and the First Amendment

Juliet Dee

This reading looks at one of the most important areas of First Amendment law: The media's responsibility for inciting action that harms others.

In this reading, Juliet Dee, who teaches communication at the University of Delaware, Newark, summarizes sixteen cases of alleged media negligence, cases ranging from the now-familiar "Born Innocent" lawsuit to several more recent, lesser-known cases. To facilitate class discussion, each case is individually numbered.

Professor Dee's examination of these cases provides fuel for one burning issue that worries many: that the worst threat to the First Amendment comes from the media itself, in the form of irresponsibility.

Reading Difficulty Level: 7. Easy in spots, such as where cases are being summarized, but slow down for passages in which distinctions are being made, such as between negligence and incitement, core and commercial speech, and so on.

Case #1

Television network NBC airs "Born Innocent," a drama about a girls' reform school. At 8:17 P.M., the "new girl" in the reform school is assaulted by four girls who rape her with a mop handle. Four days later, nine-year-old Olivia Niemi and her seven-year-old friend are raped by four teenagers wielding a beer bottle at a San Francisco beach. The teenagers say that "Born Innocent" gave them the idea. Olivia Niemi's mother sues NBC for neglience.

In one case, a rock station encouraged teenagers to chase a DJ on the freeway, and a man was killed because of it.

Case #2

A "Mickey Mouse Club" actor encourages children to put a BB in a balloon and rotate it, suggesting that it will sound like a revolving tire on a car. Eleven-year-old Craig Shannon follows the actor's advice, but uses a piece of lead and a long, thin balloon that bursts, blinding him in one eye. His parents sue Walt Disney Productions for negligence. More Protected

Case #3

KHJ, a Los Angeles rock station, encourages its teenage listeners to chase its DJ, "The Real Don Steele," who is driving the city's freeways and will pull off at exits and give the first teenager to catch him $25. Two teenagers spot him at the same time, accelerate to 80 and 90 miles per hour, respectively, and run the innocent Ronald Weirum onto the

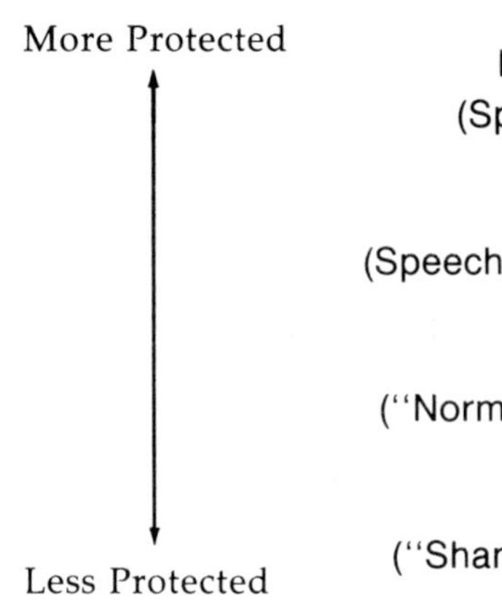

Pure "Core" Speech
(Speech for its own sake)

Commercial Speech
(Speech in promotion or advertising)

Indecent Speech
("Normal, healthy sexual desires")

Obscene Speech
("Shameful and morbid" desires)

FIRST AMENDMENT HIERARCHY

center divider, where he is killed. His wife and four children sue KHJ and its owner, RKO General, for negligence.

Case #4

Robert Black finds John Hearn through a classified ad in *Soldier of Fortune* magazine. Black pays Hearn $10,000 to murder his wife. When Sandra Black returns home from her work at the day-care center she runs, Hearn shoots and kills her. Her parents and 18-year-old son sue the magazine for negligence.

Case #5

Twelve-year-old Brian Thompson listens to more than two hours of dial-a-porn messages and rapes a four-year-old girl two weeks later. He testifies that the phone messages gave him the idea. His parents and those of the girl he assaulted sue Tele-Promo, the producer of the sex tapes, for negligence.

Negligence vs. Incitement

These cases are only a few of the growing number of negligence suits against various forms of media. The plaintiffs allege that a television show, radio contest, telephone message, or some other content triggered a viewer or listener to hurt himself, herself, or someone else and they sue for damages. Using the terms of negligence law, they argue that the media content created a "foreseeable" risk to the injured person, meaning that the producers should have foreseen that someone would imitate the media scene and cause damage. By not foreseeing that their content created a danger to the public, the media were negligent.

These cases are only a few of the growing number of negligence suits against various forms of media.

Alluding to Pandora's box, the judges handling such cases look at the facts, take a legal leap to the First Amendment, and almost always grant summary judgments to the media defendants. It's easy to see

If the plaintiffs charge negligence (tort law), the judge immediately insists that the complaint be reformulated in terms of incitement (First Amendment law), and that is tough to prove.

that to do otherwise would set a precedent whereby anyone who was injured could claim that whoever was responsible got the idea from the media. If the plaintiffs charge negligence (tort law), the judge immediately insists that the complaint be reformulated in terms of incitement (First Amendment law), and that is tough to prove.

Although it *is* illegal to speak in a way that incites a riot, the Supreme Court uses the *Brandenberg* tests, which requires that there is actual violence and the speaker *intended* for the violence to occur. The latter usually exonerates the media. Television writers, film producers, or rock singers easily can argue that they never intended for anyone to imitate a TV or movie scene or act out the message in a rock song. Thus, the media nearly always win such suits, which judges rarely allow to go to trial.

The fact that they face nearly certain summary judgments does not seem to discourage the plaintiffs, who continue to file complaints against the media for specific content. The plaintiffs, who used to charge negligence, have wised up and now claim incitement.

Before we proceed further, try applying the *Brandenberg* test to the cases above and see if your judgment corresponds to that of the courts deciding these cases. Was NBC negligent for airing "Born Innocent"? Did the movie serve to incite the teenage gang to rape Olivia Niemi and her friend four days after they saw it? If you said no, you were right. The court found that there was no intent on NBC's part for the graphic violence to be imitated in real life.

How would you rule in the case of Craig Shannon, who had lost an eye when he responded to the "Mickey Mouse Club" actor's encouragement? This case was a bit tougher for the courts. In the language of neligence law, the court admitted that encouraging children to put a BB in a balloon indeed created a foreseeable risk of injury. However, with some verbal gymnastics, the court reframed the case in terms of First Amendment law and, while admitting a "foreseeable" risk of injury, said there was no "clear and present danger" of injury.

The clear and present danger interpretation is a forerunner of the *Brandenberg* test. Although the *Brandenberg* case was decided in 1969 and the *Shannon* case was ruled on in 1981, the Georgia Supreme Court preferred to use the "clear and present danger" test for some reason. It justified its decision by arguing that, of the 16,000,000 children who watched "The Mickey Mouse Club Show" that day, Craig Shannon was the only one the court knew of who lost his eye trying to do what the TV actor was encouraging its young viewers to do. Since only one child out of 16,000,000 was injured, the program did not create a clear and present danger to children. Such reasoning could be interpreted to mean that if someone shouts "Fire!" in a crowded theater and only one person is trampled to death, it's okay—there was no clear and present danger because just one person was killed. The court was afraid of setting a precedent that would make it easy to recover damages against the media for content, *despite* the fact that the "Mickey Mouse Club" actor was encouraging children to do something dangerous.

As for the third case, should radio station KHJ be liable for the death of Ronald Weirum because of its contest encouraging teenagers to search for their disk jockey on the freeways? Did that create a foreseeable risk to other drivers because anyone should have known that some teenagers would speed to catch DJ Don Steele? If you said yes, you were right, but this case is one of the big exceptions. The California court was so appalled at KHJ's inability to foresee the consequences of its contest that it found the station negligent and awarded $300,000 to Weirum's wife and children.

How would you rule in the case of the classified ad run by *Soldier of Fortune* that enabled Robert Black to find the hit man who killed his wife? Although the first three cases cited were considered by the judges to be "a matter of law," meaning that the courts resolved them without allowing them to go to trial, the judge in the *Soldier of Fortune* case did allow it to do so. During the trial, the plaintiffs' attorney, Ronald Franklin, showed that at least nine classified ads printed in the magazine during the past 10 years had served as links in criminal plots ranging from extortion to attempted murder. Thus, he argued, printing such "gun-for-hire" ads resulted in foreseeable harm. The jury agreed and awarded Sandra Black's parents and son a $9,400,000 judgment against *Soldier of Fortune,* but this was overturned by the Court of Appeals.

Courts are generally afraid of setting a precedent that would make it easy to recover damages against the media for content.

In its decision, although the court acknowledged that "Hearn's ad presents a risk of serious harm," it still ruled in favor of *Soldier of Fortune* because it was afraid that finding the magazine guilty of negligence would force all newspaper and magazine publishers to investigate every classified ad. Again, the court did not want to set a precedent whereby anyone who was injured from using an advertised product could sue the publisher of the ad for damages.

Finally, how would you decide the fifth case? Brian Thompson testified that most of the two hours of dial-a-porn messages he listened to depicted a man forcing a woman to perform oral sex or a father forcing his 10-year-old daughter to have sex with him. In his testimony, he said: "After hearing the messages, I continued to think about having sex with a child. [The father molesting his daughter] stands out in my mind. I wanted to find out what it was like." Two weeks later, he forced four-year-old Rebecca Callen to perform oral sex on him. His attorneys charged Tele-Promo, the producer

Advertisements for pornography are handed out on the street, where they become litter that children can pick up. Is this "protected speech?" (Photo by Bruce Cotler.)

of the messages, with incitement. When it looked likely that the California Superior Court judge would refuse to grant Tele-Promo a summary judgment, meaning that the case would go to trial, the company agreed to an out-of-court settlement.

Of the five cases above, score three for the media, one win for the plaintiffs (Weirum—the radio contest case), and one out-of-court settlement that may have been for the plaintiffs, although we'll never know for certain because all those involved are bound not to discuss it. With an out-of-court settlement, one only can speculate that Tele-Promo feared it would lose if the case went to a jury; thought it might win, but was afraid of even more negative publicity; or chose to settle out of court because it estimated the costs of litigation and opted to pay the children and their parents less, but without admitting any wrongdoing.

We've had a glimpse of how judges decide whether a case involves negligence as opposed to incitement law. Now, add three more variables to the equation. The first two cases involved pure or "core" speech—*i.e.*, speech for its own sake, as in television entertainment. The purposes of "Born Innocent" and "The Mickey Mouse Club Show" were merely to entertain. This form of speech has the full protection of the First Amendment. These "pure speech" cases illustrate the two types of problems with which judges must deal. The *Niemi* case involved four teenagers who were instigated by "Born Innocent" to harm two innocent children. In other words, a third party was harmed. The *Shannon* case concerned a boy who, in trying to imitate a TV stunt, hurt himself by accident. Nevertheless, both cases involve core speech.

The *Weirum* case involving KHJ's radio contest was not identified formally in 1975 as involving commercial speech, but no doubt would be considered today as a commercial speech case because the "speech" involved was for the purpose of drawing more listeners to the radio station. The *Soldier of Fortune* case clearly involved commercial speech, which does not enjoy the unconditional protection of the First Amendment. Although it is protected, it is slightly lower on the hierarchy than core speech.

Commercial speech does not enjoy the unconditional protection of the First Amendment.

The *Brian Thompson* case involved dial-a-porn messages that were either obscene or indecent. Obscene speech is not protected by the First Amendment, but indecent speech is, although it is slightly lower on the hierarchy that commercial speech. What's the difference between obscene and indecent speech? This is one of those fine distinctions that is difficult to make, but the Supreme Court took a stab at it in a 1989 case, *Sable v. FCC*, which dealt with the entire question of whether dial-a-porn was legal or not. It determined that indecent speech appeals only to "normal, healthy sexual desires," as opposed to "shameful or morbid" desires, the latter being obscene and illegal. In other words, dial-a-porn messages can be indecent, but not obscene.

Having established the difference between negligence and incitement law and between pure, commercial, and indecent and obscene speech, let's examine some additional cases. We'll start with core speech cases where an innocent third party was harmed.

Case #6

A girl goes to a "gang movie" called "Boulevard Nights" and is shot while walking to a bus stop after seeing it. She survives, and her mother sues the film producer for negligence, arguing that he knew that violence could break out after the movie because he suggested to Warner Brothers, its distributor, that guards should be hired to stand outside the theater after it was shown.

Case #7

A 16-year-old boy is stabbed to death by a juvenile who has just seen the gang movie "The Warriors." The boy's parents sue Paramount for negligence, arguing that violence following the film was foreseeable because, three days before their son was killed, there were both a fatal stabbing and a fatal shooting by gang members who had seen the movie in two California cities.

Should the producers and distributors have been liable for these injuries? If you said no, you were right. The courts in both cases did not want to set a precedent whereby filmmakers could be found liable for acts of violence allegedly triggered by their works. The courts seemed to arrive at their decisions in favor of the filmmakers fairly easily. They clearly concluded that to rule otherwise indeed would open a Pandora's box in which anyone who was injured could sue the media for giving whoever hurt them the idea.

The courts are hesitant to open a Pandora's box in which anyone who was injured could sue the media for giving whoever hurt them the idea.

You Be the Judge

What about other cases involving the media and children and teenagers? Consider the following:

Case #8

Carolyn Carter and Christine Bertrand, students in an eighth-grade chemistry class, misread the instructions in their textbook and add methyl alcohol to a beaker of ice over a lighted Bunsen burner, causing a flash fire that results in second- and third-degree burns over 40% of their bodies. They sue Rand McNally, the publisher of the textbook, for negligence.

Case #9

Fourth-grader Christopher Walter follows the instructions in his textbook directing him to use a ruler and a rubber band in an experiment to demonstrate pitch. The ruler is propelled into his eye, causing serious damage to his sight. His father sues the textbook publisher for negligence.

Case #10

Thirteen-year-old Nicholas De Filippo watches a stunt hanging of Johnny Carson and hangs himself. His parents sue NBC for negligence.

Case #11

Six-year-old Jeremy Nezworski imitates a cartoon hanging on "The Scooby Doo Show" and kills himself. His mother sues ABC and Hanna-Barbera for negligence.

Case #12

Sixteen-year-old Irving Pulling apparently undergoes "extreme emotional and psychological stress" when his high school English teacher puts a curse on him during a game of Dungeons and Dragons. He fatally shoots himself in the chest with his father's gun. His mother sues the makers of the game for negligence.

Case #13

Fourteen-year-old Troy Dunaway reads a *Hustler* article on autoerotic asphyxiation. When he attempts what is described in the article, he accidentally hangs himself. His mother sues the magazine for incitement.

Case #14

Nineteen-year-old John McCollum listens to Ozzy Osbourne's "Suicide Solution" and other songs for five hours, then shoots himself in the head. His parents sue the rock musician for incitement.

Case #15

Sixteen-year-old Michael Waller shoots himself after listening to Osbourne's music for several hours. His parents sue the singer, accusing him of incitement.

Case #16

James Vance and Ray Belknap, aged 19 and 18, respectively, make a suicide pact after listening to the music of rock group Judas Priest for several hours. One of them shoots himself and dies instantly; the other survives with his face blown off and insists that "the music made us do it."*

How would you decide these cases?

How would you decide the cases above? In only one case did the plaintiffs win, and one other case was settled out of court. The two girls who were burned during the chemistry experiment were awarded $155,000 by a Massachusetts jury in a judgment against Rand McNally. This was the first and only case where a textbook publisher has been found liable for injuries suffered by students conducting an experiment described in a book.

However, in the case in which the boy followed instructions in his textbook and nearly lost his eye, the court found in favor of the publisher, explaining that to rule otherwise would have a serious "chilling effect" on freedom of speech. Because courts are not always consistent from state to state, some plaintiffs may have the false hope that they can win a case against the media in their own state, even though everyone before them has lost in other states.

Settled out of court was the case in which a six-year-old imitated a hanging on "The Scooby Doo Show" and killed himself by accident. His mother won an out-of-court settlement from ABC and Hanna-Barbera Productions. Although the defendants might have won this case in court, they no doubt preferred to

*A closer examination of this case may be found in Chapter Nine, page 221.

settle to avoid negative publicity. In all the other cases above, the media defendants prevailed.

It would be difficult to argue with the courts' findings in favor of the media defendants in the core speech cases. To find in favor of the plaintiffs doubtless would set a dangerous precedent that would encourage increasing numbers of people to try to recover damages, claiming that they had hurt themselves or were injured as the result of some scene in the media. In some of the core speech cases, there were underlying causes of violence far more powerful than any media influence. For example, the 14-year-old girl who led three others to assault Olivia Niemi and her friend with a beer bottle had been sexually abused by her stepfather. The two young men who shot themselves after listening to Judas Priest had been beaten by their parents as young children.

Shouldn't we ask why our society should be so eager to protect the speech of a publication whose classified ads have linked hit men to victims in at least nine cases, one of which indeed resulted in murder?

The easy availability of the guns with which Irving Pulling, John McCollum, Michael Waller, James Vance, and Ray Belknap shot themselves also must be questioned. Should the media be liable for their speech when gun manufacturers are not liable for providing weapons that cause about 22,000 deaths in the U.S. each year?

On the other hand, one could argue that the media did function to some degree as a catalyst in the cases cited. For example, although Robert Black and John Hearn caused Sandra Black's murder, *Soldier of Fortune* was the catalyst linking them. The Court of Appeals tried to balance the risk of harm from "gun-for-hire" ads such as Hearn's against the burden on publishers to check out every classified ad, and ruled in favor of *Soldier of Fortune.* Yet, if we were to balance the value of Sandra Black's life against the "life" of *Soldier of Fortune* as a continuing publication, shouldn't we ask why our society should be so eager to protect the speech of a publication whose classified ads have linked hit men to victims in at least nine cases, one of which indeed resulted in murder?

The Cost of Free Speech

What Brian Thompson "learned" from the dial-a-porn messages is that women and little girls do not mind being sexually abused—the messages always portrayed them as resisting at first, but then acquiescing. If dial-a-porn providers continue to disseminate "indecent" (but legal) portrayals of women being coerced into sex or fathers raping their daughters, we should not be surprised as a society to have many more cases in which adolescent or adult males abuse young girls and women.

Nevertheless, such images are pervasive. Rap group 2 Live Crew does a number about a man who tells how much he enjoys raping a baby girl in her crib. Although a Florida court found their album "As Nasty as They Wanna Be" to be obscene, the court ruled that it could not be banned from record stores without a proper hearing. As a society, we can choose to protect speech about raping baby girls in their cribs or pornography showing women being tortured and mutilated, and, aside from generally debasing our quality of life, it probably won't have any effect on most men except to offend them.

If such images are protected, however, we should be aware that more and more research is showing that dial-a-porn, rap porn, and graphic pornography reinforce and "legitimize" the idea that it's okay to abuse women and children. While the vast majority of the public may be offended, but otherwise unaffected, by such images, there will be men who *are* influenced, ranging from Brian Thompson to serial murderers such as Ted Bundy and Steve Pennell, who apparently were stimulated by pornography depicting women being tortured and mutilated.

We can protect speech such as dial-a-porn and thinly veiled classified ads for hit men, but let's not do it with our eyes closed. The price may be a human life. When NBC aired "Born Innocent," was it worth showing an extremely graphic rape at 8:17 P.M. to entertain 20,000,000 people and get good ratings enough to risk a case of copycat violence in which two young girls were sexually assaulted? If the price for free speech is the emotional well-being of rape victims like Olivia Niemi and Rebecca Callen and the lives of people like Sandra Black, is free speech worth it?

What's the answer? Should graphic rape scenes on television and/or dial-a-porn be censored? Should all classified ads selling guns-for-hire be banned? I personally would volunteer to play God and decide what children and adults in our society should be exposed to. The problem, however, is that I would not be able to monitor *all* the media, and other people might volunteer to help me decide what goes, and I might not agree with them. For example, should all rock lyrics dealing with suicide be banned? Does this mean that the "M*A*S*H" theme song, "Suicide Is Painless," should be banned? What about "Romeo and Juliet" and "Hamlet"? Could someone interpret these plays as encouraging suicide? Some of the lines get fuzzy.

Dial-a-porn, rap porn, and graphic pornography reinforce and "legitimize" the idea that it's okay to abuse women and children.

Even when the lines are clear, there's a problem. For instance, I would argue that the socially redeeming value of dial-a-porn messages and most pornography ranges from nil to dangerous to women, but most prosecutors have neither the time nor the money to prosecute pornographers when there are so many violent crimes to deal with. Even though the Supreme Court says that obscenity is illegal, no one seems to be able to define it.

The best solution is discussion and education. In other words, "more speech" always is better than banning speech, but it could take a generation or a millenium for our society to evolve to the point where violence is so passé that the media no longer can use it to attain higher ratings.

Censorship probably is unworkable and re-education will take a long, long time. In the meantime, the media will hide behind the First Amendment whenever they are criticized for the countless sensationalized scenes of sexual and nonsexual violence. However, as long as sex and violence produce money, they will be sensationalized. There is growing evidence that scenes of highly graphic, unusual violence are the most likely to be imitated in copycat cases. The problem is that no one can predict *who* will imitate these scenes in real life.

Maybe the mere threat of a lawsuit will lead a Hollywood studio or television producer to think twice.

As it stands, the media have the right to be as vile and disgusting as they please, and plaintiffs who believe that the media content was the "proximate cause" of their injury have the right to sue the media. Perhaps because there is nowhere else to turn, people are turning to the courts for redress of grievances against the media. The latter almost always will win before the case ever goes to trial, but who knows? Maybe the mere threat of a lawsuit will lead a Hollywood studio or television producer to think twice. One thing is certain—just because the plaintiffs rarely win in court does not mean that these cases will disappear. ♦

Questions for Discussion

1. Review the cases mentioned in this article. If you were the judge, would you have found for the plaintiff (the person harmed) or the defendant (the media)?
2. "Should the media be liable for their speech when gun manufacturers are not liable for providing weapons that cause about 22,000 deaths in the U.S. each year?"

Majorities versus the First Amendment: Rationality on Trial

Franklyn S. Haiman

Franklyn Haiman is a well-known expert in the field of freedom of speech. The following is a keynote address which was presented before the 1990 annual conference of The Speech Communication Association, an organization composed of speech professionals, teachers, and students.

In this speech, Professor Haiman discusses the constitutional protection of minority opinions. He concentrates his remarks on three recent issues:

1. *The flag-burning amendment to the constitution which was proposed in congress,*
2. *The controversy surrounding several "obscene" art exhibitions and musical entertainments, and*
3. *The control of "hate speech" on college campuses.*

Franklyn S. Haiman is John Evans Professor Emeritus of Communication Studies at Northwestern University and a Vice President of the American Civil Liberties Union. He is the author, among other works, of Speech and Law in a Free Society *(University of Chicago Press, 1981).*

Reading Difficulty Level: 10. Difficult: contains some jargon ("communitarianism," "majoritarianism"), and sentence structure tends to be complex.

Four years ago, on the eve of the Bicentennial anniversary of the U.S. Constitution, I had the privilege I am once again enjoying of delivering the keynote address to the Speech Communication Association's annual convention. My repeat appearance occurs as we enter another Bicentennial year—that of the first ten amendments to the Constitution, the Bill of Rights. But we have had an unusual kind of prelude to our observance of the 200th anniversary of the First Amendment, and instead of celebrating its birth we might well have been attending its funeral. The President of the United States, along with a majority of both houses of the Congress, was ready to make that happen by urging and enacting the first amendment to the First Amendment in our history—all for

On the 200th anniversary of the First Amendment, we might have been attending its funeral.

the purpose of ensuring that one particular mode of symbolic behavior that was said to threaten the foundations of the republic, the so-called desecration of an American flag, would be banished from the marketplace of ideas. Happily it takes more than a majority of the Congress to amend our Constitution, and a little more than a third of our senators and representatives found the unaccustomed political courage to beat back this surge of allegedly patriotic passion.

Democracy and Anti-majoritarianism

The Bill of Rights is a counter-majoritarian document.

The two-thirds rule for amending our Constitution is not the only anti-majoritarian element of our democratic system, nor even the strongest. The Bill of Rights itself is a counter-majoritarian document of the toughest fiber, confirming the view of John Stuart Mill that "if all mankind minus one, were of one opinion, and only one person were of the contrary opinion, mankind would be no more justified in silencing that one person, than he, if he had the power, would be justified in silencing mankind." And the justices of the Supreme Court of the United States are not chosen by a majority of the people nor subject to being voted out of office, but are appointed from an elite corps of judges and lawyers who serve life terms as presumptive guardians of individual liberty against encroachments by the two elected branches of government.

We have heard a lot of talk in recent times about Supreme Court justices who, in fulfilling that function, are not supposed to "legislate from the bench," as Chief Justice Earl Warren and Justice William Brennan allegedly did, but only to "interpret" the words that our Founding Fathers wrote in the Constitution, as Chief Justice William Rehnquist and Justice Antonin Scalia allegedly do. Count Alfred Korzybski, Irving Lee, Wendell Johnson and Stuart Chase must turn over in their graves every time that assertion is made.[1] Did the Founding Fathers have sit-com television in mind when they wrote the freedom-of-speech clause of the First Amendment, or helicopter surveillance of a marijuana plot in a back yard when they penned the "unreasonable searches and seizures" clause of the Fourth Amendment? It seems unlikely. So, are justices "legislating" or "interpeting" when they write those phenomena into or out of our Constitution? Justice Scalia thinks that flags are protected speech; Chief Justice Rehnquist and almost-Justice Robert Bork think

Reprinted by permission of the author.

1. Korzybski, Lee, Johnson, Chase and Hayakawa wrote about General Semantics, a form of communication study whose guiding principle is that "meanings are in people, not in words." General semanticists would reject the idea that we could elicit the meanings of the founders from their words alone, without taking into consideration changes between their time and our own.

otherwise. Which of these stalwarts of the originalist, literal interpretation school of thought have defected from the true faith and which have not? Or are they *all* fallible human beings like the rest of us, endowing words with some mixture of what others *seem* to have meant by them at the time they were uttered, what they might have meant by them if they were uttered today, and what we *want* them to mean for today and tomorrow?

I must not pursue this by-way into General Semantics and Supreme Court jurisprudence any further, but return to my original point that the Supreme Court, the Bill of Rights, and the two-thirds rule for constitutional amendments are all testimony to the fact that our democracy is not simply a system of majority rule, but a society in which *some* important areas of life are preserved for individual autonomy, and *some* fundamental decisions require, if not unanimity, at least a closer approach to it than 51% of those present and voting.

Communitarianism and Freedom of Speech

Unfortunately, the anti-majoritarian nature of democracy is not well understood by many people, at least not until their own ox is gored, and too many of our sister and fellow citizens are prone to believe that *their* values, their beliefs, their ways of living and expressing themselves, are or should be universal. Although we are a long way from anything that might fairly be characterized as a tyranny of the majority, I would like to suggest that we are heading too much in that direction and, what is much more troubling, are being offered intellectual justifications for that course which are more sophisticated, more persuasive, and supported by more political power than has been true in the past. Gathering under the banner of what is being called "communitarianism," and no doubt reacting against what is perceived as individualism run amok, we are seeing and hearing a flood of appeals in speeches, columns, books, and prestigious law journal articles for greater "civility" in our discourse, more deference to the sensibilities of the so-called "community," more rationality—as these advocates define that term—in public debate.

We are headed too much in the direction of a tyrany of the majority.

Let me illustrate this thesis with three freedom-of-speech controversies that have been raging across the land for the past two or three years. I will begin with the one that has generated the most heat and least light, the flag burning issue; proceed to the battles over alleged obscenity and government funding of the arts; and end with an issue that has evoked both deep passion and serious intellectual analysis on college and university campuses all over the nation—that of how to deal with the incidents of racist, sexist, and homophobic expression that have been erupting in that arena.

Too many citizens are prone to believe that their values, their beliefs, their ways of living and expressing themselves should be universal.

The Flag Burning Issue

The idea that the nation's flag is a sacred symbol is not new.

The idea that the nation's flag is a symbol so sacred to the American people, or perhaps, more accurately, to about 85% of them, that it must not be defaced or mutilated in public, did not originate with George Bush and his 1988 presidential campaign. Such behavior, if engaged in to communicate contempt for the flag or what it represents, has been outlawed by *state* governments for most of this century and was made a *federal* crime as well, in 1968, in response to protests against the Vietnam War. Nor is the idea a new one that such laws should be considered violative of the First Amendment because they prohibit symbolic behavior, and nothing more, on the basis of its political offensiveness, and not because they protect against any substantive evil which a legislature has the right to prevent. Justice Brennan said just that in 1981 in dissenting from a decision of the Supreme Court not to review the conviction of two protesters who had burned a flag on a sidewalk in front of the federal building in Greensboro, North Carolina. It took eight more years for Justice Brennan to persuade a majority of his colleagues, including Justices Scalia and Anthony Kennedy, that he was right; and in June of 1989 the decision was handed down in *Texas v. Johnson* that unleashed the barrage of jingoism which demanded a constitutional amendment to undo this dastardly deed. The tone for that campaign was set by the Chief Justice's dissenting opinion, which did not even pretend to be in the realm of rational discourse, starting out as it did with the unabashed assertion that "a page of history is worth a volume of logic." He then proceeded to invoke every image of the flag fluttering through wartime that he could muster—from the marines hoisting it to the top of Mount Suribachi on Iwo Jima to quoting in their entirety the words of the Star Spangled Banner and of John Greenleaf Whittier's poem, "Barbara Fritchie." Even the moderate and normally reasonable Justice John Paul Stevens was swept along in this tide of chauvinism, writing in his dissenting opinion that "a country's flag is more than a symbol of 'nationhood and national unity'. . . . It is a symbol of freedom, of equal opportunity, of religious tolerance. . . . The value of the flag as a symbol cannot be measured . . . sanctioning the public desecration of the flag will tarnish its value."

Cooler heads in the Congress managed, in the Summer of 1989, to stave off the stampede by offering their colleagues a face-saving, if politically cynical, alternative to amending the First Amendment—a new federal statute which would remedy the most glaring defect in the 1968 law with a viewpoint-neutral ban against *all* public mutilation of the flag, not just against those who do it to express contempt. But the five-person majority of *Texas v. Johnson* courageously, and some thought recklessly, since they had to know they were inviting a renewed effort to amend the Constitution, held their ground and struck down the new law (*U.S. v. Eichman*) on June 11, 1990, finding it still an intrusion, without justification, on purely symbolic behavior that is protected by the First Amendment. Predictably, the proposed amendment to the Constitution was back on the floor of Congress virtually overnight, and now our representatives and senators had nowhere to hide. Threatened by Republican Senate leader Robert Dole with the retribution of 30-second TV campaign spots for any who dared to vote as they knew they should, a substantial enough minority of them, with crucial backing from the Democratic leaders of both houses, banded together in mutual support to successfully defend the First Amendment from this majoritarian assault. They will surely survive this act of principle, majority passions being the fickle and fleeting phenomena they so often are and other issues having moved to the forefront of public attention in the meantime. But we had an uncomfortably narrow escape.

Obscenity, Art, and Government Funding

The criminal prosecutions during 1990 for exhibiting the photographs of Robert Mapplethorpe in Cincinnati, Ohio,[2] and for selling and performing 2 Live Crew's "As Nasty As They Wanna Be" in Broward County, Florida, following on the heels of the struggle over restrictions on grants by the National Endowment for the Arts, re-awakened public interest in another perennial free-speech issue—that of obscenity. But there are new twists that make the problem considerably more difficult for those of us who, along with former Supreme Court Justices Hugo Black and William O. Douglas, believe that so-called obscene speech and images are as much entitled to protection by the First Amendment as other kinds of communication.

Are obscene speech and images entitled to First Amendment protection?

The first complication is the entirely valid point made by Senator Jesse Helms and his supporters that there is a difference between criminal punishment by the government of communicative activities of private citizens, on the one hand, and affirmative government support, with the taxpayers' money, of the same acts of communication, on the other hand. Where the First Amendment may prohibit the former, it surely does not require the latter. From this undeniable premise it is then argued that while offensiveness to majority sensibilities may not be a sufficient justification for governmental suppression of words and pictures, it is certainly a reasonable basis for government refusal to

2. See George Will's article, "America's Slide into the Sewer," (page 218) for his reaction to 2 Live Crew's lyrics.

Offensiveness to the sensibilities of others is not a criterion for decision-making about government grants.

pay for their production and dissemination. But this is a classic non-sequitur. Offensiveness to the sensibilities of others, be they a majority of 90% or a minority of 10%, is no more appropriate a criterion for decision-making about government grants to the arts, humanities, and sciences than it is for the county sheriff to raid a local bookstore. Once the government decides, on an admittedly discretionary basis, that it will fund certain categories of intellectual or cultural activities—be they public schools, libraries, museums, symphonies, dance troupes, or individual artists—there must, of course, be criteria established for selecting who will benefit from the finite amount of money that is available and who will not. Qualitative judgments by peers and professionals, free insofar as humanly possible of ideological bias, are one such appropriate set of criteria. Geographical and cultural diversity, development of new talent, and maintenance of those with established records of accomplishment, may be among some other legitimate considerations. And the exclusion of illegal activity is certainly appropriate, *so long as* the determination of what constitutes illegality is left to the judicial system, where it belongs. The flaw in the 1989 Helms amendment, even as it was watered down by its opponents who still felt some need to throw Jesse a bone, was not that it went beyond the present state of the law in declaring obscenity to be beyond the pale of acceptable public communication, but that it imposed an obligation to make the decision as to what is and is not obscene on the National Endowment for the Arts, on an *a priori* basis, rather than in a court of law, with full due process safeguards. That defect has, fortunately, now been corrected by the Congress.

Whether or not so-called obscene material *should* be illegal in the first place is a question that goes far beyond Senator Helms and the National Endowment for the Arts dispute. It is a question that has been seriously debated, at least since 1957, when the Supreme Court definitively took the position that obscenity is *not* protected by the First Amendment, if not since 1873, when Anthony Comstock, leader of the Committee for the Suppression of Vice, persuaded the Congress to enact our first federal law against sending obscene literature through the U.S. mail. But that debate has taken on new complexity in the recent past, for it is now not only the prudes and Philistines who think that the Robert Mapplethorpes and 2 Live Crews of this world have gone too far, but calm and thoughtful legal scholars who invoke a facially responsible communitarian point of view to justify restraints on words or images that violate the community's standards of decency.

One such scholar, political scientist Richard Randall, in a provocative 1989 volume entitled *Freedom and Taboo: Pornography and the Poli-*

tics of a Self Divided, proposes that the Supreme Court should abandon its requirement that before something can be found obscene it must be lacking in serious literary, artistic, political, or scientific value, and should rely solely on the criterion of "patent offensivensess" to contemporary local community standards. To the critic's response that offensiveness is an immeasurably subjective standard, entirely in the eye of the individual beholder, Randall replies that patent offensiveness *to a community* is objectively measurable. "We are not speaking here of public opinion polls," he says. "More to the point are actual communications. The chief evidence of existing community standards on any matter is what has actually been done or practiced and what the community's response has been to departures from the customary. What sorts of sexual material have been openly available? . . . Was there protest or complaint, indifference, or approval? If so, by whom and in what number?" What Randall fails to appreciate is that what he has suggested be added together in an objective way are subjective judgments to begin with. Adding zero to zero still makes zero.

Randall's (1989) preference for community standards of decency as the boundary line for sexually oriented speech is largely a pragmatic one:

> Liberty as an absolute value negates the legitimacy and prudence of all opposing interests. . . . Individual liberties must co-exist with the equality principle and its operating agent, majority rule. . . . In theory, a free speech society works because its members are wise enough, mature enough, or simply self-controlled enough to check their natural inclination to silence troubling views and disagreeable expression. . . . Yet few members of any society can consistently reach such heights of political wisdom and temperance. . . . The question is not whether freedom of speech should submit to popular preferences and majority will . . . but whether the inevitable and continuing conflict between these two vital elements of liberal democracy has been managed as well as it might be . . . protecting necessary freedom and preventing unnecessary reaction.

I assume from this that Professor Randall would applaud the senators who threw Jesse Helms his bone in 1989, and look at the agony that brought us for a year.

Offensiveness is an immeasurably subjective standard, entirely in the eye of the individual beholder.

"Hate Speech" and Equality of Opportunity

But there is much more than mere pragmatism lurking in Randall's (1989) assertion that "liberty as an absolute value negates the legitimacy of all opposing interests" and "must co-exist with the equality principle and its operating agent, majority rule." Although he may not have contemplated this extrapolation, I would point out that the very same principle he has enunciated with respect to obscenity has been the bedrock on which the advocates of campus restrictions on racist, sexist, and homophobic expression have built their case. Equality of opportunity, they have argued, is denied by a concept of freedom of speech which includes the utterance of racially or sexually derogatory remarks or the display of symbols which denigrate their targets on the basis of their race, religion, sex, or sexual orientation. A 1988 *Harvard Law Review* article explains the rationale as follows:

> From the communitarian perspective, permitting group vilification causes significant harm both to individuals and to the political community as a whole. Toleration of group vilification injures individuals because it fails to respect fully the personhood of its targets . . . [It] harms the political community as a whole because it denigrates the idea of equality . . . den[ying] the targets of such expression equal membership in the political community.

John Stuart Mill believed that error of opinion must be tolerated and countered with more speech.

As to the old-fashioned notion of John Stuart Mill that error of opinion must be tolerated and countered with more speech in a free marketplace of ideas, Law Professor Mari Matsuda, in an emotionally powerful 1989 *Michigan Law Review* article, which relies on the new narrative style of legal argument and is entitled "Public Response to Racist Speech: Considering the Victim's Story," offers this Marcusian answer:

> What is argued here . . . is that we accept certain principles as the shared historical legacy of the world community. Racial supremacy is one of the ideas we have collectively and internationally considered and rejected.

It would be insensitive, unfair, even arrogant of me to imply that Professor Matsuda and other reputable leaders of the movement for restrictions on racist speech, such as Professor Charles Lawrence of the Stanford Law School, Professor Richard Delgado of the University of Wisconsin Law School, and Dean Mark Yudof of the University of Texas Law School, have abandoned rationality on this issue in the same way as have the proponents of a flag-burning amendment to the Constitution or the prosecutors of the Mapplethorpe exhibit. There *is* a serious problem of racism and sexism on our college campuses; it *does* cause emotional pain and suffering to its targets; and it may indeed hinder their academic performance and opportunities. The narratives that are told of harassment and victimization cannot be dismissed as lacking in authenticity, nor is the point without merit that intelligent women and men regard racist and sexist ideas as anathema to a civilized society. Where reason breaks down is in the leap to the conclusion that it is freedom of *speech* which is in conflict with equality, rather than the racist and sexist *behaviors* and *practices* that underlie the verbal expression of racial and sexual bigotry.

Freedom of speech and equality of opportunity are, and always have been, allies, not enemies. We must not allow them to be divided and conquered. What equality we have achieved in this country—for women, for racial and religious minorities, for gays and lesbians, and for the physically handicapped—has been significantly advanced by the exercise of freedom of speech; and freedom of speech, in turn, has been strengthened and enriched by the increased empowerment of previously disempowered groups. The truly serious problems in our system of freedom of expression today—problems such as access to the mass media and competitiveness in our political campaigns—stem primarily from gross inequalities in the distribution of wealth rather than from excesses of speech, and would be ameliorated by a more equitable economy rather than by limitations on expression.

It is also misleading to suggest, as some do, that the voices of minorities have been silenced, and equality thereby denied, as a result of racist speech, or that the voices of women have been silenced, and equality thereby denied, as a result of violent pornography. That some are intimidated, I do not doubt. But that most are driven into a state of submissive quiescence is simply contrary to the observable facts. Happily the free-speech system works in this respect as it is theoretically supposed to work—people who are insulted and denigrated find the strength within themselves, and in concert with others, to talk back, to insist on being respected, to demand their rights. If they fail it is not because their oppressors have too many words, but because they have too much power. Shutting up those oppressors will not solve the problem; sharing their power will.

The Irony of Communitarianism

One of the ironies of the new communitarianism is the pride it takes in its reasonableness—reasonable in its deference to the standards of decency of the so-called community, reasonable in its recognition of the supposed limits of human tolerance, reasonable in its willingness to exclude from the marketplace of ideas the rhetoric of grunts and groans—such as flag burnings, pornographic images, and racial slurs—a rhetoric which allegedly makes no contribution to rational discourse.

Should we exclude from the marketplace of ideas the rhetoric of grunts and groans?

I say this is ironic because it is a corruption of rationality. What is a community if not a composite of *all* of its members, not 51% nor two-thirds nor 95%, but everyone? What, therefore, is a so-called community standard of decency if 5%, one third, or 49% of that community do not share it? It is a *majority* standard, perhaps even the standard of an overwhelming majority, but let us not pretend it is unanimous and try to pass it off as that of the entire community. The substitution in recent discourse of the word "communitarianism" for "majoritarianism" is a bit of verbal legerdemain, intentional or not, which masks the fact that a community and a majority are not identical. Not that there is anything wrong with majority standards for some purposes, and that they cannot or should not be used as a basis for the outlawing of murder, rape, and robbery, even if the murderers, rapists, and robbers do not agree. But we must not be taken in by the fallacy that because such standards are justifiably invoked for murder, rape, and robbery they are similarly justified as a basis for the banning of words, pictures, or other symbols of which the majority does not approve. Rather let us hold to the time-tested premise of Thomas Jefferson that "It is time enough for the rightful purposes of civil government for its officers to interfere when principles break out into overt acts against peace and good order."

If people are taught that ideas they find disagreeable can be made to go away, they will try to make them go away.

As to the supposed limits of human tolerance, I would maintain that people learn to tolerate what they have to tolerate. If they are taught from an early age that people and ideas they find disagreeable can be made to go away, they will try to make them go away, and with each success they will be emboldened to go farther the next time. But if they learn, through moral suasion and the steady hand of the law, that they should not and will not be allowed to try to rid the world of whatever they find offensive, they will accept that, even if grudgingly, and may even grow to appreciate that such a policy is in their own enlightened self-interest, since they too may someday be deviants.

Finally, we confront the claim that what I have facetiously called the rhetoric of grunts and groans makes no useful contribution to a marketplace of ideas; that, indeed, it undermines the processes of rational discourse. That notion is not original with the new majoritarians. The U.S. Supreme Court itself, almost half a century ago, held that there are certain categories of speech—for example, the obscene, the libelous, and fighting words—which are of "such slight social value as a step to truth that any benefit that may be derived from them is clearly outweighed by the social interest in order and morality" (*Chaplinsky v. New Hampshire*, 1942). That ruling, significantly, was in unanimous affirmation of the fighting words conviction of a Jehovah's Witness by the name of Chaplinsky for calling a police officer a "damned Fascist" and a "god damned racketeer." There were no important ideas in this utterance of Chaplinsky? No insight into his feelings? No expression of a political or religious ideology? A rather cramped view, I would suggest, of what constitutes rational discourse or a useful contribution to the search for truth.

Justice John Marshall Harlan had it much straighter in 1971 when he said, on behalf of a more clear-headed majority of the Court in *Cohen v. California:*

Surely the state has no right to cleanse public debate to the point where it is grammatically palatable to the most squeamish among us. . . . Words are often chosen as much for their emotive as their cognitive force. We cannot sanction the view that the Constitution, while solicitous of the cognitive content of individual speech, has little or no regard for that emotive function which, practically speaking, may often be the more important element of the overall message sought to be communicated.

What We Can Do

As one who has been concerned and written about ethics and rationality in communication for a long time, even before I became a First Amendment junkie, I do not stand here to urge you to rush to your next meeting and call everyone a "son of a bitch" or pull out a pocketful of dirty pictures, and I do not plan to go out in front of this Hilton Hotel on Michigan Avenue, burn an American flag, and chant, as they did on this very spot 22 years ago, that "The Whole World is Watching." I am only saying that if anyone should *choose* to engage in those symbolic acts, I would hesitate, before knowing a great deal about the social and political context, to label the behavior irrational, and I would certainly not want anyone to call the Chicago cops.

I would like to conclude on a somewhat parochial and personal note. Forty-four years ago, as a graduate student at Northwestern University, I had the great good fortune, for one summer session, of coming under the influence of a visiting professor by the name of James M. O'Neil—a key figure in the renaissance of the classical rhetorical discipline in 20th century America, the prime mover in the founding of the Speech Communication Association, its first president, and, for four years, the first editor of its journal. At the time our paths crossed some thirty years after those events, Professor O'Neil was serving as chairman of the Academic Freedom Committee of the American Civil Liberties Union—a unique role in those days for a prominent lay leader of the Roman Catholic church and self-appointed respondent to the attacks on the political power exercised by the Catholic church in America written by Paul Blanshard, among others. But just as James M. O'Neil was stalwart in the defense of his church, so was he uncompromising in his defense of freedom of expression and vigorous in his advocacy of the central responsibility of teachers and scholars of speech to be engaged in that defense.

He viewed the functions of teacher of speech and guardian of the First Amendment as virtually synonymous. Indeed, it was from him that I first learned about the ACLU, was motivated to become a card-carrying member, and when the opportunity arose a dozen years later, to become even more deeply involved in its work. But it is not my intention here to become a recruiter for the ACLU (although that result would not disappoint me) nor even to engage in boosterism for the Speech Communication Association (which I assume to be superfluous

If anyone should choose to engage in symbolic acts, I would hesitate, before knowing a great deal about the social and political context, to label the behavior irrational.

in this place). It *is* my purpose to propose that the women and men of our profession, like Professor O'Neil, constitute one of the elites of our nation—and let us not blink from the label—whose mission, by virtue of training and position, is to stand up and do battle whenever the tides of majoritarianism threaten to drown out the voices of dissent. We cannot depend on the Supreme Court of the United States to do that job for us. The struggle will be won or lost in the court of public opinion where we will surely be out-numbered but hopefully not out-smarted nor out-talked. True rationality is indeed on trial as we enter the third century of the First Amendment. I hope that you will be in the court-room to testify. ♦

We should stand up and do battle whenever the tides of majoritarianism threaten to drown out the voices of dissent.

References

Chaplinsky v. New Hampshire, 315 U.S. 568 (1942).

Cohen v. California, 403 U.S. 15 (1971).

Jefferson, T. (1779). Virginia act for establishing religious freedom. In L. Pfeffer (Ed.), *Religious freedom* (p. 19). Skokie, IL: National Textbook Co.

Matsuda, M. (1989). Public response to racist speech: Considering the victim's story. *Michigan Law Review, 87,* 2320–2381.

Mill, J. S. (1859). On liberty. In C. W. Eliot (Ed.), *The Harvard classics* (p. 219). New York: PF Collier & Sons.

Note: A communitarian defense of group libel laws. (1988). *Harvard Law Review, 101,* 682–701.

Randall, R. (1989). *Freedom and taboo: Pornography and the politics of a self divided.* Berkeley, CA: University of California Press.

Texas v. Johnson, 57 U.S. Law Week 4770 (1989).

U.S. v. Eichman, 58 U.S. Law Week 4744 (1990).

Questions for Discussion

1. Do you believe that the burning of the American Flag should be a protected form of political expression? Why or why not?
2. Haiman believes that "offensiveness to the . . . majority" should not be the basis for deciding which works of art will be given government money. Do you agree or disagree?
3. Should speakers who express racist, sexist and homophobic views be allowed to speak on college campuses?

Suggested Readings

If you are interested in the various First Amendment battles currently raging, you will be interested in the historical statements presented in the next chapter. Many of these statements set up the parameters of today's conflicts.

You might be interested in some of the articles in other chapters, also. These include Victor Navasky's "Minority Voices: The Role of the Critical Journal" (page 122), George F. Will's "America's Slide into the Sewer" (page 218), Ben Bagdikian's "The Calculus of Democracy" (page 341), and Irving Kristol's "Pornography, Obscenity and the Case for Censorship" (page 442).

On Government Restrictions of the First Amendment

Curry, Richard O., ed., *Freedom at Risk: Secrecy, Censorship, and Repression in the 1980s* (Philadelphia: Temple University Press, 1988).

Demac, Donna A., *Liberty Denied: The Current Rise of Censorship in America*, Revised Edition (New Brunswick, N.J.: Rutgers University Press, 1990).

Demac, Donna A., "The Future of Free Expression in America," *Editor and Publisher*, July 2, 1988, p. 56 (2).

"Flag Burning Amendment," *Editorials on File*, June 1–15, 1990. (This collection of recent editorials can be found in most library reference rooms. The newspapers around the country were predictably upset about this proposed amendment.)

Lewis, Anthony, "Staving Off the Silencers," *New York Times Magazine*, December 1, 1991, p. 72 (4). The ups and downs of the First Amendment over the years.

Pell, Eve, *The Big Chill: How the Reagan Administration, Corporate America, and Religious Conservatives are Subverting Free Speech and the Public's Right to Know* (Boston: Beacon Press, 1984).

Traub, James, *Freedom of Speech: Where to Draw the Line* (Dubuque, Iowa: Kendall/Hunt, 1987). An even-handed discussion of First Amendment limits, prepared by the Public Agenda Foundation for a series of pamphlets they call the National Issues Forums.

Zinn, Howard, "Second Thoughts on the First Amendment," *The Humanist*, November/December 1991, p. 15 (7). Reviews the history of government infringement on free speech and free press.

On Threats to the First Amendment from the Public, and from the Media Itself

Cuomo, Mario, "Preserving Freedom of the Press," *USA Today*, January 1988, p. 32 (4).

Garneau, George "Press Freedom in Deep Trouble," *Editor and Publisher*, April 20, 1991, p. 11 (2). Survey finds support for free speech protections so weak that the First Amendment would fail a ratification vote if taken today.

Garneau, George, "Some Editors Say Press Should Not Be So Free," *Editor and Publisher*, May 4, 1991, p. 17 (2). A survey taken among members of the American Society of Newspaper Editors shows editors disagree on how much legal protection the media should have.

On the History of the First Amendment

Ingelhart, Louis Edward. *Press Freedoms: A Descriptive Calendar of Concepts, Interpretation, Events, and Court Actions, from 4000 B.C. to the Present*. Reviewed by Richard F. Hixson, *Journal of American History*, March 1990, p. 1353 (2).

Leahy, James E., *The First Amendment, 1791–1991: Two Hundred Years of Freedom* (Jefferson, N.C.: McFarland & Co., 1991).

Levy, Leonard Williams. *Emergence of a Free Press* (New York: Oxford University Press, 1985).

Shumate, T. Daniel, ed., *The First Amendment: The Legacy of George Mason* (Fairfax: George Mason University Press, 1985).

Wagman, Robert J., *The First Amendment Book: Celebrating 200 Years of Freedom of the Press and Freedom of Speech.* Reviewed by Hiley Ward, *Editor and Publisher,* June 22, 1991, p. 28 (1).

On First Amendment Law

Carter, T. Barton, Marc A. Franklin and Jay B. Wright, *The First Amendment and the Fifth Estate: Regulation of the Electronic Mass Media,* 2nd ed. Reviewed by Robert Bellamy, *Journal of Broadcasting and Electronic Media,* Fall, 1989, p. 464 (3).

Carter, T. Barton, Marc A. Franklin and Jay B. Wright, *The First Amendment and the Fourth Estate: the Law of Mass Media,* 4th ed. Reviewed in *Journal of Broadcasting and Electronic Media,* Fall, 1988, p. 502 (1).

Moretti, Daniel S., *Obscenity and Pornography: the Law Under the First Amendment and State Constitutions* (New York: Oceana Publications, 1984).

Powe, Lucas A., *American Broadcasting and the First Amendment* (Berkeley: University of California Press, 1987).

Historical Statements

2

The founders of American democracy were geniuses. Through some great accident of history, this group of brilliant minds, skilled in the art of persuasion and cognizant of the timeless nature of human motivation, existed at the same moment in history and somehow had the same great objective. The importance of the U.S. Constitution, and especially the Bill of Rights, has to be regrasped by every new generation of Americans. It is part of the wizardry of this document that it thrives in spite of the fact that the great majority of the people who live under it do not have the wisdom to appreciate it for what it is.

The following documents are a sampling of some of the historical statements that can be found that help explain the philosophical underpinnings of the First Amendment, as well as its growth and influence over the years. John Milton's *Areopagitica* helps explain how the Puritan backgrounds of the founders lead them to think in terms of the benefits of free speech; Benjamin Franklin's *Apology for Printers* show how their wisdom was tempered by personal experience; Thomas Jefferson's statement on press censorship shows how his ideas about free speech reflected political pragmatism; statements by the great editors Horace Greeley and Joseph Pulitzer show how gatekeepers who learned their trade within the tradition of free speech came to see newsgathering as a noble calling; Theodore Roosevelt's statement on "muckraking" is symptomatic of the dilemma free speech has always created for our presidents, and Edward R. Murrow's eloquent conclusion to his program on Senator Joseph McCarthy shows that the potential nobility of newsgatherers did not die with the beginnings of electronic journalism.

Areopagitica

John Milton

John Milton (1608–1674), author of Paradise Lost, *was one of the greatest English Poets. Although best remembered for his poetry, he also wrote essays and pamphlets on the subject of politics and religion. He was a Puritan, which in his time was a political party as well as a religion. (The Puritans overthrew the King of England in 1649 and had him beheaded.)*

When Milton was 34 he married a 16 year-old girl who left him almost immediately. He wrote a series of pamphlets in favor of divorce and was criticized by the Puritan government for doing so. In response, he wrote Areopagitica, *a defense of freedom of the press, in 1644.*

Although Milton was in favor of a free press only for a certain class of citizen—educated Puritan men writing in Latin—the basic idea of Areopagitica *is still cited by legal experts today. Puritans believed that people were placed on earth to choose between good and evil. Those who chose goodness went to heaven, those who chose evil didn't. In* Areopagitica, *Milton related truth and falsehood to good and evil. Basically, he argued that the true believer couldn't be "tested" unless both truth and falsehood were allowed to be printed, so the believer could choose between the two.*

It is interesting to note that many of the framers of the U.S. Constitution were, or were descended from, Puritans. Their Puritan backgrounds are believed to have influenced their creation of a democracy with free speech.

Reading Difficulty Level: 10. After all, the man was writing in allegory three and a half centuries ago. A good dictionary might help, and maybe an encyclopedia if you don't know who Isis and Osiris were. Still, this is one of those historical documents that you should at least be able to say you read while you were in college.

. . . Truth indeed came once into the world with her divine master, and was a perfect shape most glorious to look on: but when he ascended, and his apostles after him were laid asleep, then straight arose a wicked race of deceivers, who . . . took the virgin Truth, hewed her lovely form into a thousand pieces, and scattered them to the four winds. From that time ever since, the sad friends of Truth, such as dare appear, imitating the careful search that Isis made for the mangled body of Osiris, went up and down gathering up limb by limb still as they could find them. We have not yet

---

By John Milton, 1644, in Henry Morley, ed., *English Prose Writings of John Milton* (London: George Routledge and Sons, 1889).

found them all, Lords and Commons, nor ever shall do, till her Master's second coming; he shall bring together every joint and member, and shall mold them into an immortal feature of loveliness and perfection. Suffer not these licensing prohibitions to stand at every place of opportunity forbidding and disturbing them that continue seeking, that continue to do our obsequies to the torn body of our martyred saint. . . .

. . . Give me the libery to know, to utter, and to argue freely according to conscience, above all liberties. . . .

And though all the winds of doctrine were let loose to play upon the earth, so truth be in the field, we do injuriously by licensing and prohibiting to misdoubt her strength. Let her and falsehood grapple; who ever knew truth put to the worse, in a free and open encounter? ♦

Let truth and falsehood grapple; who ever knew truth put to the worse, in a free and open encounter?

An Apology for Printers

Benjamin Franklin

Benjamin Franklin (1706–1790) was a statesman (he was one of the founders of American democracy), a scientist (he proved that lightning was electricity), an inventer (he invented an efficient heating stove, the lightning rod and bifocal glasses), and publisher (we still quote sayings from his Poor Richard's Almanac*). His first profession, however, was that of printer. He founded his own 569print shop at the age of 24, and the following year established* The Pennsylvania Gazette, *which became one of the most successful newspapers of its time. Early in the paper's history, however, a controversy erupted when Franklin published an ad for an ocean voyage that warned, "No sea hens or black gowns will be admitted. . . ." The expression "black gowns" was taken as a slur on the clergy. Franklin wrote "An Apology for Printers" in response to the criticism he received for running the ad.*

Reading Difficulty Level: 9. The grammar is different from what we're used to, and it's difficult to figure out his rules for capitalization. But you can't help but realize that this was written by a brilliant mind, and one with a sense of humor.

The opinions of men are almost as various as their faces. If all printers were determin'd not to print anything till they were sure it would offend no body, there would be very little printed.

Being frequently censur'd and condemn'd by different Persons for printing things they say ought not to be printed, I have sometimes thought it might be necessary to make a standing Apology for my self, and publish it once a Year, to be read upon all Occasions of that Nature. Much Business has hitherto hindered the execution of this Design; but having very lately given extraordinary Offence by printing an Advertisement with a certain N.B. at the End of it, I find an Apology more particularly requisite at this Juncture, tho' it happens when I have not yet Leisure to write such a Thing in the proper Form, and can only in a loose manner throw those Considerations together which should have been the Substance of it.

I request all who are angry with me on the Account of printing things they don't like, calmly to consider these following Particulars.

1. That the Opinions of Men are almost as various as their Faces; an Observation general enough to become a common Proverb, *So many Men so many Minds.*
2. That the Business of Printing has chiefly to do with Mens Opinions; most things that are printed tending to promote some, or oppose others.
3. That hence arises the peculiar Unhappiness of that Business, which other Callings are no way liable to; they who follow Printing being scarce able to do any thing in their way of getting a Living, which shall not probably give Offence to some, and perhaps to many; whereas the Smith, the Shoemaker, the Carpenter, or the Man of any other Trade, may work indifferently for People of all Persuasions, without offending any of them: and the Merchant may buy and sell with Jews, Turks, Hereticks and Infidels of all sorts, and get Money by every one of them, without giving Offense to the most orthodox, of any sort; or suffering the least Censure or Ill will on the Account from any Man whatever.
4. That it is unreasonable in any one Man or Set of Men to expect to be pleas'd with every thing that is printed, as to think that nobody ought to be pleas'd but themselves.
5. Printers are educated in the Belief, that when Men differ in Opinion, both Sides ought equally to have the Advantage of being heard by the Publick; and that when Truth and Error have fair Play, the former is always an overmatch for the latter: Hence they chearfully serve all contending Writers that pay them well, without regarding on which side they are of the Question in Dispute.

From *Voices of the Past: Key Documents in the History of American Journalism,* Calder M. Pickett (Ed.) Columbus, Ohio: Grid, Inc., 1977. Originally published in the *Pennsylvania Gazette,* June 10, 1731.

6. Being thus continually employ'd in serving both Parties, Printers naturally acquire a vast Unconcernedness as to the right or wrong Opinions contain'd in what they print; regarding it only as the Matter of their daily labour: They print things full of Spleen and Animosity, with the utmost Calmness and Indifference, and without the least Ill-will to the Persons reflected on; who nevertheless unjustly think the Printer as much their Enemy as the Author, and join both together in their Resentment.

7. That it is unreasonable to imagine Printers approve of every thing they print, and to censure them on any particular thing accordingly; since in the way of their Business they print such great variety of things opposite and contradictory. It is likewise as unreasonable what some assert, "That Printers ought not to print any Thing but what they approve," since if all of that Business should make such a Resolution, and abide by it, an End would thereby be put to Free Writing, and the World would afterwards have nothing to read but what happen'd to be the Opinions of Printers.

8. That if all Printers were determin'd not to print anything till they were sure it would offend no body, there would be very little printed.

9. That if they sometimes print vicious or silly things not worth reading, it may not be because they approve such things themselves, but because the People are so viciously and corruptly educated that good things are not encouraged. I have known a very numerous Impression of Robin Hood's Songs go off in this Province at 2s. per Book, in less than a Twelve-month; when a small Quantity of David's Psalms (an excellent Version) have lain upon my Hands above twice the time.

If they sometimes print vicious or silly things not worth reading, it may not be because they approve such things themselves.

10. That notwithstanding what might be urg'd in behalf of a Man's being allow'd to do in the Way of his Business whatever he is paid for, Yet Printers do continuously discourage the Printing of great Numbers of bad things, and stifle them in the Birth. I my self have constantly refused to print any thing that might countenance Vice, or promote Immorality; tho' by complying such Cases, with the corrupt Taste of the Majority, I might have got much Money. I have also always refus'd to print such things as might do real Injury to any Person, how much soever I have been solicited and tempted with Offers of Great Pay; and how much soever I have by refusing got the Ill-will of those who would have employ'd me. I have

hitherto fallen under the Resentment of large Bodies of Men, for refusing absolutely to print any of their Party or Personal Reflections. In this Manner I have made my self many Enemies, and the constant Fatigue of denying is almost insupportable. But the Publick being unacquainted with all this, whenever the poor Printer happens either through Ignorance or much Persuasion, to do any thing that is generally thought worthy of Blame, he meets with no more Friendship or Favour on the above Account, than if there were no Merit in't at all. Thus, as Waller says,

Poets lose half the Praise they would have got Were it but known what they discreetly blot.

Poets lose half the Praise they would have got Were it but known what they discreetly blot; Yet are censur'd for every bad Line found in their Works with the utmost Severity.

I come now to the Particular Case of the N.B. above mention'd, about which there has been more Clamour against me, than ever before on any other Account.—In the Hurry of other Business an Advertisement was brought to me to be printed; it signified that such a Ship lying at such a Wharff, would sail for Barbadoes in such a Time, and that Freighters and Passengers might agree with the Captain at such a Place; so far is what's common: But at the Bottom this odd Thing was added, "N.B. No Sea Hens or Black Gowns will be admitted on any Terms." I printed it, and receiv'd my Money; and the Advertisement was stuck up round the Town as usual. I had not so much Curiosity at that time as to enquire the Meaning of it, nor did I in the least imagine it would give so much Offence. Several good Men are very angry with me on this Occasion; they are pleas'd to say I have too much Sense to do such things ignorantly; that if they were Printers they would not have done such a thing on any Consideration; that it could proceed from nothing but my abundant Malice against Religion and the Clergy. They therefore declare they will not take any more of my Papers, nor have any farther Dealings with me; but will hinder me of all the Custom they can. All this is very hard!

I believe it had been better if I had refused to print the said Advertisement. However, 'tis done, and cannot be revok'd. I have only the following few Particulars to offer, some of them in my behalf, by way of Mitigation, and some not much to the Purpose; but I desire none of them may be read when the Reader is not in a very good Humour.

1. That I really did it without the least Malice, and imagin'd the N.B. was plac'd there only to make the Advertisement star'd at, and more generally read.
2. That I never saw the Word Sea-Hens before in my Life; nor have I yet ask'd the meaning of it; and tho' I had certainly known that Black Gowns in that place signified the Clergy of the

Church of England, yet I have that confidence in the generous good Temper of such of them as I know, as to be well satisfied such a trifling mention of their Habit gives them no Disturbance.

3. That most of the Clergy in this and the neighbouring Provinces, are my Customers, and some of them my very good Friends; and I must be very malicious indeed, or very stupid, to print this thing for a small Profit, if I had thought it would have given them just Cause of Offence.
4. That if I had much Malice against the Clergy, and withal much Sense; 'tis strange I never write or talk against the Clergy myself. Some have observed that 'tis a fruitful Topic, and the easiest to be witty upon of all others; yet I appeal to the Publick that I am never guilty this way, and to all my Acquaintances as to my Conversation.
5. That if a Man of Sense had Malice enough to desire to injure the Clergy, this is the foolishest Thing he could possibly contrive for that Purpose.
6. That I got Five Shillings by it.
7. That none who are angry with me would have given me so much to let it alone.
8. That if all the People of different Opinions in this Province would engage to give me as much for not printing things they don't like, as I can get by printing them, I should probably live a very easy Life; and if all Printers were everywhere so dealt by, there would be very little printed.
9. That I am oblig'd to all who take my Paper, and am willing to think they do it out of meer Friendship. I only desire they would think the same when I deal with them. I thank those who leave off, that they have taken it so long. But I beg they would not endeavor to dissuade others, for that will look like Malice.
10. That 'tis impossible any Man should know what he would do if he was a Printer.
11. That notwithstanding the Rashness and Inexperience of Youth, which is most likely to be prevail'd with to do things that ought not to be done; yet I have avoided printing such Things as usually give Offence either to Church or State, more than any Printer that has followed the Business in this Province before.
12. And lastely, that I have printed above a Thousand Advertisements which made not the least mention of *Sea-Hens* or *Black Gowns;* and this being the first Offence, I have the more Reason to expect Foregiveness.

I take leave to conclude with an old Fable, which some of my Readers have heard before, and some have not.

I got Five Shillings by it. None who are angry with me would have given me so much to let it alone.

I consider the Variety of Humors among Men, and despair of pleasing every Body; yet I shall not therefore leave off Printing.

A certain well-meaning Man and his Son, were travelling towards a Market Town, with an Ass which they had to sell. The Road was bad; and the old Man therefore rid, but the Son went a-foot. The first Passenger they met, asked the Father if he was not ashamed to ride by himself, and suffer the poor Lad to wade along thro' the Mire; This induced him to take up his Son behind him: He had not travelled far, when he met others, who said, they are two unmerciful Lubbers to get both on the Back of that poor Ass, in such a deep Road. Upon this the old Man gets off, and let his Son ride alone. The next they met called the Lad a graceless, rascally young Jackanapes, to ride in that Manner thro' the Dirt, while his aged Father trudged along on Foot; and they said the old Man was a Fool, for suffering it. He then bid his Son come down, and walk with him, and they travell'd on leading the Ass by the Halter; 'till they met another Company, who called them a Couple of senseless Blockheads, for going both on Foot in such a dirty way, when they had an empty Ass with them, which they might ride upon. The old Man could bear no longer; My Son, said he, it grieves me much that we cannot please all these People. Let me throw the Ass over the next bridge, and be no further troubled with him.

Had the old Man been seen acting this last Resolution, he would probably have been called a Fool for troubling himself about the different Opinions of all that were pleas'd to find Fault with him: Therefore, tho' I have a Temper almost as complying as his, I intend not to imitate him in this last Particular. I consider the Variety of Humors among Men, and despair of pleasing every Body; yet I shall not therefore leave off Printing. I shall continue my Business. I shall not burn my Press and melt my Letters. ♦

On Press Censorship

Thomas Jefferson

Thomas Jefferson (1743–1846) was, like Franklin, a Renaissance man and a brilliant statesman. His inventions ranged from the dumb waiter to our decimal system of coinage. He was the foremost American architect of his day. He authored the Declaration of Independence and was largely responsible for the Bill of Rights. Without the genius of men like Jefferson and Franklin, it is doubtful that other legislators of the day could have been convinced of the importance of free speech and free press to a true democracy. The following statement was contained in a letter Jefferson wrote to a friend who had complained that a free press might be more trouble than it was worth.

Reading Difficulty Level: 7. We still have the different grammar, but it's just a short nugget.

. . . The people are the only censors of their governors; and even their errors will tend to keep these to the true principles of their institution. To punish these errors too severely would be to suppress the only safeguard of the public liberty. The way to prevent these irregular interpositions of the people is to give them full information of their affairs thro' the channel of the public papers, & to contrive that those papers should penetrate the whole mass of the people. The basis of our governments being the opinion of the people, the first object should be to keep that right; and were it left to me to decide whether we should have a government without newspapers or newspapers without a government, I should not hesitate to prefer the latter. But I should mean that every man should receive those papers & be capable of reading them. I am convinced that those societies (as the Indians) which live without government enjoy in their general mass an infinitely greater degree of happiness than those who live under the European governments. Among the former, public opinion is in the place of law, & restrains morals as powerfully as laws ever did anywhere. Among the latter, under pretence of governing they have divided their nations into two classes, wolves & sheep. I do not exaggerate. This is a true picture of Europe. Cherish therefore the spirit of our people, and keep alive their attention. Do not be too severe upon their errors, but reclaim them by enlightening them. ♦

Were it left to me to decide whether we should have a government without newspapers or newspapers without a government, I should not hesitate to prefer the latter.

Letter to Edward Carrington, Paris, January 16, 1787, in Adrienne Koch and William Peden, eds., *The Life and Standard Writings of Thomas Jefferson* (New York: Modern Library, 1944), pp. 411–12.

On "Satanic" Newspapers

Horace Greeley

Greeley was one of the great publishers of the popular press. He founded the New York Tribune *in 1841, and he used that paper and his other publications to crusade against slavery, alcohol, and everything else that he considered "satanic"—including his competition.*

Greeley is most remembered for his advice to New York unemployed, "Go west, young man." The following editorial, however, better captures the spirit of the man.

Reading Difficulty Level: 2. No problem—two paragraphs, written in the vocabulary of the penny press.

***THE SATANIC PRESS* has one sole aspiration—to achieve notoriety and coin gold by pandering to whatever is vile and bestial in a corrupted and sensual populace.**

The age we live in is remarkable for its multiplication and enlargement of all the agencies alike of good and evil. Life is more intense, more active, more eventful with us than it was with our grandfathers, and he who lives to see sixty years has really lived longer than the man who lived to eighty a century ago. Steamships, Railroads, Electric Telegraphs, Power-Presses, render communication so rapid that ideas circulate from mind to mind like the lightning, and are received in all the vivid energy of their fresh conception. . . . The moral world shares the new momentum of the intellectual and the physical, and transcendent virtues and revolting crimes are alike less rare than formerly. Philanthropy, Charity, Religion impel their votaries to unvented exertion; so do Lechery, Selfishness and Impiety. And foremost among the instrumentalities of these last stands THE SATANIC PRESS. . . .

[It] had its foreshadowings among the darkest days of atheistic butchery and terror in Revolutionary France. . . . [It is the] perverted product of a diseased Civilization wherein debauched and prurient appetites gloat upon the unripe and poisonous fruit of the Tree of Knowledge. . . . It has one sole aspiration—to achieve notoriety and coin gold for its director by pandering to whatever is vile and bestial in a corrupted and sensual populace. ♦

From *Voices of the Past: Key Documents in the History of American Journalism,* Calder M. Pickett (Ed.) Columbus, Ohio: Grid, Inc., 1977. Originally published in *The New York Tribune,* New York, February 17, 1849

The Platform of the Post-Dispatch

Joseph Pulitzer

Joseph Pulitzer (now pronounced PYOO-lit-sir, although he pronounced it POOL-it-sir) (1847–1911), was also one of the great and influential American publishers. He was a poor, uneducated Hungarian immigrant who went on to publish two of the great newspapers of his day, the St. Louis Post-Dispatch *and the* New York World. *His competition with William Randolf Hearst's* New York Journal *ushered in the age of sensationalism (and color comics) that gave rise to the term "Yellow Journalism," but Pulitzer was always the crusader. He established the graduate school of journalism at Columbia University, as well as the Pulitzer prizes for achievements in journalism, literature, music and art.*

Always in poor health, Pulitzer was legally blind from 1887, but he continued to direct his papers from aboard his yacht for 24 years. He finally retired in 1907, and this was his last published editorial.

Reading Difficulty Level: 2. Piece of cake, although you should be advised that "plutocracy" does not mean "rule by a Disney character."

I know that my retirement [from the *Post-Dispatch*] will make no difference in its cardinal principles, that it will always fight for progress and reform, never tolerate injustice or corruption, always fight demagogues of all parties, never belong to any party, always oppose privileged classes and public plunderers, never lack sympathy with the poor, always remain devoted to the public welfare, never be satisfied with merely printing news, always be drastically independent, never be afraid to attack wrong, whether by predatory plutocracy or predatory poverty. ♦

The* Post-Dispatch *will always fight for progress and reform.

This originally appeared on April 10, 1907. From *The Story of the St. Louis Post-Dispatch* (St. Louis: Post-Dispatch booklet, 1968, 9th ed.).

Clear and Present Danger

Justice Oliver Wendell Holmes

First Amendment purists cite the following statement by Justice Oliver Wendell Holmes to support the idea that speech should be free unless it represents a "clear and present danger." Many forget that this opinion, which Holmes wrote for the unanimous Supreme court, sent defendant Charles Schenck to jail for publishing an anti-draft flyer during World War I. Schenck's flyer expressed opinions that are mild by today's standards, but in the view of the court they created a great enough danger in 1919 to fall outside of the protection of the First Amendment.

Reading Difficulty Level: 6. Not one of Holmes's best pieces stylistically, but an important milestone in First Amendment law.

From Schenck v. U.S., 249 U.S. 47 (1919)

Holmes, J., for the Court

The document in question said that a conscript is little better than a convict.

The most stringent protection of free speech would not protect a man in falsely shouting fire in a theater and causing a panic.

This is an indictment in three counts.[1] The first charges a conspiracy to violate the Espionage Act . . . by causing and attempting to cause insubordination, etc., in the military and naval forces of the United States, and to obstruct the recruiting and enlistment service of the United States, when the United States was at war with the German Empire. . . .

The document in question recited the first section of the Thirteenth Amendment,[2] said that the idea embodied in it was violated by the Conscription Act and that a conscript is little better than a convict. In impassioned language it intimated that conscription was despotism in its worst form and a monstrous wrong against humanity in the interest of Wall Street's chosen few. . . . It described the arguments on the other side as coming from cunning politicians and a mercenary capitalist press, and even silent assent to the conscription law as helping to support an infamous conspiracy. It denied the power to send our citizens away to foreign shores to shoot up the people of other lands, and added that words would not express the condemnation such cold-blooded ruthlessness deserves, etc., etc., winding up, "You must do your share to maintain, support and uphold the rights of the people of this country." Of course the document would not have been sent unless it had been intended to have some effect, and we do not see what effect it could be expected to have upon persons subject to the draft except to influence them to obstruct the carrying of it out. The defendants do not deny that the jury might find against them on this point.

But it is said, suppose that that was the tendency of this circular, it is protected by the First Amendment to the Constitution. . . . We admit that in many places and in ordinary times the defendants in saying all that was said in the circular would have been within their constitutional rights. But the character of every act depends upon the circumstances in which it is done. The most stringent protection of free speech would not protect a man in falsely shouting fire in a theater and causing a panic. It does not even protect a man from an injunction against uttering words that may have all the effect of force. . . . The question in every case is whether the words used are used in such circumstances and are of such a nature as

---

1. Essentially the first count was for writing the flyer. The other two counts were for using the mails to distribute it.

2. The Thirteenth Amendment, which was adopted in 1865, read: "Neither slavery nor involuntary servitude, except as a punishment for crime whereof the party shall have been duly convicted, shall exist within the United States, or any place subject to their jurisdiction."

to create a clear and present danger that they will bring about the substantive evils that Congress has a right to prevent. It is a question of proximity and degree. When a nation is at war many things that might be said in time of peace are such a hindrance to its effort that their utterance will not be endured so long as men fight. . . . ♦

Muckraking

Theodore Roosevelt

Theodore Roosevelt (1858–1919) was a great reformer who, as president, fought big business "trusts" and defended labor unions. He generally enjoyed investigative journalism. In fact, in 1906, after reading Upton Sinclair's novel The Jungle, *which described unsanitary conditions and the mistreatment of labor in the meat-packing industry, Roosevelt started a government investigation of the industry that eventually lead to reform. That same year, however, some other investigative journalists hit a little too close to home in investigating Roosevelt himself. He termed these journalists "muckrakers" in the following speech.*

Reading Difficulty Level: 3. Roosevelt liked to say what he had to say pretty directly, and get on with his next manly activity.

Over a century ago Washington laid the cornerstone of the Capitol in what was then little more than a tract of wooded wilderness here beside the Potomac. We now find it necessary to provide by great additional buildings for the business of the government. This growth in the need for the housing of the government is but a proof and example of the way in which the nation has grown and the sphere of action of the national government has grown. We now administer the affairs of a nation in which the extraordinary growth of population has been outstripped by the growth of wealth and the growth in complex interests. The material problems that face us today are not such as they were in Washington's time, but the underlying facts of human nature are the same now as they were then. Under altered external form we war with the same tendencies toward evil that were evident in Washington's time, and are helped by the same tendencies for good. It is about some of these that I wish to say a word today.

From *Voices of the Past: Key Documents in the History of American Journalism,* Calder M. Pickett (Ed.) Columbus, Ohio: Grid, Inc., 1977. Speech originally given in Washington D.C., April 14, 1906.

The Man with the Muckrake fixes his eyes only on that which is vile and debasing.

In Bunyan's *Pilgrim's Progress* you may recall the description of the Man with the Muckrake, the man who could look no way but downward, with a muckrake in his hands; who was offered a celestial crown for his muckrake, but who would neither look up nor regard the crown he was offered, but continued to rake to himself the filth of the floor.

In *Pilgrim's Progress* the Man with the Muckrake is set forth as the example of him whose vision is fixed on carnal instead of on spiritual things. Yet he also typifies the man who in this life consistently refused to see aught that is lofty, and fixes his eyes with solemn intentness only on that which is vile and debasing. Now, it is very necessary that we should not flinch from seeing what is vile and debasing. There is filth on the floor, and it must be scraped up with the muckrake; and there are times and places where this service is the most needed of all the services that can be performed. But the man who never does anything else, who never thinks or speaks or writes save of his feats with the muckrake, speedily becomes, not a help to society, not an incitement to good, but one of the most potent forces of evil. . . .

I hail as a benefactor every writer or speaker, every man who, on the platform or in book, magazine or newspaper, with merciless severity makes such attack, provided always that he in his turn remembers that the attack is of use only if it is absolutely truthful. . . .

♦

See It Now—A Look at Joseph McCarthy

Edward R. Murrow

Edward R. Murrow of CBS was the most respected broadcast journalist of his day. His live broadcasts from London during air attacks are legendary. He brought respectable journalism to television with the advent of his program "See It Now."

The early-to-middle 1950s were a dark period for American politics. At center stage was a senator from Wisconsin, Joseph McCarthy, whose strategy for political fame was to make false, hypocritical charges about Communists taking over federal agencies. Anyone who disagreed with McCarthy was in turn accused of being a Communist or a Communist sympathizer, and many people lost their jobs—in fact, were blacklisted from their professions—on the basis of unfounded accusations. Edward R. Murrow was one of the few people to stand up to McCarthy. He did so by devoting an entire episode of his program to McCarthy's speeches and cross-examinations before his congressional committee. Murrow did not interrupt or comment upon the footage of McCarthy—he simply allowed the senator's actions to speak for himself. At the end of the hour, Murrow gave the following summation.

Reading Difficulty Level: 2. Murrow's prose was as clear and true as a crystal prism.

. . . No one familiar with the history of this country can deny that congressional committees are useful. It is necessary to investigate before legislating. But the line between investigation and persecuting is a very fine one, and the junior senator from Wisconsin has stepped over it repeatedly. His primary achievement has been in confusing the public mind as between the internal and the external threat of Communism. We must not confuse dissent with disloyalty. We must remember always that accusation is not proof and that conviction depends upon evidence and due process of law. We will not walk in fear, one of another. We will not be driven by fear into an age of unreason if we dig deep in our history and our doctrine and remember that we are not descended from fearful men, not from men who feared to write, to speak, to associate and to defend causes which were for the moment unpopular.

This is no time for men who oppose Senator McCarthy's methods to keep silent, or for those who approve. We can deny our heritage and our history, but we cannot escape responsibility for the result. As a nation we have come into our full inheritance at a tender age. We proclaim ourselves, as indeed we are, the defenders of freedom—what's left of it—but we cannot defend freedom abroad by deserting it at home. The actions of the junior senator from Wisconsin have caused alarm and dismay amongst our allies abroad and given considerable comfort to our enemies. And whose fault is that? Not really his; he didn't create this situation of fear, he merely exploited it and rather successfully. Cassius was right. "The fault, dear Brutus, is not in our stars but in ourselves." ♦

We must not confuse dissent with disloyalty.

Cassius was right. "The fault, dear Brutus, is not in our stars but in ourselves."

From Edward W. Bliss, Jr., *In Search of Light: The Broadcasts of Edward R. Murrow 1938–1961* (New York: Knopf, 1967), pp. 247–248. Originally broadcasted from New York, March 9, 1954.

Questions for Discussion

1. In your opinion, which of the historical statements best represents the spirit of the First Amendment as it is perceived in the U.S. today?
2. From your own study of history, what other figures or statements might be included in a list of importance to the First Amendment?

Suggested Readings

Altschull, J. Herbert, *From Milton to McLuhan: The Ideas Behind American Journalism* (Longman, 1990). Reviewed in *Columbia Journalism Review*, September/October 1990, p. 55 (3). This is an historical look that concerns itself with "what journalism should do and how it should be practiced."

Levy, Leonard Williams, *Emergence of a Free Press* (New York: Oxford University Press, 1985).

Pratte, Alf, "Recalling Ben Franklin's Contributions to Modern Journalism," *Editor and Publisher*, April 28, 1990, p. 76 (2).

Smith, Jeffery Alan, *Printers and Press Freedom: The Ideology of Early American Journalism* (New York: Oxford University Press, 1988).

Values and Culture

3

"Values" are ideas that people find to be personally important, and that guide their behavior in some way. A Gallup Poll conducted in the 1980s found that "having a good family life" was the most important social value in the United States. After that came "good physical health," "having a good self-image or self-respect," "personal satisfaction or happiness," and "freedom of choice to do what I want."[1]

A group of philosophers, historians, and other observers of the American character came up with these five values Americans seem to traditionally share:[2]

1. Citizenship: Americans believe, at least theoretically, that informed participation in government is the key to democracy. The power of this value is revealed in everything from our willingness to vote or serve on juries to our insistence on full disclosure about political scandals.
2. Work ethic: For Americans, work isn't just a way to make money, it's a virtue—something we believe makes us better people.
3. Tolerance: The acceptance of a wide variety of views and traditions is America's oldest value. It is the reason the Pilgrims arrived on the *Mayflower* and the reason immigrants flock to our shores today.
4. Justice for All: Americans believe in the importance of a fair and effective legal system. We believe that the guilty should be punished and the innocent should go free.
5. Individualism: Americans believe people should be able to do what they want, to "be themselves," to fail or succeed through their own efforts.

1. Peter Kerr, "Rating the Things Americans Value," *The New York Times*, January 28, 1982, p. C3.
2. Leah Eskin, "Five American Values," Scholastic Update, Feb. 26, 1988, pp. 6 (4).

One researcher identified six different types of people based on their dominant values:[3]

Theoretical types: These are people who value the pursuit and discovery of truth, people who appreciate the intellectual life.

Economic types: These are people who value that which is useful and practical.

Aesthetic types: These people value form, harmony, and beauty.

Social types: These people value love, sympathy, warmth, and sensitivity in relationships with people.

Political types: These value competition, influence, and personal power.

Religious types: These value unity, wholeness, a sense of being part of something larger than worldly human concerns.

Values tend to be abstract and relatively few in number, which make them a valuable target for advertisers and any media that wants to gather audience numbers. The three articles in this chapter all examine possible media effects on American values.

These are think pieces. The study of mass media has traditionally included such pieces. There's not much here in the way of hard facts that you can take to the job-interview bank, but there's much to think about, such as the implications of cultural fantasy, the public's need to escape, and even, if you're feeling philosophical, the nature of reality.

What Are Our Real Values?

Nicols Fox

Americans have a problem with their cultural values, and the media have something to do with it.

For example, many Americans claim to have values that their behavior seems to deny. As Nicols Fox points out, our real values are shown in what we do, and much of what we do involves reading, watching and listening to various media.

Nicols Fox is a writer and editor who lives in Maine.

Reading Difficulty Level: 2.

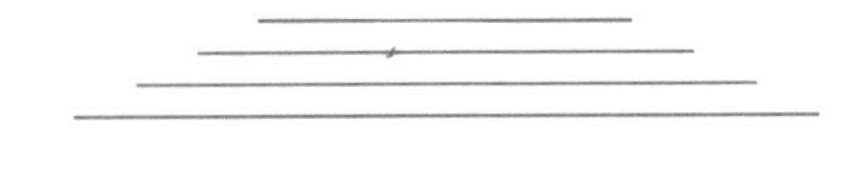

3. Michael W. Gamble and Teri Kwal Gamble, *Introducing Mass Communication,* 2nd Ed. (N.Y.: McGraw-Hill, 1989), p. 330.

The recent presidential election, according to the chorus of political pundits on both sides, was a referendum on American values. The candidate who most clearly represented our collective vision of ourself as a people, who promised most convincingly to nurture and protect that vision, was elected. But what are American values? They would appear to be the same fantasies we use to sell soft drinks, phone services and color film—and they have proved equally adaptable to selling presidents.

We value, so we like to think, families and fireplaces and front porches with swings; a picture-perfect landscape in which people sit down to eat together and worship together; a place where old folks live at home and young folks don't talk back. We value friendships. We value thrift. We value history and tradition, culture and continuity. We value childhood—a wonderful and mysterious period free from care and full of optimism. We value baseball games on hot summer nights and high-school reunions and holidays.

It is a healthy and a happy vision. But like most of the fantasies conjured up by the advertising world, it doesn't really exist. Not really—not in America in the 1990s. And maybe it never existed. What we have come to love is an image of ourselves created by artists like Winslow Homer and Norman Rockwell. And the nostalgia for this America is so strong that for those who have no genuine memory of it, we have created one. Through advertising, even the young can participate in the dream they cannot recall—a pretelevision era where lemonade came from lemons and pizza was an exotic dish, where Grandmother hadn't had a face-lift and Dad didn't have a girlfriend and 7-year-olds had no idea what a condom was. And the greater the gulf between reality and fantasy, the more we seem drawn to the dream.

Through advertising, even the young can participate in the dream they cannot recall.

The trouble is real American values are expressed not by what we say we wish for, but by what we really do. We love our families but we can't count many friends with intact ones anymore. We love our old people but not for more than an hour or two at a time. And they don't care much for us, either. They seem to prefer their child-free retirement communities to life in extended families. We are a people full of compassion but it extends more freely to three trapped whales than to the homeless huddled over heat grates on the streets of our richest cities. We love our children, but how many children come home to empty houses during the day? We believe in families, but how many families sit down to eat together anymore? Although more of us today say we believe in God, how many of us attend church regularly? We believe in fiscal responsibility but our own balance sheets look pretty much like the federal government's.

Real American values are expressed not by what we say we wish for, but by what we really do.

From *Newsweek*, February 13, 1989, p. 8. Reprinted by permission of the author.

Look at our heroes and what we watch on TV—that's what we value.

We complain about the invasion of drugs but our culture tells us that no discomfort can be tolerated and that every desire deserves to be satisfied.

What are the real American values?

Look who our heroes are. They aren't the people who volunteer in the soup kitchens; they aren't struggling writers and artists; they aren't the librarians or the nurses or the social workers. Mainly they are the rich and the famous and the successful and the beautiful, the film and sports stars, the Wall Street barons, even the articulate convicts who charm us on talk shows once they've done their time. Perhaps the best indicator of what we really are is what we spend our money on or what we watch on television. Look at what we read. Look at what we choose to do with our spare time. That's what we value.

We complain about the invasion of drugs but our culture tells us that no discomfort can be tolerated and that every desire deserves to be satisfied. We complain about crime but our system demonstrates that good guys finish last—that crime pays. We complain about the moral decadence of our young and the high incidence of teen pregnancies but our young have been carefully taught, by example, that responsibility is old-fashioned. We'd like to do something about pornography and violence but we buy it and we tolerate it and that makes our protests pretty empty.

The problem is, changing things is a problem. It's not a question of hoeing at the weeds on the surface of society, but of a real root job. Who makes the rules these days that determine how our society is going to work—the code of ethics behind the laws that determines our values and decides how we are going to live together in community?

Judgment Day

It isn't the churches. It's not so much that their moral leadership is being ignored as that, to a great extent, they've abdicated the role. Collectively they seem to exude the same relativism and insecurity about right and wrong as the rest of us. The fact is, we all have a pretty good idea of what is right and what is wrong, but deprived—as the 20th century is—of the ever-handy threat of Judgment Day, we just can't seem to find a good enough explanation for why we should do one thing and not do another. Simply saying "Because God says so" doesn't work very well anymore.

And so we are left yearning for the old order. And yearning seems all we're capable of. In spite of what President Bush says, we do seem to have lost our wills. What we'd really like is for someone else to do something about the homeless and the violence and the drugs and the sick and the old. And we'd like for it to be done without a tax increase because we don't want to pay for it. "I share your values," the new president said time and time again during the campaign, but I suspect what he was really saying was "I share your dreams, I share your nostalgia, I share your fantasies and your wishful thinking." But government in a free and democratic society, as Senate Majority Leader George Mitchell has said, is not the enemy of the people. It is ours to do with as we will, to shape and form with our collective resources in order to create a real American Dream—not a hazy, romantic vision from the past to which we pay read-my-lips service.

It's time that we started looking at ourselves as we really are because a healthy future will be based on reality, not on ad copy.

Questions for Discussion

1. If you were to list your five most important values, what would they be?
2. How do these values relate to your actions?
3. Is there a relationship between your values and the newspapers, books and magazines you read, the music you listen to, the films and television programs you watch?

Marketing Cynicism and Vulgarity

John Leo

John Leo, who writes for U.S. News and World Report, *is a cogent observer of media and values. In this piece he deals with the same issue that Nichols Fox spoke about, but Leo concentrates on the book publishing industry. We'll have more to say about the current state of this industry in Chapter Seven.*

Reading Difficulty Level: 2.

Christopher Hitchens wrote a wonderful column in the *Nation* about Ronald Reagan's alleged autobiography. Like most of us, Hitchens realizes that Reagan did not write the book, that in fact it was a marketing "concoction" rather than a genuine memoir. Under these circumstances, Hitchens writes, the editors, publishers and agent involved are "accomplices to a fraud" who "should make a public apology and give all the money to a charity other than themselves." This outcome is improbable, but fitting. If the rock group Milli Vanilli is being disgraced and stripped of its Grammy

The writers of Ronald Reagan's alleged autobiography are "accomplices to a fraud."

From *U.S. News and World Report*, December 3, 1990, p. 23, reprinted by permission.

Award because it did not actually sing the vocals on the record that won the award, it seems logical that a good-sized cloud of public disgrace should descend upon Simon & Schuster for publishing such a deception.

Hitchens's column is particularly striking because criticism from the left about the morality or social impact of any form of cultural expression is rare, and berating a publishing house for accepting a book is unheard of. As it happens, there is another current case, also involving Simon & Schuster, in which arguments for not publishing a book are even stronger. The book is *American Psycho*, by Bret Easton Ellis, 26-year-old post-yuppie novelist. It is the most gruesomly violent book on the horizon, and it is likely to remain so for at least one more publishing season, or until some imitator notices that distinguished publishing houses are now offering big money for grisly, upscale slasher novels.

Pots of money can be made by brutalizing the culture.

Not a Book for Reading

This is not the sort of book you would want to leave around the house. Somebody might pick it up. In it, endless numbers of women are nailed to the floor, then carved up, drilled or cannibalized. We can imagine the diligent Ellis slogging through research for his *magnum opus:* "Say, Doc, what happens when you hook up a woman's breasts to a car battery? Do they burn first and then explode, or is it the other way around?" In one scene, a starving rat is inserted into a living woman and left to eat a path out through her flesh. The book is totally hateful—in effect, a how-to manual on the torture and dismemberment of women. Perhaps Sonny Mehta of Knopf, who bought the book for the Vintage paperback line when Simon & Schuster dropped it at the last moment, will want to speed sales along by offering a free nail gun or chain saw with every carton of books purchased.

Why is Knopf dealing in violent junk? Because pots of money can be made by brutalizing the culture. All you have to do is push the envelope too far, thus provoking a response that will drive your feeble effort onto the best-seller lists. This is a profoundly cynical process that taints everyone involved. Knopf is an even more prestigious house than Simon & Schuster, and Mehta is a man of great learning and taste. I daresay he knows very well that this book has little literary merit. In my judgment, it has no discernible plot, no believable characterization, no sensibility at work that comes anywhere close to making art out of all the blood and torture. The book is so bad it will probably disappoint even sadists. Ellis displays little feel for narration, words, grammar or the rhythm of language. Given his early success, it is difficult to explain his desperate lurch toward splatter other than as a marketing tool.

Charges of censorship have been raised by the author and others, but this is a diversion and a bogus issue. There is no censorship issue here because no governmental body is involved telling us what to see or read. No one has a constitutional right to have his splatter fantasies published. Thousands of grotesquely violent novels are rejected by publishers every year, and this one should have been among them.

Pop Brutality

The real issue is our increasingly degraded and brutal popular culture. The fact that our rape and murder rates are triple those of other Western nations has a lot to do with the violent images and fantasies flooding our culture. The connection between the amount of violent entertainment and the amount of real-life violence is no longer seriously doubted among social scientists. Many studies show, for instance, that children exposed frequently to violent TV programs show more anger and less inhibition than other children and that they grow up to be more violent adults, too.

Sexual violence against women, particularly, is being pumped into the culture at an astonishing rate. Many rock bands now sing about dismembering females. The same theme is a staple not only in horror movies but in mainstream movies, television and even once-sedate detective novels. One woman, judging a contest for best detective novels, complained about the "increasingly more graphic and furious material about the destruction of women" in private-eye novels and in the culture at large.

How can we get this dangerous junk out of the culture? Short of censorship, everything possible ought to be done, beginning with a serious national debate. Maybe it will eventually come down to boycotts. In the meantime, maybe we should recycle Nancy Reagan's slogan, "Just say no." The career of Andrew Dice Clay began to unravel the day that Nora Dunn and Sinead O'Connor stood up and refused to perform with him on "Saturday Night Live." That touched off a chain reaction of noes that included Jay Leno, David Letterman, MTV and more and more of the public. Nan Graham of Penguin Books said no on the Ellis book. So did many of the women at Simon & Schuster, some of the sales staff and George Corsillo, who was supposed to do artwork for the jacket but refused. Perhaps some people at Knopf and Vintage might like to be counted too. ♦

The fact that our rape and murder rates are triple those of other Western nations has a lot to do with the violent images and fantasies flooding our culture.

Violence against women, particularly, is being pumped into the culture at an astonishing rate.

Questions for Discussion

1. Rather than just analyzing the problem, John Leo suggests a solution. What is that solution? In your opinion, will it work?

Elvis Alive? The Ideology of American Consumerism

Peter Stromberg

There have been many reported sightings of Elvis Presley since his death.

Peter Stromberg points out that our interest in these sightings is not "random or bizarre." After reading this article, you might believe that he's at least half right.

Stromberg, who teaches at the University of Tulsa, explains what it means when we say, "Americans live in a fantasy world," and what many critics mean when they say that media use in America is a form of religion.

Reading Difficulty Level: 7. Which is about as good as you're going to get in an academic journal such as the one this came from.

A substantial proportion of the population is interested in the topic of Elvis' survival beyond the grave.

The spring and summer of 1988 witnessed an astounding upsurge in the popularity of a ten year old folk story, the story that Elvis Presley is alive. As witnessed by the frequency of newspaper and tabloid articles, books, and programs on radio and TV talk shows, a substantial proportion of the population is—whether or not they believe the rumors—terribly interested in the topic of Elvis' survival beyond the grave.

Elvis as Symbol

As with the perennial topics of the check-out line press—alien invasions, odd births, premature burials, etc.—the myth that Elvis Presley lives is not random or bizarre. There are reasons why this story has captured the interest of the public.[1] The reason Elvis lives has to do with what Elvis stands for, what sort of symbol he is in a popular ideology that is so much a part of American life that it has for the most part escaped systematic description. As a result, it turns out to be a rather revealing exercise in the study of con-

From the *Journal of Popular Culture*, Winter, 1990, pp. 11–19. Reprinted by permission.

[1]Whitehead (1974) argues that a society such as ours, with rigid and prestigious "modes of knowing" such as science, generates a need to believe in propositions that would expand the nature of reality beyond the rational. To use her term, members of our society seek elements of the "reasonably fantastic" that would indicate that the world out there really is not so predictable as we have been led to believe. And of course, students of popular culture such as Barthes (1977) have demonstrated again and again that popular beliefs are not random superstitions but rather constitute coherent systems of signs.

temporary American popular culture to analyze why Elvis lives beyond the grave.

In order to do this it will be necessary to describe, in outline at least, the popular ideology in which Elvis occupies such a prominent place. For the purposes of this essay, this ideology will be designated consumerism.

Consumerism

The central belief of consumerism is that the mundane existence that constitutes the day-to-day life of the believer is not the ultimate reality. Rather, there is a world beyond this one, a perfect world in which unfulfilled desire is unknown. It is to this second world that the believer is ultimately oriented, for it is believed that it is fully possible to enter the second world from the first one. The believer encounters evidence of the second world countless times in each day: it is present in advertisements, in movies, in television programs and in magazines. The accurate description of this second world is a project far beyond the scope of this paper, but it is a world close to this one, yet happier, more comprehensible, and more exciting.

How does one enter the second world? One attempts to enter it first of all through consumption. After all, it is not possible to avoid the message that is relentlessly drummed into the consciousness of every sentient American, the message that by consuming product X one will become like those happy and beautiful people depicted in the advertisement (Berger, 1972). The person in the advertisement is you, depicted as you *could* be.

Advertising must endlessly repeat the message because, of course, it is untrue. No matter what one buys, one's life stays pretty much the same. But the faith in the promise remains undimmed, in part because of the repeated assurances, in part because of the fervent wish that the message be true, in part because the believer is confronted with the evidence of actual persons who have, indisputably, entered the second world. These enviable and enormously important people, who will be discussed below, are celebrities like Elvis Presley.

The central belief of consumerism is that the mundane existence that constitutes the day-to-day life of the believer is not the ultimate reality.

Consumerism as Religion

All this should make it clear that consumerism is in fact more than a popular ideology. By some definitions consumerism may be accurately termed a religion. Starting with Emile Durkheim (1915), many sociologists have been reluctant to define religion as a set of beliefs about supernatural beings. After all, many traditions that are undoubtedly religions do not consist of beliefs about supernatural beings; Theravada Buddhism is an oft-cited example.[2] An alternative definition of religion is that it is the process of placing one's experience in a larger

---

[2]Luckmann (1967) has argued against all "substantive" definitions of religion, those that would tie religion to a particular empirical characteristic such as "belief in supernatural beings."

Consumerism is a religion, in that it is a framework that imparts meaning to experience.

framework, a framework that imparts to that experience some sort of meaning.[3] From this point of view all human beings are religious because all human beings must, by their nature, work out some system for converting the flux of experience into something that transcends that flux and thereby gives it meaning.

From this point of view a person's religion is whatever lends meaning to his or her everyday existence. Mr. Green may attend church regularly and think himself a Methodist, but if his everyday experience is organized by the goals, categories, and concerns of the ambitious businessman, it is the ideology of business capitalism that constitutes his real religion.

Like Mr. Green, Americans attend churches on Sunday mornings, and they do so in numbers that are unparalleled in the rest of the Western world. But one could argue that it is not this Sunday morning Christianity that constitutes the most socially significant American religion. The message of the true faith is rather that of consumerism, the message that through consumption one may enter the second world, the world depicted in advertising.

The extent to which the fundamental belief of consumerism draws upon the image of salvation in Christianity should be no surprise. It is to be expected that new religions will develop atop the ruined foundations of old ones. What is surprising, initially at least, is that the simple tenets of this religion that our society practices with such piety remain for the most part unformulated, either by observers or adherents.

The reason for this is that we are all believers. Consumerism is so convincing that it seems not an ideology but simple fact. Is it not true that wealth can purchase comfort? Is it not then reasonable to believe that through consumption a person can enter a more comfortable world—a relative utopia? Have we not seen it ourselves, to some extent perhaps even experienced such a transformation as our own fortunes have improved?

Comfort, however, must be distinguished from perfection. The world of the advertisement is not so much comfortable as lacking any discomforts. Thus while the ideology of consumerism seems reasonable in the face of actual experience—indeed every religion must do this—it offers a perfect version of the future that belongs not to the realm of economic realism but rather to that of fantasy.

By now this fantasy is so closely interwoven with our reality as to be indistinguishable from that reality. Therefore, the ritual nature of our economic activity goes for the most part unnoticed.

[3]The definition of religion I suggest here is very similar to the one developed by Berger (1967).

Advertising as Scripture

The central sacrament of consumerism is the purchase, its daily ritual is entertainment, and its scripture is advertising. Through advertising, adherents learn not so much about products as about themselves. They learn what they could be if they consumed the product. Commentators such as John Berger (1972) and Stewart Ewen (1976) have observed that modern advertising is based on the principle that the most effective way to convince the potential consumer that he or she needs the product is to show the consumer that he or she will be a changed person if the product is acquired. Ewen locates the origin of this principle in the period around 1920. At this time a new sort of ad copy began to appear which sought to sell the product not on the basis of its qualities but on the basis of how the consumer would be changed by the product. Ewen quotes sociologist Robert Lynd, who observed in his classic *Middletown:*

> [modern advertising is] concentrating increasingly upon a type of copy aiming to make the reader emotionally unwary, to bludgeon him with the fact that decent people don't live the way he does. . . . This copy points an accusing finger at the stenographer as she reads her motion picture magazine and makes her acutely conscious of her unpolished finger nails." (Lynd, 1929, 82, cited in Ewen, 1976, 37–38)

The new advertising presented the potential consumer with the possibility, or the necessity, of a transformed self. From the perspective on religion adopted above, the extraordinary efficacy of this new strategy can be traced to the fact that it converts an economic activity into a religious one. The buyer is reoriented to consumption; rather than the satisfaction of immediate physical needs, consumption becomes the ritual whereby a transcendent meaning will be added to experience. Advertising offers the image of the transformed self, consumption the means of effecting that transformation. One need only look at a soft-drink ad on television to observe the process at work. Consumers of the soft drink, young, gorgeous, and often glistening, are presented in an orgiastic frenzy of enjoyment, careening across the screen in a thirty second explosion of exuberance. This, thinks the potential consumer, is fun. This is what my life should be. I will certainly bring Pepsi to my next beach party.

The central sacrament of consumerism is the purchase, its daily ritual is entertainment, and its scripture is advertising.

Karl Marx (1978), when he wrote of commodity fetishism in *Capital*, could not have foreseen the extent to which the phenomenon would develop in the years after his death. He observed the mystical properties that were ascribed to commodities in capitalist society, and traced this confusion to a process analogous to that which had led to the idea of Gods. Religion was born when human beings in an alienated condition disowned their own powers, projecting these powers into the universe and then worshipping them as Gods. Likewise commodities become mystical objects under a capitalist system of production, for people ascribe to the commodities themselves the power that in fact inheres in the labor which created the commodities. Today the fundamental faith in the mystical power of the commodity has been so far extended that another world has taken shape, the world, always just out of reach, that the transformed self might inhabit through the commodity.

Transformations in Another World

It is this other world that accounts, in the end, for such facts as resurrected celebrities.

It is this other world that accounts, in the end, for such facts as resurrected celebrities. This discussion must be delayed a little longer, however. To this point, consumerism has been depicted as a function of advertising, but this is to vastly underestimate the scope and significance of the phenomenon. Much of the print and broadcast media are heavily involved in the dissemination of the fundamental tenets of consumerism. Here, the effort is not usually tied to the promotion of a particular product, but rather to the much more important task of sustaining the belief that the other world exists and is accessible. It is only the faith in this proposition that can sustain the consumerism which is so central to our culture and economy.

Many examples could be cited here; for the purposes of this argument, an interesting approach is to consider the sorts of magazines intended to be read by women.[4] Take, say, *Glamour,* oriented primarily to younger women with professional aspirations. In a subscription-soliciting letter of 1985 the editor writes, "If you'll give me just a few minutes of your time *now,* I honestly believe that I can help you change almost anything about yourself that you want to—for a *lifetime. . . . Begin the great and continuing makeover of you—and save $8.43!*" Turning to the pages of the magazine itself, one is indeed impressed by the single-minded dedication with which the magazine pursues its goal of the transformation of its readers. The articles, one after another, are dedicated to the goal of changing the self, physically, mentally, and emotionally. A few article titles:

"Shorts Makeovers: Better Legs for Every Body."

"Clip it and Carry It: Glamour's Ultimate Get-Organized Guide."

"Rewriting Your Romantic Resume."

"18 Real-Life Hair Dramas: What Works and Why."

A regularly appearing feature over several years has been "the makeover." A woman, an ordinary reader, is chosen from among many applicants to be transformed. Hair

[4] I am not considering "men's magazines" here in conjunction with "women's magazines" simply because such a juxtaposition raises issues that cannot be considered in the context of this paper. I hope to treat the obvious differences between men's and women's magazines in a later paper.

stylists, make-up and clothing experts go to work, and the woman appears on the pages of the magazine, replete with "before" and "after" photographs that document the miracle. In *Glamour*'s more ambitious "makeover" projects the woman's appearance is not the only target of transformative effort. Career advice and assistance may be given; for example, the magazine's connections might be activated to land an aspiring actress a bit part in a major motion picture.

The woman who is made over is living testimony to the reality of the other world. She starts in this world, the mundane reality we all inhabit, and is ushered into the other world. It can happen! The average woman can be rendered indistinguishable from the fashion models who appear in the hundreds of advertisements contained in each issue of *Glamour.*

In one sense, then, a magazine like *Glamour* is a meta-advertisement, an advertisement for advertising. Those hundreds of opportunities for transformation are made more plausible, more desirable, and more necessary by articles that present various techniques of transformation. But to concentrate on the economic aspects of the magazine is to overlook its far more significant religious function. Every page of the magazine, whether advertising or article, offers the reader the possibility of salvation and the means for attaining it. I too can enter the world of beauty without imperfection, of luxury beyond anything in experience, of romance and tantalizing sex.

So Close, and Yet So Far

The template for all types of transformative techniques is the diet. The diet article is a genre which *Glamour* has developed into an art form by mating it with the strategy of the makeover. An overweight woman is chosen and is placed under the tutelage of *Glamour*'s experts. Her goal is to lose 50 pounds. Each month we will be informed of her progress, and photographs will record her transformation. In early months, she is pictured in black and white photographs, in frumpy clothes. As pounds are shed, the photographs are in color and eventually—near the end of her pilgrimage—in soft focus as we observe her holding a wine glass, surrounded by attractive and admiring men. Having begun as a noticeably imperfect denizen of this world, this woman has crossed over to the other side, and we have seen the step-by-step process whereby it occurred. Are any of those steps beyond our own abilities? They are not, and it is therefore impossible to deny the reality of the other world.

A magazine like Glamour *is a meta-advertisement, an advertisement for advertising.*

Whether in advertisements or in magazines such as *Glamour*, the other world of consumerism is always depicted as being so close to the believer that it is just out of his or her grasp. The disadvantage of having an image of heaven that is so close to mundane reality is that there is very little tension between this world and that one. No profound image of a better world informs the moral vision of consumerism. On the other hand, the nearness of the other world means that the believer's faith in that world is virtually unshakable. In a magazine such as *Glamour,* the world of perfection is so close, the techniques of attaining it so many and so detailed, that the other world seems fully as real as this one. The attainment of bliss really is so simple as a new diet, learning to budget one's time, or a new approach to romance.

Celebrities as Divine Mediators

Elvis is one of the most well developed examples of the general class of mediators in consumerism, mythic creatures we call "celebrities."

It is above all in entertainment that the other world is depicted and brought into juxtaposition with this one, and this at last brings me back to Elvis. Elvis is one of the most well developed examples of the general class of mediators in consumerism, mythic creatures we call "celebrities." When one reckons together the time our average citizen spends watching TV or movies and reading about or looking at pictures of celebrities in publications such as *National Enquirer* or *People,* one is forced to admit a fascination with celebrities that is literally insatiable. Why are celebrities so appealing? They are appealing because they exist from day to day in the fabulous beyond, yet they are undoubtedly humans no different from you or I. Every celebrity is touched with the qualities of the divine mediator, and in the case of Elvis Presley circumstances have developed in such a way as to make this particularly obvious.

Elvis Presley had a talent for interpreting the "race music" of the early fifties, and the characteristic of a white skin. This combination, together with the astute promotion of Colonel Tom Parker, made Elvis the paradigmatic rock 'n' roll celebrity. Then, best of all, Elvis died at a relatively early age; this brought the facts of his life into close enough conjunction with mythological patterns to render his deification inevitable. At the time of his death 80,000 people showed up at his home in Memphis to pay their respects; the first year the home was opened to the public a million visitors filed through. (Cocks, 1977)

Elvis always had a lot of devoted fans, men and (particularly) women who, as we say, "worshipped" him. Each passing year seems to augment the myth that although Elvis died, he lives. In the early years after his death, bumper stickers and t-shirts proclaimed "Elvis lives in my heart" or simply "Elvis lives." As the years passed, the evidence of Elvis' resurrection has accumulated: mysterious irregularities surrounding his death, phone conversations taped from beyond the grave, testimonies of sightings and visions.

Elvis' ability to survive his own death, of course, is only a small part of the picture. Since the time of his death, countless of his fans have worked their way into newspaper and magazine articles about Elvis' continuing legacy. A stock feature of the interview with the devoted fan is the assertion that Elvis was perfect or otherwise like a messiah; probably the most common metaphoric term for Elvis is "the king." And of course, Elvis relics are of great value. Exhibits of Elvis relics tour the country and are shown, predictably, in places like shopping malls. There fans can observe objects such as the RCA TV with a plaque on it that reads "especially crafted for Elvis A. Presley." What makes the relic particularly appealing is that it bears the mark of Elvis' intervention: It has no picture tube because Elvis shot it out with his .44 magnum when he was watching a program and Robert Goulet started singing.[5]

The point is, as many have noticed, that since his death Elvis Presley has taken on many of the characteristics of Jesus Christ. Various unconvincing attempts have been made to explain this phenomenon, based largely on the peculiar characteristics of Elvis' career, life, and personality. The fact is, however, that the deification of Elvis is only a particularly obvious instance of what is true to at least some extent of any celebrity. Celebrities are deities because they are the most significant mediators in American consumerism; like the Christian deity Jesus Christ they are at once human and God. They are the ones who participate in two worlds, the world we all live in and the world we all aspire to. Although they started out as mortals like you and me, they live their current lives in our idea of heaven, the world that is depicted in advertisements, where people are happy, beautiful, witty, satisfied, adventurous, friendly, and so on. We are all the more convinced that heaven is real, and that it can be reached, by the existence of celebrities who live in the world of fabulous beauty, wealth and fame. This is why we are so interested in personal details about celebrities—these details prove both that celebrities are like us and that they are different from us, that they do indeed mediate between the two worlds. The minor setbacks that do occur even in paradise—divorce, addictions, at times even a suicide—are fascinating because they reveal these celestial creatures to be just like us.

The public's insatiable interest in mediators is thus not much different from the fascination that such figures have evoked since the shamans of the Paleolithic; these figures attest to the reality of the other world and may, if properly petitioned, bring the favors of that world back to this one. In the ideology of consumerism, the favored method of obtaining such blessings—short of becoming a celebrity oneself—is to marry or simply have sex with the mediator, a fantasy that is surely a stock piece in the repertoire of American daydreams.

Celebrities are deities because they are the most significant mediators in American consumerism; they are at once human and God.

Elvis as Messiah

Elvis Presley sold hundreds of millions of records and used a portion of his wealth to employ a retinue of

[5]San Francisco Examiner & Chronicle, June 22, 1980, p. 7.

Americans have come to believe that the existence they live from day to day can be transformed through the transformation of themselves.

relatives and old friends who isolated him from the mundane world in which the rest of us move. Yet his continuing appeal to the white working and lower middle class was based in no small part on the theme of loyalty: interviews with fans continually stress the importance of the fact that he never forgot his origins, his own basis in the working class. Elvis, as his income increased, was not seduced by the status symbols of the upper class. His values, in terms of his taste in consumer goods such as cars and clothes, in terms of the importance of loyalty to old friends and relatives, in terms of his continual stress on the primacy of God and country, remained rooted in the working class, although these values were inflated to a degree that often made the aging Elvis seem a self-caricature. It is the fact that Elvis remained so rooted in the world of his origin while ascending the heights as the greatest rock and roll celebrity of all time that made, and makes, him such a potent mediator.

The extraordinary popularity of the various aspects of the Elvis saga is attributable to a powerful religious ideology that goes virtually unremarked, in spite of its importance in shaping economic and social conditions in America. The influence of this ideology can by now be observed across all of American culture, as traditional religions, art, literature and popular music are reshaped to better conform to the aspirations and convictions generated by consumerism.

Americans have come to believe, some vaguely and some fervently, that the existence they live from day to day can be transformed—must be transformed—through the transformation of themselves. The self can be changed through consumption and through the proper application of technique. Those persons who have undergone the transformation give solace and hope to all who believe, and in an extreme case like that of Elvis Presley, the transformed begin to merge with the great paradigm for all mediators in American culture.

♦

References

Barthes, Roland, *Image, Music, Text.* New York, Hill and Wang, 1977.

Berger, John, (and others), *Ways of Seeing.* Harmondsworth, Penguin, 1972.

Berger, Peter L., *The Sacred Canopy.* Garden City, Doubleday, 1967.

Cocks, Jay, "Last Stop on The Mystery Train." *Time,* (August 29, 1977: 56–59).

Durkheim, Emile, *The Elementary Forms of the Religious Life.* New York, Macmillan, 1915.

Ewen, Stuart, *Captains of Consciousness.* New York, McGraw Hill, 1976.

Luckmann, Thomas, *The Invisible Religion.* New York, Macmillan, 1967.

Lynd, Robert S. and Helen Merrill Lynd, *Middletown: A Study in Contemporary American Culture.* New York, Harcourt, Brace and Company, 1929.

Marx, Karl, "Capital, Volume one" The Marx-Engels Reader (second edition). Edited by Robert C. Tucker. New York, Norton, 1978. pp. 294–442.

Whitehead, Harriet, "Reasonably Fantastic: Some Perspectives on Scientology, Science Fiction, and Occultism." *Religious Movements in Contemporary America.* Edited by Irving I. Zaretsky and Mark P. Leone. Princeton, Princeton University Press, 1974. pp. 547–587.

Questions for Discussion

1. Do you agree that consumerism is a form of religion in America?
2. Do you believe in transformation through consumption? Does the rest of America?

Suggested Readings

For Those Who Want to Learn Even More about Elvis's Life After Death

Greil Marcus, *Dead Elvis: A Chronicle of a Cultural Obsession,* N.Y.: Doubleday, 1991. Marcus is a writer for Rolling Stone and The Village Voice, and this is a collection of articles and essays about Elvis as cultural phenomenon.

Those Who Are Interested in "Media As Religion" Will Be Interested in the Following

Goethals, Gregor T., *The TV Ritual: Worship at the Video Alter* (Boston: Beacon Press, 1981).

More On The Media's Role In Shaping American Values

"Ads, Violence and Values," *Advertising Age* Vol. 61, April 2, 1990, p. 12 (1). Editorial dealing with the slaying of inner city teens over their Nike Air Jordan tennis shoes.

Baran, Stanley J., Jin Ja Mok, Mitchell Land and Tae Young Kang, "You Are What You Buy: Mass-Mediated Judgements of People's Worth," *Journal of Communication,* Spring, 1989, p. 46 (9).

"Beyond Dreams: The Mysterious Power of the Movies," *Life* Vol. 10, April, 1987, p. 22 (1). Column; special issue, The Movies.

Dorris, Michael, "Why Mister Ed Still Talks Good Horse Sense: An Anthropologist Explains How Reruns, Like Old Tribal Tales, Can Link Generations and Teach Enduring Values," *TV Guide,* May 28, 1988, p. 34 (3).

Edel, Richard, "American Dream Vendors," *Advertising Age* Vol. 59, November 9, 1988, p. 152 (4). The role of advertising and popular culture. Special issue: The Power of Advertising.

Entman, Robert, "How the Media Affect What People Think: An Information Processing Approach," *The Journal of Politics* Vol. 51, May, 1989, p. 347 (24).

Ewen, Stuart, *All Consuming Images: The Politics of Style in Contemporary Culture.* Reviewed by Todd Gitlin in *Tikkun* July–August 1989 p. 110 (3).

Funkhouser, G. Ray, and Eugene F. Shaw, "How Synthetic Experience Shapes Social Reality," *Journal of Communication* Vol. 40, Spring 1990, p. 75 (13).

Goldberg, Gary David, and Jayne Anne Phillips, "The Intimacy of Mass Culture," *New Perspectives Quarterly* Vol. 7, Winter 1990, p. 58 (2). Mass media is destroying the family.

Kalter, Joanmarie, "How TV Is Shaking Up the American Family," *TV Guide* Vol. 36, July 23, 1988, p. 4 (8). Television as a value-setter, part 1. The second part ran July 30, 1988.

Karp, Walter, "Where the Media Critics Went Wrong," *American Heritage* Vol. 39, March 1988, p. 76 (4). He traces early predictions about the effect of television, and finds that it did not make Americans passive and obedient. An excerpt of this can be found in Walter Karp, "Uncle Miltie v. Mass Man," *Harper's Magazine* Vol. 277, July 1988, p. 30 (3).

Martin, Jay, "Caught in Fantasyland: Electronic Media's Hold on Society," *USA Today* Vol. 117, July, 1988, p. 92 (2).

Neuman, W. Russell, "The Threshold of Public Attention," *Public Opinion Quarterly* Vol. 54, Summer 1990, p. 159 (18). Media coverage of events and resultant public opinion.

Peterson, Eric E., "The Technology of Media Consumption," *American Behavioral Scientist* Vol. 32, November–December 1988, p. 156 (13).

Squiers, Carol, "The Future of Delusion," *Artforum* Vol. 28, February 1990, p. 19 (3).

Zoglin, Richard, "Home Is Where the Venom Is: Domestic Life Takes a Drubbing in TV's Anti-family Sitcoms," *Time* Vol. 135, April 16, 1990, p. 85 (2). The real significance of programs such as Married with Children, Roseanne, and The Simpsons.

America's Global Influence

4

Stan Le Roy Wilson, in *Mass Media/Mass Culture,* defines *culture* as follows:

For anthropologists, culture includes everything that occurs in a society—all the customs and practices handed down from generation to generation. Culture covers the various forces that contribute to our behavior in society. These contributions usually come from our formal institutions, such as churches, the state, and now, the media; mores, or standards of behavior; laws; and conventional practices and customs.

Wilson goes on to point out that *popular* culture (what some might call *low* culture) can be so pervasive that it is difficult for us to observe it. As true as this is, we still have an innate sense of the difference between high culture and low culture. Most opera is high culture, most rap music is low culture. Tuxedos are high culture, jeans are low culture. Coke is not champaign, etc., etc. Before we begin to sound like a Cole Porter song, let's state it plainly: High culture *defines* a society; it is those customs and practices that make a people what they are.

Throughout the world today, there is fear that American popular culture is taking over, leaving little room for the high culture that makes each country unique. Proud foreign nationals see CNN on their TVs, American rock music on their radios, McDonald's and Kentucky Fried Chicken on their streets, and Levis on their children. Critics here and abroad denounce this tendency as "cultural imperialism."

The readings in this chapter examine the concept of the globalization of American media, and how this affects cultural imperialism. In the first reading Michael Eisner, the chairman of The Walt Disney Company, assures us that the globalization of American culture is nothing to worry about. Then Jack Lang, the Minister of Culture of France, takes the opposing view. Finally Stuart Emmrich analyzes the effects of globalization on the American movie industry, effects which include many of our major studios being bought by foreign corporations.

It's a Small World After All

Michael Eisner

Michael Eisner is one of the world's highest-paid and most successful corporate executives. He has made the Walt Disney Company a truly global corporation, including the construction of Disneylands in Japan and France. It is no wonder that he is not threatened by the idea of American cultural imperialism. He is downright eloquent, in fact, when he points out that "The Berlin Wall was destroyed not by the force of Western arms, but by the force of Western ideas."

This article was adapted from a conversation Eisner had with Nathan Gardels, editor of New Perspectives Quarterly.

Reading Difficulty Level: 3. The man didn't get where he is today by being misunderstood.

The American entertainment industry plays a far more important role in international relations than many of our government leaders recognize.

It can be argued without exaggeration that Mickey Mouse is known by more people around the world than any other American. And it can also be argued without too much disagreement that Mickey is one of the best good-will ambassadors this country has ever had.

Mickey Mouse is known by more people around the world than any other American.

The fact is that Mickey achieves instant friendship with almost every child he meets. To Italian children he is Topolino, in Spain he is El Raton Miki. For many years he co-starred with Donald Duck in China, where he was seen by an estimated two hundred million people a week. There he is known as Mee-La-Shoo.

During 1987 alone, more than 200 million people watched a Disney film or home video; 395 million watched a Disney TV show every week; 212 million listened or danced to Disney music, records, tapes, or compact discs; 270 million bought Disney-licensed merchandise in fifty countries.

More than fifty million people from all lands passed through the turnstiles of Disney theme parks—in California, Florida, and Tokyo—bringing the total since they opened to over half a billion people.

Such figures would mean little in themselves except that they are similar to the figures of other American entertainment companies, demonstrating the universal appeal of American culture. In fact, after the

From *New Perspectives Quarterly*, Fall, 1991, pp. 40–42. Reprinted by permission.

aircraft industry, the American entertainment industry generates the largest American trade surplus with the rest of the world.

At present, motion pictures made in the United States account for less than one-tenth of the world's annual production of feature-length films. Yet these American films account for 65 percent of box office receipts worldwide.

Out of the top ten films showing in any European country, including along St. Germain des Pres in Paris, at least seven, and often more, will have been produced in the U.S. Seventy percent of movie box-office receipts in Greece go to American films. That figure is 80 percent for the Netherlands and 92 percent for Britain.

India creates far more movies than any other country, and Brazil is the volume leader in television production. But in both countries, the majority of moviegoers, music listeners, and TV viewers prefer American entertainment. And I haven't even mentioned the explosion in home video, where the same pattern maintains.

Why is there such vast appeal? There are several reasons.

The Economic Edge

The massive, assured English-language market in America—and increasingly elsewhere—enables Hollywood studios to raise the necessary financing for production and marketing that is not possible for studios in a much smaller, say, French- or German-language, market. This has given the American entertainment industry the ability to pick up the stories, stars, songs, and talent from across the world.

I would argue that because of this, the entertainment industry of this country is not so much Americanizing the world as planetizing entertainment.

The entertainment industry of this country is not so much Americanizing the world as planetizing entertainment.

Exporting the American Dream

For viewers around the world, America is the place where the individual has a chance to make a better life, and to have political and economic freedom.

Diversity of individual opportunity, individual choice, and individual expression is what American entertainment imparts—and that is what people everywhere want.

Our cultural product makes fun of the government and the establishment. Not once in my career have I had to give thought to what the government might think of something I was producing. Can you imagine trying to produce a farce like *Police Academy* in North Korea?

Originality

As a result of the unhindered freedom to create, the American entertainment industry generates originality unlike that seen any other place on earth. Originality attracts interest, and to me it is the es-

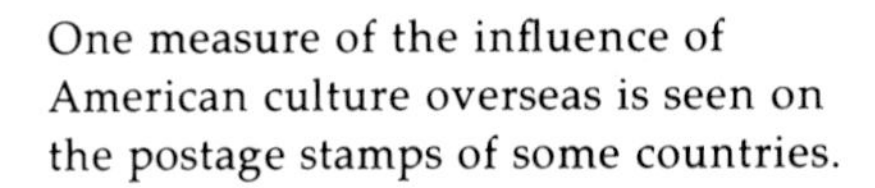

One measure of the influence of American culture overseas is seen on the postage stamps of some countries.

sence of American pop culture. Madonna is so original she recreates herself every two years, as does Michael Jackson.

America's cultural diversity contributes in important ways to this phenomenon. In homogeneous societies, as in homogeneous companies, the grass never seems greener on the other side and every idea kind of blends into the next.

In a culture as ethnically heterogeneous as the U.S.—over fifty languages are spoken at Hollywood High School—something new is always emerging. Rap music is not the same as rock, which is not the same as jazz. Steven Spielberg is not the same as Walt Disney.

The Contagion of Innocence

The specific appeal of Disneyland, Disney films and products—family entertainment—comes from the contagious appeal of innocence. Obviously, Disney characters strike a universal chord with children, all of whom share an innocence and openness before they become completely molded by their respective societies. For the whole family, as anyone who has ever visited Disneyland or Walt Disney World knows, these places respond to the child within us.

I know that some intellectuals around the world fear that what they call "American cultural imperialism" will level distinct cultures into a kind of lowest-common-denominator amalgam of mass entertainment. On these grounds, one French avant-garde theater director, in fact, attacked our construction of Euro-Disney, to open soon twenty miles outside Paris, as a "cultural Chernobyl." Although he probably shared the late French premier Georges Clemenceau's view that "America is one nation in history that has gone miraculously directly from barbarism to degeneration without the usual interval of civilization," the theater director was surely unaware of how *Frenchified* Disney has been from the beginning. Disney's first live-action feature was French science-fiction writer Jules Verne's *Twenty Thousand Leagues Under the Sea.* And while American classics like *Paul Bunyan* and *Johnny Appleseed* were mere short-subject films, the French fairy tales *Cinderella* and *Sleeping Beauty* received full-length feature-film treatment.

In the first place, such a concern is technologically outdated. *Least-objectionable-programming,* to use the industry term, was a real concern in the U.S. when there were only three TV networks, but with the end of the telecommunications oligopoly, that went out the window.

Now that there are four networks, a plethora of cable channels, PBS and video to boot, virtually any opportunity for the viewer is possible, from the highest quality to the lowest. At any given moment, the viewer can tune in to a performance of *Candide,* end-to-end coverage of the Russian parliament deliberations, or Mickey Mouse cartoons.

One French theater director attacked our construction of Euro-Disney as a "cultural Chernobyl."

France has moved away from two government-regulated stations to five stations that are less regulated; Italy has hundreds of TV stations. In such a situation, if American entertainment still attracts the most viewers, it is far less

If American entertainment attracts the most viewers, it is far less a matter of imperialism than consumer choice.

a matter of *imperialism* than consumer choice. To be sure, when Saddam Hussein chose Frank Sinatra's globally recognized "My Way" as the theme song for his fifty-fourth birthday party, it wasn't as a result of American imperialist pressure.

"If they go to see one of my plays," Voltaire wrote, "it is probably a good play. If they don't go, it is probably not a very good play." The same is true for American entertainment in general, and for Euro-Disney in particular.

Yes, Euro-Disney will have the hallmark castle at its center—a French castle, it should be noted—and Main Street and Frontierland.

Inherent in our media is a sense of individual freedom and the kind of life liberty can bring.

But in place of Tomorrowland there will be Discoveryland, inspired by Jules Verne. In Fantasyland, the fairy tale characters will all be heard in their native tongues, with Snow White speaking German, Pinocchio speaking Italian and Cinderella speaking French.

I have every confidence that, like Tokyo Disneyland, Euro-Disney will be a smashing success. And it's because of my boss, Mickey Mouse.

It would, of course, be absurdly exaggerated to say that Euro-Disney could replace the Berlin Wall as an emblem of freedom and harmony instead of conflict and division. But it may not be such an exaggeration to appreciate the role of the American entertainment industry in helping to change history.

The Berlin Wall was destroyed not by the force of Western arms, but by the force of Western ideas.

And what was the delivery system for those ideas? It has to be admitted that to an important degree it was by American entertainment. Inherent in the best and the worst of our movies and TV shows, books and records is a sense of individual freedom and the kind of life liberty can bring. It's in the movies of Steven Spielberg; it's in the songs of Madonna; it's in the humor of Bill Cosby.

The unspoken message to the world is, "We choose to make this product." And in a world where nationalist barriers are being resurrected, "you should have the choice to watch it." ♦

Question for Discussion

1. Should we be concerned that our best known citizen overseas is a cartoon mouse?

The Higher the Satellite, the Lower the Culture

Jack Lang

That the French even have an official "Minister of Culture" bespeaks how concerned they are about preserving theirs. Jack Lang is the French Minister of Culture, and as such he is one of the loudest critics of American cultural imperialism. This interview was also conducted by New Perspectives Quarterly *editor Nathan Gardels.*

Reading Difficulty Level: 6. The interview format and the French flavor makes it more difficult than it might be.

Universality. Freedom. Technology. What beautiful words. But we know that words can sometimes betray us.

Universality is a word that makes us vibrate. As an internationalist, I hate all forms of chauvinism. With Vittorio Freddi, I believe "the world itself is my homeland."

"Stars are visible from all windows of the universe," Katarina Von Bulow, a German intellectual who lived at the frontier of her divided country, has written. These universal lights are the protector of us all, no matter where we reside.

But at the same time, behind the glorious word *universality* there are always forms of domination. The Soviet empire that proclaimed—and enforced—a false universality has only just crumbled.

From *New Perspectives Quarterly*, Fall, 1991, pp. 42–44. Reprinted by permission.

Yet shouldn't men and women of culture also fear that in the name of a new universality, vast financial groups and entertainment industries will impose cultural uniformity on a global scale?

For the word not to betray us, universality must be reached through the recognition of the identity of each and every one of us, not by the criminal displacement of linguistic treasures and other diverse cultural forms.

Federico Fellini is one of the great master filmmakers of the century. He has reached the status of a master not only because he is a genius, but because his work has remained very close to the deepest, most profound experiences of Italy. But when can he be seen on American or European television?

Behind the glorious word "universality" there are always forms of domination.

Dante, another universal artist, spoke to the world through the figures of Tuscan mythology. The great

Carlo Goldoni wrote his comedies in Venetian. But in the *Locandiera*, when he placed Tuscan personalities in a scene, they spoke the Tuscan language. And when he was in exile in France, he wrote his memoirs in French.

So, today, when we speak of universality we should do so not with the idea of creating a Brave New Culture, but a global Andalusia. When that civilization flourished, culture and especially poetry flowered in the rich soil of a mixture of populations, including Arabs and Jews.

What about the word *freedom?* The world rejoices at the liberty that has come to the former Soviet empire. But what about the freedom of artists, there and elsewhere?

Are we only to choose between a state that dominates, shatters, and crushes, and a system that is run by market criteria alone? Poland rightly celebrates its newfound freedom, but without public financing of the arts not one Polish film has been made in a whole year! The same goes for Hungary. And what has happened to the great film studios of East Germany?

When in the name of liberty there is an absence of rules that protect and sustain culture, it will be the death of civilization.

When in the name of liberty there is an absence of rules that protect and sustain culture, it will be the death of civilization. Don't we need public institutions to keep civilization alive? Don't we see too many countries where small museums, little theaters, galleries, and publishing houses are allowed to be come extinct, like some unfortunate minor species in the Brazilian rainforest?

(Photo by Bruce Cotler)

Art and culture can't be produced like widgets. It takes time to create; it takes time for a new artist to reach his public. Cultural creation is not instantaneous. Yet few markets will subsidize time. More than a heartache, this is a cultural crime.

And what about technology? Will technology enrich us by creating a diversity of channels for artistic expression, or might the truth be more ominous: the higher the satellite, the lower the culture?

The disappearance of languages and cultural forms is the great risk today. Diversity threatens to be replaced by an international mass culture without roots, soul, color, or taste.

NPQ When you say that domination lurks behind universality, I assume you are talking mainly about

American mass culture. The financial capacities of Hollywood, especially now with Japanese backing, surpass by far what any individual European nation can muster.

And, given the near collapse of public financing of the arts in the eastern part of Europe, the *common language* of global culture has a distinctly American non-accent.

Jack Lang As Number One in cinema and audio-visual production, America is the mass-culture superpower. It is not scandalous to mention this fact.

America is the mass-culture superpower.

But the problem is not just America. What I object to is the system of industrialized culture. My dream is of a society in which ordinary soups are not dished up for the majority while only a minority tastes the superb broth.

In a recent interview in *Le Monde,* even Woody Allen complained about the difficulty of searching for new creative forms in the entertainment industry.

In much of Europe, I admit, there is an absence of will to counter the onslaught of industrialized culture.

In France, of course, we have made every effort to maintain public funding of artistic diversity. We are also co-producing films and working on other projects with Russian, Czechoslovakian, and Polish filmmakers.

And, at the level of the European Community, France has pushed for a policy that insures that at least a third of audio-visual production is of European content.

For me, it is vital to maintain a distinct European cultural space and, within that, a distinct space for each and every language and culture. It is our duty to encourage European artists.

NPQ You speak of a global Andalusia, yet France has increasingly become the most protectionist power in Europe—you seek not only to keep American entertainment out, but now also immigrants and Eastern European exports.

Lang I don't see it in these terms. On the contrary. France is probably the most open country in Europe. In Paris it is possible to see an Albanian film, a Brazilian film, and an American film—films from all over the world.

Paris has always been a mecca of creativity for artists from across the planet, from American novelists to Japanese fashion designers. Milan Kundera writes there. Garcia Marquez wrote there. Carlos Fuentes lived there as an ambassador. James Baldwin, too, when he felt oppressed in America. And, of course, Hemingway.

It has been our tradition for centuries.

NPQ So why are America's trade representatives, from Carla Hills to Jack Valenti of the American Motion Picture Association, always trashing French protectionism?

Lang You tell me.

A year ago, Carla Hills came to my office to talk to me about "French cultural protectionism." It was five o'clock in the afternoon.

I turned on the TV for her. On the first channel was an American television series, and on the second, the third, and the fourth. How is this protectionism?

I would be happy if only 3 or 5 percent of American television programming featured French or European series.

NPQ Well, that is up to the American audience, not the motion picture industry, and I guess that audience doesn't care for what Europe produces for TV.

Lang It's an attitude, not a question of rules. In this sense, the U.S. may be one of the most culturally protectionist countries.

A book coming from South America or Europe has a far easier time finding an audience in Moscow than in San Francisco or Los Angeles. It is much easier for a European filmmaker to be seen in Tokyo than Atlanta. Even Japan, so heralded as a closed society, has more curiosity about the cultures of Europe and Africa.

America would be so much richer if it opened its mind to the world of diverse cultures.

NPQ America is full of the kind of diverse immigrants, though, that the present prime minister, Edith Cresson, doesn't want to let in.

Lang Our immigration policy has been exploited by the right for political reasons. We consider that when the laws of immigration, which relate to work and legal status, are respected, the immigrant shares the same rights in France as a native.

The presence of foreigners in France, as I have said, is a great source of our richness. But we also have rules.

NPQ So, you don't see your arts subsidies and domestic-content legislation for TV programming as protectionist, but as a means to protect civil society from the mass market?

Lang Yes. Our schools are publicly financed and our textbooks are written in French. Is that protectionism? No. It is a duty for a nation to teach its children their own language. It is a minimum duty of a nation to preserve its culture. Indeed, it is criminal to destroy or dilute a culture. ♦

It is a minimum duty of a nation to preserve its culture. Indeed, it is criminal to destroy or dilute a culture.

Questions for Discussion

1. Do you agree with Lang when he says that "America would be so much richer if it opened its mind to the world of diverse cultures?
2. Within the catalog of your own cultural background and interests, what do you consider "high culture" and what do you consider low or "popular culture"? Which has a greater impact on your life?

Foreign Intrigue: They Come, They Romance, They Buy—Hollywood

Stuart Emmrich

Stuart Emmrich is a London-based writer, editor, and observer of the global media scene. In this article he analyzes the effects of the global influence of the American film industry, and points out that at least one of those effects is that American studios are being bought up by Japanese and other foreign companies.

Reading Difficulty Level: 5.

When writer Pico Iyer was traveling through rural Asia in the fall of 1985, he was struck by the omnipresence of a single icon: Rambo. The movie *First Blood* seemed to be everywhere, as were reverential images of its gun-toting star. The film was an unprecedented phenomenon in Asia. In China, a million people flocked to *First Blood* within 10 days of its opening, with black-market scalpers hawking tickets at seven times their official price. In India, five separate rip-offs of the Stallone picture went instantly into production, one of them even recasting Rambo as a sari-clad superwoman. And in Indonesia, not only were street vendors offering posters of the American hero, but a Rambo amusement arcade was doing gangbuster business.

The presence of Rambo was inescapable, even in the most unlikely places. "I took an overnight bus across Java," writes Iyer in *Video Night in Kathmandu*, "and, soon enough, the video screen next to the driver crackled into life and there—who else?—was the Italian Stallion. As the final credits began to roll, my neighbor, a soldier just returned from putting down rebels in the jungles of East Timor, sat back with a satisfied sigh. 'That,' he pronounced aptly, 'was very fantastic.' "

Rambo isn't the only American film character cutting a swath through the world's theaters. There seems to be a growing, almost insatiable, demand for American movies overseas, and international box-office receipts are becoming as important—and in some cases more so—to movie studios as domestic rentals. In the past four years, for instance, revenues from distribution of American films abroad have grown from $800 million annually to $1.13 billion. Overseas box-office

There seems to be a growing, almost insatiable, demand for American movies overseas.

From *American Film*, September, 1989. Reprinted by permission.

returns have become so crucial a part of studio earnings that many pictures are being made with the international audience in mind. Universal and Warner Bros., for instance, decided to gamble $20 million on *Gorillas in the Mist* because they saw the foreign marketplace as a financial cushion.

The boon provided by overseas revenues has raised the stakes in what is increasingly becoming a global film industry.

The boon provided by overseas revenues has done more than just fill the coffers of U.S. studios. It has also raised the stakes in what is increasingly becoming a global film industry. Foreign media companies are no longer content with their own small piece of this global pie. They want to be major players on the world stage. And that means taking a starring role in Hollywood.

In the past couple of years, the foreign invasion has become an onslaught. In 1985, Australia's Rupert Murdoch snapped up 20th Century Fox for $575 million, while in the past two years, Italy's Giancarlo Parretti took control of the troubled Cannon Group, Britain's Television South PLC and the French pay-television station Canal Plus bought MTM Entertainment, and Australia's Network 10 joined forces with Westfield Capital Corporation to buy a controlling interest in Barris Industries, once known as the creator of *The Gong Show,* but under Jon Peters and Peter Guber makes such films as *Rain Man.* Most recently, Australia's Qintex Group agreed to buy the United Artists studio and its 4,000-film library from MGM/UA for $600 million.

But the biggest outside threat to Hollywood comes from the Japanese. Sony is said to be actively seeking a movie studio to add to its vast communications holdings—one day the target is supposed to be Columbia, the next MCA Universal.* Nippon Steel (already partnered with MCA for a planned Japanese theme park) and Fuji-sankei Communications are also said to be on the prowl. But even if none of these three giants ends up owning a piece of a U.S. movie studio—and executives at all three companies have denied such plans—the Japanese have become as ubiquitous in Hollywood as sushi bars. Since 1987, roughly a dozen Japanese companies have set up film divisions, brandishing checks in front of American producers, bankrolling noted filmmakers and even setting up a small studio of their own, Apricot Entertainment.

Venture capitalist Shigeru Masuda has brought together a group of 10 Japanese investors to create a $20 million pool that was to have helped finance a slate of films to be distributed by its American partner, Vestron Pictures. Two films, including *Blue Steel,* were completed and a third started before Vestron ran into financial problems and disbanded most of its film operation. The balance of the financing will be invested elsewhere on a picture-by-picture basis. Shochiku-Fuji, an entertainment con-

*Sony bought Columbia; Matsushita, another Japanese corporation, bought MCA.

glomerate that distributed *The Last Emperor,* has promised $50 million to that film's producer, Jeremy Thomas, in a six-picture deal. Shochiku-Fuji is also investing in at least two films for independent producer Edward Pressman, the first of which is *Reversal of Fortune,* a film based on the Claus von Bulow case, starring Glenn Close. Fujisankei Communications Group invested $10 million in David Puttnam productions. Other Japanese investors include the Tokuma Group and Dentsu, the huge advertising agency. Dentsu recently entered into a $20 million coproduction pact with producer Jonathan Taplin. The Tokyo real estate development firm Central Kousan Ltd., newcomers to motion pictures, is also part of the deal.

Two large Japanese trading companies, Mitsubishi Corp. and Mitsui & Co., have recently opened offices in Los Angeles and are said to be interested in film properties. Perhaps most astonishingly, two Japanese media companies, NHK Enterprises and Gakken Publishing Co., have arranged $50 million in financing for producer Richard Edlund (he's best known as a special-effects man for George Lucas) to spend on his first feature film, *Crisis 2050.*

Even failure doesn't daunt these Japanese speculators. Three cash-rich companies—C. Itoh, Suntory and Tokyo Broadcasting System—last year signed a three-picture deal with MGM/UA, providing $15 million in financing for three films: *Fatal Beauty; Bright Lights, Big City* and *Last Rites.* All three flopped. But the Japanese consortium, called CST, is going to finance more films this year. (The box-office sting was considerably softened by the revenues received from broadcast, video and merchandising rights.) "CST is taking the long-term view that is typical of Japanese companies," one advisor told *Business Week* last year.

Hollywood's Appeal

Why the overwhelming interest in Hollywood, even in the face of such failure?

Part of Hollywood's appeal is its relative affordability. With the dollar on the decline against most other currencies, foreigners can buy in at a bargain rate. That is especially true of capital-rich Japanese companies looking for a place to park their excess yen. (The dollar's decline does have its up side: It increases the importance of overseas revenues for American films. "Five years ago, you could get 240 yen to the dollar. Now you get about 130," explains Kevin Hyson, senior vice president of Buena Vista International, Disney's distribution arm. "So, compared to five years ago, if you had a film that did the same amount of business {in Japan}, you are still doubling your revenues.")

With the dollar on the decline, foreigners can buy into Hollywood at a bargain rate.

As one American executive explained, "This is one of the few industries left where our technology is the world's best."

Technology, too, is a drawing card. As William Moses, senior vice president of CL GlobalPartners, the New York investment banking arm of Credit Lyonnais, and an adviser to Qintex's Christopher Skase, explains, "This is one of the few industries left where our technology is the world's best. If you are going to make a movie, the ability to create that movie exists in greater abundance in the Hollywood community than anywhere else in the world."

But a more important factor—and one that isn't dependent on the vicissitudes of currency fluctuations—is the enormous demand for video software in overseas markets, particularly that on foreign broadcast stations. In Japan, for instance, box-office attendance is slumping but television viewing is on the upswing, with the nation's five private stations playing to record audiences, and two new satellite stations will provide an even greater market for programming next year. The addition of privately owned commercial stations to the previously state-run TV industries in Europe has had a similar effect on those markets. In the past few years, France has gone from three to six stations, England from two to four and Germany from two to five. By next year, once Rupert Murdoch's commercial satellite stations are up and running and Spain privatizes its TV stations, Europe's TV stations will reach more than 120 million households and will consume an estimated 500,000 programming hours a year. And as that market has grown, it has created an additional market for the sale of theatrical product. Especially American product.

American films are an important source of programming for foreign TV stations, says PaineWebber entertainment analyst Lee Isgur, not only because English is commonly a second language in many countries, but also because the production values of U.S. films are generally better than their overseas counterparts. "When you are making a film in the United States, you have a built-in audience of 220 million people," Isgur explains. "Thus the production qualities are higher. It isn't the same as making a film in Austria for an Austrian audience. {There} you are not going to get as good a product."

It's not just American films, but their small-screen counterparts that are foreign favorites. The international appeal of American TV programming has become such a financial consideration that many producers decide whether or not to make a show based on potential foreign sales. *The New York Times* recently reported that two years ago, when 20th Century Fox decided to scrap its plans for the series *Rags to Riches,* New World Television agreed to make it for NBC because it believed the show had foreign potential. More recently, French channel TF 1 paid $11 million for 200 episodes of *Knots Landing*, a sharp reversal from two years ago when Lorimar came up empty in its search for a French outlet.

These overseas markets for homegrown products have certainly fattened the bottom lines of American studios, but they have also urged foreigners to become major players in the globalization of Hollywood. As *Forbes* asked in a recent article about the explosion of foreign investment in Tinseltown, "Why rent when you can own?"

Overseas markets for home-grown products have urged foreigners to become major players in the globalization of Hollywood.

And this is not going to be a game for small players. Analysts agree that major studios—those that have geared their distribution systems to best exploit the opportunities of a global marketplace—will benefit most in the next few years. "The studios of today are not the studios of old," says Moses. "Their power doesn't come from control of the creative product; it comes from control of the distribution system. It is the power to book, bill and collect on their movies."

Qintex chief financial officer Jonathan Lloyd says the Australian-based company had a simple reason for buying into Hollywood. "We decided that we wanted to be one of the major players in the world and the only way to do that was to buy a studio. The global market is still driven by U.S. film production and will be for some time to come," he says. "The mass appeal is there; the dollars are there. The numbers speak for themselves. This now makes us one of the seven major players on the world stage." One side benefit is the cash flow provided by an extensive film library that includes the James Bond, Rocky and Pink Panther series. "If we followed a rate of production of about 15 films a year, it would take us 50 years to create a film library of this size," says Lloyd. *Variety* recently reported that Qintex estimates that UA's library of pre-1982 films could bring in a cash flow of $76 million this year and as much as $134 million by 1998.

More important, Lloyd says that if Qintex wants to compete with such studios as Paramount and Disney, it has to be prepared to do battle with them on a global basis. It's a strategy that has many believers in Hollywood. "The philosophy of most companies these days is that bigger is better," says analyst Joseph DiLillo. "The world is just one big marketplace. That has rubbed off on the entertainment industry." But the cult of size has its detractors as well. A recent *Wall Street Journal* piece wondered if bigness was simply the latest fad, "doomed to go the way of 1960s-style conglomerates."

Even those media companies that profess to be uninterested in getting bigger for bigger's sake seem to eventually come around. In April, soon after the Time-Warner merger was announced, Gulf + Western chairman Martin Davis played down the importance of megamedia companies. "From our standpoint, we think we are well positioned to compete effectively," he said. "We

It may seem surprising to some observers that Hollywood has become such a hot investment. Only about three or four out of every 10 pictures are likely to be profitable.

don't think size means a better company." Two months later, with Gulf + Western operating under its new Paramount Communication, Inc. banner, Davis made his own bid to block the Time-Warner merger and take control of Time himself.

And although the Time-Warner deal has many facets to it, the global market is, once again, a key consideration for American entertainment software. When explaining to reporters why he thought Warner and Time made a good fit, Warner chairman Steve Ross pointed out that 40 percent of Warner's revenues came from abroad, compared to only 10 percent for Time. Warner, he implied, could help Time maximize its overseas potential. "We are the only motion picture company that owns all forms of distribution over the world," he said, "theatrical, video, magazines, records, tapes, compact discs. We can use our distribution people to push Time business products throughout the world. That's where the ball game is."

To some extent, the Time-Warner merger is an American defense against the onslaught of foreign entertainment and publishing giants. But as Dennis McAlpine, an analyst for Oppenheimer & Co., suggested to *The Wall Street Journal*, "If you look at the synergies of Paramount and Time or Time and Warner, most of the stuff they are saying about synergy is great PR meanderings—it sounds good on paper but I don't know if you'll ever see any of it."

It may seem surprising to some observers that Hollywood has become such a hot investment. Only about three or four out of every 10 pictures are likely to be profitable, says Merrill Lynch analyst Harold Vogel, and that includes revenues from ancillary sources. Perhaps only one in 20 movies turns a profit at the box office alone. Certainly there are easier ways to make money.

But then, these are not companies that are turning away from investment banking or real estate to dabble in filmmaking. They are already in the business—even if, like Sony, tangentially—and are convinced that if you are going to be in the business at all, then you have to be in Hollywood. "Sony has all the hardware players," says William Moses, referring to its computer-controlled cameras, tape-editing machines and VCRs. "Now they want to control the software. They want to be vertically integrated."

And, of course, there is the undeniable allure of making a killing on that blockbuster. For years, when a movie hit gold, like *The Sound of Music* or even *Love Story*, it was gold in the $50–$80 million range. Then, in 1977, came *Star Wars,* a movie that made $194 million and suddenly made people realize that there was a killing to be made in the movie business if you had the right movie. This year alone, there have been three such blockbusters—*Ghostbusters II, Indiana Jones and the Last Crusade* and *Batman*—the latter pulling in $100 million in just 10 days.

Moses asserts that buying into Hollywood is not quite the gamble it may appear. "An entertainment-company deal is a good economic deal," he says, explaining that the balance sheet can be "misleading" because it understates the value of a film library. "After a five-year period, a film's costs are written off, and it is carried at zero value on the books," he explains. "Yet, because of its library value, it is still generating income." Speaking of the Qintex deal for MGM/UA, Moses says, "People may say that Christopher Skase overpaid for the company, but come back to me in five years and I'll show you he didn't. It's like real estate; the value is bound to go up over time."

Moses suggests that the library value of movie studios—those long-term cash cows—are one reason that "so many American companies are in play," but one other factor that may make the studios vulnerable to outsiders is the very economics of filmmaking. As the cost of making movies continues to escalate—the typical Hollywood film costs $20 million to produce and $6.6 million to promote, and studios are now routinely greenlighting movies in the $30–$60 million range—it creates the need for an infusion of cash. And sometimes that cash is going to be in a foreign currency.

Analyst Harold Vogel says that while most of the major studios are well-enough positioned to keep foreign investors at bay, the same is not so true of the smaller independent studios. "They clearly need money," he says, "and they will take it from wherever they can get it."

Some observers warn that globalization of the film industry has its dark side. "Small" pictures will get lost in the shuffle.

Some Hollywood observers have warned that the globalization of the film industry has its dark side. They warn that "small" pictures will get lost in the shuffle and only those that have broad, cross-cultural appeal will get the financing and distribution necessary to reach an audience. There is some evidence to suggest that the "small" film may indeed be harder to find. According to *Daily Variety*, there were 126 independent features released through the first five months of 1989, compared to 180 films during the same period in 1988. Meanwhile, the major studios had released 63 pictures, up three from a year ago.

Certainly, the big global hits are movies that often seem more packaged than produced. At Disney, the foreign market provided a boost to two films that were already big winners at home, *Who Framed Roger Rabbit* and *Cocktail*. Although Disney executives count on their films taking in roughly 55 percent of their box-office receipts domestically and the other 45 percent internationally, both of those films broke out of that pattern to become enormous global hits. *Roger Rabbit*, for instance, earned $155 million at home and $198 million abroad, while *Cocktail*, starring Tom Cruise, took in $80 million domestically and $103 million internationally. "*Cocktail*," says Disney executive Kevin Hyson, is an example of a movie that "had everything you want for a film to do well overseas: It was a very glossy picture, with a popular star, a good soundtrack, and it was filmed in exotic locations."

As the importance of the international market grows, studios try to maximize the global appeal of their movies.

As the importance of the international market grows, studios sometimes try to maximize the global appeal of many of their movies by casting stars with broad international appeal and tailoring their marketing programs to the specific cultural biases of individual countries. "Production people are always looking at the international numbers to see what types of films work overseas," says Hyson. Sean Connery, for instance, may be a big star in the United States, but he is a huge one overseas. Connery was used by UIP (Paramount's overseas distributor) to sell *The Untouchables* to European audiences two years ago even though he played only a supporting role. (Sometimes, however, the taste of foreign audiences can be inexplicable. Mickey Rourke, for example, is a huge star in Germany, largely due to the popularity there of *9½ Weeks*.)

At least one independent producer argues that fears over Hollywood's loss of unique character may be overstated.

But at least one independent producer argues that fears over Hollywood's loss of unique character may be overstated. Kevin McCormick (*Saturday Night Fever*, *Burglar*) says that globalization has been a positive trend because it has created within these megastudios a number of separate fiefdoms, each with its own miniboss, who is more accessible than the studio heads of old yet can still command the distribution and marketing expertise of a huge operation. "As the studios gobble up each other, accompanying that is an ability to do different things," says McCormick. "There are more people you can go to with a project."

As an example, McCormick points to a project with Sally Field that he has finally been able to get off the ground. "Sally always loved this book, *Saint*, by Christine Bell, which is sort of a cross between Gabriel Garcia Marquez and *Private Benjamin*. It's about a woman who marries her college sweetheart, who happens to be an exchange student, and ends up 15 years later on a hacienda in South America, wondering how she got there. The project had been around for a while. Everyone said they liked the book, but they didn't quite get it. We jumped in, got the money and optioned it. Then people started calling. The story had all the ingredients {for global marketing}: an American character—as well as a major American star—yet was knowledgeable about Latin American life and culture, and how an American related to the rest of the world."

After weighing several offers, including one from Pedro Almodovar, McCormick and Field decided to go with Pathe Entertainment, the Giancarlo Parretti-controlled company that is now being run by Alan Ladd Jr.

McCormick, like others who have made deals with the new global titans, also dismisses the idea that the new Hollywood is any more money-oriented than the old. After all, Louis B. Mayer and Harry Cohn may have run their studios with an iron hand, and they may have had more personal visions of what movies to make than the bottom-line media executives now running Hollywood, but they still had to answer to the money men back east. And it's a bit hard to wax poetic about the potential loss of small, creative films in the global marketplace when Hollywood itself churns out a summer of movies that are either sequels, retreads or big-screen treatments of comic-book heroes with a built-in audience.

Money is still what makes Hollywood hum. The odds against a huge hit may be long but clearly improve when computed on an international scale. A film may have to recoup its money not through box office sales but through repeated TV viewings in Australia and Belize. And thanks to ancillary and library sales, a film that lost money at the box-office may ultimately end up in the black. In the long run, if film-making wasn't profitable, "then you wouldn't have all this interest," says analyst Joseph Di Lillo. "There is a certain glamour in being associated with Hollywood, but in the end, cash flow overshadows glamour." ♦

The odds against a huge hit may be long but clearly improve when computed on an international scale.

Question for Discussion

1. Is the purchasing of American movie studios by foreign companies a good thing or a bad thing? Explain.

Suggested Readings

For More on Michael Eisner of the Disney Company

Joe Flower, *The Prince of the Magic Kingdom: Michael Eisner and the Re-Making of Disney* (New York: Wiley, 1991).

For More on American "Cultural Imperialism"

Brookman, Faye, "U.S. Gameshows Fit Foreign Slots: Or, What's Ulrika Wearing Tonight?", *Variety* Vol. 339, April 18, 1990, p. S8 (2).

Edwards, Henry and Peter Rainer, "Sex-Rated," *Vogue* Vol. 179, April, 1989, p. 236 (4). Love scenes in movies are a measure of national style and taste.

Engelhardt, Tom, "Bottom Line Dreams and the End of Culture," *The Progressive* Vol. 54, October, 1990, p. 30 (6). Multinationalism and publishing.

Mahler, Richard, "A Tough Sell in Asia: Television Shows from America," *The Philadelphia Inquirer,* November 3, 1991, p. H-13. In Japan and other parts of Asia, American television programs are much less popular than they are in other areas of the world.

McLuhan, Marshall and Bruce Powers, *The Global Village: Transformations in World Life and Media in the 21st Century.* Expanding on what the late Marshall McLuhan said years ago about the implications of electronic media on international relations. This book is reviewed by A. J. Anderson in *Library Journal,* March 15, 1989, p. 76 (1).

Miller, Jim, "Pop Takes a Global Spin: Exotic Sounds Play from Bulgaria to Zaire," *Newsweek,* June 13, 1988, p. 72 (3). Includes related article.

Ryback, Timothy W., "Raisa Gorbachev Is an Elvis Fan, and Other Reasons Why Scholars Should Study the Role of Rock in Eastern Europe," *The Chronicle of Higher Education,* June 6, 1990, p. B1 (2).

Schneider, Cynthia, and Brian Wallis, *Global Television* This book is reviewed by Herbert I. Schiller in *Art in America,* January 1990, p. 41 (2).

Thomas, Marlo, "Soviet and American Kids: They Share a Common Language—Rock 'n' Roll," *TV Guide* Vol. 36, December 10, 1988, p. 9 (2).

Vargas Llosa, Mario, "A Cultural Battle," *UNESCO Courier,* September, 1990, p. 44 (2).

On the Business Dimensions of International Media

Bagdikian, Ben H., "Conquering Hearts and Minds: The Lords of the Global Village," *The Nation* Vol. 248, June 12, 1989, p. 805 (13). Includes related profiles of Rupert Murdoch, as well as Reinhard Mohn, the late Robert Maxwell, and Jean-Luc Lagardere.

Hoffman, Gary M., and George T. Marcou, "The Costs and Complications of Piracy," *Society* Vol. 27, September–October 1990, p. 25 (10). Countries such as Thailand where international criminals sell bootleg books and tapes.

Huey, John, "America's Hottest Export: Pop Culture," *Fortune,* December 31, 1990, p. 50 (7).

Magiera, Marcy and David Kilburn, "Hollywood Gets World View," *Advertising Age* Vol. 60, October 2, 1989, p. 2 (2). Foreign ownership of movie studios may change film marketing rules.

Paluszek, John, "Public Relations in the Coming Global Economy; Changes of Epic Proportion Are Happening, *Vital Speeches* Vol. 56, October 15, 1989, p. 22 (5).

Zonana, Victor F., "Global Media," *Los Angeles Times,* January 5, 1992, p. D1 (2). With many major players heavily indebted, some observers wonder anew about the viability of worldwide enterprises.

On the Role of American Media in International Politics

"Did TV Undo an Empire?," *World Monitor: The Christian Science Monitor Monthly* Vol. 3, March, 1990, p. 28 (3). TV's influence in the fall of Communist governments in Eastern Europe.

Schorr, Daniel, "How TV Helped Tear Down the Berlin Wall," *TV Guide* December 23, 1989, p. 10 (2).

"TV's Role in Global Political Turmoil," *USA Today* Vol. 119, August 1990, p. 13 (1).

International Aspects of American Advertising

"Look But Don't Touch," *The Economist*, Vol. 315, June 16, 1990, p. 80 (2). Advertising in Russia.

Magiera, Marcy and David Kilburn, "Hollywood Gets World View," *Advertising Age*, Vol. 60, October 2, 1989, p. 2 (2). Foreign ownership of movie studios may change film marketing rules.

Part II

THE PRINT MEDIA

5

Newspapers

Newspapers are our oldest mass medium, and there has been much talk of late about their imminent demise. With all the wonders of electronic communication around us, the conventional wisdom goes, how can this curiously old-fashioned medium survive?

Actually, the industry is surprisingly healthy. The newspaper business generates more than 30 billion dollars a year in ad revenues—about twice that of the television industry.

Newspapers are unique as a medium of communication. They are inexpensive and, compared to television, relatively portable, permanent, organized, in-depth and recyclable. They can be carried along to work on any form of transportation, they can be kept for weeks if they aren't read immediately, they are generally indexed so you can easily look up information such as weather, sports scores, movie times, stock quotations, and classified ads. They can provide much more information than even the longest television or radio newscast, and they provide that information in a format that makes it possible for you to go back and go over it if you didn't understand it the first time. And even after they have been used to line the bird cage and bring the fish home from the lake, they can be recycled into useful paper products like egg cartons and cardboard boxes. (Unfortunately, they don't make very good newsprint, because recycled newspapers have a tendency to disintegrate in large high-speed presses.)

Total daily newspaper circulation in the United States is a respectable 63 million. Newspaper circulation has remained pretty constant for most of this century, although there is cause for alarm in the way it has not increased with our increase in population. Since 1950, for example, the population has increased by 53%, but newspaper circulation has increased only by 17%.

Many observers have decried the death of the great afternoon papers, and indeed many have died in cities that are choked by daytime traffic. But there are still more afternoon papers (1,150) than morning papers (525), although circulation is greater in the morning (40 million) than afternoon (23 million). There are also far more weekly papers than daily papers (7,606 to 1,675) although the circulation of the dailies is still somewhat greater (63 million to 53 million).

Competition is also a problem in the newspaper industry, as the great majority of urban papers now operate as secure monopolies. In recent years we have seen the death of several great competing papers, including the *Chicago Daily News, Los Angeles Herald Examiner, New York Herald Tribune, Philadelphia Bulletin,* and the *Washington Star.* There is also a sharp concentration of chain ownership. About two-thirds of U.S. papers are owned by chains. The ten largest are as follows:

10 Largest Newspaper Chains

Company	**Daily Circulation**	**Properties**
Gannett	6 mil.	*USA Today* and 92 others
Knight-Ridder	3.8 mil.	*Philadelphia Inquirer, Miami Herald,* and 26 others
Newhouse	3 mil.	*Staten Island Advance, Portland Oregonian,* and 24 others
Times Mirror	2.6 mil.	*Los Angles Times* and 7 others
Tribune Company	2.6 mil.	*Chicago Tribune* and 7 others
Dow Jones & Co.	2.4 mil.	*Wall Street Journal* and 22 others
Thomson	2.1 mil.	122 dailies
New York Times	1.9 mil.	*New York Times* and 26 others
Scripps-Howard	1.5 mil.	*Pittsburgh Press* and 20 others
Cox	1.2 mil.	*Atlanta Journal* and 17 others

In this chapter, we will look at the newspaper business, the "image" of newspapers today, and at what has come to be known as "the new sensationalism." Thus, we have three articles: an inside look at the effects of big-business control (Doug Underwood, "When MBA's Rule the Newsroom"), a look at the lack of credibility some papers suffer from (Walker Lundy, "Why Do Readers Mistrust the Press?") and a look at how two competing papers dealt with a series of particularly graphic photographs (Don Fry's "The Shocking Pictures of Sage").

When MBAs Rule the Newsroom

Doug Underwood

When local papers are taken over by a giant conglomerate, changes happen. Not all of these changes are necessarily negative. A large corporation provides financial support, "economies of scale" for national and feature coverage, and managerial expertise. Some consider that last benefit a detriment, however. As managers concentrate on making a paper profitable, news becomes briefer and flashier (more like television) and reporters are given a new list of rules so they can be more productive (more like, say, factory workers). Many critics feel that the primary informative function of newspapers is co-opted by the move toward "fluff" and "safe journalism." And even though papers are generally promised by their parent corporations that there will be no interference in their editorial policies, their editors are given profit goals that increase each year. Even an editor who is committed to quality journalism has to make some tough choices in the face of these profit goals.

In the next reading Doug Underwood, who is currently on the faculty of the Department of Journalism at the University of Washington, analyzes the effects of managerial leadership that values profits over good journalism. Underwood was formerly a reporter for the Gannett News Service, as well as for The Seattle Times, *so he speaks not just from his extensive research, but from personal experience as well.*

Reading Difficulty Level: 6.

When executive editor Michael R. Fancher outlined his "1986 goals" for *Seattle Times* publisher Frank Blethen, he sounded like any other striving young organization man on the fast track, fresh from the University of Washington with an MBA in hand.

Bottom-line editors are radically changing American journalism.

In the memo, Fancher talked about overseeing a reorganization of newsroom management, establishing priorities for the development of senior editors, and serving as liaison with the circulation department to help the *Times* meet its circulation goals. Forty percent of his time, he said, would be spent coordinating the news department's role in marketing and keeping the newsroom budget in line.

Nowhere in the memo did Fancher talk about the news—either overseeing the direction of the newspaper's coverage, participating in news decisions, or helping to develop story ideas.

Reprinted from the *Columbia Journalism Review* March/April 1988, with permission.

Welcome to the world of the modern, corporate newspaper editor, a person who, as likely as not, is going to be found in an office away from the newsroom bustle, immersed in marketing surveys, organizational charts, budget plans, and memos on management training.

It's not surprising that, as corporations have extended their hold on U.S. newspapers, the editors of those newspapers have begun to behave more and more like the managers of any other corporate entity. It's understandable, too, that in an age enthralled by the arcana of scientific business management—and at a time when the percentage of the population reading newspapers has declined—newspaper executives have reshaped their newspapers in the name of better marketing, more efficient management, and improvement of the bottom line.

The editors of newspapers have begun to behave more and more like the managers of any other corporate entity.

So maybe we shouldn't be worried as the pressures grow on newspapers to treat their readership as a market—to use the words of the business consultants who have proliferated throughout the industry—and the news as a product to appeal to that market.

Well, after spending more than a dozen years as a reporter with *The Seattle Times* and the Gannett Company, I'm plenty worried. And, after interviewing more than fifty reporters and editors around the country, I find a lot of others who believe that profit pressures and the corporate ethic are fundamentally transforming—and not necessarily for the better—the nature of the newspaper business as generations of reporters and editors have known it.

In fact, many of the people I talked to say they feel increasingly unwelcome in a business that once was a haven for the independent, irreverent, creative spirits who have traditionally given newspapers their personalities.

Frank McCulloch, a longtime McClatchy executive who is now managing editor of the *San Francisco Examiner,* notes the "invidious pressure in top management of the MBA mentality," and says, "What has begun here is an inexorable process. Companies have increasingly come under the guidance of professional managers. I can't think of many companies that haven't drifted or consciously moved in that direction. Maybe what I'm expressing is nostalgia. But I still hold a deep suspicion that a lot of the strength of those companies lies in their idiosyncrasies. And professional managers can't tolerate idiosyncrasies."

The strength of many papers lies in their idiosyncracies. And professional managers can't stand idiosyncracies.

David Burgin, the editor of the *Dallas Times Herald,* concedes that newspapers have a problem on their hands because, as survey after survey has shown, many younger people simply aren't very interested in reading newspapers. But he deplores the growing dominance of marketing managers.

The newsroom of the *New York Post*, as reporters waited to hear more about the release of Terry Anderson in 1991. (Photo by Bruce Cotler.)

"I don't think editors are as good or as powerful as they were ten or fifteen years ago," Burgin says. "The new power in the industry is the marketing director. I want to see more swashbuckling editors, like Ben Bradlee or Jim Bellows. But those days are dead. Now it's target marketing and target marketing and more marketing."

Burgin adds, "It's leading to the homogenization of American newspapers. They look alike. They feel alike. It's me-too journalism all over the country."

And many reporters—including some who have been in the business for less than a dozen years—say they already feel like relics in a profession that reminds them more and more of IBM or the insurance industry.

Many reporters say they feel like relics in a profession that reminds them more and more of IBM or the insurance industry.

Laura Berman, a former *Detroit Free Press* reporter who now writes a column for *The Detroit News*, says that since Gannet's purchase of the *News* two years ago, the *News* and the Knight-Ridder-owned *Free Press* have competed to see which paper can produce the better "packaged journalism," with its emphasis on color, graphics, and splashy layouts. "The written word—it isn't as important anymore," she says. "If you're a writer you can't like the trend. Everything becomes like *People* magazine and *USA Today*. Basically, it's not as much fun.

"All the editors have come up in the corporate environment," she adds. "That's a symptom of the times—the growing acceptance that you work for a Fortune 500 company that has marketing interests."

Modern corporation management and packaging theories are sapping the vitality of creative editors and reporters.

Changing Times—and *The Seattle Times*

In many respects, my own career has been a retreat from the trends of the new corporate journalism—until it ran me right out of the business and into teaching. When I began my career at the Lansing, Michigan, *State Journal* in 1974, my managing editor was a fellow named Ben Burns, an irreverent, aggressive, shoot-from-the-hip newspaperman who helped to launch a probe of the Michigan State University football recruiting program, angered the paper's advertising director by his hard-hitting coverage of local business problems, encouraged in-depth investigations of important local government issues, and took delight in overspending his newsroom budget.

Burns, who went on to become executive editor at *The Detroit News*, was demoted when Gannett purchased the paper. His replacement as editor was Bob Giles, the prototypical Gannett editor, who has just published a 700-page tome, complete with charts on motivation, models of conflict resolution, and graphs on leadership behavior, called, *Newsroom Management: A Guide to Theory and Practice*.

Burns, who has since joined the faculty at Wayne State University in Detroit, doesn't mince words in describing what he thinks is happening to the business. "Modern corporation management and packaging theories are sapping the vitality of creative editors and reporters," he says. "It's the General Motors syndrome. In order to survive, newspapers try to look like everybody else. People who stand out from the crowd are at risk. And what you breed out of editors is the willingness to take risks with their careers. Now we think we can create good editors by management training. You end up with a CPA mentality among midlevel editors."

When I joined the Gannett News Service's Washington, D.C., bureau in 1976, we served about fifty-five Gannett newspapers out of cramped and cluttered offices in the old National Press Building. Five years later, when I left, Gannett had about eight-five newspapers and we were working in a modern, hermetically sealed, downtown office cube, complete with nouveau art, glitzy furniture, and the corporate logo stuck on everything in sight. I found it highly symbolic that, a few months before my departure, the company tore out the Gannett News

Service library to make way for offices for the executives planning *USA Today*—the quintessential corporately planned and packaged, market-driven newspaper.

My former colleagues, many of whom worked at *USA Today* before fleeing back to the Gannett News Service or leaving for other jobs, report that news meetings at *USA Today* are only half-jokingly referred to as marketing meetings by some staffers. Reporters' copy, they say, is simply grist for editors, who hack it and reshape it into the brief, graphically oriented copy that gives the paper its television feel.

USA Today "was managed to the point where what appeared under your name was irrelevant to what you wrote," says *San Francisco Examiner* reporter Eric Brazil, a former *USA Today* bureau chief in Los Angeles and a former Sacramento bureau chief for the Gannett News Service. "At a managed newspaper it beats you down. You either do it their way or you leave."

But it wasn't until I came to *The Seattle Times* in 1981 that I realized how ubiquitous the corporate influence had become and how futile it was to try to escape the changes in the business.

Even though the *Times* is controlled by the local Blethen family (Knight-Ridder owns a 49 percent share of the company), executive editor Fancher has come to epitomize the business-oriented style of editor found at so many corporately managed newspapers. As part of his grooming for the top editor's job, he was encouraged to go back to the University of Washington for a business degree. And, soon after getting it, he began applying his business training to the newsroom organization.

While Fancher entrusts the day-to-day decision-making to his newsroom lieutenants, he keeps a secure grip on the system through a pervasive newsroom bureaucracy. Under Fancher, there has been a proliferation of mid-level editors in the newsroom. These editors, few of whom have much reporting experience, keep a tight leash on the reporters, who work from computer lists of proposed stories that have been approved by committees of editors—and, to a large extent, have already been shaped and packaged by them. Strict oversight of the entire newsroom operation is maintained through countless editorial meetings and memos and by using computers to check out each staff member's lists of projects, which must be constantly kept up to date.

USA Today *"was managed to the point where what appeared under your name was irrelevent to what you wrote."*

The *Times*'s approach to management "scrubs the life out of everything," says Dick Clever, who recently left the *Times*, to become an editor at the *Seattle Post-Intelligencer*, the *Times*'s A.M. partner in a joint operating agreement.

Last year, Clever, a well-respected street-savvy veteran reporter, was passed over for a job as an assistant city editor at the *Times*, at least in part, he says, because a

The commitment to local news clearly seems to have waned.

company psychologist who interviewed him during the job selection process reported that he showed little interest in paperwork or bureaucratic routine. (A spokesperson for the *Times*-declined to speak about Clever's case specifically, but did say that the interview "was a useful part of the process that was one aspect of the decision.")

"The impulse of their system is to quantify and manage and control all the elements of the product," Clever says, "There are limits to how much you can do that in a newsroom and still have a product that reflects the vitality of a community. As much as Fancher talks about change, I think he's adopted a very rigid approach to newsroom structure. You either adapt to it or get crunched."

People involved in the look of the newspaper—artists, graphic designers, layout editors—are thriving.

While some reporters have misgivings about Fancher's approach, people involved in the look of the newspaper—artists, graphic designers, layout editors—are thriving under it. And, in fact, under Fancher's direction, the *Times*—a drab, dully written, chamber-of-commerce-oriented newspaper throughout much of its history—has put a pretty face on its once-gray pages.

The newspapers's new emphasis on appearance and bright writing has won it a series of design and news- and feature-writing prizes. As part of Fancher's "margin of excellence" program, readers of the *Times* have been inundated with colorfully packaged special projects and special sections.

At the same time, however, the newspaper's commitment to local news clearly seems to have waned. The amount of local news space is often ridiculously small—sometimes only three pages a day. The newspaper brims with light features, food sections, and special "how-to" sections—how to manage your personal finances, say, or how to repair your car. But the lack of aggressive local news coverage, combined with the slick, preplanned news product, gives the feel of a newspaper that doesn't really know what's going on in the community.

Fancher, for his part, strongly defends what he calls "a consensus style" of management that involves all the key editors in the decision-making process, and he counters those who challenge his commitment to hard news by pointing to the number of awards the *Times* has won in recent years, including two Pulitzers (both entries written by reporters who, incidentally, have since left the *Times* and the daily newspaper business). "This newspaper is phenomenally better than it was five years ago," Fancher says, "It isn't better *despite* the system, but *because* of the system."

A recent editor of *Presstime*, the journal of the American Newspaper Publisher's Association, noted that five of the *Times*'s top executives—the company president, the controller, the treasurer, the vice-president in charge of circulation, and executive editor Fancher—have MBAs. And it cited the *Times* as an example of a newspaper at which the finance manager consults with all department heads and is the key player in all management decisions.

Fancher admits that the *Times*'s financial people have played a big role in allocating news resources. "I think you'll see it even more in the future," he adds. "The era when I, the editor, could say, 'This goes because I'm the editor,' is gone."

In fact, Fancher has become something of a proselytizer on the subject of blending the news and financial sides of newspapers. In a piece that appeared recently in the *Gannett Center Journal,* titled "Metamorphosis of the Newspaper Editor," Fancher wrote that the "modern newspaper editor is expected to be a marketing expert as well as an editor. . . . Some editors resist getting involved in the *business* of newspapering, fearful they will be tainted by filthy lucre. I believe those editors are doomed. Sooner or later, their journalistic options will be proscribed by someone else's bottom line. It's a fact of modern business life."

This point of view is shared by many in the industry—indeed, it has virtually become gospel—and in academic circles as well. Steve Star, an influential media marketing consultant who teaches at the Massachusetts Institute of Technology's Sloan School of Management, says, "The senior marketing official is the editor—that's what a good editor instinctively does." And, in fact, several editors have assumed the dual role of editor and circulation director.

"It's an excellent trend," says Philip Meyer, a former Knight-Ridder reporter and the author of *The Newspaper Survival Book,* who teaches journalism at the University of North Carolina. "I believe in the total newspaper concept. You can't be an excellent editor unless you understand the business side. Some editors—but only foolish ones—are proud they don't know what their budget is."

Corporate Newsrooms, Tailored 'Products'

The move toward corporatization of the newsroom received impetus back in the mid-1970s, when publishers and editors began worrying about studies showing that young people weren't reading newspapers and that sales per household were declining. The American Newspaper Publishers Association hired Star to conduct a series of marketing and strategic planning seminars for editors and senior newspaper executives: The American Society of Newspaper Editors sponsored readership surveys by marketing researcher Ruth Clark, which persuaded newspapers to make greater use of briefs, graphics, anchored features, and interpretive and "help-me-cope" pieces.

Some editors resist getting involved in the business of newspapering. Those editors are doomed.

A later Clark study found that, while readers wanted "coping" information, they did not want it at the expense of hard news. Some editors saw this as a welcome sign that readers wanted the pendulum to swing back to traditional news coverage. Others thought that the industry's preoccupation with market studies had become obsessive. "Newspapers can put research to good use—and should," says Eugene Patterson, chairman and c.e.o. of the *St. Petersburg Times*. "But we lose our way and mistake our mission if we think our business is only to give the public what it wants. We're not in this business to lick the public's hand; we're here to tell people what they need to know."

We lose our way and mistake our mission if we think our business is only to give the public what it wants. We're here to tell people what they need to know.

During the seventies, too, newspapers were caught up in the same economic turbulence that was wrenching the rest of U.S. industry. Rapid technological change came to both the newsroom and the back shop. Big-city newspapers did battle with the suburban press, shoppers, television, and cable television for advertisers and affluent readers. From 1977 through 1985, an average of about fifty dailies a year changed hands, many of them purchased by newspaper groups—and the profit pressures on publicly traded newspaper companies escalated.

All in all, the last decade left an indelible message in the minds of many newspaper owners and editors: to survive they must more aggressively manage their finances and tailor their "product" to conform more closely to the interests of their readers.

Indicative of the fixation on finances and newsroom management, and of the role played by the new technology, are the seminars that have been developed for the American Press Institute in Reston, Virginia. At these seminars, which were scheduled to begin in February, newspaper executives will learn how to make decisions affecting all departments by manipulating advertising, circulation, and production data contained in a computer-simulated newspaper operation. Meanwhile, at the myriad industry conferences held each year, editors repeatedly hear about all the latest technological developments—and about the techniques for winning their acceptance in the newsroom.

At last year's Associated Press Managing Editors convention in Seattle, Louis LeHane, of Thompson Group, a consulting firm, urged editors to "create a culture" in their newsrooms that will ensure that reporters and mid-level executives will not resist the application of new business management practices. To achieve this end, he suggested that management should set up teams, develop lots of dialogue, and create "win-win situations." LeHane ended his remarks on this note of eerie managementese: "Some of the people may be forced to learn by peer pressure, because in a participatory system, the noncontributors—those who can't go from the rejection to the acceptance stage—really aren't tolerated." (Translation: the new newsroom is no place for nonconformists.)

What the Troops Are Saying

So how are the folks in the trenches—the reporters and mid-level editors who put the newspapers together—holding up in this era of test-marketing, readership surveys, audience targeting, and budget planning?

Not always so well, it seems.

• Drex Heikes, a former metro editor at *The Fresno Bee* who is now city editor of the *Los Angeles Times*'s San Fernando Valley edition, describes a budgeting and personnel process at McClatchy Newspapers that has become so burdensome that some editors have little time to do anything else. McClatchy's financial people, he points out, for example, require that newsroom budgeting—once an annual exercise—be continually updated.

"It seems like the bureaucratic and corporate requirements have reached down to the department heads and editors like me," he says. "Those people are swimming in paperwork. It's a tremendous frustration to deal with that, because we're the people who are the guardians of the quality of the newspaper."

• Ivan Weiss, a veteran wire editor at *The Seattle Times,* is outspokenly critical of the kind of management system that has been imposed on members of The Newspaper Guild at the *Times,* among other papers, in an era when many unions are being forced to make concessions. The *Times* now ties pay raises directly to job evaluations, and reporters and copy editors are graded not only for professional skills but also for what in elementary school would be called deportment—e.g., punctuality, cooperativeness, willingness to respond to authority. "Morale is shot," Weiss says. "This system has nothing to do with journalism. It has everything to do with bureaucratic control, and bureaucratic control is the enemy of all journalists."

Bureaucratic control is the enemy of all journalists.

• John F. Persinos, a former business reporter for *The Orlando Sentinel* who is now an associate editor at *Venture* magazine, says the *Sentinel* has evolved into a market-driven, slickly packaged cash machine. In the business department, he says, this means that the staff spends an inordinate amount of time producing copy for two new weekly supplements devoted to business and to consumer money-management.

"It's a pernicious trend," he says. "Marketing always came first. You felt like you were a copywriter for the marketing department, cranking out stories so they could sell ads for the sections."

• In Dallas, the once-aggressive news competition has evolved into a marketing battle in which the city's two dailies are trying to appeal to upscale North Dallas readers. The *Morning News* has been particularly solicitous of affluent readers, with its "High Profile" section, featuring

Newspapers used to offer an intelligent alternative. Now we're writing for the lowest common denominator.

pieces about Texas's rich and powerful people, and "Fashion! Dallas," another puffy special section.

"I'm afraid that the *News* and papers like it run the risk of appearing to be slavishly adoring of the power structure," says Brad Bailey, formerly a reporter at the *Dallas Morning News* and now a freelancer. "The effect on [newsroom] morale was to realize we weren't part of an art or a sacred responsibility but a business to put out a package that was attractive to a market segment. If most journalists realized they were going into that, they'd go into real estate."

• John Kolesar, ex-night news editor at *The Record* in Bergen County, New Jersey, says that packaging and graphics requirements at a place like *The Record* can also make life on the desk pretty unrewarding. "I think what we do with this packaging can get very damaging," says Kolesar, who is now managing editor at the *Courier-Post*, in Cherry Hill, New Jersey. "All the time that's spent in planning and packaging and detail work is time that's taken away from the news and the substance of news. It's a very corrosive thing. My mother didn't raise me to be an interior decorator. I was interested in the news."

All the time that's spent in planning and packaging is time taken away from the news and the substance of news. It's a very corrosive thing.

Kolesar's views are echoed by reporters who complain that their jobs have become circumscribed by management's obsession with packaging, marketing, and tight writing.

"I don't write anything readers can't get on television," says one *Record* reporter who requested anonymity. "The thing about newspapers is they used to offer an intelligent alternative. Now we're writing for the lowest common denominator. *The Record* and papers like it are running a terrible risk of insulting the readers who've stuck with them for years."

• Even at Knight-Ridder—long hailed as a corporation that manages its newspapers for quality—some reporters believe that the marketers and the corporate types have gotten the upper hand. Knight-Ridder pioneered the use of personality tests for new employees and of executive pay raises geared to the attainment of "management-by-objective" goals. Now one reporter at the chain's flagship paper, *The Miami Herald*, says that his newsroom bosses make it clear to feature reporters, through their market research, what kinds of stories they want. Stories that appeal to the yuppy market, suburban readers, and Hispanics are encouraged, he says. "Stories that aren't seen as targeted to a particular audience get short shrift."

This reporter, who entered the business during the social activist days of the 1960s, finds the trend very discouraging. "The change-the-world style of journalism is waning to the point where it's an endangered species," he says. "I don't know but a handful of my friends who are still in the business to make the world a better place."

A closely related theme is sounded by mid-career newspaper people, particularly those who got into journalism during Watergate and Vietnam. They say they are finding it tougher to question authority out in the world when they themselves are being pressured to become loyal corporate soldiers inside their own organizations.

"You don't see a lot of Watergate-inspired stories in papers in the U.S. anymore," says John Kolesar. "I guess the editors are like the readers: they've apparently changed the kinds of stories they like. They'd rather read about sugarless desserts than about the Democrats who have padded the payroll in the courthouse."

Ironically, many reporters are feeling that way at a time when newspapers—at least, the better ones—are devoting more resources than ever to investigate teams and big, expensive projects designed to win prestigious prizes. Winning such prizes is, of course, a marketing tool. Kolesar, for example, tells about sitting on a committee at the Bergen *Record* that set up a plan for trying to divine what kind of project might win a Pulitzer.

Some reporters feel that their papers are becoming factories at which editors neglect basic, day-to-day reporting so they can put their resources into high-profile, prize-winning projects. Richard Morin, a former editor and reporter at *The Miami Herald* who is now polling director at *The Washington Post*, says he was afraid this might happen at the *Herald* as its profit picture dimmed. "I don't want to reach a point where every newspaper will have a ten-person investigative team and one person covering everything else," Morin says.

Reporters also note that the character of investigations is changing. Michael Wagner, an investigative reporter for the *Detroit Free Press*, says that newspapers are a "perfect mirror" of a pro-business government and of a population focusing on personal problems.

"The appetite these days is for fairly safe, less controversial, sociological investigative stories," Wagner says. "If you look across the country, you see papers doing a great job of covering prisons and juvenile crime and child abuse. But you don't see people asking how Exxon got to be bigger than five or six countries in the world."

Brad Bailey, formerly of *The Dallas Morning News*, puts it this way: "Do you see a corporation that's in the business of making money going out and investigating other corporations? I don't."

Still, whether bottom-line management has led to better—or worse—journalism is an open question. People like Larry Fuller, the publisher of Gannet's Sioux Falls, South Dakota, *Argus Leader*, make a strong case that many of the country's newspapers, particularly those in smaller cities, have been invigorated by chain ownership.

"We have to change as society changes and everybody has to recognize that," Fuller says. "In my opinion, the problem isn't the newspapers that *have* changed; it's

Reporters say they are finding it tougher to question authority out in the world when they themselves are being pressured to become loyal corporate soldiers inside their own organizations.

the problem of newspapers that *haven't*. You look at many newspapers and they're still frighteningly dull."

Advocates of change, like Fuller, say, as you'd expect, that history, economics, and technology are on their side. But those of us who worry about the future of the newspaper business protest that we aren't just a bunch of romantic nostalgics, longing for an era of green eyeshades, sloppy management, and hack journalism. What worries us is whether the true values of the business—the craft of writing, the vigor of investigating, the sense of fairness and equity, the gut-level impulse to want to right wrongs—will survive in the new MBA-run, market-driven newsroom.

Eugene Patterson shows how this debate can cut both ways—even in the mind of the same person. Patterson has long been a vocal critic of chain-owned newspapers for letting their concern for short-term earnings replace journalistic concerns. But Patterson is also an advocate of what he calls "whole journalism," the integration of words and images by blending text, illustrations, and page design into a total concept—something that the new technology, by means of which pages can be designed on the computer screen, has already made a reality in many newsrooms.

A lot of reporters got into the business to be writers. If you take that away from them, they might as well have another job.

I want to close this piece with the words of Jim Renkes, a veteran reporter at the *Quad-City Times* in Davenport, Iowa, where the executives have taken the "whole journalism" philosophy to heart. The newspaper, which is filled with lots of boxes, big headlines, swaths of color, and "bite-sized nuggets of information," is designed to appeal to the busy, modern reader who tends to scan newspapers rather than read them.

The thirty-six-year-old Renkes, who has been with the paper ten years, says he doesn't think many of his younger, newly hired colleagues miss writing the longer, in-depth pieces—but he does.

"A lot of reporters, I think they got into the business to be writers," Renkes says. "They sure didn't get into it for the money. If you take that away from them—well, they might as well have another job. I'm almost melancholy about the whole thing." ♦

Questions for Discussion

1. In your opinion, are good journalism and corporate control mutually exclusive, or can they peacefully coexist?
2. Should editors, as a matter of course, have business training?
3. Let's say you get a job as a reporter at a paper where the packaging of the news is more important than the substance. How would you handle it—by fighting the system or going with the flow?

Why Do Readers Mistrust the Press?

Walker Lundy

Walker Lundy is the Executive editor of the St. Paul (Minn.) Pioneer Press. In this reading, Lundy points out another effect of corporate ownership: people tend to distrust monopolies and big businesses. Lundy also believes people lose faith in their local newspapers for other reasons that have little to do with corporate control: the papers make too many errors, they employ mostly young liberal reporters and editors, their operating procedures are mysterious, and if they're aggressive they simply tend not to be likable.

Lundy presented his remarks before a group of newspaper editors. His warning, in short, is that these editors need to help people view their papers with trust.

Reading Difficulty Level: 4.

How do you feel about the phone company? Or the oil companies? Or politicians? Think about it. Chances are you don't trust those guys very much, and you're not alone.

Rightly or wrongly, lots of people see them as too big, too powerful and not answerable to anybody most of the time. They think the phone company's arrogant, the oil companies are greedy, and the politicians are lazy or incompetent or both.

Well, brace yourselves, brother and sister editors: *Lots of readers put newspapers right up there with those other guys.* And in lots of ways, we deserve it.

From the *Asne Bulletin* (March, 1982). Reprinted with permission.

Newspapers *are* arrogant sometimes. "You ever try to talk to a newspaper?" Paul Newman asks rhetorically in *Absence of Malice.*

Lots of readers think newspapers are too powerful, arrogant and incompetent.

Many readers think complaining to a newspaper is pointless. We don't tell them whom to complain to, and if they do telephone us, they usually get a gruff, overworked news clerk who's making the minimum wage and doesn't give a hoot in hell about their beef. If they manage to get through to an editor, they often find that editor defensive and patronizing. Too often, it's like arguing with the umpire.

Sometimes it's a question of just plain good manners. For instance, when a newspaper takes a photo of someone and, for whatever reason, doesn't publish it, the person photographed—who perhaps went to some effort for the photo to be shot—is left wondering what happened. No one from the newspaper has time to call. That makes us look rude.

Most of us are the only unregulated monopoly in town, so we sure look greedy to lots of people.

Newspapers are greedy sometimes, too. Most of us are the only unregulated monopoly in town, so we sure look greedy to lots of people. And we act greedy when we charge the highest advertising rates for such noncommercial items as death notices and political advertising. (And then editorialize sanctimoniously against the high cost of campaigning.)

Talk about greedy? Some papers even make a few bucks by charging to print wedding announcements. They aren't news, the editors claim. (It also has the unfortunate effect of eliminating poor people's nuptials from the paper.)

Even papers as prestigious as the *New York Times* and the *St. Petersburg Times* peddle part of their front page for ads.

Newspapers are lazy sometimes, too. Journalists can get pretty damned impressed with themselves. Why else do we have to wear black ties to the ASNE banquet? It is a fact that many journalists stop hustling at an early age. I know some who even have taken up *golf.*

Newspapers are incompetent sometimes, too. You ever listened to the complaints of people misquoted in your paper? You ever try to get Circulation to stop your paper when you go on vacation?

Perhaps we should all put aside our First Amendment speeches for a few moments and own up: We journalists will never see the newspaper business with anything but a warm, life-long affection. That's our blind spot. Readers, however, don't have that handicap. To many of them, we're just another Big Business to be viewed with the same suspicions and mistrust. Some even think we're the worst of the bunch.

What reasons do we give readers to mistrust us? I can think of six. Some we can't avoid. But some we can:

1. We make too many errors.

Who's in charge of checking the facts **before** ***they're printed?***

Why don't newspapers have fact checkers? We have graphics editors and assistant managing editors for administration and ombudsmen for hearing about mistakes *after* they happen. But who's in charge of checking the facts *before* they're printed? Everyone, you say? We all know what happens when *everyone*'s in charge of something.

Our concern for accuracy often amounts to writing that mother up and shoving it in the paper pronto. If it's wrong, we'll run a correction the next day on page 2. Give us "100" for honesty and "0" for accuracy. Average grade: "50."

If we expect to keep the readers believing us, we'd better develop a deeper commitment to getting things right the first time. We'd also better quit making up stories and using nameless sources, whose truthfulness is unknown to the readers.

Suggestion: Now that the writing revolution is old hat, why don't we adopt accuracy as the next Great Newsroom Cause?

2. We employ almost exclusively young reporters and editors who are liberal—politically and otherwise—and who don't reflect the range of our readership.

Mortgage rates are a big story for many of our readers, but how many members of your staff own homes? Education is an important issue, but how many members of your staff have children?

If I were a political conservative, I'd suspect the nation's press of bias. (How many anti-ERA columns have you read on editorial pages?) If I were a member of the Moral Majority, I'd be convinced we're biased. (How many pro-Moral Majority cartoons have you seen on editorial pages?)

If I were older than 50 and visited the average newsroom, I'd wonder how that paper possibly could relate to people my age. If I were black and attended the news meeting, I'd wonder why only white people were in charge. If your staff doesn't reflect the community, some readers will be less likely to believe what the staff has to say.

Suggestion: List balancing the staff as one of your recruiting goals and try to broaden the range of employees.

3. Most of us are monopolies.

Who doesn't love to hate a monopoly?

Who doesn't love to hate a monopoly? For a newspaper, it's impossible sometimes not to rub people's noses in it. What do advertisers do when we make them so angry they want to take their business elsewhere? Where do readers go when they want to do the same thing? Some editors might say those people are free to quit us any time they want. But not in most communities, at least not if the advertiser wants to stay in business. And not if the reader wants to remain half-way informed about local news, or even what's playing at the movies or what supermarket has a special on toilet paper.

Suggestion: Have a system for making sure every complaint to the paper gets answered. Work hard at developing staff telephone manners. Demand that all employees be polite to everyone. Make it easy for complaining readers to get to the editors on the phone. When a reader phones, does your secretary ask, "Who's calling?" What difference does it make who's calling?

4. Most of us are large corporations.

Who doesn't love to hate Big Business?

Who doesn't love to hate Big Business?

Suggestion: Take time and space in the paper to explain yourself and your business decisions to your readers and customers. If you're having a subscription rate increase, make sure the story explains where the extra money's going and why.

5. We're our own sacred cow.

A newspaper is a pretty mysterious business for most people, and who trusts what he doesn't understand? Over the years, we've done a decent job of reporting on everyone's business but our own. Most people get their impressions of us from Hollywood.

Suggestion: The editor should write a regular column that tries to explain how the newspaper operates. Reporters should be assigned to cover the paper's news just like anyone else's.

A good, aggressive newspaper is often not a very likable institution.

6. A good, aggressive newspaper is often not a very likable institution.

Eventually, we get around to angering most people and organizations in town. We can't really avoid that, but we need to recognize that it also affects our credibility.

Suggestion: Insist that your staff be fair. Before you lambast somebody in an editorial, make sure you know in advance what that person's explanation is. Always get both sides. Check to make sure followup stories about the charges being dropped get the same play as the earlier arrest story. Do periodic spot checks to make sure your news report has balance. For example, pull the school beat reporter's byline file and see whether he's written any stories about what the school system's doing right.

We editors need to realize that many readers—perhaps a growing number—do not view our newspapers with the same warm trust that we do. They see us more as we see the other too-big, too-powerful monopolies in this country.

That's a problem we'd all better start trying to solve. ♦

Question for Discussion

1. Analyze your local paper in terms of the criticisms listed by Lundy. Is it guilty or innocent on each count?

The Shocking Pictures of Sage: Two Newspapers, Two Answers

Don Fry

American newspapers, since their very beginnings, have been guilty of sensationalizing the news. In recent times this sensationalization has taken on ugly overtones, as some newspapers offend sensibilities, invade privacy, and publish unsubstantiated rumors to increase sales. Different newspapers have re-

acted to this trend in different ways. Don Fry, the associate director of The Poynter Institute for Media Studies in St. Petersburg, Florida, analyzes one such case in the following reading.

Reading Difficulty Level: 3. The photographs have a much higher viewing difficulty level, however.

One night, as Sage Volkman slept, a spark from a wood stove set her father's camper on fire. The flames burned the five-year-old girl over 45 percent of her body, destroyed her eyelids, nose, and left ear, fused her toes together, and melted the skin on her legs, arms, chest, and face. Later, doctors had to amputate her fingers.

Two local newspapers, the Albuquerque *Journal* and *Tribune,* faced a series of decisions on printing photographs of the scarred girl as she struggled through operations, therapy, and her return to public view. One paper eventually decided not to risk offending its readers with shocking pictures, while the other printed gruesome photographs large in a special section. Why would two newspapers, edited for the same city, published in the same building under a joint operating agreement, reach such opposite conclusions on essentially the same materials?

Reprinted by permission of *Washington Journalism Review.* From the April, 1988 issue.

The Journal

The *Journal* initially ran three stories, illustrated only with a school photo of Sage *before* her accident. Then, six weeks after the fire, it sent reporter Steve Reynolds and photographer Gene Burton to the Shriners Burn Institute in Galveston, Texas, to report on Sage's treatment. Initially, Burton had some problems with feeling intrusive in the therapy sessions but he began to think, "What wonderful pictures." He soon came to regard the Volkmans as "one of the strongest and most courageous families I've ever been involved with," the universal reaction among people who have met them.

Two local newspapers, the Albuquerque Journal *and* Tribune, *faced a series of decisions on printing photographs of the scarred girl as she struggled through operations, therapy, and her return to public view.*

For the December 25th issue, Reynolds wrote a story on the Volkmans' emotional struggles. Asked how the Volkmans felt about the paper's coverage, he told his editors that the family was "open to publicity." Indeed, counselors at the Burn Institute had told the Volkmans that Sage would face major problems with public reactions. The institute's former nursing director, James Winkler, had said, as reported in Reynolds's story, "She's

Sage Volkman before the accident that would focus the attention of two Albuquerque newspapers.

When Sage returned to Albuquerque the* Journal *ran a large picture on the front page.

going back into the street for the first time as an entirely different person. . . . Society is going to be very cruel to her and it's going to, not intentionally, stop and stare and she's going to be ostracized." He recommended preparing Sage's schoolmates for her new appearance.

Burton offered a portfolio of pictures, which his photo editor took to higher editors for consultation. Eventually they settled for a color picture of the parents with Sage wrapped up in her Jobst suit, an elasticized body covering. A mask covered her face. This picture ran on page A-1, accompanied on A-13 by a black-and-white of the family without Sage. Reporter Reynolds, who did not participate in the photo deliberations, called the color picture "the least offensive photo we had [of her], and the safest."

This decision matched the style of the *Journal,* a statewide paper with a morning circulation of 117,000 daily and 153,000 on Sunday. The *Journal* considers itself a paper of record, and favors hard-news treatments. Its editor, Jerry Crawford, a short, neat, cautious man, has won wide respect for his courageous stands against corrupt politicians. He consults often and broadly, and runs an aggressive paper. Crawford characterizes the *Journal* as "very careful with pictures," always cautious about its "responsibility to anticipate what the public can deal with."

When Sage returned to Albuquerque the *Journal* ran a large picture on the front page. Totally covered up by her Jobst suit and mask, Sage reaches toward her brother, who smiles back. Crawford called it "the most appealing picture we had taken . . . with the greatest impact in terms of tugging the heart." The editors had rejected all the other pictures as "much too graphic."

During this period, the *Journal* discussed the pictures in editors' meetings, and Crawford often took them upstairs to Tom Lang, publisher of the *Journal.* Lang manages the joint operating agreement between the *Journal* and the *Tribune.* He also heads the Albuquerque Publishing company, which owns the building and prints the two papers. Lang rejected some of the pictures as "too graphic."

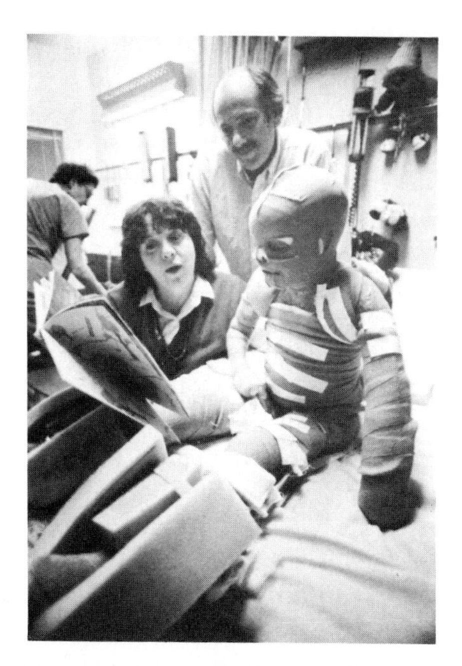

The *Journal* ran this photograph on page one. (Photo by Gene Burton.)

The photographer got complete cooperation from the Volkmans, who were willing to unbandage and disrobe Sage in the hospital. Although the family had preferred photos in Texas with Sage's mask on, after her return they began taking her out in public without it, as the Galveston counselors had advised. Reporter Reynolds told his editors that the family did not mind the coverage, indeed welcomed it.

The Shriners agreed to cover most of Sage's medical costs until her 18th birthday, estimated to run as high as $1 million. But the Volkmans faced other expenses far beyond Michael's means as a tree planter and Denise's salary as a kindergarten teacher. A whole series of fund-raising events helped build a trust fund for Sage.

Five of the stories in the *Journal* ended with a detailed notice on where to send contributions. Editor Crawford and Publisher Lang had several discussions about the family's need for publicity. Lang worried that the Volkmans were trying to make the paper into their advertising agency: "We didn't want to be their solicitor of funds." Crawford also suspected that the family wanted more explicit pictures in the paper.

Lang worried that the Volkmans were trying to make the paper into their advertising agency: "We didn't want to be their solicitor of funds."

By the summer months, Sage improved remarkably, learning to walk again and even riding her bike with training wheels. The family wanted to prepare Sage and her classmates for her return to school.

On July 27, the *Journal* made a decision that affected the coverage of Sage in unexpected ways. Although staff members remember the sequence of events with slight variations, a picture of the key meeting emerges.

Burton shot a new series of photographs, mostly at a therapy clinic. He brought both black-and-white and color pictures to Dan Ritchey, the Metro Plus section editor, while reporter Reynolds worked on a long story about the many people who voluntarily helped Sage and her parents.

Dan Ritchey found the pictures shocking, but "very warm, as warm as you could shoot." He and the photographer spread the prints on a slant table outside the office of Frankie McCarty, the managing editor for news, and asked her opinion. McCarty looked them over and said "They're pretty shocking, but we might be able to get by with this one," indicating one of the black-and-whites. She found the other pictures "gruesome," likely to offend readers, even outrage them. But she decided to consult the editor, Jerry Crawford.

Crawford came out and immediately rejected the color photos. He looked over the others, and said: "I see only one picture we can publish," paused, and said, "No, not even that one." Crawford pronounced all the pictures "too graphic." He took the pictures to his assistant editor, Kent Walz, for a second opinion, returned, and said, "Not even this one." Managing Editor McCarty left.

***The Journal* rejected the pictures as too graphic.**

Crawford felt amazed that the staff had proposed such photos, because he had turned down "less gruesome" ones before. He "thought the family wanted the paper to run shocking photos to educate potential classmates." He worried about the paper's reputation, as he always does, and "didn't want to be considered reckless." But he stayed and debated the issue with Ritchey and Burton.

Crawford brought up a page-one photo in the *Journal* several weeks before, showing an injured cyclist lying in the street. Paramedics had slit the rider's pants to treat his wounds, and Crawford had to field calls about revealing the underpants. He said, "I could tell the news value overrode the shock value *there,* but what is the news value *here?*" Section editor Ritchey argued that the family wanted people prepared for what Sage looked like; with the start of school coming up, they needed the pictures to break the ice. Photographer Burton argued: "Here's a story about a little girl. We should publish a picture. If it's okay with the family, why not with us?" Both stressed their desire to help the Volkmans. Crawford countered: "No, we've done that. . . . There's a fine line between our responsibility to our readers and helping this little girl."

The discussion ended.

Crawford did not think he had made a hard decision, "no big deal." But he sympathized with the disappointment he anticipated: "The staff was so close to it, so they felt let down. I felt sorry for Gene [Burton] and the writer because they wanted their work out." Managing Editor McCarty also worried about her staff's reaction, but she approved of the decision although she felt that "any story about a person is better with a picture of that person."

Crawford saw his decision as simple: "we would not run *those* photographs on *that* story." But as the decision began to reverberate through the newsroom, staff members separately interpreted its implications for their own work. Burton, the photographer, thought the decision meant that "we can never publish another picture of that girl in this newspaper." He received no further assignments on the Volkmans, and generated none himself.

Ritchey, the section editor, felt upset by the decision, but he thinks he got a fair hearing. Like the photographer, he took the finding to mean that the *Journal* would run no further pictures of the girl. He thought: "To have stories [on Sage], we have to have photos." Ritchey concluded: "It seemed dishonest to write stories about the child being accepted while saying the child's face is too gruesome to run in the newspaper." He assigned no further stories on Sage Volkman.

Reynolds, the reporter, learned of the debate, and thought: "If you're not going to use those pictures, you're not going to use any." As a writer, he worried that describing Sage's disfigurement would seem "exploitive and sensational." Only pictures could capture "the way she is in public." He felt disillusioned, and lost interest in the Volkman story. Apparently no one in the newsroom thought a policy on Sage had been announced, but many other staffers were upset by the implications.

The next day, July 28, Reynolds's story appeared in a zoned section, with no pictures. In a later edition, the main section of the *Journal* picked it up and ran it with the old file photo taken before the fire. Section editor Ritchey angrily sealed the library copy of the mug shot in an envelope so it could never run again. He thought it was "insensitive to remind people how cute and beautiful she was." Despite a series of fund-raising events, the *Journal* published no further stories on Sage until December 4, seven weeks after the *Tribune's* special section came out.

The Tribune

Meanwhile, the *Tribune* had published nothing on Sage beyond a few city briefs. Vickie Lewis, a staff photographer, began shooting pictures with the Volkman family on her own time. One day in February or March (no one seems to remember), she tossed a half-dozen difficult photos onto Editor Tim Gallagher's desk and proposed a pictorial essay. Tim says he made no formal decision on what would become a major project involving controversial photographs; he just told Vickie "to take all the time you need." The casual style of this interchange tells a lot about the contrast between the two papers an their editors.

The reporter worried that describing Sage's disfigurement would seem "exploitive and sensational."

The *Tribune,* an afternoon daily owned by Scripps-Howard, has a circulation of 43,000, about one-third of the *Journal's,* with only 15 percent overlap in readership. The *Journal's* editor, Jerry Crawford, characterizes the rival paper as "less cautious . . . more likely to rush into print." He thinks "the *Tribune* has to gain attention. They're number two, so they try harder."

The *Tribune's* managing editor, Jack McElroy, agrees with that assessment, praising the rival *Journal* as complete, thorough, methodical, and tenacious as a government watchdog. But he adds: "They're a tortoise; we're a hare."

At the Tribune, *the question never arose of* not *publishing the photographs.*

The two papers differ markedly in their handling of photographs. In January 1987, when Pennsylvania state treasurer Bud Dwyer committed suicide at a press conference, the *Journal* ran two AP wirephotos inside on page A-3, one with Dwyer reaching into an envelope for his gun, and the other, waving the pistol. But the *Tribune* ran the two most disturbing wirephotos on page one above the fold, of Dwyer with the weapon in his mouth, and just after he pulled the trigger. Managing Editor McElroy says he "would like to take that one back," but concedes that it shows "the direction we tend to err in."

The *Tribune's* Tim Gallagher looks nothing like his rival editor, Jerry Crawford. Tall and rumpled, he hunches his shoulders and looks at you out of the top of his eyes. He shouts comic remarks across the newsroom and laughs a lot. In January 1987, Scripps-Howard sent him to Albuquerque to revive a stagnant and boring paper, suffering disastrously from bad advice and falling circulation.

Gallagher recalls his older brother Charlie, who suffered from Down's Syndrome. Like the Volkmans, his parents braved the reactions of others, taking Charlie out with them in public. Other children mocked his brother, and Gallagher felt "a deep desire to have people understand Charlie, to explain why staring hurt my brother's feelings." Later, as a reporter, he wrote a highly regarded series on mainstreaming the handicapped. This concern stayed in the front of his mind throughout the Volkman project.

Managing Editor McElroy says the "question never arose of *not* publishing the photographs." Indeed, all the discussions seemed to concern packaging the pictures and the story in ways to make them acceptable and powerful for the reader. Mike Davis, the photo editor, says the *Tribune's* style is to ask *how* photos and text should run. The staff tends to make decisions in casual and mostly technical discussions among the players, rather than in editors' meetings. Generally, Gallagher says go and leaves them alone. Managing Editor McElroy had little direct involvement in the project, and none in the photo screening.

Through the year, the team kept adding players as Gallagher hired his new staff. Vickie Lewis, the photographer, privately recruited Julie Klein, a new reporter whose style she liked. Klein gathered materials for Sage's story on her own time, before she got the formal assignment. Eventually the team decided on a special tabloid section with no advertisements, designed to ease the reader into accepting very difficult pictures. The package included a letter from the parents printed twice, an emotional editorial, excerpts from the mother's diary, and a careful sequencing of photographs.

Sage's father, Michael, helped her get reacquainted with her classmates. (Photo by Vickie Lewis.)

One night late in the process, reporter Klein sat around the kitchen table with the Volkmans and took dictation while they composed a letter to the public (see box, page 114).

Printed on page A-1 of the main paper and reprinted on page two of the special section, accompanied by an appealing photograph of Sage before her accident, the letter obviated all arguments about privacy and exploitation. Kent Walz, the *Journal's* assistant editor, believes the letter muted potential negative reaction, because criticizing the paper would amount to criticizing the family.

The photographs and the text each follow their own logic, and seldom correspond on individual pages. The staff designed the photo sequence to ease the reader in toward the middle. On the cover, Sage's mother smiles and snuggles her. The reader sees Sage smiling and getting along with her schoolmates before coming to the harshest picture in the double truck. The *Journal's* editor, Jerry Crawford, would later praise the *Tribune* for their "extraordinary pains to diminish the impact" on readers.

Two weeks before publication, Vickie Lewis took one final photograph that provoked the strongest reaction and the most debate, both before and after publication. This photograph will become a classic case in photo ethics debates for years to come. The double truck depicts Sage and her mother after her painful nightly bath. The naked, scarred girl sobs while her mother comforts her (see page 115).

One photograph depicts Sage and her mother after her painful nightly bath. The naked, scarred girl sobs while her mother comforts her.

Tim Gallagher confesses he had "an anxiety attack" over this picture, "so graphic you couldn't help but feel her pain." But it reminded him of his parents' struggles with his disabled brother, and he knew he had to use it. He thought: "This is the private side of Sage. People have to know it." Lewis feared she had lost her objectivity as a photographer, and worried about exploitation of private grief. But the mother convinced her, and Lewis decided that "this photo tells so much from the woman's face about how she accepts her daughter." The graphics editor, Randall Roberts, held out, worried that the picture was "too strong," but he finally gave in. He then decided it "was the strongest picture, so we ran it big." But he paired it with a smaller photo of Denise cuddling Sage in her Jobst suit.

Two days before the section ran on October 16, the values of the two organizations collided in the backstop. Persistent rumors say that two engravers, Dennis Gardner and Jeff Micono, tried to stop the pictures, even in one version taking their case directly to Tom Lang, owner of the press and a man of legendary inaccessibility. Technicians in production do not normally question editorial judgments, especially in organizations involved in a joint operating agreement. In an interview, with his production director present, Gardner insisted that he merely pointed out "excessive grain" to his supervisor.

Persistent rumors say that two engravers tried to stop the pictures.

Tom Lang gives this official explanation: the engravers called attention to a technical problem, which was then solved. That problem came to the attention of Hugh Sarrels, operations director of the Albuquerque Publishing Company, who expressed misgivings about the pictures to Tim Gallagher, and suggested he run them by Lang.

***The following is the letter Sage's parents wrote for the October 16* Tribune:**

Dear Readers:

We wanted this article written to make our daughter Sage's adjustment to her new life as easy as possible.

We would like you to be aware of her struggle from when she was first burned and almost through death's door to her return to us as a 6-year-old girl with feelings who sees life in terms of Barbie dolls and her Brownie troop.

When you come upon Sage unexpectedly in a store or restaurant, your first reaction may be one of sadness.

But if you do run into her, we hope you will see her as we do—as a brave little girl.

Thank you.

From Sage's family: Michael, Denise and Avery Volkman.

P.S. We would like you to share these thoughts with your children.

Gallagher and Lang discussed Lang's worries about the family exploiting the newspapers, the proximity of publication to Halloween, and the very graphic double truck. Lang spoke of the balance between "offending the reader versus tugging the heart." Gallagher described the various efforts to soften the impact for the readers, concluding: "This is a story about a little kid who has more courage than any of us will ever have." Lang said, as he usually does, "It's your call."

The presses rolled, and all the players braced themselves for phone calls and cancellations. To every-

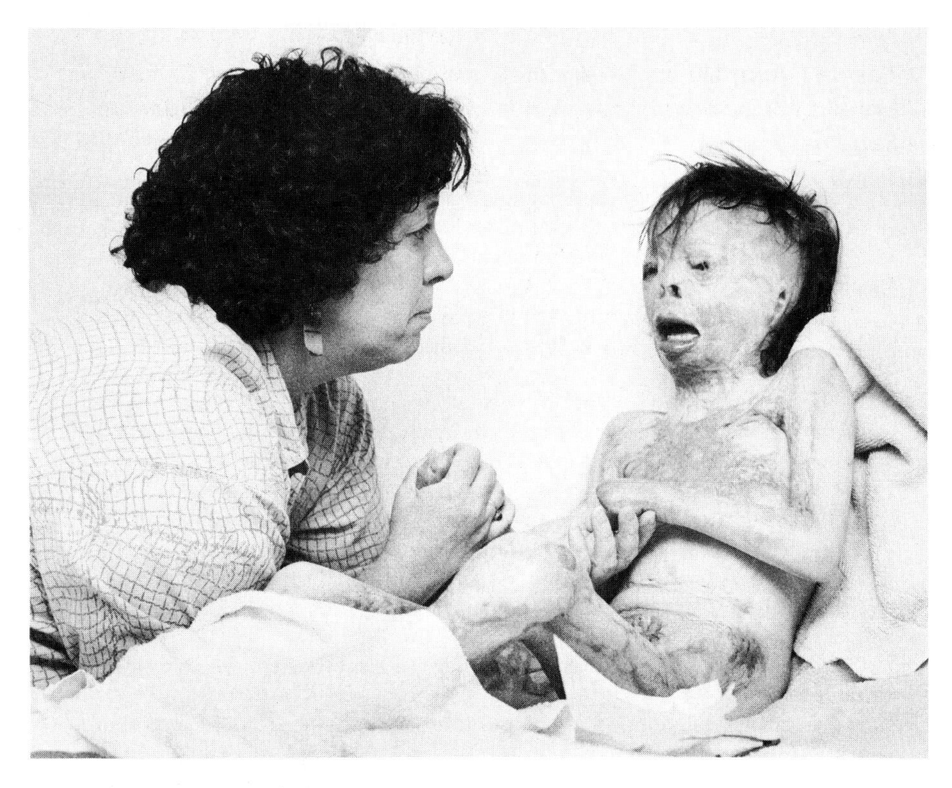

(Photo by Vickie Lewis.)

Mother and daughter share a moment before bedtime. Sage wears a skin-tight suit to prevent scarring. (Photo by Vickie Lewis.)

one's surprise and relief, the *Tribune* got no negative reactions at all; in fact, quite the opposite. Readers deluged the newspaper with praise. Contributions poured into Sage's trust fund. The section sparked a whole new series of fund-raising events. And parents showed the pictures to their children and discussed them, as the Volkmans' letter suggested. Even Sage liked the pictures.

The Tribune *got no negative reactions at all; in fact, readers deluged the newspaper with praise.*

The *Tribune* newsroom responded joyously. George Baldwin, a columnist, called it "the best thing in my 52 years with this newspaper." On the other side of the building, the *Journal* staff reacted

The picture at the top of the previous page accompanied this story by Julie Klein, which appeared in the* Tribune's *special section on Sage on October 16:

Bath time for Sage is a time-consuming ritual that begins daily at 7 p.m. For months, a typical bath took three hours. Now it's down to an hour and a half, and friends of the family sometimes schedule their evenings to help Sage with her bath.

Scabs consume the evening. They're a welcome sign that her skin is healing. But each scab must be picked with forceps. Then, the open wounds are scrubbed with anti-infection soap.

"Michael picks and I scrub," Denise said. "I'm a pretty good scrubber."

After bathing, Sage is propped up in her hospital bed in her bedroom. Her parents break pustules and cleanse them with hydrogen peroxide.

The peroxide stings more than usual. Her skin feels as if it is on fire and Sage cries about the excruciating pain.

"We don't mean to do things that make you cry," Denise said.

She reminds Sage about another burned little girl whose parents stopped giving her home therapy because she wept too much. Now, that little girl can't walk.

Sage stops sobbing. Minutes later, her sullenness is followed by uncontrollable tears.

"I wish I could give my body or anything so that little girl could walk again," Sage said through her tears.

variously, some with surprise and fascination, some with anger, and some with dismay. Assistant editor Kent Walz thought: "I'm glad we didn't do that."

Which paper made the right choice? Each remained true to its own identity and values.

Which paper made the right choice? Both editors stand by their decisions, and neither would have done what the other did. In my opinion, both newspapers chose correctly, in that each remained true to its own identity and values. Journalism school classes and professional seminars debate photo choices like these at length and in rather high-flown ethical terms, but the two staffs made quick operational decisions, more on grounds of credibility than ethics.

But how could they come to such opposite conclusions? We can see some obvious reasons in the story above:

- The traditionally feisty P.M. chasing the traditionally gray A.M.,
- a newsroom culture of risk versus a newsroom culture of restraint, and
- two editors as different as two editors could be.

This list leaves out what I consider the most important difference: the way the two papers frame questions. The *Journal* tends to talk in images of a balancing act, or of drawing lines. State editor Bruce Daniels, for example, spoke of the "fine line between arresting photos

Sage back at school. (Photo by Vickie Lewis.)

and pornography." They try to judge whether a decision would cross those fine lines or upset a balance. They ask "yes or no" questions, and they settle for "yes or no" answers. The *Tribune*, on the other hand, tends to ask process questions, not "*should* we put this in the paper? but "*how* can we present this to the reader?"

"Yes or no" questions serve a restrained newsroom culture well, because in sticky situations, the answer usually turns out "no." But answering "no" repeatedly tends to stifle creativity and injure morale. Process questions serve a more adventurous newsroom culture well, because they get the staff deep into a project before anyone asks hard questions that might stop the project. Unfortunately, the players tend not to ask the hard questions at all, or too late. As the *Tribune's* Jack McElroy puts it: "We're more aware today of how the ice can get thin out where we skate." ♦

Questions for Discussion

1. Judging from the styles of the two newspapers Fry discusses, where would you prefer to work? Would you have run the photo on the top of page 115, if you were the story editor?
2. Observe the stories covered in your local paper for several days. Observe also the way these stories are covered. Is your paper guilty of sensationalization?

Suggested Readings

More on That Nasty Image Problem

Robinson, Michael J. and Andrew Kohut, "Believability and the Press," *Public Opinion Quarterly* Vol. 52, Summer, 1988, p. 174 (16).

On Newspaper Chains

Bagdikian, Ben H., "Conquering Hearts and Minds: The Lords of the Global Village," *The Nation* Vol. 248, June 12, 1989, p. 805 (13). Includes related profiles of Rupert Murdoch, Reinhard Mohn, the late Robert Maxwell, and Jean-Luc Lagardere.

Bagdikian, Ben H., "Global Media Corporations Control What We Watch (and Read)," *Utne Reader*, July–August 1990, p. 84 (6).

Cose, Ellis, *The Press: Inside America's Great Newspaper Empires.* Reviewed by Ron Rosenbaum, *The New York Times Book Review*, April 9, 1989, p. 9. Reviewed by Michelle Lodge, *Library Journal*, June 1, 1989, p. 120. Reviewed by Genevieve Stuttaford, *Publishers Weekly*, Feb. 24, 1989, p. 216.

Fitchett, Joseph, "Media Empires: A Necessary Evil?", *UNESCO Courier*, September, 1990, p. 38 (5).

Lichter, S. Robert, Stanley Rothman and Linda S. Lichter, *The Media Elite: America's New Power Brokers.* Reviewed in *The Annals of the American Academy of Political and Social Science,* January 1988, p. 184 (2), and *Commentary*, January 1987, p. 78 (3).

Prichard, Peter. *The Making of McPaper: The Inside Story of USA Today* (Kansas City, KS: Andrews, McMeel and Parker, 1987).

Remnick, David, "Good News is No News: Al Nueharth, USA Today, and the Revenge of the Flying Class," *Esquire*, October 1987, p. 156 (7).

Simon, Simon A. and David Wagenhauser, "Can Rupert Murdoch Have It All?", *The Nation* Vol. 247 February 13, 1988, p. 181 (4). Concerning media cross ownership rules.

Schiller, Herbert, *Culture Inc.: The Corporate Takeover of Public Expression.* Reviewed by Saul Landau, *The Progressive,* November, 1989, p. 39 (2).

What Is News?—How Do Gatekeepers Decide Which of the Innumerable Events of the Day Will Be Winnowed Out and Reported to the Public?

Gaunt, Philip, *Choosing the News: The Profit Factor in News Selection* (Westport, Conn.: Greenwood Press, 1990). A comparative study of foreign news coverage in regional newspapers in the United States, Britain, and France.

Karp, Walter, Charlotte Hays, Jonathan Rowe and Michael Parenti, "Who Decides What Is News? (Hint: It's Not Journalists)," *Utne Reader*, November–December 1989, p. 60 (9).

Pinsky, Mark I., "Cops and Robbers—And a Secrecy Pledge," *Columbia Journalism Review,* September/October 1990. Short but interesting case study concerning the ethics of the media withholding information from the public at the request of the FBI.

More On the Newspaper Business

Holusha, John, "The Tough Business of Recycling Newsprint," *The New York Times,* January 6, 1991, Section 3, p. F9, Col. 1, 50 Col. in. It's not as simple as it sounds.

Jones, Alex S., "Rethinking Newspapers," *The New York Times,* January 6, 1991, Section 3, page 1 (2) 80 Col. in. The newspaper industry's current problems—fewer readers, fewer ads—and what's being done about them.

Magazines

6

Magazine circulation has grown steadily throughout the twentieth century. Although hundreds of magazines fail each year, new ones spring up in their place.

Eleven thousand periodicals are currently published in the U.S. About 2,000 of these are consumer publications. The rest are professional or business periodicals.

A list of the top ten magazines (see Table 1) might surprise you. While *TV Guide* and *Reader's Digest* battled for the top of the heap for the last decade, a new contender called *Modern Maturity,* published by the American Association of Retired Persons, was climbing steadily. The fact that *Modern Maturity* now ranks number one demonstrates the tie between magazines and demographics. The American population has gotten older, and as more and more people reach retirement age they need the type of information published in *Modern Maturity.*

Table 1.

Top 10 Magazines	Circulation, in millions
1. Modern Maturity	20.3
2. Reader's Digest	16.4
3. TV Guide	16.3
4. National Geographic	10.8
5. Better Homes and Gardens	8
6. Family Circle	5.2
7. Good Housekeeping	5.1
8. McCall's	5.1
9. Ladies' Home Journal	5.1
10. Woman's Day	4.4

Source: Gale Directory of Publications and Broadcasting Media (Detroit: Gale Research, 1990).

Of course, there are different ways to determine the top magazine. The list above refers to total paid circulation. In single-copy newsstand sales and ad revenue, *TV Guide* is the perrennial leader.

Magazine audiences tend to be fragmented, however. If we look at the top magazines for a particular age group, the titles would be completely different, and they would be mostly different for men and women. Take, for example, the top magazines for readers 18 to 29 years of age outlined in the following table.

Top magazines for readers 18 to 29 years of age

Men	Women
1. Rolling Stone	1. Rolling Stone
2. Muscle & Fitness	2. Mademoiselle
3. Gentlemen's Quarterly	3. Seventeen
4. Skiing	4. Self
5. Cycle World	5. Shape
6. Hot Rod	6. Glamour
7. Audio	7. Cosmopolitan
8. Popular Hot Rodding	8. Omni
9. Ski	9. Ski
10. Cycle	10. Vogue

Source: Conrad C. Fink, "Inside the Media," (N.Y.: Longman, 1990), p. 143.

In this chapter we look at three types of magazines and their characteristics. As it happens, these characteristics all relate to the way magazines have become specialized and their audiences have become fragmented. In the first reading Victor Navasky discusses the role of the political or "critical" journal. In Navasky's view, the fragmented, specialized nature of these journals is essential to democratic debate. In the second reading David Owen tells of his adventures through the trade magazine industry, whose diversity testifies to the diversity of American business. In the final reading Laurie Oullette discusses the varieties of small, underground magazines, or " 'zines," which make it possible for anyone with something to say to find a place to say it.

Minority Voices: The Role of the Critical Journal

Victor Navasky

Victor Navasky, a former editor of The New York Times Magazine *and a winner of the American Book Award, has been the editor of* The Nation *magazine since 1978. In this article, Navasky discusses the role of what he calls "the critical journal," although we could substitute the word "political" for "critical" in his title. Navasky's magazine, like* The Progressive, *is one of the best-known liberal journals. Conservative journals include* National Review *and* The American Spectator.

Much of what Navasky tells us about critical journals is true for specialized magazines in general. Navasky tells us, for example, that "even if it were true that we always tell our readers what they want to hear, there would still be value in that, since many readers need and want facts, figures and a vocabulary to document and articulate their intuitions."

All specialized magazines, political or not, contribute to the multiplicity of voices that was so important to the democracy that was envisioned by Thomas Jefferson. But political journals could rightfully be called the most important, as they give birth to and nurture those political ideas that would die without them.

The battleground of the political journals is a fiery one. We could say, in fact, that today's political journals have taken the place of the Partisan Press of the early nineteenth century. The Partisan Press died when objectivity became the goal of American newspapers, but polemics in the spirit of that era continue in today's "critical journals."

Reading Difficulty Level: 5. Grasp the main point, and it's all downhill.

It is an inauspicious moment for the small-circulation anything.

It is an inauspicious moment for the small-circulation anything. Bookstores and newspapers are increasingly in chains. Even before Mortimer Zuckerman has completed payments for *The Atlantic,* he acquires *U.S. News & World Report.* S. I. Newhouse buys *The New Yorker* under circumstances that compel editor William Shawn to announce—his first public announcement of anything, ever, I believe—that he had nothing to do with it. Capital Cities Communications is in the process of swallowing ABC, three times its size. And Jesse Helms and Ted Turner have made their move on CBS, which itself owns considerable book and magazine subsidiaries, while General Electric waits patiently in the wings to "rescue" the network from such a fate.[1]

Those media mergers and takeovers are merely the latest examples of a trend toward concentration documented by Ben Bagdikian in his book *Media Monopoly.* According to Bagdikian, six corporations account for more than 50 percent of the annual sales of magazines in the United States, from a total of 10,830

1. CBS successfully fought this takeover attempt, although this required a change in corporation management that resulted in reforms very much like what one would expect following a corporate takeover. And GE did, in fact, take over NBC and its parent corporation, RCA, in 1986.

publications with combined revenues of $12 billion. "By the 1980s," he writes, "the majority of all American media—newspapers, magazines, radio, television, books and movies—were controlled by 50 giant corporations." Those corporations, financially interlocked with massive industries and a few international banks, constitute what he calls a Private Ministry of Information and Culture. "It is more difficult than ever," he observes, "for society to hear minority voices in the majority thunder."

It is a misconception that circulation is a measure of the influence of journals of opinion.

The journal of critical opinion is, one hears, a nineteenth-century conception, a doomed attempt to preserve the outmoded metaphor of the marketplace of ideas, when in fact we get our dominant images of reality from the electronic media. Other communications scholars argue persuasively that the mass media, with its links to advertising, consumer marketing and big finance, serves as an instrument of social control reinforcing the status quo. But whether the mass media really represents what Marxists call the bourgeois hegemony of society, there is little doubt that the media scene is newly electronic, highly concentrated, increasingly bureaucratized, advertising-dependent and bottom-line oriented.

Beyond the quality of the readership is the intensity with which these publications are read.

Moreover, we are told by a chorus which has been holding forth for at least twenty-five years that these journals of opinion never had much going for them anyway. Their circulations are too small, they preach only to the converted, they are perpetually on the brink of bankruptcy, their shrill tone is calculated to limit their audience to the faithful, and they lack credibility. Besides, their day is past, they are anachronisms, relics from the age of print.

It seems to me we've heard that song before. It is a misconception that circulation is a measure of the influence of journals of opinion. Every small magazine has its equivalent of Frank Walsh's famous story about how he wrote a series on railroads for the Hearst papers which reached 10 million people and not one reader said a word to him. Then he published the same material in an article for *The Nation,* whose circulation was then 27,000. "The day *The Nation* went on the Washington newsstands," he said, "my telephone started ringing. I heard from editors, broadcasters and congressmen."

Beyond the quality of the readership is the intensity with which these publications are read. Dwight Macdonald made this point in 1957, when he wrote that

> While I was editing *Politics* I often felt isolated, comparing my few thousand readers with the millions and millions of nonreaders. . . . But in the last eight years I have run across so many nostalgic old readers in so many unexpected quarters that I have the impression I'm better known for *Politics* than for my articles in *The New Yorker,* whose circulation is roughly seventy times greater. This is curious but should

not be surprising. A "little magazine" is often more intensively read (and circulated) than the big commercial magazines, being a more individual expression and so appealing with special force to individuals of like minds.

Even the proprietors of these magazines don't always remember that the influence of the journal of opinion extends well beyond the range of its readership, whereas mass magazines have more circulation than influence. *The New Republic's* Martin Peretz once tried to dismiss *The Nation* by referring to its "tiny" circulation.

The widespread notion that, as William Henry III recently put it in *Time,* "Traditionally, the opinion magazines have preached to the converted, offering the dependable pleasures of a party line," is false. These magazines are read by diverse publics. As Jim Curran, former editor of *New Socialist,* a British publication in the orbit of the Labor Party, told me, "We perform a knitting function, bringing together groups with very different ideas—the peace movement, feminists, trade unionists, civil libertarians and members of the Labor Party." Each of these groups has its own belief system, and agendas are frequently at cross-purposes. Thus a reader who agrees with *The Nation's* stand on abortion may disagree with its First Amendment defense of the right to publish pornography. And even if it were true that we always tell our readers what they want to hear, there would still be value in that, since many readers need and want facts, figures and a vocabulary to document and articulate their intuitions.

The fact that small-circulation journals are perpetually on the brink of bankruptcy is outshone by the more amazing fact that, at least for those of us here today, there always appears a patron or a foundation or a spouse or subscribers or friends of the magazine to bail us out in the nick of time. Consider, for example, that a couple of years ago—i.e., the last time anyone counted—*National Review,* which announced it was going out of business back in 1957, reported a loss of $600,000. Jimmy Weinstein, the proprietor of *In These Times,* told a panel at the Socialist Scholars Conference, held in April in New York City, that he "started the paper to be an editor and ended up being a beggar." Correct me if I'm wrong, but of all the magazines here, only *The Washington Monthly* claims to break even as often as not.

The influence of the journal of opinion extends well beyond the range of its readership.

The complaint that we are shrill, captious or carping can, of course, be a euphemism for the fact that journals of critical opinion are critical—that most of them have rejected the myth of objectivity (also called fairness, but it amounts to the same thing) that pervades the mass media. The media still purports to separate facts from values and opinions, ghetto-izing the latter on editorial and Op-Ed pages. Interpretation is often banished to a no man's land, labeled News Analysis so as not to be mistaken for the real stuff.

Ever since Zenger, the government has paid small publications the compliment of a kind of attention that presumes an important influence.

Credibility these days is confered largely by a moderation of tone, the appearance of evenhandedness.

Because the journal of opinion so often makes political assumptions at odds with those in the mainstream media, even its factual reports are said to lack credibility and are dismissed as ideology. When *The Village Voice* reported that novelist Jerzy Kosinski got more help Englishing his novels than he had publicly acknowledged—a report based on interviews with a number of those who participated in the process—*The New York Times* responded by attributing the charges to a Polish K.G.B. plot to smear Kosinski because of his anti-Stalinism.

Precisely because these publications declare their biases, opinions, assumptions and attitudes, presumably neutral critics discredit them as nonobjective, nonneutral and therefore noncredible. Of course, even publications in the (shifting) center operate on political premises; it is simply that their assumptions remain unexamined. In that way, the conventions of ostensibly objective reporting reinforce the status quo. Credibility these days is conferred largely by a moderation of tone, the appearance of evenhandedness. Independent magazines—left *and* right—exist to violate this conspiracy of coolness, the false equation, which has become today's dogma, between moderate and credible.

There are those who say that the journal of critical opinion had more influence in an earlier day. It was said of Kingsley Martin, editor of the *New Statesman,* that "His influence on the generation which came of age in the 30s is incalculable. It is probably no exaggeration to claim that for better or worse, it changed the course of history as well as the patterns of dissenting thought throughout the British empire." Historian Charles Beard credited U.S journals with helping to bring about women's suffrage, old-age pensions, state and Federal housing, the regulation of securities, wages and hours, and public ownership of water supplies, among other reforms.

Ever since the incarceration of John Peter Zenger in 1734 for seditious libel, the government has paid small publications the compliment of a kind of attention that presumes an important influence. The State of Georgia once offered a reward for the arrest and conviction of the abolitionist editor of the *Liberator.* John Dean reported how the Nixon Administration conspired to put *Scanlan's Monthly* out of business (or at least keep it out of the country) by seizing its last issue on the Canadian border. *The Nation* recently acquired its F.B.I. files, which run to nine thick volumes of recorded surveillance, including a two-inch comparison of *The Nation*'s and *The New Republic*'s adherence to a party line. Did the Reagan Administration's attempt to deprive *Mother Jones* of its tax-exempt status have anything to do with such *M.J.* muckraking pieces as "Investigating Reagan's Brain . . . And Other Dark Regions of the New

Right"? And, of course, when the Central Intelligence Agency wanted to co-opt intellectuals, its first impulse was to fund a journal of opinion, *Encounter.* "In the Great Chain of Opinion that ends with network television," Nick Lemann of *The Atlantic* has written, "the first link is the highbrow periodicals and faculty clubs."

The question of influence comes down to how one defines it, what one regards as indicators. Some cite the sort of things Murray Rothbard had in mind when he reported in *Inquiry,* which, incidentally, expired last year, that in the mid-1950s "*National Review,* edited by Bill Buckley, filled the power vacuum, and with [William] Rusher as point man in the political arena, it managed, in a scant few years, to transform the American right wing beyond recognition." Erwin Knoll, editor of *The Progressive,* tells of a woman who approached him brandishing an umbrella and shouting, "I hold you and your magazine responsible for my son failing to register for the draft." (He replied," I hope you are as proud of him as I am.") Others, by way of demonstrating the power of small-circulation journals, point to articles that have found their way into the mass media. Irving Louis Horowitz notes that a report of his on the treatment of prisoners printed in *Transaction/Society* was picked up for a twenty-minute segment by CBS, was seen by 25 million people and led to improvements of prisoners' rights. There is also what we might call the Loom Factor. The looming presence of a muckraking magazine like *The Texas Observer* forces other Texas publications to undertake stories they might otherwise avoid.

In the Great Chain of Opinion that ends with network television, the first link is the highbrow periodicals.

Even though journals of opinion exert their influence primarily through other media, no mechanistic one-on-one test can adequately convey the relationship of these publications to the intellectual climate they shape and the climate of opinion in which they operate. Again, the man who puts it as well as anyone is Carey McWilliams, who wrote that their function is more varied than is generally supposed:

> To provide a home for new ideas and young writers. To prepare, so to speak, an agenda of items requiring national attention and discussion. To flush out new points of view. To support unpopular causes and issues. To focus a consistent and intelligent criticism on prevailing attitudes, policies and dogmas. To expose the exaggerations, omissions and distortions of the press and media. To offer sound and impartial criticism of books and the arts and the performance of the media. To break the taboo on particular subjects. . . . Above all, the small-circulation magazines provide the seedbed for ideas which are often fragile at birth and require nurture, pruning and careful editorial cultivation, all as part of the mysterious, never fully understood process by which they are finally projected out into the society for discussion, debate and possible testimony. These are vital, indispensable functions which the mass media cannot perform.

The small-circulation magazines provide the seedbed for ideas which are often fragile at birth and require nurture, pruning and careful editorial cultivation.

In addition, he argued, such journals have a capacity for survival precisely because they don't get caught up in the circulation numbers game or the advertising trap—the danger of becoming overdependent on advertising. Most big magazines go under not because readers don't read them but because advertisers stop advertising in them. Small-circulation magazines attempt to please advertisers at their peril. Our character, our identity, is our prime asset.

Carey wrote before the latest wave of media merger mania. The incessant recycling of the same stories by the conglomerated, homogenized dailies, weeklies and networks creates opportunities for small magazines and enhances rather than reduces their importance. To the extent that the mass media appropriates and consumes ideas rather than generates and considers them, it may have handed over a monopoly to the journal of opinion.

The incessant recycling of the same stories by the conglomerated, homogenized dailies, weeklies and networks creates opportunities for small magazines.

When I asked Deirdre English, executive editor of *Mother Jones,* how she saw the role of her magazine she said,

> Part of our job is being a carrier of a certain aspect of the political culture. We are contributing to the culture but we are the culture, not just commenting on it. For example, we present feminism to a mixed audience. The left culture has got to assimilate feminism in the next few years and we're part of that. We are a place where movements came together, a coalition-builder, a synthesizer.

In other words, each of us has a politics; each publication in its own way is trying to identify, advance and speak to the culture, and there's nothing wrong with that. It's an honorable role. Buckley may think that if *The Nation* closed down, the Republic would be a better place, but the real danger to *National Review, Socialist Review* and *Partisan Review,* to *The American Scholar* and *The Black Scholar,* to *Present Tense, Commonweal, Christianity and Crisis* and the rest of us is the concentration of media power which will limit the number of voices that are heard. My thought is that we have a common interest in preserving and extending our ability to be heard. ♦

Questions for Discussion

1. Do you agree or disagree that circulation is not a measure of the influence of a magazine?
2. Do you agree with Navasky that the mainstream media incessantly recycle the same stories?
3. Navasky states that most critical journals have "rejected the myth of objectivity." In your mind, is this a good or a bad thing?

The Fifth Estate: Eavesdropping on American Business Talking to Itself

David Owen

David Owen is a professional writer who likes to look into things that interest him. One of his books, for example, was all about the Educational Testing Service and what he called "The Myth of Scholastic Aptitude."

One topic that caught Owen's interest was the vast array of professional trade magazines. Looking into them, he discovered that our economy is "almost inconceivably various." What he learned about trade magazines could be said to be true for all magazines: they increasingly appeal to small, fragmented audience segments that are characterized by narrow interests.

Owen's article also provides a good look at the world of trade magazines without requiring the actual reading of a whole bunch of them. Judging from some of the articles he found, that might be the biggest blessing of all.

Reading Difficulty Level: 3. This is mostly for fun; you don't have to memorize the titles of all the magazines.

"If the bird is tame," Freud wrote, "I like to place him on a stand and then, while telling him what a good bird he is, I get behind him and lift one of his feet. . . . Birds which are not tame will generally require handling by two individuals with one holding the patient in a towel and the other doing the cutting."

There's a lot more to it than that. I'm just touching on the major points. Before trying this yourself you'd want to read Arthur Freud's entire article, "Proper Nail Clipping of Birds," in the January issue of *PSM*. *PSM* is a magazine for pet-store owners. Its name stands for Pets Supplies Marketing. Say that aloud a few times and you'll understand why they use only the initials.

Let's see. On August 4, 1984, nearly 300 people in Las Vegas stood up and said, "Bowling belongs in the Olympic Games, and I pledge that I will do everything I can for that goal," according to *Bowling Proprietor*. The bowling industry's Olympic aspirations are "rapidly becoming the talk of the town," the magazine says. Still, bowling linage was down a bit last year. Perhaps hoping to reverse that trend, residents of Indiana last year contributed $296 to B-PAC, the bowling

From *The Atlantic Monthly*, July 1985, pp. 80–85. Reprinted by permission.

political-action committee. B-PAC tries to entice politicians to adopt a more pro-bowling stance. One of its beneficiaries is my own congressman, Bill Green, of New York City, whose district contains exactly one bowling alley.

Most trade magazines don't attract much public attention. When people talk about "the media," they are usually not referring to Laundry News.

Here are a few of the magazines that are piled up on the table in my dining room: *Turkey World, Iron Age, American Carwash Review, National Jeweler (edited by S. Lynn Diamond), Fur Rancher, Lab Animal, Hosiery & Underwear, Weeds Trees & Turf* (incorporating *Golf Daily*), *Infections in Surgery, American Cemetery.* I also have *Kitchen & Bath Business, Ground Water Age, Beverage World* (the average American drank 43.2 gallons of soft drinks last year), *National Mall Monitor, Quick Frozen Foods, Lodging Hospitality, Hardware Age, The National Notary* ("Only in Florida, Maine and South Carolina may Notaries join couples in matrimony"), *Meat Plant, Pulp & Paper, Pizza Today,* and a couple of hundred others.

The specialized focus of trade magazines assures a certain privacy; they can speak to their readers with a candor that is impossible in the popular media.

Although according to my wife it is now impossible to sit down in our apartment without landing on a copy of *Cemetery Management,* my collection of trade and professional magazines is really just the tip of the iceberg in terms of what's available. Standard Rate & Data Services' directory of business publications, which comes out monthly and is larger than the Manhattan Yellow Pages, has more than 5,000 entries. The largest single publisher is Harcourt Brace Jovanovich, whose hundred or so titles include *Plastics Focus, Pit & Quarry,* and the brand-new *Food Sanitation.* Though little known outside their fields, such magazines can be enormously profitable. Last year Rupert Murdoch bought twelve of Ziff-Davis's trade magazines, including *Meetings & Conventions* and *Aerospace Daily,* for $350 million.

Rupert Murdoch notwithstanding, most trade magazines don't attract much public attention. When people talk about "the media," they are usually not referring to *Laundry News.* In fact, aside from the 15,387 people who receive it every month, how many Americans are even aware that there is an entire magazine devoted to laundry? (Actually, I saw in the February Standard Rate & Data directory that such magazines abound; they include *American Coin-Op, American Drycleaner, American Laundry Digest, Clean Scene Quarterly, Coin Launderer & Cleaner, Coinamatic Age, Drycleaners News, National Clothesline, New Era Laundry & Cleaning Lines, Textile Maintenance Reporter,* and *Western Cleaner & Launderer.*) The specialized focus of trade magazines assures their editors a certain privacy; they can speak to their readers with a candor that is impossible in the popular media. One could never find out from reading *Time* or *Newsweek,* for example, that people who make pretzels are considered to be somewhat boring by people who make potato chips. This is a fact that to the best of my knowledge can be found in print nowhere except in the pages of *Snack Food.*

Before I started piling up trade magazines, I had a vague, free-floating sense—derived mostly from watching the evening news—that there were only about a dozen different jobs in the United States: my job, Dan Rather's job, the President's job, steelworking, farming, banking, law enforcement, driving taxis, several others. But now I realize that the economy is almost inconceivably various and that in addition to the occupations just mentioned there are jobs involving, for example, the building of clam bunk skidders, the marketing of feller-bunchers, and the repairing of log forks (*World Wood*). I also know that 43 percent of men believe that they have sensitive skin (*Progressive Grocer*) and that the 1973 Arab oil embargo, though disastrous for almost everybody else, was about the best thing that ever happened to the people who make chain saws (*Chain Saw Age*, not to be confused with *Chain Store Age*).

Before I started piling up trade magazines, I had a vague, free-floating sense that there were only about a dozen different jobs in the United States.

Trade and professional magazines make some of the most esoteric reading in the world. They are the forum where American business talks to itself. Flipping through them is like eavesdropping on private conversations.

Flipping through trade magazines is like eavesdropping on private conversations.

If keeping up with all these magazines didn't take so darned much time, I might be tempted to start a magazine of my own. It would be a sort of compilation of the best parts of all my favorite trade and professional publications. I wouldn't be able to call it *Magazine Age*, *Communication World*, or *Editor & Publisher*, because there are already magazines with those names. Perhaps I would call it *The Other Media* or *The Fifth Estate*. It would be filled with page after page of arresting facts. For example:

• Coffee aroma consists of 100 to 200 volatile chemical compounds derived from the thermal degradation of primarily sucrose in the process of roasting the coffee bean. [*Tea and Coffee Trade Journal*]

• Astronaut Sally Ride's recent space mission not only advanced the space program, but also prosthetic dentistry. Material used to make her urinary catch device is now being used to make soft denture liners. [*Dental Management*]

• Some people call it polish. Others say class. We term it professionalism. Trying to sum up just what professionalism is, is somewhat like trying to define beauty or honesty. It's either there, or it isn't, but its presence adds a very special lustre. And Uniforms by Mindy has it. [*Uniforms & Accessories Review*]

• Ironically, Notaries are rarely seen in modern American dramas and musicals—although this nation has more Notaries than any other and their role is an important one. The reason is that the office of Notary is viewed as an auxiliary rather than a primary vocation in modern America (except in Louisiana, with its French heritage), and characters are identified by their primary vocations—as in Arthur Miller's "Death of a Salesman." [*The*

National Notary. This may be the world's most self-absorbed magazine. An article in a recent issue explained that Vanessa Williams lost her Miss America title because she "violated the morals provision of a notarized agreement."]

• Finally, combining the edible with the collectible, Freelance will introduce Goofy Pops®, a lollypop on a "squiggly straw." The candy will be wrapped in a cellophane which will have a puffy sticker with rolly eyes attached to it. Extra stickers will come with the Goofy Pop. [*Giftware Business*]

Every now and then my magazine would cover certain stories in greater depth. I might, for example, consider running an entire article about Goofy Pops, which in the taxonomy of giftware are classified as "stationery." (So are Mello Smello Mini Duffles, stick-on Mello Smello scratch-and-smell tattoos, Wild & Wacky Mello Smellos, Smell & Spell fragranced message stickers, and Smellopads.)

Stationery is a category of giftware, but it isn't the same thing as a gift. Before I started reading *Giftware Business,* I was a little confused on this point. Now I understand that a gift in the giftware sense isn't something like a fishing rod, a set of golf clubs, or anything else you wish someone would give you. Rather, it is something like a pewter figurine of a scuba diver, a tiny panda sculpted from "hydrostone," a pencil sharpener in the shape of a monkey standing in a shoe, or a ballpoint pen packaged with a color-coordinated lady's bow tie. It is, in brief, a thing that no sensible person would every buy for himself or herself. It is a thing that is generally thrown away shortly after it is received.

One place where people buy a lot of giftware (according to a recent issue of *Souvenirs & Novelties,* a magazine whose readership overlaps somewhat with that of *Giftware Business*) is the souvenir shop at the Oklahoma City Zoo. (Another place is the gift shop at almost any hospital. In fact, hospital gift shops have their own trade magazine, called *Hospital Gift Shop Management.*) In an article titled "Zoo Shop Employees Create Functional Displays," Judy Rowe, the manager of the zoo shop, explains the secret of her success: "When someone walks in and asks for something penguin- or tiger-themed, we'll show the shopper whatever is currently in stock. We don't stop after showing one item. I prefer to take a few extra moments and make sure my customer is aware of everything—the plush, statues, and pictures." *Plush* is the giftware word for fuzzy stuffed things. According to *Giftware Business,* teddy bears led the plush list last year, "but lambs did pick up momentum."

The line between gifts and souvenirs is thin. Souvenirs are generally a bit less inhibited: a baseball cap covered with golf-ball-sized plastic peas and a huge plastic pat of melting butter; "underwear that's funtawear," from British Bulldog, Ltd.; toilet paper printed with sayings like "Show business is my life"; a pair of hat-wearing Maw and Paw 'Zarky Doodler Hillbilly Character Pens, sold in a "2-holer outhouse display-gift package"; Famous Amish Dolls; fake tomahawks made by Cherokee Indians from North Carolina ("We're on the warpath to bring you fast selling items that bring high profits for you!").

Cherokee tomahawks aside, gifts and souvenirs tend to be made on islands in the pacific. This sometimes causes tension. An article in *Souvenirs & Novelties* discusses the perceived indelicacy of selling Japanese-made souvenirs in American battleship museums. The problem can usually be overcome. "In the past three years I have had only one person who, after discussing this issue, still refused to buy," reports Hattie Horton, the retail manager of the gift shop at Battleship Alabama Memorial Park.

If you just bought up your local battleship museum's entire supply of Bother Me greeting cards (for example, "It bothers me when you eat with your mouth open") but don't have anyone in particular you want to send them to, you might consider buying a mailing list consisting of the names of, say, all the people who between January and August of 1984 bought the phonograph record *Floyd Cramer Piano Favorites,* "featuring World Famous Love Songs and a Treasury of Favorites." There are 59,000 such people, 90 percent of them female. Finding out who they are costs fifty dollars per thousand names.

Selling names and addresses is a very big business. Popular lists, according to recent issues of *Direct Marketing* and *Fund Raising Management,* include people in the state of California who have rented or purchased wheelchairs, canes, walking chairs, or crutches; women who subscribed to *Redbook* after responding to a sweepstakes offer; members of the Association of Handicapped Artists; Americans "concerned about the growing Soviet military threat to peace"; buyers of the Thompson chain Reference Bible; buyers of the Perry County Pizza Kit; and "people interested in the welfare of children and who support building character, teaching valuable skills, providing adequate education and suitable housing, along with developing networks to help abused, lost, stolen and abandoned children." (Another popular mailing list consists, apparently, of the names of people who subscribe to magazines dealing with popular mailing lists. Shortly after I began reading *Direct Marketing* and *Fund Raising Management,* I received a piece of junk mail urging me to buy three books by someone named Cecil C. Hoge, Sr.: *Mail Order Survival & Success, Mail Order Know-How,* and *Mail Order Moonlighting.*)

One popular mailing list consists of the names of people who subscribe to magazines dealing with popular mailing lists.

It is a general rule that the more carefully a trade magazine is read by its trade, the more stultifying its content is to outsiders.

For a couple of summers when I was in college, I worked as a reporter for a trade magazine called *Milling & Baking News.* Shortly before I took the job, the magazine had come to something resembling national prominence by breaking the story on the famous Russian wheat deal—the Soviet Union's enormous purchase of American grain in 1972. For several weeks that year Walter Cronkite, *The New York Times,* and the rest of the popular media relied on *Milling & Baking News* for virtually all their information about the transaction. This information was uncannily accurate. The magazine's editor, Morton I. Sosland, was getting it from an anonymous source, who, Sosland gradually realized, was probably a Soviet official (the source always addressed Sosland as "Mr. Morton," something an American Deep Throat wouldn't do). Excitement about the wheat-deal story had mostly died down by the time I signed on, although work in the office was still occasionally disrupted by a British or Japanese television crew looking for an offbeat American feature story.

As is true of many trade publications, *Milling & Baking News* has a tiny circulation—just a little over 5,500. Even so, *The Wall Street Journal* once described the magazine as "indispensable" to its industry. Its influence derives not from the number of people who read it but from who those people are. About a fifth of the magazine's readers are the chief executives of milling or baking companies. Most of these people read every issue carefully, and advertisers pay a premium to reach them. A full-page, full-color ad in *Milling & Baking News* costs about $2,500. That's not much money in absolute terms, but it works out to nearly half a dollar per subscriber, or about what it would cost to read the ad aloud to each one over the phone. A similar advertisement in *Time,* in contrast, has a cost per paying reader of less than three cents.

It is a general rule that the more carefully a trade magazine is read by its trade, the more stultifying its content is to outsiders. Indispensable or not, *Milling & Baking News* is pretty grim reading for anyone who doesn't care deeply about milling and baking. "In the face [of] sharply higher prices last week," begins a typical article in a recent issue,

> shortening business was very sluggish. Soybean oil for nearby jumped 2 1/2@3 1/8c a lb on the heels of 1 1/4c gain the previous week. Deferred prices rose 1 1/8@3 7/8c. Virtually all other oil varieties also were considerably higher. Loose lard finished up 1 1/2@2c and edible tallow gained 3 1/2c. . . .

The magazine can keep this up for pages and pages. Still, trade writing is not without its charms. *Milling & Baking News*'s use of the symbol @ in place of a dash in price ranges is, I believe, unique. The *News* is also the only publication I know of that consistently uses the word *firm* precisely. Most business writers treat *firm* as a synonym for *company* or *corporation.* It is not, in strict usage. A firm, according to *Webster's Third New International Dictionary,* is "a partnership of two or more persons not recognized as a legal person distinct from the members composing it." Editor Sosland—who once had a brand of flour named after him (Big Boy)—also maintains an idiosyncratic but absolute ban on the word *however.*

As a summer intern at *Milling & Baking News,* I wasn't qualified to write the dense grain-market analyses that are the heart of the magazine (I was, though, once allowed to contribute an editorial praising an astronaut who had smuggled a sandwich into outer space). My usual beat was much humbler: obituaries, new-product announcements, rewritten press releases. Most trade magazines depend heavily on press releases, often printing them verbatim. It was a matter of pride at *Milling & Baking News* that a press release was never run without our at least switching around the order of the clauses and changing all the "he stated"s to "he said"s.

New-product announcements are the most fascinating part of almost any food-related trade magazine. "*Ex-Cel,* a microcrystalline cellulose powder, adds bulk to food products without adding calories," the January issue of *Prepared Foods* reports. "When mixed with water, *Ex-Cel* forms a ribbon paste ideal for low-calorie spaghetti, macaroni and other formed products." Another issue of the same magazine announces "a fluid, oil-based coloring" ingredient that "yields a butter color on popcorn or extruded snacks." Butter color has what the prepared-food industry calls "eye appeal." A closely related concept is that of "mouth-feel," as in "Our formulary explains how to use Avicel MCC [another cellulose bulking additive] to make a cole-slaw dressing with controlled flow, cling, and improved creaminess without sacrificing high-fat mouthfeel." (Eye appeal and mouthfeel are often difficult to improve without sacrificing yet another desirable quality—"consumer labeling appeal.")

Some of the most popular new food products are ones that enable manufacturers to replace expensive ingredients. "HOW TO MILK CHOCOLATE," reads the headline on an advertisement in *Candy Industry* for Durkee's line of "coating fats," "cocoa butter equivalents," and other chocolate extenders and substitutes. A similar product is Viobin Cocoa Replacer, which, according to an announcement in the January issue of *Food Technology,* "is made from defatted wheat germ and 5% added carbohydrate which is pressure toasted to a rich brown. It is then ground to a fine powder which is similar in color and texture to processed cocoas."

Most trade magazines depend heavily on press releases, often printing them verbatim.

Even better than new-product announcements are patents for new processes and ingredients. Here are a few garnered from recent issues of *Food Technology:*

U.S. 4,473,592. . . . Process for producing a meat-based product having a meat core of substantially constant cross-section of relatively dense compacted meat and an outer coating of fat which is mobile in the uniform state.

U.S. 4,477,476. . . . Method for converting salmon green eggs into a roe product in which the green eggs is agitated in a saturated aqueous solution of salt containing a nitrite to impart a scarlet color, after which the salted egg is dried and agitated in a saturated aqueous solution of a malate containing sufficient nitrite to impart scarlet coloring.

U.S. 4,478,861. . . . Method of preparing a frozen food product in which a plurality of cooked pieces is treated to remove free water to form voids after which food mass is subjected to a freezing gas to surface freeze pieces while leaving some unfrozen moisture thereon. Dry powder additives are then introduced with agitation to uniformly coat pieces, after which they are fully frozen throughout and transferred to a storage container for later reconstitution.

Most people probably think they would never eat a frozen food product in which a plurality of cooked pieces had been treated to remove free water to form voids. But in fact almost everybody cheerfully eats stuff like this. Much of the food that is served in modern restaurants traces its ancestry directly to the patents page of *Food Technology.* "Precooked," "pre-browned," and "portion-controlled" frozen-food items are "microwaved" and either 'plated" immediately or, in the fancier establishments, gussied up with inexpensive "profit-makers" like olive bits or almond slivers before being "menued" as expensive, "signature" entrées. There isn't much need for chefs anymore. Kitchen technology has advanced to the point at which a pre-browned slice of portion-controlled prime rib can be microwaved in a minute or two and then keep in a holding oven for eight hours or more without losing eye appeal.

"Eye appeal," according to an advertisement in the January issue of *The Director,* "is still the main reason people buy!" The ad is for "Aurora's new 18 gauge 1500 shell with accent stripes. . . . This new ACCENT series features a stripe on the top and base moldings that color coordinates with the shell finish. Notice how the interior shade completes this color combination. The striping has been marker tested and found to be widely accepted." The ACCENT series also features "adjustable bed, seam welded bottom, metal gimp and material-lined foot end."

Aurora is the Aurora Casket Company, of Aurora, Indiana. *The Director* is the official publication of the National Funeral Directors Association. Food-related publications are a lot of fun, but for pure, bone-chilling enjoyment there's nothing like a funeral magazine. *The Director, Casket & Sunnyside, American*

For pure, bone-chilling enjoyment there's nothing like a funeral magazine.

Funeral Director, Stone in America (gravestones, that is), *Cemetery Management, Morticians of the Southwest, American Cemetery, Southern Funeral Director*—if I had to choose a single trade magazine to accompany me into an 18-gauge 1500 shell, it would probably be one of these.

"Silver Taupe with Ash Grey Crepe interior, it does sound exciting, doesn't it?" Gene C. Hunter, the president of the Marshfield Casket Company, asks in a recent issue of *Morticians of the Southwest.* "More families are wanting caskets with new interior designs that are different and stand out over others."

A modern casket is a remarkable piece of merchandise. It is the single most expensive piece of furniture that many people will ever own, yet its only real function is to be lowered into the ground and covered with dirt. Its numerous optional features serve no purpose except to increase the final bill. With racing stripes, or plain? How firm a Sealy mattress? Should the interior upholstery coordinate or contrast with the exterior finish? Persuading grieving relatives to buy these unnecessary amenities is known to the trade as "loading the casket." It is the mainstay of the funeral business.

Many expensive casket features are seemingly meant to prevent or delay what has already occurred. Batesville caskets are treated with "an exclusive Chemgard coating" intended to provide "additional protection," according to advertisements in various funeral magazines. Marshfield's premium Signature caskets (the Monarch Blue, the West Coast Blue, and the Silver Taupe) offer a "one-piece rubber gasket" and a "50-Year Warranty." Belmont's Bronze Masterpiece caskets are protected by "a lustrous 4-millimeter, twice-baked, hand-rubbed Dupont finish" applied over a generous coat of "Dupont Adhesion Promoting Primer." Batesville's Sapphire, Mediterranean, and Tourmaline models have both inner and outer lids, the better to protect a loved one from—well, from what?

Loading the casket doesn't stop with the casket. Most caskets, even ones with two lids, aren't buried in the ground; they're buried in other caskets, known as vaults. Wilbert's Monticello, Continental, Venetian, and Tribune models (with Strentex and Marbelon liners) all provide "the very finest in underground protection." According to an ad in *The Director,* Wilbert tests these vaults in an "immersing tank" that subjects them to

> a side wall force of over 18,000 pounds at a depth of twelve feet. In another test, a freeze/thaw machine takes Wilbert burial vaults to temperatures of 30° below zero. And Wilbert's instrumented burial vault provides accurate technical data from a Wilbert burial vault buried at a normal depth, through sensing devices attached to an external digital readout device.

Sozonian's top-of-the-line vault is made of twelve-gauge steel and "designed like a real I-Beam to give it plenty of self-supporting strength"; optional " 'Electro-Shield' protection" is also available.

Another profit-maker for funeral directors is burial clothing. "A Thing of Beauty, a Joy Forever" is the motto of Willingham Tailoring Company, manufacturers of funeral dresses and jobbers of burial underpants. Morticians can also order the second revised edition of *Desairology: Hairstyling for the Deceased.*

Reading the funeral magazines, you can almost begin to believe that the color or texture of the inside of your casket is something that might one day make a difference to you.

It's all an elaborate rip-off. And yet these magazines are fascinating, no? The best of them is *American Funeral Director,* a monthly journal that contains, in addition to advertisements for caskets, vaults, burial clothes, and other paraphernalia (including SnFF, the nonformaldehyde arterial chemical that "has no smell!', and King Tut, the popular cavity fluid from Egyptian Chemical & Funeral Supply), articles with headlines like "LUNG CANCER IN WOMEN UP 152.6% IN TENNESSEE," "FIND BONES IN ATTIC," and "JOB-RELATED DEATHS HIT RECORD LOW IN '83" (I've got some good news and some bad news). A chart in the February issue reveals that Hawaii, Nevada, Rhode Island, and South Dakota suffered no weather-related deaths in 1983, while Texas led the nation, with sixty-six. Like all good trade magazines, *American Funeral Director* is obsessed with its subject; unlike most trade magazines, it has a subject that lends itself to obsession.

Reading the funeral magazines can be a peculiar experience. They make mortality seem simultaneously vivid and unreal: vivid because nothing could be more vivid than a bottle of SnFF, unreal because you can almost begin to believe that the color or texture of the inside of your casket is something that might one day make a difference to you. As Freud wrote, "No one believes in his own death."

That's the other Freud, incidentally—the one who didn't know anything about birds. ♦

Questions for Discussion

1. Like the trade magazines Owen discusses, the magazine industry in general is fragmented into periodicals that appeal to people with very specific interests. In your opinion, is this a beneficial or detrimental trend?
2. Analyze your favorite magazine in terms of its specialization and the narrowness of its audience. To whom is the magazine targeted? Do the articles fulfill an important need for this target audience?

'Zines: Notes from the Underground

Laurie Oulette

In a typical media class, we tend to discuss specialized consumer magazines along the lines of American Baby, American Hunter, *and* Skateboarding, *along with* Pen and Quill *(a magazine for collectors of autographs),* Blue and Gray *(a magazine of Civil War nostalgia—"For those who still hear the guns"), and* Renalife *(a quarterly publication of the American Association of Kidney Patients). As Laurie Oulette points out in the following reading, these are just the beginning of what's available out there.*

Laurie Oulette was formerly the librarian for Utne Reader, *a sort of* Reader's Digest *of the alternative press. She is currently studying media criticism at the New School for Social Research in New York City.*

Reading Difficulty Level: 2. No problem. You'll love some of the titles of the 'zines.

You're as likely to find copies of **Profane Existence, Holy Titclamps,** or **Twisted Image** at the local newsstand as you are to find their respective subject matter (anarchist politics and punk music, Queer culture, radical comics) in the latest issue of *Women's Day* or *U.S. News & World Report.* Cantankerous, outrageous, and completely uncensored, these publications are radically removed from the established press and even from the alternative press. Virtually invisible to mainstream America, they belong to a growing genre of do-it-yourself publishing that is integral to today's counterculture. Within subcultures that are most alienated and marginalized by conventional society—radical youth, gays and lesbians, political and social non-conformists—you'll find thousands of similar underground publications: homemade, self-published musings known as fanzines, or more often just as 'zines.

Within subcultures that are alienated and marginalized by conventional society, you'll find thousands of underground publications.

Embodying grass-roots democracy, mailbox comradeship, and flagrant freedom of expression, 'zines are a product of the recent communications revolution. Ever since the printing press was invented, independent thinkers have struggled to publish their own alternatives to mainstream viewpoints. Today, anyone with something to say and access to a photocopy machine can publish a 'zine on any topic, no matter how unconventional or obscure.

From *Utne Reader,* November/December 1991, pp. 139–142. Reprinted by permission.

For every passion there is at least one 'zine circulating somewhere for like-minded aficionados.

And they do. It's impossible to know exactly how many 'zines are currently being published, but estimates range into the tens of thousands. For every passion there is at least one 'zine circulating somewhere for like-minded aficionados: Alternative bowling (**Baby Split Bowling News**), urban witchcraft (**Enchanté**), cross dressing (**Girlfriends**), punk gender issues (**Girl Germs**), and working-class biography (**People's Culture**) are but a few examples.

'Zines are unpredictable and individualistic by definition, but there are certain characteristics that define 'zine publishing as a genre. Most 'zines are produced by one person in his or her spare time, using a pen-and-typewriter, cut-and-paste, photocopy-and-staple method. Most have a rough, crowded, amateur look that can be visually interesting and highly creative. 'Zines are written in a voice that suggests personal correspondence more often than journalism and that cares less about grammar and spelling than it does about honestly and spontaneity. Many 'zines defy a regular schedule, but are published whenever time, energy, and cash allow. And almost all 'zines are distributed free or for the cost of postage—or in exchange for other 'zines—to a readership that numbers from the low thousands to the hundreds and even the teens.

Almost all 'zines are distributed free or for the cost of postage—or in exchange for other 'zines.

'Zines tend to cover a diverse range of subjects that are usually ignored by (or sometimes unknown to) the mainstream media. Since 'zines are not controlled by advertising, they are free to be as shocking, accusatory, or nasty as they like. According to Mike Gunderloy, a 'zine expert who publishes an authoritative 'zine on 'zines, 'zines often cover controversial topics—HIV as a cause of AIDS and U.S. dealings in the Middle East are two examples—long before the mainstream media. Since they're on the fringes of society, where trends are often conceived, 'zines can be trendsetters themselves. Recycling was a popular 'zine topic years before the mainstream caught on. But there is a flip side to all of this. While 'zines do provide an alternative, they should be viewed as passionately opinionated rather than objective. "Zines can't always be counted on as a reliable source of information, and many have lost credibility by printing wild conspiracy theories and unresearched stories, Gunderloy explains.

Some of the most quirky 'zines are one-of-a-kind publications that focus on offbeat subjects: **Frostbite Falls Far-Flung Flier** is devoted to the Rocky and Bullwinkle cartoon characters, and **Three Twenty-Seven** is "by and for people born on 3/27." Most 'zines, however, can be classified into loosely defined subgenres that sometimes overlap.

Alternative music, mainly punk music, inspires more 'zines than any other subject. **Ben is Dead, Break-**

(Photo by Bruce Cotler.)

fast Without Meat, and **Yoko Only,** a 'zine devoted to Yoko Ono, are just a few of many 'zines in this category. Comics 'zines, such as the popular **Twisted Image,** are often political, but some are sexually explicit at the expense of women. Radical politics is another impetus behind many 'zines. Appropriate to the do-it-yourself 'zine philosophy, anarchist views—promoted by the feisty **Instead of a Magazine** and **Dumpster Times**—are the most popular.

Many frustrated writers and poets turn to 'zines as a vehicle of expression and a way to get published. Talent is variable, but as titles like **Shattered Wig Review** and **Poems Inspired by Poverty and Beer** suggest, these literary 'zines are not exactly out to emulate *The Paris Review.* Feminist 'zines—such as **Not Your Bitch** and **Girl Germs,** two 'zines that question sex roles in male-dominated punk culture, **f/Lip,** a feminist literary 'zine, and

Many frustrated writers and poets turn to 'zines as a vehicle of expression and a way to get published.

Femzine, mini *Ms.* of the micro-press—constitute another subgenre of the 'zine community.

Ecology-oriented 'zines such as **The Deep Ecologist** and Pagan 'zines such as **Harvest,** which is devoted to urban witchcraft, sometimes overlap. Alternative art, graphics, performance art, and mail art are featured in 'zines like **Art Police,** the photography-oriented **Shots,** and the beautifully designed **Maximum Traffic.**

Girl Jock **is a 'zine "for the athletic lesbian with a political consciousness."**

Diseased Pariah News, a 'zine for HIV-positive gay men, and **Girl Jock,** "for the athletic lesbian with a political consciousness," are just two of the many 'zines serving the gay and lesbian communities. TV and other types of popular culture also inspire 'zine commentators. Titles like **Popular Life** and **Teenage Gang Debs,** a clever 'zine devoted to *The Brady Bunch* and other '70s television shows, can often interpret mass culture better than any stuffy volume of academic theory.

Violence and dark humor are perhaps the most shocking subjects found in 'zines. **Murder Can Be Fun** (the latest issue focused on "Death at Disneyland"), **Weekly World Noose** (it pokes fun at suicide), and **Skag Rag** (a violet literary 'zine containing poetry about self-cannibalism) are 'zines that have worried some readers.

Science fiction 'zines, which began in the 1940s as the original "fanzines" and from which the current concept of 'zines was derived, keep perhaps the most insular company of any subgenre within the 'zine community. **The Fandom Directory** (Fandata Publications, 1991) details a spectrum of science fiction 'zines and is an excellent resource on fandom, the organized fan groups who worship celebrities like Jack Kerouac (**Moody Street Irregulars**), obscure interests and hobbies like poetic lawn care (**Leaves of Grass**), and cult films and television shows such as *Star Trek* (too numerous to mention).

People usually discover 'zines through their association with an alternative social group. Queer culture is bursting with 'zines like **Holy Titclamps** and the militant **Bimbox.** The alternative music scene relies on 'zines just as Madison Avenue relies on *Advertising Age.* Fandom cultures, including the group that worships Jim Morrison and publishes the 'zine **The Deadly Doorknell: The Organ of the First Church of The Doors,** would be lost without their 'zines.

In the world of 'zines, there are few distinctions between publishers and readers—everyone's an equal member of the 'zine community. Readers contribute most of the 'zines' material by sending passionate and personal letters of comment (known in 'zine lingo as LOC's). 'Zine enthusiasts often form friendships with each other through the mail, and many readers eventually start their own 'zines. Publishers regularly trade 'zines with one another. 'Zines review and encourage readers to send for samples of other 'zines, a circular process that steadily feeds the growth and furthers the reach of amateur publishing.

At the center of the 'zine network is **Factsheet Five,** a publication that has earned an esteemed reputation as the 'zine of all 'zines. Started nine years ago by 'zine connoisseur Mike Gunderloy as a single photocopied sheet intended to inform friends about interesting 'zines, *Factsheet Five* has evolved into the indispensable bible of the 'zine community. For the uninitiated reader, *Factsheet Five* offers an excellent way to sample 'zine culture and connect with thousands of 'zines. Each issue contains more than 100 pages of reviews and other news for the underground publishing community.

Gunderloy, who sees more 'zines than probably anyone else in the world, believes that 'zines are a growing phenomenon. In addition to new technology, he cites the conservative climate of the 1980s and people's desire to shape their own lives instead of relying on cultural institutions as major factors in the 'zine boom over the past ten years.

For his booklet **Why Publish** (Pretzel Press, 1989), Gunderloy conducted a series of interviews with dozens of 'zine publishers, who explain their compulsion to publish:

"Well, why NOT publish? Maybe it's the only way, doing it yourself . . . it feels good knowing you have at least a semblance of a voice in the madness out there."

"Because it's fun, and you meet interesting folks, plus you get to say exactly what you want to say."

"To bring relief . . . a small 'zine brings out a new world for people like me to escape to."

Troll, a 20-year-old from Minneapolis, started the anarchist/punk music 'zine **Profane Existence** about two years ago. He got into 'zines because he wanted to be a part of the punk music scene but wasn't in a band. Publishing a 'zine seemed another way to contribute to the punk culture. He financed his 'zine with money originally intended for college; he dropped out because he felt he wasn't learning anything. *Profane Existence* has grown quickly and is now considered one of the largest and best of its kind, distributed to about 4,000 readers across the United States and even overseas.

Troll is representative of the people most frequently involved in the 'zine scene, according to Gunderloy. The same people who flocked to earlier counterculture movements like the hippies and the Beats—namely young, white, middle-class urban males who are rebelling against both liberal and conservative culture—also dominate 'zine culture. "The 'zine scene isn't real open to other groups," explains Gunderloy. There are few 'zines coming from minority or working-class communities. Gunderloy notes that proportionately

The same people who flocked to earlier counterculture movements like the hippies and the Beats also dominate 'zine culture.

fewer women publish 'zines than men, and when they do, they tend to be feminist- or Pagan-oriented.

Gunderloy feels that 'zines, even though they're usually published by middle-class white males, can be an important tool in promoting social change. "Even when ['zine publishers] think they're just writing or reading about punk music, kite-flying, the revival of Asatru, or new sculpture, these people are part of a phenomenon," he wrote in **Whole Earth Review** (Fall 1990). "Presented with access to an inexpensive means to say things, people have found things to say, and, better yet, they have discovered that other people will listen."

While commercial mass media become increasingly homogenous, 'zines add new alternative views to the publishing spectrum.

And in an age when a very small number of corporate conglomerates own the majority of the world's media outlets, 'zines take on an even greater importance. While commercial mass media become increasingly homogenous, 'zines add new alternative views to the publishing spectrum. Along with cable-access video and computer bulletin boards, 'zines are paving the way toward media decentralization, empowering people at the grass-roots level to take media into their own hands. ♦

Suggested Readings

More On Small Magazines

Dunkel, Tom, "The Fringes of the Magazine World," *Insight* Vol. 6, July 16, 1990, p. 54 (2). Self-published magazines.

Kiely, Thomas, "In Praise of Smallness," *The Nation* April 13, 1985, p. 417. Small-circulation periodicals are vital to intellectual life.

On the Joys of Magazine Reading and Publishing

Atlas, James, "A Magazine Junkie," *The New York Times Magazine* Vol. 136, November 1, 1987, p. 22, Col. 3, 20 Col. in.

Boynton, Robert S., "How to Make Love to a Magazine," *Manhattan, Inc.* Vol. 7, July 1990, p. 48 (6). Alexandra Penney, author and editor of *Self* magazine.

Byron, Christopher M., *The Fanciest Dive* (New York: New American Library, 1986). The story of how Time Inc. lost $47 million dollars in just six months trying to launch a new magazine called *TV-Cable Week*. An inside view of decision-making within a media conglomerate. Reads like a novel.

Janello, Amy and Brennon Jones, *The American Magazine* (N.Y.: Abrams, 1991). A lushly illustrated history. Reviewed by Brendan Gill in *The New York Times Book Review*, December 1, 1991, p. 50.

Trends in Magazine Publishing

Fabrikant, Geraldine, "Wooing the Wealthy Reader," *The New York Times,* October 14, 1987, pp. D1, D5. New magazines are being designed to attract readers from the upper income brackets, and older magazines are changing for the same group of readers.

Grune, George V., "Challenges to the Magazine Industry: Some Plain Talk," *Vital Speeches of the Day* Vol. 56, January 15, 1990, pp. 202–204.

Kagan, Daniel, "Magazines That Befit the Times," *Insight,* December 28, 1987. The newest publications aim at market segments that are the product of modern times: successful middle-aged women, divorced people and low-profile travelers.

McDowell, Edwin, "Women Move to the Top in Publishing: A Gentleman's Profession No Longer," *The New York Times,* October 25, 1987, p. E 24.

Books

"One thing about books: they are objects, like lamps, ashtrays, vases. They last, they hang around."

—John Garvey

Books are our least used mass medium, and yet they are the most important. It is through books that truly revolutionary ideas are developed and enter into public consciousness. It is through books that we transmit our cultural heritage from one generation to the next. As Kurt Vonnegut has pointed out, when we read, "we are meditating with minds other than our own, often minds better than ours, surely minds that have seen things we will never see."[1]

Although as individuals we use books less than we use other media, book publishing is still a thriving, $13 billion a year business. Book sales break down roughly as follows:

Texts (includes elementary, secondary and college)	4 Bil.
Trade (includes adult and juvenile, hardbound and paper)	3 Bil.
Professional (includes business, law, medicine, technical and scientific books)	2.5 Bil.
Mass market paperback (includes rack-sized paperbacks marketed in stores such as supermarkets and pharmacies as well as bookstores.)	1 Bil.
Other (includes religious book, book clubs, mail order publications, university presses)	2.5 Bil.

Source: American Association of Publishers estimated sales, 1988–1991.

1. "Kurt Vonnegut Eyes Things Magical, Ghastly, and Literary," *The Pennsylvania Gazette*, December, 1990, p. 13 (2).

Tina Turner signs copies of her autobiography, *I, Tina.* (Photo by Bruce Cotler.)

The top U.S. book publishers are all huge corporations. The top five all have sales in the billion-dollar range. Their names are familiar:

1. Simon & Schuster
2. Time Inc.
3. Harcourt Brace Jovanovich
4. Random House
5. Reader's Digest

In this chapter, we deal exclusively with the question of quality in book publishing today, although in doing so we will look at three different types of books. In Steve Weinberg's "The Kitty Kelley Syndrome," we look at the high-stakes world of nonfiction trade books. In Katha Pollitt's "Canon to the Right of Me . . ." we examine what are known as "the Great Books" or "the canon," by which we mean those books that all educated Americans (read that, "undergraduates") should be required to read. Finally, Harriet Tyson Bernstein looks at the shape of textbooks published for public schools, and finds some real problems.

The Kitty Kelley Syndrome

Steve Weinberg

Kitty Kelley is best known for dropping the dirt on Frank Sinatra and Nancy Reagan, but she is merely the most recent in a long line of gossip writers passing themselves off as biographers. In Elvis, *Albert Goldman exposed "the king" as a pervert. Bob Woodward and Carl Bernstein, in* Final Days, *show Richard Nixon as severely mentally troubled. Christina Crawford, in her biography of Joan Crawford,* Mommie Dearest, *shows Crawford as a child abuser ("No wire hangers!"). The list goes on and on. What Steve Weinberg would like to make clear is that the difference between a biographer and a gossip-monger is that the former deals with facts, and the latter deals with unsubstantiated rumors, some of which originate from untruthful sources with axes to grind. Weinberg would also like us to know that the huge success of these books jeopardizes the quality of nonfiction trade books in general.*

Weinberg, a contributing editor of the Columbia Journalism Review, *has been on both sides of the book-accuracy fence. He has investigated the accuracy of books as an editor, a reviewer, and as an author. In that last capacity he was sued by the industrialist Armand Hammer for libel. The suit ended when Hammer died in 1990.*

Reading Difficulty Level: 4.

"In any nonfiction book . . . it is presumed by the reader that the facts have been checked and are accurate, and that the book therefore is to be relied on. In most publishing houses, however, a copy editor simply cannot check everything. . . . A lot of very famous authors are really quite sloppy, and both editor and copy editor simply have to live with it and keep as many obvious errors as possible from slipping through to final copy."

from *Who Does What and Why in Book Publishing,* by veteran editor-publisher Clarkson N. Potter

"Neither the editor nor the copy editor should be expected to serve as researcher or co-author. You are the authority . . . don't expect your editors to check every fact, as they would in a newsmagazine."
Samuel S. Vaughan of Doubleday, addressing authors in Editors on Editing

"Out there, where folks are reading their papers and cruising their shopping mall book marts, they're

Reprinted from the *Columbia Journalism Review,* July/August 1991, by permission.

scratching their heads. How could the nation's biggest publisher print nearly a million copies of a bare-knuckles attack on a former First Lady without knowing for certain that everything between the covers was true? Isn't Simon and Schuster accountable for the accuracy of the books it publishes?"
from an article by Paula Span, part of *The Washington Post*'s coverage of Kitty Kelley's *Nancy Reagan: The Unauthorized Biography*

All the media attention devoted to Kitty Kelley's biography of Nancy Reagan, published by Simon & Schuster, had some beneficial fallout: a few news organizations examined not only what Kelley wrote, but also how she knew it. It was a rare instance in which journalists examined a book's accuracy on the news pages.

From the first sentence of the biography, Kelley began taking liberties.

From the first sentence of the biography, Kelley began taking liberties. That sentence reads: "Two entries on Nancy Reagan's birth certificate are accurate—her sex and her color." Actually, it appears that all the items on the birth certificate are accurate. What Kelley apparently meant is that Nancy Reagan later may have told lies about certain items.

Item after item in Kelley's book has been questioned. A *Newsweek* team led by Jonathan Alter stated: "Sarah Brady, wife of former Reagan press secretary James Brady, convincingly denies they were excluded from White House social functions to avoid reminding Nancy of the assassination attempt on her husband." Alter and team also noted, "Mike Wallace, an old friend of Nancy's who despises Kelley, says her third-hand story about his encounter with Nancy's foulmouthed mother in Arizona is partially accurate but wrongly dated by about ten years." The article also convincingly questioned a date-rape allegation against Ronald Reagan that Kelley included, uncritically, in her book.

The same week Simon & Schuster shipped Kelley's book it published a Ronald Reagan biography by *Washington Post* reporter Lou Cannon. The contrast was stark. *Newsweek* noted: "No one has to ask whether to believe Cannon when he writes that Reagan preferred watching *The Sound of Music* to studying his summit briefing books. Kelley's credibility is much shakier. Good biographies depend on more rigorous standards than quotation marks around the word luncheon to suggest a White House affair with [Frank] Sinatra."

Cannon's biography was praised in part because his book is painstakingly documented and because he has built a reputation for accuracy. That raises the question of where to place Bob Woodward on the spectrum. Woodward is the author or co-author of six important best-sellers—*All the President's Men, The Final Days, the Brethren, Wired, Veil,* and *The Commanders.* Only *Wired*, a biography of John Belushi, contains end notes. The sourcing on the other books is impossible to determine on most pages unless the reader is an insider at, respectively, the White House, the Supreme Court, the Central Intelligence Agency, and the Pentagon. Even Kelley's copious but imprecise sourcing on her biographies of Frank Sinatra and Nancy Reagan is better than Woodward's. Woodward, however, has a better reputation for accuracy because (tautology noted) nobody has proved that his books contain inaccuracies. Should his publisher let him play by his own rules? Woodward insists that on-the-record interviews and other specific sourcing would impede his efforts, but other authors—such as James Bamford writing about the National Security Agency in *The Puzzle Palace*—have covered controversial public affairs topics while providing copious end notes.

Controversy over the veracity of Kelley's Nancy Reagan biography should have been no surprise, for two reasons—Kelley's past performance and the frequent disregard for accuracy in trade book publishing.

Reviewing Kelley's biography of Jackie Onassis twelve years ago in *The Nation,* Richard Gilman wrote that "almost nothing she claims to be quoting has the slightest ring of authenticity," then went on to provide examples. Published in 1978 by Lyle Stuart, *Jackie Oh!* contains no footnotes or end notes; the bibliography is superficial. In the acknowledgments, Kelley thanks forty-five sources, but it is usually difficult, and sometimes impossible, to determine who told her what.

Kelley's 1986 biography of Frank Sinatra, while more thoroughly documented—it contained chapter notes, a fuller bibliography, and 857 interviews as tabulated by the author—promoted questions about accuracy nonetheless. Some of the research was brilliant; she demonstrated more fully than previous authors the crooner's influence at the White House during various administrations, his violent streak, and his links to organized crime figures, for example. Some of her findings, however, were unsubstantiated gossip or came from others' work previously published in newspapers, magazines, or books—work that may have contained inaccuracies to begin with and that was used by Kelley without question. Because of the imprecise way Kelley constructed her chapter end notes, much of her information cannot be verified by the average reader.

Controversy over the veracity of Kelley's Nancy Reagan biography should have been no surprise.

After the Sinatra biography was published, by Bantam, journalist Gerri Hirshey produced a three-part unauthorized profile of Kelley for *The Washington Post.* Kelley failed to cooperate in any way. The series revealed Kelley's fabrications about her own life and convincingly cast doubt on parts of her Sinatra research.

Window display at B. Dalton bookstore in New York City. (Photo by Bruce Cotler.)

The sometimes shaky factual foundation of the Sinatra book did not prevent it from becoming one of the biggest-selling biographies in publishing history. So Kelley, despite her less-than-sterling reputation among sundry reviewers, journalists, and publishers, commanded a multimillion dollar contract for the Nancy Reagan book.

Publishing's Dirty Secret

Kelley's most recent bestseller is symptomatic of publishing's dirty secret – few nonfiction books are checked for accuracy.

Kelley's most recent bestseller is symptomatic of publishing's dirty secret—few nonfiction books are checked for accuracy. As a result, inaccuracies abound.

It could be worse, of course. Because many authors possess not only pride, but also research skills and high standards, numerous books that purport to be serious nonfiction are indeed mostly accurate, serving as imperfect but nonetheless indispensable research material.

That said, far too much inaccuracy makes it into print. Almost every edition of *The New York Review of Books* and the book sections of *The Washington Post*, *The New York Times*, and the *Los Angeles Times* contain reviews that expose factual errors.

Meanwhile, book publishers have little incentive to change their ways. Trade publishing is a for-profit endeavor; spending money for fact-checking would cut into profits. Moreover, few readers pay attention to which publishers are responsible and which are not; for whatever reasons, there is little brand-recognition among consumers of books. Many consumers are aware that the *National Enquirer* is an unreliable newspaper, but they have no idea which book publishers are the industry's *National Enquirer* equivalents.

Trade publishing is a for-profit endeavor; spending money for fact-checking would cut into profits.

Publishers have plenty of "good" excuses for their failure to check for accuracy besides bottom-line considerations. It is hard to find outside experts to vet manuscripts and, even when the right expert is available, the process is time-consuming. The proper comparison, some publishers contend, is not with newspaper or magazine articles but with columnists, who blend fact and opinion to disseminate a point of view. If publishers brought out only those books they knew beyond question to be completely accurate, the argument goes, many would never reach readers, thus inhibiting the free flow of ideas. Finally, publishers say, truth established beyond a reasonable doubt, truth with a capital T, is unachievable; readers will believe what they want anyway—if they are skeptical, let them prove error.

If publishers brought out only those books they knew beyond question to be completely accurate, many would never reach readers.

Chapter and Verse: Getting Down to Cases

There are instances of publishing house editors knowing about inaccuracies but pushing ahead anyway. Brad Miner made a rare public confession to such a sin in *National Review* six years after the deed:

> In 1984, I spent a week locked in an office with David Yallop, editing *In God's Name: An Investigation Into the Murder of Pope John Paul I;* this so my then employer, Bantam Books, could publish it as an "instant hardcover". . . . Yallop knew I thought his book proved none of its fantastic claims. . . . He never actually named the murderer, you see, and nervously feigned opacity whenever I pointed it out. The book was published, sold well, and received a lot of attention, most of it (as I'd predicted) negative.

In God's Name lacks source notes and a bibliography. Despite Miner's misgivings, it also lacks any warning to readers. As for Yallop, he explained away his heavy reliance on anonymous sources by raising the specter of murder should their names be revealed. But, Yallop asserted, there was no need to worry about accuracy: "I can assure the reader that all the information, all the details, all the facts have been checked and double-checked to the extent that multiple sources were available. I take the responsibility for putting the evidence together and for the conclusions reached."

Publishers have occasionally withdrawn books from the market, at least temporarily, when they get caught out.

A handful of book industry observers took that assurance with a shovelful of salt. Edwin McDowell, the book beat reporter at *The New York Times,* commented that Yallop "does not always say which fact came from which source, and therefore some people consider such 'documentation' pointless. Worse yet, it suggests that his shocking conclusions may have come from some perfectly reputable library included in his list, without giving the reader a way to check this information. The Vatican press office last week denounced the book's conclusions as 'absurd fantasies,' adding, 'It is shocking and deplorable that anyone could so much as think let alone publish theories of this kind.' " In the post-Watergate age, however, during which official denials have come to be regarded as automatically suspect, the Vatican's statement may well have added to Yallop's credibility among many readers.

In the same 1984 article, McDowell questioned the credibility of *Vengeance: The True Story of an Israeli Counter-Terrorist Team* by George Jonas, published by Simon & Schuster. After reviewing the evidence against the credibility of the two books, McDowell wondered, "What are the responsibilities of book publishers in a democratic society for maintaining standards of evidence, proof, and disclosure in the books they publish?"

"What are the responsibilities of book publishers in a democratic society for maintaining standards of evidence, proof, and disclosure in the books they publish?"

Publishers have occasionally withdrawn books from the market, at least temporarily, when they get caught out. That happened to *Poor Little Rich Girl,* a biography of Woolworth heiress Barbara Hutton written by C. David Heymann and published by Random House in 1983.

Like Kitty Kelley, Heymann had written previous biographies that were suspect in some of their specifics. Like Kelley in her Reagan book, Heymann trumpeted his extensive research on Hutton. Like Simon & Schuster, Random House thought it had a bestseller on its list.

Then Random House received a call from a lawyer representing a Beverly Hills physician mentioned in the book as having overmedicated Hutton in 1943. The lawyer presented proof that his client had been only fourteen years old in 1943. Random House executives began to do the kind of checking nobody had insisted upon before publication. That checking led to the book's recall.

Publisher Lyle Stuart bought the discredited manuscript, reworked it, and got it back into stores. Heymann's only quasi-admission of inaccuracy appeared in a disingenuous footnote on page 193.

Instead of shunning Heymann, the book world embraced him. Lyle Stuart signed him up for a new biography of Jackie Onassis, just as Stuart had signed Kitty Kelley to write about the same subject the previous decade. In 1989, Heymann's *A Woman Named Jackie* shot to the top of the bestseller list, despite questions about accuracy.

Probably the most searing indictment came from *Miami Herald* reporter Mike Wilson, who wrote, in part:

> The two-pound, twelve-ounce book bulges with steamy new stories about the Kennedy's. . . . But much in the book is not new. And much, Heymann's sources are saying, is not true. Heymann, whose last book was recalled by Random House because of a serious error, defended *A Woman Named Jackie* in a 45-minute phone interview with *The Miami Herald*, saying he had most of the interviews on tape. Then, refusing to answer any more questions, he hung up. Heymann's publicist, Sandra Bodner, said later that the *Herald* is 'attacking the author's credibility on really peripheral issues.' She said that, unless someone sues him, Heymann will not play his tapes for the *Herald* or anyone else.

Wilson's investigation of Heymann's book yielded convincing evidence that the author had wrenched a key direct quotation out of context, thereby altering its meaning. Furthermore, Wilson demonstrated that Heymann had borrowed heavily from previous books without adequately crediting their authors.

Several of Wilson's sources questioned whether Heymann had even interviewed some of the people he said he had, including people who died before publication. Heymann insisted he had conducted the interviews, but, he said, he had not taped some of the particular ones at issue. His chapter notes were of little help—like Kelley's, they looked extensive at first glance, but some turned out to be vague and unverifiable upon closer study.

Neither Heymann nor his publicist nor his publisher produced new evidence to validate the book's accuracy. Yet the book stayed in stores and on library shelves. Signet, an imprint of New American Library which in turn is part of Penguin Books USA, published the book in mass market paperback without disclaimers.

The annals of contemporary trade publishing are filled with similar cases. Among the more notable was *The Underground Empire: Where Crime and Governments Embrace* by James Mills, published by Doubleday in 1986. This 1,165-page blockbuster received lots of attention, mostly favorable, upon publication. Mills, touted by Doubleday as having "won a reputation as one of America's most respected journalists," had written for *Life* magazine. His books included fiction and nonfiction.

To a discerning reader, there were immediate warning signs that *The Underground Empire* might contain elements of fiction. The book lacked footnotes, end notes, a bibliography, and an index. Such omissions make fact-checking nearly

Several sources questioned whether one author had even interviewed some of the people he said he had, including people who died before publication.

The Problem with Memoirs and Other Tell-All Tales

Almost no serious nonfiction work is without merit for future researchers, especially journalists and historians. But when a researcher discovers a documentable error (a misspelled name, a wrong date, a sequence of events that could not have happened), how is he to know what portions to trust and what portions to distrust without a great deal of further checking?

Certain categories of books are especially troublesome—autobiographies and memoirs, for example. Most contain little or no documentation. Even if a reader were to check the facts, how is an average reader to know what is omitted? I learned about this the hard way while researching the first independent biography of industrialist-philanthropist-citizen-diplomat Armand Hammer. It took me about a year to fact-check his 1932 memoir, his 1987 autobiography, his 1975 commissioned biography, and his 1985 authorized picture book. It took me several more years to discover which significant episodes he had omitted, and there may well be others of which I am unaware.

John P. Roche, a Kennedy and Johnson administration insider, once tried to evaluate the accuracy of the memoirs from that era. "I know what I thought was happening, what others on the staff thought was happening, what the press thought was happening. But I cannot fully document what happened. And I have seen enough highly classified documents to know that what most of the observers thought was happening was at best half-right, at worst dead wrong," Roche wrote in *The New York Times Magazine* a score of years ago. After providing examples to support that assertion, he concluded, "So, farewell to instant history and God help the poor souls who try to put the jigsaw puzzle together when all the precincts have reported. As for me, I'm going to write it as I saw it—but with a candid admission that any resemblance to events as they in fact occurred may be coincidental."

There have been at least twenty insider memoirs of the Reagan administration; they contradict each other at the turn of each page.

There have been at least twenty insider memoirs of the Reagan administration; they contradict each other at the turn of each page. Yet, read in isolation, any one of those books might seem accurate. It is often necessary to read one after the other (a task almost nobody performs) before it becomes plain that something is rotten on publishers row.

Another troublesome category is first-person books about espionage. In researching this article, I examined a dozen highly publicized books, all allegedly true, about the CIA, the KGB, and other intelligence services. I found compelling evidence that some of the biggest-selling, most important espionage books contain major, multiple errors amidst their pearls of fact. I found evidence of inaccuracy nearly as distressing while researching espionage books written by journalists and academics. A number of those belong to a subcategory of espionage—books about the John F. Kennedy assassination.

If authors and publishers can't guarantee accuracy before publishing, perhaps they should consider using the backdoor approach taken by the publisher of David Rorvik's *In His Image: The Cloning of a Man.* The publisher J. B. Lippincott, provided readers with a warning that concluded: "The account that follows is an astonishing one. The author assures us it is true. We do not know. We believe simply that he has written a book which will stimulate interest and debate on issues of the utmost significance for our immediate future."

S.W.

impossible, and thus can be used by authors and publishers to evade responsibility. Those signs, among others, made Jack Miles and David Johnston suspicious. Miles was the book editor at the *Los Angeles Times;* Johnston was one of the paper's investigate reporters.

Johnston's eventual page-one story said that "forty-three people involved with events described in the book have told the *Times* that what Mills wrote about those events is untrue. Four people named or identified in the book say that Mills twisted their innocent and normal actions to make it appear that they are criminals or knowingly do business with major drug traffickers. All four said they would have explained their side if Mills had given them a chance."

After listening to those sources and checking the book page by page as thoroughly as he could, Johnston concluded that "government records, court papers, newspaper clippings, and other documents directly contradict numerous . . . facts covering scores of pages throughout the book that are crucial to Mills' stated premise."

Mills and Doubleday defended the book's accuracy, without providing any proof. But, as Johnston wrote, Mills acknowledged "that he made no attempt to interview many people he writes about negatively. He said that because government agents were the sources of most of the allegations of criminal activity, he was under no journalistic obligation to let the suspects and others tell their side of the story."

Johnston was not the only critic. Law professor Alan Dershowitz, writing in *The New York Review of Books,* cited example after example showing why he found Mills's work nearly worthless as a guide to reality. The Federal Bureau of Investigation wrote to Doubleday, detailing errors. Doubleday did not respond.

This seeming indifference by a major publisher to well-documented charges of inaccuracy infuriated *Times* book editor Miles. In a column, he asked rhetorically, "Aren't there errors in any book? Couldn't a smart and determined reporter find flaws almost anywhere? Does it matter that the credibility of a given book is not total? Yes, there are errors of detail in every book. But no, there are not errors of this magnitude. And no, the smartest, most determined reporter would not get far against a carefully researched book. . . . *The Underground Empire* . . . has debased the intellectual currency of its publisher. As with disinformation in the political arena, so with this example of public discourse—Mills's distortions and errors make it harder to take future Doubleday books at face value."

The smartest, most determined reporter would not get far against a carefully researched book.

The *Los Angeles Times* exposé had little impact. Dell published *The Underground Empire* in paperback; reviewers of the paperback edition praised it, perhaps unaware of the Johnston-Miles debunking.

Often when books on the same topic appear more or less simultaneously, they are reviewed together. Inevitably, the conscientious reviewer, feeling compelled to compare and contrast, discovers passages in one book that contradict passages in the other. It happens even when both authors are respected researchers. A recent example involves two generally well-researched accounts of Manuel Noriega's rise and fall in Panama: *Our Man in Panama* by John Dinges, published by Random House, and *Divorcing the Dictator* by Frederick Kempe, published by Putnam. Reviewing the books together in *The Washington Post, Miami Herald* reporter Jeff Leen (whose expertise is based partly on research conducted for *Kings of Cocaine,* of which he was a co-author) commented:

The multiple books on how Elvis Presley, Marilyn Monroe, Sylvia Plath, Pablo Picasso, and John Lennon lived and died contradict each other wildly.

> Although Kempe out-reports Dinges, he's also given to making snap judgments in the face of scant facts. His most vivid scenes are often the products of unnamed sources. Time after time, he makes small errors. He estimates the cost of a cartel cocaine lab in Panama at $1 billion—Dinges' $500,000 is much closer to reality. He convicts a cartel boss in Tampa—it was Jacksonville. He has cartel drug flights overflying Cuba very soon after 1982—the evidence shows it was five years later. He has DEA agents unaware that the cartel bosses were in Panama in 1984—in fact, the DEA was running an informant who was meeting with those bosses personally. . . . In many unintended ways, these books illustrate how fragile our knowledge is of these events. The authors conflict on an amazing number of details, small and large. The disagreements range from the trivial (Noriega's favorite liquor—Old Crow or Johnny Walker Black Label?) to the significant (Dinges says Noriega's father acknowledged paternity. Kempe says he did not) to the crucial ([source José] Blandon's credibility, the cartel's connections to Noriega).

Other cases in point: the multiple books on how Elvis Presley, Marilyn Monroe, Sylvia Plath, Pablo Picasso, and John Lennon lived and died contradict each other wildly.

Causes and Solutions

Book publishing is a strange business indeed. Most editors are educated people who presumably depend on books for much of their own knowledge. Yet they do virtually nothing meaningful to promote accurate knowledge for their house's customers.

Why is that? Publishers do not expect authors to be perfect spellers or grammarians: copy editors make hundreds, even thousands of alterations in a typical manuscript. Publishers do not expect authors to be omniscient about libel and privacy; in-house publishing lawyers or outside counsel fire off multiple queries at the manuscript stage. But most publishers seem willing to assume that authors are somehow pillars of diligence and wisdom when it comes to finding facts, evaluating information, and drawing conclusions. The contractual burden for accuracy is by tradition primarily the author's. Yet authors are frequently unequipped to get everything right—because of poorly developed research skills, because of time and money pressures, because of laziness.

Some authors would welcome fact-checking assistance from their publishers; a few beg for it. The absence of a safety net is especially scary for authors who also write for magazines at which fact-checking is a tradition. *The New Yorker*'s fact-checking operation is perhaps best-known to non-journalists, but fact-checkers at numerous other magazines are in the same league. They regularly catch errors. Everybody benefits—author, magazine publisher, and readers.

Kitty Kelley knows this. Seven years ago, during the controversy over the accuracy of a different biography by a different author, *Publishers Weekly* quoted Kelley as saying. "I take full responsibility for what I write, but when publishers have vast investments in writers, they should do all they can to help the book. They have an obligation to at least make an effort to fact-check."

Trade publishers do have alternatives to the current situation. They could pay in-house or outside researchers to request documentation from the author, then judge its worthiness. At the very least, they could pay for a spot check, then decide whether a full-scale review is necessary. (Models already exist in university presses, which traditionally send manuscripts to two or more outside readers knowledgeable in the subject area, paying those readers a stipend for their documented opinion.)

Reviewers, for their part, can be doing something, too. If a book lacks end notes, a bibliography, or an index, the reviewer should take the publisher to task. Newspapers, magazines, and broadcast outlets that use book reviews ought to increase their compensation so that reviewers can afford to take the time required to check accuracy.

Theodore Draper is living proof that it can be done. An independent journalist/historian, Draper is an assiduous checker of other authors' facts, convincingly exposing their transgressions in such publications as *The New York Review of Books, The New Republic, The New York Times Book Review*, and *Dissent*. Draper understands the special status books hold in the minds of readers, in the institutional memory of the nation: "A newspaper can report one thing one day and revise or revoke the

Authors are frequently unequipped to get everything right—because of poorly developed research skills, because of time and money pressures, because of laziness.

report the next day; a book makes a promise of much longer duration and far greater authority. The scale and presentation make a vital difference."

In book publishing houses, accuracy is supposedly everybody's responsibility, but we all know what usually happens when a task is "everybody's responsibility"—ultimately, it becomes nobody's responsibility. As a result, the saying "You could look it up" doesn't always hold true, since the book you look it up in is not necessarily the final word. ♦

Questions for Discussion

1. Do you feel that you can trust the accuracy of the books you read?
2. Why, in your opinion, are people so attracted to idle gossip about celebrities?

Canon to the Right of Me . . .

Katha Pollitt

The current controversy over the canon could be boiled downed and stated politically as follows: Conservatives would like to return to a list of "great books" for all college students, books such as those by Homer, Plato, Virgil, Milton and Tolstoy, as well as Aeschylus, Danti Alighieri and Shakespeare. Liberals would like to open the canon up to more works by women, blacks, and writers of other countries. As the battle rages on, Katha Pollitt takes a step back and takes a look at why we read in the first place. When she does so, she decides that all this fuss about required reading does more harm than good.

Reading Difficulty Level: 5. You would think it would be more difficult, considering her subject matter, but it isn't.

For the past couple of years we've all been witness to a furious debate about the literary canon. What books should be assigned to students? What books should critics discuss? What books should the rest of us read, and who are "we" anyway? Like everyone else, I've given these questions some thought, and when an invitation came my way, I leaped to produce my own manifesto. But to my surprise, when I sat down to write—in order to discover, as E. M. Forster once said, what I really think—I found that I agreed with all sides in the debate at once.

What books should be assigned to students? What books should critics discuss? What books should the rest of us read, and who are "we" anyway?

Take the conservatives. Now, this rather dour collection of scholars and diatribists—Allan Bloom, Hilton Kramer, John Silber and so on—are not a particularly appealing group of people. They are arrogant, they are rude, they are gloomy, they do not suffer fools gladly, and everywhere they look, fools are what they see. All good reasons not to elect them to public office, as the voters of Massachusetts recently decided.* But what is so terrible, really, about what they are saying? I too believe that some books are more profound, more complex, more essential to an understanding of our culture than others; I too am appalled to think of students graduating from college not having read Homer, Plato, Virgil, Milton, Tolstoy—all writers, dead white Western men though they be, whose works have meant a great deal to me. As a teacher of literature and of writing, I too have seen at first hand how ill-educated many students are, and how little aware they are of this important fact about themselves. Last year I taught a graduate seminar in the writing of poetry. None of my students had read more than a smattering of poems by anyone, male or female, published more than ten years ago. Robert Lowell was as far outside their frame of reference as Alexander Pope. When I gently suggested to one student that it might benefit her to read some poetry if she planned to spend her life writing it, she told me that yes, she knew she should read more but when she encountered a really good poem it only made her depressed. That contemporary writing has a history which it profits us to know in some depth, that we ourselves were not born yesterday, seems too obvious even to argue.

Some books are more profound, more complex, more essential to an understanding of our culture than others.

But ah, say the liberals, the canon exalted by the conservatives is itself an artifact of history. Sure, some books are more rewarding than others, but why can't we change our minds about which books those are? The canon itself was not always as we know it today: Until the 1920s, *Moby-Dick* was shelved with the boys' adventure stories. If T. S. Eliot could single-handedly dethrone the Romantic poets in favor of the neglected Metaphysicals and place John Webster

This article is reprinted from *The Nation* magazine/The Nation Company, Inc. © 1991. From the September 23, 1991, issue, pp. 328–332.

*John Silber, president of Boston College, ran for Governor of Massachusetts and lost.

Doonesbury copyright © 1991 G. B. Trudeau. Reprinted with permission of Universal Press Syndicate. All rights reserved.

alongside Shakespeare, why can't we dip into the sea of stories and fish out Edith Wharton or Virginia Woolf? And this position too makes a great deal of sense to me. After all, alongside the many good reasons for a book to end up on the required-reading shelf are some rather suspect reasons for its exclusion: because it was written by a woman and therefore presumed to be too slight; because it was written by a black person and therefore presumed to be too unsophisticated or to reflect too special a case. By all means, say the liberals, let's have great books and a shared culture. But let's make sure that all the different kinds of greatness are represented and that the culture we share reflects the true range of human experience.

Alongside the many good reasons for a book to end up on the required-reading shelf are some rather suspect reasons for its exclusion.

If we leave the broadening of the canon up to the conservatives, this will never happen, because to them change only means defeat. Look at the recent fuss over the latest edition of the Great Books series published by Encyclopedia Britannica, headed by that old snake-oil salesman Mortimer Adler. Four women have now been added to the series: Virginia Woolf, Willa Cather, Jane Austen and George Eliot. That's nice, I suppose, but really! Jane Austen has been a certified Great

Writer for a hundred years! Lionel Trilling said so! There's something truly absurd about the conservatives earnestly sitting in judgment on the illustrious dead, as though up in Writers' Heaven Jane and George and Willa and Virginia were breathlessly waiting to hear if they'd finally made it into the club, while Henry Fielding, newly dropped from the list, howls in outer darkness and the Brontës, presumably, stamp their feet in frustration and hope for better luck in twenty years, when *Jane Eyre* and *Wuthering Heights* will suddenly turn out to have qualities of greatness never before detected in their pages. It's like Poets' Corner at Manhattan's Cathedral of St. John the Divine, where mortal men—and a woman or two—of letters actually vote on which immortals to honor with a plaque, a process no doubt complete with electoral campaigns, compromise candidates and all the rest of the underside of the literary life. "No, I'm sorry, I just can't vote for Whitman. I'm a Washington Irving man myself."

Well, a liberal is not a very exciting thing to be, as *Nation* readers know, and so we have the radicals, who attack the concepts of "greatness," "shared," "culture" and "lists." (I'm overlooking here the ultraradicals, who attack the "privileging" of "texts," as they insist on calling books, and think one might as well spend one's college years deconstructing *Leave It to Beaver*.) Who is to say, ask the radicals, what is a great book? What's so terrific about complexity, ambiguity, historical centrality and high seriousness? If *The Color Purple*, say, gets students thinking about their own experience, maybe they ought to read it and forget about—and here you can fill in the name of whatever classic work you yourself found dry and tedious and never got around to finishing. For the radicals the notion of a shared culture is a lie, because it means presenting as universally meaningful and politically neutral books that reflect the interests and experiences and values of privileged white men at the expense of those of others—women, blacks, Latinos, Asians, the working class, whoever. Why not scrap the one-list-for-everyone idea and let people connect with books that are written by people like themselves about people like themselves? It will be a more accurate reflection of a multifaceted and conflict-ridden society, and will do wonders for everyone's self-esteem, except, of course, living white men—but they have too much self-esteem already.

Who is to say what is a great book? What's so terrific about complexity, ambiguity, historical centrality and high seriousness?

Reading and Self-esteem

Now, I have to say that I dislike the radicals' vision intensely. How foolish to argue that Chekhov has nothing to say to a black woman—or, for that matter, myself—merely because he is Russian, long dead, a

How foolish to argue that Chekhov has nothing to say to a black woman.

The notion that one reads to increase one's self-esteem sounds to me like more snake oil.

Why is everyone so hot under the collar about what to put on the required-reading shelf?

man. The notion that one reads to increase one's self-esteem sounds to me like more snake oil. Literature is not an aerobics class or a session at the therapist's. But then I think of myself as a child, leafing through anthologies of poetry for the names of women. I never would have admitted that I needed a role model, even if that awful term had existed back in the prehistory of which I speak, but why was I so excited to find a female name, even when, as was often the case, it was attached to a poem of no interest to me whatsoever? Anna Laetitia Barbauld, author of "Life! I know not what thou art/But know that thou and I must part!"; Lady Anne Lindsay, writer of languid ballads in incomprehensible Scots dialect; and the other minor female poets included by chivalrous Sir Arthur Quiller-Couch in the old *Oxford Book of English Verse:* I have to admit it, just by their presence in that august volume they did something for me. And although it had nothing to do with reading or writing, it was an important thing they did.

Now, what are we to make of this spluttering debate, in which charges of imperialism are met by equally passionate accusations of vandalism, in which each side hates the others, and yet each one seems to have its share of reason? Perhaps what we have here is one of those debates in which the opposing sides, unbeknownst to themselves, share a myopia that will turn out to be the most telling feature of the whole discussion: a debate, for instance, like that of our Founding Fathers over the nature of the franchise. Think of all the energy and passion spent pondering the question of property qualifications or direct versus legislative elections while all along, unmentioned and unimagined, was the fact—to us so central—that women and slaves were never considered for any kind of vote.

Something is being overlooked: the state of reading, and books, and literature in our country at this time. Why, ask yourself, is everyone so hot under the collar about what to put on the required-reading shelf? It is because while we have been arguing so fiercely about which books make the best medicine, the patient has been slipping deeper and deeper into a coma.

Let us imagine a country in which reading is a popular voluntary activity. There, parents read books for their own edification and pleasure, and are seen by their children at this silent and mysterious pastime. These parents also read to their children, give them books for presents, talk to them about books and underwrite, with their taxes, a public library system that is open all day, every day. In school—where an attractive library is invariably to be found—the children study certain books together but also have an active reading life of their own. Years later it may even be hard for them to remember if they read *Jane*

Eyre at home and Judy Blume in class, or the other way around. In college young people continue to be assigned certain books, but far more important are the books they discover for themselves—browsing in the library, in bookstores, on the shelves of friends, one book leading to another, back and forth in history and across languages and cultures. After graduation they continue to read, and in the fullness of time produce a new generation of readers. Oh happy land! I wish we all lived there.

In that other country of real readers—voluntary, active, self-determined readers—a debate like the current one over the canon would not be taking place. Or if it did, it would be as a kind of parlor game: What books would *you* take to a desert island? Everyone would know that the top-ten list was merely a tiny fraction of the books one would read in a lifetime. It would not seem racist or sexist or hopelessly hidebound to put Hawthorne on the syllabus and not Toni Morrison. It would be more like putting oatmeal and not noodles on the breakfast menu—a choice part arbitrary, part a nod to the national past, part, dare one say it, a kind of reverse affirmative action: School might frankly be the place where one reads the books that are a little off-putting, that have gone a little cold, that you might pass over because they do not address, in reader-friendly contemporary fashion, the issues most immediately at stake in modern life, but that, with a little study, turn out to have a great deal to say. Being on the list wouldn't mean so much. It might even add to a writer's cachet *not* to be on the list, to be in one way or another too heady, too daring, too exciting to be ground up into institutional fodder for teenagers. Generations of high school kids have been turned off to George Eliot by being forced to read *Silas Marner* at a tender age. One can imagine a whole new readership for her if grown-ups were left to approach *Middlemarch* and *Daniel Deronda* with open minds, at their leisure.

Of course, they rarely do. In America today the assumption underlying the canon debate is that the books on the list are the only books that are going to be read, and if the list is dropped no books are going to be read. Becoming a textbook is a book's only chance; all sides take that for granted. And so all agree not to mention certain things that they themselves, as highly educated people and, one assumes, devoted readers, know perfectly well. For example, that if you read only twenty-five, or fifty, or a hundred books, you can't understand them, however well chosen they are. And that if you don't have an independent reading life—and very few students do—you won't *like* reading the books on the list and will forget them the minute you finish them. And that books have, or should

The assumption underlying the canon debate is that the books on the list are the only books that are going to be read.

How strange to think that people need professorial help to read John Updike or Alice Walker.

have, lives beyond the syllabus—thus, the totally misguided attempt to put current literature in the classroom. How strange to think that people need professorial help to read John Updike or Alice Walker, writers people actually do read for fun. But all sides agree, if it isn't taught, it doesn't count.

Let's look at the canon question from another angle. Instead of asking what books we want others to read, let's ask why we read books ourselves. I think the canon debaters are being a little disingenuous here, are suppressing, in the interest of their own agendas, their personal experience of reading. Sure, we read to understand our American culture and history, and we also read to recover neglected masterpieces, and to learn more about the accomplishments of our subgroup and thereby, as I've admitted about myself, increase our self-esteem. But what about reading for the aesthetic pleasures of language, form, image? What about reading to learn something new, to have a vicarious adventure, to follow the workings of an interesting, if possibly skewed, narrow and ill-tempered mind? What about reading for the story? For an expanded sense of sheer human variety? There are a thousand reasons why a book might have a claim on our time and attention other than its canonization. I once infuriated an acquaintance by asserting that Trollope, although in many ways a lesser writer than Dickens, possessed some wonderful qualities Dickens lacked: a more realistic view of women, a more skeptical view of good intentions, a subtler sense of humor, a drier vision of life which I myself found congenial. You'd think I'd advocated throwing Dickens out and replacing him with a toaster. Because Dickens is a certified Great Writer, and Trollope is not.

Am I saying anything different from what Randall Jarrell said in his great 1953 essay "The Age of Criticism"? Not really, so I'll quote him. Speaking of the literary gatherings of the era, Jarrell wrote:

> If, at such parties, you wanted to talk about *Ulysses* or *The Castle* or *The Brothers Karamazov* or *The Great Gatsby* or Graham Greene's last novel—Important books—you were at the right place. (Though you weren't so well off if you wanted to talk about *Remembrance of Things Past.* Important, but too long.) But if you wanted to talk about Turgenev's novelettes, or *The House of the Dead,* or *Lavengro,* or *Life on the Mississippi,* or *The Old Wives' Tale,* or *The Golovlyov Family,* or Cunningham-Grahame's stories, or Saint-Simon's memoirs, or *Lost Illusions,* or *The Beggar's Opera,* or *Eugen Onegin,* or *Little Dorrit,* or the *Burnt Njal Saga,* or *Persuasion,* or *The Inspector-General,* or *Oblomov,* or *Peer Gynt,* or *Far from the Madding Crowd,* or *Out of Africa,* or the *Parallel Lives,* or *A Dreary Story,* or *Debits and Credits,* or *Arabia Deserta,* or *Elective Affinities,* or *Schweik,* or—any of a thousand good or interesting but Unimportant books, you couldn't expect a very ready knowledge or sympathy from most of the readers there. They had looked at the big sights, the current sights, hard, with guides and glasses; and those walks in

the country, over unfrequented or thrice-familiar territory, all alone—those walks from which most of the joy and good of reading come—were walks that they hadn't gone on very often.

I suspect that most canon debaters have taken those solitary rambles, if only out of boredom—how many times, after all, can you reread the *Aeneid*, or *Mrs. Dalloway*, or *Cotton Comes to Harlem* (to pick one book from each column)? But those walks don't count, because of another assumption all sides hold in common, which is that the purpose of reading is none of the many varied and delicious satisfactions I've mentioned; it's medicinal. The chief end of reading is to produce a desirable kind of person and a desirable kind of society. A respectful, high-minded citizen of a unified society for the conservatives, an up-to-date and flexible sort for the liberals, a subgroup-identified, robustly confident one for the radicals. How pragmatic, how moralistic, how American! The culture debaters turn out to share a secret suspicion of culture itself, as well as the antipornographer's belief that there is a simple, one-to-one correlation between books and behavior. Read the conservatives' list and produce a nation of sexists and racists—or a nation of philosopher kings. Read the liberals' list and produce a nation of spineless relativists—or a nation of open-minded world citizens. Read the radicals' list and produce a nation of psychobabblers and ancestor-worshipers—or a nation of stalwart proud-to-be-me pluralists.

But is there any list of a few dozen books that can have such a magical effect, for good or for ill? Of course not. It's like arguing that a perfectly nutritional breakfast cereal is enough food for the whole day. And so the canon debate is really an argument about what books to cram down the resistant throats of a resentful captive populace of students; and the trick is never to mention the fact that, in such circumstances, one book is as good, or as bad, as another. Because, as the debaters know from their own experience as readers, books are not pills that produce health when ingested in measured doses. Books do not shape character in any simple way—if, indeed, they do so at all—or the most literate would be the most virtuous instead of just the ordinary run of humanity with larger vocabularies. Books cannot mold a common national purpose when, in fact, people are honestly divided about what kind of country they want—and are divided, moreover, for very good and practical reasons, as they always have been.

The canon debate is an argument about what books to cram down the resistant throats of a resentful captive populace of students.

The culture debaters turn out to share a secret suspicion that there is a simple, one-to-one correlation between books and behavior.

For these burly and energetic purposes, books are all but useless. The way books affect us is an altogether more subtle, delicate, wayward and individual, not to say private, affair. And that reading is being made to bear such an inappropriate and simplistic burden speaks to the poverty both of culture and of frank political discussion in our time.

On his deathbed, Dr. Johnson—once canonical, now more admired than read—is supposed to have said to a friend who was energetically rearranging his bedclothes, "Thank you, this will do all that a pillow can do." One might say that the canon debaters are all asking of their handful of chosen books that they do a great deal more than any handful of books can do. ♦

Questions for Discussion

1. Is it important to agree upon a list of books that all college students should read?
2. If you were going to add a book to "the canon," what would it be?

America's Textbook Fiasco: A Conspiracy of Good Intentions

Harriet Tyson-Bernstein

Harriet Tyson-Bernstein is one of many educators concerned about the quality of today's textbooks. She believes that adoption policies that lead publishers to "custom tailor" text content has resulted in books that are boring, misleading, and generally just don't do the job they are supposed to do.

This article is included here for a variety of reasons. On one level it will help to inform students on the text publishing business, which is the mainstay of today's book publishing. But it is also hoped that the article will encourage students to become more critical readers of the textbooks they are currently using. It might also help them analyze the effectiveness of their own education, to date.

Tyson-Bernstein has served as president of the Montgomery County (Md.) Board of Education and director of the project on textbook reform sponsored by the National Association of State Boards of Education. This article is adapted from The Textbook Fiasco: A Conspiracy of Good Intentions, *a report published by the Council for Basic Education, an organization that promotes a rigorous liberal arts education for all students.*

Reading Difficulty Level: 4.

"If the customer wants a pink stretch Cadillac, I may think it's tacky and wasteful, but I would be a fool to produce a fuel-efficient black compact if nobody is going to buy it."

—textbook executive

"The most frustrating part of the job is that the user isn't the buyer."

—textbook author

"The books are all alike anyway, so we don't even bother to read them. We go for the publisher who gives us the biggest freebie package."

—curriculum supervisor

"They have broken up learning into bits no larger than an eyelash, and the kids aren't able to sweep up the pieces."

—textbook editor

"All I know is we can make those publishers do what we tell them to do. They support our curriculum, and our scores are going up."

—city superintendent

Imagine a public policy system that is perfectly designed to produce textbooks that confuse, mislead, and profoundly bore students, while at the same time making all of the adults involved in the process look good, not only in their own eyes, but in the eyes of others. Although there are some good textbooks on the market, publishers and editors are virtually compelled by public policies and practices to create textbooks that confuse students with non sequiturs, that mislead them with misinformation, and that profoundly bore them with pointlessly arid writing.

None of the adults in this very complex system intends this outcome. To the contrary, each of them wants to produce good effects, and each public policy, regulation, or conventional practice was intended to make some improvement or prevent some abuse. But the cumulative effects of well-intentioned and seemingly reasonable state and local regulation are textbooks that squander the intellectual capital of our youth.

The cumulative effects of well-intentioned regulation are textbooks that squander the intellectual capital of our youth.

Some critics of the American textbook system would disagree with our "good intentions" hypothesis. It could be argued that adoption policies that fail to secure serious reviewers, fail to give them adequate time to review materials, and fail to compensate them are not well intended. The case could be made that special-interest groups that fight for their own particular views to the exclusion of others are not well intended. Publishers who concern themselves only with sales could be accused of bad intentions. But more likely, most school boards, and perhaps even top administrators, are simply unaware of the relationship between superficial adoption policies and superficial textbooks. Zealots and idealogues, however distasteful they may be to their opponents, generally believe they are protecting children from harm. And publishers, as businessmen, cannot be expected to be idealists; their first obligation is to return a profit, not to render a public service.

Imagine a public policy system that is perfectly designed to produce textbooks that confuse, mislead, and profoundly bore students.

You might suppose that such a system could not exist. If it did, wouldn't those responsible for the educational system change it? Or if not, you might suppose that citizens would rise up in sufficient force to create a better way. But you would be mistaken; such a system does exist, and there is at the moment no noticeable effort to change it.

What Is a Good Textbook?

The very first textbook given to young children in school ought to be so delightful that they want to read more books.

The very first textbook given to young children in school ought to be so delightful that they want to read more books. Children would not only be thrilled by their growing ability to crack the code of written language, they would also be ushered into the riches of our culture. The skills taught in reading books would be closely related to, and not divorced from, the content of the stories. Mathematics books for young children would help them think mathematically and let them practice their skills on problems worth solving. *All* books written for elementary students ought to contain information that is important to adults as well as children. Parents, as well as students, would enjoy reading them.

Books for older students ought to have a theme or purpose that is crystal clear. Topics and facts would support, and not distract from, the overall theme. Important and difficult topics—gravity, for example, or the constitutional system of checks and balances—would be presented with enough depth for students to understand. Information about the lives and cultures of minorities, women, workers, or ordinary people would not be stuck on gaudily, but integrated into the text. Controversy—so essential to both democracy and intellectual growth—would be embraced rather than avoided. Students would share in defeats as well as triumphs of those who shaped history or built bodies of knowledge.

Facts ought to be accurate. Questions and exercises ought to encourage students to think rather than force them to hunt down trivial details. Chapter summaries would forge essential connections between ideas; they would not merely be cheat sheets for the questions at the chapter's end.

Good textbooks for any grade level or subject ought to be written so students can benefit from the book independently. If students miss a lecture, are absent from school, or merely want to review what was covered in class, they would read the book with some prospect of gathering meaning. The author ought to give students reason for persisting through inevitable patches of drudgery. Most important, the book would be written so students can remember what they read.

Sadly, very few of today's textbooks meet such criteria. Although the flaws in today's textbooks vary according to grade level and subject, two serious flaws afflict the vast majority of commercially prepared materials for schoolchildren: writing is poor, and books treat most topics so superficially that students can't make sense of what they are reading.

The Bad Writing Problem

> Rabbit said: "I can run. I can run fast. You can't run fast." Turtle said, "Look Rabbit. See the park. You and I will run. We'll run to the park."
>
> Rabbit said, "I want to stop. I'll stop here. I can run, but turtle can't. I can get to the park fast." Turtle said, "I can't run fast. But I will not stop. Rabbit can't see me. I'll get to the park."

In this nearly unrecognizable version of "The Hare and the Tortoise," the main points of the fable—the danger of cockiness and the value of persistence—are utterly lost. Its repetitions are pointless at best and boring at worst. Unfortunately, this kind of editorial mangling is typical of material our children are forced to read in the early grades of school.

Susan Ohanian, in "Ruffles and Flourishes," (*Atlantic Monthly*, September 1987) says, "Basal readers can be criticized on lots of grounds. Their worst fault, I think, is that for no good reason, they squeeze the juice out of some very fine tales." Comparing a passage from the Paul Leyssac translation of Hans Christian Anderson's "The Emperor's New Clothes," she finds the following:

> "Magnificent!" "Excellent!" "Prodigious!" went from mouth to mouth, and everyone was exceedingly pleased.

had been changed to:

> "How marvelous," they echoed the emperor. "How beautiful."

And in "How the Camel Got His Hump," Ohanian notices that Kipling's "a great big lolliping humph" has been changed to "a great big humph." "You lose a great big lolliping lot when you lose the humph's gerundive," she writes.

Beatrix Potter, whose judgment about what children can and will read is substantiated by the choices made by children at libraries and parents at bookstores, said that children "like a fine word occasionally." Researchers have also demonstrated that kids, as well as adults, like an occasional big word that is delicious to say.

The basic elements of good storytelling often get lost in the editing process.

Not only have the fine words been taken out. The basic elements of good storytelling often get lost in the editing process. In his study of elementary readers, Bertram Bruce of Bolt, Beranek and Newman, Inc., found that the conflict essential to any good story has often been suppressed. Moreover, the engaging voice of a narrator, which can bind readers to the story and give them glimpses into characters' thoughts, is often missing.

Comparing the original Judy Blume story "Freckle Juice" with the textbook version, Bruce shows what happens to an otherwise-good story about a freckled boy who thinks his life would be happier if he could get rid of his freckles. In the story, a friend sells the boy some "freckle juice," a vile concoction to smear on his face. In the textbook version, the reader gets little information about why the boy doesn't like his freckles or why he allows himself to be gulled by his friend. "Without these elements," says Bruce, "the story makes little sense."

In general, the writing in elementary schoolbooks is choppy, stilted, and monotonous.

In general, the writing in elementary schoolbooks is choppy, stilted, and monotonous. Worse still, the words and the phrases that help a novice reader infer the correct relationships between ideas and events are often stripped away.

Authors and editors do not willingly chop and flatten sentences, nor do they thoughtlessly mangle storylines. The source of the writing problem is not in the publishing house, but in the public agency. Legislators, educational policymakers, and administrative regulators have unintentionally drained the life out of children's textbooks in several ways.

First, they have rejected textbooks that fail to achieve a mandated numerical score on a readability formula, a number they believe will guarantee a proper match between the text's difficulty and the reading ability of children at a given grade level.

Second, they have favored books that present a particular list of vocabulary words or teach a particular list of abstract skills (e.g., "finding the main idea") over books that might ignite children's imaginations.

Third, they have discouraged publishers from investing the time and effort it takes to produce carefully written material by failing to buy from publishers who do produce well-written textbooks.

Readability Formulas

Readability formulas were developed over 60 years ago to help educators choose textbooks written at the appropriate level of difficulty. The designers of readability formulas, then and now, operated on the assumption that long words, unfamiliar words, and long sentences are the primary causes of reading difficulty. Judging the difficulty of a text by such formulas is easy. Some formulas count syllables in words and words in sentences and calculate averages. Others rely on lists of words deemed to be familiar to children at various ages, adding points for words children are not believed to know. These mechanical labors yield a score that represents the grade level of a passage or a textbook.

When educators used readability formulas informally, along with common sense, to judge reading difficulty, these formulas had no harmful effects. But when policymakers and regulators began to make them part of official policies and procedures, the picture began to change. Publishers discovered they could lose a sale if an adoption committee subjected a randomly chosen passage to a formula analysis and found that the score was too high or too low. Defensively, textbook authors and editors began to write or adapt text so that it would survive a readability formula check. Short words ("it," for example) had to be substituted for long words. ("elephant," for example).

The popular phrase, "dumbing down," aptly describes the effect of readability formulas on not only elementary books, but also junior high textbooks. Even the simple cadence of language can be cruelly monotonous. To add confusion to boredom, short and vague words are often substituted for longer, precise ones. Instead of "esophagus," there will be "food tube." Instead of "protoplasm," there will be "stuff."[1]

Compound or complex sentences have been chopped in two, often at the expense of the reader's comprehension, in order to lower the score. For example:

ORIGINAL: "If given a chance before another fire comes, a tree will heal its own wounds by growing new bark over burned parts."
ADAPTED: "If given a chance before another fire comes, the tree will heal its own wounds. It will grow new bark over the burned parts."

In this instance, the way in which trees heal themselves—by growing new bark—is unstated in the edited version. "[A]n inexperienced reader, or one who does not know very much about trees, might make an incorrect guess and see healing wounds and growing new bark as separate processes, simply ordered in time," writes Andee Rubin, a textbook researcher.[2] This butchery is clearly attributable to an editorial effort to bring down the readability score.

Readability formulas are blind to both meaning and style.

The limitations of readability formulas have been exposed by contemporary researchers. It is clear that readability formulas are blind to both meaning and style. Although their purpose was to provide a gross indication of grade level, the paradoxical effect of their misuse as a formula for writing has been to make texts harder to understand. Moreover, the required use of words that children are presumed to know already puts too tight a rein on the growth of their vocabulary.

Despite the mounting evidence that writing to meet a formula is educationally unsound, specified formulas and scores are required in some states by law and in others by regulation. Even in states and localities with no formal requirements, judging the difficulty of a textbook by formula is still common practice.

Research has shown that at least five experienced teachers (five is the number needed to offset out biases and poor judgment), if given a modicum of training, are quite good at judging the reading difficulty of a text. Yet teachers have also become increasingly reluctant to exercise "subjective" judgment, preferring the safety of an "objective" measure. With so many dimensions of a book to consider in an adoption process, this one—Is the book easy enough?—can be nailed down without much effort. A committee member can check the "readabilities" with one eye on the TV or with the help of a computer program.

Skills Mongering

Readability formulas are only one of the causes of bad writing. Another is the current accountability movement. Increasingly, educational accountability has become synonymous with student achievement on standardized tests of rudimentary skills. Few states or localities test subject knowledge, but virtually all schools test the skills said to be critical to a mastery of content. Not surprisingly, textbook publishers have also begun to emphasize skills more than subject content.

Instead of designing a book from the standpoint of its subject or its capacity to capture the children's imagination, editors are increasingly organizing elementary reading series around the content and timing of standardized tests.

Even when testing is limited to skills, the most available form of mass testing—the multiple-choice test—limits even skills to those that accommodate a short-answer form. Thus, even though writing is a "skill," it will rarely be tested by asking students to write a composition, but by asking them to identify correct usage from among several options, to fill in blanks in sentences, to correct punctuation and capitalization, or other recognition tasks.

Similarly, reading is a "skill," but the multiple-choice format shrinks most test passages to a paragraph. In the early grades, children are expected to learn letter sounds in certain sequences, and are tested accordingly on their ability to recognize similarities and differences in letter sounds in the test passages. Increasingly, textbooks are designed to help children pass such tests. "Too often," says Andee Rubin, "the books for children in grades one through three are full of stories "whose claim to coherence is that they use the same vowel in almost every word."

Instead of designing a book from the standpoint of its subject or its capacity to capture the children's imagination, editors are increasingly organizing elementary reading series around the content and timing of standardized tests. If commas are taught in September, but not tested until April, the book will administer a little comma dose every few lessons from October through May so children will be able to answer questions about commas on the test.

Frequently, says Diane Ravitch of Columbia University, the stories are being written by people who have never been heard of outside of textbook publishing houses. Under present policy, though, it could hardly be otherwise. Gifted writers of children's trade books are reluctant to write for textbook companies, or even to surrender their already-published work to the technocratic editors concerned with readability formulas, vocabulary controls, and standardized multiple-choice tests.

The emphasis on testable skills is not limited to elementary textbooks. Books written for junior and senior high school students are laced with exercises claiming to develop "critical thinking skills" even though the text itself may do very little to stimulate thinking. Nobody would suggest that children should not learn how to think, but the dynamics of the textbook market encourage publishers to feature an almost content-free approach to "thinking," rather than allowing the content to drive children to think about what they are reading.

As these skills become imbedded in the "scope and sequence" charts, or "curriculum frameworks" of major states and cities, publishers are pressed to plan skills to be "taught" on each page, even before the text has been written. Publishers must also provide an index to the required skills, by page number, so that curriculum directors who don't have time actually to read the books can satisfy themselves that the skills are being "taught." A long string of page references behind "main idea," for example, impresses some curriculum directors who don't have time to discover that the main idea might not be worth finding. Clearly, many books are planned to satisfy the superficial selection process rather than to satisfy the curiosity of students.

The "Mentioning" Problem

Another pervasive textbook sin is "mentioning," a term coined by researcher Dolores Durkin at the University of Illinois. The term refers to textbook prose that flits from fact to fact, statement to statement, and topic to topic, without giving the reader the context that would make sense of the factual information. Books accused of "mentioning" are generally long on facts and terms but short on ideas and explanations. Without the necessary context, readers often fail to see the significance of the connections between statements. Metaphors and similes, which would help readers grasp a complicated concept, are remarkably infrequent, even when we allow for how difficult it is to find metaphors that immature readers can understand. Examples and counterexamples that would give a concept some roundness are rare.

In an effort to satisfy the content requirements of so many adoption authorities, the text must be compressed into incomprehensibility. In science books, the density of new, italicized (but poorly explained) technical terms on each page is a good measure of the extent of mentioning. Entire books, like the biology example below, are often glossaries masquerading as textbooks.

NUCLEIC ACIDS New vocabulary: chromosome, nucleic acid, DNA, RNA nucleotide.

Books written for junior and senior high school students are laced with exercises claiming to develop "critical thinking skills" even though the text itself may do very little to stimulate thinking.

Many books are planned to satisfy the superficial selection process rather than to satisfy the curiosity of students.

> In the nucleus of a cell are thread-like strands called *chromosomes,* (KRO-muh-somz). They are composed of proteins and *nucleic acids* (noo-KLAY'-ik). The proteins in nucleic acids make up two important chemicals, *DNA* and *RNA.* Nucleic acids are organic compounds that are made up of carbon, hydrogen, oxygen, nitrogen, and phosphorus.
>
> DNA and RNA are not the only nucleic acids, but they do have special roles in the cell. RNA is involved in making proteins. DNA is involved in controlling the cell's activities. *Both are involved in passing on characteristics from parents to offspring.*
>
> Each nucleic acid is made up of units called *nucleotides* (NOO'-klee-uh-tidz). In turn, each nucleotide is composed of three parts: a chemical group containing phosphorus, a group containing nitrogen, and a simple sugar.

If you find this incomprehensible, pity the poor ninth grader. In this tangle of passive voice sentences, cause and effect relationships become lost. The author switches back and forth between parts and chemical compounds without warning. The signals— "are composed of" and "are made up of"—are inconsistently applied. The intelligent response to such "mentioning" and bad writing is "So what?" or "Who cares?"

The "mentioning" problem, like the bad writing problem, is directly attributable to public policies and procedures. Adoption states that generate excessively detailed textbook specifications seldom take into account the time it would take to teach all their required items, or the space available in a standard-sized textbook. Typical selection procedures seldom take into account the critical mass of information a student needs to understand an unfamiliar topic.

The problem of too many topics in too little space is especially severe in social studies, history, and science books. The Thirty Years' War will be "covered" in a paragraph; the Nixon presidency in two sentences. Nucleotides will be mentioned, and the glossary will contain a circular definition, but the student will not learn much about them. All of the small facts and terms that can be tested on a multiple-choice test will appear in the index, because that is where adoption committees usually check on curricular and test "congruence"—if they check at all.

Special-interest groups pressure policymakers to include more material in the curriculum (and therefore the textbooks) about their favorite subjects.

In recent decades, the "mentioning" problem has become more acute. Special-interest groups pressure policymakers to include more material in the curriculum (and therefore the textbooks) about their favorite subjects. Policymakers find it difficult to resist these pressures because, for the most part, the additions sound reasonable. A state or local school board can submit, without a troubled conscience, to demands from environmentalists, the health food lobby, advocates of the work ethic, and any organized minority group.

Even where good causes are not involved, there are adult pressures to teach more and more academic material as the scope of knowledge within disciplines expands. School systems, test developers, and textbook publishers often ask university professors to serve on advisory committees, and in that setting, professors generally defer to one another, cheerfully adding each other's suggestions to the list of what should be taught.

With so much to stuff into the book, editors make sacrifices. Since publishers are held to account for a jumble of topics and facts, but not for coherence, coherence suffers. A thoughtful reader finds it tough to detect the pattern that has determined an author's choices.

Since publishers are held to account for a jumble of topics and facts, but not for coherence, coherence suffers.

Lacking any firm basis for choosing material, and required to include so much, textbook authors easily fall into the "mentioning" trap. A student may be told, for example, that Aristotle "studied the political organization of 150 city states and put down his conclusions in a book called *Politics*." He won't be told, however, what Aristotle's conclusions were.

At the moment, school officials prefer mentioning to coherence because they are obsessed with the idea that the textbook must cover as many of the facts and topics in the curriculum and tests as possible. With so little time to examine books, adoption committees check up on textbook/curriculum/test congruence by checking the labels, captions, index, and glossary. Knowing how superficially books are examined, publishers are best advised to sacrifice depth and comprehensibility and concentrate on coverage, however inadequate it may be.

Publishers also sacrifice material that may cause them to be criticized or to lose sales. Pressures from the politically organized, religious right have made it risky for publishers to discuss evolution. If evolution is discussed at all, it is often confined to a chapter at the end of the book. Students are conducted on a forced march through the phyla, and given no understanding of the overarching theory (evolution) that gives taxonomy life and meaning. Touchy subjects, like dinosaurs, the fossil record, genetics, natural selection, or even the scientific meanings of the words "theory" and "belief" are treated skimpily or vaguely in order to avoid fundamentalist ire.

Bad writing and the "mentioning" problem are intimately related. It is hard to write well about a vast span of history in one paragraph. A scientist might call a one-page explanation of photosynthesis "inaccurate" while a writer will call it "badly written." They are both right, but they have examined the text from different perspectives. Sense and style are intimately related, and so are space and accuracy, as every newspaper reporter knows.

Some teachers defend today's outline-style textbook on the grounds that they can fill in whatever information the textbook omits.

Such a defense suggests that the book is not even expected to be comprehensible on its own. Many teachers no longer see the book as material for students to read, but as a reference guide to the material that is supposed to be covered in class. They have, in effect, given up on the possibility that a textbook can be an independent source of learning. ♦

References

Armbruster, Bonnie B., J. Osborn, and A. Davison, "Readability Formulas May Be Dangerous to Your Textbooks," *Educational Leadership*, April 1985, p. 18–20.

Rubin Andee, "What Can Readability Formulas Tell Us About Text? In R. C. Anderson and J. Osborn (eds.): *Foundations for a Literate America*. Lexington, MA. Lexington Books, 1984.

Questions for Discussion

1. In your experience, were your school textbooks guilty of the problems this author claims for them?
2. According to this author, many teachers now use textbooks only as reference guides. In your opinion, should textbooks be independent sources of learning?

Suggested Readings

More On Kitty Kelley

Alter, Jonathan, "Wretched Excess," *Newsweek*, April 22, 1991, p. 52 (6).

On the Effects of the Declining Book Readership

Cohen, Roger, "The Lost Book Generation," *The New York Times*, Sec. 4A ("Education Life" Supplement), January 6, 1991, p. 34 (2). People ages 15 to 25 are computer-literate but book shy. Television and time constraints are the main culprits.

Garvey, John, "Creeping Dimness: When the Past Is Marginalized," *Commonweal* Vol. 115, October 21, 1988, pp. 552 (2). Television discourages reading, and makes people concentrate on the present and forget history. Today's racism might be caused by ignorance of history.

On the Importance of Books

Rushdie, Salman, "Is Nothing Sacred?", *New Perspectives Quarterly*, Spring, 1991, p. 8. The author who the Ayatolla Khomeini put a hit out on discusses literature as a means of secular transcendence.

Yardley, Jonathan, "Ten Books That Shaped the American Character," *American Heritage*, May/June 1985. This reading was included in the last edition of *Mass Media Issues*. Although we don't have room for it here, you might be interested in his list:

Walden, by Henry David Thoreau (1854)
Leaves of Grass, by Walt Whitman (1855)
Ragged Dick, or *Street Life in New York*, by Horatio Alger (1867)

The Adventures of Huckleberry Finn, by Mark Twain (1884)
The Boston Cooking School Cookbook, by Fannie Farmer (1896)
The Theory of the Leisure Class, by Thornstein Veblen (1899)
The Souls of Black Folk, by W. E. B. DuBois (1903)
In Our Time, by Ernest Hemingway (1925)
How to Win Friends and Influence People, by Dale Carnegie (1936)
The Common Sense Book of Baby and Child Care, by Benjamin Spock (1946)

On the Declining Quality of Books

Aldridge, John, "The New American Assembly-Line Fiction: The Empty Blue Center," *The American Scholar* Vol. 59, Winter, 1990, pp. 17–38. Modern fiction is changing, and not for the better.

Hoban, Phoebe, " 'Psycho' Drama," *New York* December 17, 1990, pp. 32–37 (6). This is the inside story of what happened when the publisher decided that Bret Ellis's *American Psycho* was too loathsome to print.

Rosenblatt, Roger, "Snuff This Book! Will Bret Easton Ellis Get Away With Murder?", *The New York Times Book Review,* December 16, 1990, p. 3 (2). Nice argument, making the point that Simon and Schuster's decision is not censorship. "You remember censorship. Censorship is when a government burns your manuscript, smashes your presses and throws you in jail. When an artist is unable to get a government grant, it may be inconvenient, but censorship it ain't."

Solotaroff, Ted, "The Paperbacking of Publishing," *The Nation,* October 7, 1991. The "paperback mentality" now pervades hardcover publishing.

Tom Wolfe, "Stalking the Billion-Footed Beast: A Literary Manifesto for the New Social Novel," *Harper's Magazine* Vol. 279, November 1989, p. 45 (12). Wolfe suggests that the contemporary American novel is not all it should be.

Towers, Robert, "The Flap Over Tom Wolfe: How Real Is the Retreat from Realism?", *The New York Times Book Review,* January 28, 1990, p. 15.

More On "The Canon" Controversy

"The Derisory Tower," *The New Republic,* February 18, 1991, p. 5 (2). The editors explain why they are opposed to the current "multiculturalist" trend.

Goodman, Matthew, "Who Says Which Are Our Greatest Books: The Politics of the Literary Canon," *Utne Reader,* May/June 1991, p. 129 (5). This includes Goodman's list of "28 more great books" that could be added to a multicultural canon.

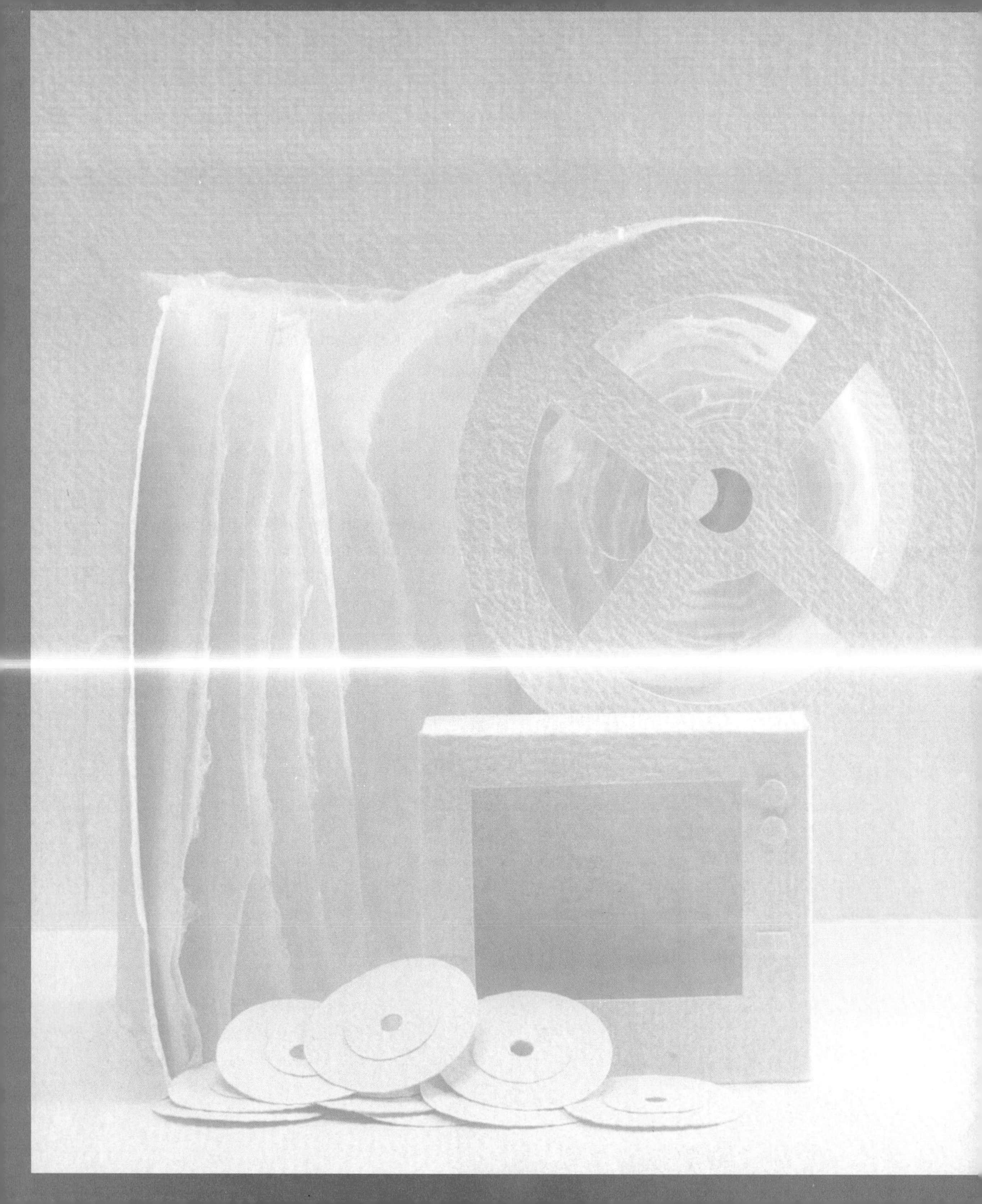

Part III

THE SIGHT AND SOUND MEDIA

The Movies

8

The fact is I am quite happy in a movie, even a bad movie. Other people, so I have read, treasure memorable moments in their lives.

—Walker Percy, *The Moviegoer*

The movies might be the closest we come to a dream state during our waking moments. We wait in line, sometimes in the cold and sometimes for considerable amounts of time, and we pay a good percentage of our entertainment budgets to sit in a darkened theater with strangers to experience the escapism inherent in the light show before us. Here we view our fantasies played out by characters who are physically and emotionally larger than life.

Anyone who doubts the basic fantasy function of the film experience need only peruse the following list of the top 10 money-makers of all time.

Film, Year of Release	Earnings up to 1990
1. E.T.: The Extra-Terrestrial (1982)	229 mil.
2. Star Wars (1977)	194 mil.
3. Return of the Jedi (1983)	168 mil.
4. Batman (1989)	151 mil.
5. The Empire Strikes Back (1980)	142 mil.
6. Ghostbusters (1984)	130 mil.
7. Jaws (1975)	130 mil.
8. Raiders of the Lost Ark (1981)	116 mil.
9. Indiana Jones and the Last Crusade (1989)	116 mil.
10. Indiana Jones and the Temple of Doom (1984)	109 mil.

Films are an important part of our cultural history, and it's an area in which you can educate yourself enjoyably. One path to enlightment is to view classic films, many of which are available on late-night TV and at your local video store. The Library of Congress recommends the following 25 films as "culturally, historically, or esthetically significant."

Best Years of Our Lives	1946
Casablanca	1942
Citizen Kane	1941
The Crowd	1928
Dr. Strangelove	1964
The General	1927
Gone with the Wind	1939
The Grapes of Wrath	1940
High Noon	1952
Intolerance	1916
The Learning Tree	1969
The Maltese Falcon	1941
Mr. Smith Goes to Washington	1939
Modern Times	1936
Nanook of the North	1922
On the Waterfront	1954
The Searchers	1956
Singin' in the Rain	1952
Snow White and the Seven Dwarfs	1937
Some Like It Hot	1959
Star Wars	1977
Sunrise	1927
Sunset Boulevard	1950
Vertigo	1958
The Wizard of Oz	1939

Another way to become literate in American films is to seek out the films of selected directors. Film is considered a director's medium; by viewing two or three of a director's films you can become aware of that director's style or "message." Here is a list of six great American directors and some of their representative films:

D. W. Griffith

The Birth of a Nation (1915)

Intolerance (1916)

Frank Capra

- It Happened One Night (1934)
- Mr. Deeds Goes to Town (1936)
- You Can't Take it With You (1938)
- Mr. Smith Goes to Washington (1939)
- It's a Wonderful Life (1946)

Howard Hawks

- Bringing Up Baby (1938)
- To Have and Have Not (1944)
- The Big Sleep (1946)

Alfred Hitchcock

- Strangers on a Train (1954)
- Rear Window (1954)
- North by Northwest (1959)
- Psycho (1960)
- The Birds (1963)

John Huston

- The Maltese Falcon (1941)
- The Treasure of the Sierra Madre (1948)
- Key Largo (1948)
- The Asphalt Jungle (1950)
- The Man Who Would Be King (1976)

Orson Welles

- Citizen Kane (1941)
- The Magnificent Ambersons (1942)

One final way to become "film literate" is to track current trends in today's cinema. The articles in this chapter look at two such trends. Julia Cameron, in "Sex for Kicks," points out what she considers to be a dangerous increase in the mixture of sex and violence in today's movies. Then Mark Crispin Miller looks at the ramifications of the placement of advertisers' products within movies.

Sex for Kicks

Julia Cameron

In September, 1990, The Motion Picture Association of America changed its "X" designation to "NC-17," meaning no one under 17 admitted. The change was made necessary because the hard-core pornography industry had co-opted the "X" rating, which led many theaters to refuse to show the films, and many newspapers refuse to advertise them. For a legitimate film, the "X" rating had become the financial kiss of death.

The new rating opens the door for movies of even greater sexual and violent content to be shown in neighborhood theaters. In the following reading, film writer/director Julia Cameron suggests that this trend will be especially dangerous if movies continue to mix sex with violence. This mixture, she says, leads to an increase of sexual addiction in society.

Along with her film work, Cameron is coauthor of The Money Drunk, *a book on money as an addictive substance.*

Reading Difficulty Level: 5. It's a short reading but there's a number of provocative ideas compressed into it.

We learn a great deal at the movies but, just as we did with those clandestine kisses and fondlings that happened in the balcony, we pretend that nothing really goes on.

A friend of mine says facetiously that she learned everything she could need in life at the movies: how to stand up under Nazi interrogation, how to smoke a cigarette, how to behave in Congress, how to conduct a cross examination, how to go mad. As it happens, I do believe we learn a great deal at the moves but, just as we did with those clandestine kisses and fondlings that happened in the balcony, we pretend that nothing really goes on. We pretend that what plays on the screen stays on the screen and has nothing to do with us. This is nonsense. The truth is that movies fill up our collective psyche and we respond. We wriggle, we groan, we laugh, we shriek and then, when we leave the theater, we pretend it didn't really happen. We like to deny that what we watch is a projection of ourselves as well as the work of a singular artist. "Artists are the antennae of the race," claimed Ezra Pound. And, yes, as a culture we do love to kill our messengers. Often a film is savagely reviewed not for its artistry, but for its uncomfortable implications. I am thinking now of the late, great Michael Powell, who scuttled his career with a single chiller, *Peeping Tom.* A creepy masterwork about a voyeuristic serial killer, the film links violence and

From *American Film,* October, 1990. Reprinted by permission.

pornography, and points to their darkest intersection: death as a sexualized experience. It is this same yoking of sex to domination that marks the current media message. Over the past decade, the link has grown more and more explicit—just like the sex itself. Increasingly, the message from our films is that ours is a society focused on sex—and more disturbingly, the combination of sex and violence—not as a part of human expression but as a drug that gets us high and becomes a substitute for real human connection.

Movie Sex and Safe Sex

It is a chilly day in winter. I am sitting in a New York loft talking with a well-known gay pornographer whose business is booming as the AIDS epidemic spreads its daily toll to include the rich, the famous and the merely luckless.

"Sex is no longer safe," the pornographer is telling me, "And that's good business."

What he means by that, I learn, is that if people "can't do it safely," they like to watch other people do it while they watch at a "safe" remove.

"My business has quadrupled," he says. (His profit rate is nearly as exponential as the AIDS death rate.) But the pornographer has an ethical problem. His "actors" don't practice "safe sex."

Why? "It's not a turn-on. People don't get off on it. Look, if people can't do sex anymore, they at least want to be able to watch it."

Just as the Depression yielded movies about the rich, our current sexual depression is offering a bumper crop of films that are specifically sexual in theme and/or explicitly sexual in execution.

These days when movies are pitched, screenwriters make sure to add: Oh, yeah. There's this other character, a nice-girl virgin type who happens to be working in this sort of strip-joint brothel.

Ours is a society focused on sex as a drug that gets us high and becomes a substitute for real human connection.

True, the virginal girl with the vaginal ache has always been a celluloid staple. Long before we had centerfolds to moon over, we had the stars. Alone, in the dark, we savored their kisses, felt their charisma and their caresses. Alone, in the dark, we had our fantasies. We still do, but they are growing darker.

In 1983's *Flashdance*, the nice-girl virgin type was Jennifer Beals. She "happened" to be working in a place like a go-go bar. In this year's megahit, *Pretty Woman*, that girl is Julia Roberts, who happens to be working in this Hollywood Boulevard sort of brothel. In the brutal *Miami Blues*, the yuppie hooker is Jennifer Jason Leigh.

It can be argued that we've always met whores with hearts of gold at the movies—if not so often in real life. It's just that this year we seem to be meeting an awful lot of them.

"It just really bothers me that two films at the same theater at the same time had hooker heroines," complains one female producer.

These days the R rating is regarded by many filmmakers to be less a "sure death" at the box office than a G might be.

"And they were at the neighborhood multiplex." Even worse, these are bad girls you *could* take home to mother. Watching adorable Laura San Giacomo cuddle up to that teddy bear in *Pretty Woman* makes hooking look as dangerous as a bad college weekend.

"A Cinderella story," cheered the press. Did Cinderella give Prince Charming head?

"I wanted to do something a little different," is how director Garry Marshall explains his first two sex scenes in *Pretty Woman*, the oral-sex scenes. Wanting to do something a little different is a time-honored sexual tradition and so is fellatio, the "something" Garry Marshall chose. "It's the 1990s," he points out, correctly. "The original script was a lot darker. He left her at the end—and she was on drugs. But the script was very well-written. Disney saw something in the script, and they wanted my Pollyanna sensibility. I wanted to do something a little more . . . ," he breaks off. "Something a little more." He grins.

Mixing sex with violence, like mixing alcohol with certain drugs, is very dangerous.

Art films have long teetered between experimentation and exploitation. (In the international film market, soft-porn films are even called "art" films.) We expect a certain modicum of flesh from them—just as we expect "flash" from Hollywood product. What we are seeing these days, however, from the art film to the mainstream movie house, is *more*. More tits. More ass. "More . . . more," as Marshall succinctly says.

Consider titles like *Tie Me Up! Tie Me Down!* and the very wild *Wild at Heart*. Consider the proliferation of X ratings, however arbitrarily meted out. Consider that these days the R rating is regarded by many filmmakers to be less a "sure death" at the box office than a G might be. Make no mistake, sex sells. Family multiplexes offer smorgasbords porn palaces might once have envied. (Which movie did your child sneak into?)

Mixing Sex and Violence

What is disconcerting about all of this is less the sheer sexual content, which barely rivals daytime TV and pales next to cable, than the unsettling and increasing mix of sexuality and violence. Mixing sex with violence, like mixing alcohol with certain drugs, potentiates (makes more potent and explosive) the high. Taken alone, sex and violence are extremely powerful and, as sexologists will tell you, extremely addictive. These days we are doing something very dangerous. We are combining the two.

In *Blue Velvet* (1986), we watched Isabella Rossellini succumb to both her masochism and Dennis Hopper's abuse. Slouched in our seats, just like the young hero crouched in the closet, we watched in fascinated horror, seeing her grovel, yield and open herself to assault. When later, we saw her stumble, arms out stretched, trembling with vulnerability in full frontal nudity toward the ogling lens, who didn't feel privy to something more and other than mere sexuality?

What was this movie saying to us? What was our fascination with it saying about us? Occupying the same ambiguous terrain as Robert Mapplethorpe's photography, it made the play of light and shadow less cinematic than spiritual.

In the past couple of years, it seems nearly every other release has enlisted sex as its central subject: *Scandal; sex, lies, and videotape; Sea of Love; Dangerous Liaisons, The Cook, The Thief, His Wife & Her Lover*—the list goes on. And according to the National Coalition on Television Violence, one out of every eight movies these days depicts a rape scene.

Too often, sensational films draw us like the scene of a bad accident. We *have* to look. Very often, artists claim to be pandering to our lowly audience tastes. Is it possible, as audience, that we may be pandering to theirs?

Even in less "serious" entertainments, sex, and sexual objects, tend to get slapped around. We know from Madonna's recent "eat me" tour and the tabloids chronicling her personal exploits that the rock provocateur likes to flirt with violent sex. In *Dick Tracy*, she takes it on the chin, and so do we. Predictably, it will be argued that it's just the bad guys who would do such a thing to a "dame" like Madonna, but this nicety may be lost on the kids in the peanut gallery. After all, Madonna doesn't seem surprised by it, so why should they?

In *Pretty Woman*, Roberts is roughed up by Gere's lawyer and no cops are called. The bully is out of line, not outside the law. (We're light years away from the time when a grapefruit in the face of a female was a criminal's offense.) Many moviegoers, when questioned, do not even remember watching this scene. They display an alarming "desensitization factor," as experts on media violence call it: Did somebody beat her up? Oh, yeah, I guess so. I forgot all about it.

Many moviegoers display an alarming "desensitization factor."

In *Blue Steel*, sex and violence fuse when a psychopath (Ron Silver) witnesses a rookie cop (Jamie Lee Curtis) blow away an armed robber. Dressed to kill, Curtis becomes his favorite erotic fantasy, a woman with a great big gun. This is death as the Big Orgasm instead of orgasm as *le petit mort* (the little death).

In *Sea of Love*, Manhattan singles, even those practicing safe sex, find themselves playing a game of sexual roulette. A serial, sexual killer is on the loose, and loose woman Ellen Barkin plays the part full steam ahead, making a celluloid wet dream into a sanguinary adventure. Al Pacino, lusting after Barkin, lusting after the killer and lusting after death itself, follows his sexual obsession into the realm of the senseless.

As moviegoers, we may wish to support freedom of expression for our film artists, but find ourselves repulsed by the "freedom" expressed.

In the cop movie *Internal Affairs,* sexual addiction drives the entire plot. Richard Gere is a compulsive womanizer and a cool, conscienceless killer. Andy Garcia is a too-much-testosterone Latin with a red-hot wife and a quick backhand.

Gere is the bad guy who seduces his friend's wife, kills his friend, seduces his enemy's wife, sodomizes her, kills her and then kills his enemy as well. As the good guy, Garcia merely roughs up his wife in public and berates her in private. The motivating force for all of this is sexual insatiability in Gere's character and sexual insecurity in Garcia's. In this movie, sex and violence seem to go together like Molotov and cocktail. The unsettling fact is that perhaps they do.

In his death-row confession, Ted Bundy revealed that violent pornography threw a trigger in his mind which made his compulsion to sexually assault and then kill an irreversible urge. The linking of sex and violence has long been a staple in pornography, reaching its nadir in the infamous "snuff" films. Surfacing in the late '70s, said to emanate from South America, these films showcased young women who were sexually used and then murdered—right on film. Decried as a hoax or an aberration by the defenders of pornography, snuff films marked the ultimate in sexual abuse—and the ultimate in eroticism for some pathologically ill sex offenders.

As moviegoers, we may wish to support freedom of expression for our film artists, but find ourselves repulsed by the "freedom" expressed. *Liberty* is, after all, a word with several meanings.

A Society Addicted to Sex

Just what, you may ask, is "sex addiction?" Put simply, it might be described as a life-distorting obsession with sex. Over the years, we have described sexual compulsivity as Don Juanism or womanizing.

Heterosexual multiplicity is only one familiar form that sexual addiction may take. (In *Pretty Woman,* Gere is dumped by his girlfriend and picks up Julia Roberts as a "feel good" much the way he might have taken a stiff drink.) An addiction to pornography, to anonymous sex, to adult bookstores, compulsive masturbating, voyeurism, exhibitionism, use of prostitutes, pederasty or sadomasochistic sexual practices—all are aspects of a compulsive sexual focus.

While the addict may think of his/her sexualizing as "normal"—and indeed may engage in practices that *are* normal when used normally—an outsider may see clearly that sex plays an inordinately large and important role in the addict's life, often at great cost to career, family and health. Consider the celebrities—and the politicians—who have cost themselves credibility by their sexual behavior. Gary Hart and

Ted Kennedy may have cost themselves the White House. Warren Beatty's considerable creative accomplishments have never received the same press as his sexual escapades. (We may joke at his expense, but, in the case of an authentic artist like Beatty, such dimunition of his career constitutes an artistic tragedy.)

Dr. Patrick Carnes, author of *Out of the Shadows: Understanding Sexual Addiction*, considered by many the pioneering work in the field of sexual addiction, describes it as a progressive disorder and divides it into three escalating levels of behavior.

Level-one addiction includes many behaviors often considered normal and used by many members of our society. "Light" pornography and multiple sex partners are examples of level-one behaviors. (*Shampoo, I Love You to Death* and *Mo' Better Blues* are level-one films.)

Level-two behaviors are less "normal" in their rage and often illegal. (*Taxi Driver, Klute, 9½ Weeks* detail level-two behaviors. *Pretty Woman*, despite its seeming innocence, is at least level two.)

Level-three behaviors would strike almost anyone as toxic, clearly abnormal and highly illegal as well. At level three, sex and violence are inextricably intermingled. (*The Cook, the Thief; Wild at Heart* and *Internal Affairs* might be called level-three films.)

While filmmakers have a right to explore whatever artistic territory they choose, it is important to note that what they choose increasingly falls into level-three territory, where sex and violence intersect to potentiate each other and create an inflammatory, volatile and highly addictive mix.

What does all of this have to do with us as moviegoers?

Plenty. With the NEA under fire for the way it disburses funds to artists who quite literally piss people off with their urine-soaked Christs and desecrated flags, where do we draw the line between responsibility and censorship? Between pandering to pornographers and pandering to muckraking moralists?

How patronizing is "protection"? If we are a nation of sexual addicts, conditioned by our media to sexualize our every encounter, should screen sexuality be sanitized? Where do we cross the line between violating First Amendment rights and violating human rights? Perhaps what is called for is not more *control* but more honesty. Let's stop pretending that it is the artistic and not the erotic content that we, as a nation, may be after. Do we go to a Mapplethorpe show to view black-and-white photography or black-and-white physicality? Is it art or is it Tom, Dick and Harry that we're after?

Are we a nation of sexual addicts, conditioned by our media to sexualize every encounter?

In other words, is the sex in the movies really getting any dirtier or is it just our minds?

The answer is, both. ♦

Questions for Discussion

1. Do movies affect sexual behavior?
2. Is mixing movie sex with movie violence more dangerous than treating sex and violence individually?

Hollywood, the Ad

Mark Crispin Miller

Mark Crispin Miller is well known for looking beneath the surface of media phenomena that others take for granted. It is often amazing to see how much he finds there.

In this reading, he looks at the tendency for today's movies to include "product placements"—which means selling advertisers the right to show their products within the movie.

If Miller seems to be inordinately concerned, it is only because he considers film an important cultural form, and he believes this practice weakens the moviegoing experience.

Reading Difficulty Level: 6. A fairly long article, and the connections he makes require some extra thinking time.

The techniques and the cartoon-like moral vision of television advertising are exerting more and more influence over American moviemaking.

"This approach to human beings strikes me as utterly cynical, and directly contrary to the democratic ideal." Such was the sharp response of Dr. Lewis Webster Jones, the head of the National Conference of Christians and Jews. Other clergymen agreed: this new technique could mean the twilight of democracy. It was not only God's ministers who sensed a threat. This technique, Aldous Huxley declared, made "nonsense of the whole democratic procedure, which is based on conscious choice on rational ground." The public protest was immense. The National Association of Radio and Television Broadcasters felt obliged to ban the use of the technique by any of its members, and the three major television networks also publicly rejected it. The New York State Senate unanimously passed a bill outlawing the technique. When KTLA, an independent TV station in Los Angeles, announced that it would soon start using the invention to discourage littering and unsafe driving, the station "received such a torrent of adverse mail," *Life* magazine reported, "that it cancelled the campaign."

Meanwhile, there were some who were not emitting "yelps of alarm," according to *The Wall Street Journal.* Indeed, certain forward-looking managers were rather taken with the idea, despite its dangers, or perhaps because of them. "Chuckles one TV executive with a conscious eye on the future," *Time* magazine reported in its coverage of the controversy, " 'It smacks of brainwashing, but of course it would be tempting.' "

The invention that sparked the national panic, and that was also quietly thrilling certain corporate salesmen, was "subliminal advertising"—a phrase coined by the first of its practitioners, James M. Vicary, "a young motivational researcher and amateur psychologist," as the *Journal* called him. On September 12, 1957, Vicary, the vice-president of the Subliminal Projection Company, held a press conference to tout the results of an experiment that he had just concluded at a neighborhood movie theater in Fort Lee, New Jersey. For six weeks, using special equipment, he had flashed imperceptible allurements onto the screen during the theater's showings of *Picnic,* a Columbia release. Projected every five seconds for one three-thousandth of a second, those unnoticed coaxings, Vicary said, had dramatically boosted concession-stand sales of the items subliminally hyped on the big screen. Vicary had projected two terse bits of copy: "Hungry? Eat popcorn" and "Drink Coca-Cola."

Blatant Impositions

Today what matters most about Vicary's experiment is not his "findings"—which Vicary fabricated. His invention turned out to have had no effect at all on how much Coke or popcorn people swallowed, but was a mere sales gimmick to promote the Subliminal Projection Company itself. Although his "results" were valueless, the outrage stirred by his announcement is important. Back then the rumor that one movie had been temporarily polluted with an advertising pitch— "Drink Coca-Cola"—was enough to elicit a great wave of angry protest. That was in 1957. Let us now look at two clips from movies of the 1980s—movies that nobody protested.

Subliminal advertising had no effect at all on how much Coke or popcorn people swallowed.

In *Murphy's Romance,* released by Columbia in 1985, Sally Field is a youngish divorcée, poor but plucky, who has just moved with her sweet pre-adolescent son to a friendly little Texas town. At the start of the film she wanders into an old-fashioned drugstore, owned, we soon discover, by James Garner, a very benevolent curmudgeon ("Murphy"). On her way in, Field passes, and so we see (she's moving slowly so that we'll see), not one but *three* bright Coca-Cola signs (the merry red, the bold white script)—one on each front window, one on the front door. And then, as Field plunks herself down cutely at the soda counter, and as the seemingly brusque but really very kindly Garner comes to serve her, there is the following exchange:

Field: I'll have a banana split. No, I won't. I'll have a Coke.
Garner: A Coke?
Field: A lemon Coke.

Much is later made of Garner's cherished 1927 Studebaker, which sits out front; Garner refuses to put it elsewhere, despite a daily parking ticket. Although this business does say something obvious about Garner's character ("That Murphy! Stubborn as a mule!"), the car's visual function is to say "Drink Coca-Cola," because it shares the frame with, and is the same deep merry red as, those three prominent Coca-Cola signs. (The movie, incidentally, has a happy ending.)

Coca-Cola bought 49 percent of Columbia Pictures and began at once to plug (its own) products in (its own) movies.

Toward the beginning of *Who's Harry Crumb?*, a 1989 Columbia release, John Candy sits next to Jim Belushi on a bus. A fantastically inept detective, Candy is on his way to meet his employers in a big kidnapping case. Here, in all its comic brilliance, is the entire scene with Belushi:

Candy (eating cherries, offers one): Cherry?
Belushi (reading): No fruit, thank you.

Candy pulls a can of Diet Coke (silvery cylinder, red block letters) out of his bag.

Candy: Coke?
Belushi: No, thank you.
Candy: Mix 'em together, ya got a cherry Coke. Ah ha ha ha ha ha! A cherry Coke, ha ha ha ha!

Later, dining with his wealthy clients, Candy pours a can of Diet Coke into a brandy snifter full of ice cream, holding the (silvery) can up high so that its (red) name is not just legible but unavoidable.

What is the difference between James Vicary's ploy and these later cinematic tricks to make an audience "Drink Coca-Cola"? In 1957 Vicary tried to boost his business by implanting a commercial message in a Columbia release (and then by making false claims for the failed experiment). In 1982 Coca-Cola bought 49 percent of Columbia Pictures and began at once to plug (its own) products in (its own) movies—trying, just like Vicary, to profit by turning movies into advertising. (The company kept it up until it sold Columbia Pictures to Sony, in 1989.) Certainly there is a difference in degree. Whereas Vicary's method was a furtive imposition on the movie, used in only one theater, and only temporarily, the come-ons embedded in Coke's movies are there forever, in whatever prints or tapes you choose to see, because those messages are worked—overtly—right into the movies' scripts and mise-en-scène.

In this overtness, one might argue, these later exhortations to drink Coca-Cola differ crucially from Vicary's gimmick, because his appeal was "subliminal," whereas the later cans and signs beckon us openly, like illuminated billboards. Such a distinction, however, rests on too crude an understanding of subliminal effects—which result not from invisible implants but from words or images that are, in fact, explicitly presented yet at best only half perceived. These latter-day plugs for Coca-Cola, for example, work as subliminal inducements because their context is ostensibly a movie, not an ad, so that each of them comes sidling toward us dressed up as non-advertising, just as other kinds of ads now routinely come at us disguised as "magalogues" and "advertorials"; rock videos; "educational" broadcasts, newsletters, filmstrips, and posters; concerts, art exhibits, sporting events, magazines, newspapers, books, and TV shows; and a good deal of our daily mail—in short, as anything and everything but advertising.

The subliminal impact of the Coke plugs arises not only from their cinematic camouflage but also from the pleasant welter of associations that in each movie efficiently glamorize every Coca-Cola can or logo: Garner's personal warmth and fine old car, John Candy's would-be riotous antics (and, in each case, the very fact of stardom itself), are attractions serving as oblique (that is, subliminal) enhancements to the all-important product. Precisely because of this benefit Coca-Cola has understandably been very careful in its choice of cinematic vehicles—and has also used them to stigmatize the competition.

In *Murphy's Romance*, Field's nice son goes looking for a job; and while "Coca-Cola" sheds its deep red warmth throughout Murphy's homey store, in a big supermarket where the kid is told abruptly that he isn't needed, two (blue) Pepsi signs loom coldly on the wall like a couple of swastikas. In fact, the company used such tactics before it bought Columbia. In Costa-Gavras's *Missing*, a Universal picture made just before the purchase, Jack Lemmon plays a very decent father searching Chile for his son, who has been kidnapped by Pinochet's soldiers. In one scene this haggard, loyal dad, while talking things out, takes rare (and noticeable) solace in a bottle of Coke—whereas inside the nightmare stadium where the army does its torturing and murdering there stands a mammoth Pepsi machine, towering in this underworld like its dark idol.

Subliminal effects result not from invisible implants but from words or images that are explicitly presented yet only half perceived.

Although Pepsico owns no movie studio (yet), its officers began fighting back at once. A special manager tackled the job of keeping Pepsi on the silver screen, and from that moment the spheric Pepsi logo (white/blue/red) became a film presence almost as prevalent as big handguns. In the movies Pepsi is the choice of a new generation—that is, of every generation. The suburban kids are drinking Pepsi in *Ferris Bueller's Day Off*, like the poor kids in *Stand and Deliver* and *Lean on Me*, and like the old folks in *Cocoon: The Return*. Jennifer Beals is drinking Diet Pepsi in *Flashdance*, Kathy Baker

In return for the plug the advertiser will help defray the ever-rising costs of filmmaking by mounting a tie-in promotional campaign.

is buying Pepsi in *Clean and Sober,* in *Always* a brightly lit Pepsi logo lengthily upstages Holly Hunter, and in *Legal Eagles* Debra Winger keeps her Pepsi cold and blatant in a refrigerator otherwise full of blank containers. Pepsi glides through the Texas of the fifties in *Everybody's All-American,* pops into the cute Manhattan of *Crossing Delancey,* and drops in on Norman Bates's milieu in *Psycho II* and *Psycho III.* And Pepsico, too, has tried to move against its major rival, declining to place a Pepsi ad on the cassette of *Dirty Dancing* unless Vestron, the video company, cut every scene that showed a Coca-Cola sign. Vestron passed. (All these movies have happy endings.)

Product Placement

Such subliminal tactics are certainly not peculiar to the mighty cola rivals. They are also used today—aggressively—by every other major advertiser. Indeed, cinematic product placement became so common in the eighties that it now sustains a veritable industry. Formerly plugging was a marginal (if common) practice in the movie industry, the result of direct bartering between studio and advertiser. In the eighties the plugging process became "rationalized," as dozens of companies formed to broker deals between advertisers and film producers. Usually the advertisers—and sometimes the studios themselves—keep the brokers on retainer with an annual fee; the advertisers are then charged extra for specific "placements." In return for the plug the advertiser will help defray the ever-rising costs of filmmaking, not only by providing props or costumes but often—and more important—by mounting a tie-in promotional campaign that will sell the movie in many ads, in thousands of bright aisles, on millions of clean boxes.

Cinematic product placement became so common in the eighties that it now sustains a veritable industry.

The arrangement seems to work wonders for the budgets of all concerned. The advertisers love it: "More and more companies now recognize that movies are an alternative advertising and promotional medium," a plugster exults. And this offer is one that financially pressed filmmakers can't refuse. "Obsessed with the bottom line, studios no longer snub promotion tie-ins—much to the delight of marketers eager to reach the last captive media audience," *Incentive* magazine reports. An executive at Walt Disney Pictures and Television says, "Add the magic of movies to a promotion, and you can rise above the clutter to get people's attention."

Always in search of the perfectly closed-off setting, advertisers have for decades been eyeing cinema, whose viewers can't flip the page or turn their chairs away. It is this interest in a captive audience that has the marketers delighting in the movies—which, now crammed with plugs, offer about as much magic as you would find at K-Mart, or at Lord & Taylor. Watching them, there is no way that you "can rise above the clutter," because they *are* "the clutter."

Consider one of Sylvester Stallone's big hits, *Rocky III*, which showcases in passing Coca-Cola, Sanyo, Nike, Wheaties, TWA, Marantz, and Wurlitzer, and—in actual ads within the film (with Rocky, now a big celebrity, as endorser)—Nikon, Harley-Davidson, Budweiser, Maserati, Gatorade, and American Express. Or consider *Over the Top*, a box-office disaster in which Stallone plays a humble trucker who, estranged from his son, must win the lad back by taking first prize in a major arm-wrestling tournament. Even before the opening credits are over, the movie has highlighted Budweiser, Colgate shaving cream, and Michelin tires; and daubed across the side of Stallone's giant rig is a huge full-color ad for Brut cologne, which shows up grandly in the film's big landscape shots. (Brut and the film's producers had a tie-in deal.) Moreover, each of the many arm wrestlers who roar and shudder at the Big Event bears the imprint of some corporate sponsor, so that the movie displays not only Hilton Hotels, TWA, Alpine car stereos, Leaseway Transportation, Nintendo—and Pepsi—but also Volvo *and* Toyota, Nike *and* Adidas, and Valvoline, Duracell, Soloflex, and Alka-Seltzer. (Both films have happy endings.)

These are two examples of Hollywood's new commercialism at its most grotesque, and there are many others—for example, the latest 007 entry, *License to Kill*, in which James Bond ostentatiously smokes Larks, a plug for which Philip Morris paid $350,000; or *Back to the Future II*, a very loud and manic "romp" that lovingly showcases the futuristic wares of at least a dozen corporate advertisers; or *The Wizard*, a children's movie that is essentially a long commercial for Nintendo; or, in what may be (you never know) the most glaring case of rampant plugging yet, the children's movie *MAC & Me*, a shameless *E.T.* knock-off in which a handicapped child befriends an alien, MAC, who lives on Coca-Cola. (In just over a month this movie grossed $34 million.)

The practice of plugging is just as obvious in movies that do not resemble comic books. Take *Bull Durham*, which begins with the cute rookie pitcher Nuke LaLoosh (Tim Robbins) on the mound, the Pepsi logo plain as day on the outfield wall behind him, its colors reproduced exactly on his uniform. As the film proceeds, it also plugs—repeatedly—Budweiser, Miller, Jim Beam, Oscar Mayer, and a host of Alberto-Culver products. (*Bull Durham* has a happy ending.) Or take *Mr. Mom*, a feeble "issue" comedy about the travails of a green house-husband, which showcases McDonald's, Domino's pizza, Terminix exterminators, Folgers coffee, Lite beer, Jack Daniels, Van Camp's chili, Ban deodorant, Windex, Tide, Spray 'n Wash, Borax, Clorox 2, and Downy fabric softener. (*Mr. Mom* has a happy ending.) Or, finally, take *Murphy's Romance*, which showcases (aside from Coke) Purina, Heinz 57 Steak Sauce, Wesson Oil, Nike,

***Bull Durham** begins with Nuke LaLoosh on the mound, the Pepsi logo plain as day on the outfield wall behind him, its colors reproduced exactly on his uniform.*

In the latest 007 film James Bond smokes Larks, a plug for which Philip Morris paid $350,000.

Producers say product placements give the movie greater reality.

Usually, however, product placement does not seem natural at all but is deliberately* anti-*realistic.

Huggies, Vanish toilet-bowl cleaner, Fuji film, and Miller beer. There are also *two* bottles of Ivory Liquid at Sally Field's kitchen sink, and at one point she asks James Garner, "Could I have two Extra-Strength Tylenol and a glass of water, please?" At another point she shouts enticingly, "Campbell's tomato soup!"

Such bald intrusions into dialogue are no longer rare. Usually the spoken plug comes in the form of a casual request: "Want a Coke?" Eliot asks E.T. "Gimme a Pepsi Free," Michael J. Fox tells the soda jerk in *Back to the Future*—and since they didn't have that choice back in 1955, the jerk's snide retort is really funny. To the advertisers, such a soft gag is ideal, especially if it quotes an established piece of copy. For instance, in *Vice Versa,* one of the late 1980s' several comedies about adults and children swapping bodies, the apparent child, in line at the school cafeteria, betrays his inner maturity in this way: "I don't suppose you have any Grey Poupon?" (All these movies have happy endings.)

TV programs, routinely interrupted by pure ads, need not themselves display the labels quite so often, or so dramatically (although they do display them). American movies nonetheless have a televisual counterpart: Brazilian soap operas, a daily spectacle in which the products play so large a role that some multinationals, among them Coca-Cola, sign annual contracts with Brazil's largest television network, TV Globo, to keep their products constantly written into the shows' ongoing "stories." Down there in Rio the practice, which the Brazilians call by the English word "merchandising," is defended just as Hollywood defends the practice here—by attesting to its powerful naturalism. "Most soap operas are about daily life in which people go shopping and drive cars and drink beer," TV Globo's head of product placement says. "That's why it is so natural." Likewise, a Hollywood plugster argues that since films "are pushing more toward reality," plugging is imperative: "A can that says 'Beer' isn't going to make it anymore."

In a few recent movies—the eerie satire *Heathers,* the exquisite *Drugstore Cowboy*—the subtle use of products does make the fictive milieu more believable than generic items would. Usually, however, product placement does not seem natural at all but is deliberately *anti*-realistic: its sole purpose is to enhance the product by meticulously placing it within the sort of idealized display that occurs nowhere in real life but everywhere in advertising—which is itself just such display. In the world as advertised, the label or logo always shines forth like the full moon, whereas in our world, where "people go shopping and drive cars and drink beer," the crucial symbols reach us (if at all) with none of that sudden startling clarity—for the very ubiquity of advertising has paradoxically also worked to hide it from us. To live the daily life in which people go shopping is to be bombarded into numbness; and it is this stupefaction that movie plugs, like advertising proper, have been devised to penetrate.

As such plugs are anti-realistic, so also are they antinarrative, for the same movie-glow that exalts each product high above the clutter of the everyday also lifts it out of, and thereby makes it work against, the movie's story. Even when half turned toward us, coquettishly, or placed in some marginal position, the crucial can or box or bottle tends (as it were) to make a scene. An expert rhetorical missile in the first place, and with its force enhanced a thousandfold by advertising, the product cannot even sneak by without distracting us at least a little, its vivid, pleasant features calling, "*Hey!* It's *me!*"

And when shoved right into the spotlight, the product doesn't just upstage the actors but actually stops the narrative. In *Uncle Buck,* John Candy appears sitting on a sofa, holding a big box of Kellogg's Frosted Flakes at his side, as prominent and boldly hued as an armorial shield—and on that sight the camera lingers. At such a moment the loud package wipes out its costars and surroundings, becoming the only thing we notice. (*Uncle Buck* has a happy ending.)

The rise of product placement has, however, damaged movie narrative not only through the shattering effect of individual plugs but also—more profoundly—through the partial transfer of creative authority out of the hands of filmmaking professionals and into the purely quantitative universe of the CEOs. All the scenes, shots, and lines mentioned above represent the usurpation by advertising of those authorial prerogatives once held by directors and screenwriters, art directors and set designers—and by studio heads, who generally cared about how their films were made, whereas the managers now in charge are thinking only of their annual reports. "Hollywood has changed," says Ed Meyer, of the ad agency Saatchi & Saatchi DFS Compton. "Unlike the old days, the bankers and M.B.A.s are calling the shots."

Thus the basic decisions of filmmaking are now often made, indirectly, by the advertisers, who are focused only on a movie's usefulness for pushing products. Take the case of costume designers, who have often in the eighties been displaced by "promo-costuming"—an arrangement that, according to *Premiere* magazine, either showcases the wares of name designers (Oscar de la Renta did *Bright Lights, Big City,* Giorgio Armani did *The Untouchables*) or, more frequently, "involves manufacturers of such branded staples as jeans and sneakers, which have visible logos that make them much easier to promote." In 1987, for example, Adidas shod and clad many of the characters in some sixty movies.

The basic decisions of filmmaking are now often made, indirectly, by the advertisers, who are focused only on a movie's usefulness for pushing products.

The plugging process is as thorough and exacting as the work of those professionals whose skill it has long since superseded.

The plugging process is as thorough and exacting as the work of those professionals whose skill it has long since superseded. The pre-production effort is exhaustive: "Friendly producers," *The Wall Street Journal* reports, "send scripts to [Associated Film Promotions] weeks and even months before filming starts, and the company analyzes them scene by scene to see if it can place a product—or advertising material, a billboard perhaps—on, under or behind the stars." While the advertisers may not be as idealistic above movies as, say, David O. Selznick, they are just as dictatorial: "We choose projects where we have maximum control," says one plugster. "We break a film down and tell the producers exactly where we want to see our clients' brands."

Such subordination of the movie is essential to plugging, which is based on the assumption that the movie will in no way contradict—will, indeed, do nothing but enhance—the product's costly, all-important aura. The plug, in other words, must not just "foreground" the crucial name or image but also flatter it—that is, brightly reaffirm the product's advertising. When its brokers argue that plugging enhances realism, they are implying that reality is only where the products mean just what their advertising says they mean: "power" or "safety" or "old-fashioned goodness."

Advertisers seek to give movies the same tranquilizing atmosphere as TV, theme parks and shopping malls.

Now and then in the eighties an American movie has invoked products critically, or at least in a way that is poetically telling and not just promotional. In Garry Marshall's *Nothing in Common*, a surprisingly grim and moving (if uneven) comedy about a successful young adman (Tom Hanks) and his dying scoundrel of a father (Jackie Gleason), the same product appears in two shots—not to sell it but as a chilling metaphysical implication and a visual hint that father and son, despite their mutual loathing and antithetical life-styles, are fundamentally alike. Placed casually in each man's kitchen—the one tidy and state-of-the-art, the other bare and slovenly—is a box of the same cereal: Life. (*Nothing in Common* does not have a happy ending.)

Such dark suggestiveness is precisely what advertisers do not want, and so they, or their brokers, will back away from any movie that might somehow cast a shadow on their advertising. For advertisers are obsessed not just with selling their own specific images but also with universalizing the whole hermetic ambience for selling itself—the pseudo-festive, mildly jolting, ultimately tranquilizing atmosphere of TV and its bright epiphenomena, the theme park and the shopping mall.

Crossovers

Even if, armed with some marvelous zapping gizmo, you could sit and blast away every obvious product as it passed through the frame or glowed in close-up, today's

Hollywood movie would still seem like an ad. This is in part because movies now tend to look and sound a lot like TV commercials, as if the major film schools were teaching not, say, the best movies out of Warner Brothers but the latest campaign by the Saatchi brothers. Like ads, movies now tend to have a perfectly coordinated total look, as if they'd been designed rather than directed—a tendency so marked, in some cases, that the movie and some well-known ad can hardly be distinguished. Thus *The Color Purple,* with its lush score, hazy golden images, and long climactic round of teary hugs, leaves you thinking not that you should read the novel but that you really ought to call your mother ("Reach out—"), while the parodic *Raising Arizona* uses precisely the same wide-angle distortion and hyped-up, deadpan acting that Joe Sedelmaier used in his famous ads for Federal Express ("When it abso*lute*ly, posi*tive*ly—"), while *Top Gun,* the blockbuster salute to navy fliers, is in its action sequences identical to those spectacular commercials that allured the young with "It's Not Just a Job: It's an Adventure!" or (yes!) "Be All You Can Be!"—expert recruitment propaganda that was probably well known to the firm's director, Tony Scott, who came to the movie business as a famed director of TV ads, most notably for Diet Pepsi. (These three movies leave you feeling good.)

Such crossovers are the usual thing in today's media industry, many of whose filmmakers learned their craft (and continue to work) in TV advertising. Ten years ago a stellar group of such professionals migrated from the ad shops of London to the studios of Hollywood, where they helped to alter modern cinema. Like his brother Tony (who, the year after *Top Gun,* directed the repetitious *Beverly Hills Cop 2*), Ridley Scott is a prolific admaker, most notably for Chanel, W. R. Grace, and Apple Computer. He is also the auteur of the inspired and nauseating *Alien;* the brilliant *Blade Runner;* a thriller designed, as if by computer, to stroke lonely women, *Someone to Watch Over Me;* and finally the unforgivable *Black Rain.* The ad-maker Hugh Hudson has turned out such gorgeous, empty films as *Chariots of Fire* and *Greystoke: The Legend of Tarzan, Lord of the Apes.* Having made hundreds of short ads, Adrian Lyne came to Hollywood and made such ad-like films as *Flashdance, 9 1/2 Weeks,* and also the gynophobic crowd-pleaser *Fatal Attraction.* Alan Parker, whose films include *Midnight Express, Fame,* and *Mississippi Burning,* is easily the most successful of the British émigrés, because the most adept at stirring out worst impulses. Many American ad-makers have also become filmmakers, including Stan Dragoti, the director of the "I Love New York" ads and the plug-ridden *Mr. Mom;*

Movies now tend to look and sound a lot like TV commercials.

Many American ad-makers have become filmmakers.

Howard Zieff, the director of Alka-Seltzer's "Spicy Meatball" ad and the incoherent *Private Benjamin;* and Joe Pytka, the director of numerous Pepsi ads and the deadly racetrack comedy *Let It Ride.*

As more and more admen direct films, more and more filmmakers are directing television ads.

Meanwhile, as more and more admen direct films, more and more filmmakers are directing television ads—simply in order to keep working, now that the huge costs of moviemaking have made it nearly impossible to get a project going. Directors can no longer afford to scorn the sixty-second pitch: "There *was* a stigma in the past," Jerry Bernstein, the head of the Association of Independent Commercial Producers, observed in 1988. "The feeling was [that the ad] was not a great art form." That feeling is passé, if not extinct, now that Robert Altman, Martin Scorsese (Armani), Federico Fellini, Jean-Luc Godard, Francis Ford Coppola (Fuji), John Frankenheimer, John Badham, Tony Bill (Bud Light), John Schlesinger, David Lynch, Penny Marshall (Revlon), David Steinberg, Stephen Frears, and Errol Morris (7-Eleven), among others, are making ads. Cinematographers, too, have turned to advertising: Sven Nykvist, Nestor Almendros, Gordon Willis, Eric Saarinen, and Vilmos Zsigmond, among others. And filmmakers have even been doing celebrity turns in ads: Richard Donner for Amaretto di Saronno, George Lucas for Panasonic (in Japan), Bernardo Bertolucci for Pioneer, Spike Lee for the Gap, and for Nike (which he plugs throughout his movies) in a commercial that he also directed.

Now that TV has induced a universal taste for TV's pace and tone, the new "filmmaking" takes its lead primarily from those who create the small screen's most hypnotic images.

If movies look like ads, then, the transformation may owe something to this exchange of personnel—which delights the powers of advertising, who want their ads to look like movies (so that the restless TV viewer won't zap them). "Advertisers and agencies want their commercials designed with the look of the hottest features," one ad producer says. Crossovers have helped erase the old distinctions between movies and commercials: "The two disciplines—feature films and commercial films—have blended together to the point now where it's just filmmaking," says a senior vice-president at the ad agency DDB Needham, in Chicago. It might seem that through this convergence each "discipline" would somehow benefit the other—but in the era of the VCR it is advertising that has affected cinema, and not the other way around. Now that most movies are produced with an eye toward their eventual re-release on videocassette for the home audience, and now that TV, moreover, has induced a universal taste for TV's pace and tone, the new "filmmaking" takes its lead primarily from those who create the small screen's most hypnotic images. "There's not a good filmmaker alive who doesn't look to us for inspiration," Bob Giraldi, the director of ad spots for GE, Sperry Rand, McDonald's, Miller Lite, and many other corporations, claimed in 1984.

Grabbers

Just as the product plug halts or weakens the movie narrative, so has this general drift toward ad technique drastically reduced the movies' narrative potential, for cinematic narrative works through a range of visual conventions or devices, and the recent rise of ad technique has all but wiped out that earlier diversity, coarsening a various and nuanced form into a poundingly hypnotic instrument—a mere *stimulus,* and an ugly one at that.

There is, first, the all-important difference in scale. "This is just like doing a small feature," Ridley Scott assured his crew on the set of a Pepsi ad in 1984. "I see commercials as short films," Adrian Lyne told *Advertising Age* in 1985. But to suggest that commercials are just like movies, only smaller (in both space and time), is to negate the crucial ground of cinematic art: an expansive visual field, broad enough to imply a world beyond, behind, more varied than, the glamorous item in midframe. TV is, to say the least, different. Watching *The Last Emperor* on your set is like trying to survey the Sistine Chapel ceiling by peeping at it through a toilet-paper roll. TV, however, has reduced the movies not just by putting blinders on the viewers of wide-screen epics but also by establishing a compositional norm of close-ups, two-shots, and other setups whereby the action is (just as in advertising) repetitiously *foregrounded.*

Such is now the norm of cinema. Today there are few scenes shot in deep focus (as in Renoir and Welles, *Vertigo* and *The Godfather Part II,* or, for that matter, *The Night of the Living Dead*). Likewise, we rarely see the kind of panoramic composition that once allowed a generous impression of quasi-global simultaneity, as (most elaborately) in the movies of Robert Altman and Jacques Tati, and that also, more subtly, enriches the frame in most great movies, whose makers have offered *pictures,* composed of pleasurable "touches" and legible detail. These moving tableaux often, as André Bazin argued, gave their viewers some choice, and required some (often minimal) interpretive attention. Only now and then, and in films that don't come out of Hollywood—Terry Gilliam's *Brazil,* Stanley Kubrick's *Full Metal Jacket*—do we perceive such exhilarating fullness. In contrast, today's American movies work without, or against, the potential depth and latitude of cinema, in favor of that systematic overemphasis deployed in advertising and all other propaganda. Each shot presents a content closed and unified, like a fist, and makes the point right in your face: big gun, big car, nice ass, full moon, a chase (great shoes!), big crash (blood, glass), a lobby (doorman), sarcasm, drinks, a tonguey, pugilistic kiss (nice sheets!), and so on.

Today's American movies work without, or against, the potential depth and latitude of cinema, in favor of that systematic overemphasis deployed in advertising.

Thus today's movie not only foregrounds but also serializes, for just as TV's narrowness has super-

Marketing and advertising always aim directly at the lowest levels of the mass (that is, your) brain, seeking a reaction that is not just "positive" but unconscious and immediate.

Ad techniques encourage cutting and discourage dissolves and fades to black.

annuated deep focus and the movies' (sometime) lateral complexity, so has the speedy pace of TV's ads superannuated most of cinema's earlier transitional devices. As John Frankenheimer (*The Manchurian Candidate*, Fiat, AT&T) told *Advertising Age* in 1988, "No longer do films use the fade to black and the slow dissolve the way they used to." This laconic, and correct, observation hints at a grievous cinematic loss, because the fade and the dissolve are no quaint old movie mannerisms. Rather, the dissolve is a succinct and often beautiful means of conveying the passage of time or the onset of a memory; although it has no exact linguistic counterpart, to drop it from the movies would be somewhat like dropping the past tense from verbal language. The fade to black works like a curtain to cover some event too painful or intimate for exhibition, or as a means of conveying loss of consciousness, or as a somber sort of visual cadence, a way of saying, "It's over: now consider what you've seen." In today's ad-saturated "filmmaking" these devices not only seem too slow but are, in different ways, too suggestive of mortality for the movies' bright mall atmosphere, and so they have been dumped in favor of that most basic of connectives, the simple cut, the overuse of which has helped transform the movies into ad-like serial displays.

Such displays show us nothing—not only because each image in the series is as unambiguous as a brand-new belt but also because the serial rush itself is mesmerizing, and so it blinds us to the flashing items that compose it. Large, stark, and fast, the mere contrast stuns us pleasantly—a response that is, as it were, subvisual, as the ad-makers know very well. Thus both marketing and advertising always aim directly at the lowest levels of the mass (that is, your) brain, seeking a reaction that is not just "positive" but unconscious and immediate. Although the pillars of the ad world still use the word "persuasion" to (mis)represent their business, the whole selling project now depends on moves that are less rhetorical than neurological: "Color goes immediately to the psyche and can be a direct sales stimulus," one typical package designer says. Such blithe and simplistic Pavlovianism is wholly characteristic of the ad-makers and marketers, who like it when we respond without even knowing it, much less knowing why. Thus Philip Dusenberry, of the ad agency BBDO, in New York, claims to have learned (from making Pepsi ads) "that it wasn't important that the viewer read every scene—just that they get the impact of the message."

That last remark could as easily apply to the movies, which now, like advertising, rely heavily if not exclusively on techniques that work directly on the nervous system. Of course, the movies have always used gratuitous tricks to keep viewers riveted: pointless close-ups of a baby's smile to get the women cooing, martial music to tense up the men, sad violins to get the whole house sniffling. Indeed, some of cinema's basic rhetorical devices, it could be argued, are inherently nonnarrative, subvisual: cross-cutting for suspense, say, or the weepy reaction shot (which moves the viewers to weep). The point, however, is not that such tricks are new but that they are now all-important—for their power has been fantastically augmented by computer science, Dolby sound, great strides forward in the art of mock mayhem, and other technological advances.

Music, for example, has long been overused by Hollywood, as James Agee noted in 1945. Watching John Huston's war documentary *San Pietro,* which he admired immensely, Agee found it "as infuriating to have to fight off the emotional sales pressure of the Mormon Choir as it would be if all the honored watches and nasal aphrodisiacs insisted on marketing themselves against a Toscanini broadcast." At its pushiest, movie music "weakens the emotional imagination both of maker and onlooker, and makes it virtually impossible to communicate or receive ideas. It sells too cheaply and far too sensually all the things it is the business of the screen itself to present."

Watching the movies that Agee found overscored, most people now would probably agree with him, since the aesthetic errors of the past are easy to laugh at decades later. What may be less obvious today is the persistent relevance of Agee's argument, for the movies have, as visual events, been largely devastated by their "music"—a vast and irresistible barrage of synthesized sound, a hyper-rhythmic full-body stimulus far more effective, and a whole lot louder, than the old choral yawpings or symphonic sweeps that now seem so corny. Starting somewhere out there and back to the left, the "music" thrums and zooms and jumps and jangles right on through you, clearing out your head with such efficiency that not only is it impossible to receive ideas but the whole movie, once over, seems to have gone in one ear and out the other—except that it's not just your head that has functioned as a throughway but every vital organ.

Movies, like ads, now rely too heavily on music and special effects.

It is the Dolby system, sometimes enhanced by George Lucas's more recent THX Sound System, that gives the music such prostrating force. Even on cassette, however, the music works an antivisual effect (just as it does throughout TV's shows and ads), imposing an upbeat mood on images that are, per se, so mundane that they would bore or even depress you if the music weren't there telling you to dance. In *St. Elmo's Fire,* Emilio Estevez drives off in a car, and the music makes it sound as if he's just won gold at the Olympics. At the end of *Private Benjamin,* Goldie Hawn walks down a lonely road, and the score exults as if she were attending her own coronation. (Both those movies have happy endings.)

More and more, the movies' very images are also—paradoxically—nonvisual, because, like the music, they try to force our interest or reaction through a visceral jolt that stuns the mind and shuts the eyes. Some of the movies' latest grabbers are very old, like the gooey close-up of some wondering baby ("Awwww!"), a device no less sickening in *Ghostbusters II* (1989) than it was in *Bachelor Daddy* (1941). Generally, however, the latest grabbers are more technologically sophisticated and (a lot) more violent than those sentimental moments—and far more commonplace, now that movie narrative has been supplanted by such blinding jabs.

As special effects have since *Star Wars* become more mind-blowing and yet more believable, they have also grown more important to the spectacle—and have changed in tone. In many instances the effects now *are* the movie, whether it's *Indiana Jones and the Last Crusade* or *A Nightmare on Elm Street 3,* films you can sleep through for twenty minutes without then having to ask, "What did I miss?" And as the effects have become the whole show, they have ceased to represent some ambiguous looming force, uncanny or apocalyptic—as they did in the first *King Kong, The Day the Earth Stood Still,* and *2001: A Space Odyssey*—and have instead become the tools for a light show that both stimulates and reassures, like fireworks on the Fourth.

Movies are becoming antivisual and non-narrative.

In other words, whereas the effects were once used by and large to fake some scary threat to all humanity, they now routinely fake, in one way or another, someone's annihilation—and it is *good.* The wipeout might be violent, as at the end of *Raiders of the Lost Ark,* when the Nazis are melted down or shriveled up by the wrathful ark light, or as in the horror movies, where, say, Jason burns, zaps, and mangles several teens, until some teen burns or zaps or mangles Jason. Whether the killing force is righteous or demonic, the spectacle of its, his, or her destructiveness or destruction invites your rapt gaze of wondering assent, just like those movies that present the wipeout as a sweet translation into outer space (that is, heaven): *E.T., Close Encounters of the Third Kind, Cocoon, Cocoon: The Return*—films whose (grateful) characters finally disappear into the all-important light show, just like the films themselves.

For all their visual sophistication, these effects are meant to move us beyond, or back from, visual experience, by either having us nearly *feel* those razors rake that throat or having us *feel* as if we, too, were dissolving in a celestial bath of light. The same kind of experience—antivisual, non-narrative—is commonplace even in films that have no supernatural or "alien" component. In the eighties the car chase, for instance, became the movies' main story substitute, offering the illusion of dreamlike forward speed and the gratifying sight, sound, and feeling of machinery bucking, squealing, blowing up—elements that have become so frequent that to catalogue them here would fill a page, since they compose whole sections not only of the cop films (*The Presidio, Cobra,* the two *Lethal Weapons,* the two *Beverly Hills Cops, Red Heat*) but also of many comedies, even ones that didn't need such filler (*Midnight Run, The Blues Brothers, Throw Momma From the Train*). The pleasure here is not visual but physically empathic—the centrifugal tug, that pleasing *crash!*: mock thrills that have only gotten punchier and more elaborate as the car stuff has become routine. Likewise, screen violence in general, a relentless story substitute, has become both commonplace and often horribly sadistic. (The movies named in the above two paragraphs all have happy endings.)

The Imperative of Violence

The empathic function of today's screen violence has changed the character of movie heroics. In *Bullitt* (1968) and *The French Connection* (1971), in *The Searchers* (1956), and in the movies of Sam Peckinpah, the violence, however graphic, was muted by a deep ambivalence that shadowed even the most righteous-seeming acts of vengeance, and that therefore suppressed the viewer's urge to join in kicking. In contrast, screen violence now is used primarily to invite the viewer to enjoy the *feel* of killing, beating, mutilating. This is most obvious in the slasher films, in which the camera takes the stalking murderer's point of view, but the same empathic project goes on throughout the genres. There is no point to Rambo's long climactic rage, or Cobra's, or Chuck Norris's, other than its open invitation to *become him* at that moment—to ape that sneer of hate, to feel the way it feels to stand there tensed up with the Uzi. The hero's inner kinship with the villain used to seem uncanny, as in Hitchcock's and Fritz Lang's movies, and in Clint Eastwood's excellent *Tightrope*—whereas Stallone's Cobra gets a charge out of being *exactly* like the psychopaths he chases, just as we are meant to feel *exactly* like him.

Screen violence now is used primarily to invite the viewer to enjoy the feel *of killing, beating, mutilating.*

Screen violence, a relentless story substitute, has become both commonplace and often horribly sadistic.

Moreover, it is not just the overt paeans to machismo that thus incite us but also films that seem politically unlike, say, *Rambo III*—and like *Mississippi Burning.* Hailed for having a plot based on a key event in the history of the civil-rights movement, it actually has no plot, nor is it even slightly faithful to that history. The movie is, in fact, nothing more than one long grabber. After an hour of watching white trash inflict atrocities on helpless blacks (and a nice white woman), we watch the kick-ass Gene Hackman argue hotly with his FBI superior, the tight-assed Willem Dafoe, who has from the outset rebutted Hackman's vigilantist urgings with the boring creed of rules and regulations. They fight at length (shouts, punches; a

The primacy of stimulation has made the movies increasingly cartoonlike.

gun is even pulled)—and then, suddenly, Dafoe just up and *changes:* "New rules. We nail 'em any way we can. Even your way." This absolute reversal, although absurd in terms of character, makes sense rhetorically, since it's now time to have the three of us (audience, Dafoe, Hackman) all fold into Hackman, who is thereby freed to punish all those ugly rednecks in the ugliest of ways—crushing their testicles, threatening them with castration, maiming them with straight razors, and otherwise permitting "us" to act, through him, just like the Klansmen we presumably detest, while the blacks remain helpless throughout. (*Mississippi Burning* has a happy ending.)

Over and over, conventional narrative requirements are broken down by the imperative of violence—which need not be inflicted by "us," through the movie's hero, but is just as often used *against* us, by the movie's anti-hero, for what matters above all, it seems, is that we feel the stimulus. Thus we are victimized by the "sight" of the vampires in *The Los Boys* biting off bright red gobbets of their victims' heads ("Ow!"), and by the sight and sound of the good guy having his fingers broken (*Blade Runner, Blue Thunder*) or receiving a ballistic kick between the legs (*Shoot the Moon, Black Moon Rising*). Likewise, the movies now more than ever shock us with the old nonvisual trick of going "Boo!"—a crude startler once used mainly in horror films but now recurring in thriller after thriller (and often heightened by the deep "*lub*-dub-*lub*-dub" that simulates your fearful heartbeat).

The primacy of stimulation has, in short, made the movies increasingly cartoonlike. In the cartoon world nothing stands between the wish to look at violence and the enactment of that violence: no demands of plot or character, no physical limitations (space, gravity), no mortality. Ingeniously, and with cruel wit, the cartoon presents a universe wherein the predatory are punished again and again for their appetite by the very hills and trees, the doors and crockery. Full of rage and purpose, those victim-predators get nowhere, and yet never die, pushing on forever, despite the anvils falling on their heads, the steamrollers flattening their bodies out like giant pancakes, the cannonballs caroming down their throats—torments at once severe and harmless, and which occur exclusively because we want to see them happen.

In cartoonlike movies the human characters appear just as indestructible as Wile E. Coyote or Yosemite Sam.

It is not just *Batman* and *Who Framed Roger Rabbit* that invoke the cartoon but all those movies that present a universe wherein the stimulus is gross, never-ending, and immediate, the human "characters" appearing just as easily tormentable, and yet (usually) as indestructible, as Wile E. Coyote or Yosemite Sam. Thus *Lethal Weapon II,* which begins with the old Looney Tunes theme playing over the familiar Warner Brothers logo, includes several scenes in which Mel Gibson casually brutalizes Joe Pesci—squeezing his badly injured nose, for instance. And thus in *Dragnet*, as a car runs over Dan Ackroyd's feet there is a sound as of the crushing of a bag of walnuts, and Ackroyd pales and winces. And thus Jason, although dead, keeps coming back to life, like Freddy Kreuger, like Michael Myers, and, for that matter, like the dead ballplayers in *Field of Dreams*, like the vanished old folks in *Cocoon: The Return*, like the dead E.T.—all of them coming back forever and ever, because the cartoon always has a happy ending.

Surplus Wish Fulfillment

The convergence of the movies with both ads and cartoons makes sense, because the ad and the cartoon each present a fantasy of perfect wish fulfillment: that is, wish fulfillment that seems both immediate and absolute, arising, on the one hand, from a purchase (which will make life perfect *now*) or, on the other hand, from the animated spectacle itself (in which the universe appears responsive to one's wishes). This effect has been compounded in the movies, which now purvey a wish-fulfillment fantasy as extreme as, and far more compelling than, any Coke spot or Tom and Jerry free-for-all. ♦

The convergence of the movies with both ads and cartoons makes sense, because the ad and the cartoon each present a fantasy of perfect wish fulfillment.

Questions for Discussion

1. Why does Miller make a point of stating that many of the movies he uses as examples have happy endings?
2. Do you believe that product placements hurt the narrative flow of movies?
3. Using the most recent movies you have seen as examples, attack or defend Miller's thesis that movie commercialism has made movies cartoon-like.

Suggested Readings

More On the Changing Moral Universe of the Movies

Almendros, Nestor, "Spots of Art: How Commercials Are Changing the Movies," *The New Republic* Vol. 198, May 23, 1988, p. 27 (4).

Chunovic, Louis, "Looking for Trouble," *American Film*, February 1991, p. 30 (4). How Hollywood searches for real-life tragedies to sensationalize.

Lejeune, Anthony, "The Way We Were," *National Review*, April 15, 1991, p. 43 (3). Asks why Hollywood stopped showing the best of America and started imagining the worst.

On the Psychological Functions that Movies Perform for People

"Beyond Dreams: The Mysterious Power of the Movies," *Life* Vol. 10, April, 1987, p. 22 (1). Column; special issue, The Movies.

Rooney, Mickey, "The Value of Villains," *Newsweek* Vol. 114, November 27, 1989, p. 12 (1).

Rosenbaum, Jonathan, "Are You Having Fun?", *Sight and Sound* Vol. 59, Spring, 1990, p. 96 (5). Commentary on recent trend in motion pictures.

Tesser, Abraham, Karen Millar and Cheng-Huan Wu, "On the Perceived Functions of Movies, *The Journal of Psychology* Vol. 122, September, 1988, p. 441 (9).

Global Domination of American Movies

Denby, David, "As the World Turns," *New York* Vol. 22, December 11, 1989, p. 116 (2).

Edwards, Henry and Peter Rainer, "Sex-Rated," *Vogue* Vol. 179, April, 1989, p. 236 (4). Love scenes in movies are a measure of national style and taste.

Magiera, Marcy and David Kilburn, "Hollywood Gets World View," *Advertising Age* Vol. 60, October 2, 1989, p. 2 (2). Foreign ownership of movie studios may change film marketing rules.

Movie Ratings and the Production Code that Preceded Them

Corliss, Richard, "Berating Ratings," *Film Comment* Vol. 26, September–October 1990, p. 3 (11).

Leff, Leonard J., Jerold L. and Simmons, *The Dame in the Kimono: Hollywood, Censorship, and the Production Code From the 1920s to the 1960s* (Grove Weidenfeld, 1990). A readable history of movie censorship.

Leff, Leonard J., and Jerold L. Simmons, "No Trollops, No Tomcats," *American Film* Vol. 15, December 1989, p. 40 (7). Film censorship in the 30s and 40s. Based on their book.

"NC-17," *Editorials on File*, September 16–30, p. 1126. A sampling of editorial opinion on the new rating category that replaced "x" for nonpornographic films.

Sheinfeld, Lois P., "Ratings: The Big Chill," *Film Comment*, June, 1986. This reading can also be found in the third edition of *Mass Media Issues*, p. 64.

Vaughn, Stephen, "Morality and Entertainment: The Origins of the Motion Picture Production Code," *Journal of American History* Vol. 77, June, 1990, p. 39 (27).

Yang, Ni and Daniel Linz, "Movie Ratings and the Content of Adult Videos: The Sex-Violence Ratio," *Journal of Communication* Vol. 40, Spring, 1990, p. 28 (15).

More On Creative "Placements"

Marin, Richard, "Products Stare Camera in the Eye," *Insight* Vol. 5, January 9, 1989, p. 60 (2). Displaying product brand names on television programs.

"Talk About Placements . . . ," *Newsweek* Vol. 114, July 31, 1989, p. 50 (1). Just an "item" about product tie-in between Lethal Weapon 2 and Ramses condoms.

Radio and Recorded Music

9

We listen to radio more than ever these days. We wake up to clock radios, catch up on the news while we make breakfast, travel to work in earphones and often stayed plugged in all day.

The average American listens to radio about 25 hours a week. The average household has five radios. In fact, Americans own more than half the radio receivers in the world, and we have about 11,000 stations to listen to.

Radio has a larger audience than television for eight hours a day (that is, during "drive times," 6 to 10 A.M., 3 to 7 P.M.), and at least one segment of the audience, high school and college students, spend more time listening to it than watching television. In fact, for that segment of the population, radio and rock music might be their most important medium.

As a society, we use radio mostly to listen to music. Most of that is rock music, which is divided into formats such as Adult Contemporary, Top 40, Classic Rock, Soft Rock, and Club Music. Other formats include Easy Listening, Country, Classical and Jazz. Radio also tends to be our first source of news in an emergency and all-news and all-talk formats have met with considerable success. And, of course, radio call-in shows are a social phenomenon of their own (where do those people come from?).

Radio is a local medium, and gets most of its revenue (around 80%) from local ads (the rest comes from national spot advertising). The radio industry makes around $8 billion a year.

Radio fuels the recorded music industry, which pulls down a healthy $9 billion a year. As we go to press in 1992, sales of each recorded music format break down approximately like this:

Cassettes:	55%
Compact Discs	40%
LP's & Singles	5%

CDs, of course, are on the rise, while LP's sell less every year, and singles are pretty much a thing of the past.

There are a number of problems that beset the record industry. The Justice Department is concerned about reports of payola—record promoters supplying money, sex and drugs to music directors for adding the promoters' products to their playlists. Piracy is a problem, too, as revenues are lost to illegal copying. And the problem of lyrics that are accused of being obscene and/or subliminally dangerous keeps popping up.

Radio and recorded music are important social phenomena. The readings in this chapter examine the effects of those phenomena. In the first reading, Allan Bloom, a cultural conservative, and Frank Zappa, one of the free spirits of the rock world, compare their ideas about the social significance of rock music. In the second reading, the commentator George Will offers his thoughts on what rap lyrics tell us about society. The third reading is an extensive analysis of the Judas Priest "Teen Suicide" case.

On Junk Food for the Soul

Allan Bloom and Frank Zappa

In spite of the coauthorship of this reading, Allan Bloom and Frank Zappa are not a writing team. Allan Bloom is one of the leaders of the conservative cultural movement. His book, The Closing of the American Mind, *was a condemnation of American education and many facets of popular culture, including rock music. It was Bloom who labeled rock music "junk food for the soul." The editors of* New Perspectives Quarterly, *subscribing to the "let's you and him fight" school of scholarship, asked Frank Zappa to respond to some of the passages of Bloom's book.*

The editors knew that Zappa would give a spirited response. Zappa and his group, the Mothers of Invention, were a major influence on rock music during its formative years in the 1960s. More recently, Zappa has been busy defending rock against the onslaught of would-be censors, such as the Parent's Music Resource Group, a group of congressional wives fighting for more parental control over rock.

Reading Difficulty Level: 3. A short bit of give-and-take that goes down easily.

The Nature of Music

Music is the soul's primitive and primary speech . . . without articulate speech or reason. It is not only not reasonable, it is hostile to reason. . . . Civilization . . . is the taming or domestication of the soul's raw passions. . . . Rock music has one appeal only, a barbaric appeal, to sexual desire—not love, not eros, but sexual desire undeveloped and untutored.—A. Bloom

This is a puff pastry version of the belief that music is the work of the Devil: that the nasty ol' Devil plays his fiddle and people dance around and we don't want to see them twitching like that. In fact, if one wants to be a real artist in the United States today and comment on our culture, one would be very far off the track if one did something delicate or sublime. This is not a noble, delicate, sublime country. This is a mess run by criminals. Performers who are doing the crude, vulgar, repulsive things Bloom doesn't enjoy are only commenting on that fact.

In general, anti-rock propositions began when rock n' roll began, and most of these were racially motivated. In the 50s, petitions were circulated which said, "Don't allow your children to buy Negro records." The petitions referred to the "raw unbridled passion" of screaming people with dark skin who were going to drive our children wild. Some things never go out of fashion in certain ideological camps. They are like tenets of the faith.

Music's real effect on people is a new field of science called psychoacoustics—the way an organism deals with wiggling air molecules. Our ears decode the wiggling air molecules, and that gives us the information of a particular musical sound. Our brain says, "This is music, this is a structure," and we deal with it based on certain tools we have acquired.

Rock music has one appeal only, a barbaric appeal, to sexual desire. —Allan Bloom

I personally make music because I want to ask a question, and I want to get an answer. If that question and answer amuse me, then statistically, there are a certain number of other people out there who have the same amusement factor. If I present my work to them, they will be amused by it, and we will all have a good time.

I need to be amused because I get bored easily and being amused entertains me. If I could be easily amused, like many people who like beer and football, I would never do anything because everything that would be beautiful for my life would already be provided by American television.

Performers who are doing the crude, vulgar, repulsive things Bloom doesn't enjoy are only commenting on the fact that this is not a noble, delicate, sublime country. —Frank Zappa

But beer and television bore me, so what am I going to do? I am going to be alive for X number of years. I have to do something with my time besides sleep and eat. So, I devise little things to amuse myself. If I can amuse somebody else, great. And if I can amuse somebody else and earn a living while doing it, that is a true miracle in the 20th Century!

From *New Perspectives Quarterly*, Winter, 1988, pp. 26–29.

Rock music has risen to its current heights on the ashes of classical music.
—Allan Bloom

Music and the Dark Forces of the Soul

To Plato and Nietzsche, the history of music is a series of attempts to give form and beauty to the dark, chaotic, premonitory forces in the soul—to make them serve a higher purpose, an ideal, to give man's duties a fullness.—A. Bloom

This is a man who has fallen for rock's fabricated image of itself. This is the worst kind of ivory tower intellectualism. Anybody who talks about dark forces is right on the fringe of mumbo jumbo. Dark forces? What is this, another product from Lucasfilm? The passions! When was the last time you saw an American exhibit any form of passion other than the desire to shoot a guy on the freeway? Those are the forces of evil as far as I am concerned.

If there are dark forces hovering in the vicinity of the music business, they are mercantile forces. We meet the darkness when we meet the orchestra committees, when we get in touch with funding organizations, when we deal with people who give grants and when we get into the world of commerce that greets us when we arrive with our piece of art. Whether it's a rock n' roll record or a symphony, it's the same machinery lurking out there.

Whether it's a rock n' roll record or a symphony, it's the same machinery lurking out there.
—Frank Zappa

The reason a person writes a piece of music has got nothing to do with dark forces. I certainly don't have dark forces lurking around me when I'm writing. If someone is going to write a piece of music, in fact they are preoccupied with the boring labor and very hard work involved. That's what's really going on.

What Makes Music Classical

Rock music . . . has risen to its current heights in the education of the young on the ashes of classical music, and in an atmosphere in which there is no intellectual resistance to attempts to tap the rawest passions. . . . Cultivation of the soul uses the passions and satisfies them while sublimating them and giving them an artistic unity. . . . Bach's religious intentions and Beethoven's revolutionary and humane ones are clear enough examples.—A. Bloom

This is such nonsense. All the people recognized as great classical composers are recognized at this point for two reasons:

One, during the time these composers were alive and writing they had patrons who liked what they did and who therefore paid them money or gave them a place to live so that the composers could stay alive by writing dots on pieces of paper. If any of the compositions these men wrote had not been pleasing to a church, a duke, or a king, they would have been out of work and their music would not have survived.

There is a book called *Grove's Dictionary of Music and Musicians*, with thousands of names in it. You have never heard of most of the people in that book, nor have you heard their music. That doesn't mean they wrote awful music, it means they didn't have hits.

So basically, the people who are recognized as the geniuses of classical music had hits. And the person who determined whether or not it was a hit was a king, a duke, or the church or whoever paid the bill. The desire to get a sandwich or something to drink had a lot to do with it. And the content of what they wrote was to a degree determined by the musical predilections of the guy who was paying the bill.

Today, we have a similar situation in rock n' roll. We have kings, dukes, and popes: the A&R guy who spots a group or screens the tape when it comes in; the business affairs guy who writes the contract; the radio station programers who choose what records get air play.

The other reason the classical greats survived is their works are played over and over again by orchestras. The reasons they are played over and over again are: 1) all the musicians in the orchestra know how to play them because they learned them in the conservatory; 2) the orchestra management programs these pieces because the musicians already know them and therefore it costs less to rehearse them; 3) the composers are dead so the orchestras pay no royalties for the use of the music.

Today, survivability is based on the number of specimens in the market place—the sheer numbers of plastic objects. Many other compositions from this era will vanish, but Michael Jackson's *Thriller* album will survive because there are 30 million odd pieces of plastic out there. No matter what we may think of the content, a future generation may pick up that piece of plastic and say, "Oh, they were like this."

I suppose somewhere in the future there will be other men like Bloom certifying that the very narrow spectrum of rock n' roll which survives composes the great works of the later half of the 20th Century.

The Difference Between Classical Music and Rock n' Roll

Rock music provides premature ecstasy and, in this respect, is like the drugs with which it is allied. . . . These are the three great lyrical themes: sex, hate and a smarmy, hypocritical version of brotherly love. . . . Nothing noble, sublime, profound, delicate, tasteful or even decent can find a place in such tableaux.—A. Bloom

Rock music provides premature ecstasy and, in this respect, is like the drugs with which it is allied. —Allan Bloom

Again, Bloom is not looking at what is really going on here. The ugliness in this society is not a product of unrefined art, but of unrefined commerce, wild superstition and religious fanaticism.

The real difference between the classics and rock n' roll is mostly a matter of form. In order to say we have written a symphony, the design we put on a piece of paper has to conform to certain specifications. We have an exposition that lasts a certain amount of time, then modulation, development and recapitulation. It's like a box, like an egg carton. We must fill all the little spaces in the egg carton with the right forms. If we do, we can call it a symphony because it conforms to the spaces in that box.

Compare that creative process to rock n' roll. If we want to have an AM hit record, we have another egg carton to fill. We have an intro, a couple of verses, a bridge, another verse, and then a fade out. All of which requires a "hook." That's a very rigid form. If we wander away from that form, our song's not going to go on the radio because it doesn't sound like it fits into their format.

Now, whether the person writing the song graduated from a conservatory or whether they came out of a garage, they know that in order to finish a piece they have to do certain things to make it fit into a certain form. In the classical period the sonata or a concerto or symphony had to be that certain size and shape or else the king was not going to like it. One could die. These were literally matters of life and death, but not in the way Bloom defines them.

Today, rock n' roll is about getting a contract with a major company, and pretty much doing what the company tells you to do. —Frank Zappa

The Rock Business

The family spiritual void has left the field open to rock music. . . . The result is nothing less than parents' loss of control over their children's moral education at a time when no one else is seriously concerned with it. This has been achieved by an alliance between the strange young males who have the gift of divining the mob's emergent wishes—our versions of Thrasymachus, Socrates' rhetorical adversary—and the record-company executives, the new robber barons, who mine gold out of rock.—A. Bloom

There is some truth to that, but how did we get to this point and what do we do about it?

We got here because teenagers are the most sought after consumers. The whole idea of merchandising the pre-pubescent masturbational fantasy is not necessarily the work of the songwriter or the singer, but the work of the merchandiser who has elevated rock n' roll to the commercial enterprise it is.

In the beginning, rock n' roll was young kids singing to other kids about their girlfriends. That's all there was. The guys who made those records came from Manual Arts High School. They went into a recording studio, were given some wine, $25 and a bunch of records when their song came out as a single—which made them heroes at school. That was their career, not, "Well, we're not going to sing until we get a $125 thousand advance."

Today, rock n' roll is about getting a contract with a major company, and pretty much doing what the company tells you to do. The company promotes the image of rock n' roll as being wild and fun when in fact it's just a dismal business.

Record companies have people who claim to be experts on what the public really wants to hear. And they inflict their taste on the people who actually make the music. To be a big success, you need a really big company behind you because really big companies can make really big distribution deals.

Even people who are waiting to go into the business know it's a business. They spend a great deal of time planning what they will look like and getting a good publicity photo before they walk in the door with their tape. And the record companies tend to take the attitude that it doesn't make too much difference what the tape sounds like as long as the artists look right, because they can always hire a producer who will fix up the sound and make it the way they want it—so long as the people wear the right clothes and have the right hair.

Retaining Classical Music

Classical music is dead among the young. . . . Rock music is as unquestioned and unproblematic as the air the students breathe, and very few have any acquaintance at all with classical music. . . . Classical music is now a special taste, like Greek language or pre-Columbian archeology, not a common culture of reciprocal communication and psychological shorthand. —A. Bloom

On this point, Bloom and I can agree, but how can a child be blamed for consuming only that which is presented to him? Most kids have never been in contact with anything other than this highly merchandised stuff.

When I testified in front of the Senate, I pointed out that if they don't like the idea of young people buying certain kinds of music, why don't they stick a few dollars back into the school system to have music appreciation? There are kids today who have never heard a string quartet; they have never heard a symphony orchestra. I argued that the money for music appreciation courses, in terms of social good and other benefits such as improved behavior or uplifting the spirit, is far less than the cost of another set of uniforms for the football team. But I frankly don't see people waving banners in the streets saying more music appreciation in schools.

When I was in school, we could go into a room and they had records there. I could hear anything I wanted by going in there and putting on a record. I won't say I enjoyed everything that was played for me, but I was curious, and if I had never heard any of that music I wouldn't know about it.

Once we're out of school, the time we can spend doing that type of research is limited because most of us are out looking for a job flipping hamburgers in the great tradition of the Reagan economic miracle. When all is said and done, that's the real source of America's barren and arid lives. ♦

Classical music is dead among the young.
—Allan Bloom

How can a child be blamed for consuming only that which is presented to him?
—Frank Zappa

Questions for Discussion

1. Frank Zappa claims that the only reason young Americans have no taste for classical music is because they are not exposed to it in music appreciation classes. Do you agree or disagree?
2. What do you think of Allan Bloom's contention that rock music is "junk food for the soul"?

America's Slide into the Sewer

George F. Will

During the summer of 1990, America was numbed by the testimony heard emanating from the trial of a group of young men accused of raping a woman in New York City's Central Park. Around the same time, a rap group called 2 Live Crew was on a concert tour that left a string of shocked cities behind them, and resulted in their arrest for obscenity in Florida.

All this happened a few years after Allan Bloom had written The Closing of the American Mind. *George Will, a fellow cultural conservative, made the same connection between the rape and rap that Bloom would have.*

Reading Difficulty Level: 2. Which is pretty standard for Newsweek.

I regret the offensiveness of what follows. However, it is high time adult readers sample the words that millions of young Americans are hearing.

Which words are lyrics, which are testimony?

Which words are lyrics, which are testimony?

In a Manhattan courtroom testimony continues in the trial of young men accused of gang rape and other sadistic violence against the Central Park jogger in last April's "wilding" episode. "We charged her and we got her on the ground. Everybody started hitting her and stuff, and she's on the ground and everybody's stomping and everything . . . I grabbed one arm, and this other kid grabbed one arm and we grabbed her legs and stuff. And then we took turns getting on her." They did it for fun, for entertainment.

"After she was hit on the head with the pipe, did someone take her clothes off?"

"Yeah."

"OK, who took her clothes off?"

"All of us."

"Did somebody have sex with her?"

From *Newsweek,* July 30, 1990. Reprinted by permission.

"Yeah."

"Did a lot of people have sex with her?"

"Yeah."

When arrested a defendant said, "It was something to do. It was fun." Where can you get the idea that sexual violence against women is fun? From a music store, through Walkman earphones, from boom boxes blaring forth the rap lyrics of 2 Live Crew:

To have her walkin' funny we try to abuse it

A big stinking p—y can't do it all

So we try real hard just to bust the walls

That is, bust the walls of women's vaginas. 2 Live Crew's lyrics exult in busting women—almost always called bitches—in various ways, forcing anal sex, forcing women to lick feces. *"He'll tear the p—y open 'cause it's satisfaction." "Suck my d—k, bitch, it makes you puke."* That's entertainment.

This is medicine. The jogger lost most of her blood, her temperature plunged to 85. Doctors struggling to keep her alive had to tie down her arms and legs because, even hours after the attack, while in a coma that would last weeks, she was flailing and kicking as if "in a fighting stance." Her face was so disfigured a friend took 15 minutes to identify her. "I recognized her ring."

Do you recognize the relevance of 2 Live Crew?

I'll break ya down and d—k ya long

Bust your p—y then break your backbone

The furor (if anything so evanescent can be called that) about 2 Live Crew has subsided, for two reasons. Saturation journalism, print and broadcast, around the clock, quickly wrings the novelty out of subjects, leaving them dry husks. Then, if someone raises the subject again, the answer is a journalistic shrug: "Not again. We've already done that." But for 2 Live Crew the tour rolls on and the money rolls in.

Where can you get the idea that sexual violence against women is fun? From a music store.

Anyway, the "fury" over the lyrics was feigned. It had to be because everyone dependent on journalism did not learn what the offending words were. Media coverage was characterized by coy abstractness, an obscuring mist of mincing, supercilious descriptions of the lyrics as "explicit" or "outrageous" or "challenging" or "controversial" or "provocative." Well, now. Provoking what, precisely?

From the jogger trial: "Steve was holding her with his leg and someone was ripping off her clothes and pulling her down. She screamed and Steve held her while Kevin pulled down his pants and had sex with her. Steve hit her with a brick twice."

Fact: Some members of a particular age and social cohort—the one making 2 Live Crew rich—stomped and raped the jogger to the razor edge of death, for the fun of it. Certainty: the coarsening of a community, the desensitizing of a society will have behavioral consequences.

The coarsening of a community, the desensitizing of a society will have behavioral consequences.

Juan Williams of The Washington Post is black and disgusted. The issue, he writes, is the abuse of women, especially black women, and the corruption of young blacks' sensibilities, twisting their conceptions "of good sex, good relationships and good times." Half of all black children live in single-parent households headed by women. The black family is falling apart, teen pregnancy regularly ruins lives, the rate of poverty is steadily rising and 2 Live Crew "is selling corruption—self-hate—to vulnerable young minds in a weak black America."

No Morals

In such selling, liberals are tools of entertainment corporations. The liberals and the corporations have the morals of the marketplace. Corporations sell civil pollution for profit; liberals rationalize it as virtuous tolerance in "the marketplace of ideas." Not to worry, yawn The New York Times editorialists, "The history of music is the story of innovative, even outrageous styles that interacted, adapted and became mainstream." Oh, I see: First Stravinsky's "Rite of Spring," now 2 Live Crew's "Me So Horny." ("*I won't tell your momma if you don't tell your dad /I know he'll be disgusted when he sees your p—y busted.*" Innovative. When that is "mainstream," this will be an interesting country.)

2 Live Crew, who are black, resemble the cretinous Andrew Dice Clay, the white "comedian." There is nothing new about selling the talentless to the tasteless. What is new is the combination of extreme infantilism and menace in the profit-driven degeneration of popular entertainment. This slide into the sewer is greased by praise. Yes, praise. When journalism flinches from presenting the raw reality, and instead says only that 2 Live Crew's lyrics are "explicit" and "controversial" and "provocative," there is an undertone of approval. Antonyms of those adjectives are "vague" and "bland" and "unchallenging." Somehow we never reach the subject of busting vaginal walls.

A confused society protects lungs more than minds, trout more than black women.

America today is capable of terrific intolerance about smoking, or toxic waste that threatens trout. But only a deeply confused society is more concerned about protecting lungs than minds, trout than black women. We legislate against smoking in restaurants; singing "Me So Horny" is a constitutional right. Secondary smoke is carcinogenic; celebration of torn vaginas is "mere words."

Words, said Aristotle, are what set human beings, the language-using animals, above lower animals. Not necessarily. ♦

Questions for Discussion

1. Should obscene rap lyrics be censored?
2. Do you agree with George Will that our society seems to protect trout more than Black women?

Heavy Metal Goes On Trial

Mary Billard

Two days before Christmas in 1985, Ray Belknap shot and killed himself with a shotgun. His best friend, Jay Vance, then picked up the gun, shot himself in the face, and survived, at least for a few horrible years. Nearly five years later, the parents of these two young men were preparing to enter a courtroom to argue that their sons had been driven to these actions by subliminal messages on the Judas Priest album they had been listening to.

As the trial approached, Mary Billard, a producer with American Lawyer Media, a cable channel devoted to trial coverage, filed the following report.

Reading Difficulty Level: 1. It's gritty, but you won't be able to put it down.

A young man turned a shotgun on himself after listening to Judas Priest. Did the music make him do it?

On the day after Christmas, in 1985, Jay Vance's family gathered around his bed in the intensive-care unit of the Washoe County Medical Center, in Reno, Nevada. Detectives David Zarubi and Robert Cowman of the Sparks Police Department arrived at 11:30 that morning, escorted by members of the hospital staff. Zarubi explained that he wanted Jay to answer a few questions, which was going to be somewhat difficult as Jay couldn't talk. His face was bandaged up to his eyes.

The young man in the hospital bed nodded that he understood. His eyes—bright, blue, expressive above the bandages—told the detectives he was ready to begin. They handed him a clipboard and pen to use if he needed to elaborate beyond a simple yes or no.

Zarubi asked Jay if he knew that his best friend, Raymond Belknap, had died from a shotgun blast to the head on December 23rd. Jay nodded. He nodded in agreement to the subsequent questions: Yes, he and Ray had been drinking prior to the shooting, and Ray had also been smoking grass. Yes, Ray was the owner of the sawed-off shotgun that killed him.

Jay counted off on his fingers to indicate that it was a twelve-gauge weapon. He confirmed that the two friends had taken the gun to a nearby playground with the idea of killing themselves.

In the report filed later that day, Zarubi wrote: "He was questioned about reloading the weapon after BELKNAP, Raymond, shot himself, and he replied that when he observed BELKNAP, Raymond, shoot himself and lose much of his head

---

and brains, he reloaded the weapon, stood approximately (2) feet away and fired it into his own jaw."

Though it seemed unlikely to be the case, Zarubi had to ask whether the injured young man had shot his friend before turning the gun on himself. Jay tossed his head violently from side to side and waved his arms to indicate no. When the officers asked him why his best friend would want to kill himself, he raised a hand and with his index finger began drawing letters in the air. At first Zarubi and Cowman did not understand.

When the officers asked him why his best friend would want to kill himself, he raised a hand and with his index finger began drawing letters in the air: "Life sucks."

Finally, one of them figured it out: "Life sucks."

For Jay Vance and Ray Belknap, that sentiment was something of an understatement. The two had met six years earlier at Dilworth Middle School, in the Reno suburb of Sparks. They went on to Reed High, where they hung with the stoners, drinking and getting high, cutting classes, getting into trouble. They both dropped out after their sophomore year, and both lived at home while they bounced from one dead-end job to another. Jay, 20, worked at a dirty, part-time job in the bindery of a printing plant. Ray, 18, had just started working for a local contractor.

Their friends remember the boys as loners, lost boys who hovered at the periphery of life.

Neither one owned a car; their most valuable possessions were their stereos, their guns and their record collections. Both had police records for a variety of offenses, Jay's mostly violent in nature, Ray's involving stealing and exposing himself to women. Both were the products of violent families, the victims of childhood beatings and abuse. Ray, according to his friend, had tried suicide once before.

Facing a dismal future of unskilled jobs, the two friends dreamed of becoming mercenaries and practiced shooting at small animals and bottles. They played "cops and criminals" in their parents' homes, at least once with real guns. Their drink of choice was beer, and plenty of it—Jay drank a twelve-pack a day—and they abused a variety of drugs, including pot, cocaine, methamphetamine, angel dust and hallucinogens. In July of 1985, Jay checked himself into the New Frontier drug-treatment center. He told the intake counselor that he'd suffered from blackouts and hallucinations. To the question "What is your favorite lesiure-time activity?" he responded: "Doing drugs."

Their friends remember the pair as loners, lost boys who hovered at the periphery of life at Reed High. At six feet two and 141 pounds, Ray was a gangly, freckle-faced kid whose red hair had faded to brown in his teen years. He was shy and gentle. His mother says he was something of a mama's boy; she has snapshots of him carefully cradling his baby sister. Everybody said Ray was the follower, led around by Jay, a classmate, who though two years older had been left back twice as a kid.

Also skinny but a few inches shorter, Jay was a cocky, handsome kid, sure of himself, especially with girls. His mother says he was an angry and violent teenager who would storm through the house smashing things and punching walls if he didn't get his way. His photograph in the *Galleon*, the Reed High yearbook, shows a handsome, thin-faced boy with longish blond hair and a shadow of a mustache on his upper lip. Like most of the kids in their crowd, the two friends dressed in jeans, boots and cropped T-shirts, often souvenirs from rock concerts. They listened to KOZZ-FM, and from their early teens they were devoted fans of heavy-metal music, especially the albums of the English metal band Judas Priest.

It is for that last reason that on July 16th, in a courtroom in Reno, Nevada, a jury will decide whether the members of Judas Priest—along with their label, CBS Records—are responsible for Raymond Belknap's suicide. The lawsuits filed almost four years ago by Aunetta Roberson, Ray's mother, and Jay and his family allege in no uncertain terms that Judas Priest's music caused Ray to shoot himself.

The tragedy of youthful suicide invariably leaves the victim's family searching for the reasons why. In this case, however, there was a survivor. And, in the weeks and months after Ray's death, Jay Vance found comfort in believing it was Judas Priest's evil, hypnotic music that compelled them to carry out their suicide pact.

In the families' "wrongful death" complaint, the plaintiffs allege that Judas Priest's "suggestive lyrics combined with the continuous beat and rhythmic nonchanging intonation of the music combined to induce, encourage, aid, abet and otherwise mesmerize plaintiff into believing the answer to life was death."

The original suit claimed that Judas Priest's lyrics filled the young men with dire thoughts, urging them to pull the trigger. But when the lawyers for the families, Timothy Post and Kenneth McKenna, learned that similar suits had been thrown out of court on constitutional grounds, they wisely changed their strategy. In August 1988, recording engineers claimed to have found "subliminal messages" on the *Stained Class* album—directives that they theorize can unleash overpowering *subconscious* feelings. The suit is now a product-liability case, alleging that the product—Judas Priest's 1978 LP *Stained Class*—is dangerous to unstable individuals like Ray Belknap.

The suit is alleging Judas Priest's LP Stained Class *is dangerous to unstable individuals like Ray Belknap.*

CBS Records has pushed for dismissal on a number of legal grounds. The company spent a year arguing unsuccessfully that the members of Judas Priest, as British citizens, could not be sued in the United States. Then CBS invoked the First Amendment, which protects virtually all forms of speech. But Reno judge Jerry Carr Whitehead ruled that subliminals are not protected by the Constitution. No matter what the jury decides, both sides vow to take the case to the U.S. Supreme Court.

Jay Vance found comfort in believing it was Judas Priest's music that compelled them to carry out their suicide pact.

Yeah I have left the world behind
I am safe now in my mind
(I'm) free to speak with my own mind
This is my life this is my life and
I'll decide not you
Keep the world with all its sin
It's not fit for living in.

—Judas Priest, "Beyond the Realms of Death"

For Aunetta Roberson, the morning of December 23rd, 1985, started with happy holiday chores. She picked up a Christmas turkey from her husband's workplace and took Ray's four-year-old half sister, Christie Lynn, for her first real haircut. The family went to the Happy Looker beauty parlor in a shopping center around the corner from their modest home on Richards Way. Once there, they decided to document the occasion, and Ray drove home to get a camera.

In the small, smoky room, the two got worked up about a fight Ray had gotten into the night before.

After Christie Lynn's haircut, Ray borrowed his mother's car and went to the Vance residence on Glen Meadow to pick up his friend. They went back to the salon to get Ray's hair trimmed a little shorter in imitation of Jay's new haircut. Back at Ray's house, Ray handed Jay a Christmas present, a copy of *Stained Class.* Jay had once owned the album, but at a former girlfriend's urging, he'd sold his entire collection of heavy-metal music. A die-hard fan who had once owned all thirteen of the band's albums and who had five Judas Priest tattoos on his body, Jay appreciated the gesture.

"We caught the beer buzz, and we started getting amped on the music."

In Ray's bedroom, the young men talked, drank beer and smoked some marijuana that Ray had stolen, arguing briefly over what to put on the turntable. Ray wanted Lynyrd Skynyrd, but Jay insisted on an afternoon of Priest.

"I had a mild beer buzz," Jay told lawyers at a deposition for the lawsuit. "I wasn't out of my senses at all." The marijuana was so mild that they hardly bothered to smoke it. "We weren't going to waste our time on it."

In the small, smoky room, the two got worked up about a fight Ray had gotten into the night before. Drinking and playing pool at Doc and Eddy's tavern, Ray lost his day's wages of fifty dollars to his boss in a bet. Jay offered to "persuade" the man to give back the money. He later told police what he meant: "I was going to stomp on him in the back of his knee, and I would crunch his knee to the concrete and then karate chop him in the back of the neck, and he would pretty much be helpless at that moment, because I knew karate."

That afternoon the two played selected cuts from four of Ray's Judas Priest albums while they got wasted on beer and pot. "We caught the beer buzz, and we started getting amped on the music," Jay said. "And when I say *amped,* we started getting this feeling of power, and it was something that we got often, you know, and we started rocking out, you know, and we started getting really involved in the music."

Then some decisions were made. They would quit their jobs—Ray over the fight, Jay because he hated his. "You would spend twelve hours on the press," Jay said, "and about three hours washing the ink off, and the ink never came off. It looked like you had leprosy."

The plan to fight Ray's boss, like much in their lives, was a flight of macho fancy. In a deposition taken in 1987, Jay told attorneys what he did while listening to Judas Priest:

Q: What are those things that you and Ray did or you did alone?

A: Fantasies. Just, you know, being under—sitting there and listening to a song and using your imagination with it is all you needed to do, is all I ever did.

Q: These would be the fantasies of killing people or being a mercenary?

A: Right.

But as the afternoon of December 23rd wore on, the mood in the room darkened. Jay said that the music that they loved was now giving them directions: "All of a sudden we got a suicide message, and we got tired of life." He was referring to lyrics from the song "Beyond the Realms of Death": "He couldn't take any more/Keep the world with all its sin/It's not fit for living in."

They left the room to get more beer from the garage and ran into Ray's pregnant sister, Rita Skulason, who also lived at the house. A little high and drunk, Jay playfully pinched her breast. Ray hugged his sister and told her that he loved her. Then Jay asked Rita if she would name the baby after her brother if something happened to him.

"Not unless it's a goddamn redhead," she said.

Then she heard Jay say, "Let's go finish it." She said later that she thought they were talking about the beer.

Suddenly, Jay's mother and stepfather were at the door. They'd come to drive him to work. "They argued with me to go, and I told them no," Jay said. "I was rocking out." He told them he was going to quit. Phyllis Vance asked her son how he was going to buy his own cigarettes and do the things that he wanted to do for himself. The argument spilled out into the living room. Voices were raised, and finally Jay shouted, "Leave me alone!" He went back into the bedroom, and his parents left.

As the afternoon wore on, the mood darkened. Jay said that the music was now giving them directions.

Ray and Jay finished the last of a twelve-pack of beer and changed the record. Now *Stained Class* was playing, Jay remembered: "And I said, 'This guy is saying, "Leave this life with all its sin, it's not fit for living in."' And I started listening to the vibrations, and for myself, you know, I said this after the fact, that I more or less believed in the answer to life was death. It was like, you know, 'I finally understand,' and so we did the suicide pact and then Ray . . . was in the same frame of mind that I was. . . . And we got the same burst of energy at the same time."

Over the strains of "Heroes End," Jay said to his friend, "Let's see what is next." They hugged each other goodbye.

"Let's see what is next, let's leave this world, let's go."

"Let's see what is next, let's leave this world, let's go."

But first they demolished the room, breaking glass, punching through the walls, kicking holes in the door. Alarmed, Rita Skulason called her mother, who rushed home. While she pounded on the door, Ray grabbed his sawed-off shotgun from beside the stereo and jumped out of the window. Jay was right behind him.

They ran behind the house, over a fence and into an alley that led to the deserted playground of the Community First Church of God preschool. Ray stood up on the merry-go-round and said to his friend: "I sure fucked my life up." Then he sat down, wedged the stock of the gun into the ground and steadied the muzzle under his chin. Jay watched in amazement as his best friend blew his head off.

Jay stared at the lifeless body on the dirt. Then he picked up the bloody shotgun.

Jay stared at the lifeless body on the dirt; the writing on the gray Miami Super Bowl XIX T-shirt was covered with blood, as was the brass belt buckle in the shape of a marijuana leaf.

Then he picked up the bloody shotgun. "It felt like it had grease on it," he later said. "There was so much blood I could barely handle the gun, and I reloaded it, and then it was my turn, and I readied myself." He propped the gun against the merry-go-ground and counted to thirty. "My whole life flashed before my eyes," he said. "My mother, my father . . . I thought about Ray, who was already gone. I don't know how long I stood there, a minute, two minutes." But something went wrong; as he pulled the trigger, the muzzle of the gun moved. The blast ripped through his chin and out through his nose, missing his brain.

Why do you have to die if you're a hero? When there are still so many things to say, say?

—Judas Priest, "Heroes End"

Before he lost consciousness, Jay remembered an awful stinging sensation on his face, as if he had been slapped very hard. While the police moved his friend's body to the morgue, an ambulance took Jay to Washoe Medical Center's emergency room. At the hospital his mother talked to Detective Zarubi, who filed his report later that day. "I learned from her that both subjects were seriously depressed prior to the holidays," he wrote, "both using controlled substances, specifically cocaine, marijuana and alcohol. Both had made her aware of their feelings towards their own life by making the statement, 'Life sucks.' Further, both were distraught in regard to their employment prospects. Further, it was her belief that if one decided to commit an act such as suicide, the other would follow suit without question."

Within days, the police felt comfortable calling Ray's death a suicide, but his mother wouldn't believe it. She sifted her memories, looking for signs that she might have missed. "There were no appetite changes," she says. "No giving things away. None of those mood swings. Just nothing." A week later, still searching for understanding, Roberson went into her son's room. On the stereo was *Stained Class.* She turned on the stereo and listened to it several times. "I couldn't understand it," she says. "Not a word. But I didn't like it."

The survivor was also trying to figure out what had happened. Jay had lost his jaw, tongue, nose and gums, and all but one tooth; he was undergoing hundreds of hours of reconstructive surgery at Stanford University. Part of his scalp had been moved to his forehead, a large, fleshy bulb that surgeons planned to swing down and mold into a nose later on. He had to shave the lump, since it still grew hair. Part of his shoulder was made into a chin. He drooled and wore a towel under his chin. He did not have a gag reflex, and at times had to manually dig what was left of his tongue out of his throat.

But now Jay wanted to live more than ever. He tried to figure out what had driven him. Three months after the suicide attempt, he told Detective Zarubi that he had found Christ and was avoiding drugs, alcohol and heavy metal. For a few months, he actually did stop doing illegal drugs and became a born-again Christian like his mother. He reunited with an old grilfriend, Lisa Davis, and a year or so later fathered a daughter, Athena, who was born in September 1987. He wrote Ray's mother a letter trying to explain their actions. "I believe that alcohol and heavy-metal music such as Judas Priest led us to be mesmerized. . . ."

In early 1986, Mrs. Roberson contacted Kenneth McKenna, a self-described "slip and slide" personal-injury lawyer and a friend of the family. McKenna listened to the album *Stained Class* again and again. A cherub-faced family man, McKenna was disturbed by the music. He had trouble sleeping at night. He agreed to pursue the suit against CBS Records and Judas Priest. McKenna contacted the Vance family to see if they would be interested in joining the suit. Phyllis Vance retained a born-again Christian attorney named Timothy Post as cocounsel. The complaints, which were filed on May 8th, 1986, attracted much media attention. The *Sparks Gazette-Journal* titled its story LAWSUIT: ROCK LYRICS LED TO YOUTH'S SUICIDE. McKenna was free with his views, suggesting that the album *Stained Class* carry a warning sticker saying, IF YOU'RE EMOTIONALLY DISTURBED, DON'T LISTEN TO THIS ALBUM.

The local paper titled its story ***LAWSUIT: ROCK LYRICS LED TO YOUTH'S SUICIDE.***

McKenna hired a crew of technicians from a Sacramento, California, recording studio to scour the records for hidden messages. They testified that they turned up "masked lyrics" on the song "Better by You, Better Than Me," on *Stained Class*—words they said could be heard only through attentive listening—telling the listener to "do it." What "it" is, is not specified, but McKenna argues that if the listener is contemplating suicide, the "do it" command will reinforce that desire.

The technicians testified that they found lyrics that appear to have another meaning when played in reverse.

The Sacramento team also testified that they found "backward sounds," lyrics that appear to have another meaning when played in reverse. A line on *Stained Class*—"Deliver us/From all the fuss"—sounds to his experts like "Fuck the lord; fuck [suck] all of you." Another line—"Faithless continuum/Into the abyss"—is supposed to sound like "Sing my evil spirit." The backward-masking hypothesis claims that as the music plays forward, the listener's subconscious perceives the masked message. It's a theory that even the conservative Parents' Music Resource Center doesn't buy. "There is no scientific proof that you pick up the lyrics that way," says PMRC executive director Jennifer Norwood.

Nevertheless, McKenna changed the case's focus to subliminals in August 1988. During pretrial hearings, McKenna played his experts' tapes in Judge Whitehead's chambers. The judge, a tough hardliner who had expressed his disdain for heavy metal in a pretrial hearing, set a trial date.

The jury in Reno will decide for the first time whether subliminals exist and whether heavy-metal music is responsible for the deaths. The trial promises to be a full-scale media circus. There will be television cameras in the courtroom. A reporter for the *Reno Gazette* has been asked by three London newspapers to cover the trial. It will also be a field day for the so-called experts on subliminals, like Wilson Bryan Key, a professor of marketing formerly at the University of Denver, who will testify as a friendly witness for the families. Key, an anti-heavy-metal crusader, has consulted in twenty-two separate cases involving homicide, suicide and acts of violence. Heavy metal is Key's primary target, but in *The Clam Plate Orgy* and his other books on subliminal persuasion, he claims to have found satanic or sexual messages on five-dollar bills, Howard Johnson's place mats and Ritz crackers.

McKenna, who says he is anxious to show the conservative Nevada jury MTV videos of Judas Priest, will have to proceed without his star witness, Jay Vance. Within months of his suicide attempt, Jay went back to using drugs, shooting cocaine intravenously. He was hospitalized intermittently for severe depression, and in late 1988, with the Christmas holidays approaching, he admitted himself to the psychiatric unit at Washoe Medical Center. A suicide watch was ordered, and he was given a series of antidepressants and painkillers, including methadone. During the early hours of November 24th, he stopped breathing, and six days later, he died.

Lethal, deadly, hung, drawn and quartered
He slaughtered and faltered and altered the world.
But by doing so smashed all his hopes and utopian dreams.

—Judas Priest, "Stained Class"

Phyllis Vance was seventeen when she gave birth to her only child, James Matthew, on October 12th, 1965. His biological father denied parentage and saw the boy only once shortly after his birth. While pregnant with Jay, Phyllis married Emmit "Tony" Vance, who raised the boy but didn't legally adopt him until Jay was eighteen.

Raymond Belknap's parents had also split up before his birth in 1967. Kerry Belknap didn't see his son until the child was sixteen months old, then not again until Ray was about twelve. At forty-three, Aunetta Roberson, a pretty brunette with blue eyes, has had four husbands, which she knows will look bad to outsiders in the upcoming trial.

Her son Ray never got along with this third stepfather, Jesse Roberson, who, according to Mrs. Roberson, was a violent alcoholic who sometimes whipped Ray and his stepbrother with his belt. In 1981, according to a Sparks police report, while Ray watched, his stepfather threatened his mother with a gun.

Jay was also raised in a violent home. His mother admitted to beating him when he was a child. In rages of anger, she remembered, her blows fell on the young boy "just wherever my hands hit." Both of Jay's parents were alcoholics during his childhood. A sickly kid, Jay was diagnosed as hyperkinetic at the age of four, and in second grade he was sent by his school to a therapist for pulling out his hair and tying a belt tight around his head. He repeated the first and second grades. Phyllis put him in therapy briefly but stopped treatment when the counselor suggested that she come in for a session as well. Six years later, she admitted to another counselor that she may have taken her anger with her husband out on her young son. "When Tony frustrates me," she said, "I tend to take it out on James."

Both of Jay's parents were alcoholics during his childhood.

At the age of thirteen, in a minor disagreement, Jay tried to choke his mother while she was driving on the freeway. In 1978, a school psychologist visited Mrs. Vance at home and filed this report: "I indicated to her that I felt a high probability existed for James to respond violently to stressful situations and that this probability might increase as James is subjected to the additional stresses of adolescence."

As boys, both got into trouble with school authorities. Jay was suspended for fighting with a fellow student and arrested for making threatening phone calls to a former girlfriend. Ray was suspended from school for indecent sexual behavior. "I think him and his cousin flashed some ladies," says his mother. At the

As boys, both got into trouble with school authorities.

Sparks Police Department, Ray's rap sheet listed a series of minor transgressions, including petty theft and truancy. "Ray never got away with anything in his life," says his mother. "He was not sneaky."

The boys took consolation in drugs and music.

The boys took consolation in drugs and music. The music was a sore point with Jay's parents. His stepfather recalls hating the loud, blasting music that gave his wife headaches.

One time, Phyllis went into Jay's room, where he was listening to music with a headset. He came at her and pointed a pistol at her head, saying. "I'm going to shoot you." His threats of violence were not always idle. He hit his mother frequently, bruising her skin with his fists. In the two years before his suicide attempt, Jay ran away from home—thirteen times by his mother's count.

Neither friends nor family were surprised when Ray and Jay dropped out of school after their sophomore year. In 1983, Reed High must have seemed like alien territory to them, a complete time warp. The student plays that year were *Arsenic and Old Lace, The Odd Couple* and *Wait Until Dark.*

Both found work at low-paying jobs, living for their off hours, when they would listen to Judas Priest and dream of exotic adventures. Jay wanted to leave Sparks and become a soldier of fortune. He told people he was training in the martial arts with a black belt. Jay bragged that he had surpassed the master with his own brand of "American street-fighting karate."

They got stoned and drunk and dreamed of becoming professional hit men.

"[Ray] was one of my favorite sparring partners," Jay said. In his self-designed training program, Jay also said, he learned how to shoot from a Vietnam veteran, a man who, according to Jay, was still involved in secret government activities. "We used to play war sometimes," Jay said. "TV is a really good teacher."

Nineteen-eighty-four was a big year for Judas Priest. The band released its album *Defenders of the Faith* and went on a six-month U.S. tour. Ray and Jay caught the band in July at the Lawlor Events Center, in Reno. Jay kept the ticket stubs, bought a T-shirt at the concert and hung in his bedroom a poster of the group from the magazine *Hit Parader.*

The summer before the suicide, both boys reached crucial junctures in their lives. Ray stole $450 from an employer and traveled by bus to Oklahoma to visit the father who had rejected him. The visit could not have been successful; Ray never saw his father again. He was caught and put on probation.

Meanwhile, Jay felt his drug use had gotten out of hand and checked into the New Frontier Treatment Center for alcoholism and drug addiction. The director recommended a detox center for at least three months, but Jay checked out after several days.

So they got stoned and drunk and dreamed of becoming professional hit men. The reality of their lives was sadly different. The week before his death, Ray was caught by the police shooting darts from a blowgun at a neighbor's cat. They wrote him up for animal torture. Only a few months before, Jay told a drug counselor about the bleakness of his existence. Asked to name one good thing in his life, he came up empty. Asked to name his ideal job, Jay the mercenary wrote, "Janitorial work."

The walls in Aunetta Roberson's pleasant home are covered with photographs and plants, the shelves filled with china figurines. Country-western music plays on the radio, and ribs are cooking in the oven. In the living room, a sunlightened snapshot shows Ray at a family picnic. Long and lean, he smiles shyly at the camera.

Roberson has grown weary of the lawsuit that she says hasn't allowed her to heal. She says she didn't know what she was getting into when she started these proceedings a few months after Ray's death. "I will be happy when it is over" is what she says now. Roberson speaks haltingly, choosing her words carefully. She has had practice, but she is clearly uncomfortable with all the scrutiny of her family life.

She would prefer not to speak to the press but forces herself to protect the memory of her son. She talks about his favorite foods, escargot and rack of lamb, and his terrible luck with cars. "Once he had a van, one he bought himself, and made a wrong turn," she says. "He totaled that." Another time, he rolled over in a truck. "He just had no luck," she says.

Roberson wants people to know that Ray was a loving son, part of a close family. "We use to go to hunt and fish at Pyramid Lake," she says. "One time, Ray got a deer.

Only a few months before, Jay told a drug counselor about the bleakness of his existence.

"He loved his little sister," she continues. "He was closest to her, even though he used to tease her, and they would fight like cats and dogs. Him and Jay were real close, too."

Roberson has moved away from the house on Richards Way where Raymond spent his last afternoon. Now she lives in a two-family dwelling nearby. She is single again and shares the place with her mother and Ray's stepsisters. Her son Tony Roach lives several blocks away. Her daughter Rita Skulason lives around the corner. Rita named her son Raymond Dakota, but she calls him Dakota.

One of Ray's earliest wood-shop efforts hangs on a wall in the master bedroom, a handful of nails pounded into a flat piece of wood. Dangling from the nails are a few gold chains and coral necklaces. Burnt into the wood is the inscription I WUV YOU.

Roberson has trouble looking at that sometimes. The son she remembers bought ice-cream cones for the baby, ran home to get the camera for the baby's first haircut and raked leaves. He was a good son. His problems were like all other teenagers'. It had to be the music. ♦

Her son's problems were like all other teenagers'. It had to be the music.

Ozzy: Read My Lyrics

Wine is fine, but whiskey's quicker
Suicide is slow with liquor
Take a bottle, drown your sorrows
Then it floods away tomorrows.

—Ozzy Osbourne, "Suicide Solution"

Rock and roll has, of course, been the target of periodic witch hunts in the forty or so years of its history, but the moral hysteria—and litigation—has never reached so fevered a pitch as it has today.

In three widely reported incidents, Ozzy Osbourne's "Suicide Solution" is the common denominator. Osbourne maintains that the song's lyrics are an anti-alcohol eulogy for his friend Bon Scott of AC/DC, but the song's misinterpretation has become so widespread that John Cardinal O'Connor of New York City recently called the song a "help to the devil."

In California, in 1984, John McCollum, 19, spent a solitary Friday night in his family's living room, listening to three Osbourne albums, including *Blizzard of Ozz,* which contains "Suicide Solution." Wearing only a pair of black pants and the stereo headphones, he went to his bedroom and shot himself with his father's pistol. His family filed a wrongful-death lawsuit against Osbourne and CBS Records, seeking an undisclosed amount for damages.

In 1986, Michael Waller, 16, of Ben Hill County, Georgia, was found dead in his van, the victim of a self-inflicted gunshot. *Blizzard of Ozz* was found in the van's cassette deck. In 1988, Walter Kulkusky, 16, of Edison, New Jersey, killed himself behind his high school early one morning. In the pocket of his denim jacket was a cassette of Osbourne's concert album *Tribute,* which also contains "Suicide Solution."

Headlines like SUICIDE SOLUTION: COUPLE LINKS SON'S DEATH, ROCK MUSIC, ***were typical of the media's angle.***

The newspaper coverage of these tragedies focused almost exclusively on the music. Headlines like SUICIDE SOLUTION: COUPLE LINKS SON'S DEATH, ROCK MUSIC, from Georgia's *Albany Herald,* were typical of the media's angle. What was hardly ever reported was that the victims—like Ray Belknap and Jay Vance—had far sadder, less exotic reasons for taking their lives. McCollum, it was conceded by his family, suffered from psychological problems and a history of alcohol abuse. The lawyer for the Waller family admits that Michael was a disturbed kid as well as a drug user. And though Walter Kulkusky, a poor student who often seemed depressed to his friends, apparently did not abuse drugs, he left another indication of his motives in his denim jacket: a note about the loss of a girlfriend.

None of these cases has come to trial. In the McCollum case, lawyers for CBS argued in a pretrial hearing that literature like Hamlet's "To be or not to be" soliloquy and Arthur Miller's *Death of a Salesman* deals with the theme of suicide. The California District Court of Appeal ruled that Osbourne's music is protected by the First Amendment and dismissed the suit. The heavy-metal connection in the Kulkusky case was the product of an overheated prosecutor; not even the victim's parents agreed with him. And in Georgia, the attorney for the Waller family has recently amended the complaint to center on so-called "masked lyrics" that allegedly say, "Shoot, shoot, shoot." This case is pending. —M.B.

Editor's note: After a month-long trial in 1990, Judge Jerry Carr Whitehead ruled that Judas Priest bore no legal responsibility for the suicides of Jay Vance and Ray Belknap. The judge also ruled that there was "no scientific evidence presented to suggest that subliminal messages could lead someone to attempt suicide." (Kim Neely, "Judas Priest Gets Off the Hook," *Rolling Stone,* October 4, 1990, p. 39.)

Questions for Discussion

1. In your opinion, do record producers place subliminal messages in recorded music?
2. What would be the effect of such messages?

Suggested Readings

More On What Allan Bloom Would Call the Antisocial Aspects of Rock Music

Marsh, Dave, "Rocking Racism," *Playboy* Vol. 37, March, 1990, p. 74 (6). Heavy metal bands flaunt racist lyrics, stations discriminate against black groups.

Toufexis, Anastasia, "Our Violent Kids: A Rise in Brutal Crimes by the Young Shakes the Soul of Society," *Time* June 12, 1989, p. 53 (6). And rock music has something to do with it.

Of Course, Not Everyone Thinks Rock and Radio Are All Bad. Here's a Few Readings from Frank Zappa's Side: The Prosocial Effects

Cosgrove, Stuart, "The Hum of Humanism," *New Statesman and Society* Vol. 3, April 13, 1990, p. 41 (2). Social causes in rock music. Column.

Pareles, Jon, "Righteous Rock: Issues You Can Dance To," *The New York Times* Vol. 139, August 26, 1990, Section 2 p. H23 (N and L) Col. 1; 31 Col. in.

"Radio Stimulates Imagination; Television Enhances Recall," *Society* Vol. 25, September–October 1988, p. 3 (1).

Sinclair, A. J., D. Symington and S. N. Winn, "Eco Rock: Environmentalism in Music," *Alternatives* Vol. 16, March–April 1990, p. 22 (2).

The Subtext of Comments by Zappa and Bloom Has to Do with the Idea of the Censorship of Radio and Rock Music; Here's Some Readings On That Topic

"Get Thee Hence!", *The Nation* Vol. 250, March 26, 1990, p. 401 (1). Anti-Satanism, rock music, abortion and the Catholic Church. Editorial.

Goldberg, Michael, "At a Loss for Words: Record-Industry Acceptance of Stickering is Already Having a Chilling Effect," *Rolling Stone,* May 31, 1990, p. 19 (3). Parental-warning labels.

Koen, David, "Fear of Music," *Harper's Magazine* Vol. 281, August, 1990, p. 29 (1). Excerpt from "Who Wants to Stop the Music? We Talked to Some of Them."

"The Issue Is Fear," *Rolling Stone,* August 9, 1990, p. 24 (1). Editorial.

Neely, Kim, "Rockers Sound Off," *Rolling Stone,* August 9, 1990, p. 27 (2). Opinions on the censorship of 2 Live Crew.

"O'Connor Links Rock Music and the Devil," *National Catholic Reporter* Vol. 26, March 16, 1990, p. 3 (1). Cardinal John O'Connor.

Poland, Larry W., "What to Do About Shock Radio: Even One Well-Placed Letter Can Hush Up Foul-mouthed Announcers," *Christian Herald* Vol. 111, April 1988, p. 20 (5).

"Rock Music—Worse Than Pornography?", *USA Today* Vol. 118, September, 1989, p. 11 (1). Random survey in Mecklenburg County, North Carolina.

More On the Judas Priest/Teen Suicide Case

Henry, William A. III, "Did the Music Say 'Do It'? A Trial Tests Whether a Rock LP Subliminally Prompted Suicides," *Time* Vol. 136, July 30, 1990, p. 65 (1).

"It's Only Rock 'n' Roll but It Kills People," *The Economist* Vol. 314, February 17, 1990, p. 28 (1). American Survey.

Kuipers, Dean, "Executioner's Song," *Spin Magazine* Vol. 6, November 1990, p. 63 (6). The Judas Priest trial from the perspective of a heavy metal fan. The language is harsh, but the attitude is youth—nonacademic, headbanger.

Neely, Kim, "Judas Priest Gets Off the Hook," *Rolling Stone,* October 4, 1990, p. 39 (1). The judge found no evidence that subliminal messages can lead anyone to commit suicide.

Quindlen, Anna, "Suicide Solution," *The New York Times,* Sept. 20, 1990, p. A19 (N), p. A21 (L), Col. 5., 18 Col. in. Rock and roll music is becoming a scapegoat in parents' search for someone to blame for teenage suicide. Column.

Rohde, Stephen F., "The Sounds of Lawsuits: Rock Lyrics on Trial," *USA Today* Vol. 118, July, 1989, p. 86 (2).

On Radio Formats and How They're Changing

Barone, Michael, and Joannie Schrof, "The Changing Voice of Talk Radio," *U.S. News and World Report* Vol. 108, January 15, 1990, p. 51 (3).

Norman, Geoffrey and Steve Wulf, "Yak Attack," *Sports Illustrated* Vol. 73, October 8, 1990, p. 108 (11). Radio airwaves are rolling with rage, obsession and absurdity: Call-in sports programs.

Murr, Andrew and John Schwartz, "Unusual, but Not Crazy: All-anything AM Radio Tries to Win Back Listeners," *Newsweek* Vol. 112, December 19, 1988, p. 47 (1).

"O.K., Caller, You're On the Air," *U.S. News and World Report* Vol. 106, February 29, 1989, p. 12 (1). Radio talk-show hosts mobilize opinion against a proposed Congressional pay raise.

Zoglin, Richard, "Bugle Boys of the Airwaves: Talk-Show Hosts Stir Up a Storm of Political Action," *Time* Vol. 133, May 15, 1989, p. 88 (2). Radio hosts lead protests against Cat Stevens, Exxon and Congressional pay raises.

On the International Influence of Rock Music

Miller, Jim, "Pop Takes a Global Spin: Exotic Sounds Play from Bulgaria to Zaire," *Newsweek,* June 13, 1988, p. 72 (3). Includes related article.

Thomas, Marlo, "Soviet and American Kids: They Share a Common Language—Rock 'n' Roll," *TV Guide* Vol. 36, December 10, 1988, p. 9 (2).

One Last Issue, Brought to You as a Public Service: Does Rock Music Make You Deaf? or, "What's That You Say? I've Had This Ringing in My Ears Since 1957"

Cardinal, David, "Cover Your Ears," *Men's Health,* August, 1990, p. 40 (3). Includes related information.

Jaret, Peter, "The Rock & Roll Syndrome: From Elvis to the Stones to Def Leppard, the Music Has Taken Its Toll on Your Hearing. But You Don't Have to Lose What's Left," *In Health* Vol. 4, July–August 1990, p. 50 (8). Includes articles on hearing aids, hearing hazards, and hearing testing.

Television

10

Television is our most pervasive and powerful medium, and it is also the one that is most rapidly changing. Sometimes it doesn't *seem* to be changing all that much—as we go to press in 1992 the most-watched programs seem eerily familiar:

1. 60 minutes
2. Roseanne
3. Murphy Brown
4. Cheers
5. Designing Women
6. Full House
7. Coach
8. Major Dad
9. Murder, She Wrote
10. Home Improvement

By the time you read this the list of the top 10 programs might have changed considerably, but chances are they will be the same type of programs—mostly sitcoms about families and synthetic families of friends and coworkers, with a touch of drama and news thrown in. The highest rated program so far this year has been the Superbowl. In fact, a list of the 10 top-rated shows of all time will include six Superbowls.

If programming hasn't changed much, the *amount* of programming and its means of delivery to the home has changed dramatically. Whereas once "television" meant the big three broadcast networks—ABC, CBS, and NBC—today it also means a wealth of independent stations, station groups, cable systems and cable networks. The networks once garnered more than 90% of the audience; as we go to press, that figure is barely 60%. We'll deal with cable in the next chapter.

Television viewing is our most time-consuming activity, next to sleeping. The average home has two television sets which are on for more than seven hours a day. The average person watches more than four hours a day. It is difficult to capsulize the importance and meaning of this kind of cultural attention, but that is exactly what the first reading in this chapter, William A. Henry's "The Meaning of Television," attempts to do.

The second reading, Mark McGinnis's "Television is Numbing Creativity and Sensitivity," points out one of the many criticisms of television. The third reading, Adam Snyder's "Adventures in Neilsenland," is an industry perspective on the trouble that today's TV organizations are having measuring their audience.

The Meaning of Television

William A. Henry III

Currently a senior writer at Time *magazine, William A. Henry III won the 1980 Pulitzer Prize in criticism for his writing about television. He was the youngest person ever to win that prize; the unique perspective that separated him from older critics was that Henry was a member of the television generation. He grew up with television, and his observations culminated in this essay for* Life *magazine.*

What follows is his explanation of why he believes television is the discovery that has made the greatest difference in human history.

Reading Difficulty Level: 5. Whereas his prose is as clear and commanding as a top-of-the-line high-definition TV image, there's a lot of ideas packed into this short essay.

A vision of the ascent of man from ape to couch potato.

What discovery has made the greatest difference in human history? Fire is one traditional answer. Some say the wheel. Others, the alphabet and its happiest logical consequence, the printing press. To suggest that a mostly maligned newcomer—the Boob Tube, the Idiot Box, the Electronic Babysitter, the Plug-in Drug—might belong in that hallowed archaeological company could seem trivial, or even depressing: a vision of the ascent of man from ape to couch potato. Yet in the half century since NBC undertook the first regular U.S. television broadcasts—from the 1939 World's Fair—TV has spread its influence among humankind far faster than those earlier landmarks of insight. It also has had as deep an everyday impact in shaping how we live, interact, govern ourselves and comprehend our world.

Television is now the hearth around which we meet, the cool fire of domestic evenings and the tribal gathering place for moments of ritual celebration or mourning. TV transports us around the world faster than any two-wheeled chariot, or jet for that matter, and it is the invaluable link that gives earthbound meaning to the flotilla of satellites up in the skies. TV has replaced print as the primary means of communication and in the process restored the spoken word to preeminence over the written one.

Television has come to dominate our politics, to set our national agenda for debate and action. It brings us together for moments of solemnity (an assassination, a *Challenger* disaster) and for moments of joy (a baby rescued from peril, a release of hostages, a champagne shower in a winning team's locker room). It makes electronic onlookers feel that they are part of every happening, and in a way they are: Their presence, million upon unseen million, gives events a sense of pomp and circumstance.

Television has speeded up awareness of everything, compressing into months, weeks or even days the arc of publicity from unknown to overexposed. It gives us our myths, our stories, the very means by which a nation defines itself. In its range of series and stars it offers us a choice of dozens of surrogate homes and workplaces, hundreds of surrogate friends; in many cases they are more real to us, or at any rate more convivial, than the people we know. In a nation sprawled across six time zones, 12 or more climates and several dozen regional economies, a nation of persistent localism in language and attitude, custom and cuisine, television has made us truly national, giving people from Maine to Monterey the same experiences at night, the same context for conversation around the water cooler in the morning.

Television brought the civil rights struggle into American living rooms, and also, in succession, the Vietnam war, the sexual revolution and women's movement and the upheavals of the Middle East. More than just a mirror, it turned out to be a maker of social change, because it turned other people's battles into personal contests in which the viewer felt an important emotional stake. Through the camera and its capacity to reach beyond reason to the most basic emotions, TV has made people vastly more compassionate toward trouble far from home, whether it is an earthquake in Armenia or dioxin poisoning in Times Beach or a couple of whales trapped in an Alaskan ice pack. During almost every disaster story, TV provides instant heroes: the brave TWA stewardess who saves the lives of hijacked passengers, the proud old man who will not be driven out of his home by the threat of a volcano. And yet, at the same time, television has fostered a permanent cynicism by stripping away the symbolic and ceremonial aura surrounding leaders of church and state to reveal what the TV generation holds to be most human about human beings, their flaws.

More than just a mirror, television turned out to be a maker of social change.

TV has given the world the concept of a "celebrity," someone well known for being well known.

The publicity culture, which TV has fueled if not precisely created, has given the world the curious concept of a "celebrity," only half-jokingly defined as someone well known for being well known. Television has equated in the popular mind the celebrity status of a statesman or artist with that of a talk show host or spokesmodel. It has turned the business of choosing a leader for the nation, and not incidentally the free world, into a process of selecting the most confidence-inspiring video personality, and thereupon entrusting him or her with a nuclear arsenal.

Once in office, candidates look to television to sell their messages by arousing public sympathy and concern about particular issues. The result is in a way more democratic, but at the cost of courage, leadership, long-range thinking and that sine qua non of statesmanship, the willingness to be unpopular now in favor of the greater good later on. Television has made American politics, in effect, a permanent campaign. Yet, ironically, while the populace is far more involved in the process, people vote less and less. Television may emphasize the "pretty factor" in politics, may reward good looks and glibness more than wisdom. Yet almost no one, maybe not even Teflon-coated Ronald Reagan, has been able to survive the persistent scrutiny of the camera with a larger-than-life aura intact. Unable to mythologize leaders who are visible warts and all, much of the televiewing public has opted out of participation. The late Marshall McLuhan, Canada's guru of the video generation, may have been right that television would create a global village. But many people choose not to come to its town meetings.

Television has made American politics, in effect, a permanent campaign.

Television's intrusive, transportable cameras and relentless demands for access have stripped away the privacy of public people and, perhaps, the respect for privacy in a nation that has come to think of itself as being foremost an audience. The medium has imposed on all the famous, kings and courtesans alike, the expectation that they will be interviewed, and will in the process reveal their innermost selves to a viewership seemingly addicted to confessional insight. It has also largely taken from them, leaders even more than the entertainers, the opportunity for the discreet white lie. When George Bush claimed, after becoming Ronald Reagan's 1980 running mate, that he had never accused his erstwhile rival of "voodoo economics," videotapes of those very words came back to haunt Bush. Thus what began as a graceful gesture of cooperation turned into a damaging display of deceit.

TV has come to seem a perfect reflection of our national character, quintessentially American, part of every citizen's birthright. Whereas a generation ago skeptics ritually wisecracked about welfare families owning color sets, hardly anyone raised eyebrows when *The New York Times* reported a few months ago about some homeless people passing the time in Manhattan's Port Authority Bus Terminal by watching their own miniportable.

This phenomenon of rapt viewership is truly global. TV is becoming central to political, cultural and economic life in the Soviet Union; it, too, has been liberated by Mikhail Gorbachev's glasnost, and his style so suits the medium that some Kremlin-watchers believe he could not have achieved and sustained power without television. China is moving more slowly down the same path. And elsewhere in the pauperized third world, TV is often as favored a tool of politicians as it is in the industrial democracies. Some of the programs are locally made. Many are American ambassadors to the world. The VCR is as hot a consumer item in the Islamic Mideast as it is in Beverly Hills, and so are cassettes of Hollywood movies and TV shows. *I Love Lucy* has reached screens in more than a hundred countries.

The best measure of how much television has changed the world is that when people speak of politics or pageantry, of calamity or combat, they do not mean the thing itself so much as the video experience of it. The electronic image has become the reality, not only for audiences but also for participants. Any activity that can attract camera crews is soon reshaped to serve foremost as a media event, from the Olympics and national political conventions to county fairs and neighborhood protests. Indeed, if something does not get reported on television, it is deemed not to have happened, not only by the intended audience but by the organizers themselves. And video spectatorship often seems preferable to being there. At live sports the eye yearns for instant replay; at the theater, for a close-up; at a parade, for the panoramic overhead view. From the cradle onward, television teaches us how to see and, upon seeing, how to feel. It teaches us to expect to receive events already filtered—selected, analyzed, visually displayed to maximum advantage—and then to treat as raw reality what is in fact a finished product, one in which the thinking has already been done for us.

If something does not get reported on television, it is deemed not to have happened.

We tend to talk about television as though it has already been there, as though it provides the same experience for everyone, as though it were a single, living organism. In conversation almost everyone speaks of "television" doing this or that, intending this or that. A moment's thought is enough to recall that "television" is made up of a score and more broadcast and cable networks, some 1,300 local stations and countless production companies. The medium is collaborative; there are few if any *auteurs*. Yet TV is so potent a presence that it seems to have a mind, and personality, of its own.

The best measure of how much television has changed the world is that when people speak of politics or pageantry, of calamity or combat, they do not mean the thing itself so much as the video experience of it.

If TV has changed over time, we take it mostly as a reflection of how we who view it have changed, and

If television were a personality, it would qualify as almost everyone's closest friend.

in a sense that is right. While TV may not sense our moods and respond to them like a friend or family member, the people who administer, advertise on and program television all devote themselves to research that tracks each zig and zag of national mood. Their goal is to keep television exactly in step with mainstream taste, so that in most homes it will resemble a family member or a congenial neighbor. If television really were a personality, it would qualify as almost everyone's closest friend.

The average American watches TV about four hours a day; the average household has the set on for seven hours in all. Even people who say they "don't watch much television" turn out to be forgetting to count news, or sports, or Mister Rogers with the toddlers, or old movies, or vintage reruns, or something or other that they somehow consider to be not mere TV. Just why do people in all walks of life feel such guilt about watching TV, or assert such superiority in pretending that they do not? Because, despite their affection for TV, they think watching it is too passive, an inert substitute for exercise or reading or conversation—or study.

In both its programs and its commercials, TV has proved the most effective selling mechanism for envy and materialism that mankind has yet known.

The reality is that TV can provide plenty of learning, and not merely on *Sunrise Semester.* For every schoolchild whose reading problems might be blamed on an excess of TV, there is probably another who learned the alphabet from *Sesame Street* and began see-and-say reading with the on-screen words of commercials. High school students may have trouble spotting South America on a map, but through TV they have grapsed some basic truths about the planet. Wherever they live, they were shaken last summer by images of beaches closed to bathers because the sands were strewn with toxic hospital waste. Among television's diehard critics, the print journalists, it is an open secret that the most important source of news flow during any election night or political crisis is the television set, around which editors and reporters cluster to stay abreast and to test their news judgment. And the same scholars and opinion-makers who profess to view television with disdain are nearly always avid to appear on it—fully expecting that their friends will see them. Most of the nation's elite seem to live by at least the latter half of Gore Vidal's reported dictum: "There are two things in life one must never refuse. One is sex, and the other is television."

In both its programs and its commercials, TV has proved the most effective selling mechanism for envy and materialism that mankind has yet known. The Bulova watch company paid $9 for the first commercial ever aired, a 10-second spot on July 1, 1941, that reached about 4,000 homes. Spots on this January's Super Bowl telecast, watched in 39.3 million homes, cost as much as $1.35 million per minute. Why? Some corporations choose TV to burnish their images: IBM and Xerox do not do all that much business with the average household, but sponsoring highbrow, or even middlebrow, programs enhances general goodwill and thus helps in everything from negotiating deals to lobbying Congress.

Most companies, however, advertise on TV because it measurably boosts sales. With a shrewd set of commercials, an unknown product can become famous overnight. The bulk of the commercials, as former NBC News president Reuven Frank once ruefully noted, are for items that can be bought with pocket change. That is because many other articles are bought infrequently enough, or with enough other research involved, that TV commercials cannot be cost effective. But TV itself, especially in prime time, is in a sense one continuous advertisement for the whole notion of consumption. While the earliest sitcoms—*The Honeymooners, The Goldbergs, The Life of Riley*—sometimes depicted modest blue-collar life, the action soon shifted to sylvan suburbs, where the furniture was spotless, the lawn manicured and the car new. On *Leave It to Beaver*, mom June Cleaver wore pearls in the kitchen. On *Family Affair*, the household budget provided for a British butler, on *Bachelor Father* for a Japanese manservant. *The Brady Bunch* settled for a plain old American housekeeper. Archie Bunker was determinedly working class on *All in the Family*, but even so, his living room looked cavernous. The current season's hit, *Roseanne*, is considered noteworthy at least partly because its blue-collar family admits to occasional money problems.

What impact does the relentless display of possessions have on the young? Or, for that matter, on their elders? Theories abound, blaming TV's fascination with the lifestyles of the rich and famous for everything from urban burglary and crack dealing to insider trading and larceny by computer. Does commercial TV's emphasis on get-it-all-now have anything to do with the U.S. savings rate, the lowest among the leading industrial powers? Or is the urge to spend the very impulse that propels people into working and thus keeps the economy afloat? Both are probably true. Whatever the moral value of our consumer culture, TV has made its plethora of pleasures visible, and keenly desirable, to all social classes. The cause and effect is hard to prove, but the combination of TV and the post-World War II economic boom seems to have created ever-expanding expectations that the next generation may find it equally hard either to relinquish or to fulfill.

What impact does the relentless display of possessions have on the young? Or, for that matter, on their elders?

One of TV's clearest contributions to greed, and perhaps its most disillusioning, has come in sports. Television and athletics has been such a successful marriage that it sometimes seems hard to remember there was a sporting world before the instant replay. There was, of course. But it was a lot smaller, and nostalgia tells us it was a world more motivated by simple love of the

One of TV's clearest contributions to greed has come in sports.

game. Then came the contracts in the millions, and eventually billions, of dollars, turning team owners into tycoons and utility infielders into plutocrats. For a price, almost every sport proved willing to accommodate itself to the demands of the camera and the advertising schedule—adding time-outs, juggling schedules, even adjusting the rules. The whole nation of South Korea changed its clocks to daylight savings time for the Seoul Olympics, the better to provide the U.S. with prime-time events in exchange for NBC's $300 million.

The great civilizing effect of all literature is that it takes people's vision beyond the immediate, the clan and the tribe. Television simply does this more effectively.

Perhaps TV's deepest power is not the change it works on sports or commerce or any other branch of reality, but the way its innocuous-looking entertainment reaches deep into the national mind. TV has the ability to generate, or regenerate, national mythology. The great characters of television embody human truths as profound as the great characters in Molière or Ibsen, and for vastly bigger audiences. The viewership for even one modestly successful airing of a prime-time series would fill every theater on Broadway, eight performances a week, for a couple of years. These characters linger in memory because they epitomize what the nation feels about itself. They teach behavior and values. They enter the language. Say the name Falstaff, and some minority of the population will know that you mean a vainglorious coward; say Ralph Kramden, and everyone will know what you mean: The Mary Richards character created by Mary Tyler Moore summed up their own lives for a whole generation of thirty-something single women who could have any careers they wanted, but often at the expense of satisfaction at home. This is not new with television. The great civilizing effect of all literature is that it takes people's vision beyond the immediate, the clan and the tribe. It enables them to make the philosophical leap that Jean-Paul Sartre described as "seeing the other as another self." Television simply does this more effectively, more touchingly, than any kind of art that went before. Unlike the stage and movies, the episodic TV series does not end in catharsis. The characters come back week after week, evolving at the slow pace of ordinary life, exposing themselves more fully than most relatives or friends. Other literature provides occasional experiences. Television becomes an ongoing part of life and for some susceptible people is only barely distinguishable from real life itself.

The great characters of television embody human truths as profound as the great characters in Moliere or Ibsen, and for vastly bigger audiences.

It is hard to imagine a world without television, harder still to imagine what the world of the last half century would have been without those first flickering images from NBC and all that followed. We might have fewer terrorists, because there would be no worldwide pulpit for their propaganda. We might have a less violent society, because the typical child would not have been exposed to tens of thousands of actual and simulated violent crimes on news and entertainment by the time he or she reached adulthood. We might have a society in which people still felt respect for established institutions and their leaders, instead of one in which TV-bred skepticism had lowered the approval rating for Congress, business executives and even judges to between 20 and 40 percent. We might have a healthier society, one in which children played outside instead of watching the box hour after hour, one in which meals cooked from scratch at home had not been outdistanced by snacks and fast food loaded with sugar, salt and fat, all enticingly advertised. We might have a more restrained, less libertine world, one in which virginity and marriage were still revered while premarital pregnancy and divorce were still treated with distaste rather than sympathy. All of these effects have been attributed, sometimes convincingly, to TV. But we effects have been attributed, sometimes convincingly, to TV. But we might also have a less alert world, one in which citizens were not so widely informed about the economy, about medical matters, about foreign military adventures that run the risk of war. We might have a less concerned world, one in which starvation in Ethiopia could never inspire Live Aid, one in which the homeless of Manhattan or Chicago might remain unseen by the rest of the nation. We might have a lonelier, more isolated world in which the old lived without much entertainment, without much company, without the sense of involvement in life that can be conferred even by watching Donahue.

Only one thing can be said for certain. Whatever world we would have, it would be different in many and unimaginable ways from this one. Like fire and the wheel and the alphabet, television has changed the world that humans live in. And more, perhaps, than any invention or discovery before it, television has changed the definition of what it means to be human. ♦

More than any invention before it, television has changed the definition of what it means to be human.

Questions for Discussion

1. Do you agree that television has changed the definition of what it means to be human?
2. Having read Henry's essay, do you feel that television has been a detriment or a benefit to humankind?

Television Is Numbing Creativity and Sensitivity

Mark W. McGinnis

Television has been blamed for a wide variety of social ills. Research suggests that it helps make us biased and violent, both of which we will deal with in later chapters. In this reading Mark McGinnis, a professor of art at Northern State University in Aberdeen, South Dakota, explains why he believes television also deadens the visual imagination.

Reading Difficulty Level: 4.

Everything we see in our ordinary life undergoes to a greater or lesser degree the deformation given by acquired habits, and this is perhaps especially so in an age like ours, when cinema, advertising, and magazines push at us a daily flood of images which, already made, are to our vision what prejudice is to intelligence. The necessary effort of detaching oneself from all that calls for a kind of courage, and this courage is indispensable to the artist who must see all things as if he were seeing them for the first time. All his life he must see as he did when he was a child.

—Henri Matisse, 1953

The "FLOOD OF IMAGES" Matisse referred to in the early 50's has become an unending torrent. To say that the vision of the young is prejudiced by this constant bombardment is an understatement; "numbed," "desensitized," maybe even "deadened" are more appropriate terms.

To my horror, "gifted" children produced stiff drawings of Garfield cats, Snoopy dogs, and Transformer cars.

An incident in my own teaching drove this point home with frightening clarity. Several years ago I served as a guest mentor for a group of gifted 8- to 10-year-olds who had expressed a special interest in the visual arts. I started out by showing them examples of what artists and designers are producing now, including paintings, sculptures, crafts, architecture, advertising, and new technologies such as computer graphics. Then I distributed art materials and asked the children to create pictures of what they would like to make if they were to become artists or designers. To my horror, these "gifted" children produced stiff drawings of Garfield cats, Snoopy dogs, and Transformer cars; many of them could not produce any images at all. It was as if their visual imagination had been extinguished.

I'm sure this episode could be interpreted in many ways, but for me it partially explained the visual lethargy and lack of imagination of

Reprinted by permission of the author. Originally published as "An Overdose of Television Has Deadened the Visual Imagination of Our Students," *Chronicle of Higher Education*, February 20, 1991.

many students in my college classes. Since the late 1970's I have felt the need to structure more tightly the art projects I assign to students, to give them more direction and guidance, especially in subject matter. If I attempted to structure only a project's technique and leave the subject matter open, many students would flounder or—worse yet—produce facile variations on commercial imagery, such as the death's-heads, muscle men, and huge-breasted women in heavy-metal motifs.

Early in my teaching career, I assumed that students would produce works that drew upon their own unique backgrounds and imaginations, and generally they did. They and I took individualism for granted as part of the art student's personality. But students' individualism seems to have diminished over the years, replaced by a conformity born of having had the same visual experiences: Whether they come from cities, small towns, suburbia, or farms, students have seen—and embraced—the same television programs, films, videos, and fashions.

Today's college art students clearly are creatures of the mass media, especially television. In the last sentence of the Matisse quotation he states that we must see as we did when we were children; but what are children seeing? Researchers tell us that by the age of 18, most young people have spent more time watching television than doing anything else, except sleeping. And in this age of the video-cassette recorder, time spent watching television may even exceed sleeping time for some. The primary focus of research on television viewing has been on the effects of television violence, stereotyping, and commercialization, but art educators need to consider how the torrent of television images is affecting students' visual sensitivity and imagination. The challenge for art educators is to develop and refine the knowledge and approaches needed to foster these qualities in an age when television is deadening them.

Research has established that television watching is a one-way experience: The viewer takes in sensory material and gives back little or none. It is an undemanding, passive activity in which viewers have no opportunity to interact or to create fantasies, since television supplies them ready-made, complete with auditory and visual effects. Watching replaces doing, thinking, touching. Matisse encourages us to return to the visual experiences of our childhood for aesthetic stimulation and inspiration, but children today are being visually programmed by television rather than experiencing the sensory world around them. For them the world is what television tells them it is. Individual experience is replaced by mass experience. The common experience—at best mediocre, at worst detrimental—enters the child's memory as real.

Television watching is a one-way experience: The viewer takes in sensory material and gives back little or none.

Research also shows that heavy television watching correlates with low levels of imaginative play; certainly my art students have shown an increasing lack of imagination over the years. They seem to have the will to create but often lack the experiences and knowledge with which to produce imaginative work. For example, when I ask students to apply techniques and principles to a subject of their choice, students often choose subjects like cars, demons, rock stars, or unicorns—subjects they have seen treated commercially. But what should we expect after they've watched television for at least 16 years? Can we expect them to be excited by Matisse's joyous paper cut-outs after years of watching MTV?

Television numbs not only visual imagination but also deadens another faculty critical for creative reactions—emotions.

Television numbs not only visual imagination but also deadens another faculty critical for creative reactions—emotions. Violence on television has been widely researched. The fear in the 1970's and 1980's that detective and cowboy shows would incite children to aggressive behavior now pales in the 1990's, when cable-television and video movies are bringing sadistic and gruesome imagery and behavior into living rooms across the country. One videotape popular with teen-agers, called "Faces of Death," shows seemingly endless scenes of *actual* deaths, mutilations, autopsies, executions, and blood rituals. This bombardment of video violence helps to densensitize us to the violence that permeates our country and the world. The use of poison gas in Iraq, the death squads in El Salvador, the murder across town, the child abuse next door are all accepted as part of everyday life rather than as outrages against humanity.

Most college freshmen react passively to Picasso's "Guernica" or Goya's "Disasters of War" series. Can students perceive the horrors of war in Picasso's abstractions? Are Goya's depictions of atrocities merely grotesque and perversely humorous after all students have seen on video and movie screens? I fear they can't see the horror. I fear that the snickers I hear when showing Goya's work are not nervous laughter.

Another danger that television and film present to the potential artist is that they can limit the attention span. Images flash before the eyes at a phenomenal rate—a trend seen in music videos, film, and advertising. Young people become habituated to this manic, mesmerizing barrage. As a result, many of them find it hard to concentrate on a static image. And when I ask students to think about what they are seeing they become confused. Their expressions say, "Think about what?" Looking and thinking no longer seem related, since looking so often is accompanied by oral explanations or an onslaught of images that drowns out thought. Looking has become a passive experience in which information is given, instead of being an active experience that requires thought.

How will this desensitization affect the artists and designers who grow up with it? We may be seeing part of the results now. My generation, born in the early 1950's, was the first to grow up with television. Although the television we watched was radically different from that viewed by today's college students, we nevertheless were influenced by it through the common visual experiences it provided. Certainly many artists in their 30's and 40's are creative and imaginative, but too many are producing variations on what they have already *seen*, not what they have *thought* about. I do not claim that we can blame television entirely for a decline in imaginative art over the past two decades, but I do claim that television has contributed to it.

Despite the pervasiveness of television in American life, I hold some hope for art students. Though visually desensitized, few are completely deadened. Most show an interest and will to learn in spite of their visually "prejudiced" past. Art educators need to give students the opportunity that Matisse was talking about: to see with the eyes of a child. We must teach students how to actively look and think about what they see. This can be done best through basic design and drawing classes in which a student's eyes, hands, and mind must work together.

For example, drawing every individual needle on a pine branch can help students develop their ability to observe and explore the visual world as well as their capacity to see line, space, shape, texture, color, and mass not simply as artistic concepts but as elements of life itself. And by working with color schemes and color properties, students can learn not only to see color but also to experience the emotions it communicates.

A clever post-modern artist would find it easy to dismiss my suggestions as naïve. But the problem is too serious and the artistic price too great to disregard students' needs that casually. Faculty members should begin now to develop the knowledge and approaches needed to resensitize students to the visual world around them. We must ask students to dissect, analyze, and criticize their mass culture. Using the tools of design analysis, students can take apart an advertisement, video, or film, piece by piece. They can explore the underlying concepts of these productions, what makes them work, what makes them good or bad. In this way, critical observation can give students power over what in the past has manipulated them.

It will take courage for students and teachers to overcome the desensitization caused by our electronic culture, but the goal—fostering artists capable of producing the art of sensitive human beings—is worth it. ♦

Many artists in their 30's and 40's are creative and imaginative, but too many are producing variations on what they have already* seen, *not what they have* thought *about.

Questions for Discussion

1. Do you agree or disagree that television deadens visual imagination?
2. Do you feel that your own creativity has been harmed by television viewing?

Trouble in Nielsenland

Adam Snyder

Whereas the first two readings in this chapter look at television from the audience's point of view, this last article looks at television looking at its audience, in the form of ratings. For the last few years, with the growth of independent stations, groups, cable systems, VCRs and remote controls, there has been a dramatic shift in the patterns of television viewing. Whereas the three broadcast networks once commanded 90% of the viewing audience, their share is down to just over 60%. As the networks and the newer program sources scramble for their share of advertising revenue, the ratings services have come under ever-increasing scrutiny. As Adam Snyder, a writer specializing in media concerns, explains in the next reading, the obsession with ratings affects the audience as much as the industry.

Reading Difficulty Level: 5. Read purely for entertainment it would be even easier, but you'll be expected to remember some of the details of how ratings work.

Are Nielsen ratings accurate?

The Push-Button Players Present "An Evening at Home," With Tom, Jane, Bobby, Grandpa and, Yes—The People Meter!

After dinner, Jane walks into the living room while her husband, Tom, loads the dishwasher. She turns on the TV and a red light on the "people meter"—a small box on top of the set—lights up. She presses her assigned button on the remote control until a green light flashes. She presses the "OK" button and the flashing stops. Three minutes into "Cheers," Tom enters the living room. He begins staring at the TV, so Jane quickly hands him the remote so he can punch in his own code, then hit the "OK" button to signify everything has registered correctly.

Tom offers to make coffee, then presses his buttons to tell the meter he isn't watching. Now son Bobby

From *Home: The Newsday Magazine*, April 21, 1991. Reprinted by permission.

bounds downstairs. Jane hears the basketball game on his TV upstairs, and asks if he remembered to log off his meter. He runs back up to log off, then returns and presses his buttons on the living-room meter. At the next commercial, Jane switches to a movie on Ch. 11, then a few minutes later to CNN. When Tom returns with the coffee, he sees three red lights blinking on the meter because Jane switched channels. He presses four buttons and the blinking stops.

The doorbell rings. It's Jane's father dropping off a gift. He begins watching, too, so Jane presses the "visitor" button on the remote, then punches in her father's age and gender.

If you believe that scenario, you'll believe anything, some people say—some powerful, influential people at America's three major networks.

But if you believe the A. C. Nielsen Co.—which is supposed to be the No. 1 authority on such things—that's precisely the kind of TV-watching routine followed by its 4,000 "Nielsen families"—those randomly selected button-pushing folk who remain publicly anonymous while providing the raw data that Nielsen transforms into this country's TV ratings.

If you listen to Nielsen's strongest critics—including all three networks, some TV programers and independent researchers—no human being could possibly watch TV this way. It's just not reasonable, they say, to expect people to punch two buttons on a tiny remote control every time they turn on the TV or change a channel or get up to grab some ice cream from the freezer.

As a result, there are complaints about the accuracy of Nielsen's figures. "There's really no telling how closely Nielsen's numbers correspond to reality," says J. Ronald Milavaky, an communications-science professor at the University of Connecticut. He is a former NBC researcher who spent several months analyzing Nielsen's procedures.

Still, Nielsen is no stranger to TV measurement, having dominated the ratings scene ever since Arthur Charles Nielsen began tracking radio listening in 1936. In 1950, as soon as network programming began, Nielsen issued the nation's first TV ratings. For the next 40 years, its word was gospel. Nielsen became a part of our language—like Xerox and Kleenex.

As soon as network programing began, Nielsen issued the nation's first TV ratings.

Today, when "Cheers" and "60 Minutes" are running neck and neck in popularity, everyone knows that Nielsen is the one keeping the score. Once a week, newspapers across America deliver that score in detail. In fact, not a day goes by when "the Nielsens" aren't mentioned in one way or another in the press. This continuous publicity helped turn the ratings into cash. In 1984 Nielsen looked like such a juicy plum that the business-information giant, Dun & Bradstreet, proceeded to gobble it up for $1.3 billion.

For years, Nielsen's clients—every top cable and broadcast channel and advertising agency—seemed perfectly satisfied with Nielsen's virtual monopoly.

Each year advertisers use the Nielsen ratings to place 50 million commercials at a total cost of more than $21 billion—more than the gross national product of Kuwait before the Iraqis invaded.

But the Nielsens influence far more than the direction of the nation's advertising dollars. They help determine the stock prices and prosperity of the nation's giant media conglomerates. They dramatically affect the fortunes of the major Hollywood studios (which make the shows that live or die by them), to say nothing of the 200 million Americans who can watch only shows the ratings allow to survive.

For years, Nielsen's clients—every top cable and broadcast channel and advertising agency—seemed perfectly satisfied with Nielsen's virtual monopoly. After all, the TV business wasn't all that complicated in its early decades.

It seems hard to believe now, but as recently as 1979 the average American home received fewer than seven channels and the big networks—ABC, CBS and NBC—accounted for more than 90 percent of all viewing. But then cable TV came along and jumped the average number of channels to 35. Today, Nielsen says the percentage of viewers watching the three networks has plummeted below 40 percent.

So now the Manhattan-based Nielsen ratings service not only has many more channels to measure, but is in the awkward position of delivering bad news to its biggest customers, the networks. And they must decide how to satisfy many new clients as well, all with different self-interests to protect.

Channels such as MTV want to make sure teenagers are pushing the right buttons. Nickelodeon is worried about children who can't even read Nielsen's meter instructions. Sports programers want Nielsen to count viewers in bars and restaurants. And the networks—oh, the networks!—are really up in arms. They want to bring their slide to a screeching halt, and they blame Nielsen for some of that slide.

Like many of us, Nielsen's clients have begun to wonder how accurately 4,000 families can portray the habits of the nation's viewers. They've formed committees with odd-sounding names—CONTAM, COLTAM, CONCAM—that keep firing off all kinds of recommendations telling Nielsen how to improve its system.

If you're like most of the TV-watching public, you look at Nielsen's weekly results and root for your favorite show, hoping it will rank high enough to avoid cancellation. But that's about the last consideration of Nielsen or its clients.

In fact, those who rely on ratings as their bread and butter disdainfully refer to the hot-program list you read every week as "the popularity contest." They not only aren't overly concerned about which TV programs are better; they refuse to worry about which ones make the public happy. They're so far inside their own groove of inquiry that they almost don't understand questions about how accurately Nielsen gauges the popularity of specific programs.

Here's what *does* interest them: *Who* is watching. Not how many, or how enjoyably. That's because (surprise) the TV business is motivated by dollars. And it's ratings that are the product. Don't believe it? "We sell ratings, not TV programs," says Nicholas Schiavone, vice president of media and marketing research at NBC. How unambiguous can you get?

As a result, Nielsen and its clients talk almost reverently about a TV program's demographics, or "demos." They want to know whether the viewers advertisers want most—women 18 to 49, for example—are watching. That's why the networks dwell on fancy research terms such as "cooperation rate" and "fatigue factor" instead of how the public really feels about "Twin Peaks" or "China Beach" getting axed for low Nielsens.

What's that? You've never been approached by Nielsen? No one you know has been contacted? Well, be patient. Nielsen is in 4,000 of 90 million households—which means you have a one in 22,500 chance of being selected.

But sample size is the least of the networks' worries. They have been Nielsen's most aggressive critics because they have the most to lose. The Big Three were incensed when, during the first quarter of 1990, Nielsen shocked the industry by reporting that almost 2 million households had suddenly stopped watching TV and that viewing by key segments was sharply off as well.

This was a dropoff unprecedented in TV history, and the networks bore the brunt of it. On the other hand, Nielsen had a few customers who were more satisfied than before—a lot of cable stations and the new Fox network were delighted. They had numbers that showed their viewing was steady or growing.

Not so the Big-Three networks. They had to refund from $150 million to $200 million in "make-goods"—giving advertisers free rides to make up for audience guarantees they hadn't met. The ratings were so low that all three networks adopted a controversial audience-measurement system in attempts to cut their losses.

Instead of setting advertising prices on the basis of current Nielsen ratings alone, as had been the practice for years, the network plan used a complex mathematical model involving eight years of viewing. But advertisers rejected the plan, and the networks eventually abandoned it.

"There's never been a satisfactory explanation for the dip," says Bill Rubens, former research head at NBC and now a consultant to all three networks.

"It just doesn't make sense that households using TV would dip during the cold months and then suddenly go back up again as the weather got warmer."

Advertisers want to know whether the viewers they want most—women 18 to 49, for example—are watching.

Nielsen is in 4,000 of 90 million households—which means you have a one in 22,500 chance of being selected.

Button-pushers all suffer from a "fatigue factor."

Nielsen has another answer. "We're not sociologists," says John A. Dimling, Nielsen's executive vice president for ratings. "All we can do is record a drop in TV-watching as it occurs. We spent countless hours and [lots] of dollars to find out what happened, and we concluded that viewing *really was* down."

Is this what the networks want to hear? Not for a minute. They're under big pressure to boost their ratings, and they've got two choices: improving programs or pressuring Nielsen to make changes. They say they're doing both.

How are they applying that pressure? They formed the Committee on Nationwide TV Audience Measurement (CONTAM, hereafter referred to as "the committee"). And, after spending more than $1 million and 18 months on a 600-page report, the committee's members are none too subtle or diplomatic about the committee's conclusions, either. Take this little blast from its chairman, NBC's Schiavone: "The system is not accurate. We have demonstrated that Nielsen has no apparent commitment to responsible methodological research."

It's impossible to get meaningful data from "grazers"—people who constantly flip from program to program.

Gulp. The committee's members say that Nielsen's flaws run deep—and it has made a list of the worst of them:

- The people meters go against human nature. No one can watch TV that way.
- There's no way children press the right buttons.
- Button-pushers all suffer from a "fatigue factor." After a few months of obediently pressing the right buttons, they get tired of the whole business and lie down on the job.
- Out-of-home crowds (such as viewers at restaurants and bars) aren't counted at all.
- Nielsen doesn't take into account the effect of all the new gadgets. VCRs are the big offenders here. Not only is a taped show recorded as a watched show ("Ha!" say the networks) but watching videotapes allows viewers to speed past commercials.
- And then there are split screens (which screen is being watched?) and miniature TVs (not recorded at all).
- Nielsen's incentives to viewers, a mere few hundred dollars a year, aren't enough to make most people push all those buttons.
- It's impossible to get meaningful data from "grazers"—people who constantly flip from program to program.

Dimling, for his part, says Nielsen is moving to improve its operations. He reports Nielsen is working on using former panel members to persuade new families to participate. It is also checking whether those who agree to become Nielsen families are different from those who refuse. The problem, says the committee, is that no one knows. Says Dimling: "It's very difficult to get direct evidence . . . You're trying to get information from people who have already refused to respond."

Nielsen is removing the word "voting" from its instructions—so families understand they're recording their viewing, not voting. The company is also providing material to teach children how to use people meters and is testing an electronic diary to measure out-of-home viewing.

Unlike the networks with their "High Noon" attitude, six-guns blazing, Nielsen is eerily peaceful toward all the Huns storming its gates. After all, the Huns are its customers—its biggest-paying customers. The Big Three pay about $6.5 million each to Nielsen every year. That's about half of what Nielsen makes from its ratings business.

No wonder Nielsen executives are relucant to talk to the press these days. They can't bash their best customers, can they?

But Dimling does say Nielsen is responding to all of the committee's complaints. "The networks sincerely felt there was something wrong and . . . they needed assurances that the system was working properly," he says diplomatically. "I really believe we've made substantial improvements."

The committee makes Nielsen's cooperation sound like part of the problem. "They were responsive and open to our CONTAM study, that's true," says Schiavone. "But that only made their methodological flaws more apparent."

"Why was it up to us to find these problems?" says the committee's Alan Wurtzel, who is ABC's research chief. "Why didn't Nielsen come up with the flaws in their system and propose solutions? If we hadn't spent a million dollars to identify that something was seriously wrong, would Nielsen have ever done it?"

The networks aren't the only ones grousing. Marshall Cohen, executive vice president of MTV, which also owns the children's channel, Nickelodeon, says Nielsen's methods are biased against programming aimed at young people. "You'll never see a Nielsen meter on a college campus," he says. "Nielsen has decided it isn't going to meter those kinds of living situations. But what are college kids always watching? MTV. We're forced to show our advertisers other kinds of research to prove that our numbers are higher than [our Nielsens]."

Why is it you never see a Nielsen meter on a college campus?

As a result of low ratings in the Nielsen surveys, the networks have talked about abandoning children's programs on Saturday mornings, Cohen says. "The big losers would be children . . ."

Since *who* is watching is critical, everybody complains about errors in age and gender categories. After all, advertisers buy ads based on how old or rich a program's viewers are. If important groups such as 18-to-35-year-olds don't push their people-meter buttons (as many in the TV industry suspect), their favorite programs can't get their fair share of ad revenues.

The networks and some independent researchers say Nielsen's research methods are so sloppy they make the weekly hot-program list questionable.

The networks and some independent researchers say Nielsen's research methods are so sloppy they make the weekly hot-program list questionable. "I wouldn't count on much of a relationship between what Nielsen reports and the true popularity of programs," says Milavsky, the communications-science professor. "The point is, nobody knows for sure."

Most people in the business think the programs Nielsen lists as far ahead of the pack—"60 Minutes," for example—are at least very popular. But that's as far as they'll go. It's the vast middle ground that doesn't get a fair shake, they say. "The TV show that Nielsen ranks as 50 is probably not No. 1," says Milavsky. "But as far as programs that are separated by only a percentage point or so, all bets are off."

Schiavone says: "It's not just a demographic problem. The publicity that occurs when programs like 'Fresh Prince' and 'Uncle Buck' are supposedly running neck and neck is a joke. Nielsen has no idea which program is actually being watched by more Americans."

Nielsen's overall strategy appears to be to lie low until it can unveil its new technology: the passive system.

So where do advertisers stand in all this? Mostly, they've stayed on the sidelines, and that's good ammunition for Nielsen, because advertisers are the ones who fork over their dollars based on Nielsen's numbers. And, if those numbers are wrong, they'd surely be squawking. Wouldn't they?

"One can't help feeling there is at least a little bit of a 'kill-the-messenger' syndrome going on here," says Bob Warrens, senior vice president of media research and resources at J. Walter Thompson. He is also chairman of the American Association of Advertising Agencies.

"I generally believe, and I think the advertising agency community generally believes, that the [people meter] is better than the old diary/household meter system," says Jayne Spittler, vice president for media research at the Leo Burnett agency. "We all sometimes lose sight of that."

But then advertisers, too, are looking out for their own interests. As network viewing falls, they pay less for network commercials. Schiavone is unhappy that ad folks don't speak up. But here's the way he says it, because now he's talking about *his* customers: "Passivity on the part of the ad community is in part a function of what is at stake for certain players."

Nielsen is cearly sensitive to all the criticism it has received, but its overall strategy appears to be to lie low until it can unveil its new technology: the passive system. This is the new wonder in Nielsen's back rooms, and many of its people believe it will miraculously make Nielsen, broadcasters and advertisers one big happy family again. The passive system will sit on the TV set just like the people meter, but with one big difference. A very big difference. By Nielsen's description, the passive system will actually be able to "see" who is in the room. The new-tech meter uses an infrared image-recognition system that can actually recognize every individual in viewing range. Even if your head is turned away from the set, Nielsen says, the meter will *know*.

The passive system will be able to "see" who is in the room.

The passive meter is still in the prototype stage, but when it's placed in Nielsen's 4,000 households, there will be no more button-pushing. Nielsen families won't have to do anything to record who's watching what.

Dimling says his "image-recognition system" will not only be much more accurate, but will dramatically increase "cooperation rates" (the percentage of people willing to become Nielsen families). Since nobody will have to do anything, goes this thinking, who could object?

Actually, it's the networks that object. They say the expense and reliability of the passive system remains questionable, and that a fear of "Big Brother" invading the home could actually lower cooperation rates. "It's still an open question whether people will allow these things to 'watch' them in their bedroom," agrees Milavsky.

Nielsen's best estimate is that an image-recognition system is at least two years and billions of advertising dollars away. The networks say they can't wait that long because Nielsen's system is costing them money now. Since the introduction of people meters in 1986, the committee says, its audience share has regularly been "underreported," particularly among groups important to advertisers such as children and young adults.

And there's one more thing. Many Nielsen clients believe that more technology is the last thing the audience-measurement business needs. Even people meters bother Schiavone: "[They] were sold on their ability to provide a tremendous amount of data, much of it overnight. But who uses all this data, and why do we need it the next day except as a popularity contest?

"I guarantee you that TV stations and advertisers all over the country have mounds of information lying unopened under someone's desk. Nielsen provides more than 75 demographic categories. No one cares about most of them."

So what would he prefer? Schiavone says the committee would like to see a return to the system of checks and balances that existed before 1986. Meaning what? Meaning a combination of meters and diaries, and probably telephone surveys as well. "The answer is simplicity itself," says Schiavone.

Broadcasters would like to see a return to the system of checks and balances that existed before 1986.

So if the networks want less gadgetry, is that what they're going to get? Not a chance, if Nielsen and its competitors have their way. They're moving toward even more high-tech solutions that would provide an even higher pile of information.

Troubled Diaries

Nielsen rushed people meters into operation in 1986 after its primary European competitor, AGB, began to put them in U.S. homes.

AGB claimed the meters were much more reliable than Nielsen's old dairy system. But Nielsen had a system of checks and balances built into those old procedures. One set of families filled out a weekly diary while another set used a metering device. The two samples, combined, produced the ratings.

This system is still used in 25 local markets during "sweeps" periods (four a year), when Nielsen measures local ratings. But the diaries had problems, too. They were usually filled out by the woman of the house, who often "voted" for her favorite programs—whether anybody watched them or not.

The diaries frequently weren't filled in until days later, when the diarist had to "remember" what her family watched. Given human memory and all the possibilities, this was fairy-tale stuff. "I wouldn't want General Foods basing its decisions on my diaries," says a New Yorker who regularly filled one out (for Arbitron) a few years ago.

AGB said people meters would cure these ills, so Nielsen caved in and rushed its own meters into the breach. That move paid off for Nielsen—AGB lost $67 million and fled the field.

—*A. S.*

For instance, Arbitron—Nielsen's major competitor in local ratings—has staked its future on its "ScanAmerica" system. It's the "Scan" that's crucial here.

"ScanAmerica" would keep people meters, but add an in-home scanner that reads the bar codes of grocery products.

"ScanAmerica" would keep people meters, but add an in-home scanner that reads the bar codes of grocery products. Its participants would not only have to press people-meter buttons; they'd have to scan every grocery item they unload in their kitchens. This system is being tested in Denver—and is supposed to go nationwide next year, telling Arbitron's clients not only who is watching, but what viewers are buying.

Arbitron has some major advertisers sold on ScanAmerica's potential to become an invaluable marketing tool. The company says it will be able to tell Campbell's Soup, for example, that " 'L.A. Law' had a rating of 19 in the Denver market and a 41 share, and 49 percent of those watching were heavy soup drinkers. Thirty-nine percent regularly bought Campbell's and 16 percent did most of their shopping at Albertson's."

Then there's Information Resources Inc., with its BehaviorScan, which will allow two different commercials to be sent to adjacent cable households. They will check to see who bought what—in other words, which ad worked better.

Here, too, the networks are naysayers. Buying habits and viewing data are two completely separate pieces of the pie, they say, and so ScanAmerica is exactly what they *don't* need. "Asking people to scan and push buttons will obviously only compound the problem," says Schiavone. "We want to simplify the process."

So the networks have taken their best shot, and Nielsen is still standing. They've asked other research companies for new proposals and come up empty. No matter what AGB, the leading ratings company in Europe, and Arbitron say about their methods being superior, both rely on the same people meters that the networks hate.

After absorbing Scudball after Scudball, Nielsen appears firmly in control. With all their dissatisfaction, network executives admit they'll probably sign a new contract with Nielsen before the fall season begins. And although the contract is expected to include a few specifics about Nielsen's planned improvements, that probably won't make a dent in the intensity of the networks' frustration.

What kind of business is this? As long as Nielsen was serving the self-interest of all its clients, no one complained about its research. Now the networks are trying to shoot holes even in its "new, improved" methodology.

The networks have taken their best shot, and Nielsen is still standing.

This frontal assault by the networks is bound to take its toll on the credibility of the ratings. And as that begins to happen, no one—not the networks, not the advertisers, not the viewing public—stands to benefit.

Nevertheless, Nielsen still holds a monopoly in the ratings business, and for the foreseeable future will continue to decide what the American public gets to see on TV. That much is certain.

Keeping track of the nation's viewing habits, it seems, looks like a job for Superman. In his absence, Nielsen will have to do. ♦

Question for Discussion

1. In your opinion, is the current system for collecting ratings data all that it could be? How would you change it, if you could?

Suggested Readings

The Meaning of Television

Edgerton, Gary, "Clio Beckons Us to the Looking Glass," *Journal of Popular Film and Television* Vol. 17, Summer 1989, p. 43 (3). Introduction to special issue on television history.

Karp, Walter, "Where the Media Critics Went Wrong," *American Heritage* Vol. 39, March 1988, p. 76 (4). He traces early predictions about the effect of television, and finds that it did not make Americans passive and obedient.

Kubey, Robert and Mihaly Csikszentmihalyi, *Television and the Quality of Life: How Viewing Shapes Everyday Experience* (Hillsdale, N.J.: Lawrence Erlbaum, 1990). A scholarly approach to the question of how television viewing both contributes to and detracts from the quality of everyday life. There will be a quiz on the spelling of the second author's name in the morning.

Miller, Mark Crispin, "Boxed In: The Culture of TV." Reviewed by Jackson Lears, *The Nation,* January 9, 1989, p. 59 (4).

Russell, David, "A World in Inaction," *Sight and Sound* Vol. 59, Summer 1990, p. 174 (6). TV Drama.

Television and Children

Carlsson-Paige, Nancy, and Diane E. Levin, "Why Children's Television Should Be Regulated," *Education Digest* Vol. 55, September 1989, p. 37 (3).

Dorr, Aimee, "Television and Children: A Special Medium for a Special Audience," reviewed by Marilyn Kaye, *Library Quarterly,* January 1988, p. 113 (1).

Luke, Carmen, *Constructing the Child Viewer: A History of the American Discourse on Television and Children, 1950–1980* (N.Y.: Praeger, 1990). Examines three decades of U.S. research on television's effect on children.

Zoglin, Richard, "Is TV Ruining Our Children? Reforms Are at Hand, but the Way Kids Grow Up Has Already Been Profoundly Changed," *Time* Vol. 136, October 15, 1990, pp. 75 (2). On the occasion of the 1990 Children's Television Bill.

Television and the Family

Goldberg, Gary David, "The Intimacy of Mass Culture," *New Perspectives Quarterly* Vol. 7, Winter 1990, p. 58 (2). The producer of "Family Ties" gives his opinion about the effect of television on the American family.

Kalter, Joanmarie, "How TV Is Shaking Up the American Family," *TV Guide* July 23, 1988, p. 4 (8). Television as a value-setter, part 1.

Zoglin, Richard, "Home is Where the Venom Is: Domestic Life Takes a Drubbing in TV's Anti-family Sitcoms," *Time* Vol. 135, April 16, 1990, p. 85 (2). An analysis of the significance of programs such as Married with Children, Roseanne, and The Simpsons.

Television Ratings

Buzzard, Karen S., *Chains of Gold: Marketing the Ratings and Rating the Markets* (Metuchen, N.J.: Scarecrow Press, 1990). An exploration of the evolution of broadcast ratings. The title derives from congressional representative Oren Harris's statement that "Broadcasters are bound to ratings with chains of gold which they are reluctant to break . . ."

On the Censorship of Television Programming

Berkman, Dave, "If I Don't Like It, You Can't See It," *USA Today,* March 1990, p. 50 (3). Criticism of religious fundamentalists who want to censor television broadcasting.

Gold, Philip, "As TV Races to the Edge, Society Pulls in the Reins," *Insight* Vol. 5, May 8, 1989, p. 12 (3). Organized protest against sex, violence and offensive topics influences advertisers.

Beneficial Effects of Television

Adams, Don and Arlene Goldbard, "Steal this TV: How Media Literacy Can Change the World," *Utne Reader,* July–August 1990, p. 66 (11). Rethinking TV: includes related article on using TV for social use.

Atkinson, Robert, "Respectful, Dutiful Teenagers: Out of TV's Wasteland, Here's the First Generation. They're Global Villagers." *Psychology Today,* October 1988, p. 22 (3).

Dorris, Michael, "Why Mister Ed Still Talks Good Horse Sense: An Anthropologist Explains How Reruns, Like Old Tribal Tales, Can Link Generations and Teach Enduring Values," *TV Guide* Vol. 36, 28, 1988, p. 34 (3).

Maynard, Joyce, "Talkin' 'Bout My G-G-Generation," *New York Times,* January 20, 1991, p. H.31 (2). Children who grew up in the 60s were granted unprecedented access to current events.

"Radio Stimulates Imagination; Television Enhances Recall," *Society* Vol. 25, September–October 1988, p. 3 (1).

Detrimental Effects of Television

Good, Stephen, "The World in a Fun House Mirror," *Insight* Vol. 5, November 27, 1989, p. 46 (2). Two USC professors lambaste television as a misleading force in society.

Hamill, Pete, "Crack and the Box," *Esquire* Vol. 113, May 1990, p. 63 (3). Blaming drug addiction on television.

Norton, Clark, "What TVs Recommend Most," *Hippocrates* Vol. 3, January–February 1989, p. 24 (2). Television pushes prescription medication.

Pooley, Eric, "Grins, Gore and Video Tape: The Trouble with Local TV News," *New York* Vol. 22, October 9, 1989, p. 36 (9).

Synnestvedt, Justin, "TV—No! Let's Get Off the Couch," *Vital Speeches* Vol. 55, January 15, 1989, p. 209 (3).

Television and International Politics

"Did TV Undo an Empire?," *World Monitor: The Christian Science Monitor Monthly* Vol. 3, March 1990, p. 28 (3). TV's influence in the fall of Communist governments in Eastern Europe.

Schorr, Daniel, "How TV Helped Tear Down the Berlin Wall," *TV Guide,* December 23, 1989, p. 10 (2).

Cable and the New Electronic Media

11

We will deal with both cable and the "new" media in this chapter, but we really can't consider cable a new medium. Cable is really just a newer delivery system for the older medium of television. And it's not even all that "new" anymore. In fact, as an industry it's rather established and downright arrogant, as the first reading in this chapter points out.

We deal with cable here because, like other forms of new media, the growth of cable has been explosive.

The growth of cable is an example of how communications technologies change very quickly these days. Guttenberg published his bible in 1456, and for the next 430 years the technology remained pretty much the same, until the linotype machine began to be used in 1886. Within the last few years, however, print news has begun to be distributed via satellite and delivered via on-line data bases, electronic bulletin boards, information services such as teletext and videotext, CD-ROM (compact disc—read-only memory), and fax machines, while the photographs that appear with the news can be changed through digital image manipulation. As Edward Tenner points out in the second reading in this chapter, these combinations of telecommunications and computer technology might be creating some problems that we should be aware of.

We Don't Have to Care, We're the Cable Company

Pat Aufderheide

According to Pat Aufderheide, cable companies have become too arrogant, they charge too much money and give too little service. The following reading analyzes the governmental and industry actions that allowed this to happen.

Pat Aufderheide teaches Communication at the American University, and is also senior editor of In These Times.

Reading Difficulty Level: 5. Discussing the cable industry and our governmental bureaucracy necessitates the use of some specialized vocabulary, but everything is understandable in context.

How Raymond Beckett discovered the secrets of the universe in Boston, touts the Time/Warner ad featuring a charming African-American boy. The answer: the Discovery Channel. "Since Congress passed the 1984 Cable Act, the cable industry has exercised its freedom with care and concern," reads the copy. But care and concern isn't what the cable industry is famous for. Consider:

Care and concern isn't what the cable industry is famous for.

• In Louisville, Kentucky, subscribers' rates have risen 204 per cent in four years. In Tucson, Arizona, subscribers ate a 70 per cent cost increase over six years, even though the cable company's worth more than doubled in the course of four spectacular buyouts. And in Henderson, Tennessee, rates rose 40 per cent in one year alone—with no increase in channels or in quality of service. The Consumer Federation of America estimates that consumers are being overcharged $6 billion annually.

• In Austin, Texas, it took the Time-owned company just two weeks after deregulation went into effect to announce that it couldn't afford to meet its franchise obligations—especially its promises to provide $400,000 a year for access television and to deliver programming on eight channels. It took eleven months and some $800,000 to get the company to restore the provisions.

• When NBC got the bright idea of providing a cable news service, CNBC, it tried to place the programming on the systems of Tele-Communications, Inc. (TCI), the cable giant that controls 24 per cent of U.S. cable systems. But TCI would only carry it if NBC promised that the service would not compete with Cable News Network, in which TCI owns a major stake.

"This is a First Amendment horror," says communications lawyer and former regulator Henry Geller. "Would you be happy if the only broadcast news service was ABC?"

Cable companies have become the arrogant bullies of consumer television.

Since 1986, when the Act's provisions went into effect, cable companies have become the arrogant bullies of consumer television. Last fall, constituents' complaints finally persuaded Congress to try to pass

Reprinted by permission from *The Progressive*, 409 East Main Street, Madison, WI 53703. From the January, 1991, issue.

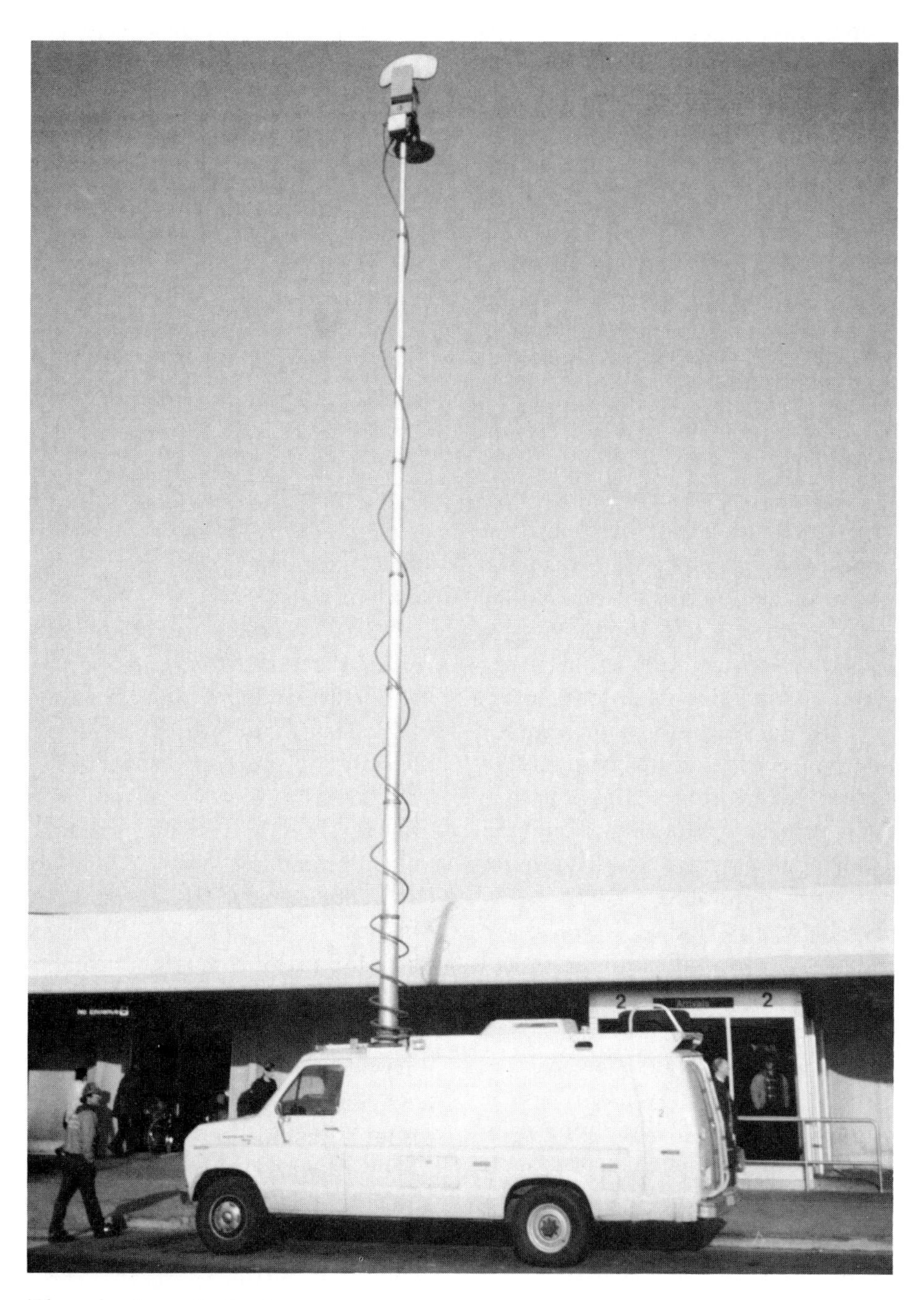

(Photo by Bruce Cotler.)

reregulation. That's why there was a sudden flurry of cable ads praising the industry's public-interest work. But the legislation flopped, and many public-interest and consumer advocates are breathing a sigh of relief, because the proposed bills raised key issues about our communications future and then buried them under ineffective, silly, and sometimes counterproductive provisions.

At stake is something as crucial as freedom of speech in the electronic age.

The problems, however, won't go away.

Cable looks like a luxury compared with broadcast television, but not to the residents of Madelia, Minnesota, a rural community where the only signals that come in clearly come through cable wires. And not to residents of Manhattan, where dense building makes for poor reception. And certainly not in Laredo, Texas, where three-quarters of the citizens speak Spanish and can only get Spanish-language programming on cable.

Now that cable wires reach some 85 per cent of American homes, and nearly 60 per cent of those homes subscribe to it, cable is likely to be the main pipeline of televised information for the immediate future. Telephone companies have launched a formidable public-relations campaign to let them into the business too. And one day, cable may be rendered obsolete by a fiber-optic pipeline of information to our living rooms and offices. But for now, cable is America's informational highway.

More than 99 per cent of cable households have no alternative to cable.

"At stake are not *I Love Lucy* reruns or better movies on HBO or the ability of our young people to watch more video music." Tucson Mayor Thomas Volgy told Congress. "At stake is something as crucial as freedom of speech in the electronic age."

When you're dealing with information, the have/have-not issue always takes on more-than-marketplace proportions. Supreme Court Justice Felix Frankfurter once put it succinctly in a case that linked the First Amendment with antitrust enforcement: "Truth and understanding are not wares like potatoes and peanuts."

But in cable, they're being treated just that way. Cable is now, as Senator Howard Metzenbaum of Ohio says, an "unregulated monopoly," an unrivaled supplier. It's also creeping steadily toward monopsony—being a single purchaser of programming.

Cable enjoys local monopoly because it is prohibitively expensive for a rival company to come in and wire an entire area in the hopes of beating out the competition, and because other ways of delivering service (broadcast, microwave, direct-broadcast satellite) can't offer what cable can. More than 99 per cent of cable households have no alternative to cable, unless you count "competition" the way the Federal Communications Commission does—as access to three broadcast signals.

Cable is moving toward monopsony because cable systems (and often other media) increasingly insist on owning part of any programming they let on their systems. They basically hold programmers hostage until they get a piece of the action. Then they keep rival programmers off their systems and refuse to sell their programming to rival delivery systems.

This is the situation antitrust legislation was invented to prevent: letting the common-carrier—say, the owner of a railroad or pipeline or telephone system—have a grip on what's carried and for how much. But today's Justice Department thinks there are benefits to monopoly and vertical integration, and so it looks the other way. In practice, cable is neither regulated nor subject to antitrust laws.

Access is the key to understanding the public issues at stake: for consumers, access to see; for commercial competitors and alternative voices, access to show. For consumers, this usually means cost and quality. For competitors, it means being able to get on a cable system or to offer a rival service without getting into bed with a cable company. And for alternative voices, it means reserved channels, whether for public television or for noncommercial public access.

If Lily Tomlin were doing her telephone-operator routine today, she'd say, 'We don't have to care, we're the cable company,' " says Andrew Jay Schwartzman, head of Media Access Project, a public-interest group. Subscribers complain that when they call their local cable company to report blackouts or billing errors, the phone just rings and rings. But price and quality problems are more than consumer issues. They're symptoms of cable's near-monopoly grip, because people go on signing up despite them.

In 1990 the General Accounting Office surveyed cable rate increases since deregulation and found that prices for the cheapest service had increased by 43 per cent since 1986, and by 10 per cent in 1989 alone. Compliance with the GAO survey was voluntary, so the worst price gougers may have simply thrown the questionnaire away.

In practice, cable is neither regulated nor subject to antitrust laws.

Subscribers had been offered a few more channels—like home shopping, and the low-quality E! Entertainment channel—but cable companies' profits had risen faster than their investments.

And when it looked in 1989 as if cable might be reregulated, with lids on basic rates, the cable companies suddenly invented a "basic-basic" tier—usually just broadcast channels and C-SPAN, with maybe an access channel or two. Almost nobody bought just the "basic basic," but if cable gets price reregulation, the cable companies are betting that's all that will be affected.

Skyrocketing rates put cable beyond the reach of poor consumers, but cable companies don't worry much about the poor. In fact, they're notorious at dragging their feet when servicing less-than-upscale neighborhoods. For instance, in New York City, most residents of Harlem, Chinatown, and the Lower East Side finally have access to cable—a mere sixteen years after the deadline by which the Time (now Time/Warner) company promised to deliver it, and only under the threat of reregulation.

A mere five corporations now control half of all U.S. cable subscribers.

Cable companies have been centralizing power for some time. A mere five corporations now control half of all U.S. cable subscribers. Profits per subscriber have ballooned, though the value of service has remained relatively constant. And the major cable operators—the companies that string the wire to your home—are also eagerly buying up shares of program services so they can carry what's good for their bottom line, keeping competitors out and saving the best (lowest) channels for their own stuff.

Take behemoth TCI: It owns a piece of programming services ranging from Black Entertainment Television to the Discovery Channel to Home Sports Network to Showtime and CNN. Or take Time/Warner: It also owns a chunk of BET and CNN, as well as owning HBO and the Comedy Channel. When Viacom wanted to get Showtime for its New York cable company, it had to sue Time, Inc., to get it. Jones Intercable bumped the USA Network off its systems to make room for Turner Network TV; sure, Turner was more expensive, but Jones owned a piece of it.

These days, if you want to start a new program service—and there are a host of hopefuls, from live court proceedings to comedy shows—you try to get a cable company (preferably TCI) to buy into it. That way, you'll get your programming on cable. If not, forget it. In theory, cable companies with more than thirty-six channels have to keep between 10 and 15 per cent of their space open for any purchaser. But "leased access," as it's called, is a dead letter, because the cable companies also get to set the price and terms, and don't have to bill the consumer for the programmer. Nobody uses leased access; hopeful programmers just try to strike a deal with the cabler.

In some cases, stations had to pay cable companies—effectively, bribe them—to carry their signal.

Along with stifling competing cable programmers, cablers also sabotage broadcasters. A Federal Communications Commission report found, again in a voluntary survey, that 20 per cent of the cable systems surveyed had denied carriage to broadcast stations. In some cases, stations had to pay cable companies—effectively, bribe them—to carry their signal. And 23 per cent of the cable systems admitted changing the channel number, which at best confuses viewers and at worst—among nearly half the current television sets—can put a signal into "cable Siberia" by bumping it up past the set's ability to receive it. Some cable operators even move broadcast signals to make room for their own look-alike-broadcast "stations," without any of the public-service requirements broadcasters have to meet.

Why sabotage broadcast stations—which are still the most-watched cable programming? Because the lowest (and most popular) channels are where the advertising money is. Ask big-time cable operator Jones Intercable. It boasted to advertisers that moving down its own most popular cable programming at the expense of broadcast signals "means that the advertiser's exposure to area consumers increased greatly without additional cost." That logic is also behind the creation of cable look-alike "stations"; they're cash cows for advertising.

When the likes of NBC, Showtime, and HBO are bickering over market share, it's easy to shrug your shoulders. After all, they're all in the commercial universe whose idea of excellence is *Fresh Prince of Bel Air* and the MTV Music Awards. For some of us, the difference between Showtime and HBO isn't much. Lawyer Schwartzman says, "Why trade a headache for an upset stomach? Why care? Because it shows you the power that TCI and others have acquired, and how the big guys fight over us without letting us into the process."

He's right. The slugfest over cable's power has largely been fought on commercial turf, and by the big-time players. The place to see how impoverished our cable future might be is embattled access cable—the public, educational, and government channels known together as PEG. They were carved out, franchise by individual franchise, mostly since 1978.

"Cable is a true community medium, a technology that allows you to direct a message at specific people at low incremental cost and stop that message at the city boundaries," explains lawyer Nicholas Miller, whose firm represents many municipal franchise authorities. "So it gives us a possibility of community programming unlike anything else."

When you tune in to a PEG channel—if you're among the lucky cable subscribers to have one—you'll be watching America's hidden television. On government channels, you might find the city council meeting, or the local high school's basketball game. On community channels, you might be watching a five-site hookup from senior-citizen centers, or a rummage-sale announcement on a community billboard or religious programming. Some colleges have sponsored oral history sessions that illuminate immigrant history. Most often, these channels have some professional staff.

When the likes of NBC, Showtime, and HBO are bickering over market share, why should we care? Because it shows their power, how the big guys fight over us without letting us into the process.

Public-access channels are usually funkier, an open-to-all, perpetual amateur hour. They exist in only about a quarter of the cable systems; often they're more promise than substance—a studio with one camera and no production budget.

Ever since the 1984 Cable Act, cable access has been in trouble.

They've been a source of scandal, for instance, when the Ku Klux Klan started circulating its own programs for local viewing. In a few places—New York City, for instance, where Paper Tiger Television regularly produces sharply critical programs on the media—public access has become an offbeat alternative voice. And in many, as a Benton Foundation study recently reported, they support apple-pie American community programming ranging from a Humane Society adopt-a-pet program in Fayetteville, Arkansas, to a musical education series sponsored by the Los Angeles Jazz Society.

Grass-roots activists left and right love public access. For instance Deep Dish TV, formed by a hardy band of left-wing media activists, has founded a national, satellite-fed service of anthologized local cable programming—farm problems, AIDS, and labor issues are typical topics—to be used in conjunction with local programs and community tie-ins.

Political skeptics cast a cold eye on cable access. A lot of the programming looks as home-made as it is.

Arch-conservative Representative Newt Gingrich, Georgia Republican, also sees opportunity in public access. He's the host of the half-hour shows produced by American Citizens' Television (ACTV), promoting his take on issues ranging from education to crime, drugs and housing. ACTV sponsors workshops to teach locals how to make their own programs, and to use ACTV's program in grassroots activism; ACTV head Mark Colucci counts some 200 sites and is working hard on getting more.

But ever since the 1984 Cable Act, cable access has been in trouble—both from cable companies and from cities. The Act put a ceiling on the amount of revenues a city could collect from a cable company, and furthermore didn't require the city to return those revenues to access channels. In austerity times for cities, the money has rarely been funneled back to access. "If it's between potholes and video freaks, you know who's going to win," says Miller.

In Nashville, when the city found itself in a budget crisis in 1988, a program by a gay and lesbian alliance on public access triggered a city-council slugfest. The cable company, a Viacom operator, acted as cheerleader for council members trying to rechannel access funds into general operating funds. The upshot was near-total defunding of the access center. Access director Elliott Mitchell finally quit in disgust. "They were out to get us in concert, both the city and the cable company," he said.

Political skeptics cast a cold eye on cable access. Indeed, even people who can get the channels often don't tune them in. A lot of the programming looks as home-made as it is. Moreover, access programming works best when it's part of a community-organizing effort. Overworked, underpaid, or volunteer access producers often don't have time to be community organizers as well.

"But you have to ask yourself, 'Where was public television in 1962?' " says lawyer Miller. "That's the relevant comparison. We need assured funding, in the hands of professionals, with local accountability. Then we'll find out what access can do for a community."

When the House and Senate took up the problems of cable last fall, many of cable's problems—cost, quality of service, shutout of competitors—surfaced scandalously. But in the typically ugly process of bill-making, in which major industry rivals duked it out on paper, the basic issues got lost. And the public interest in cable was simply never addressed.

Pricing proposals established a basic package so basic it was barely more than what you can get on "free" broadcast television—similar to the cable companies' "basic basic" tiers that nobody wants. Cable companies would then be free to raise prices at will above that first tier. Conglomeration and vertical monopoly were addressed by proposing slightly revised standards for measuring "effective competition"—standards so loose that they wouldn't affect the majority of cable systems. Cablers blocked proposals to force them to make their programming available to competitive services (such as microwave and the largely hypothetical direct-broadcast satellite).

Access channels simply lost out. In fact, proposals would have undermined them further. For instance, public television stations would have been permitted to take over "unused" access slots, but no provision was made for getting those channels back if someone wanted to use them. Public-interest advocates and access lobbyists protested, but their outcries were nothing compared to the quiet chat of big money.

Worst of all, Congress would have handed responsibility for enforcing reregulation to the FCC, which openly opposes it. And even if the FCC wanted to enforce legislation, it doesn't have the staff. Andrew Blau at the United Church of Christ's Office of Communication figures that if just 20 per cent of the cable companies asked for price increases, the FCC would be processing them at the rate of one an hour throughout the year.

When Congress took a look, many of cable's problems surfaced scandalously. But in the ugly process of bill-making, the public interest was never addressed.

Are there workable solutions for cable's tight grip on our information future? Yes, although they're not ideas that the big players would like very much. Making cable a common carrier would help. It's even possible to imagine letting the phone companies become rivals—if they, too, were required to be common carriers, and were prohibited from buying and shutting down their cable rivals.

Even setting price caps on a truly basic tier—one that required well-funded PEG channels—and throwing some power to rate-payers and municipalities would control prices, if not eliminate the problem

Cable isn't just a business. It's a way of understanding our communities, our culture, and our political system.

of the low-income subscriber who "falls off" the cable service in a bad month. (Daring policymakers might even consider the innovation of "cable stamps" for the poor.)

Most imaginatively, policymakers might require cable programmers, like broadcasters, to perform public service, in trade for their use of public right-of-way and in recognition of the fact that "truth and understanding are not wares like potatoes and peanuts."

These proposals require viewing cable as an essential public service. If we're to see anything but the Big Five's version of reality, it's time to insist that cable isn't just a business, but a way of understanding our communities, our culture, our political system, and our own relationship to them. ♦

Questions for Discussion

1. What are the advantages and disadvantages of cable television as a monopoly?
2. Should cable be regulated by the government? If so, in what way?

The Impending Information Implosion

Edward Tenner

Much has been written about the "Information explosion," and indeed today's computer/telecommunications technology has vastly increased the amount of information that has been recorded in one form or another. In the next reading Edward Tenner, contributing editor of Harvard *magazine, suggests that what is actually occuring is an implosion, or "bursting inward." The analogy suggests that as the amount of information has increased it has become more difficult and costlier to find.*

Reading Difficulty Level: 6. It's not an easy concept to get your mind around, but it's nicely laid out here.

Questioning the information explosion seems to be as willful as recruiting for the Flat Earth Society. One major astronomy project alone, the Digital Sky Survey, will store and analyze ten million megabytes of information over the next ten years to produce a three-dimensional map of one million galaxies and a million stars in the earth's own galaxy, among other objects. The *abstracts* of a recent London meeting on sequencing the human genome take up 350 printed pages.

Questioning the information explosion seems to be as willful as recruiting for the Flat Earth Society.

From 1980 to 1989, public electronic mailboxes increased from 210,000 to 1.8 million, institutional mailboxes from 220,000 to 6.8 million. Traffic on the National Science Foundation Network (NSFNET) alone increased from about 190 billion characters in July 1989 to 645 billion characters in July 1990. Palmtop organizers surpass the processing power and memory of the first personal computers of a decade ago at a tenth the price. A single CD-ROM disk can replace two thousand library-card-catalogue drawers. So crucial are information networks to profits that in 1986 the president of American Airlines said that if he had to divest the airline or its Sabre reservation system, he would keep Sabre.

Print media, too, seem to be multiplying. Richard De Gennaro, Larsen librarian of Harvard College, predicts that the College library holdings will double from the present seven million volumes in twenty years. Widener Library is already 500,000 books above its three-million-book capacity. To make room for the 70,000 volumes added each year to Widener and Pusey libraries, Harvard has begun to build massive outlying depositories for environmentally sensitive, less frequently used materials.

A University of Texas publication reports one estimate that "the amount of knowledge generated by man [sic] throughout history will more than double by the end of the twentieth century" and that Americans consume "approximately 7 trillion words a day" in written and electronic forms.

Even so, many people are wondering whether information overload is the only problem. As early as 1984 the political scientist Langdon Winner questioned the "revolutionary" rhetoric of computer people as "Mythinformation" in the electronic engineering magazine *IEEE Spectrum:* "Exhausted in Madison Avenue advertising slogans, the [revolutionary] image has lost much of its punch." And in 1986, the media scholar Brian Winston could call the information revolution "an illusion, a rhetorical gambit, an expression of profound ignorance, a movement dedicated to purveying misunderstanding and disseminating misinformation." Even the author of *The Right Stuff* himself re-

Even so, many people are wondering whether information overload is the only problem.

From *Harvard Magazine,* November-December 1991, pp. 30–34. Reprinted by permission of the author.

cently turned technology critic. On a 1990 Public Broadcasting Service (PBS) symposium, Tom Wolfe wondered aloud whether electronic advances had made information more available. "I seriously doubt that there has been any information explosion," he said.

"I seriously doubt that there has been any information explosion," said Tom Wolfe.

What if the information *ex*plosion is driving an equal and opposite information *im*plosion (a word apparently first used by the French critic Jean Baudrillard), affecting have-nots most severely, as all shortages do, but also touching middle-class and even well-off people? A college classmate who teaches at a leading law school recently pointed out that his library could deliver superb legal bibliographies in minutes but that he had written to the Louisiana Highway Department four times in vain for a map. My friend had discovered that the total quantity of information and the number of channels for delivering it matter less than how hard it is to get when one needs it.

What about the cost, ease of access, variety, and clarity of information?

Even the Flat Earthers have a point. Sometimes the local picture matters as much as the global one. Who takes a great-circle route to the supermarket? And since it's well known that the long run is a series of short runs, it's time to pay as much attention to the *present* of information as to its future.

Nobody has a definition of information satisfactory for both theoretical and everyday use. But when any of us wants to know something, we recognize information when we see it. It is easy to quantify—as pages or minutes or square inches or bytes—but difficult to measure. John Maddox, editor of *Nature,* recently compared scientific information to a salami that can be cut in thick or thin slices. Who can quantify the importance of the results in papers? They are like blips on a radar screen that do not disclose whether the craft is a two-seat trainer or jumbo jet. And many scientists and librarians are now convinced that the salami is not growing as fast as the number of slices.

The new *Encyclopedia Britannica* isn't much longer than the fabled eleventh edition of eighty years ago. The years required for schooling at all levels have not changed significantly, though more people do of course get higher degrees now. Some subjects have been cut back to make room; societies forget things as they learn others.

There are at least four ways to judge whether we have better or worse information: cost, ease or difficulty of access, variety of sources or viewpoints, and clarity. None of these has improved unambiguously over the last generation.

Consider cost. Processing and storing information electronically is cheaper than it ever was, and it is getting cheaper all the time. But the lower cost of hardware is leading to more powerful computers at the same price points, running fancier releases of the same software, rather than to cheaper machines.

New information technologies, even those that decrease in real cost, increase the cash and (equally important) time cost of information. We have more mailboxes to maintain and check. Fax and electronic mail are parallel channels with their own hardware and service expenses, and neither reduces the national overhead of postal and express shipping routes. First-class postage increased from 6 cents in 1970 to 29 cents in 1991.

New information technologies increase the cash and time cost of information.

It is true that the marginal cost of long-distance telephone calling has decreased significantly after the breakup of AT&T in 1984—a savings offset for many people by higher local rates and a smorgasboard of costs from "access" to "wire maintenance." Competition among long-distance carriers now seems to be in marketing rather than in price cuts or technical improvements. Long-distance information itself, once free, now costs 65 cents per inquiry after the first two for AT&T residential customers. Out-of-town telephone books are also no longer supplied gratis. This may or may not work to the benefit of telephone customers, but it hardly represents cheaper information. (At least we had Reaganism rather than Thatcherism. One British columnist recently had fifteen minutes to find a telephone book or get directory assistance near Trafalgar Square. He failed.)

The toll-free 800 information services of the 1970s and 1980s remain an outstanding accomplishment but are threatened by the 900-line concept. *The Wall Street Journal* reports that the French government's regular (toll) tourist information number now offers only a recording that gives another 900 number at fifty cents a minute—presumably plus tax and service. Other foreign tourist offices may follow. "Clearly, companies are looking to migrate 800 services to 900 numbers to produce revenue," a telecommunications consultant at Booz Allen & Hamilton told *USA Today*.

Similarly, pay-per-view television threatens even premium cable as we have known it. Scott Kurnit, president of the Viewer's Choice division at Showtime, has declared in *Entertainment Weekly* that "free TV is no more than a fluke, a lack of technology forty years ago, rather than a birthright. They just didn't have a viable means of scrambling signals back then, or they would have."

Free TV is no more than a fluke. They just didn't have a viable means of scrambling signals back then.

Print media prices have also been headed upward. The daily *New York Times'* new 50-cent price compares with 15 cents in the early 1970s, and *The Wall Street Journal* has quintupled in price from 15 to 75 cents. (The national edition of the *Times* also sells for 75 cents in the Midwest and Southwest.) Most other dailies are expected to increase in price from between 25 and 35 cents to between 35 and 50 cents. *The Economist* has calculated that its own British after-inflation price more than doubled between 1960 and 1990.

It's true that there are more journals, but information can hardly be called more affordable.

Many paperback publishers began repricing aggressively in autumn 1990, but the trend is older. In the twelve years from 1977 to 1989, according to the 1990–91 *Bowker Annual*, average cloth prices increased by 108.7 percent, but paperback prices grew by 179.9 percent and are now 41.4 percent rather than 30.9 percent of clothbound averages.

Prices of professional and technical journals rose two and three times faster than the Consumer Price Index in the 1980s and are expected to rise even more sharply in the 1990s, according to a recent *Publishers Weekly* article. The Association of Research Libraries (ARL) reports they increased by 51 percent between 1985 and 1990 alone. It's true that there are more journals, and that some, though not all, have more pages annually, but information can hardly be called more affordable.

Electronic databases are still for deep-pocketed researchers. *InfoWorld* reports that most services charged between ten and fifteen dollars for retrieving a single *Business Week* article that would cost sixty cents to photocopy.

The jump in the number and price of journals has helped convert the problem of price in public and academic libraries to one of access. To maintain their serials budgets, libraries have cannibalized book acquisition funds. The 94 members of the ARL bought 570,000 fewer books in 1989 than in 1985, a 16 percent decline. The Berkeley university library reports a drop of nearly 50 percent both between 1981 and 1992, and between 1990 and 1991. Berkeley has canceled more than $400,000 worth of journals subscriptions. Yes, there are interlibrary loans, but despite electronic networking, they can still take weeks; and, of course, users at the lending library lose access during the term of the loan.

Washington hasn't been setting a good example for the private sector. In 1988 the Washington, D.C., office of the American Library Association published a chronology of the eighties called *Less Access to Less Information by and about the U.S. Government*, deploring "a continuing pattern of [the] federal government to restrict government publications and information dissemination activities." Among other things, it reported that since 1982, one fourth of the government's sixteen thousand publications had been eliminated.

According to *The New York Times*, Bill Kovach, curator of the Nieman fellowships at Harvard, believes the popularity of restrictions on the press's coverage of the Persian Gulf war "has established a new standard in terms of the amount of information the government is willing to give its people." The total number of official secrets created by the U.S. government did, it is true, decline from an all-time peak of 15 million in 1985 to 6.8 million for the year that ended September 30, 1990, but the 1990–91 statistics should see a big jump again. Of course, the exact number, compiled by the Information Security Oversight Office, is classified.

Thinking of calling for information in the civilian sector? Don't count on finding the number. Seventeen percent of the telephones in New York City and about 40 percent of those in Los Angeles are now unlisted—partly as a reaction to automatically dialed, recorded sales spiels, another Information Age blessing. Many of the published L.A. numbers list no address. And don't assume that a professional directory is an alternative. The fax and electronic switchboard explosions have increased the demand for new telephone numbers, making old area codes and exchanges obsolete.

Cities, for all their misery, were once fountains of information for ordinary people. Now they are becoming ground zero of the information implosion. In the words of one New York City school administrator recently reported in *The Washington Monthly:* "Extant data systems contain an abundance of information which is underutilized due to deficit staff knowledge and abilities due to inaccessibilities." But the situation of New York's and other urban libraries is no joke; it's a tragedy to the children and adults who depend on them. The president of the New York Public Library reports that budgets for books and periodicals have been cut by almost 40 percent. Most of the branches of the Brooklyn Public Library now are open only part of the day, three or four days a week. Even sidewalk newsstands have decreased in number from 1,325 in 1950 to 298 in 1991, according to a spokesman for their operators, with almost none outside Manhattan.

At the New York Public Library budgets for books and periodicals have been cut by almost 40 percent.

And as Brooklyn goes, so evidently goes Bakersfield. *The Los Angeles Times* has abandoned home delivery and newsstand sales in central California and in other Western cities like Phoenix, Tucson, and Salt Lake City. Sociologists at the University of Minnesota say that urban newspapers throughout North America are discontinuing rural delivery at the very time when farms and small towns need economic and political information most. A 1990 article in the Minneapolis-St. Paul *Star Tribune,* one of these papers, acknowledged a rural "information shortage" as a result of these very policies.

Whatever might be said of price and accessibility, variety would seem to be improving. The number of books in print continues to grow. After years of losing ground to chains, independent bookstores are thriving again. Fiber optics will soon

Whatever might be said of price and accessibility, variety would seem to be improving.

make it possible to view 150 channels of cable television. Samir Husni, a journalism professor at the University of Mississippi, has found that an average of more than five hundred new magazines a year (out of a total of more than three thousand in the United States) were started in the four years beginning in 1987.

Viewed close up, the range of choice is not quite so appealing.

Viewed close up, the range of choice is not quite so appealing. Fewer antiquarian booksellers can afford to maintain open shops. Of the nine books I considered assigning when developing a course at Princeton University in the history of information in spring 1990, five were out of print or out of stock. The greater efficiency of computerized book ordering, both for retailers and for individuals, doesn't help much of the book isn't available. And if you think on-demand publishing is the answer, look at the prices, which can be more than one hundred dollars for a paperbound microfilm printout of a four-hundred-page history book.

It's true that the variety and quality of professional publications are at an all-time high. In fields like law, medicine, education, engineering, and, of course, computers, there is a feast of material—much of it remarkably jargon-free. If only media for presenting public issues were so diverse! When Albert Robida founded *La Caricature* in the early 1880s, there were over eighty daily newspapers in Paris. Freedom of entry into publishing for the ordinary journalist may have reached an all-time peak, extending to a petit bourgeois artist from the provinces. But even in New York City a hundred years ago there were fifteen daily newspapers in addition to the weekly and foreign-language press.

We take for granted that only the largest studios can assure national distribution of a feature film, but this wasn't always so. The University of Southern California historian Steven Ross has pointed out in *The American Historical Review* that in the days of the two-reel film before the First World War, labor unions and other organizations could produce films for only a few thousand dollars, and did. It was the growing expense of films in the postwar years that shut dissenting voices from the motion picture marketplace. Higher production standards arrived at the expense of variety. (Cable television may reverse this process, but it's still too early to tell.)

For all the marvels of desktop production, the cost of entry into trade publishing has also soared.

For all the marvels of desktop production, the cost of entry into trade publishing has also soared. In the late teens and twenties, the brash young publishers Albert Boni and Horace Liveright were able to start the Modern Library with a capital of $12,500. Richard Simon and Max Schuster had only $4,000. Of course small publishers are starting now with even less money in real terms, but it is far more difficult for them to bootstrap their way out of niche markets. Whether opportunities in cable television can offset the losses of independent publishing houses and general-interest magazines remains to be seen.

While we usually don't give the clarity of information the same priority as its cost, accessibility, and variety, we recognize it when it's changing. With increasing computer power, resolution of video terminals and letter quality of printers have been increasing as costs have been dropping. The problems of high-definition television (HDTV) are now more political and legal than technical.

While we usually don't give the clarity of information the same priority as its cost, accessibility, and variety, we recognize it when it's changing.

At the same time, underlying data are becoming less clear. A 1989 poll of business economists found an increasing majority, 72 percent, dissatisfied with the quality of data. They named inadequate staffing of government statistics-gathering agencies more than any other factor.

But we are also losing clarity because users lack the background knowledge to display properly the statistics they do have. In his provocative book *How to Lie With Maps* (University of Chicago Press, 1991), the Syracuse University geographer Mark Monmonier points out the serious problems that computerized mapmaking has introduced, including distortions of gray scales by laser printers and confusing use of bright hues by amateurs overwhelmed by their color publishing capabilities. "With no guidance and poorly chosen standard symbols," he writes, "users of mapping software are as accident-prone as inexperienced hunters with hair-trigger firearms."

Sometimes making things clear to computers indirectly makes them more opaque to people—as when prices are not marked on electronically scanned merchandise. The customer who remembers a lower posted price may then have to stroll with the cashier across aisle after aisle to the shelf in question. For years, postmarks have revealed only A.M. or P.M., and now they may say something like "Northern New Jersey" rather than an actual post office. Unlike their mechanical or even electric ancestors, electronic alarm clocks generally don't display the actual time and the alarm setting simultaneously. Already consumers have been turning away from digital-only wristwatches to analogue displays and digital-analogue hybrids.

As more information is transferred to nonprint media, clarity becomes a major issue. "One of the biggest banes of my existence," said Tom Wolfe at the PBC symposium, ". . . is microfilm. . . . [T]he research that I now don't do because of the existence of microfilm . . ."

As more information is transferred to nonprint media, clarity becomes a major issue.

The real pitfall is not to overvalue or undervalue information but to be mesmerized and anesthetized by it.

In fact the average public or university library microfilm user benefits from few of the impressive but expensive advances that corporate librarians and archivists have been using. An article from a back issue of a magazine that would take a few minutes to find in a bound volume now requires tedious threading and rewinding.

Even more advanced technology may not offer more clarity. The computerized directories of some large office buildings are actually more difficult to use than the conventional kind. A visitor must approach them and usually scroll through a few screens before finding the right name instead of simply spotting it on a listing on the wall. This feature may appeal to building managers intent on barring salespeople for rival developments, but it's hard to see how it benefits tenants or visitors.

If there is an information implosion, how serious is it? Many professional people are now much more concerned about their skills than about their all-around knowledge. Of the graduate students in leading economic programs surveyed a few years ago, 65 percent rated "being good at problem-solving" and 57 percent rated "excellence in mathematics" as "very important" in economics, while only 10 percent gave the same status to "having a broad knowledge of the economics literature" and 3 percent to "having a thorough knowledge of the economy." (Fully 68 percent said the last was "unimportant.") As if to prove their point, the best-compensated employee of Salomon Brothers last year was a 31-year-old mathematician who earned a bonus of $23 million.

The real pitfall is not to overvalue or undervalue information, or the amount of information available, but to be mesmerized and anesthetized by it. George Orwell wrote in *The Road to Wigan Pier* (1937) of "the queer spectacle of modern electrical science showering miracles upon people with empty bellies. You may shiver all night for lack of bedclothes, but in the morning you can go to the public library and read the news that has been telegraphed for your benefit from San Francisco and Singapore. . . . What we have lost in food we have gained in electricity. Whole sections of the working class who have been plundered of all they really need are being compensated, in part, by cheap luxuries which mitigate the surface of life."

The good news is that the problems of information are transitional. The bad news is that the transition appears about to go on indefinitely. ♦

Questions for Discussion

1. What's the difference between an information explosion and an information implosion?
2. Do you agree that an information implosion is taking place?

Suggested Readings

On Cable

Alter, Robert H., "Cable Is Making TV Even Better," *USA Today*, January 1990, p. 25 (2). Network vs. Cable Television.

Baig, Edward C., "Had It With Cable? Satellite Dishes Up an Alternative," *U.S. News & World Report*, June 25, 1990, p. 63 (2).

Barnes, John A., "Why Cable Costs Too Much: How Local Politicians and Cable Companies Conspire to Make Cable TV Overpriced," *Washington Monthly*, June 1989, p. 12 (5).

"Cable Television Rates and Services," *Congressional Digest* Vol. 70, February 1991, p. 37 (2).

Gabelmann, Chuck, "The Networks are More Important than Ever," *USA Today*, January 1990, p. 22 (3).

Grossman, Andrew, "Public Enemy Number One: In Some Cities, Operators Are as Popular as the Tax Auditor. Here's Why," *Channels: The Business of Communications*, September 24, 1990, p. 37 (2). In Focus: Managing Cable's Future.

Hickey, Neil, "Would You Pay to Watch the Super Bowl? That Day May Be Getting Closer, as Cable Continues to Gobble Up Sports," *TV Guide*, November 25, 1989, p. 31 (3).

Hong, Peter, "Fires, School Board Meetings, and Accidents—24 Hours a Day: Local All-News Cable TV Is Springing Up Around the Country," *Business Week*, December 17, 1990, p. 32 (1).

"Instant Messengers of the Global Village," *U.S. News and World Report*, February 12, 1990, p. 16 (2). Concerning Cable News Network.

Jaffee, Larry, "Whatever Happened to Sex on Cable TV?", *The Humanist*, July–August 1991, p. 33 (2). Cable television programs appear increasingly similar to network broadcasts—column.

Jessell, Harry A., "Survey Says: Cable Rates Doubling, Competition Nil," *Broadcasting*, April 29, 1991, p. 49 (1).

Lambert, Peter D., "How to Grow Competition for Cable," *Broadcasting*, June 24, 1991, p. 56 (2). Report on the House Subcommittee on Telecommunications hearings.

Mason, Donna M., "Vancouver, Washington: On Camera! How One City Made Public-Access TV Big Time for Citizens," *Nation's Cities Weekly*, August 27, 1990, p. 3 (2).

Miller, Ron, "Unhappy with Your Cable Service? Dial B-U-Z-Z O-F-F," *Nation's Cities Weekly*, July 1, 1991, p. 4 (1).

Moshavi, Sharon D. "Cable Rates Rising Faster Than Perceived Value," *Broadcasting*, January 14, 1991, p. 108 (2). Customer perceptions.

"Not a Pretty Picture," *Time*, March 18, 1991, p. 69 (1). Cable television industry.

Rosen, Jay, "The Whole World Is Watching CNN," *The Nation*, May 13, 1991, p. 622 (3). Cable News Network.

On the Effects of New Media and the Information Explosion

Carlson, Richard W., "When Words Collide: Legal Ethics and the Coming Information Wars," *Vital Speeches* V. 54, July 15, 1988, p. 578 (6).

Cordell, Arthur J., "Preparing for the Challenges of the New Media," *The Futurist*, March–April 1991, p. 20 (4).

Diener, Richard A. V., "Comments on an Information Age," *Bulletin of the American Society for Information Science* Vol. 16, August–September 1990, p. 29 (3).

Entman, Robert, "How the Media Affect What People Think: An Information Processing Approach," *The Journal of Politics* Vol. 51, May 1989, p. 347 (24).

Feder, Barnaby J., "Toward Defining Free Speech in the Computer Age," *The New York Times*, November 3, 1991, p. E 5 (1). The special problems of public bulletin boards for personal computers.

Gumpert, Gary, "The Media: Structural Changes and Personal Choice," *ETC.: A Review of General Semantics* Vol. 44, Summer 1987, p. 174 (6). Excerpt from *Talking Tombstones and Other Tales of the Media Age.*

Karp, Walter, "Uncle Miltie v. Mass Man," *Harper's Magazine* Vol. 277, July 1988, p. 30 (3).

Lavery, David, "Remote Control: Mythic Reflections," *Journal of Popular Film and Television* Vol. 18, Summer 1990, p. 65 (7). Demonstrates the significance of a device most of us take for granted.

Levine, Joshua, "The Last Gasp of Mass Media?", *Forbes* Vol. 146, September 17, 1990, p. 176 (4).

Martin, Jay, "Caught in Fantasyland: Electronic Media's Hold on Society," *USA Today* Vol. 117, July 1988, p. 92 (2).

McLuhan, Marshall and Bruce Powers, *The Global Village: Transformations in World Life and Media in the 21st Century*. Reviewed by A. J. Anderson, *Library Journal*, March 15, 1989, p. 76 (1).

Mowlana, Hamid, "Implications of the Information Explosion," *USA Today* Vol. 117, September 1988, p. 91 (2).

Neuman, W. Russell, "The Threshold of Public Attention," *Public Opinion Quarterly* Vol. 54, Summer 1990, p. 159 (18). Media coverage of events and resultant public opinion.

Peterson, Eric E., "The Technology of Media Consumption," *American Behavioral Scientist* Vol. 32, November–December 1988, p. 156 (13).

Rogers, Everett M., and Francis Balle, *The Media Revolution in America and Western Europe.* Reviewed in *Public Opinion Quarterly,* Spring 1987, p. 138 (3).

Rosen, Jay, "The Messages of 'The Medium Is the Message'," *ETC.: A Review of General Semantics* Vol. 47, Spring 1990, p. 45 (7). Media supplement.

"The Search for Knowledge," *The Economist* Vol. 315, June 16, 1990, p. 619 (2). A survey of information technology.

Szykowny, Rick, "Bewildering the Herd," *The Humanist* Vol. 50, November–December 1990, p. 8 (10). Interview with Noam Chomsky on the mass media industry.

Uncapher, Willard, "Trouble in Cyberspace: Civil Liberties at Peril in the Information Age," *The Humanist,* September/October 1991, p. 5 (11). More on the invasion of privacy dangers inherent in the new media.

Part IV

ADVERTISING AND PUBLIC RELATIONS

Advertising

12

In a free speech, free enterprise society such as ours, there is a perennial fear, or at least constant speculation, about the power of advertising. This has created witch hunts such as the "subliminal advertising" hysteria that Mark Crispin Miller referred to earlier (pp. 192–209). Many observers have analyzed advertising techniques to try to ferret out where advertising's power comes from. In such an analysis, it makes sense to begin with the realization that advertisers do not sell the advertised product or service, but the "end product," which is the emotional satisfaction that the product promises. In an earlier edition of this anthology, Rick Berkoff identified some of the major ad techniques[1] as follows:

1. Parity Statements—in which advertisers don't claim their product is better, just equal to the competition, as in "There's no finer razor made."
2. Borrowed Interest—in which you inject something interesting to get the audience's attention about some boring product.
3. Playing on Guilt and Fear—"Doesn't your baby deserve Pampers?"
4. Omission—"Get American Express Traveler's Checks. If *they're* lost, you can get a full refund. . . ." That's true of all other traveler's checks, too, but the ad isn't going to say so.
5. Heartstrings—the old idea of emotional appeals.
6. Joy—Have lots of happy people singing, "You got the right thing, baby," and forget about cola cleaning the rust off your fender panels.
7. Red Herrings—and other cute cartoon characters like Tony the Tiger and the Pillsbury Doughboy.

1. Rick Berkoff, "Can You Separate the Sizzle from the Steak?", in *Mass Media Issues,* 2nd ed., originally published in the *Journal of Popular Culture* (Fall, 1981).

Berkoff suggests a few other techniques, also, such as "selling you where you live," which is the specialty of motivational researchers, an area we will examine in the first reading in this chapter. Berkeley Rice's "The Selling of Lifestyles" looks at the kind of psychological research advertisers do in order to make their advertising as powerful as possible. The second reading, a set of sample ads, asks if advertising is powerful enough to sell the concept of deadly sin. The final article deals with both advertising's power to help young people become addicted to tobacco, and the tobacco industry's power over the magazines they advertise in.

The Selling of Lifestyles

Berkeley Rice

Psychographics is a type of market research that seeks to categorize members of the buying public according to their psychological make-up, including attributes such as deep-seated beliefs, unconscious motivations, attitudes and values. The idea is that if advertisers pick the correct category, they can direct their ads specifically to those people who would be likely to buy the product for some profound psychological reason.

The business community has always been interested in market segmentation. It began with geographical segmentation, since people living in different regions had different needs. Then there was demographics, which divided people by such traits as age, sex, and occupation. Demographics became extremely sophisticated with the advent of computer analysis in the 1950s, which ushered in the third type of segmentation: psychographics (literally, a "map of the mind").

The argument against psychographic research is the argument against all types of marketing research: Some feel that the business community ought to spend more time improving products and spend less time obsessing over the mind of the consumer.

Berkeley Rice is a contributing editor at Psychology Today magazine. Rice offers an analysis of the current vogue in psychographic research, VALS (which stands for "Values and Life Styles") Research.

Reading Difficulty Level: 5.

You may not care about psychographics, but psychographics cares about you. It cares about what you think, what you feel, what you believe, the way you live and, most of all, the products and services that you use.

Are you what you buy? Madison Avenue wants to know.

Ever since the snake convinced Eve to sample an apple in the Garden of Eden, advertisers and marketers have been trying to discover why consumers buy what they do. A few years ago, marketers thought the reason was demographics, and that buying was governed by consumers' age, sex, income, education, occupation and other characteristics. They also tried to divide the purchasing world up according to social class.

These mass-marketing strategies, however, are now considered crude and overly general. Marketing researchers today want to get into the individual consumer's head, so that companies can aim their products at more specific segments of the population. Some think that psychographics is their ticket inside.

Psychographic analyses for Schlitz beer, for example, revealed that heavy beer drinkers were real macho men who feel that pleasures in their lives are few and far between, and they want something more, according to Joseph Plummer, the researcher who conducted the study. This insight led to Schlitz commercials that told people "You only go around once," so you might as well "reach for all the gusto you can."

When the current walking-shoe boom began, the athletic-shoe industry assumed that most walkers were simply burned-out joggers. Psychographic research, however, has shown that there are really several different groups of walkers: Some walk for fun, some walk with religious dedication, others walk to work and still others walk the dog. Some really want to exercise, and some want the illusion of exercise. As a result, there are now walking shoes aimed at several groups, ranging from Nike Healthwalkers to Footjoy Joy-Walkers.

When Merrill Lynch learned through psychographics that the bulk of its clients saw themselves as independent-minded, upwardly mobile achievers, the investment firm changed the image in its commercials. Instead of the familiar thundering herd of bulls from the 1970s, Merrill Lynch ads portrayed scenes of a solitary bull: "a breed apart."

Marketing researchers want to get into the consumer's head. They think psychographics is their ticket.

The term "psychographics" first began to pop up in the business community during the late 1960s, referring to attempts to classify consumers by their beliefs, motivations and attitudes. In 1970, psychologist Daniel Yankelovich, who headed his own social-research firm, launched an annual survey of changing values and attitudes called the Yankelovich Monitor. It tracks more than

Psychographics tracks more than 50 trends in people's attitudes toward aspects of their life-style.

50 trends in people's attitudes toward time, money, the future, family, self, institutions and many other aspects of their life-style. By measuring these shifts in attitudes, Monitor researchers claim to have spotted or predicted trends such as the shift to white wine and light alcoholic beverages, and the rising sales of supermarket-chain brands and generic drugs. About 100 companies now pay $28,500 a year to subscribe to the Monitor survey.

By the mid 1970s, "life-style" had become a popular buzzword in advertising and marketing circles. Many advertising agencies began to do their own psychographic research: Needham, Harper and Steers (now DDB Needham), for example, divided consumers into 10 life-style categories typified by characters such as Thelma, the old-fashioned traditionalist; Candice, the chic suburbanite; and Fred, the frustrated factory worker. A flurry of ads tried—often blatantly—to pitch products by appealing to the life-style of people commonly referred to as the "upscale market." An ad for Chrysler's 1979 LeBaron, for example, featured an attractive young couple engaged in typically active, upscale pursuits such as tennis and sailing. The ad copy gushed: "It's got style. It's got life. Put some life in your style."

An ad for Chrysler's LeBaron, for example, featured an attractive young couple engaged in typically active, upscale pursuits such as tennis and sailing.

While all of this was going on, a researcher named Arnold Mitchell wrote a series of reports analyzing the way people's basic needs and values influenced their attitudes and behavior, particularly as consumers. Working at what is now SRI International in Menlo Park, California, he had administered a lengthy questionnaire to nearly 2,000 people. Using the results, Mitchell divided consumers into categories based in part on the theories of the late psychologist Abraham Maslow and his hierarchy of "needs growth." (See Figure 12.1).

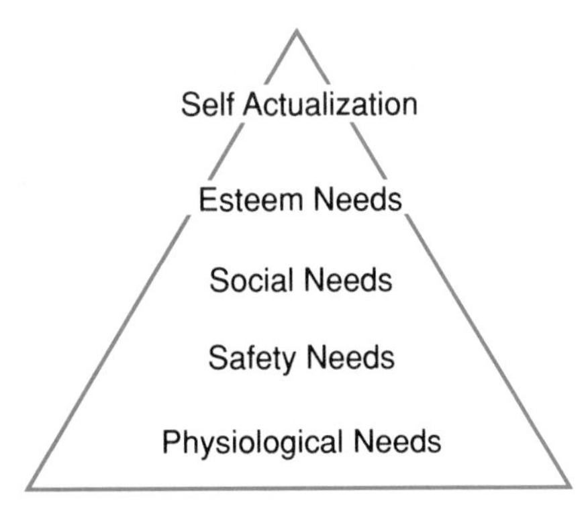

Figure 12.1. Maslow's Hierarchy of Needs.

Maslow believed that most human behavior is based on certain internal drives or needs, and that personal development consists of stages of maturity marked by fulfillment of these needs. Until the needs of one stage are satisfied, an individual cannot progress to the next level of maturity. At the lowest level are basic bodily needs such as hunger and sleep, followed by needs for safety, shelter and comfort. The next levels consist of psychological needs to belong, to have self-esteem and to be respected by others. Near the top comes the need for self-actualization: fully developing one's potential. People who reach this level are likely to be more creative, successful and influental than people who haven't attained it. Finally, Maslow said, the needs for spirituality and sensitivity lead to the highest level of consciousness.

Mitchell also claimed that each stage of an individual's development is marked by a "particular pattern of priorities . . . a unique set of dominating values and needs." He used his survey findings to create nine psychologically graphic portraits of consumers, one for each pattern he identified. By 1983, when Mitchell published a book called *The Nine American Lifestyles,* his work had attracted considerable interest from marketers and advertisers. Based on his work, SRI had formed a commercial marketing-research program called VALS, an acronym for Values and Lifestyles. Before he died in 1985, Mitchell saw VALS become the country's most widely used system of psychographic research.

The VALS typology (See Figure 12.2) begins with two life-styles, the Survivors and the Sustainers, both small groups with limited financial resources. Survivors are typically elderly and poor: Most feel trapped in their poverty, with no hope of escape. Sustainers, only slightly better off, are struggling at the edge of poverty. Although they often bitterly blame "the system" for their troubles, Sustainers have not quite given up.

VALS then divides into two pathways, Inner-Directed and Outer-Directed, terms drawn from the work of sociologist David

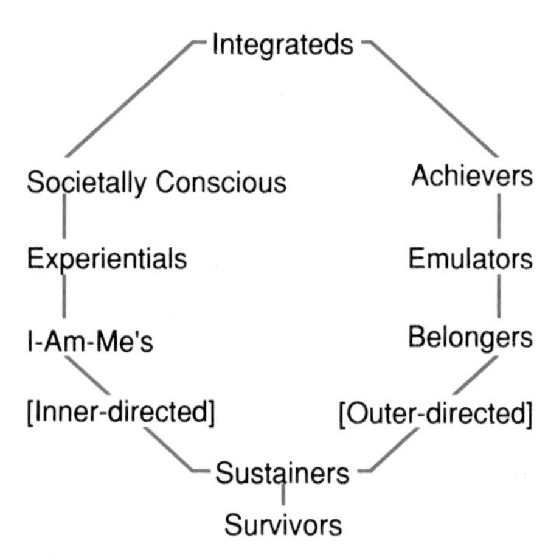

Figure 12.2. Nine VALS Lifestyles.

Riesman. There are three Outer-Directed types: Belongers, Emulators and Achievers. Belongers are the largest VALS group of all, making up 38 percent of the country's population. These stable, hard-working blue-collar or service-industry workers are conservative and conforming; they know what's right and what's wrong, and they stick to the rules because they want to fit in.

VALS is the country's most widely used system of psychographic research.

Emulators are more ambitious, more competitive and more status conscious than Belongers. They also make more money, but they envy the life-style of the Achievers, one level above them. Emulators would like to feel they're "on the way up," but most will never make it. They wonder if they're getting a fair shake from the system.

Achievers, who make up 20 percent of the population, are the successful business managers and professional people. Competent and self-reliant, "they know what they want and they make it happen."

They want the trappings of success—expensive homes, cars, and vacations—and most expect to get them. Having achieved the American Dream, they are generally staunch defenders of the society that rewarded them.

Parallel to but quite different from the Outer-Directed types are the three Inner-Directed VALS categories. The first, the I-Am-Me's, is a tiny group: generally young, highly individualistic, very egocentric and often confused about their goals in life. As their outlook broadens and they become more sure of themselves, they tend to mature into Experientials. If they then extend their view to include society as a whole, they become the Societally Conscious. This is the largest of the Inner-Directed groups; its members tend to be knowledgeable and concerned about social causes such as conservation. Many earn a good deal of money, but their life-styles emphasize simplicity and involvement.

The idea that basic psychological needs or drives affect consumer behavior makes a good deal of sense, and few researchers would quarrel with it.

At the pinnacle of VALS is the tiny group of psychologically mature Integrateds, the lucky few who have put it all together. They combine the best of Inner and Outer Direction: the power and drive of the Achievers and the sensitivity of the Societally Conscious. They have a sense of balance in their lives and confidence in their place in the world.

SRI has produced a half-hour video that provides brief looks at people in different VALS categories. Estelle, an elderly Survivor in the film, lives alone, scraping by on a tight budget. Moe is a Hispanic Sustainer who spends his afternoons at the racetrack hoping for a big win. Dave and Donna, a young Belonger couple who believe in God, family and country, live in a small house in a development of similar homes. Art, the Emulator, is a door-to-door salesman who drives through a fancy neighborhood and wonders, "What did they do right?" Steve, a lawyer-entrepreneur Achiever who's pictured soaking in his hot tub with his attractive wife, insists that money's "just a way of keeping score."

Mitchell's idea that basic psychological needs or drives affect consumer behavior makes a good deal of sense, and few researchers would quarrel with it. It's less clear, however, that VALS survey methods really tap into the things that Maslow was talking about. VALS "does not measure basic psychological characteristics, but social values which are purported reflections of these characteristics," says psychologist Joseph Smith, president of the market-research firm Oxtoby-Smith. Those values, Smith contends, don't predict consumer behavior very well: "Maslow was working in the world of clinical and developmental psychology. To try to adapt his theories and language from that world, as VALS has done, is an engaging idea but bound to be fruitless."

But bear fruit VALS has. Since SRI began marketing psychographic research, 250 corporate clients or "members," as SRI calls them, have used VALS data. Most VALS clients sell consumer products and services: packaged goods, automobiles, insurance, television, publishing and advertising. Depending on how much customized service they want, 150 current VALS members pay from $20,000 to more than $150,000 per year, producing reported annual revenues of more than $2 million for Mitchell's brainchild.

Since SRI began marketing psychographic research, 250 corporate clients clients have used VALS data.

Member companies can combine VALS profiles with much larger marketing systems that provide information on specific product brands and media use. Or they can link VALS to several "geodemographic" marketing services that group people by ZIP codes or neighborhood, according to the demographic features of typical households.

Advertising agencies such as Young & Rubicam, Ogilvy and Mather and J. Walter Thompson have used VALS information to place ads on TV shows and in magazines that draw the right psychographic segments for their clients' products or to design commercials and print ads that target specific consumer groups. They have learned, for example, that TV's daytime soap operas draw heavily among Survivors, Sustainers and Belongers, because they're often home alone. Achievers watch a lot of sports and news shows, while the Societally Conscious prefer dramas and documentaries.

Magazines such as *Time* and *The New Yorker* have a lot of Achiever readers, while *Reader's Digest* has more Belongers (*Psychology Today*, which uses a different psychographic system, has readers who are broad-minded, style conscious and experimenters—probably more Inner- than Outer-Directed).

VALS has attracted many clients from the auto industry, including GM, Ford, Nissan, Honda and Mercedes-Benz. VALS studies show what you might expect: that Belongers tend to buy family-sized domestic cars, while Emulators and I-Am-Me's prefer "muscle" cars like the Chevy Camaro. Achievers usually buy luxury cars, often foreign models like Mercedes or BMW, not so much because of their superior quality but because they represent achievement and status. Societally Conscious types might also buy a Mercedes, but more for its technical excellence than what it "says" about them.

To complicate matters, nearly half of all couples are "mixed" marriages of two VALS types.

To complicate matters for advertisers, nearly half of all couples are "mixed" marriages of two different VALS types. Ads for minivans, therefore, may need to carry a double message: one to appeal to an Achiever husband who might use it for golfing or fishing expeditions with his buddies and another to appeal to his Belonger wife, who sees it primarily as a vehicle for ferrying the children.

Corporate clients can use a 30-item VALS questionnaire to survey their own markets and have SRI classify the results into VALS types. The questionnaire asks people to indicate their agreement or disagreement with statements such as "What I do at work is more important to me than the money I earn" or "I would rather spend a quiet evening at home than go out to a party" or "I like to be outrageous."

By using such research methods, client companies can construct VALS profiles for their own markets or those of their competitors; position products or design packaging to appeal to particular groups; or spot trends in product use and consumer needs.

By using VALS, companies can design packaging to appeal to particular groups; or spot trends in product use and consumer needs.

Ray Ellison Homes, a big real estate developer and builder in San Antonio, Texas, took advantage of this type of VALS research. The company began by mailing a VALS questionnaire to 5,000 home buyers in the area and also asked them how much they valued items such as wallpaper or landscaping. "We needed to find out their values," says Jim Tilton, vice president of merchandising and advertising, "so we could really build to their needs and desires."

The company then conducted in-depth group interviews with the three VALS types most likely to buy its homes—Belongers, Achievers and Societally Conscious—to probe for further insights. When a group of Achiever women saw pictures of a big country kitchen, one of them exclaimed, "There's no way I'd clean all that tile!" A similar display of tile in the luxurious master bathroom, however, did not put her off. Apparently, the kitchen made her think of work, but she viewed the bathroom as a place of relaxation.

On the basis of these interviews and the survey results, Tilton says, "we took our standard houses apart and started from scratch, putting them back together piece by piece." To attract Achievers, for instance, the company added impressive facades, luxury carpeting and elaborate security systems. For the Societally Conscious, they designed energy-efficient homes. "What we've done," executive vice-president Jack Robinson explains, "is really get inside the consumer's head, into what his perceived values are, and give them back to him—in land, in financing and in the features of a home."

While VALS is the best-known and most successful psychographic research program around, it is hardly the only one doing this kind of work. Yankelovich's Monitor is still going strong, and many smaller firms do custom-tailored research for individual clients or specific markets. Some large consumer-goods companies and TV networks now do their own psychographic studies.

Despite this popularity, psychographics has plenty of doubters. Some critics, like Smith, question its utility: "We can't really measure the important personal attributes based on surveys," he says. "Psychographic research gives you a lot of superficial, inconsequential and titillating material but very little of pointed use to the guy who is designing products or trying to advertise and sell them." Because psychographic research firms guard their methods very carefully, as trade secrets, outsiders have been unable to test the data's validity and reliability (most firms claim they do their own validity testing).

Russell Haley, a professor of marketing at the University of New Hampshire who heads a market-research firm, points out that decisions to buy some products are simply not closely related to personal values. "If you're dealing with paper towels," he says, "personal values are not likely to be that relevant. On the other hand, if you're selling cosmetics or insurance, VALS may be quite useful because people's attitudes toward beauty or money are very relevant." He concludes: "I have some clients who like it, and some who don't."

Some companies that have used VALS and other psychographic research in the past no longer do so, having decided it's not worth the extra cost. Some claim that psychographics merely reveals the obvious or that it duplicates what demographic data show more clearly. In demographic language, Belongers are 57 years old on average, and the majority earn less than $20,000 per year; 72 percent of them are married, and only 3 percent have graduated from college. Experientials are 28 years old and earn $32,000 per year, on average; only 31 percent of them are married, and 40 percent attended college.

"When VALS first came out," says Bob Hoffman, president of Mojo MDA, a San Francisco advertising agency, "it enlightened us and described behavior in certain ways that some people hadn't thought of before. But now it makes people think in boxes." Hoffman and others argue that psychographics tries too hard to categorize everyone into discrete types, ignoring the fact that most people have traits and behavior common to several types. People also don't always think and behave consistently in every context. Some individuals may vote as Belongers but think like Achievers when they walk into the automobile showroom. Some Achievers may act like Belongers when pushing a baby's stroller through a supermarket.

According to one ad exec, "VALS makes people think in boxes."

In response to such critics, VALS marketing director Jack Tyler insists that "We've never claimed that all individuals fit neatly into one category, like cookie-cutter types, or that they have a stereotypical response to every situation. We provide our clients with secondary VALS scores that indicate these other characteristics." VALS simply claims that people's general behavior fits the profile of a given category, Tyler says, and that these categories offer valuable insights into the consumer.

Some claim that psychographics merely reveals the obvious or that it duplicates what demographic data show more clearly.

What VALS and other life-style studies have done is provide vivid portraits of American consumers;

while the accuracy of the pictures is debatable, psychographics still has many believers. Says Jerry Hamilton of Ketchum Advertising in San Francisco, "VALS makes it possible to personalize marketing and to understand the target we're trying to reach better than any other piece of research. Sure, it may oversimplify. No matter what classification system you use you're distorting everybody's individuality. But the alternative is to tailor advertising to 80 million individual households." ♦

You Can Have It All: Seven Campaigns for Deadly Sin

The Creative Staffs of Seven Top Advertising Agencies.

The following seven ads are the result of a challenge that Harper's *magazine sent out to seven of the world's most prestigious ad agencies: show us how you would advertise one of the seven deadly sins.* Harper's *proposed this exercise with tongue firmly in cheek, "in the interest of moral instruction and clarification," and "to provide grist for tomorrow's sermonizers."*

Although Harper's *motive was just to have fun, the ad agencies replied mostly to show off, and what we have before us is a primer of advertising technique. Each ad is a good example of the style of the ad house that presented it.*

The article is also an example of how creativity can be used for purposes which are, by definition, immoral.

Reading Difficulty Level: 1. But it's not all for fun. There's a serious point here.

With sweet words, Madison Avenue seeks to profit from our longing to lead ourselves into temptation.

The recent public debate on our nation's scandals exposes a fundamental irony. Amid the moralizing columns of pundits and two-minute homilies by newscasters warning "Thou Shalt Not" fall the whispers of advertisers: "Who Says You Can't Have It All?" and "Obsession" and "You Deserve a Break Today" and "The Pride is Back!"

With sweet words, Madison Avenue seeks to profit from our longing to lead ourselves into temptation. The schizophrenia of public puritanism and private libertinism creates a host of charming—and uniquely American—effects. Ivan Boesky cloisters himself with the

GLUTTONY

Agency: Fallon McElligott. *Art Director:* Dean Hanson. *Copywriters:* Jarl Olson, Mike Lescarbeau. *Clients:* Federal Express; Wall Street Journal; Lee Jeans.

Do you remember all of the things you told me you wanted as a child?

Well, your list may have changed, but I'll bet it hasn't gotten any shorter.

Perhaps you shouldn't be worried about that.

Greed has always motivated men and women. It has motivated inventors to make better mousetraps, artists to create greater art and scientists to find cures for diseases and pathways to the moon.

Just be sure to use your greed to good ends. Be greedy for knowledge. Be greedy for the kind of success that helps you, your family and your friends. Be greedy for love.

Just don't be greedy in ways that hurt others.

Remember, I'll always be the first one to know if you've been bad or good. So be good for goodness sake.

The world's foremost authority speaks out on the subject of greed.

AVARICE

Agency: The Martin Agency. *Art Director:* Hal Tench. *Copywriter:* Mike Hughes. *Photographer:* Jim Erickson. *Production:* Chet Booth. *Clients:* State of Virginia, "Virginia Is for Lovers"; General Motors; Reynolds Aluminum.

ENVY

Agency: NW Ayer, Inc. *Art Director:* Keith Gould. *Copywriter:* Patrick Cunningham. *Clients:* AT&T, "Reach Out and Touch Someone"; DeBeers, "A Diamond Is Forever"; U.S. Army, "Be All That You Can Be."

The only emotion powerful enough both to start a war—

and stop one.

WRATH

Agency: Saatchi & Saatchi DFS Compton. *Creative Director:* Dick Lopez. *Copywriter:* Jeff Frye. *Clients:* Toyota, "Who Could Ask for Anything More? Toyota"; PaineWebber, "Thank You, PaineWebber"; Wendy's, "Where's the Beef?"

SLOTH

Agency: J. Walter Thompson. *Art Director:* Jean Marcellino. *Copywriter:* Chuck Hoffman. *Clients:* Ford, "Have You Driven a Ford Lately?" Pepsi Slice, "We Got the Juice"; U.S. Marine Corps, "We're Looking for a Few Good Men."

It's Time To Start Feeling Good About Yourself–*Really* Good!

"PRIDE goeth before a fall"—we've all heard it. But how *TRUE* is it?

It's mostly *BUNK*, agree today's top mental health experts.

Pride: the sin you can feel good about

You've heard all the bad-mouthing.

At home. In Sunday school. In literary magazines. "Pride's a sin!" they proclaim. Well, don't you believe it.

"Pride's gotten a bad rap," says psychiatrist/ornithologist Bernard Warbler.

"It's time this country wakes up and faces facts. Pride, *to whatever extent,* is healthy and natural. The psychiatric community is in complete agreement on this point."

So stick out your chest, for heaven's sake. PRIDE—it's today's "buzz word" for mental health!

Henry VIII

Failure after romantic failure, it was Henry's pride that kept him searching for Mrs. Right. At 52, he finally found her—the lovely Catherine Parr.

William Plover
Dictionary Editor

The most misunderstood word in the English language? "Hubris," or excessive pride, is a word that's quickly leaving our vocabulary. *Good riddance!* The concept of "excessive" pride no longer works—and people are taking notice.

Dictionary editor William Plover: "'Hubris,' of course, comes to us from ancient Greece, and most word-watchers think it's come far enough. It's quite clear, early translators misunderstood the sense of 'wellness' implied by the Greeks. Resulting in centuries of lexicological slander, if you will. To me, hubris is a rather pleasant word."

Next time you run across "hubris" in the dictionary, cross it out—or write a new definition. You'll feel better for doing so!

A poet celebrates pride

And on the pedestal these words appear:
My name is Ozymandias, king of kings:
Look on my works, ye Mighty, and despair!

—*Percy Bysshe Shelley, "Ozymandias"*

Shelley was an early advocate of prideful living. His famous king Ozymandias wasn't afraid to put his words—or himself—up on a pedestal.

Shelley's wife, Mary Wollstonecraft Shelley, believed pride enabled men to do the extraordinary. Her novel Frankenstein was a classic celebration of a doctor's pride so great, it was larger than life itself.

Dr. Frankenstein's pride allowed him to create a human being—a task no fictional character had ever before accomplished.

Putting yourself on a pedestal—it's never been more convenient

But how can *you* live more pridefully?

It's easier than you think. We're the Pride Council. A trade association dedicated to bringing fine products—"Prouducts™"—to the American people. At prices that make pride easy to swallow.

ACT NOW! HERE'S HOW!

Just read the coupon below. You'll find carefully screened and selected companies that can help you design the look-down-your-nose lifestyle you've always dreamed of having.

Don't dally—send in your coupon today!

It would be a sin not to.

The Pride Council
Pride. It's not a sin anymore.™

Mail today to:
The Pride Council
666 Broadway
New York, NY 10012

You've got me convinced! Rush me FREE information on the following prideful products and companies, please!

- ☐ Your Face in Bronze, Inc.
- ☐ Old World Family Crests
- ☐ Roots to Royalty Ancestor Investigators
- ☐ The Freelance Biographers Guild
- ☐ Acme Pedestal Co.

Name ....
Address ....
City .... State .... Zip ....

PRIDE

Agency: Ogilvy & Mather. *Creative Director:* Jay Jasper. *Art Director:* Carrie Wieseneck. *Copywriter:* Jim Nolan. *Clients:* Hathaway, "The Man in the Hathaway Shirt"; American Express, "Don't Leave Home Without It"; Pepperidge Farm, "Pepperidge Farm Remembers."

Any Sin That's Enabled Us to Survive Centuries of War, Death, Pestilence and Famine Can't Be Called Deadly.

Lust

Where Would We Be Without It?

LUST

Agency: TBWA Advertising, Inc. *Art Director:* Geoff Hayes. *Copywriter:* Evert Cilliers. *Clients:* Absolut Vodka; Bombay Gin; Laughing Cow Cheese.

Torah. The President publicly offers his urine for official inspection. Mafia bosses make a public show of attending church. Preachers swear off adultery.

In the interest of moral instruction and clarification, *Harper's Magazine* asked leading advertising agencies to develop a campaign *promoting* the seven deadly sins: Wrath, Lust, Avarice, Gluttony, Sloth, Envy, and Pride. Each agency pitted in-house teams against one another to perform this public service, to provide grist for tomorrow's sermonizers and to reconcile God and Mammon. ♦

Questions for Discussion

1. In your opinion, which ad is most effective? Which techniques within the ad *makes* it most effective?
2. Do advertising campaigns today promote sin? If so, is that necessarily a detriment to society?
3. Do any of these ads actually make one of the seven deadly sins seem . . . less deadly?

Buying Silence: Self-Censorship of Smoking and Health in National Newsweeklies

Joe Tye

Cigarette advertising is an interesting case. Here we have an industry implicated in the deaths of 350,000 Americans each year, that spends $2 billion each year on advertising and promotion. This advertising is designed to replace whatever percentage of the industry's 50 million addicts have recently died or quit.

The following reading confirms what many observers had suspected: magazines that accept cigarette advertising don't do a very good job reporting on the health hazards of smoking.

The author of this piece, Joe Tye, is the chief operating officer of the Bay State Medical Center in Springfield, Massachusetts. He is also the president of an organization called STAT, which stands for "Stop Teenage Addiction to Tobacco."

Reading Difficulty Level: 2. But don't let that stop you from thinking about the implications of what he's saying.

When the tobacco companies shifted their broadcast advertising to print, magazines stopped covering the health effects of smoking.

The media's self-censorship on smoking and health may well be contributing to the occurrence of avoidable illnesses and premature deaths among tens of thousands of Americans.

Kenneth E. Warner, PhD
New England Journal of Medicine, 1985

Quite likely, publishers will feel increasing moral pressure to drop cigarette ads.

Time, 1969

On December 18, 1953, John C. Whitaker, then-chairman of the RJ Reynolds tobacco company, was infuriated by an article in the *Charlotte Observer* which stated that lung cancer deaths in South Carolina were up 25% in the past six years, and that "recent medical reports have indicated smoking may be connected with lung cancer." He grabbed his pen and scrawled across the page: "Carolina *contacts:* Can't such outbursts as the attached be silenced?"

The tobacco industry was well-experienced at using its contacts to prevent the media from reporting on smoking and health issues. As reported by Thomas Whiteside in his landmark 1971 book, *Selling Death*, results of the 1954 Hammond & Horn study on smoking and lung cancer "made the front pages of the press in this country but were virtually ignored on network television news shows—which, as it happened, were nearly all sponsored by cigarette companies."

On January 1, 1971, cigarette commercials were outlawed on television and radio, and tobacco companies transferred hundreds of millions of dollars in advertising to the print media. As the national newsweeklies began to depend on cigarette advertising revenues, one would expect to see a significant decline in their coverage of smoking and health issues.

To test this conclusion, STAT (Stop Teenage Addiction to Tobacco) researchers examined coverage of smoking and tobacco issues in *Time*, *Newsweek*, and *US News & World Report* from 1950 to 1985. Each article listed in the *Reader's Guide to Periodic Literature* under "tobacco," "cigarettes," and "smoking" was examined.

As shown in the charts, a clear drop in coverage of smoking and health topics by all three newsweeklies followed the elimination of broadcast cigarette advertising in 1971.

The 63% decline in the number and length of articles between 1960–69 and 1970–79 substantially understates the reduction in coverage of smoking and health issues. During the 1950s and 1960s most articles were about smoking and lung cancer or other diseases, but after 1970, most focused on business or political matters.

In defending *Time* magazine's acceptance of cigarette advertising, then-publisher Ralph P. Davidson said, "In our Medicine section, we take special care to report fully on

Reprinted from *Tobacco and Youth Reporter*, vol. 4, no. 1, Spring 1989. Reprinted by permission.

any statistical and laboratory evidence which may link smoking with cancer and heart and respiratory disease." (*Business and Society Review*, Winter 1977–78.)

However, we were unable to find a single article on statistical or laboratory evidence linking smoking with any of these diseases in *Time* magazine from 1971 until that statement was made. During all of the 1970s, in fact, *Time* ran only 17 articles on smoking, one-third of which concerned business issues and were unrelated to health.

Evidence suggests that the ignoring of smoking and health issues by these magazines is a direct result of publishers not wishing to offend cigarette advertisers.

A Smokescreen?

Perhaps more important than the reduction in the number of articles is the exclusion of smoking from articles about diseases caused by smoking. A study by the American Council on Science and Health showed that from 1981–86, *US News & World Report* did not mention smoking in 18 stories about cancer and mentioned it only once in 19 stories about heart disease. During the same period, *Time* mentioned smoking only once in 22 stories about heart disease and not at all in five articles about cancer.

In 1979, *Newsweek* carried a two-page article about the boom in smokeless tobacco use but did not hint that adverse health consequences might be associated with the product. A *Newsweek* cover story in August 1988 on the "Medical Mystery of Miscarriages" did not mention maternal cigarette smoking, although this has been identified as a major cause of miscarriage and spontaneous abortion.

A Newsweek cover story on the "Medical Mystery of Miscarriage" did not mention maternal smoking as one of the causes.

Evidence suggests that the ignoring of smoking and health issues by these magazines is a direct result of publishers not wishing to offend cigarette advertisers. For example, in October 1984, *Time* included a personal health supplement written by the American Academy of Family Physicians. According to the Academy, all references to smoking and health were excised by *Time* without the Academy's approval. The only reference to smoking was a statement that smoking in bed should be avoided.

In November 1983, *Newsweek* ran a 16-page special supplement written by the American Medical Association, which virtually ignored smoking and health, although the original AMA manuscript included information on the subject. According to the AMA science editor, *Newsweek* "resisted any mention of cigarettes." That issue of *Newsweek* had 12 full-page cigarette advertisements.

The following October, *Newsweek* ran another personal health supplement written by the AMA. This one had a brief but hard-hitting section on smoking and health. That issue had only four cigarette ads. Evidently, the publishers got the message because in September 1985, a third personal health supplement said only that heavy smokers should see their physicians

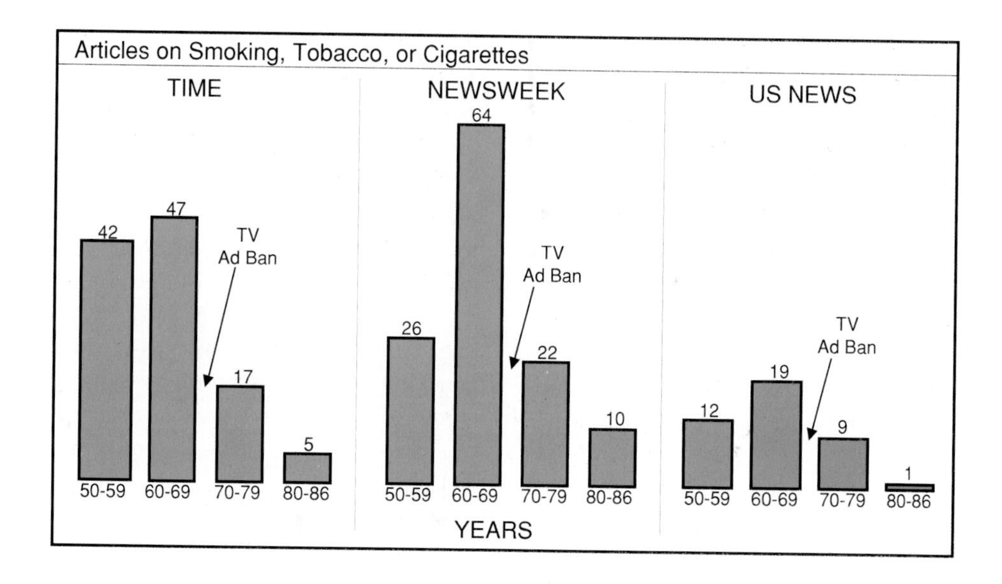

before exercising, and it downplayed the role of smoking and lung cancer in women's cancer mortality.

The publishers and editors of magazines justify their acceptance of cigarette advertising on the grounds that they are able to maintain a "Chinese Wall" between editorial policy and advertising policy.

This study supports earlier work concluding that this separation is more of a Japanese paper house wall and that from the beginning of the broadcast ban on cigarette ads until 1985, the major national newsweeklies systematically failed to accurately and completely report on smoking and health issues.

Although this study does not cover the period since 1985, these three newsweeklies appear to have increased their coverage of smoking and health issues during the past several years.

Ignoring the Issues

No editor ever acknowledges that many cigarette ads are deceptive. Many do not even meet the minimal standards of the tobacco industry's own code of advertising ethics which prohibits depiction of vigorous athletic activity and of smoking as essential to social or sexual success. Nor will editors comment on the implicit health claims made in many cigarette ads which are unproven, false, and deceptive.

Nowhere could we find any article or editorial critical of the efforts of the tobacco industry to promote smoking or offering an alternative point of view. On the other hand, a number of editorials criticized "self-righteous" nonsmokers' rights advocates, and, not surprisingly, opposed any restrictions on tobacco advertising on freedom-of-speech grounds.

The publishers and editors of magazines justify their acceptance of cigarette advertising on the grounds that they are able to maintain a "Chinese Wall" between editorial policy and advertising policy.

When the AMA called for a total ban on all advertising for tobacco, the three newsweeklies did not even cover the proposal.

In 1985, when the AMA called for a total ban on all advertising and promotion of tobacco, marking a reversal of a decades-long hands-off position, the action should have been a major news story. The three newsweeklies, however, did not even cover the proposal. Also absent have been articles and editorial condemnation about the tobacco industry's efforts to develop cigarette markets in lesser developed nations.

Although the publishers and editors of *Time*, *Newsweek*, and *US News & World Report* claim that their editorial policies are totally uncompromised by the acceptance of cigarette ads, evidence suggests that receiving millions of dollars in tobacco advertising fees every year has resulted in a systematic self-censorship on the issue of smoking and disease.

Articles on the nation's leading cause of preventable death have averaged less than two per year per magazine, which contrasts sharply with the coverage given AIDS, drugs, cholesterol, and other health-related issues. When cancer, heart disease, complications of pregnancy, and other diseases are covered, the role of smoking is minimized or eliminated.

A conflict of interest has prevented the major newsweeklies from appropriately covering the worldwide epidemic of cigarette-caused diseases. So long as these publications benefit from tobacco industry advertising revenues, it is unlikely that the public will be adequately informed of all important smoking and health and public policy issues. ♦

Editor's note: *After publication of this article in* Tobacco and Youth Reporter, *Joe Tye sent the editors of* Time, Newsweek, *and* US News & World Report *a copy of the issue and offered to print their respones. No one answered.*

During February and March 1990, the three newsweeklies—to their credit—covered the events surrounding RJR's proposed introductions of Uptown and Dakota cigarettes which were specifically targeted at minority consumers. Whether this signifies a change of policy remains to be seen.

Magazines That Have No Tobacco Advertising

The *Journal of the American Medical Association* publishes a list of magazines with a policy against tobacco advertising. Following is the list from the September 8, 1989 issue (Vol. 262, No. 10).

Adirondack Life
Air & Space
Alaska Magazine
American Baby
American Health
American Heritage
American History Illustrated
Animal Kingdom
Arizona Highways
Audubon
Aviation Week & Space Technology
Backpacker
Bicycling
Boy's Life
Business Week
Consumer Reports
Cyclist
Dance Magazine
Down East Magazine
Farm Journal
Fishing Facts
The Futurist
Golf Illustrated
Good Housekeeping
Hadassah Magazine
Harvard Business Review
Harvard Medical School Health Letter
Health
Highlights for Children
Historic Preservation
Horticulture
Humpty Dumpty's Magazine
International Travel News
Isaac Asimov's Science Fiction
Jack and Jill
MAD Magazine
Maine Fish & Wildlife
Maine Life Magazine
Mayo Clinic Health Letter
Model Railroader
Modern Maturity
Montana Magazine
Mother Earth News
Mother Jones
Nation
National Geographic
National Parks Journal
Nation's Business
Natural History
The New Yorker
North American Review
Nutrition Action Healthletter
Oceans
Old House Journal
Organic Gardening
Parenting
Parents Magazine
Personal Computing
Petersen's Hunting
Popular Communications
Prevention
Railfan and Railroad
Ranger Rick
Reader's Digest
Runner's World
Sail
Saturday Evening Post
Science
Science News
The Sciences
Scientific American
Sesame Street
Seventeen
Sierra
Smithsonian
Sports Afield
Stork
Sunset Magazine
Theatre Crafts
Travel Holiday
Utah Holiday
Vegetarian Times
Venture Magazine
Vermont Life
The Washington Monthly
Western Outdoors
Writer's Digest
Yankee

Questions for Discussion

1. In your opinion, does advertising for tobacco products deserve First Amendment protection?
2. Do you agree or disagree that an all-out ban on cigarette advertising would be in the best interests of the American public?

Suggested Readings

On Motivational Research Within the Advertising Industry

Kanner, Bernice, "Mind Games: How Advertising Agencies Use the Latest Research to Get You to Buy the Products They're Hawking," *New York* Vol. 22, May 8, 1989, p. 34 (7).

Miller, Annetta and Dody Tsiantar, "Psyching Out Consumers: In the Quest to Divine Shopper's Motivations, Marketers Are Returning to the Social Sciences," *Newsweek* Vol. 113, February 27, 1989, p. 46 (2).

Moore, Suzanne, "Insider Trading: Inner Selves for Sale," *New Statesman* Vol. 115, April 15, 1988, p. 14 (1). Lifestyle advertising and VALS.

Trachtenberg, Jeffrey A., "Beyond the Hidden Persuaders," *Forbes* Vol. 139, March 23, 1987, p. 134 (3). Psychological aspects of marketing.

A Sampling of Articles Dealing with the Power and Effects of Advertising

"Ads, Violence and Values," *Advertising Age* Vol. 61, April 2, 1990, p. 12 (1). Editorial dealing with the slaying of inner city teens over their Nike Air Jordan tennis shoes.

Almendros, Nestor, "Spots of Art: How Commercials Are Changing the Movies," *The New Republic* Vol. 198, May 23, 1988, p. 27 (4).

Bogart, Leo, "The Multiple Meanings of Television Advertising," *Society* Vol. 25, May–June 1988, p. 76 (5).

Cohen, Stanley E., "Don't Let Advertising Take the Rap for Social Ills," *Advertising Age* Vol. 61, June 11, 1990, p. 34 (2).

Edel, Richard, "American Dream Vendors," *Advertising Age* Vol. 59, November 9, 1988, p. 152 (4). Advertising and popular culture. Special issue: The Power of Advertising.

Galbraith, John Kenneth, "Economics and Advertising: Exercise in Denial," *Advertising Age* Vol. 59, November 9, 1988, p. 80 (3). Special issue on the power of advertising.

Kanner, Bernice, "Big Boys Don't Cry," *New York* Vol. 23, May 21, 1990, p. 20 (2). The stereotyping of men in advertising.

Landler, Mark, Walecia Konrad and Teresa Y. Wiltz, "Consumers Are Getting Mad, Mad, Mad at Mad Ave.," *Business Week*, April 30, 1990, p. 70 (3).

Miller, Mark Crispin, "How Dow Recycles Reality," *Esquire* Vol. 114, September 1990, p. 110 (1). Using the environment as an advertising ploy.

Norton, Clark, "What TVs Recommend Most," *Hippocrates* Vol. 3, January–February 1989, p. 24 (2). Television pushes prescription medication.

On "Subliminal Advertising" and Subliminal Persuasion.

Beatty, Sharon E., and Del E. Hawkins, "Subliminal Stimulation: Some New Data and Interpretation," *Journal of Advertising* Vol. 18, Summer 1989, p. 4 (5). Hawkins's 1970 article on subliminal stimulation has been used for nearly 20 years as empirical evidence that subliminal advertising can directly affect consumption-relevant behavior. This study presents new evidence that casts doubt on Hawkin's conclusion that a simple subliminal stimulus can serve to arouse a basic drive.

Bornstein, Robert F., Dean R. Leone and Donna J. Galley, "The Generalization of Subliminal Mere Exposure Effects: Influence of Stimuli Perceived Without Awareness on Social Behavior," *Journal of Personality and Social Psychology* Vol. 53, December 1987, p. 1070 (10).

Bower, Bruce, "Subliminal Deceptions," *Science News* Vol. 138, August 25, 1990, p. 124 (1). Effectiveness of audio tapes containing alleged subliminal messages.

Caputi, Jane, "Seeing Elephants: The Myths of Phallotechnology," *Feminist Studies,* Fall 1988, p. 489 (39).

Davis, Lisa, "Secret Suggestions," *Hippocrates* Vol. 2, September–October 1988, p. 90 (2).

Gable, Myron, Henry T. Wilkens, Lynn Harris and Richard Feinberg, "An Evaluation of Subliminally Embedded Sexual Stimuli in Graphics," *Journal of Advertising* Vol. 16, Winter 1987, p. 26 (6). Findings indicate that subliminally embedded, sexually oriented stimuli do not influence consumer preference.

Goleman, Daniel, "Research Probes What the Mind Senses Unaware: New Findings Fuel Debate about the Power of Messages Directed to the Unconscious," *The New York Times,* August 14, 1990, p. B5 (N), p. C1 (L), Col. 1, 26 col. in. Science pages.

Hill, Doug, and Ken Sobel, "Could that ALF Cartoon Be Flashing a Hidden Message? Yes, Said a Sharp-Eyed Viewer—Who Pursued the Case to Its Surprising Conclusion," *TV Guide* Vol. 37, August 12, 1989, p. 6 (3).

Kanner, Bernice, "From the Subliminal to the Ridiculous," *New York* Vol. 22, December 4, 1989, p. 18 (3). A Column.

Key, Wilson, *The Age of Manipulation: The Con in Confidence, the Sin in Sincere.* Although widely discredited, Key's ideas receive mixed reviews. Reviewed by Phil Dorado, *New Statesman and Society* Vol. 2, October 27, 1989, p. 43 (3). Also reviewed in *Advertising Age,* Oct. 2, 1989, p. 26 (1) and *Publishers Weekly* May 26, 1989, p. 51 (1).

Krajick, Kevin, "Sound Too Good to Be True? Behind the Boom in Subliminal Tapes," *Newsweek* Vol. 116, July 30, 1990, p. 60 (2).

Natale, Jo Anna, "Are You Open to Suggestion? Subliminal Persuasion Is Back—In a Big Way for Big Bucks. But Does It Work?", *Psychology Today* Vol. 22, September 1988, p. 28 (2).

"Subliminal Learning: A Fraud?", *USA Today* Vol. 118, September 1989, p. 8 (1). Behavior modification tapes.

On Cigarette (and Alcohol) Advertising

"Advertising Pleads the First: The Great American Smoke-in," *Commonweal*, February 13, 1987, p. 75 (5).

Castro, Janice, "Volunteer Vice Squad: The Outcry Over Tobacco and Alcohol Marketing Reaches a Fever Pitch," *Time* Vol. 135, April 23, 1990, p. 60 (2).

"Cigarette Ads and the Press," *Nation*, March 7, 1987, p. 283 (7).

Dollisson, John, "Advertising Restrictions: A Threat to the Open Society," *Vital Speeches* Vol. 56, September 1, 1990, p. 689 (3).

Fleishman, Diana and Norman Fleishman, "Beer Ads: Fuel for the Drug Bonfire," *The Humanist* Vol. 49, November–December 1989, p. 18 (3).

"The Intolerance Spreads," *The Economist* Vol. 315, April 28, 1990, p. 28 (2). American Survey, smoking.

Ramirez, Anthony. "Debating Cigarette Ad Curbs," *The New York Times* Vol. 140, Sept. 20, 1990, p. C6 (N), p. D19 (L), Col. 1, 16 col. in.

"Smoke and Mirrors," and "Smoking 'em Out," *The Economist* Vol. 316, September 15, 1990, p. 84 (1) and p. 83 (2).

On the Wider Area of "Health Advertising"

Schiller, Zachary, Russell Mitchell, Wendy Zellner, Lois Therrien, Andrea Rothman and Walecia Konrad, "The Great American Health Pitch," *Business Week*, October 9, 1989, p. 114 (6). Also includes related article on eating right even when you are busy.

"The Top Ten Health Frauds," *Consumers' Research Magazine* Vol. 73, February 90, p. 34 (2). Includes related article.

On the History of American Advertising

Collins, Julia M., "Image and Advertising," *Harvard Business Review* Vol. 67, January–February 1989, p. 93 (5).

Goodrum, Charles and Helen Dalrymple, *Advertising in America: The First 200 Years* (Abrams, 1990). Lavishly illustrated, provides an anecdotal as well as a visual history of advertising in the U.S.

McCauley, Lucy A., "The Face of Advertising," *Harvard Business Review* Vol. 67, November–December 1989, p. 155 (5). How advertising images have changed over the years.

Public Relations I: The Corporate Sector

13

Public relations is something that large organizations do to stay in touch with the rest of the world. It is defined as the management function that seeks to influence public opinion in ways that are favorable to the organization, while gathering data about the public that will be useful to the organization. The organization could be of any type, from a small nonprofit office to a huge corporation or national government. In this chapter we look at the way public relations is practiced in the corporate world. In the next two chapters we will look at this same function—influencing and keeping in touch with public opinion—as it is practiced by governments and political candidates.

One way to understand public relations is to analyze the ways it is different from advertising. First, public relations communication is two-way: unlike advertising, it has the objective of allowing the public to communicate with the organization, as well as sending the organization's message out to the public. If you have a complaint that you would like to register with a corporation, the switchboard will probably connect you to someone in the public relations office.

Second, public relations incudes the use of interpersonal communication, while advertising uses mass media exclusively. Public relations messages are delivered as speeches and lunchtime chats, as well as the more common press releases.

Third, organizations do not pay for the time and space in which public relations messages appear, as they do with advertising. P.R. messages often appear within news stories, editorials, and even entertainment programming.

The public relations industry has done much good. It has promoted full disclosure of at least some embarrassing corporate events, it has sparked at least some public debate, and it has kept corporate management in touch with the public's feelings.

But the public relations industry also has some black marks on its record, and these black marks generally have to do with the manipulation, in one form or another, of the American public. This chapter deals with three forms of manipulation.

The first reading deals with advertising that is disguised as news. The second deals with the corporate willingness to cash in on environmental concerns while doing very little to improve the environment. The final reading deals with how entertainment corporation executives manipulate the journalists who cover the Hollywood "beat."

A Word from Your Friendly Drug Company

Steven T. Taylor and Morton Mintz

This first reading is all about public relations promotions that show up on your local news—as news.

Public relations influence in the news is no secret. It is, in fact, a time-honored tradition. It has always been easy to go through your local newspaper, especially in the specialty sections such as real estate and travel, and pick out the stories that began as press releases from public relations organizations. To a certain extent, the same kind of analysis is possible with radio and television news. A relatively recent trend, however, is the use of "canned" news, in which the news item is actually written and produced by the public relations firm. As the authors of the following article make clear, this blurring of the distinction between news and advertising imperils an important function of the media: to provide accurate, unbiased information about the marketplace. This trend is particularly dangerous in the field of drugs and medications.

Reading Difficulty Level: 4.

Many local stations slip into their newscasts "news" segments about prescription drugs that are nothing more than canned promotions.

Suppose a reputable newspaper acted as a conduit for "news" articles about prescription drugs that were in fact puff pieces published as received from the manufacturers. Now suppose someone exposed the breach of trust, and television stations or magazines jumped on the story. Wouldn't there be hell to pay? But in the case of TV, unfortunately, this breach of trust is actually happening. Many local stations slip into their newscasts "news" segments about prescription drugs that are nothing more than canned promotions, called video news releases. These VNRs rarely warn viewers that unlike other consumer products, prescription drugs are potent agents that can cause nasty, even life-threatening, adverse reactions and are not always effective.

This article is reprinted from *The Nation* magazine/The Nation Company, Inc., © 1991. From the October 21, 1991 issue, pp. 480–484.

The VNRs, plucked free of charge from satellite feeds, are produced for most pharmaceutical manufacturers by public-relations outfits. The stars of the disguised commercials—usually white-coated, confidence-inspiring physicians who tout drugs knowingly and glowingly—are paid by the manufacturers.

As if this weren't abusive enough, some VNRs escalate the deception by including lead-ins and closings suggested by the P.R. firm. When these are spoken by newscasters, the effect is to trick viewers even more into assuming not only that they are hearing and seeing authentic news but that it is news produced by their admirably enterprising local station.

It gets worse. Some VNRs have blank audio and visual portions, which are designed to enable a station to compound the con with phantom interviews. In these, viewers are led to believe that they hear and see a local anchor or reporter putting questions to the hired-hand doctor. It's an illusion: No conversation actually occurs. Instead, the "interviewer" fills in the blanks with questions planted and shaped by the P.R. firm to elicit and be in sync with the canned answers of the paid doctor. In turn, he or she is stage-managed to look to one side and nod just as in a real interview. Considerately, the P.R. firms supply extra footage, known as "B roll," that enables stations to work in a local angle.

The very least stations could do would be to signal viewers that drug companies are the sources of the VNRs, which would be no more difficult than tagging old videotapes "file footage." But no clues are given to the trusting, vulnerable, manipulated viewers. VNRs "send a controlled message," a CIBA-GEIGY representative said at a Food and Drug Law Institute conference in Washington in September 1990. "They allow us to make sure we can control the message as much as possible and not depend on a journalist to interpret data that would be in a news release kit."

The ultimate goal of all this slick, collaborative fakery is blatantly obvious: to induce the maximum possible number of victims of various real or imagined medical conditions to go to their doctors and demand the covertly advertised medicines.

TV's improper use of the pharmaceutical industry's tilted VNRs has gone on for years without public scrutiny. December 1990, however, the practice finally came under sharp fire in little-noted testimony at a hearing of the Senate Labor and Human Resources Committee. The testimony came from Eugene Secunda, an expert on VNR production who is an assistant professor of marketing at Baruch College in New York City, and David Jones, a former public affairs vice president at

The stars of the disguised commercials—usually white-coated, confidence-inspiring physicians—are paid by the manufacturers.

Some VNRs have blank audio and visual portions, which are designed to enable a station to compound the con with phantom interviews.

Abbott Laboratories who had previously worked for two other leading pharmaceutical houses, CIBA-GEIGY and Marion Laboratories. He left Abbott in disgust over objectionable marketing, promotion and pricing practices.

Committee chair Edward Kennedy asked Secunda whether VNRs "are by their very nature meant to deceive the viewer." Secunda's reply was damning: "They are meant to deceive in the sense that they do not represent themselves as a promotional message. When the television audience does not recognize that there is a promotional objective to be achieved, that is inherent deception."

When the television audience does not recognize that there is a promotional objective, that is inherent deception.

Jones was equally blunt. "The news media now is a major outlet, particularly when the message you are trying to distribute is a little questionable," he told Kennedy. In a recent interview, he said, "Many VNRs are terribly misleading. The media aren't doing what the public expects them to do—which is screen, evaluate and judge the information they get. Journalistic rigor is missing."

Strikingly, the absence of journalistic rigor troubled David Bartlett, director of the Radio and Television News Directors Association, and a knowledgeable Washington TV reporter who asked not to be named. "We have no problem with a station taking a piece of B roll or soundbite out of a VNR and putting it into a story," Bartlett said. "We do have a very, very big problem with folks who use VNRs deceptively, without identifying the source, without proper context, or [referring to their airing of uncut VNRs] the most egregious sin of all."

Many in the television industry won't admit to using uncut, unedited or unbalanced VNRs. But the Washington TV reporter, when asked whether the use of VNRs is fair to the viewers, reflected for a moment before saying, "Perhaps we do the viewer a disservice when we use a VNR—even if we alter it—without identifying that the main . . . resource for this story is a pharmaceutical company. Perhaps that is a disservice."

Her "perhaps" would be deleted by Dr. George Lundberg, editor in chief for scientific publications of the American Medical Association. "Our ten A.M.A. journals require full disclosure of financial interests of authors, editors, reviewers and editorial board members," Lundberg told us. "For a television station to receive and use promotional information from a company without appropriate editing to inform the viewer of the financial interests of the producer of that information would seem to be a gross breach of good ethical practices and against the public interest."

Yet, while many specifics are elusive, there's no doubt that the use of pharmaceutical and other VNRs is widespread and growing. Last

'News' About Xanax

Early this year on its evening newscast, Detroit television station WJBK aired a "health feature" about Xanax, an anti-anxiety drug, that included portions of a video news release. Expanding on the VNR segments, the newscaster told viewers: "The Food and Drug Administration recently approved the drug Xanax for treatment of panic attacks. Panic attacks strike 2 million people each year. Experts say two out of three victims are women but famous athletes can be victims as well." The next image on the screen showed former football star Earl Campbell speaking about panic attacks and, in the next image, in action on the field. Viewers then saw two sets of slick graphics listing the mental and physical symptoms of panic attacks. Next, another shot of Campbell breaking tackles as he sprinted for a touchdown. Then a quick shot of Jerilyn Ross, identified only as a "panic attack expert," saying that panic attacks can strike anyone and that victims are not "wimpy people."

Ross is president of the Anxiety Disorder Association of America. The organization accepts financial contributions from The Upjohn Company, which produced the VNR in house. In fact, the Kalamazoo, Michigan, business has donated large sums of money to the A.D.A.A., including nearly $128,000 in 1988 alone. That's more than the A.D.A.A. received from all its membership dues. Campbell and Ross were filmed at an Upjohn-sponsored press conference held soon after the F.D.A. had announced approval of Xanax. They, as well as other conference participants, were paid by the drug company.

TV viewers were told none of these facts. Instead, the anchor said, "Doctors . . . believe attacks start deep in the brain and that Xanax quiets that region. . . . Doctors say there seem to be few side effects to the drug but some people may have to be on it for the rest of their lives." Actually, in some cases Xanax does have serious adverse effects, such as blurred vision, sexual dysfunction, confusion, dizziness, impaired attention and addiction.

Upjohn spokesperson Godfrey Grant says the VNR that was used to help shape the news segment was not meant to promote the drug. "It is an educational piece," he contends. "The VNR was intended to help increase public understanding of a disorder that is largely misdiagnosed."

Many pharmaceutical companies now have marketing budgets that dwarf their medical education budgets. "Medical education is now determined by what the marketing department wants, not what doctors need," according to David Jones, a former public affairs executive for three large prescription drug companies. "In fact, at CIBA-GEIGY [where Jones once worked] medical education was moved out of R&D and into public affairs to assure that education supported marketing, and that scientists did not get in the way."

Dr. Sidney Wolfe, director of the Public Citizen Health Research Group, puts it even more bluntly: "It's very embarrassing to be a scientist for a drug company and see that, despite your hard work and in many cases your ethical behavior, when push comes to shove the marketing people take over."

S. T. T. AND M. M.

year alone, various industries offered about 4,000 of them to local TV stations, by the estimate of Nielsen Media Research. In a survey of TV news departments, 51 percent of news professionals said they preferred VNRs that were medical- or health-related. And it's a good bet that most of those came from the drug industry. At the Food and Drug Law Institute conference, the CIBA-GEIGY representative said that "about 300" TV stations usually picked up its VNRs. "This is very cost-effective," she pointed out.

Among the diverse companies also sponsoring VNRs are Disneyland, McDonald's and Odor Eaters. Last year a group of wealthy Kuwaitis hired Hill & Knowlton, the high-powered P.R. firm, to produce VNRs for its anti-Iraq propaganda campaign. In addition, members of Congress field questions in VNRs that are aired in their home districts by local TV stations, which usually don't reveal that the questioners are the legislators' press secretaries.

Last year a group of wealthy Kuwaitis hired Hill & Knowlton, the high-powered P.R. firm, to produce VNRs for its anti-Iraq propaganda campaign.

Also in 1990, Nielsen Media Research and Medialink, the largest VNR distributor, surveyed television news directors and editors. Each week, according to the survey, 15.2 percent of those polled said they had used at least one unedited VNR, while 78 percent said they had used at least one they had edited. The quality of the editing, of course, varies widely.

Notably, the Kennedy committee's invitations to four leading drug companies (Abbott, CIBA-GEIGY, Wyeth-Ayerst, and Hoffman-LaRoche) to testify were spurned. But industry spokesperson Gerald Mossinghoff, president of the Pharmaceutical Manufacturers Association, did show up. He professed surprise at the extent of his industry's use of VNRs. "I honestly had not known about [P.M.A. member] companies' use of VNRs until I read [the transcript of the hearing] yesterday," he testified. "Well," Kennedy said, "it is the most dramatically new . . . promotional device that has been developed in recent years, and it is amazing to me that you are not familiar with it."

"Believe me," a committee aide said afterward, P.M.A. representatives "spent plenty of time figuring out what they were going to say, and they realized they couldn't say a damn thing about it—that anything they would say would get them screwed because VNRs are misleading stuff. So [Mossinghoff] said he's never heard of companies using them. Come on. That's ridiculous." But Mossinghoff was on the mark, albeit self-servingly, when he told *Newsday* for a June 21 article that it's ultimately the TV stations that "determine what warrants showing to the public."

Why Video News Releases Are Used

The powerful, synergistic forces that drive TV stations to use drug-industry VNRs include:

- *The weakening economics of local television, which enhances the desire for slick news segments with designer features but not designer prices.* In all but the very largest markets, such as New York and Los Angeles, few stations can afford to originate all the material used on their local newscasts. "Because of the downsizing of news staffs and the general financial crunch," says Jill Olmsted, a professor of broadcast journalism at The American University in Washington, "stations are often running VNRs in their entirety or some portion of them." Professor Secunda told Kennedy, "The harsh realities of this marketplace make it extremely likely that the use of video news releases will . . . increase." (Meanwhile, *Newsweek* has reported a related defeat for journalistic balance: TV stations throughout the country, knuckling under to advertiser pressure, are shucking their watchdog consumer reporters.)

• *The strong appeal of VNRs to marketers—so long as viewers perceive them as credible, genuine news—as an almost ideal alternative to paid commercials.* Increasingly, advertisers have tended to conclude that the seductive power of commercials is oozing away—that more and more viewers see them as signals to go to the kitchen for a beer. As Secunda testified, "Commercials are losing their ability to stimulate consumer sales. Viewers' minds began to boggle and rebel as the number of commercial minutes in each programming hour increased and the standard thirty-second commercial was replaced by a blizzard [of fifteen- and ten-second ads]." The logical corollary to Secunda's assessment was suggested by Senator Kennedy in a statement provided for this article: "VNRs are worthwhile to drug companies only if the corporate sponsor is never revealed. They would lose their value if viewers knew that the so-called news story is actually a commercial."

Said Senator Kennedy, "VNRs are worthwhile to drug companies only if the corporate sponsor is never revealed."

• *The unquenchable thirst of countless Americans for health news, most of all for happy news of the "new, breakthrough" drug that they hope will cure their maladies and maybe extend their lives.* Health is the hot topic of the 1990s, said Olmsted. "I would hope that stations would be suspicious of bias when airing anything as a health issue." she added. Distinguishing between edited and unedited VNRs, she said that the greater the reliance on canned footage, the more spurious the "news" segment.

• *The huge payoffs for the drug industry in stimulating public demand for its products.* VNRs can be a phenomenally good investment, as the CIBA-GEIGY representative pointed out. Costing a modest $20,000 to $30,000 each, they are much less expensive than the purchase of TV airtime on just a few stations. In the big picture, VNRs are part of drug-industry promotional expenditures, estimated at a staggering $5 billion a year. Inexorably, outlays of such

VNRs can be a phenomenally good investment.

magnitude have helped cause the prices of prescription drugs to skyrocket over the past decade. According to the Bureau of Labor Statistics, overall inflation rose 46 percent from 1981 to 1989, but prescription-drug prices rose 128 percent.

VNRs drive up the cost of drugs "by creating inappropriately high expectations of what a drug can do."

VNRs and other marketing tools drive up the cost of drugs "by creating inappropriately high expectations of what a drug can do, which then provides the psychological underpinnings of an extremely aggressive [i.e., inflated] price," says David Jones, the former pharmaceutical company official. All too often, the high expectations and exploitative prices are created for a "me too" drug virtually identical to, and no better than, possibly a dozen others already on the market.

• *The utter failure—up to now—of the Food and Drug Administration to develop and enforce policies to stop pharmaceutical houses from using VNRs and other promotional devices to circumvent F.D.A. regulations for prescription drugs. Those rules clearly require advertising and promotion to incorporate in brief summary the minuses as well as the pluses of a drug's officially approved labeling, including warnings and uses that are hazardous because of contraindications.* "The judgment of the F.D.A. has been terrible in terms of determining when something is violative and what you do when it is violative," Dr. Sidney Wolfe, director of the Public Citizen Health Research Group, said in an interview.

But new F.D.A. Commissioner David Kessler's surprising injection of vitality into F.D.A. law enforcement—including a doubling of the staff of enforcers of the advertising and promotion rules—changes the outlook dramatically. "It's a whole new ball game," says Wolfe. "They are now taking actions that are consistent with being a regulatory agency rather than being a patsy for the drug industry."

In a speech, Kessler said that VNRs and other "new promotional techniques" blur the line between promotion and scientific exchange. He went on to say that all information about prescription drugs must "be true and not misleading . . . [must] provide 'fair balance' [and must not] promote unapproved uses." He told *Newsday*, "And that means you're not only going to talk about the benefits of a drug, you also have to talk about the risks." By year's end, he said, he wants new regulations for drug-industry VNRs to be proposed by the F.D.A.'s Division of Marketing, Advertising, and Communications, whose new director, Ann Witt, was praised by Wolfe.

In June, Kessler told the House Subcommittee on Human Resources and Intergovernmental Relations, "In no uncertain terms let me say to the medical community that we will subject not only the manufacturers but all those involved in the manufacturers' promotion to the full force of the law." (Dr. Lundberg, the top A.M.A. editor, raised the possibility that a TV station using a drug-company VNR promoting a drug or medical device for an unapproved use "is probably in violation of federal law.")

The first hard indication of a looming crackdown came on August 1, when the F.D.A. put the drug companies on formal notice that promotional VNRs and material disseminated with them must be reported to the agency "as part of their required submissions of advertising and promotional labeling."

If the F.D.A. ultimately adopts rules that effectively deter drug companies from producing and distributing biased, violative VNR commercials, there could be an ironic collateral result: Thanks to government intervention on behalf of honest news, the ethical lapses of TV stations in relaying such propaganda could become irrelevant. ♦

Questions for Discussion

1. Monitor your local television news for a few days and see if you can pick out stories that might have originated as "canned" video news releases. Do any of these stories represent an abuse of the station's responsibility toward its viewers?
2. Do you agree that when some news reports are based on canned news, it casts doubt on everything presented as news?
3. Argue for or against: Public relations messages disguised within news reports should be made illegal.

Green Like Me

Bill Walker

You've seen the ads on television: the chemical company that suggests that college graduates can't wait to work for them, so they can help clean up the environment (in spite of the fact that we know this company to be one of America's top polluters). Or the print ads for energy companies that tell us, "Every day is Earth Day with nuclear energy," (in spite of the fact that we haven't figured out what to do with our nuclear waste yet).

According to Bill Walker, who writes for **Greenpeace** magazine, these ads are part of a corporate public relations trend in which polluters are cashing in on environmental concerns through public relations, rather than making meaningful changes in their environmental policies.

Reading Difficulty Level: 4. Reads like fiction.

I have seen the future of public-relations hype, and it is green.

Green garbage bags. Green gasoline. Computers, hamburgers, compact discs: all here, all green, already. In California, where I live, supermarket chains that refuse to stop selling pesticide-dusted grapes are trying to promote themselves as environmentally correct because their pickle jars are reusable (you know, you can stick flowers in them). They're getting away with it. The chairman of Du Pont has the *New York Times* practically comparing him to John Muir. An oil company is forced by federal regulations to put a few bucks into preserving wildlife habitat, so it spends 10 times that much to buy newspaper ads patting itself on the back for obeying the law. Do people buy it? People do. Me, I buy Natural Brown coffee filters.

Sorry to have to tell you this, but you ain't green nothing yet. Get ready for a brazen new wave of hype, half-truths and plain old lies, as the greenwashers turn their spin-cycling talents to really challenging subjects. Green chlorofluorocarbons. Green nuclear power plants. Green Agent Orange. Oil tankers, toxics incinerators, dolphin steaks—you name it, the PR flacks of America are ready to reassure you that it's green, clean, and using it is one more simple thing you can do to save the Earth.

Green CFCs. Green nuclear power. Green Agent Orange. Oil tankers, toxic waste incinerators, dolphin steaks, you name it—the PR flacks of America are ready to assure you that it's all green, clean and safe for the Earth.

I learned all of this at the 43rd annual convention of the Public Relations Society of America (PRSA), which met in New York City. The theme of the 1990 convention was "Our World in Transition," but when I looked through the program for the first time I thought it was How to Make Your Corporation Look Like a Friend to the Planet While Reaping Billions in the International Waste Trade. And getting away with it. I signed up.

What I found, I must admit, was more subtle, less cynical, than I expected. Most greenflacks, it appears, believe in what they are flacking. When the cocktail chatter turns to environmental ethics, they tend to say things like this: "I've always considered myself a child of the sixties—stop the war, save the Earth, corporations are environmental criminals. It wasn't until I started working for this company that I saw for myself how strong their commitment is to the environment."

From *Greenpeace* magazine. May/June 1991, pp. 9–11. Reprinted by permission.

"What's the company you're working for?"

"Waste Management."

I made a note for my friend Bradley, who works for Greenpeace in San Francisco and is fighting on half a dozen fronts against toxics incinerators proposed by Waste Management Inc., the largest hazardous-waste handler in the country, and among the most frequently fined: "Big news. Inside source says WMI not environmental criminals."

In the interest of full disclosure, I should admit something else. I work for Greenpeace, too, and as much as I hate to admit it, my job there is basically public relations. So I suppose I shared a certain familial guilt with the thousands of legitimate PRSA conventioneers with big plastic "hi-my-name-is" tags who queued earnestly for workshops like "Understanding Activist Publics: Making Allies Out of Enemies." (One of the most intriguing, "Emerging Public Relations Challenges in a Changing Defense Environment," was inexplicably canceled—maybe somebody noticed the world heading toward an oil war and decided that stuff about the changing defense environment was a bit premature.) But I was really there, hanging around the red-carpeted meeting rooms of the Marriott Marquis on Times Square, as a spy: Observe greenwashing, document same, report findings, eat in Manhattan on $20 a day.

The first day, I nearly blew my cover.

Sixty or so of us had been bused over to the Fordham University Graduate School of Business Administration for a symposium called "The *Exxon Valdez* Story: How to Spend a Billion or Two and Still Get a Black Eye in Public." For two hours, communications experts like William J. Small, former president of NBC News and United Press International, argued about the most notorious man-made environmental disaster in U.S. history from what seemed to me a brilliantly novel, if perverse, point of view: that the spilling of 11 million gallons of crude oil into Prince William Sound, the fouling of at least 1,500 miles of pristine Alaskan shoreline and the ensuing deaths of hundreds of thousands of sea birds, otters and salmon, was fundamentally a public relations problem. Small, now professor of communications at Fordham, wore a name tag that said "Bill."

He had a brilliantly novel, if perverse, point of view: That the spilling of 11 million barrels of crude into Prince William Sound, killing hundreds of thousands of sea birds, otters and salmon, was essentially a public relations problem.

"I won't ask how many of you are environmentalists," he began. "We are not here today to debate environmental or ethical questions. We are, at least for today, not concerned with the fate of sea otters, but with how a huge American corporation spent $2 billion on the cleanup of what was not the worst oil spill ever, yet lost the battle of public relations and more than a year later is still struggling with one of the worst tarnishings of its corporate image in American history."

Oh. Exxon's struggling, not the otters. Bill, it was clear, felt the company had gotten something of a raw deal.

"There are lots of reasons to feel sorry for Exxon," he said. "Joseph Hazelwood [the *Valdez's* captain] had a terrific reputation. Although the press made much of the fact that the first mate was not officially certified, he had met all of his qualifications to be certified. The judge who sentenced Hazelwood called the spill 'a manmade disaster not seen since the likes of Hiroshima.' Well, let's be realistic: Nobody died at Prince William Sound—no humans, anyway. Exxon failed to tell the best sides of its story."

Isn't the real question whether a company should continue engaging in actions that are inherently dangerous?

I was thinking that the only good side of Exxon's story was the fact that the oil the *Valdez* spilled didn't end up as an L.A. smog alert. But Marion Pinsdorf, a professor of communications and media management at Fordham, also took up the company's case: "There were lots of positive Exxon stories that could have been picked up that were not." And what really hurt Exxon, said Professor of Management Systems Falguni Sen, was not immediately sending its chief operating officer to the scene of the disaster to display the company's concern.

"Exxon," declared Sen, "was long ago past the point at which it could no longer afford to have an operations-oriented CEO vs. a public-relations guy. Of course, as the chairman of Union Carbide found out in Bhopal, just as important is how well you manage the perception of why the boss goes to the site." Someone asked: "What happened to the chairman of Union Carbide?"

"He spent his first 24 hours in India in jail," said Sen.

"Lesson learned," I scribbled in my official convention notebook. "Jail time harder to explain than thousands of deaths from toxic chemical leak." But I couldn't let it go at that. Bill Small said there was time for one more question, and I put my hand up. I felt like the one kid in first grade who doesn't believe in Santa Claus, but—and here's where I nearly blew it—managed what I thought was a pretty reasonable sounding hypothetical: "Isn't the, uh, real question here whether a company should continue engaging in actions that are inherently dangerous? Maybe a public relations department's responsibility should include telling the CEO that what the company is doing is not only unpopular but irresponsible, and that if there's an accident, there'll be no way to put a good face on it."

People coughed. People turned to look at me. I wished I'd worn a tie.

"Well," Bill said, finally. "What would you do? Cut off the flow of oil from Alaska?"

This notion also sounded quite reasonable to me. But there was no time left; we were not there, after all, to discuss ethical questions. The buses were leaving for the hotel. I shook Bill's hand on the way out. He assured me that his own daughter used to make the same argument I had, but she had come around to her old man's way of thinking. There was still hope for me.

Back at the Marriott, one of the other participants in the Exxon seminar sought me out. Her name tag said "Kerry," she was from Seattle, and she worked for one of those outdoor clothing companies up there. Kerry just wanted me to know how much she appreciated what I'd said, because someone had to say it, and she was feeling bad because she hadn't said it, and of course she was really into recycling and all, and she couldn't believe the attitudes of these people. Could I?

She told me about a workshop she had attended earlier: "Building Public Support by Resolving Disputes Through Consensus," billed in the program as "a hands-on exercise based on real-life applications in which a company, government agencies, environmentalists, labor and elected officials worked together to develop solutions all could live with." It struck me that the problem was that companies and government agencies were usually not interested in environmental solutions all could live with, but in those only a politically acceptable number would die from, but I had a feeling that wasn't what the people doing the workshop meant. I asked Kerry what she'd learned at the workshop.

"One of the group leaders said when you're dealing with a group of outside agitators—Greenpeace or somebody like that—they usually have a different agenda than the people in the community where you're trying to place your facility," Kerry said. "If you let them rant and rave and foam at the mouth, the community will sometimes get turned off and approach you with a compromise. She said you can short-circuit these outside agitators by letting them disrupt public meetings, then you can arrange a private meeting behind their backs."

"Where was she from?"

"Waste Management, I think."

I drifted from meeting room to meeting room, searching for the soul of the greenwasher.

I got a rather enthusiastic dose of optimism from keynote speaker Patricia Aburdene, collaborator (and wife) of *Megatrends* pop-futurist John Naisbitt. "We now have the opportunity," she said, "to create techno-topia—although we've also got to deal with poverty, homelessness, this Persian Gulf thing and, of course, the environment."

I witnessed an act of bravery by the manager of a big financial services company, who began his seminar ("Managing the Environment: A Business Perspective") by declaring, "I am an environmentalist." He handled the account for Pacific Gas & Electric Co. (PG&E), my hometown utility monopoly, so he talked a lot about "trade-offs" between environmental quality and "continuing to provide an adequate supply of energy for healthy economic growth." He later predicted that, during the '90s, "You're going to see a lot more of this radical activism—people tying themselves to redwood trees, that sort of thing. And that's probably healthy, as long as you don't have social disorder."

The problem was that companies and government agencies were usually not interested in environmental solutions all could live with, but in those only a politically accepted number would die from.

I heard Jay Hair, head of the National Wildlife Federation (the only environmentalist, incidentally, quoted in the *Times* piece on the greening of Du Pont who found something good to say about the company), bluntly tell a gang of oil company flacks that fossil fuels had to go, and safe alternatives must be urgently pursued. Perhaps unintentionally, he quickly found a chorus of supporters from the other side of the room: "Nuclear" they cried.

You can say that a new brand of gasoline will "drive away pollution" because it's not as dirty as the stuff you were selling before.

I tried to put all this together, from a flack's point of view. The future, it seems, will be great, except for war and global warming; we'll save the planet, but not enough to hurt the stock market; the environmental movement is OK because preserving redwoods keeps people from worrying about plutonium. There was a common thread there, but I couldn't put my finger on it. Then I overheard a conversation that made it clear:

A PR manager for a company named ChemLawn complained that the entire city of Columbus, Ohio, its headquarters, hated the company because it makes, you know, chemicals. "But what can you do?" she asked a couple of colleagues. They replied immediately—and in unison—"Change the name."

Of course. What did Reagan's EPA Chief Anne Gorsuch do when Congress threatened to throw her in jail? She got married! Anne Gorsuch might do time, but would Anne Burford? And after Windscale, Britain's notorious nuclear reprocessing plant, reached its fourth decade of pumping plutonium into the Irish Sea, it changed its name to Sellafield. The pollution, of course, continues. What did Exxon do when it got ready to put the *Valdez* back into service? Change the name. It hasn't worked—"ex-*Valdez*" is still shorter in a headline than "*Mediterranean*"—but you had to admire the thought behind it, because it was the very spirit of greenwashing: Things are whatever you say they are.

You can say that a new brand of gasoline will "drive away pollution" because it's not as dirty as the stuff you were selling before. You can say that your tuna is guaranteed dolphin safe when you've got all of nine certified observers working the entire North Pacific fishing fleet. You can say that nuclear energy is a safe alternative to fossil fuels if you ignore Chernobyl and Three Mile Island. You can say whatever you want, because if you send out enough press releases on brown paper, sponsor enough nature series on public television and hire enough flacks for your Department of Marketing and Publicity, you might get away with it. Just change the name: Now it's the Office of Environmental Affairs.

I was still thinking about this on the final afternoon of the conference. I was waiting for an elevator when I recognized someone from the opening night cocktail party—

the same woman from Waste Management who told me she was a child of the sixties. We said hello, and she tried to recall what company I was with.

"None," I confessed. Since I was practically on my way to the airport, I dropped my cover and told her the whole scam. "Greenpeace," she said. "What's Waste Management going to have to do to get you off our back?"

"Well, I said, "You could change the name." ♦

Question for Discussion

1. Are there any positive aspects of corporate America's attention to environmental matters?

The Hollywood Treatment

Neal Koch

Granted, it is a serious thing when corporate polluters attempt to manipulate the news media and the American public. But what about entertainment companies? If you follow Neal Koch's argument, the damage that the entertainment moguls do to journalistic integrity is just as bad.

Neal Koch writes frequently about media issues. He was an editor of **Channels** magazine until it closed in December 1990.

Reading Difficulty Level: 4

Last spring, Larry Rohter, *The New York Times*'s Mexico City bureau chief, was shuttling around Central America, covering the Nicaraguan elections and following up on the aftermath of the U.S. invasion of Panama, when Hollywood phoned. This wasn't surprising, because Rohter was about to start a new assignment as the *Times*'s Hollywood correspondent. What *was* surprising—at least to Rohter—was that the caller, the head of a movie company, asked him if he would like to write a screenplay. While the caller did not say so explicitly, he made it clear that Rohter would *not* be expected to quit the *Times* while working on the script. Rohter says he declined. But that was only the beginning.

It's hard to tell the Tinseltown story if you don't follow the studio script.

Reprinted from the *Columbia Journalism Review*, January/February 1991, by permission.

After several months on his new beat this veteran reporter of third-world coups and intrigues says, "People try to pull stuff here that no politician would ever dare pull."

People try to pull stuff here that no politician would ever dare pull.

Indeed, for all the glamour, glitz, and froth, Hollywood can pose problems of attempted media seduction and manipulation, outsized egos, arrogance, and brazen lying to a degree few journalists encounter elsewhere—except, perhaps, Washington, D.C. "Someone switching from the Reagan White House to Hollywood would feel very much at home," says Peter Bart, editor of *Variety* and a veteran of twenty years as a Hollywood executive. "There's a pathological need to manipulate. The people who run the studios are control freaks."

The people who run the studios have a pathological need to manipulate. They're control freaks.

"It's a lying industry," says Al Delugach, a Pulitzer Prize-winning journalist who spent nearly forty years covering organized crime, labor, politics, business, and entertainment companies before retiring in 1989 from the *Los Angeles Times,* where he had worked since 1970. "Sometimes it seems to me that [lying] is almost raised to the level of being socially desirable."

Regarded by some as a cushy assignment, the Hollywood beat is anything but.

Regarded by some as a cushy assignment, the Hollywood beat is anything but. Hollywood is, first and foremost, a company town, an industrial village. The industry is entertainment and it is one of the few industries in which America still dominates—the second-largest contributor to the U.S. balance of payments, behind aircraft. Film exports alone contribute an estimated $2.5 billion annually, according to the U.S. Department of Commerce. Moreover, American-made films, television programs, and music recordings have a tremendous impact on culture worldwide. They define the terms for entertainment, in the process communicating values, influencing expectations, and providing shared experiences.

Historically, however, reporting on Hollywood has consisted mainly of handouts, gossip, and virtually bought space. "There was a big wink between the parties involved in the coverage, as if to say, 'I'll take care of you and you take care of me,'" says Alex Ben Block, executive editor, special issues, at *The Hollywood Reporter.* "For many years it was the toy department and you had hacks. But today you have a lot of people who are first-rate."

Most reporters trace the change back to the late 1970s. The seminal event that created and defined modern Hollywood coverage was the David Begelman scandal, in which the head of Columbia Pictures was caught forging checks. Although Begelman eventually resigned under pressure, he has worked steadily since. The person who suffered most was the man who blew the whistle, actor Cliff Robertson. He didn't work in Hollywood for the next six years.

The *Los Angeles Times,* whose entertainment coverage before the Begelman scandal was handled mostly by critics and columnists, was scooped on the story in its own backyard by *The Wall Street Journal,* primarily, and *The Washington Post.* As a result, the *Times* (and many other newspapers) reevaluated their approach to Hollywood and committed themselves to more solid coverage. Today it is not uncommon to see articles scrutinizing studios' financial dealings and even the occasional piece probing mob influence in Hollywood.

Still, reporting as informed and candid as *How Blind Is Hollywood to Ethics?* which appeared in the *Los Angeles Times* last April, is a rarity. Written by Jack Mathews from reporting by himself, Elaine Dutka, and Nina J. Easton, it concluded with a quote from a veteran Hollywood talent agent: "People will do anything they have to do, leverage anyone they have to leverage, screw any of their friends to get what they want for themselves and that's at every level of the business. . . ."

Since the Begelman scandal, other developments have heightened the importance of Hollywood as a news story. Large publicly held companies entered the business, a trend that began with the acquisition of Paramount by Gulf & Western in 1967. In 1983, Rupert Murdoch made a run at Warner Communications, spreading takeover mania to the entertainment industry. As stock prices rose in that sector, Wall Street investment bankers began looking for new Hollywood companies to take public. The story rolled on as many of these smaller companies failed to live up to their hype, with a number of them, notably the De Laurentiis Entertainment Group, crashing and burning. Now, the story has turned into one of increasing globalization and concentration of power in the hands of a few giant media companies, such as Time Warner. With the purchase of MCA by Matsushita, more than half of Hollywood's major studios are foreign-owned.

The Hollywood story has turned into one of increasing globalization and concentration of power in the hands of a few giant media companies.

Another significant topic was the development of ancillary markets for movies and TV shows—home video, foreign sales, cable, pay TV, a burgeoning number of independent television stations—while other American industries, such as steel and autos, went into decline. As MBAs drifted into show business, stories started focusing on the art of the deal. Even the general public latched on to reports of box-office grosses, popularized by such programs as *Entertainment Tonight.* As Block of *The Hollywood Reporter* observes, Hollywood news "was no longer just in the amusement section" of newspapers, "but in the business section and often on the front page."

Today, many journalists, industry executives, and producers say that the beat that most closely resembles the Hollywood beat is the capital beat. Both require an understanding of powerful people—celebrities with big egos—and of their relationships with others; and both

Today, many journalists, industry executives, and producers say that the beat that most closely resembles the Hollywood beat is the capital beat.

involve reporting on coalition building by the players. But even experienced Washington hands have a hard time when they switch coasts.

"It differs at every conceivable level," says NBC's Tom Brokaw, who anchored a prime-time special called *The New Hollywood* last March and seems to be in no hurry to return. (The focus was on the increasing concentration of power in the hands of a few big international corporations, and the effect this has on the marketplace of ideas.) In reporting the story, Brokaw discovered a frustrating Hollywood peculiarity—namely, that otherwise sophisticated industry veterans don't seem to understand the meanings of the terms "off-the-record" and "on-the-record." And production often bogged down as press agents for sources tried to initiate extended negotiations over conditions for interviews. "We were constantly rowing through the swamps of Hollywood p.r.," says Brokaw. "There was a lot of heavy lifting. I wouldn't like to do it every day."

Producers were shocked at the notion that journalists were not cooperating.

Comparing Hollywood politics with Washington politics, Brokaw observes that in Washington "there is some clear understanding of what it means to be in the public arena. In Hollywood—and it may have something to do with those who cover Hollywood—the 'A' stars and their press agents see the press as only to be manipulated."

"The Hollywood principals have no understanding of what journalism is supposed to be," says Warren Hoge, editor of *The New York Times Magazine* and formerly that paper's assistant managing editor for culture, who scrutinized Hollywood coverage for the *Times* last winter before choosing a replacement for veteran reporter Aljean Harmetz, who had left the paper to write a book. Producers "were shocked at the notion that the journalists were not cooperating," says Hoge, who has been a newspaper correspondent both overseas and in Washington. "I've never seen anything like it anywhere else."

In her October 22, 1989, *New York Times Magazine* profile of producers Peter Guber and Jon Peters, free-lance writer Diane K. Shah incorporated into the structure of her piece the attempt by Guber and Peters to produce the story themselves, starting with a meeting with the magazine's editors: in return for shifting the focus of the piece away from the duo, the *Times* would be offered exclusive access to the set of *The Bonfire of the Vanities.* When the *Times* declined, the producers offered to arrange Shah's reporting schedule, in addition to providing a list of people for her to call. Then there was the heavy-handed hint that they would orchestrate a buzz in Hollywood about Shah's just-completed book to make it a hot property among film studios and agents.

Hollywood is hostile to virtually any reporting not seen as promoting its product.

Institutionally, Hollywood is hostile to virtually any reporting not seen as promoting its product. "Most people in Hollywood see journalists as the rough social equivalent of flacks," says William Broyles, Jr., a former editor of *Newsweek, California,* and *Texas Monthly* magazines, now a television writer-producer who co-created ABC's *China Beach.* "They are useful for promotion and semi-dangerous any other way."

Hollywood's main approach to the press is built around cadres of "planters"—seeming legions whose sole job is to get their company's version of reality into news columns and on news programs, with virtually every announcement, no matter how trivial, being trumpeted by fax, phone, and mail. Many companies go so far as to employ one media relations staff for the consumer press, another for trade and business publications, and a third for corporate matters.

Hollywood's main approach to the press is built around cadres of "planters"—seeming legions whose sole job is to get their company's version of reality into news columns and on news programs.

For a single episode of a single TV series, pitches may come from a host of flacks—publicists representing the network on which the program airs, others representing one or more of its stars, and still others employed by the studio that made the show, and, finally, those employed by the show's individual producer. In an effort to get out from under the deluge, *People* magazine's West Coast office recently changed its fax number, hoping to start all over again.

Hollywood's second-level of manipulation involves negotiating deals with the press for access to stars, sets, and executives in return for a measure of control over the resulting articles. Typically, the dickering is over the approval of quotes, photographs, and writer, the timing of the release of stories, and, most prized of all, the placement of a client on a national magazine's cover.

Some publicists will exact revenge if their clients appear in non-cover features. In some cases, profiles appear as the price of getting access to another client of the publicist or talent agent who represents both celebrities. "At most publications, you need those publicists for access," says Richard Turner, a *Wall Street Journal* staff reporter and former Hollywood bureau chief of *TV Guide,* "so some people wind up making a lot of compromises. There are lot of places that give photo approval, cover approval—who knows *what* they do with copy."

Some writers have learned that access to movie sets can depend on whether they ask unpleasant questions or produce less than flattering copy.

Some writers have learned that access to movie sets can depend on whether they ask unpleasant questions or produce less than flattering copy. Kim Masters, now a staff writer for *The Washington Post*'s Style section, says that Warner Brothers refused to allow her access to *Batman* director Tim Burton for a free-lance profile of him because of various brief items she had written as a senior writer with *Premiere* magazine. One item speculated that with all the money sunk into *Batman,* there might be changes in the Warner executive ranks if it didn't succeed at the box office. Another predicted that *Pink Cadillac,* a Warner

Brothers film starring Clint Eastwood, wouldn't be very successful. "I called Rob Friedman [president of Warner's worldwide advertising and publicity] and that was expressly stated," says Masters. "They said, 'Get another writer.' " The *Post* chose instead to forego the Burton profile. Friedman's office told CJR he was not available for comment.

"On the celebrity side, everybody is playing this access game, this horse trading," says Michael Cieply, an investigative business reporter for the *Los Angeles Times*. "You will pay dearly for those two hours with a star: they will be on your cover. It's a racket."

It's a racket that landed one of its most adept practitioners, Pat Kingsley, on *Los Angeles Magazine*'s 1990 list of the thirty most powerful people in L.A. Kingsley has used her celebrity clients to build national political influence for herself by delivering them for fundraisers for candidates and causes she favors. It was Kingsley, for example, who arranged Michael Dukakis's introduction to the Hollywood community in 1987 at a party given by Kingsley client Sally Field.

Executives of entertainment companies seem to feel less constrained to tell the truth than executives in other industries.

Such power grew out of the intense competition between news organizations that, over the last decade, began tripping over one another in their attempt to satisfy the public appetite for Hollywood news and gossip. Many publications opened or beefed up their Hollywood bureaus. New specialty magazines sprang up, such as *Premiere* and *Entertainment Weekly*, and a rash of TV shows spawned by the success of *Entertainment Tonight* appeared, including CNN's *Showbiz Today*.

Reporters found editors throughout their publications paying more attention to stories even remotely touching on Hollywood. "There was more and more of a tendency and reason to jazz up a story with celebrity names," recalls former *Los Angeles Times* reporter Al Delugach, "even though they were just straight business stories." This produced what he terms "paparazzi reporters."

"The magazine business is so competitive," publicist Kingsley told the *Los Angeles Times* in 1988, "they seem willing to promise almost anything to get what they want." In the process, says the *Times*'s Cieply, "journalists handed a big stick to the people on the other side. And, quite rationally, they decided to use it."

In fact, emboldened by their success at negotiating with mass-market magazines on access to their clients, publicists now frequently make similar demands about business stories. And when executives of entertainment companies do deign to talk to the press, they seem to feel less constrained to tell the truth than executives in other industries. "You don't often find people who will lie on the record when it's a provable lie," says Bill Knoedelseder, executive producer of Fox Entertainment News, who

The Terminator at Work?

When it comes to strong-arming the Hollywood press, some of the biggest muscle belongs to Arnold Schwarzenegger, who hasn't hesitated to use it, says author Wendy Leigh. And few journalists have been willing to cry foul.

Leigh claims that Schwarzenegger—rumored to harbor national political ambitions—has waged a heavy-handed campaign first to suppress her book, *Arnold, An Unauthorized Biography*, and then to sabotage its promotion.

Some journalists have found her reporting worthy of attention. *Time* made it part of a profile of Schwarzenegger that ran in the magazine's international edition. And accounts of the contretemps surrounding the alleged attempts to interfere with the book appeared in *New York* magazine and the *Chicago Tribune* last May and in *Newsday* last July.

But for the most part, the Hollywood publicity machine rolls on, and puffy cover stories on Schwarzenegger, timed to coincide with the release of his latest movies, continue to appear. They rarely contain more than a dismissive mention of Leigh's book, let alone an independent analysis of its content.

James Willwerth, a *Time* correspondent for twenty-three years and the author of *Time*'s profile of Schwarzenegger, says he's not a fan of Leigh's gossipy type of journalism. But, he adds, after checking out her research, using her thirty-four pages of source notes in the back of the book as a guide, he came away with respect for her thoroughness. "It was very well reported," Willwerth says. "My nose told me that the book was on target."

In *Arnold*, Leigh persuasively portrays Schwarzenegger as an often crude womanizer—perhaps a misogynist—of limited morals who has been given to expressions of racism, anti-Semitism, and admiration for Hitler's ability to lead.

Citing the Berlin Document Center as a source of documents which have further been authenticated by the World Jewish Congress, Leigh reports that Schwarzenegger's father, Gustav, police chief of the Austrian village of Thal, applied for membership in the Nazi party in 1938 and was subsequently accepted. And she reminds readers of Arnold's public support of Kurt Waldheim, even after revelations of the Austrian president's Nazi past.

Leigh says that Gustav was an alcoholic who raised his two sons, Arnold and Meinhard, as bullies who delighted in publicly humiliating friends as well as rivals. She reports further that Schwarzenegger owes much of his success in bodybuilding contests to an expertly honed aptitude for undermining his opponents psychologically, as well as to the use, according to fellow bodybuilders she interviewed, of anabolic steroids for many years.

Leigh portrays Schwarzenegger as a calculating, intense salesman who at an early age set out to create an image that would eventually propel him to wealth and international celebrity. Bodybuilding was just the first step. National political ambitions followed, with rumors that he might be angling for a run at the U.S. Senate, something that Schwarzenegger has denied. A staunch conservative Republican, he married into the Kennedy clan and was appointed chairman of the President's Council on Physical Fitness and Sports by George Bush, for whom he campaigned in 1988. Writes Leigh, "Arnold embraced . . . the ruthlessness and the dark side of the American dream."

When it comes to strong-arming the Hollywood press, some of the biggest muscle belongs to Arnold Schwarzenegger.

"All publicists make deals," says Lynn, "but this is the first time I've been censored."

Continued

Schwarzenegger's publicist, Charlotte Parker, calls the book inaccurate, but declined repeated requests for specifics and cut the interview short. Schwarzenegger himself, the publicist said, was unavailable for comment.

Leigh says that as she began researching her book here and overseas she received "strange" late-night phone calls, "whispering that I'd better be careful." She says she went into hiding to write the book, sequestering documents in a bank vault and shredding papers daily.

Her publisher, Contemporary Books in Chicago, says it received phone calls from Schwarzenegger associates, already known to the publisher, offering money and a different book, to be co-authored by Schwarzenegger, if Contemporary would drop Leigh's book. Someone claiming to be connected with the publishing firm called its printing plant eight times with questions about the book, the company says. Before *Arnold,* Contemporary says, it hadn't had a break-in in ten years. Then it had four in one month.

Contemporary says that it moved the production schedule up three weeks, shifted the printing to a hidden location, installed security guards, and began using secret passwords and a fake title.

Leigh says that when she hit the promotional circuit, television show bookings and filmed appearances were mysteriously canceled at the last minute—in one case, even as TV promos ran—as were planned newspaper features for which she had already been interviewed. In at least one case Schwarzenegger himself turned up on the show soon after. Bruce Lynn, Leigh's former personal publicist, says he believes that Charlotte Parker threatened producers of TV shows that they wouldn't get Schwarzenegger again if they put Leigh on the air. "People told me that," says Lynn. Lynn adds that a booker for one national program—which he declines to name because, he says, he still does business there—told him, "No way. We're doing Arnold for the movie [*Total Recall*], and we don't want to upset him."

"All publicists make deals," says Lynn, "but this is the first time I've been censored."

Time's Willwerth says he wasn't threatened, but did receive "urgent, demanding pleas" from Parker to avoid mentioning the book. But he says that while she called it unfair, she never claimed it was inaccurate.

Parker categorically denies any efforts by Schwarzenegger or any of his associates to inhibit either the book's publication or promotional efforts on its behalf.

Schwarzenegger is pursuing a libel suit against Leigh in Britain over information she supplied to the writer of an article about him in Rupert Murdoch's *News of the World.* Although the paper settled last spring by giving Schwarzenegger £30,000 and a published apology, Leigh's attorney says she will not settle because the information she gave was accurate. The attorney, who accuses the tabloid of having "embellished" her information and calls the suit against Leigh an attempt at harassment, points out that Schwarzenegger has attempted no court action in this country, where it is more difficult to successfully sue for libel.

started his career in journalism by writing about organized crime. "In Hollywood you will. And they don't care. It's like a badge of honor!"

To be sure, most companies, in any industry, are uncomfortable having their finances and inner workings scrutinized by the press. But entertainment companies are more secretive than most. Unlike aerospace contractors—the only industry to contribute more to this country's balance of payments than entertainment—movie studios rarely hold government contracts. So they needn't be unduly concerned that bribery scandals, cost overruns, inflated billings, or failure to present themselves to shareholders in a realistic light will result in congressional hearings or a loss of federal largess.

Moreover, even when internal financial information does become available, it's frequently of very limited use because of the industry's highly unusual accounting methods. Most notably, studios rely on complex and ever-shifting definitions of "profit" and "revenue." The terms' meanings change not only from studio to studio but from contract to contract. For example, in response to Art Buchwald's claim that the Paramount Pictures' Eddie Murphy movie *Coming to America* incorporated a Buchwald script idea and that therefore he is entitled to a share of the profits, the studio argues that although the film ranked among the top ten box office hits of 1988, it does not show a net profit.

In addition to fuzzy definitions, Hollywood numbers are notoriously hard to pin down because entertainment valuations usually depend on present-value estimates of future revenues from uncertain products to be launched into highly volatile, largely unpredictable ancillary markets. "It's a very murky sort of situation," says *Los Angeles Times* assistant business editor Stephen West, who divides his time between coverage of the entertainment, media, securities, and insurance industries. "It leaves open a wider possibility for the management of earnings than what may be the case in other industries."

To be sure, most companies, in any industry, are uncomfortable having their finances and inner workings scrutinized by the press.

Even those industry insiders who complain privately that the press doesn't cover their business with sufficient rigor rarely give out usable facts. They fear the information could be traced back to them, and within the tight little Hollywood island, nobody knows who might be involved in the next deal. "Everyone's standing in a glass house," explains the *Los Angeles Times*'s Cieply. "Sometimes you think you've gone a month without an on-the-record conversation." Says Warren Hoge of *The New York Times*, "There is an aversion to being the identified source that is more acute in Hollywood than in any place I've ever encountered."

There is an aversion to being the identified source that is more acute in Hollywood.

Last April, for instance, in an assessment of the Walt Disney company's then-long string of failures in prime-time television production, *Los Angeles Times* writer Jeff Kaye reported that not only had Disney executives declined to be interviewed, but that "Disney staffers—including Randy Reiss, executive vice-president of Walt Disney Pictures and president of its network TV division—also took the highly unusual step of calling people who have worked on Disney television programs to ask them not talk to the *Times.* Some people also were asked if they knew of anybody who had agreed to be interviewed."

Those people who write well enough to cover the story can easily become participants in the story at far higher rates than any newspaper can pay.

A beat so relationship-dependent and personality-driven produces an unusually high level of tension, given the unavoidable tradeoffs between access and independence. Editors want reporters who have a sense of Hollywood's history and its constantly shifting sands, but who haven't gone native. Too often, however, the temptation to go native proves irresistible.

It's not hard to understand why some of the best journalists have succumbed. The Hollywood beat brings reporters face-to-face with other young, highly verbal people who party with stars, drive company sports cars with cellular phones to weekends in Palm Springs, lunch in expensive restaurants, attend private movie screenings, and observe irregular hours. Admission requires no formal credentials, and even lower-level executives and mildly unsuccessful producers can earn large sums relatively quickly. "More than with any other industry they cover," notes Richard W. Stevenson, a Los Angeles-based business correspondent for *The New York Times,* "journalists probably spend more time thinking about how they could do the job better than the twenty-five-year-old kid across the desk from them making $250,000."

Observes Warren Hoge, "The main literary form in Hollywood is the screenplay, and it is not really a literary form. Those people who write well enough to cover the story can easily become participants in the story at far higher rates than any newspaper can pay."

"For a journalist, who is given an enormous responsibility," adds an experienced public relations executive who asked not be identified, "the compensation is out of whack. So it's very enticing." One result, this source says, is that "there are always some who feel there are opportunities to ingratiate themselves and so [their coverage] may not be as hard-hitting" as it might be otherwise.

One Saturday morning Los Angeles softball game, which started out as a match between reporters and editors, has evolved into a game largely played by screenwriters and industry executives, with a number of the players remaining the same. Says first-baseman David Israel, co-executive producer of NBC's *Midnight Caller* and a former newspaper columnist, "Covering Hollywood is the only job where reporters aren't sure whether to pitch or catch. All those people who, while they're doing journalism, would like to think that they're being objective, may, in the back of their minds think, 'These guys buy screenplays; maybe I have a shot.' " (Israel, incidentally, made the switch from journalism to the entertainment industry before joining the Saturday-morning players.)

Of course, there's nothing new about journalists going into industries they cover. But many insiders consider the extent of the defection in Hollywood to be one of the profession's dirty little secrets, with some reporters switching sides not long after getting transferred to the entertainment beat. This has promoted the notion that—despite denials—there are those who angle for the assignment in a deliberate attempt to cross over. While several *Newsweek* staffers have defected, the pattern has been particularly evident at the *L.A. Times.* A 1987 *Los Angeles* magazine article titled "Scooped Up" noted that six of the paper's entertainment reporters had defected to the industry in recent years. "With so many reporters leaving," wrote author Jim Seale, "editors find themselves in the same position as the Scotland Yard inspector who continued to send undercover detectives to the London whorehouse to gather evidence, only to see one after another 'go native.' "

Such losses to the industry make it that much harder for those who remain to deal with executives already confident of their ability to manage the news. "It tends to make them think that all the rest of us are waiting for the right job offer," says Larry Rohter. "It's insulting."

Many Hollywood executives seem unable or unwilling to regard journalists as professional observers, preferring instead to categorize them as either friends or foes. A favorable article frequently brings a phone call from the subject saying, "You handled that nicely. I'm your friend for life." It's a beat where people a reporter barely knows will say without cracking a smile, "I'm speaking to you off the record as your friend."

Many Hollywood executives seem unable or unwilling to regard journalists as professional observers, preferring instead to categorize them as either friends or foes.

The other side of the coin is that negative remarks in print fade from memory *very* slowly. "You talk about elephants," says Ron Grover, entertainment-industry reporter and L.A. bureau chief for *Business Week,* his voice rising. "Have these guys got memories!" Grover says that as the result of an unflattering, but accurate, article he wrote, one studio head, whom he declines to name, will communicate with him only by mail.

Many insiders consider the extent of journalistic defection in Hollywood to be one of the profession's dirty little secrets.

"The only people who are more thin-skinned," says editor-turned-producer William Broyles, Jr., "are journalists."

A final frustration in getting a story into print can come from a reporter's boss. Many say their editors seem driven to involve themselves in questioning and rewriting Hollywood stories to a degree not experienced with stories they file on other subjects. "Everybody's got an opinion," says Grover. "Everybody messes with it," says *Forbes* senior editor Lisa Gubernick.

Reporters speculate as to the reasons why. Most boil down to the old saw that when it comes to show business, everyone's a critic. One reporter suggests that New York editors in particular gravitate toward dispatches from the Coast because the Hollywood stories remind them so much of their own newsroom politics.

Said one reporter, "I have never covered a beat where your sources air-kiss you."

In the end, some prefer to look at the amusing, if surrealistic, side of covering Hollywood. Says Gubernick, "I have never covered a beat where your sources air-kiss you." ♦

Questions for Discussion

1. Analyze an entertainment report—in your local paper, on **Entertainment Tonight,** or any entertainment segment of local news. Do you recognize any area in which the reporter's ability to uncover a larger story might have been compromised?
2. Even if the manipulation of the press by Hollywood executives is as bad as Neal Koch suggests, is it really a serious problem?

Suggested Readings

Those who are interested in advertising disguised as programming might want to reread Mark Crispin Miller's "Hollywood: The Ad" in Chapter 8.

More On Disguised Advertising

"Advertising in Disguise," *Consumer's Reports,* March, 1986. This article can also be found in the third edition of *Mass Media Issues,* p. 176 (5).

Marin, Richard, "Products Stare Camera in the Eye," *Insight* Vol. 5, January 9, 1989, p. 60 (2). Displaying product brand names on television programs.

Pierre, Evans, "Infomercials Under Fire," *Consumers Research Magazine* Vol. 73, September, 1990, p. 2 (1).

Powers, Ron, "The Message Is the Medium," *GQ: Gentlemen's Quarterly* Vol. 60, June 1990, p. 67 (3). Column. Commercials that masquerade as programs. Infomercials.

"Talk About Placements . . . ," *Newsweek* Vol. 114, July 31, 1989, p. 50 (1). The product tie-in between Lethal Weapon 2 and Ramses condoms.

More On the "Greening" of Public Relations

Beers, David, and Catherine Capellaro, "Greenwash," *Mother Jones,* March/April 1991, p. 38 (5).

Miller, Mark Crispin, "How Dow Recycles Reality," *Esquire* Vol. 114, September 1990, p. 110 (1). Using the environment as an advertising ploy.

Yagoda, Ben, "Cleaning Up a Dirty Image," *Business Month,* April, 1990, p. 49 (4).

More on Public Relations Within the Entertainment Industry

Alter, Jonathan, "The Art of the Deals: How Publicists and Celebrity Mania Are Taking Journalistic Favor-Swapping to New Extremes," *Newsweek* Vol. 113, January 9, 1989, p. 58 (2).

Lapham, Lewis, "Skywriting," *Harper's Magazine* Vol. 276, May 1988, P. 12 (2). Authors and the public. Column.

More On the Art of Publicity

Landler, Mark, "Publicity? Why It Never Even Occurred to Us: Companies Are Vying to Donate Products to the Troops." *Business Week,* September 24, 1990, p. 46 (1).

Olins, Wally, "How A Corporation Reveals Itself," *The New York Times* Vol. 140, October 14, 1990, Sec. 3 p. F13, col. 3. 6 col. in. An organization's corporate identity can inspire loyalty, shape decisions, aid recognition and attract customers.

Thackray, John, "America's Corporate Hype," *Management Today,* March 1987, p. 68 (5).

There are Several Basic Texts Available in Public Relations. These are Four of the Most Widely Used

Cutlip, Scott, Allen H. Center and Glenn M. Broom, *Effective Public Relations, 8th ed.* (Englewood Cliffs, N.J.: Prentice-Hall, 1991).

Newsom, Doug and Alan Scott, *This is PR: The Realities of Public Relations, 5th ed.* (Belmont, Ca.: Wadsworth Publishing, 1991).

Seitel, Fraser P., *The Practice of Public Relations, 4th ed.* (Columbus: Charles E. Merrill, 1990).

Simon, Raymond, *Public Relations: Concepts and Practices, 5th ed.* (New York: MacMillan, 1992).

Other Readings On the Public Relations Industry

Hartman, Curtis and Leslie Brokaw, "Everything You Always Wanted to Know About PR . . . But Were Afraid You'd Have to Pay For," *Inc.* Vol. 10, October 1988, p. 90 (6). Includes a related article on business and the press.

Paluszek, John, "Public Relations in the Coming Global Economy; Changes of Epic Proportion Are Happening," *Vital Speeches* Vol. 56, October 15, 1989, p. 22 (5).

Paluszek, John, "Public Relations and Ethical Leadership: If Not Us, Who? If Not Now, When?", *Vital Speeches* Vol. 56, October 1, 1989, p. 747 (4).

Pavlik, John V., *Public Relations: What Research Tells Us.* Reviewed by James E. Grunig, *Journalism Quarterly,* Spring 1988, p. 216 (1).

Wilcox, D., P. Ault and W. Agee, *Public Relations Strategies and Tactics.* Reviewed by Dianne L. Cherry, *Communication Education,* January 1990, p. 86 (1).

Public Relations II: Government

14

In the America envisioned by Benjamin Franklin and Thomas Jefferson, the press would be an adversarial press, one that examined the actions of its government carefully and would expose those actions that should be debated by the American people.

Partly because of the adversarial nature of the press, public relations has always been a part of American government. Franklin and Jefferson had to "sell" the Bill of Rights to the American public, and Lincoln had to "handle" his strategy for freeing the slaves by making early statements that made him sound less radical than the abolitionists. But in recent years—especially since the administration of Richard Nixon—the government's use of public relations has grown increasingly cynical.

The readings in this chapter examine the current use of public relations by the U.S. government—specifically, in terms of government secrecy and the government's "management" of the press during its most recent military actions.

The Calculus of Democracy

Ben Bagdikian

A basic conflict in rights arises when the government wants to keep a secret and media want to make that secret known to the public. Oliver North's defense of covert operations during the Iran-Contra hearings was preceded by more than a decade by a statement made by former CIA director William Colby:

> Some secrets, after all, do protect the nation. Secret technology to locate and shoot down foreign nuclear missiles could be jammed if known in detail by a potential enemy. Confidential give-and-take in diplomatic negotiations would be impossible under klieg lights. And disclosure of the intelligence purpose behind an apparently commercial venture can enable a foreign nation to thwart the operation.[1]

1. William E. Colby, "How Can the Government Keep a Secret?", *TV Guide* (February 12, 1977), p. 2+.

In the next reading Ben Bagdikian, author of The Media Monopoly, *explains the other side of the argument. He proposes a formula for calculating how democratic a government is: The more secrecy, he says, the less truly democratic the democracy.*

Reading Difficulty Level: 2. As long as you realize that "calculus" and "formula" are essentially synonymous in this context.

A sinister wind is blowing through the American democratic process.

A sinister wind is blowing through the American democratic process. We began our society on the principle that government exists legitimately only with the consent of the governed and that consent without significant information is meaningless: the greater the information available to the public, the safer the democracy. But in the last generation, we have reversed that assumption. Thanks to nuclear weapons, the Cold War, and the growing militarization of America, we seem to have accepted the contrary idea that the less the public knows, the greater "the national security."

The Reagan and Bush administrations have accelerated this reversal of the democratic process. Each year the American public learns less crucial information about its most vital issues: war and peace, military budgets, and the endless struggle between corruption and rectitude in spending public money.

Each year the American public learns less crucial information about its most vital issues.

There has been debate about secrecy, as there ought to be. But it has continued so long that much of it reaches the public in exchanges of clichés, of "national security" versus "the public's right to know," or "not aiding the enemy" versus "freedom of information." Those terms have real meaning, but they soon become drained of content. As largely symbolic utterances, they obscure the damning detail.

Censors seldom need to explain their acts; the rhetoric of superpatriotism diverts attention from the losses that flow from compulsive secrecy. We have been conditioned to accept the alarming scenarios of harm that is presumed to come if a particular piece of information becomes known to the public and therefore to potential adversaries. We are seldom reminded of the disasters that occur regularly throughout history because important information has been kept from the public.

There is almost a formula for the calculus of democracy: a government that presses for zero risk from the consequences of releasing information by that act maximizes damage to the country's political process.

Most governments are tempted to minimize the short-term risks and so are inclined toward secrecy. Heads of state usually prefer to avoid political inconvenience or embarrassment by total disclosure. A president who is able to increase secrecy decreases his accountability to the public.

When secrecy is raised to an almost religious level in the name of "national security," it becomes impossible to know when a withheld fact is, in fact, militarily dangerous or merely politically inconvenient for those in power. But whether kept secret for legitimate military purposes or for self-serving political ones, every significant fact hidden from public view diminishes freedom in society. The society that is given no choices has no real freedom.

The quality of public policy, no less than the quality of science, depends on maximum exposure of data and propositions. The scientific discovery locked instantly in the scientist's safe is the equivalent of a discovery never made. If every scientific insight with potential military application had been perfectly censored, we would all be living in a world that is flat, and we would still be treating diseases by bleeding the sick and burning witches. Scientific ideas are not published mainly to benefit the ego of the investigator but to expose the ideas to the test of others, to allow them to detect errors, and to allow as many people as possible to think of opportunities for further steps. There is no identifiable closed circle of people who can guarantee the creation of scientific insights or detect errors in them. Einstein, after all, was once a mere examiner in the Swiss patent office with no official recognition and no top-secret clearance.

Every significant fact hidden from public view diminishes freedom in society.

Public policy, even more than science, is likely to be perfected by involvement with the many rather than with the few. Few scientific pursuits are as complex and subtle as formulating a public policy that is appropriate for 200 million Americans or, more demanding still, for more than 4 billion human beings and the interlocked interests of their 160 nations. Giving citizens access to the processes and information of government is not merely an elegant flourish in the Declaration of Independence. It is the only way that a national consensus can be reached in a viable and continuing way, which is to say, the only way democracy can succeed and endure.

Secrecy and censorship remove the vital information from the political process. The smaller the circle of knowledge, the greater the incidence of undetected error and of detachment from reality. The sequestered decision making of the elite has produced a succession of catastrophes in the history of the twentieth century, from World War I to Vietnam. If information is withheld because it is considered too disturbing for the public, it merely

If information is withheld because it is considered too disturbing for the public, it merely postpones society's confrontation with its problem.

postpones society's confrontation with its problem. It removes the issue from open, political resolution.

Even secrecy considered justified, such as the atom bomb project during World War II, nevertheless had a high subsequent cost. Atomic secrecy after the war made it possible to conceal the effects of low-level radiation, permitted political exploitation for massive military spending to close alleged gaps—"missile" and "bomber" and "windows of vulnerability"—that later were found to be nonexistent, withheld data that led to fateful decisions to make hydrogen bombs, and let Cold War and McCarthyist cynicism persecute people such as J. Robert Oppenheimer, who helped create the secrets in the first place.

The vast apparatus of secrecy in the United States, which began more than a generation ago, is now so large that no one any longer knows how many documents are classified or even how many thousands of government and industrial functionaries have the power to stamp documents secret. Even classifiers admit that most of what is stamped secret could safely be made public. No one has been able to find a way to discover the documents that may be needed for history that are in the tons of sealed papers. Periodically, a government leader with a sense of obligation to the ethic of democracy tries to slow the pace, to move toward a more open government. The Freedom of Information Act was passed to give the citizen some limited right to the information possessed by his government. Occasionally, an attempt is made to reduce the size of the army of people permitted to classify documents. These attempts were reversed by President Reagan. The Freedom of Information Act has been made more restrictive. Secrecy and censorship have been spread to areas of government and scholarship never before hidden from the public. These and other acts of excluding the citizens from their government usually are accomplished in innocuously numbered "Executive Orders" or little-publicized bureaucratic reorganizations. Two hundred years ago, James Madison issued a warning appropriate for our time: "I believe there are more instances of the abridgment of the freedom of the people by gradual and silent encroachment of those in power than by violent and sudden usurpation." ♦

Questions for Discussion

1. Is Bagdikian's formula for the calculus of democracy accurate?
2. Which secrets, if any, should a democratic government be allowed to keep?

TV News and the Neutrality Principle

John Corry

According to John Corry, there's a difference between "objectivity" and "neutrality." Being objective means trying to report things as they really are, rather than the way you, as a reporter, react to them. Being neutral means not taking sides. If by being neutral you blind yourself to the side that contains the truth, you do your readers a disservice.

John Corry was formerly a television critic for the New York Times. *He currently teaches communication at Boston University.*

Reading Difficulty Level: 9. He's making a rather precise philosophical point here.

Almost unremarked, we have passed a turning point in journalism, particularly as journalism is practiced on television. Exactly when this happened is unclear—although by the 1980's there were hints—but American broadcasts from Baghdad while American warplanes flew overhead finally made it certain. The old journalistic ideal of objectivity—the sense that reporting involves the gathering and presentation of relevant facts after appropriate critical analysis—has given way to a more porous standard. According to this new standard, reporters may—indeed should—stand midway between two opposing sides, even when one of the two sides is their own.

This is no academic matter. Neutrality is now a principle of American journalism, explicitly stated and solemnly embraced. After Dan Rather of CBS reported from Saudi Arabia last August that "our tanks are arriving," the Washington *Post* gave him a call: wasn't it jingoistic, perhaps xenophobic, to say "our tanks"? Rather apologized and promised he would never say such a thing again. He should have known better in the first place. After all, Mike Wallace, Rather's CBS colleague, made the new standard clear well before the Gulf crisis started. At a conference on the military and the press at Columbia University on October 31, 1987, Wallace announced that it would be appropriate for him as a journalist to

Almost unremarked, we have passed a turning point in journalism. Neutrality is now a principle of American journalism.

Mike Wallace announced that it would be appropriate for him as a journalist to accompany enemy troops into battle, even if they ambushed American soldiers.

accompany enemy troops into battle, even if they ambushed American soldiers.* And during the war itself, Bernard Shaw of CNN, explaining why he had refused to be debriefed by American officials after he left Baghdad, declared that reporters must be "neutral."

As it happens, Shaw once said that the late Edward R. Murrow of CBS was his great hero. Indeed, a whole generation of television newsmen regard Murrow as their hero, invoking his name every time they give one another an award. They ought to go back now and listen to his broadcasts. In the Battle of Britain and other engagements, Murrow was outspoken about which side he was on, and he was never a neutral reporter. It would have been unthinkable for him in 1944, say, to make his way to Berlin, check into the Adlon Hotel, and pass on pronouncements by Hitler.

"You must avoid the appearance of cheerleading," said the head of CNN. "We are, after all, a global network."

*A Marine colonel at the conference, George M. Connell, had a different perspective. "I feel utter contempt," he said when responding to Wallace, who had been supported in his declaration of neutrality, even if hesitantly, by Peter Jennings of ABC. "Two days later they're both [Wallace and Jennings] walking off my hilltop; they're 200 yards away, and they get ambushed, and they're lying there wounded—and they're going to expect that I send Marines up there to get them. . . . But I'll do it, and that's what makes me so contemptuous of them. And Marines will die going to get a couple of journalists." Colonel Connell was not being fanciful. When the correspondent Bob Simon vanished with his crew near the Kuwaiti border, CBS called the Pentagon for help.

Still, this is the New World Order, and rules everywhere are changing. The great place to be for television journalists this winter was the Al Rashid Hotel in Baghdad, in the basement of which, according to the Pentagon, was a command-and-control center, although the journalists holed up there were (neutrally) unable to find it.

Colleagues did complain when Peter Arnett of CNN stayed on in Baghdad after other journalists had been expelled; the complaints, however, were not so much about whether CNN (which has outlets in 104 countries) was acting as a broadcasting service for Saddam Hussein as about whether it was taking advantage of its competitors. When CBS, ABC, and NBC got their own correspondents into Baghdad, the complaints ended.

"You must avoid the appearance of cheerleading," Ed Turner, the vice president of CNN, said during the war. "We are, after all, at CNN, a global network." Turner, no relation to his boss Ted Turner, although obviously they think alike, went on to stress that CNN wanted to be fair to *all* nations. But the truth was that CNN had a mission. Speaking from Baghdad, Arnett told us what it was:

I know it's Ted Turner's vision to get CNN around the world, and we can prevent events like this from occurring in the future. I know that is my wish after covering wars all over and conflicts all over the world. I mean, I am sick of wars, and I am here because maybe my contribution will somehow lessen the hostilities, if not this time, maybe next time.

Old-style journalists grew sick of wars, too, although few thought their presence would prevent them. New-style neutral journalists, however, have their conceits, and the constraints that bind fellow citizens are not necessarily binding on them. At the Columbia conference, Mike Wallace was asked if a "higher duty as an American citizen" did not take precedence over the duty of a journalist. "No," Wallace replied, "you don't have that higher duty—no, no." But if a neutral journalist does not owe a higher duty to citizenship, where does his higher duty lie? Old-style journalists seldom thought about that. A story was a story, and a reporter went out and reported it. Our age is self-consciously moral, though, and higher duties now weigh on us all. Arnett was clear about his higher duty, even without being asked. "I don't work for the national interest," he asserted in another broadcast from Baghdad. "I work for the public interest."

The Public Interest

And it may be here that neutral journalism flies apart and breaks up into shards. What is this public interest, and who determines it, anyway? The national interest is determined by consensus and people are elected to serve it. The recent consensus was that the U.S. national interest lay in driving Iraq out of Kuwait and decimating its war machine. But the public interest is amorphous, and usually it turns out to be closer to the interest of its advocates than to that of the public.

Consider the performances in Baghdad. The correspondents there could not gather relevant facts, and if they had tried, they would have been expelled, or worse, from Iraq. What the correspondents did was listen to government-controlled Baghdad Radio (with a translator, presumably; none of the correspondents seemed to speak Arabic), tour Baghdad neighborhoods (with government guides and monitors), and, in the fashion of journalists everywhere, pick up what they could from other correspondents they met.

The constraints that bind fellow citizens are not necessarily binding on journalists.

There is not much chance to do real reporting in a situation like that, and most of the time, one suspects, the correspondents knew it. Anchormen pressed them on questions they could not possibly answer. Tell me, Peter (or Bill, or Tom, or Betsy), an anchor would ask, how do Iraqis feel about this statement from President Bush? And Peter (or Bill, or Tom, or Betsy), from a cubicle in a hotel, an eight-hour time difference away, in a country whose language he did not understand, would reply as best he could.

The most accurate reply would have been, "I don't know," but you cannot say that very often and keep your job in television. So the reporting from Baghdad inevitably turned into an exercise by the cor-

What is the public interest, and who determines it, anyway?

respondent in appearing to know something when he probably did not know much, while bearing in mind that he could not offend the host government.

What if a correspondent in Baghdad had discovered something the host government did not want revealed?

Obvious questions arise: what if a correspondent in Baghdad had discovered something the host government did not want revealed? What if a correspondent had uncovered news about a party purge, or an outbreak of civil disorder, or the whereabouts of Saddam Hussein? Or—and this is not far-fetched—what if a correspondent, being bused from Baghdad to Basra, had come across an artillery battery with shells loaded with nerve gas and pointed toward U.S. Marines? The profession was uncomfortable with questions like that. Nonetheless, they could not be entirely ignored, and obliquely the correspondents in Baghdad addressed them. Were they, for example, holding back information?

"There are lots of things that you can't report," Betsy Aaron of CBS acknowledged. "If you do, you are asked to leave the country, and I don't think we want to do that. I think you do a very valuable service reporting, no matter what you are allowed to report."

Neutral journalism is a symbolic act, distinguished by form and not content.

No matter what you are allowed to report? Imagine Ed Murrow saying that. Neutral journalism assumes that what the reporter reports is not nearly as important as the fact that the reporter is there to report it. Journalism becomes a symbolic act, distinguished by form and not content. Operate under that standard, and censorship will not be a problem. Here is Bill Blakemore, speaking over ABC from Baghdad:

> The script process is very normal for wartime, I would say. We write our scripts. We find one of the censors who's down in the hotel lobby, and we show it to the censor who reads it, and sometimes there's a slight change of a word here or there. Very often you may say something you didn't realize would touch a sensitivity, but there's not been any kind of heavy censorship in my experience here so far. It's a fairly easy understanding we have.

Clearly, the "fairly easy understanding" between correspondents and one of the world's most repressive governments meant that the correspondents simply censored themselves. If they were uncertain how to do this, they could always get help. Here is Blakemore again, in an exchange with his anchorman, Peter Jennings:

"Bill, are you operating on a completely uncensored basis?" Jennings whimsically asked.

No, Blakemore responded, "we got organized just now and managed to get somebody over here to listen and make sure we don't have any military or strategic information."

Neutral status means that a journalist does not report objectively; he reports selectively. Arnett, visiting what had been Baghdad's two main power plants, now destroyed by bombs and missiles, spoke of "relentless attacks on civilian installations." He did not mention that those installations had been covered in camouflage paint. When he reported on the famous target that the Pentagon said was a biological-weapons factory and the Iraqis claimed was a "baby-milk plant"—"innocent enough from what we could see," observed Arnett—he did not notice the camouflage there, either. (Visiting German peace activists, of all people, did notice it and talked about it when they got back to Europe.) After being taken to another bombed-out site, Arnett reported that "while we were there, a distraught woman shouted insults at the press and vented anger at the West." Then we saw and heard the woman, who was standing next to a crater. "All of you are responsible, all of you, bombing the people for the sake of oil," she screamed in perfect English. She also turned up on French television speaking perfect French. Several days later, a CNN anchor in Atlanta identified her as an employee of the Iraqi Foreign Ministry.

Arnett, an old hand at covering wars and seeing through propaganda, presumably knew that when the "distraught woman" was shouting. Surely he at least noticed that her jogging suit had "United Nations" printed down one leg. A neutral journalist must narrow his vision and report with one eye closed.

The Baghdad correspondents, as individuals or as a group, most likely will sweep this year's television-journalism prizes. A claque formed almost immediately for Arnett, heaping encomiums on his head (especially after his patriotism was questioned by Senator Alan Simpson). He was a "dukes-up guy," "brave," and "independent," and an ornament to his profession. In the true spirit of neutral journalism, government-controlled Iraqi newsmen joined the claque, too. "The Iraqi press wrote favorably about me," Arnett told Larry King, the CNN talk-show host, who interviewed him when the war was over. Arnett also said he had become a "third-world hero."

Certainly Arnett and the other Baghdad correspondents displayed physical bravery in placing themselves in a war zone; and they did report, loosely speaking, to the best of their abilities. On the other hand, the correspondents as individuals were incidental. If there had not been Peter, Bill, Tom, or Betsy, there would have been John, Morton, Arthur, or Susan, and the "reporting" would have been much the same. For them, the great thing was that anyone was in Baghdad at all, and it did not matter that a great many other Americans were disturbed. When a Washington *Post*-ABC News poll asked if we should bomb a communications center in the Baghdad hotel where the reporters were staying, 62 percent of the respondents said we should issue a warning and then bomb even if the reporters were still there; 5 percent said we should forget the warning and just go ahead with the bombing.

A neutral journalist must narrow his vision and report with one eye closed.

The press as a whole did not come off well in the war.

In fact, the press as a whole did not come off well in the war. Television tarred more reliable print, and polls showed a huge dislike of the media. The essential reason was captured by the headline over a story in *Time* about disenchantment with the press: "Just Whose Side Are They On?" The "they," of course, were journalists, and simply by raising the question *Time* went a long way toward providing the answer, even though the story itself predictably took a different position: "The attacks from both sides probably mean that the press is situated just about where it usually is: in the even-handed middle ground."

Well, perhaps, but the even-handed middle ground becomes an increasingly elusive place in the television age. There were no American reporters in Kuwait when Iraq salted and pillaged that country; it was not in Iraq's interest to have them there. It was in Iraq's interest, however, to have reporters in Baghdad; when the war was over, Iraq kicked them out. Could the press have found a more even-handed middle ground here? Why, yes. It could have insisted that if it was going to be in Baghdad it must also be in Kuwait. Obviously, no network did insist on that.

The principal signs of television's search for a middle ground were "cleared by censor" titles; they were even-handedly applied to film approved by either American or Iraqi censors, showing skepticism of both sides. But the new neutral journalism also went a long way toward suggesting which side it was the more skeptical of. As long ago as last August, Michael Gartner, the president of NBC News, in a piece for the op-ed page of the *Wall Street Journal,* had alerted us to danger: "Here's something you should know about the war that's going on in the Gulf: much of the news that you read or hear or see is being censored."

Actually, the American part of the war had not begun yet, but that did not deter Gartner. He went on to quote, disdainfully, from a list of things the Pentagon did not want us to know. They included:

1. Number of troops.
2. Number of aircraft.
3. Number of other equipment (e.g., artillery, tanks, radars, trucks, water "buffaloes," etc.).
4. Names of military installations/geographic locations of U.S. military units in Saudi Arabia.
5. Information regarding future options.
6. Information concerning security precautions at military installations in Saudi Arabia.

And so on, ending with "9. Photography that would show level of security at military installations in Saudi Arabia" and "10. Photography that would reveal the name of specific locations of military forces or installations."

While it would be easy to dismiss Gartner as merely frivolous, it may be assumed that his peculiar ideas about censorship and war and the military and the press got passed on to his reporters. Surely they were reflected in an NBC special, "America: The Realities of War," when Arthur Kent, the NBC correspondent in Saudi Arabia, took on Pete Williams, the Pentagon spokesman in Washington.

"Why are you trying to put your hands so far into our business?" Kent asked peevishly. "We're not trying to tell you how to run the war. We're just trying to cover it. Why do you want to control us so completely?"

Williams did not mention Gartner's laundry list of complaints, although if he had he would have made a reasonable argument not just for controlling the press but for banning it altogether. Williams did not say either that some of the television coverage was so goofy the Pentagon might have thought its higher duty was to straighten it out. In an interview when the war was over, General H. Norman Schwarzkopf remarked that he had "basically turned the television off in the headquarters very early on because the reporting was so inaccurate I did not want my people to get confused."

On the same program in which he attacked Williams, Kent also offered a choice specimen of the reporting General Schwarzkopf probably had in mind:

"Saddam Hussein is a cunning man and nowhere does he show that more clearly than on a battlefield when he's under attack," Kent told Faith Daniels, who was anchoring the special.

"And that, Arthur, really seems to be this administration's greatest miscalculation," Daniels replied.

"That's right, Faith," Kent continued. "He is ruthless, but more than ruthless. In the past eleven days, he's surprised us. He's shown us a capable military mind, and he still seems to know exactly what he's doing."

With "reporting" like that, is it any wonder that 57 percent of the respondents in one poll said the military should exercise more, not less, control over the press, and that 88 percent in another poll supported censorship? For, in addition to the other problems—moral, political, and professional—it has created, the neutrality principle has evidently turned many otherwise intelligent people into fools. ♦

Fifty-seven percent of the respondents in one poll said the military should exercise more, not less, control over the press, and 88 percent in another poll supported censorship.

Question for Discussion

1. Do you agree that American correspondents did their audience a disservice when they attempted to remain neutral during Operation Desert Storm?

Trained Seals and Sitting Ducks

Lewis H. Lapham

Among many in the media, there was a sense of anger over the government's treatment of the press during the Persian Gulf war. Lewis Lapham, editor of Harper's Magazine, was one of the angriest.

Reporters were allowed to gather information only in officially authorized "pools" that were organized and accompanied by military personnel. The reporters were forced to get most of their information from military briefings that, according to Lapham, were orchestrated to make the conflict look like a sporting event.

Lewis Lapham can be seen on PBS as moderator of "Book Talk."

Reading Difficulty Level: 5. You might not agree with everything Lapham says, but you'll not hear it said more eloquently.

Journalism consists in buying white paper at two cents a pound and selling it at ten cents a pound.

—Charles A. Dana

There were two campaigns waged by the American military command in the Arabian desert – one against the Iraqi army and the other against the American media.

Between the two campaigns waged by the American military command in the Arabian desert—one against the Iraqi army and the other against the American media—it's hard to know which resulted in the more brilliant victory. Both campaigns made use of similar tactics (superior logistics, deception, control of the systems of communication), and both were directed at enemies so pitiably weak that their defeat was a foregone conclusion.

The bombardment of Baghdad began on January 17, 1991, and within a matter of hours the newspaper and television correspondents abandoned any claim or pretension to the power of independent thought. It was as if they had instantly enlisted in the ranks of an elite regiment, sworn to protect and defend whatever they were told to protect and defend by the generals who presented them with their morning film clips and their three or four paragraphs of yesterday's news.

By the end of the first week I no longer could bear to watch the televised briefings from Washington and Riyadh. The journalists admitted to the presence of authority were so obviously afraid of giving offense that they reminded me of prisoners of war. The parallel image appeared on cue five weeks later when what was left of the Iraqi army stumbled across the desert waving the white rags of surrender.

The Iraqi troops at least had suffered the admonitions of gunfire. The American media surrendered to a barrage of propaganda before the first F-16 fired its first round at an Iraqi military target. The Pentagon's invitation to the war carried with it a number of conditions—no reporters allowed on the battlefield except under strict supervision, and then only in small task forces designated as "press pools"; all dispatches submitted to the military censors for prior review; no unauthorized conversations with the allied troops; any violation of the rules punishable by expulsion from the theater in the sand.

News organizations were encouraged to tell "feel good" stories about the Gulf War. (Photo by Bruce Cotler.)

The American media surrendered to a barrage of propaganda before the first F-16 fired its first round at an Iraqi military target.

The media accepted the conditions with scarcely a murmur of protest or complaint. Who could afford to decline even so ungracious an invitation? The promise of blood brings with it the gift of headlines, audiences, single-copy sales, Nielsen ratings, Pulitzer prizes, and a swelling of the media's self-esteem. A television network on assignment to a war imagines itself outfitted with the trappings of immortality. The pictures, for once, mean something, and everybody has something important to say.

On the fourth day of the bombing Dan Rather confirmed the Pentagon's contemptuous opinion of a media cheaply bought for a rating point and a flag. He appeared on a CBS News broadcast with Connie Chung, and after reading the day's bulletin, he said, "Connie, I'm told that this program is being seen [by the troops] in Saudi Arabia. . . . And I know you would join me in giving our young men and women out there a salute." Rather then turned to the camera and raised his right hand to his forehead in a slightly awkward but unmistakably earnest military salute.

The salute established the tone of the media's grateful attendance at what everybody was pleased to call a war. Had anybody been concerned with the accurate use of words, the destruction of Iraq and the slaughter of an unknown number of Iraqis—maybe 50,000, maybe 150,000—might have been more precisely described as a police raid, as the violent suppression of a

Dan Rather's salute established the tone of the media's grateful attendance at what everybody was pleased to call a war.

The military command provided the media with government-issue images roughly equivalent to the publicity stills handed around to gossip columnists on location with a Hollywood film company.

mob, as an exemplary lesson in the uses of major-league terrorism. Although the Iraqi army had been much advertised as a synonym for evil (as cruel as it was "battle-hardened," possessed of demonic weapons and a fanatic's wish for death, etc.), it proved, within a matter of hours, to consist of half-starved recruits, as scared as they were poorly armed, only too glad to give up their weapons for a cup of rainwater.

But the American media, like the American military commanders, weren't interested in the accuracy of words. They were interested in the accuracy of bombs, and by whatever name one wanted to call the Pentagon's trade show in the Persian Gulf, it undoubtedly was made for television. The parade of images combined the thrill of explosions with the wonder of technology. Who had ever seen—live and in color—such splendid displays of artillery fire? Who could fail to marvel at the sight of doomed buildings framed in the glass eye of an incoming missile? Who had ever seen the light of the Last Judgment coursing through a biblical sky?

Most of the American correspondents in Saudi Arabia experienced the war at more or less the same remove as the television audience in Omaha or Culver City. They saw little or nothing of the battlefield, which was classified top secret and declared off-limits to the American public on whose behalf the war presumably was being waged. The military command provided the media with government-issue images roughly equivalent to the publicity stills handed around to gossip columnists on location with a Hollywood film company. Every now and then the government press agents arranged brief interviews with members of the cast—a pilot who could be relied upon to say hello to all the wonderful folks who made the plane and the ordnance, a nurse who missed her six-month-old son in Georgia, an infantry sergeant (preferably black) who had discovered that nothing was more precious than freedom. But even this kind of good news was subject to official suspicion. A reporter who said of some pilots that the excitement upon returning from a mission had made them "giddy" found the word changed to "proud."

The pentagon produced and directed the war as a television miniseries.

The Pentagon produced and directed the war as a television miniseries based loosely on Richard Wagner's *Götterdämmerung*, with a script that borrowed elements of *Monday Night Football*, *The A Team*, and *Revenge of the Nerds*. The synchronization with prime-time entertainment was particularly striking on Super Bowl Sunday. ABC News intercut its coverage of the game in progress in Tampa with news of the bombing in progress in the Middle East, and the transitions seemed entirely in keeping with the spirit of both events. The newscasters were indistinguishable from the sportscasters, all of them drawing diagrams in chalk and talking in similar voices about the flight of a forward pass or the flare of a Patriot missile. The football players knelt to pray for a field goal, and the Disneyland halftime singers performed the rites of purification meant to sanctify the killing in the desert.

The televised images defined the war as a game, and the military command in Riyadh was careful to approve only those bits and pieces of film that sustained the illusion of a playing field (safe, bloodless, and abstract) on which American soldier-athletes performed feats of matchless daring and skill.

Like the sportscasters in the glass booth on the fifty-yard line, the newscasters standing in front of the palm tree or the minaret understood themselves to be guests of the management. Just as it never would occur to Frank Gifford to question the procedures of the National Football League, so also it never occurred to Tom Brokaw to question the ground rules of the war. When an NBC correspondent in Israel made the mistake of talking to New York about an Iraqi missile falling on Tel Aviv without first submitting his news to the local censors, the Israeli government punished his impudence by shutting down the network's uplink to the satellite. The embargo remained in force until Brokaw, at the opening of *NBC Nightly News,* apologized to Israel for the network's tactlessness.

Between representatives of competing news organizations the protocol was seldom so polite. The arguments were about access—who got to see whom, when, why, and for how long—and the correspondents were apt to be as jealous of their small privileges as the hangers-on attached to the entourage of Vanilla Ice. When Robert Fisk, a reporter for the British paper *The Independent,* arrived at the scene of the fighting for the town of Khafji, he was confronted by an NBC television reporter—a licensed member of the day's press pool—who resented the intrusion. "You asshole," the television correspondent said. "You'll prevent us from working. You're not allowed here. Get out. Go back to Dhahran." The outraged nuncio from NBC summoned an American Marine public affairs officer, who said to Fisk, "You're not allowed to talk to U.S. Marines, and they're not allowed to talk to you."

The televised images defined the war as a game, and the military command in Riyadh was careful to approve only those bits and pieces of film that sustained the illusion of a playing field

Even under the best of circumstances, however, print was no match for television. The pictures shaped the way the story was told in the papers, the newsmagazines, and the smaller journals of dissenting opinion. Although a fair number of writers (politicians as well as scholars and plain citizens) took issue with the Bush administration's conduct of the war, their objections couldn't stand up to the heavy-caliber imagery delivered from Saudi Arabia in sorties as effective as the ones flown by the tactical fighter squadrons. *Time* and *Newsweek* followed the pictures with

With Hussein, the trick was to make the sitting duck look like the 6,000-pound gorilla.

an assault of sententious rhetoric—"The greatest feat of arms since World War II . . . Like Hannibal at Cannae or Napoleon on a very good day."

At the end as in the beginning, the bulk of the writing about the events in the Persian Gulf was distinguished by its historical carelessness and its grotesque hyperbole. The record strongly suggests that the Bush administration resolved to go to war as early as last August, almost as soon as Saddam Hussein made the mistake of invading Kuwait. If the war could be quickly and easily won, the administration might gain a number of extremely desirable ends, among them the control of the international oil price, a revivification of the American military budget, a diversion of public attention from the sorrows of the domestic economy, a further degradation of what passes for the nation's political opposition, a cure for the mood of pessimism that supposedly had been undermining Washington's claims to world empire.

The media never subjected the administration's statements to cross-examination, in large part because the administration so deftly promoted the fiction of a "liberal press" bent on the spiteful negation of America's most cherished truths.

But none of these happy events could be brought to pass unless a credulous and jingoistic press could convince the American people that Hussein was a villain as monstrous as Adolf Hitler, that his army was all but invincible, that the fate of nations (not to mention the destiny of mankind) trembled in the balance of decision. It wouldn't do any good to send the grand armada to the Persian Gulf if the American people thought that the heavy guns were being wheeled into line to blow away a small-time thug.

The trick was to make the sitting duck look like the 6,000-pound gorilla. Much later in the proceedings Lieutenant General Thomas Kelly could afford to say, amidst applause and self-satisfied laughter at the daily press briefing at the Pentagon, that, yes, sending B-52's to carpet bomb a single Iraqi Scud site was, come to think of it, "a delightful way to kill a fly." But in the beginning the generals were a good deal more careful about the work of disinformation. By October, Washington was besieged with ominous reports—about Hussein's chemical and biological weapons, about the price of oil rising to $50 or $100 a barrel, about the nuclear fire likely to consume the orchards of Israel, about the many thousands of body bags being sent to Saudi Arabia to collect the American dead. All the reports derived from government sources, and all of them proved to be grossly exaggerated.

The advantage of hindsight suggests that President Bush and his advisers chose Saddam Hussein as a target of opportunity precisely because they knew that his threats were mostly bluster and his army more bluntly described as a gang of thieves. The media never subjected the administration's statements to cross-examination, in large part because the administration so deftly promoted the fiction of a "liberal press" bent on the spiteful negation of America's most cherished truths. The major American media are about as liberal as Ronald Reagan or the late John Wayne, but in the popular mind they enjoy a reputation (undeserved but persistent) for radicalism, sedition, and dissent. The administration well understood that the media couldn't afford to offend the profoundly conservative sympathies of their prime-time audience, and so it knew that it could rely on the media's complicity in almost any deception dressed up in patriotic costume. But for the purposes of the autumn sales campaign it was necessary to cast the media as an antagonist as un-American as Saddam Hussein. If even the well-known "liberal press" could be brought into camp, then clearly the administration's cause was just.

The media loved the story lines (especially the ones about their own dread magnificence), and by Christmas every network and every magazine of respectable size had designed for itself some kind of red, white, and blue emblem proclaiming its ceaseless vigilance and its readiness for war. When the steel rain at last began to fall during the second week of January, most of the national voices raised in opposition to the war had been, as the Pentagon spokesmen liked to say, "attrited." Through the five weeks of the aerial bombardment and the four days of the ground assault the version of the public discourse presented in the media turned increasingly callow. *Time* and *Newsweek* published posters of the weapons deployed in the Persian Gulf, and the newspapers gave over the majority of their editorial-page space to columnists gloating about the joy of kicking ass and kicking butt. Andy Rooney on *60 Minutes* struck what had become the media's preferred note of smug self-congratulation. "This war in the Gulf," he said, "has been, by all odds, the best war in modern history. Not only for America but for the whole world, including Iraq probably. It was short and the objectives of victory were honorable: In spite of all the placards, the blood was not for oil. It was for freedom. We did the right thing."

The return of the nation's mercenary army was staged as a homecoming weekend for a college football team, and the troops arriving in Georgia and California found themselves proclaimed, in the words of *Life* magazine, "Heroes All." Many of them had spent several uncomfortable months camping in the desert, but few of them had taken part in any fighting. The number of American casualties (125 dead in action, twenty-three of them killed by "friendly fire") once again posed the question of whether America had gone to a war or to a war game played with live ammunition. But it was a question that few people cared to ask or answer.

The return of the nation's mercenary army was staged as a homecoming weekend for a college football team.

Had America gone to a war or to a war game played with live ammunition?

In the postmodern world maybe war will come to be understood as a performing art, made for television and promoted as spectacle.

Maybe the question is irrelevant. In the postmodern world maybe war will come to be understood as a performing art, made for television and promoted as spectacle. Maybe, as the producers of the charades on MTV would have it, Madonna is Marilyn Monroe, true love is a perfume bottle, and George Bush is Winston Churchill.

Certainly the administration succeeded in accomplishing what seemed to be its primary objectives. The cost of oil went down, and the prices on the New York Stock Exchange (among them the prices paid for Time Warner, the Washington Post Company, CNN, and the *New York Times*) went up. The country welcomed the easy victories in Kuwait and Iraq with band music, ticker-tape parades, and speeches to the effect that once again it was good to be American.

How do we tell the difference between our victories and our defeats unless we insist that our media make the effort of asking questions other than the ones that flatter the vanity of the commanding general?

Still, I find it hard to believe that the American people feel quite as triumphant as they have been made to appear in the newsmagazines. The cheering rings a little hollow, as if too many people in the crowd were shouting down the intimations of their own mortality. The elation seemed more like a feeling of relief—relief that so few Americans were killed and that almost everybody, this time at least, got home safely.

Maybe the war in the desert was a brilliant success when measured by the cynical criteria of realpolitik, but realpolitik is by definition a deadly and autocratic means of gaining a not very noble end. The means might be necessary, but they are seldom admirable and almost never a cause for joyous thanksgiving. If we celebrate a policy rooted in violence, intrigue, coercion, and fear, then how do we hold to our higher hopes and aspirations? We debase our own best principles if we believe the gaudy lies and congratulate ourselves for killing an unknown number of people whom we care neither to know nor to count. How do we tell the difference between our victories and our defeats unless we insist that our media make the effort of asking questions other than the ones that flatter the vanity of the commanding general? Like the seal balancing the red, white, and blue ball on the end of its faithful nose, a servile press is a circus act, as loudly and laughingly cheered by a military dictatorship as by a democratic republic. ♦

Question for Discussion

1. Do you agree with Lapham that "We debase our own best principles if we believe the gaudy lies and congratulate ourselves for killing an unknown number of people whom we care neither to know nor to count."?

Suggested Readings

Those who are interested in the type of controversy engendered here will not want to miss the readings in Chapter 16, which deal with the question of whether the media are politically biased.

More On the Government's Management of the Media During Operation Desert Storm

Bennet, James, "How They Missed That Story," *The Washington Monthly*, December, 1990, p. 8 (7) ("The first casualty of Desert Shield was a skeptical press.").

Browne, Malcolm W., "The Military Vs. the Press," *The New York Times Magazine*, March 3, 1991, p. 27 (9). Includes a related story on Peter Arnett of CNN.

Diamond, Edwin, "How CNN Does It: Winning the Gulf War," *New York*, February 11, 1991, p. 30 (9). Includes profiles by Jeanie Kasindorf of Peter Arnett, Bernard Shaw, John Holliman, Charles Jaco, Wolf Blitzer, Richard Blystone, and Charles Bierbauer.

Diamond, Edwin, "Who Won the Media War," *New York*, March 18, 1991, p. 26 (4). Which journalists and journalistic organizations did the best job.

Nathan, Debbie, "Just the Good News, Please," *The Progressive*, February, 1991, p. 25 (3). ("The Pentagon prefers 'Hi-Mom' coverage.")

Polman, Dick, "News Media Fight Pentagon, But Fear Getting Shot in Foot," *The Philadelphia Inquirer*, February 24, 1991, p. 3C. A lawsuit brought by journalists over the rules imposed on them during the Gulf War.

On the History of Wartime Censorship

Lubow, Arthur, "Read Some About It," *The New Republic*, March 18, 1991, p. 23 (3).

O'Sullivan, Gerry, "The Free Press: Every Military Should Own One," *The Humanist*, May/June 1991, p. 39 (4). Column analyzing press coverage of wars and the military's relationship to the press during wartime.

More On the Press/Government Relationship

Cronin, Thomas E., "Kennedy was America's Best TV President, Johnson Was the Worst: A Presidential Scholar Ranks Our Leaders' Ability to Use the Medium," *TV Guide* Vol. 37, October 14, 1989, p. 22 (2).

Freedman, Tom, "While Journalists Chase 'Sexy' Issues . . ." *The New York Times* Vol. 139, September 16, 1990, sec. 4 p. E23 (L), p. E23 (N), Col. 2, 17 col. in. Column: media ignores substantive political issues such as legislative decisions leading up to savings and loan crisis.

Karp, Walter, "All the Congressmen's Men: How Capital Hill Controls the Press," *Harpers Magazine* Vol. 279, July, 1989, p. 55 (9).

Ornstein, Norman J., "What TV News Doesn't Report about Congress—And Should," *TV Guide* Vol. 37, October 21, 1989, p. 10 (4).

"Raised Eyebrow," *The Progressive* Vol. 54, July, 1990, p. 8 (2). Sam Donaldson on press adversarial role. Editorial.

Rather, Dan, "Journalism and the Public Trust," *The Humanist,* November/December 1990, p. 5 (4). ("A journalist's job isn't always to make America feel good about itself.")

Woodruff, Judy, "Can Democracy Survive the Media in the 1990s?", *USA Today,* May, 1990, p. 24 (3). ("The media must not forget that they are here to serve the public, to bring them the information they need to make informed judgments about their community, the nation, and the planet.")

Public Relations III: Politics

15

What has caused the shape of contemporary American politics? The major parties no longer seem to have clear-cut ideologies—we just don't know where they stand. They seem more interested in ferreting out emotional but meaningless issues that have the capacity to motivate people to vote, and jumping on that bandwagon. Campaigns are conducted by negative advertising, mostly because it's easier to knock down your opponent than to come up with your own proposals for change. Whereas it was once said disdainfully, "candidates are sold like soap," we now realize that no soapmaker could use these tactics and stay in business.

The readings in this chapter examine the possible role that the media play in the current shape of American politics. The first two readings—James Boylan's "Where Have All the People Gone" and Christopher Lasch's "Journalism, Publicity and the Lost Art of Argument," examine the press's role in voter apathy. The third reading—Garry Wills's "How Pure Must Our Candidates Be?", looks at the effects of the kind of scrutiny the press gives candidates' private lives.

Where Have All the People Gone?

James Boylan

In the following reading James Boylan, the founding editor of the Columbia Journalism Review, *examines the reasons that people have become politically apathetic, to the point that our largest political party today is the "party of nonvoters."*

Reading Difficulty Level: 7. The problem he's analyzing is complex.

Many members of the party of nonvoters may be making a political statement of their own.

At this point, neither of the major parties appears to have a clue as to what the current party of nonvoters is waiting for.

Although it was forecast to be a veritable hurricane of voter anger and frustration, the 1990 midterm election neither breached sea walls nor blew down trees. In fact, it came and went much like its predecessors: it returned to Congress more than 95 percent of the incumbents who chose to run; it earned the participation of only a little more than one in three Americans of voting age, a proportion that has varied little since the post-Watergate election of 1974; and it revealed the further growth, to almost 120 million souls, of what has been called the "party of nonvoters," those of voting age who do not show up at a polling place on a national election day.

Political scientists continue to provide a standard set of explanations for the phenomenon of nonturnout; the declining ability of the major parties to stimulate political activity or create agendas; the failure of new campaign marketing techniques to mobilize support; the apparent voter weariness when the big business of officeholding demands attention to year-round campaigns; and, not least, the discouragement created by the legal and procedural obstacles still placed in the way of those who might otherwise vote. Blame is also apportioned to the nonvoters themselves, for ignorance, cynicism, and—the catchall term—apathy.

Less attention is given to the possibility that many members of the party of nonvoters are not irreversibly apathetic, cynical, ignorant, or self-indulgent. Many in fact may be making a political statement of their own—that they fail to see in current politics, as presented by the media, any connection between their vote and their political interests.

Historians have discerned an earlier party of nonvoters, persisting until the New Deal called it out of hiding. The new party-in-waiting, like its predecessor in the 1920s, is a reverse image of the present American electorate. American voters are drawn disproportionately from the better educated, better off, and elderly. In contrast with electoral democracies elsewhere, the United States has failed to gain in equal proportions the participation of the less wealthy, the less educated, the young, and, most recently and curiously, the male.

At this point, neither of the major parties appears to have a clue as to what the current party of nonvoters is waiting for: sometimes they do not appear eager to find out. Indeed, the mini-electorate has its apologists, who ask what is wrong with having those who are most interested and best informed do the voting.

One thing is certain: the causes of nonvoting are deeply embedded in our political culture and their alleviation will depend on the course of political change. This is not to imply that the problem is too vast and intractable to be addressed, but

---

simply that it is too big for gimmicks. Specific measures can help. After all, federal legislation in the 1960s helped create the South's first black electorate since Reconstruction. Most of all, it appears, we need to rediscover what, if anything, politics is about or might be about.

Which brings us to journalism. Journalism fits into the problem somewhere, maybe not as obviously as many journalists (and their critics) would think. It is a given that mass communication provides most of the contact people have with candidates for major offices. And journalism supplies a good part of that contact but, what with the growth of candidate advertising on television, by no means all. Yet there is far from universal agreement that reading and viewing political news has an important relationship to voting. A recent book on nonvoters—*Why Americans Don't Vote,* by Frances Fox Piven and Richard A. Cloward—does not even mention journalism.

Still, it is probably more than a statistical curiosity that the three-decade decline in voting has coincided, almost to the year, with a similar proportionate lag in newspaper reading. Like voting, newspaper reading has become a more elite practice; in particular, the great cities are peopled with increasing numbers of nonvoters and nonreaders. This is far from saying that there is a simple causal relationship—that people stopped voting because they stopped reading or vice versa. Nor is there necessarily support for the implication that the newer dominant medium, television, has smothered electoral politics.

The two declines may share a common source—a lessening willingness by many Americans to consider themselves engaged in a national public life.

Nonetheless, the two declines may share a common source—a lessening willingness by many Americans to consider themselves engaged in what, as recently as the 1960s, constituted a sense of common enterprise, that is, a national public life. In the years since, there have been many signs of a sea change in the content and manner of national politics. A *New Yorker* writer recently watched a recording of the first Kennedy-Nixon debate of 1960; so startling was the decorum, the attention to issues, the seriousness of the content, that the writer felt "as if this presidential debate were happening in some other culture."

The three-decade decline in voting has coincided, almost to the year, with a similar proportionate lag in newspaper reading.

Perhaps it was. As late as 1960 national politics could still be understood in terms defined by the Franklin Roosevelt years—domestically, the magnitude of economic entitlements; abroad, the American obligation to police the world. This rather constricted agenda held together an electorate through the middle years of the century, but even before the end of the 1960s it had lost its force. There was too much else crowding the docket—civil rights, racial upheaval, Vietnam, the environment, and more—to which elections may have seemed too tardy and too indirect a response.

Has the press carried out its historical function of offering the raw material for public debate?

There is no longer even agreement as to what to argue about. Some scholars—the worrying kind—have turned recently to inquire into the nature of public life in America, scrutinizing in particular the question of whether the press has carried out its historical function of offering the raw material for public debate.

James W. Carey, Daniel C. Hallin, and other media scholars have noted the long association between the press and public life. Newspapers, they point out, came into existence as an important auxiliary to political debate almost with the emergence of legislative and electoral politics. Carey, in a 1987 article in *The Center Magazine,* points to James Madison's conception of the First Amendment—that the rights of free assembly, free speech, and the free press were created less specifically to guarantee individual expression than to evoke the public debate that creates a vigorous society.

The First Amendment was created to evoke the public debate that creates a vigorous society.

"The public," Carey writes, "is a group that gathers to discuss the news." Such a notion sounds a bit wistful in a time when we think of politics on a national scale as a struggle of clashing interests, causes and elites for ninety seconds on the evening news. But it has a point: that news ought not to be grist merely for consumption, but for discussion as well.

How well does news serve that purpose today? Stated in its most positive light, today's journalism operates largely to supply information; journalists gather the raw materials from sources and process it into attractive news formats. Theoretically, the system opens the news to all subjects, to all the voices in a society, and the press should thus reflect the full range of society's concerns. But the reality is something else, for the simplest of reasons. Information, the raw material of news, usually turns out to be the peculiar property of those in power and their attendant experts and publicists.

The main link with the non powerful, non expert population is supposed to be the opinion poll. The problem with polls, as David L. Paletz and Robert M. Entman pointed out a decade ago in *Media Power Politics,* is that instead of finding out what is on people's minds, poll-takers usually—barring, say, a life-and-death question such as war or peace—find out what people think about questions of primary concern to the journalistic and political elites, issues on which public feelings may be "at best casual and tentative." Harry Boyte, director of the Hubert H. Humphrey Institute of Public Affairs at the University of Minnesota, warns that poll results should not be mistaken for debate: "We have public opinion now, which is people's private reflexes. But we don't have public judgment. So everything is broken down into market segments. You have no public process."

Political journalism—that is, reporting on parties, candidates, campaigns—is a special case. Criticism of campaign reporting has chronically concentrated on the cliché that reporters focus on the "horse race" and disregard the "issues." But the difficulty may be not that politics is covered badly but that it is covered like other kinds of news and has the same constrictions. Political reporting, like other reporting, is defined largely by its sources. Political sources these days—candidates, consultants, free-floating quotesmiths—seem to be as addled about policy issues as the rest of us and prefer to deal in ethnic-cultural cant, marketing predictions, and tactical speculation.

Political reporting, like other reporting, is defined largely by its sources.

Drastic measures have been proposed to bring substance to the fore. A feasibility study by Alvin H. Perlmutter, Inc., for the John and Mary Markle Foundation proposed the creation of a company, The Voters' Channel, to stimulate new political programming, primarily through public radio and public television. The study envisioned four main types of effort: (1) to present voters' feelings and concerns; (2) to scrutinize the truthfulness of political communications; (3) to present a state-of-the-nation agenda; and (4) to provide national candidates and parties air time for direct communication. Programming is now being planned.

Robert Entman goes farther: in his *Democracy Without Citizens*, he proposes the restoration of the politically underwritten press of 160 years ago—the creation of "national news organizations run by the major parties and subsidized by the government," to foster the dissemination of "more analytical information, more diversity, more readily accessible ideas." Entman does not make clear how the palsied hand of present-day party bureaucracy can be sufficiently reinvigorated to take on such a task. Nor is there much encouragement to be found in one predecessor effort, the *Democratic Digest* of the 1950s, a pocket-size organ of no great depth designed to rally the faithful while the party was out of power.

Such proposals, while valuable in charting new political channels outside mainstream journalism, do not directly address the issue of journalism itself. In the rhetoric of journalism, "the public" is frequently invoked; functionally, however, news organizations rarely go beyond treating the public as consumer. Journalism produces news; the public eats it—or not, as it chooses.

Even when the function of journalism is considered to be education, the public role is still likely to be conceived as passive. Not uncommonly, news media try to find out what their readers and viewers have learned. Always the students are revealed to be failing; every one of the polls designed to reveal Americans' grasp of what are called, in schoolroom terms, current affairs finds that most are ignorant of such facts as the date of Earth Day or the name of the Chairman of the Joint Chiefs of Staff. The implications of such polls are alarming, not because of what the subjects answer but because of what they show about the assumptions of the press: first, that people should look to the press for correct answers rather than raw material for argument; second and worse, that the press itself thinks of news as what it too often appears to be, just a jumble of unconnected facts.

In practice, American politics has come to be run by full-time insiders, and to a degree the press has aspired to be one of the insiders.

In practice, American politics has come to be run by full-time insiders, and to a degree the press has aspired to be one of the insiders. It has taken on itself the task of scrutinizing and, on occasion, disqualifying candidates. It engages in as much speculation about campaign strategies as does any political consultant. And it has frequently made those consultants more central in the story of campaigns than the candidates themselves.

To change things around, to point the compass needle toward the public rather than the insider political networks, will be difficult, but it is a worthy challenge. Not because it implies vast upheavals in journalistic practice; it doesn't. But it proposes something more tortuous—a change in thinking.

Prescriptions from scholars of the public arena tend to be vague. What they have in common is their sense that journalism should be viewed as communication in which the recipient counts for something. Carey puts it: "The public will begin to reawaken when they are addressed as a conversational partner and are encouraged to join the talk rather than sit passively as spectators before a discussion conducted by journalists and experts." Indeed, the panel—a conversation conducted by journalists and experts—is one of the quintessential twentieth-century forms, and one of the most deadening; much of journalism is like a panel discussion in which those in the audience never get to ask a question.

The subject here, however, is not the public-access gimmicks that the news media adopted so widely in the 1970s, and often abandoned later. The question is whether political news as such can be written for a public instead of for participants, and in public language rather than codes.

It may be time to try to break up familiar patterns. There are several ideas in the air that may point in the right direction.

In an essay in *Critical Theory and Public Life* (1985), Daniel Hallin urges that reporters become more "sensitive to the underlying message their reporting conveys about politics and citizen's relation to it." The message, he contends, is that money and expertise count for everything and the citizen for little or nothing. For example, in an article in the January/February 1991 issue of the *Columbia Journalism Review* ("Whose Campaign Is It, Anyway?"), Hallin notes the virtual disappearance of voters from television campaign coverage in 1984 and 1988 and the influx of insiders and consultants.

The columnist David Broder suggests that one way to break the hold of insiders is to go first to the voters. In a speech last November, he proposed that journalists should "start each election cycle as reporters in the precincts with the voters, themselves, talking to them face to face, finding out what is on their minds. . . . Let their concerns set our agenda and influence the questions we take to the candidates . . . and help determine how we use the space in our newspaper and the air time on our broadcasts."

There may be another underlying message in political coverage—an implication that politics is either so esoteric or so dog-eat-dog that individual citizens should keep their distance. The political scientist Robert D. McClure has charged that journalism has taken on itself the task of becoming the chief interpreter of campaigns but has performed the task in a way that excludes "the reality of principle and moral purpose that forms the soul of a people's politics." Could there be a place in the political dialogue for those willing to discuss the moral-ethical dimension?

Another aspect of the problem may be journalistic specialists themselves, many of whom have long tenure and write with an air of magisterial entitlement. News organizations could vary their practice of consigning big-time politics to this aristocracy, not only by bringing in specialists from other fields but also, if such animals survive, generalists who write well, with a warning that they will be quarantined at the first sign of pontification.

It is, of course, not up to the media alone to reinvigorate American public life. But journalism remains the one nonofficial institution that is not, or at least should not be, itself a special interest. As such, it may in the long run be able to occupy a critical role in re-establishing a sense of common interests and common welfare. It can begin by seeking to emphasize its role of widening and deepening public discussion, of providing a record of its times, of doing no further harm to political life, if indeed it has done such harm. ♦

Journalism may in the long run be able to occupy a critical role in re-establishing a sense of common interests and common welfare.

Questions for Discussion

1. Are you a voter or a nonvoter? Why?
2. Do you agree with Robert Entman (p. 365) that one solution to political apathy would be news organizations run by the major parties?

Journalism, Publicity and the Lost Art of Argument

Christopher Lasch

Within the study of media history it has become a truism to say that the partisan press began to die because of the founding of the Associated Press in 1848. This nation-wide press service made it necessary for member newspapers all over the country to report objectively, so their wire releases could be used in papers anywhere.

Like James Boylan in the previous reading, Christopher Lasch believes that the press should encourage debate, not just provide information. But Lasch goes further, explaining the complex relationships between news and information, opinion and argument, and education and debate. Lasch also argues that the partisan press died partly because advertisers didn't care for the type of audience that political debate attracted. It is Lasch's contention that voter apathy and political ineffectuality might be traced back to the way public relations is used politically, and what the press does about it.

Christopher Lasch is Don Alonzo Watson Professor of History at the University of Rochester. His books include The Culture of Narcissism.

Reading Difficulty Level: 8. This one's going to require some cerebration.

What democracy requires is public debate, not information.

Let us begin with a simple proposition: What democracy requires is public debate, not information. Of course it needs information, too, but the kind of information it needs can be generated only by vigorous popular debate. We do not know what we need to know until we ask the right questions, and we can identify the right questions only by subjecting our own ideas about the world to the test of public controversy. Information, usually seen as the precondition of debate, is better understood as its by-product. When we get into arguments that focus and fully engage our attention, we become avid seekers of relevant information. Otherwise we take in information passively—if we take it in at all.

From these considerations it follows that the job of the press is to encourage debate, not to supply the public with information. But as things now stand the press generates information in abundance, and nobody pays any attention. It is no secret that the public knows less about public affairs than it used to know. Millions of Americans cannot begin to tell you what is in the Bill

From the *Gannett Center Journal*, Spring, 1990. Reprinted by permission of author.

15,000 spectators attended the fifth Lincoln-Douglas debate in 1858. (Library of Congress photo)

of Rights, what Congress does, what the Constitution says about the powers of the presidency, how the party system emerged or how it operates. A sizable majority, according to a recent survey, believe that Israel is an Arab nation. Ignorance of public affairs is commonly attributed to the failure of the public schools, and only secondarily to the failure of the press to inform. But since the public no longer participates in debates on national issues, it has no reason to be better informed. When debate becomes a lost art, information makes no impression.

Though the question at first may seem to have little to do with the issues raised by modern publicity, let us ask why debate has become a lost art. The answer may surprise: Debate began to decline around the turn of the century, when the press became more "responsible," more professional, more conscious of its civic obligations. In the early 19th century the press was fiercely partisan. Until the middle of the century papers were often financed by political parties. Even when they became more independent of parties they did not embrace the ideal of objectivity or neutrality. In 1841 Horace Greeley launched his *New York Tribune* with the announcement that it would be a "journal removed alike from servile partisanship on the one hand and from gagged, mincing neutrality on the other." Strong-minded editors like Greeley, James Gordon Bennett, E. L. Godkin and Samuel Bowles objected to the way in which the demands of party loyalty infringed upon editorial independence, making the editor merely a mouthpiece for a party or faction; but they did not attempt to conceal their own views or to impose a strict separation of news and editorial content. Their papers were journals of opinion in which the reader expected to find a definite point of view, together with unrelenting criticism of opposing points of view.

Ignorance of public affairs is commonly attributed to the failure of the public schools, but since the public no longer participates in debates on national issues, it has no reason to be better informed.

It is no accident that journalism of this kind flourished during the period from 1830 to 1900, when popular participation in politics was at its height. Eighty percent of the eligible voters typically went to the polls in presidential elections. After 1900 the percentage declined sharply (65 percent in 1904 and 59 percent in 1912), and it has continued to decline more or less steadily throughout the 20th century. Torchlight parades, mass rallies and gladiatorial contests of oratory made 19th-century politics an object of consuming popular interest. Horace Mann's account of the campaign of 1848 conveys something of the vitality of 19th-century politics, all the more impressive when we remember that this particular account came from someone who believed that the attention devoted to politics might better have been devoted to education:

> Agitation pervaded the country. There was no stagnant mind; there was no stagnant atmosphere. . . . Wit, argument, eloquence, were in such demand, that they were sent for at the distance of a thousand miles—from one side of the Union to the other. The excitement reached the humblest walks of life. The mechanic in his shop made his hammer chime to the music of political rhymes; and the farmer, as he gathered in his harvest, watched the aspects of the political, more vigilantly than of the natural, sky. Meetings were everywhere held. . . . The press showered its sheets over the land, thick as snow-flakes in a wintry storm. Public and private histories were ransacked, to find proofs of honor or proofs of dishonor; political economy was invoked; the sacred names of patriotism, philanthropy, duty to God, and duty to man, were on every tongue.

Nineteenth-century journalism served as an extension of the town meeting.

Mann's account suggests that 19th-century journalism served as an extension of the town meeting. It created a public forum in which the issues of the day were hotly debated. Newspapers not only reported political controversies but participated in them, drawing in their readers as well. Print culture rested on the remnants of an oral tradition. Print was not yet the exclusive medium of communication, nor had it severed its connection with spoken language. The printed language was still shaped by the rhythms and requirements of the spoken word, in particular by the conventions of verbal argumentation. Print served to create a larger forum for the spoken word, not yet to displace or reshape it.

The "best men," as they liked to think of themselves, were never altogether happy with this state of affairs. Horace Mann, even though he was himself elected to Congress in the 1848 election, regarded party strife as the bane of the republic. In his view, education belonged exclusively in schools; it did not occur to him that public controversy might be educational in its own right. Because it divided men instead of bringing them together, he believed, public controversy was something to be avoided. The political wars, moreover, usually ended in the victory of demagogues and spoilsmen, not of the "best men."

By the 1870s and 1880s, Mann's low opinion of politics had come to be widely shared by the educated classes. The scandals of the Gilded Age gave party politics a bad name. Genteel reformers—"mugwumps," to their enemies—demanded a professionalization of politics, designed to free the civil service from party control and to replace political appointees with trained experts. Even those who rejected the invitation to declare their independence from the party system, like Theodore Roosevelt (whose refusal to desert the Republican party infuriated the "independents"), shared the enthusiasm for civil service reform. The "best men" ought to challenge the spoilsmen on their own turf, according to Roosevelt, instead of retreating to the sidelines of political life.

The drive to clean up politics gained momentum in the Progressive era. Under the leadership of Roosevelt, Woodrow Wilson, Robert La Follette and William Jennings Bryan, the Progressives preached "efficiency," "good government," "bipartisanship" and the "scientific management" of public affairs, and declared war on "bossism." They attacked the seniority system in Congress, limited the powers of the speaker of the House, replaced mayors with city managers, and delegated important governmental functions to appointive commissions staffed with trained administrators. Recognizing that political machines were welfare agencies of a rudimentary type, which dispensed jobs and other benefits to their constituents and thereby won their loyalty, the Progressives set out to create a welfare state as a way of competing with the machines. They launched comprehensive investigations of crime, vice, poverty and other "social problems." They took the position that government was a science, not an art. They forged links between government and the university so as to assure a steady supply of experts and expert knowledge. On the other hand, they had little use for public debate. Most political questions were too complex, in their view, to be submitted to popular judgment. They liked to contrast the scientific expert with the orator—the latter a useless windbag whose rantings only confused the public mind.

Professionalism in politics meant professionalism in journalism. The connection between them was spelled out by Walter Lippmann in a notable series of books: *Liberty and the News* (1920), *Public Opinion* (1922) and *The Phantom Public* (1925). These provided a founding charter for modern journalism—the most elaborate rationale for a journalism guided by the new ideal of professional objectivity. Lippmann held up standards by which the press is still judged—usually with the result that it is found wanting.

Walter Lippmann held up standards by which the press is still judged—usually with the result that it is found wanting.

What concerns us here, however, is not whether the press has lived up to Lippmann's standards but how he arrived at those standards in the first place and what their connection to advertising and public relations is today. In 1920 Lippmann and Charles Merz published a long essay in *The New Republic* examining press coverage of the Russian Revolution. This study, now forgotten, showed that American papers gave their readers an ac-

Sex, violence and "human interest"—staples of modern mass journalism—raised grave questions about the future of democracy.

count of the revolution distorted by anti-Bolshevik prejudices, wishful thinking and sheer ignorance. *Liberty and the News* was also prompted by the collapse of journalistic objectivity during the war, when the newspapers had appointed themselves "defenders of the faith." The result, according to Lippmann, was a "breakdown of the means of public knowledge." The difficulty went beyond war or revolution, the "supreme destroyers of realistic thinking." The traffic in sex, violence and "human interest"—staples of modern mass journalism—raised grave questions about the future of democracy. "All that the sharpest critics of democracy have alleged is true if there is no steady supply of trustworthy and relevant news."

In *Public Opinion* and *The Phantom Public,* Lippmann answered the critics, in effect, by redefining democracy. Democracy did not require that the people literally govern themselves. The public's stake in government was strictly procedural. The public interest did not extend to the substance of decision-making: "The public is interested in law, not in the laws; in the method of law, not in the substance." Questions of substance should be decided by knowledgeable administrators whose access to reliable information immunized them against the emotional "symbols" and "stereotypes" that dominated public debate. The public was incompetent to govern itself and did not even care to do so, in Lippmann's view. But as long as rules of fair play were enforced, the public would be content to leave government to experts—provided, of course, that the experts delivered the goods, the ever-increasing abundance of comfort and conveniences so closely identified with the American way of life.

Lippmann acknowledged the conflict between his recommendations and the received theory of democracy, according to which citizens ought to participate in discussions of public policy and to have a hand, if only indirectly, in decision-making. Democratic theory, he argued, had its roots in social conditions that no longer obtained. It presupposed an "omnicompetent citizen," a "jack of all trades' who could be found only in a "simple self-contained community." In the "wide and unpredictable environment" of the modern world, the old ideal of citizenship was obsolete. A complex industrial society required a government carried on by officials who would necessarily be guided—since any form of direct democracy was now impossible—either by public opinion or by expert knowledge. Public opinion was unreliable because it could be united only by an appeal to slogans and "symbolic pictures." Lippmann's distrust of public opinion rested on the epistemological distinction between truth and mere opinion. Truth, as he conceived it, grew out of disinterested scientific inquiry; everything else was ideology. The scope of public debate, accordingly, had to be severely restricted. At best, public debate was a disagreeable necessity—not the very essence of democracy but its "primary defect," which arose only because "exact knowledge," unfortunately, was in limited supply. Ideally public debate would not take place at all; decisions would be based on scientific "standards of measurement" alone. Science cut through "entangling stereotypes and slogans," the "threads of memory and emotion" that kept the "responsible administrator" tied up in knots.

The role of the press, as Lippmann saw it, was to circulate information, not to encourage argument. The relationship between information and argument was antagonistic, not complementary. He did not take the position that reliable information was a necessary precondition of argument; on the contrary, his point was that information precluded argument, made argument unnecessary. Arguments were what took place in the absence of reliable information. Lippmann had forgotten what he learned (or should have learned) from William James and John Dewey: that our search for reliable information is itself guided by the questions that arise during arguments about a given course of action. It is only by subjecting our preferences and projects to the test of debate that we come to understand what we know and what we still need to learn. Until we have to defend our opinions in public, they remain opinions in Lippmann's pejorative sense—half-formed convictions based on random impressions and unexamined assumptions. It is the act of articulating and defending our views that lifts them out of the category of "opinions," gives them shape and definition, and makes it possible for others to recognize them as a description of their own experience as well. In short, we come to know our own minds only by explaining ourselves to others.

It is the act of articulating and defending our views that lifts them out of the category of "opinions," gives them shape and definition.

The attempt to bring others around to our own point of view carries the risk, of course, that we may adopt their point of view instead. We have to enter imaginatively into our opponents' arguments, if only for the purpose of refuting them, and we may end up being persuaded by those we sought to persuade. Argument is risky and unpredictable—and therefore educational. Most of us tend to think of it (as Lippmann thought of it) as a clash of rival dogmas, a shouting match in which neither side gives any ground. But arguments are not won by shouting down opponents. They are won by changing opponents' minds—something that can happen only if we give opposing arguments a respectful hearing and still persuade their advocates that there is something wrong with those arguments. In the course of this activity, we may well decide that there is something wrong with our own.

Arguments are not won by shouting down opponents. They are won by changing opponents' minds.

The press extends the scope of debate by supplementing the spoken word with the written word.

If we insist on argument as the essence of education, we will defend democracy not as the most efficient but as the most educational form of government—one that extends the circle of debate as widely as possible and thus forces all citizens to articulate their views, to put their views at risk, and to cultivate the virtues of eloquence, clarity of thought and expression, and sound judgment. As Lippmann noted, small communities are the classic locus of democracy—not because they are "self-contained," however, but simply because they allow everyone to take part in public debates. Instead of dismissing direct democracy as irrelevant to modern conditions, we need to recreate it on a large scale. And from this point of view, the press serves as the equivalent of the town meeting.

This is what Dewey argued, in effect—though not, unfortunately, very clearly—in *The Public and Its Problems* (1927), a book written in reply to Lippmann's disparaging studies of public opinion. Lippmann's distinction between truth and information rested on a "spectator theory of knowledge," as James W. Carey explains in his recently published *Communication and Culture.* As Lippmann understood these matters, knowledge is what we get when an observer, preferably a scientifically trained observer, provides us with a copy of reality that we can all recognize. Dewey, on the other hand, knew that even scientists argue among themselves. "Systematic inquiry," he contended, was only the beginning of knowledge, not its final form. The knowledge needed by any community—whether it is a community of scientific inquirers or a political community—emerges only from "dialogue" and "direct give and take."

It is significant, as Carey points out, that Dewey's analysis of communication stressed the ear rather than the eye. "Conversation," Dewey wrote, "has a vital import lacking in the fixed and frozen words of written speech. . . . The connections of the ear with vital and out-going thought and emotion are immensely closer and more varied than those of the eye. Vision is a spectator; hearing is a participator."

The press extends the scope of debate by supplementing the spoken word with the written word. If the press needs to apologize for anything, it is not that the written word is a poor substitute for the pure language of mathematics. What matters, in this connection, is that the written word is a poor substitute for the spoken word. It is an acceptable substitute, however, as long as written speech takes spoken speech and not mathematics as its model. According to Lippmann, the press was unreliable because it could never give us accurate representations of reality, only "symbolic pictures" and stereotypes. Dewey's analysis implied a more penetrating line of criticism. As Carey puts it, "The press, by seeing its role as that of informing the public, abandons its role as an agency for carrying on the conversation of our culture." Having embraced Lippmann's ideal of objectivity, the press no longer serves to cultivate "certain vital habits" in the community—"the ability to follow an argument, grasp the point of view of another, expand the boundaries of understanding, debate the alternative purposes that might be pursued."

The rise of the advertising and public relations industries, side by side, helps to explain why the press abdicated its most important function—enlarging the public forum—at the same time that it became more "responsible." A responsible press, as opposed to a partisan or opinionated one, attracted the kind of readers advertisers were eager to reach: well-heeled readers, most of whom probably thought of themselves as independent voters. These readers wanted to be assured that they were reading all the news that was fit to print, not an editor's idiosyncratic and no doubt biased view of things. Responsibility came to be equated with the avoidance of controversy because advertisers were willing to pay for it. Some advertisers were also willing to pay for sensationalism, though on the whole they preferred a respectable readership to sheer numbers. What they clearly did not prefer was "opinion"—not because they were impressed with Lippmann's philosophical arguments but because opinionated reporting did not guarantee the right audience. No doubt they also hoped that an aura of objectivity, the hallmark of responsible journalism, would also rub off on the advertisements that surrounded increasingly slender columns of print.

What advertisers did not prefer was "opinion" . . . because opinionated reporting did not guarantee the right audience.

In a curious historical twist, advertising, publicity and other forms of commercial persuasion themselves came to be disguised as information. Advertising and publicity substituted for open debate. "Hidden persuaders" (as Vance Packard called them) replaced the old-time editors, essayists and orators who made no secret of their partisanship. And information and publicity became increasingly indistinguishable. Most of the "news" in our newspapers—forty percent, according to the conservative estimate of Professor Scott Cutlip of the University of Georgia—consists of items churned out by press agencies and public relations bureaus and then regurgitated intact by the "objective" organs of journalism. We have grown accustomed to the idea that most of the space in newspapers, so called, is devoted to advertising—at least two-thirds in most newspapers. But if we consider public relations as another form of advertising, which is hardly farfetched since private, commercially inspired enterprises fuel both, we now have to get used to the idea that much of the "news" consists of advertising, too.

In a curious historical twist, advertising and publicity substitute for open debate.

Much of the press now delivers an abundance of useless, indigestible information that nobody wants, most of which ends up as unread waste.

The decline of the partisan press and the rise of a new type of journalism professing rigorous standards of objectivity do not assure a steady supply of usable information. Unless information is generated by sustained public debate, most of it will be irrelevant at best, misleading and manipulative at worst. Increasingly information is generated by those who wish to promote something or someone—a product, a cause, a political candidate or officeholder—without arguing their case on its merits or explicitly advertising it as self-interested material either. Much of the press, in its eagerness to inform the public, has become a conduit for the equivalent of junk mail. Like the Post Office—another institution that once served to extend the sphere of face-to-face discussion and to create "committees of correspondence"—it now delivers an abundance of useless, indigestible information that nobody wants, most of which ends up as unread waste. The most important effect of this obsession with information, aside from the destruction of trees for paper and the mounting burden of "waste management," is to undermine the authority of the word. When words are used merely as instruments of publicity or propaganda, they lose their power to persuade. Soon they cease to mean anything at all. People lose the capacity to use language precisely and expressively, or even to distinguish one word from another. The spoken word models itself on the written word instead of the other way around, and ordinary speech begins to sound like the clotted jargon we see in print. Ordinary speech begins to sound like "information"—a disaster from which the English language may never recover. ♦

Questions for Discussion

1. Do you agree with Professor Lasch that "When we get into arguments that focus and fully engage our attention, we become avid seekers of relevant information?" Do you have any personal experience to back up your answer to this?
2. Do you agree that "We come to know our own minds only by explaining ourselves to others"? Once again, do you have any personal experience to back up your answer?

How Pure Must Our Candidates Be?

Garry Wills

In this article, Garry Wills points out the main problem in the "distasteful questions" we now subject political candidates to: "The scrutinizing process has become," he says, "an incredible shrinking machine that diminishes all its participants—the prying reporters, the candidates shying off from the hunt, and a public torn between embarrassment and titillation."

In spite of the problems, he says, the scrutiny we subject our political candidates to serves a purpose. It allows us to bring up and openly discuss our assumptions about eligibility for candidacy. "Bringing such matters up," he says, "is the way we discover jointly that we have changed our communal attitude" about how attributes such as sexual orientation, religion, race and gender affect a candidate's appropriateness for an office.

Garry Wills is the Henry R. Luce Professor of American Culture and Public Policy at Northwestern University.

Reading Difficulty Level: 6.

"Has the press gone too far?" is a question that has been asked more frequently in this presidential campaign than any other. At a time when politicians are being canvassed on their love lives, their acquaintance with marijuana, and the originality of all their sayings, the question seems to answer itself. The "character issue" has become, in many people's eyes, a hunting license. The prey are intimidated even when they are not eliminated, made to seem vulnerable, "on the run" instead of running for office. The character issue seems to reverse its intended effect and puts in question all of a candidate's merits if he or she cannot measure up.

According to political managers like Raymond Strother (once Gary Hart's media adviser) and Robert Beckel (who ran Walter Mondale's 1984 campaign), the search for character has blighted any chance for charisma, for the kind of respect that makes governing possible. After making candidates scurry in fear from intrusive, petty, trivializing questions, how could the American public turn around and accord the winner a decent esteem?

According to political managers, the search for character has blighted any chance for the kind of respect that makes governing possible.

These are all good questions. Do we really want to know as much as we are being told about other people's (even public people's) private

(Photo by Bruce Cotler.)

The scrutinizing process has become an incredible shrinking machine that diminishes all its participants.

lives? Are we going to make it impossible for public figures to have any private lives at all? The scrutinizing process has become, in the eyes of many, an incredible shrinking machine that diminishes all its participants—the prying reporters, the candidates shying off from the hunt, and a public torn between embarrassment and titillation. There seems to be no escape from knowing about Pat Robertson's premarital sex or Albert Gore's most recent experience of marijuana (which occurred, significantly, when he was a journalist).

Nor is this kind of inquiry limited to presidential candidates, as Judge Douglas Ginsburg learned when he tried to move from a lower court to the highest one. It was found that in his various screenings for Justice Department and judicial appointments, he had exaggerated some things and minimized others. One of the things he minimized was any mention of drugs, including the putatively harmless (or at least temporarily expected) use of marijuana in his past. Widely expressed was a fear that the media would now enforce a "generational vendetta," disqualifying for public office those of a certain age bracket–that group of people coming of age in the 1960s, when custom seemed temporarily to exempt the young from the law against marijuana possession or use.

Of course, there have always been generational tests and barriers in our politics. After World War II it was almost impossible for men of a certain age to run for public office if they had not been in the armed forces. In the courts, too, it was a disqualification, for some time after the Civil War, for any judge to have served with the Confederacy. More recently, generations of Southern senators were brought up with an instilled certitude that keeping the "nigra" in his place was not only wise but the best thing for the "boy" himself. Many of these senators woke up in the 1970s to discover that

During the 1992 primaries, Gennifer Flowers held a press conference about her affair with Presidential hopeful Bill Clinton. (Photo by Bruce Cotler.)

their generation was being attacked for racial views that were accepted in an earlier time.

The rules are always changing in our politics, though never perhaps so rapidly as over the last two decades. Some lament that this changing of the rules will exclude worthy candidates. We are constantly warned that if Tendency X is allowed to run its course, no one of any self-respect will submit to the indignities of running for office.

But the changes in the rules that have occurred in recent years have worked mainly not to exclude candidates but rather to include vast new parts of the electorate. President Reagan was himself a prime instance of this. A generation ago, as a divorced and remarried man, he would have had a slim chance or none of being elected. Changing attitudes toward sexual morality—greater tolerance—made possible the Presidency of a man who called for a return to the good old days of strict sexual abstinence and just saying no. Some people, at least, counted that change a blessing.

A generation ago, as a divorced and remarried man, Ronald Reagan would have had a slim chance of being elected.

We have in our time what no American preceding us could boast of: the prospect of serious candidacies by blacks and females.

More clearly a blessing in my eyes is the fact that we have in our time what no American preceding us could boast of: the prospect of serious candidacies by blacks and females. It was not until the 1960s that a Catholic could be elected President. Now we are at the point where a Jewish candidacy will soon be viable. My own nominee for the person to fill that slot is Barney Frank, the gay congressman from Massachusetts who lost seventy pounds so he would not stick in the door while coming out of the closet. Any process that will include Barney Frank in the roll of serious candidates is clearly widening the pool of talents available, not narrowing it.

Paradoxically, the same processes that led to the election of a divorced man led to the scrutiny of adulteries committed by other candidates. The same opening up of taboo subjects, the same willingness to reassess the relevance of sexual behavior to public respectability made people bring up questions earlier suppressed. The ban on divorced men, or on Catholics, or Jews, or blacks, was never explicit in our politics. Neither Congress nor the Constitution, nor any party rules or guidelines expressly forbade the nomination of minority candidates. It was an unspoken prohibition, a gentlemen's agreement cloaked in civil reticences. The whole structure of suppression rested on an imperviousness to scrutiny or public challenge. It was simply unthinkable that a woman, for instance, could be President.

Well, now it is thinkable. But for that to happen, vast changes in our social assumptions had to take place—the entire feminist movement, for instance. That, in turn, could not have occurred without the preceding civil rights movement, during which arguments, debates, and demonstrations broke the rules of contained discourse that had countenanced Jim Crow laws.

Within the past few decades there were struggles over the most disturbing, wrenching things that went to society's inmost ties, to the makeup of the family, to relations between husband and wife, parent and child. They called into question interlocked patterns of authority, they instilled respect for parents and teachers and officers of the law. They were resisted, advocated, articulated, household by household, and the struggle is far from over. Generations overlap. The losing side has enclaves where it is still in the majority. Many try to deny that changes have taken place at all or that they are permanent.

Sexual Complications of the Presidential Kind

Did you know that John Quincy Adams pimped for the czar Alexander I of Russia while he was serving as the American minister in St. Petersburg? Some journalists claimed to know that fact during the notably scurrilous campaign of 1824. But historians have tended to remember the even more foul allegations brought against Andrew Jackson by an unscrupulous journalist, Charles Hammond, since there was a kernel of truth in the stream of filth directed at Jackson. He had (with the approval of the woman's family) taken away the vivacious wife of the man in whose home he boarded as a young bachelor and had then married her before her divorce was completed, living with her in inadvertent adultery for four years. Early in his political career, Jackson discouraged talk of that scandal with two duels, in one of which he killed a man. But it made him touchy about rumors and innuendo, a touchiness his enemies used to torment him. His first term was plagued with charges that his Secretary of War, John Eaton, had married a trollop, whom other cabinet wives would not meet socially.

The American public has always shown an interest in the sex lives of the Presidents, but the curiosity was usually thwarted by the same thing that fed it: the overkill of an irresponsible, openly partisan press. George Washington and Thomas Jefferson both declared their love for another man's wife in their youths, but only Jefferson's lapse was reported; the disreputable James Callender, in a tide of other charges—most of them untrue—accused Jefferson of being an atheist as well as the lover of his mulatto slave. This last charge, unsubstantiated, still echoes in history's whispering gallery, but it was disbelieved by the voters who reelected Jefferson in 1804.

Thomas Jefferson was accused of being an atheist as well as the lover of his mulatto slave.

The most famous sexual charge raised against a presidential candidate was the cartoonists' baby that cried, "I Want My Pa!" during Grover Cleveland's 1892 campaign. Once again the attack failed by an "overkill" reliance on false charges. Cleveland admitted that as a bachelor he had had an affair with a promiscuous widow who claimed her child as his. He had cared for the child, taking it from the woman when she proved a neglectful mother and having it brought up by respectable friends. This was before his distinguished terms as mayor of Buffalo and governor of New York. When the episode was brought up in the presidential campaign by a suspect rag, the Buffalo *Evening Telegraph,* it was included in a list of other and later (and imagined) debaucheries. Leading clergymen, taken into Cleveland's confidence declared that he had acted honorably, years before, as a bachelor and that the later charges were baseless. This was as close as sexual impropriety ever came to affecting an election before 1988.

Continued

Warren Harding had a long affair with a woman who might have been a politically relevant embarrassment in his 1920 campaign since she had been a German sympathizer in World War I, but that affair was kept so rigorously hidden that Harding's estate as recently as 1968 blocked in court the publication of his love letters. Woodrow Wilson wrote love letters (possibly platonic) to a woman not his wife, but that, too, was not known at the time. Franklin Roosevelt's affair with Missy LeHand was known to more people, as was Eleanor Roosevelt's warm friendship with Lorena Hickok; but many inhibitions, including wartime morale, kept those matters from public discussion.

John F. Kennedy was not given a similar exemption, but he was lucky that journalists went after the wrong scandal early in his Presidency. Instead of discovering his wartime affair with Inga Arvad, who had Nazi friends, critics of Kennedy chased a will-o'-the-wisp former marriage to Durie Malcolm. Kennedy's father ended and covered up the affair with Inga Arvad, as his brother Robert would end and cover up an affair with a mafioso's girl friend, Judith Exner. Both father and brother knew the danger of such liaisons, and even Kennedy himself wrote ruefully, during the 1960 campaign, that election would mean the end of his "poon days." He recognized the rules, even though he later broke them.

Only luck and bad journalism had saved other Presidents from scandal. No presidential race until the current one was decided for any candidate by his sex life, though the potential was always there. Some now think James Buchanan was homosexual. If that is true, and had been known, it would have prevented his serving as President—or even as town librarian in most towns. The requirements of sexual conformity were greater, not less, in the past.

—G. W.

But the sexual revolution, for instance, has occurred, despite those who believe that sexual roles will resume their old configuration if we just stop talking about them. Don't mention condoms in schools, these people insist, don't discuss AIDS in front of the children, keep it out of the media, don't bring it up. There is an aching desire to return to some of the social taboos, the unspoken arrangements that once kept people in their place. This is reflected in the fad for Allan Bloom's book, *The Closing of The American Mind*, arguing as it does that exposure to more than one culture system destroys the very idea of morality.

There is an aching desire to return to some of the social taboos, the unspoken arrangements that once kept people in their place.

Our society in general is questioning past attitudes toward race, gender, and authority, and sex is one of the most touchy but inevitable arenas where this self-questioning goes forward. One clear sign of that was the advice of some people to Gary Hart. They thought he should have immediately said, "Of course, I slept with Donna Rice. So what?" That reflects the attitude of many in our society, and it shows that what some see as prying into one man's privacy is seen by others as a vindication of what they believe is acceptable. After all, we live in a time when many respected figures live openly together in what used to be called sin. Barney Frank and others openly say that they are gay, that there is nothing wrong with that, that they have nothing to be ashamed of. That is not a position that would be as acceptable in many places as it is in Frank's Boston area. But it puts homosexuals in a difficult position—should they be ashamed of being ashamed? If it is all right for a gay person to be a political candidate, shouldn't one fight to establish that right rather than hide from the struggle? Yet who has the right to compel another to enlist in such a way? The questions circle aback and back on each other. And in an open society all such shifting evaluations are expressed through the media, our forum for encountering each other as members of the same large and disagreeing community. The rules are changing for everyone, whether one wants to admit that or not. Parents admit it when they accept the new sexual behavior of their children, if only by averting their eyes from it. Society's consensus is distributed, with large areas of change and equally large enclaves of resistance. That is how profound social alteration, going deep into moral attitudes, is always effected.

So candidates are rightly confused. They are caught in a social situation where conflicting signals are being sent, clashing attitudes expressed; where there is widespread disagreement on fundamental premisses. The presidential race itself is one of the ways this country decides what kind of society it wants to be, what symbols it will honor, what authority figures it finds persuasive. It always mattered that the nominee for President was male, white, Protestant, presumably happily married (but only once), and presumably heterosexual. In fact, it was always decisive to be most or all of those things. If you were not, you were simply out of the running from the outset. There were race and gender assumptions so securely in place that they never had to be brought up. There was little discussion of a candidate's private life because the range of a candidate's options in his private life was so narrow.

If it is all right for a gay person to be a political candidate, shouldn't one fight to establish that right rather than hide from the struggle?

Those who did not bring up religion in an election wanted the reigning religious exclusions to continue. So religion ruled the situation far more rigidly when it was not discussed than it does now, when the fact that Bruce Babbitt is a Catholic is somewhat relevant, but not the decisive factor, as it was with Al Smith, nor a disproportionately relevant factor, as with John Kennedy. The issue had to get more relevant, to be brought up and openly addressed, before it could become less relevant. Only in that way could society make up its mind publicly on the matter and signal a new set of presidential rules: more inclusive for Catholics (though not yet for Jews).

Bringing such matters up, even before the children, is the way we discover jointly that we have changed our communal attitude. We discover the change while making the change, in public interchanges with our fellow citizens. We could not know the shift had occurred until it was thrashed out in public forums of social acceptance—forums like the presidential race, our leading symbol of social choice and cohesion.

Does smoking pot in the sixties have any relevance to a political career today?

Does smoking pot in the sixties have any relevance to a political career today? That, too, is a question we could not know the answer to until it was brought up. For Bruce Babbitt and Senator Gore, the answer seems to be no. But this is a question on which society itself has been somewhat hypocritical. For one thing, there has been a lag in time, or a lack of fit, between behavior and the law—the sort of thing we experienced under Prohibition. Law enforcement figures still preach against marijuana; this First Lady takes her campaign against it into the schools; Justice Department prosecutors have to declare whether they themselves have broken this particular law, detailing times and circumstances. It was an institutional hypocrisy that caught Ginsburg in the anomalous position of being higher in the Justice Department than some who had been disqualified because of what he did or that put him on the way toward being a high court justice who might have to pronounce on a crime (if that is what it is) that he himself had committed. And if it is not a crime, then why have it on the books? As I say, the "youthful indiscretion" argument seems to work for a Gore or a Babbitt, who did not have the institutional procedure of the Justice Department and the specific legal mandate that Judge Ginsburg sought. The Ginsburg case posed in its most pointed way this question: How does one go from challenging authority figures—as Ginsburg did, not only by smoking marijuana and growing a beard and long hair but by demonstrating against a war being conducted by the political authorities of the United States—to becoming an authority figure oneself? Even with all these factors weighing against him, Ginsburg would not necessarily have been denied office if other matters—possible conflict of interest and misrepresentations of his experience—had not also come into play.

The question of who deserves authority is complicated and must be decided case by case, person by person, but smoking marijuana is relevant precisely because the sixties were a generation that challenged authority so effectively and had such readily identifiable symbols for doing that. We are still caught in the turmoil caused by such questioning, and the sixties generation will have to sort out its attitudes in the world it helped change, with all the doubts that follow in successful challenges to authority. How do you reestablish authority? On what grounds of agreed values? These are the large questions that underlie such apparently trivial points as whether one broke a law that is still on the books, whether one supports that law now or would favor abolishing it.

There is probably no better way to thrash out all this than in a political race. From the time of George Washington, the choice of President has been a symbolic endorsement of certain values. He, more than any other President, was chosen for character, apart from the issues. Admittedly he was chosen by an electoral college that still had real independence. Nonetheless, that college voted for a man who would be a convincing, persuasive, unifying leader of the people at large—which he proved to be. He was chosen for his war record and, even more, for his resignation of military authority, for his peacetime self-restraint during the troubled period of transition from the Articles of Confederation to the present Constitution. Washington was an embodiment of what America was striving to be as a nation when we did not yet have a cluster of symbols and institutions that made the national identity and authority.

If we have trouble finding a similar figure now, it is because we do not have as firm a consensus of our values or as easy a way of signaling our identity. It was not held against Washington that he was a slaveholder. That was no disqualification for the Presidency down through Andrew Jackson's time; after him, it became a liability, if not a disqualification. Slave-holding had by then been brought up and made relevant. Today, of course, we exclude slaveholders from running for office. We have even eliminated the electoral college except as a counting device—going more directly to more voters than ever in the search for a rallying figure in this large, heterogeneous nation. This is a risky process, and some want to reverse it. In a recent symposium sponsored by *Harper's* magazine, Raymond Strother said: "We force a man or woman to run for president of the United States as though he were a city-council candidate in Dubuque. . . . The race for it [the Presidency] should be nobler and larger."

From the time of George Washington, the choice of President has been a symbolic endorsement of certain values.

The only way to maintain the charisma and distance of the office is to avoid the demeaning process of seeking votes in Iowa, exposing oneself to endless questions that reflect the confusions of the society at

How is one person to express the character of the American people?

large. Charisma is protected (if not created) by not talking about certain things in front of the children. Robert Beckel agreed with his fellow symposiast: "These primaries don't enhance a candidate. They mold the public's opinion of a candidate and almost always mold it negatively. . . . This system has got to be overhauled, and we have to get this word 'democracy' out of the way. We have to get back to selecting delegates in a rational way that gets us our best nominee with the least amount of fighting."

Though he seems to be calling, on the face of his words, for a return to smoke-filled rooms crowded with "brokers," Beckel is actually expressing a deeper yearning for the original electoral college—for people who know what the voters *should* want, rather than what they *think* they want, and can do the choosing for them. The only trouble with this is that a modern electoral college would have to consider the same things the original one did: how to find a candidate who is convincing, persuasive, authentic in the role of speaking for America. And no candidate can be that anymore unless he or she goes directly to the people, with an open and inclusive campaign, rather than rely on an elite of the sort that ruled America in the 1780s. The "character issue" is simply the modern way of stating the abiding problem of the American Presidency: How is one person to express the character of the American people, a character that is never entirely made up, yet one that emerges (so far as that is possible) precisely through transactions like the campaigns for the Presidency?

We are always changing the rules in this process, simply by talking to each other every day. It is called self-government. And we talk to each other through the presses and the cameras, by what we read and see, or refuse to read or see, about Americans at some distance from us coping with the same questions we have. In an electronic age we must plug in to the process in order to become aware of all our fellow citizens. The community exists only so long as its parts are in electronic touch with each other. This leads us, if not toward consensus, then at least to a sense of the boundaries of our disagreement, the rules and limits within which we can keep on disagreeing, keep bringing up questions that matter to any of us, and still be conscious of ourselves as part of a larger community, one that, despite all the changes of recent years—or, rather, *because* of the changes that have brought in more women, more blacks, more gays, more of the deprived and handicapped—is a society achieving "a more perfect union." ♦

Questions for Discussion

1. Does the American public need to know about a candidate's personal life?
2. Do you agree with Garry Wills that probing questions into candidates' personal lives help contribute to changing public attitudes and increasing chances for women and minorities to run for office?

Suggested Readings

How Politicians Handle the Press, How the Press Covers Politicians

Boot, William, "Hamming It Up for the Press," *Columbia Journalism Review,* September–October 1990, p. 17 (3). Promoting members of Congress.

Cronin, Thomas E., "Kennedy was America's Best TV President, Johnson Was the Worst: A Presidential Scholar Ranks Our Leaders' Ability to Use the Medium," *TV Guide* Vol. 37, October 14, 1989, p. 22 (2).

Denton, Robert E. Jr., and Gary C. Woodward, *Political Communication in America, 2nd Ed.* (N.Y.: Praeger, 1990). A systematic and comprehensive analysis of the role of communication in American politics.

Entman, Robert, "How the Media Affect What People Think: An Information Processing Approach," *The Journal of Politics* Vol. 51, May, 1989, p. 347 (24).

Freedman, Tom, "While Journalists Chase 'Sexy' Issues . . ." *The New York Times* Vol. 139, September 16, 1990, sec. 4 p. E23 (L), p. E23 (N), Col. 2, 17 col. in. Column: media ignores substantive political issues such as legislative decisions leading up to savings and loan crisis.

Gergen, David R., "The Politics of Sound Bites," *U.S. News and World Report* Vol. 105, September 12, 1988, p. 76 (1). Presidential candidates and the press. Editorial.

Karp, Walter, "All the Congressmen's Men: How Capital Hill Controls the Press," *Harpers Magazine* Vol. 279, July, 1989, p. 55 (9).

Lee, Martin A. and Norman Solomon, "Media Con Games," *The Progressive* Vol. 54, July, 1990, p. 16 (5). Politics and the language of mainstream news reporting.

Mickelson, Sig, *From Whistle Stop to Sound Bite: Four Decades of Politics and Television* (New York: Praeger, 1989). An eyewitness account of television's complicated interaction with the U.S. political system, by a former president of CBS news.

Ornstein, Norman J., "What TV News Doesn't Report about Congress—And Should," *TV Guide* Vol. 37, October 21, 1989, p. 10 (4).

"Raised Eyebrow," *The Progressive* Vol. 54, July, 1990, p. 8 (2). Sam Donaldson on press adversarial role. Editorial.

Rothman, Stanley, and Robert Lerner, "Television and the Communications Revolution," *Society* Vol. 26, November–December 1988, p. 64 (7). Also appeared as "Politics and the Media: A TV Revolution," *Current*, March–April 1989, p. 4 (8). How television has changed political campaigns.

Shapiro, Walter, "Is It Right to Publish Rumors? In an Age of Dirty Politics, Alas, Mudslinging is Part of the Story," *Time* Vol. 134, July 10, 1989, p. 53 (1). Journalistic ethics.

Smoller, Fredric T., *The Six O'Clock Presidency: A Theory of Presidential Press Relations in the Age of Television* (N.Y.: Praeger, 1990). Argues that the "big three" network coverage of the presidency is gradually eroding public confidence in that office. Coverage of the presidency is determined by the technical and commercial nature of television, which produces a bias toward negative coverage.

Squiers, Carol,"The Future of Delusion," *Artforum*, Vol. 28, February 1990, p. 19 (3).

Stempel, Guido H. and John W. Windhauser, eds., *The Media in the 1984 and 1988 Presidential Campaigns* (Westport, Conn.: Greenwood Press, 1990.) A study of media bias in recent elections.

Taylor, Paul, *See How They Run: Electing the President in an Age of Mediacracy*, (New York: Knopf, 1990). Reviewed, in *Columbia Journalism Review*, September/October 1990, p. 54. The 1988 campaign "was as if the proceedings had been hijacked by a team of gag writers from 'Saturday Night Live.' "

Wafai, Mohamed, "Senators' Television Visibility and Political Legitimacy," *Journalism Quarterly* Vol. 66, Summer, 1989, p. 323 (10).

On Negative Political Ads

Alter, Jonathan, "The Media Mud Squad: This Year the Press Takes a Hard Look at Political Ads," *Newsweek*, October 29, 1990, p. 37 (1).

Garramone, Gina M., Charles K. Atkin, Bruce E. Pinkleton, and Richard T. Cole, "Effects of Negative Political Advertising on the Political Process," *Journal of Broadcasting and Electronic Media* Vol. 34, Summer 1990, pp. 299–311.

Hinerfeld, Daniel Slocum, "How Political Ads Subtract: It's Not The Negative Ads That Are Perverting Democracy. It's the Deceptive Ones," *Washington Monthly* Vol. 22, May, 1990, p. 12 (8).

Kern, Montague, *30-Second Politics: Political Advertising in the Eighties* (N.Y.: Praeger, 1989). An analysis of political advertising from 1972 to 1988, including considerations of campaign consultants and negative ads.

Pfau, Michael, and Henry C. Kenski, *Attack Politics: Strategy and Defense* (N.Y.: Praeger, 1990). Examines the growth of negative campaigning through the 1988 election, and examines the responses used by politicians.

Wooster, Martin Morse, "Grab a Bucket and Mop," *Reason* Vol. 21, March, 1990, p. 39 (2).

On the Private Lives of Politicians

Fenby, Jonathan, "Private Life and the Public Eye," *UNESCO Courier,* September, 1990, p. 20 (4). Special issue on "The Media: Ways to Freedom."

Mindle, Grant B., "Liberalism, Privacy and Autonomy," *The Journal of Politics* Vol. 51, August 1989, p. 575 (24).

"Privates on Parade," *The New Republic* Vol. 201, November 13, 1989, p. 7 (3). Editorial: Sex-and-morals scandals in politics are overemphasized.

Other Readings of Interest

Brownstein, Ronald, *The Power and the Glitter: The Hollywood-Washington Connection* (NY: Pantheon, 1991). Movie stars, writers, directors and producers tend to be liberals, but their leftish bias rarely evidences itself in the entertainment products that Hollywood produces. They might campaign for their favorite causes and candidates, but the movies they make are not propaganda.

Coles, Robert, "What TV Teaches Children About Politics," *TV Guide* Vol 36, February 6, 1988, p. 2 (3).

McWilliams, Wilson Carey, "A Republic of Coach Potatoes," *Commonweal* Vol. 116, March 10, 1989, p. 138 (3).

"TV's Role in Global Political Turmoil," *USA Today* Vol. 119, August 1990, p. 13 (1).

Part V

ETHICAL ISSUES

Bias

16

There are many types of bias. The media have been accused of being biased against women, minorities, gays, and just about every religious and ethnic group. We will concentrate here on political bias, with three readings: one contends that the media are too conservative, another contends that they are two liberal, and a third contends that they lean neither to the left nor the right, but they are "biased just the same."

The Right Rolodex

Marc Cooper and Lawrence C. Soley

Cooper and Soley claim that network news reporting is biased in the conservative direction, because the experts chosen for "sound bites"—those certified smart people we see so often—tend to be Republicans and conservative Democrats, former Republican officials, and members of conservative "think tanks."

Marc Cooper is a Los Angeles journalist who teaches media studies at California State University, Northridge. Lawrence C. Soley teaches at the University of Minnesota.

Reading Difficulty Level: 3. Some of the names might be unfamiliar to you.

Experts tend to be men rather than women, East Coasters rather than West, and Republicans rather than critics of the political establishment.

They are like those character actors you see on the late night movie. You know you've seen them a hundred times, you know after one glance if they are typecast as a Thug, a Lover, a Soft Touch, maybe a Cop. But you just don't know their names.

The familiar faces we're talking about here are ones you see on the evening news. They light up on the screen, dutifully squawk out a ten-second sound bite, disappear, and then pop up a few nights later on another channel. The role of these expert "news shapers" is to put complex national and world events into a context we can understand, to tell us what an event "really" means, or, often, to predict what course an evolving news story will take. And they claim to do it dispassionately, neutrally, objectively.

A two-year study documents the bias in network news reporting.

After conducting a study of every network newscast from January 1987 through June 1, 1989, we found that correspondents and producers established a pattern of returning time and again to a very small group of the same experts. Indeed, our study found that less than one-fifth of all experts used accounted for more than half of the group appearances on the air. And the cluster of experts most favored is remarkably homogenous in its composition. They tend to be men rather than women, East Coasters rather than West, and Republicans (along with a few conservative Democrats) rather than critics of the political establishment. Also favored by television news are ex-government officials (mostly from Republican administrations), and "scholars" from conservative Washington, D.C., think tanks who appear to be more steeped in political partisanship than in academic credentials.

As you go over the list that follows, keep one technical detail in mind: the number of appearances stated for each "expert" refers only to appearances on the three network evening newscasts. It does not include spots on the three morning news shows, *Nightline, This Week with David Brinkley, 20/20, Meet the Press, Face the Nation,* the entire CNN network, *The MacNeil/Lehrer NewsHour,* nor on the thousands of local newscasts broadcast daily.

Now, meet the men who helped shape our collective consciousness through the final days of the Reagan presidency, Iran-Contra, the redirection of the Supreme Court, the 1987 stock market crash, and the momentous 1988 election.

WILLIAM SCHNEIDER

He is the "Aristotle of American Politics," according to his publicity sheet at the *Los Angeles Times,* for whom he writes a column. But Wil-

---

Primary research for this article is contained in the University of Minnesota School of Journalism's *News Shapers* Study. The research paper analyzes the experts used by the ABC, CBS, and NBC evening news shows during 1987 and 1988.

Originally published as "All the Right Sources: A Two-Year Study Documents the Bias in Network News Reporting," *Mother Jones,* February-March 1990. Reprinted by permission of Lawrence Soley.

liam Schneider (64 appearances January 1987–June 1989) might more accurately be described as the Dr. Joyce Brothers of the Beltway.

Name a topic—presidential affairs, foreign affairs, or extramarital affairs—and "Bill," as the Washington press knows him, will gladly oblige the cameras.

Schneider's rise to prominence is a curious one, reflective of what constitutes Aristotelian-class credentials in the Age of The Tube. Now a "resident fellow" at the conservative American Enterprise Institute, Schneider taught politics at Harvard University from 1971 to 1979, but he left without receiving tenure. "My contract ran out there," Schneider flatly explains. From Harvard it was off to California's Hoover Institute and then AEI. Residence in these two rightist bastions offered Schneider the academic legitimacy he had not achieved at Harvard. Over the span of several years AEI's promotional literature touted Schneider as the coauthor of two books that, in fact, have not been published. Schneider has coauthored a single book, *The Confidence Gap: Business, Labor and Government in the Public Mind.* "I have an academic background," Schneider explains, "but I do want to speak to a broader audience."

"We think [Schneider] is one of the most astute analysts on the American scene," says his editor at the Los Angeles Times Syndicate. "He is not a commentator with an opinion. He rather interprets what the American people are thinking." Schneider, who told us he is a Democrat ("I'm even liberal on some issues"), says he strives for neutrality above all: "I come on as a sort of objective analyst; I try not to represent a political point of view."

Networks usually give Republican militants neutral titles. Not so with Democrats.

But it's not just Schneider's grooming by unmistakably right-wing institutions that belies his affirmation of nonpartisanship—it is also his on-air performances. Schneider is a faithful source for the most conventional, which is to say conservative, Washington wisdom:

On Pat Schroder's bid for the presidency: "I think it's risky to nominate a woman for the top of the ticket and the Democrats are probably aware of that."

On Democratic programs: "Reagan has created a new coalition in American politics and it is holding together for George Bush, because that coalition perceives one simple threat: liberals. The higher the political office, the more ideology matters. And the more ideology matters, the worse Democrats do."

On Jesse Jackson's campaign: "Most Democrats agree that it would be suicidal to put Jesse jackson on the ticket . . . it could endanger their prospects."

NORMAN ORNSTEIN

When a B-movie actor can become president, it shouldn't be a surprise that one of the media's most admired political scientists has *TV Guide* as one of his showcases. While the credentials of Norman Ornstein are even more anemic than Schneider's, Ornstein's overall penetration of the media is deeper. By December 1986, *The Washington Monthly* (religiously read by the national press corps) had already identified Ornstein as the "King of Quotes" and described his media court as "addicts." So embarrassing was the frequency with which Ornstein's quotes saw print (more than six hundred per year) that *Los Angeles Times* Washington Bureau Chief Jack Nelson called for a moratorium on their use.

Yet in our study of the two and one-half years immediately following the publication of the *Washington Monthly* article, Ornstein registered forty-eight network news appearances. Forty-two of these occurred during the period from 1987 to 1988. In addition, during the election campaign, CBS News paid him as a consultant, in Ornstein's words, to "help organize coverage and interpret election results." A commentator in one form or another on PBS since 1974, Ornstein also continues to receive a check as the only "paid news consultant" in the history of the *MacNeil /Lehrer NewsHour,* on which he has appeared twenty times between January 1987 and September 1989. "We use him to find out what's happening on the Hill," says Senior Political Producer Peggy Robinson in regard to Ornstein's off-camera contractual duties. "He makes suggestions on our coverage, on our guests, and floats story ideas."

Ornstein (like Schneider, he's an AEI "scholar") considers chumming with the press integral to his professional development. "It happens that I do spend a lot of my time with press people," he says (after returning our call almost immediately). "It is a two-way relationship, it's a way for me to keep up with ideas and events going on across the country."

Ornstein's expertise certainly isn't coming from academic research. Even though the *New York Times* credited Ornstein as the "author and editor of dozens of books and monographs," and *U.S. News & World Report* blessed him as the "author of seven books on government," describing Ornstein as the *sole author* of as much as one book is being generous. When asked to list separately the books he has single-authored, coauthored, or merely edited, Ornstein hurriedly responds: "I don't know the breakdown offhand." But the breakdown is simple: Ornstein has cowritten one book, published in 1978, entitled *Interest Groups, Lobbying and Policymaking.* He is also listed as coauthor on the 1988 volume "The People, Press and Politics," a 109-page, soft-cover summary of a nationwide Gallup poll.

Bustled after for his political-science expertise, Ornstein rarely publishes articles in scholarly or political-science journals. Instead, like Schneider, Ornstein concentrates his efforts on the popular press, regularly making his mark with such heavyweight pieces for *TV Guide* as "Which Lawmakers Are Best on TV—And Why" and "Yes, Television Has Made Congress Better." Ornstein is quoted on everything from the NFL, to Warren Rudman's honesty, to the federal deficit. The *New York Times* once tagged him as an "economist," while *Nightline* called him a "tax-policy expert" on one show, a "congressional scholar" on another, and a "political scientist" on yet one more outing.

How can you get more quotable than this: *NBC Nightly News* did a piece last March on why the same experts, like Ornstein, keep showing up on the news, and the man giving the answers was—Ornstein. "People come to me because they want to get some outside perspective, and they want to do it in a way that is pungent, that is, uh, energetic, and that can be done without spending three hours doing it," Ornstein told NBC's cameras. "I saw Tom Brokaw and he said, um, 'Sometimes I think we ought to give you residuals, you are on so much.' . . . One of the things I've found is that the more of this I end up doing, the more I end up doing."

"It must be striking to the viewer to see the same faces, like Ornstein and Schneider, over and over," says Tim Russert, a vice-president of NBC News and NBC Washington Bureau chief. "We are aware of the 'quotemeister' syndrome and I am taking steps to broaden our Golden Rolodex. Of course, I can only speak for what we are doing here out of Washington, not for the rest of the network."

And what kind of quote do you get when you call on Norm Ornstein? "Center-center," says Ornstein. "We don't put him on thinking his view needs to be offset by someone else," says *MacNeil/Lehrer*'s Robinson. "Even if he is affiliated with the conservative AEI, we think his view is straightforward."

It probably is Ornstein's proven blandness that does make him so popular with the press. Given the narrow margins within which the press debates such hallowed institutions as Congress, who is a better choice than Ornstein, who, on that particular aspect of his expertise, boasted: "In the final analysis I'm a defender of Congress." You call Ornstien, in short, to get fed back to you the perfectly predictable and safe opinion that will ruffle neither editors nor viewers. Says producer Robinson, "It's true that if you want analysis that is provocative, you don't use Norm."

You call Ornstein, in short, to get fed back to you the perfectly predictable and safe opinion that will ruffle neither editors nor viewers.

ED ROLLINS

(51 appearances 1987–1988) Here is U.S. politics come full circle. A gaggle of full-time media spin doctors have managed to disembody American political life, converting what should be grass-roots campaigning and participation into passive viewing of competing TV commercials. As their final victory,

The same hucksters who have wrecked the art of political campaigning are hired as analysts of their own mutant creation.

these same hired hucksters are anointed as the chief media analysts of their own mutant creation.

Among these media manipulators the longtime Nixon-Ford-Reagan appointee and adviser **Ed Rollins** was the network news favorite during the 1987–88 campaign, popping off more than any other news shaper except William Schneider. So dependent did network correspondents become on Rollins to frame political events that Rollins, in this same two-year period, was on two networks the same night on seven different dates. He was on one network or another for two consecutive nights or more four different times. Rollins made six appearances in one month during two separate thirty-day periods. And in one four-month period (May–July 1988), he appeared nineteen times. During 1987 and 1988, CBS reporter Bill Plante saw fit to dip into Rollins's knowledge-well seven times, as did NBC's Lisa Myers, followed by Sam Donaldson, who deferred to Rollins as an expert five times. These three reporters and others used tags such as "Ex-White House Political Director," "Ex-Reagan Aide," and simply "Political Consultant" as interchangeable descriptors for Rollins.

"Double-dippers" sell advice to political candidates and then, once they are elected, lobby them for favors on behalf of other, corporate, clients.

A former official in the last four Republican administrations, Rollins spends his out-of-office time as a lobbyist, influence agent, and consultant for such firms as the Tenneco Corporation. His firm, Russo, Watts and Rollins, specializes in what's called "double-dipping": selling advice to political candidates and then, once they are elected, lobbying them for favors on behalf of other, corporate, clients. When queried on the ethics of this practice, Rollins told the *Washington Post*: "I don't know what the response is. Actually, I guess I do—I'm going to continue lobbying anyone I can."

After leaving the White House in 1984, Rollins found his way onto the national airwaves to conduct a not-always-subtle covert campaign on behalf of Jack Kemp, while all the time maintaining the guise of disinterested expert on Republican politics. From December 1986, when Rollins signed on as Kemp campaign chair, until March 1988 when the push evaporated, Rollins made more than two dozen network appearances. Yet on less than a handful of occasions was he properly identified as a Kemp operative. Under nonpartisan cover, Rollins proceeded to chip away at the credibility of the Reagan government, which of course included Kemp's major rival, George Bush. On the November 11, 1987, *CBS Evening News*, Rollins used the busted Ginzburg nomination to comment: "It is a terrible embarrassment. I think it makes the Reagan administration look a little hypocritical."

Less than a week later, Rollins was on NBC, continuing his media guerrilla war against Bush. "Rollins was one of my favorites during the campaign," says Lisa Myers, Washington correspondent for NBC News. "He was used so heavily because he was in no way affiliated with the Bush campaign. He's also very candid, he has a lot of experience, not likely to spin his answer in any strange way, and you know who his client list is." Once Kemp withdrew from the race, Rollins's good standing within the party, George Bush's approval included, was demonstrated by his appointment as chair of the Republican Congressional Committee.

The Democrats also had a chosen few on as regular experts during the past campaign season. Pollster **Harrison Hickman** (33 appearances), was the most oft-heard from, in part because he was a paid CBS News consultant during the campaign (reporter Bruce Morton put him on the air 12 times in 21 months). Strategist **Bob Beckel** (27 appearances) was followed by **Robert Squier** (18 appearances and 10 paid appearances as a regular debater on NBC's *Today*), **David Garth** (15 appearances), and **Ann Lewis** (12 appearances).

Unlike full-time Republican militants, whom the networks usually cloak with neutral titles, the Democrats are almost always billed as Democrats, tipping off the viewership that it is listening to a partisan view. In Beckel's case, more than half of his appearances are billed as those of "Democratic Consultant," "Ex-Mondale Campaign Manager," or "Dukakis Advisor." Harrison Hickman is identified as a Democrat in two-thirds of his appearances.

But it was Ann Lewis who was singled out for truly special treatment: Of her twelve appearances during 1987 and 1988 she was called a "Jackson Advisor" six times, a "Democratic Consultant" three times, an "Americans for Democratic Action Spokeswoman" twice, and a "Dukakis Adviser" once. Zero mention as a "political analyst" or "political consultant."

DAVID GERGEN

As the nation watched Ronald Reagan struggle through the final chapters of his presidency—Iran-Contra, the Meese-Wedtech scandal, the Bork fiasco—and his Republican party strain to pull out the 1988 election, we got much of our network analysis on these subjects from two staunchly conservative journalists recast as neutral experts: **David Gergen** and **Kevin Phillips.**

Gergen (28 appearances) was one of the most sought-after observers on presidential affairs. On NBC, he appeared three times in two weeks to interpret Reagan's first Iran-Contra-era press conference. ABC's Peter Jennings had Gergen tell us on the heels of the Tower Report that Reagan could "bounce back." Sam Donaldson brought us Gergen twice in a little more than one week to cap the hearings on the same scandal, predicting that Reagan could still "improve his standing." And nearly every time that Gergen had something reaffirming to say about his former boss, Ronald Reagan, he was identified only as an editor of *U.S. News & World Report.* On rare occasions Gergen was also identified as the former White House communications director, a job he held till 1983.

A full accounting of Gergen's worship of Reagan can be found in a 1984 *New Republic* essay on the Great Communicator's coming second term: "Reagan has a chance of becoming even more of a national father figure than he already is," a misty-eyed Gergen predicts. ". . . He cannot abandon his roots either as a conservative or a Republican. . . . But the man who [has been called] the Chairman Mao of the Republican party could make himself the force that binds the country together and points it toward larger purposes." Gergen's role as a Republican mouthpiece dates back to his days as top speech writer to President Nixon. In 1973, Gergen was in-house when Nixon uttered his most memorable mendacities about the cover-up. By his own admission, Gergen was one of the last officials in the White House to accept the truth about Nixon's Watergate role. After Nixon's demise, Gergen went on to direct the 1976 Republican presidential campaign. When Carter emerged victorious, Gergen took refuge in the conservative American Enterprise Institute and helped found the rightist think sheet, *Public Opinion.* Gergen aided the 1980 Reagan campaign by helping stage rehearsals of the presidential debates, and by the next year he was President Reagan's communications director, one of the fathers of Reagan's strategy of media manipulation.

Gergen, however, never forgot the Nixonian axiom of scapegoating Oval Office staff. On February 6, 1987, responding to press stories that Reagan might be snoozing through the crash landing of his presidency, Gergen (identified only as *U.S. News & World Report*) appeared on NBC to say: "The staff is the one who helps [Reagan] understand the world around him. If the staff isn't up to that, he's not going to have the acute sense he needs to be president."

With a new president in office, Gergen continued to be a hot media commodity. His credentials to objectively analyze the Bush administration: Gergen was a paid consultant to the Bush campaign back in 1980.

The only journalist quoted more than David Gergen was the ultraconservative Kevin Phillips.

KEVIN PHILLIPS

The only other journalist quoted more than Gergen on the networks is the ultraconservative **Kevin Phillips.** During our study period, Phillips appeared as an expert a whopping forty-three times (twenty-two times on CBS alone). On three-fourths of those network cameos he was given the neutral, objective title of "Political Analyst," even though his views are patently right wing. "My background is conservative and Republican," he freely clarifies.

Phillips was the author of the strategy of appealing to the fears of white voters.

Phillips began his political career in the mid-sixties as an aide to the U.S. representative from the Bronx, Paul Fino. Phillips is credited with having steered Fino away from a traditional liberal program into becoming a vociferous critic of anything that smacked of the Great Society. By 1966 Fino was branding proposals for urban renewal as civil rights measures whose beneficiaries would be the advocates of black power.

Next came a stint as special assistant to Nixon's Attorney General John Mitchell, Watergate felon. But Phillips, like Gergen, survived the Nixon presidency and became a public advocate for a series of hard-nosed New Right social programs. Phillips, in his 1969 book, *The Emerging Republican Majority*, envisioned a new, explicitly race-based electoral strategy for the GOP. "All the talk about Republicans making inroads into the Negro vote is persiflage," Phillips elaborated for the *New York Times* in 1970. "From now on, the Republicans are never going to get more than 10 to 20 percent of the Negro vote and they don't need any more than that . . . but Republicans would be shortsighted if they weakened enforcement of the Voting Rights Act. The more Negroes who register as Democrats in the South, the sooner the Negrophobe whites will quit the Democrats and become Republicans. That's where the votes are."

To the intellectual author of that strategy of appealing to the fears of white voters, such first-string reporters as Lesley Stahl, Jeff Greenfield, John Martin, Bill Plante, and Lisa Myers turned time and again for dispassionate commentary on domestic issues and political strategies (Myers and Plante each used Phillips five times during 1987 and 1988). And some of those reporters packaged and repackaged Phillips to fit their momentary needs.

CBS's Bill Plante, for example, aired a bite from Phillips in September 1987 in which Phillips accused the Reagan administration of weakening the NATO alliance by agreeing to arms treaties with the Soviets. On that occasion, Phillips was correctly tagged as a "conservative columnist." Why then, when Plante used Phillips on four other occasions earlier that year to comment on such partisan subjects as the Republican primaries, the Iran-Contra hearings, and Reagan's relations with the press, was Phillips simply palmed off as a "political analyst"?

"We consider Phillips to be a political analyst and don't feel it is necessary to give someone's complete background each time he appears" is the terse explanation offered by Rome Hartman, *CBS Evening News* senior producer, who often produces Plante's reports. (Hartman also claims that Gergen was "always identified as a former Reagan official." Actually, on several occasions, CBS tagged him as *U.S. News & World Report*. After a few minutes of conversation on the

Henry Kissinger helped ABC News decide what political experts you should see and hear.

phone, Hartman terminates the interview, claiming that it is "unfair" to "focus in on the experts.")

When asked if the media are misleading the public by positioning him as an objective observer, Phillips argues that he is objective: "I don't think that any [of the regularly used experts], myself included, would or should be considered by the media to be talking from the point of view of a given political party. But rather with an expertise perhaps rooted or gained in a given party."

Such "party-rooted expertise" surfaced just days after the 1988 presidential vote, when CBS's Lesley Stahl turned to Phillips, of all people, to explain to the U.S. public why the Democrats had become unpopular. Arguing that the Democratic party is dominated by the heritage of sixties radicalism, Phillips summarized: "It was disorder in the streets, on the campuses, [liberals] didn't have the stomach to finish the job in Vietnam, just weak, they weren't patriotic, they didn't defend the country against criminals; I think people had the sense that was a big change in liberalism and people haven't lost that sense."

THE KISSINGER CLONES AND CRONIES

The man who engineered the carpet bombing of Cambodia and inspired the bloody overthrow of the elected government of Chile is the same man who during the Reagan era, helped ABC News decide what political experts you should see and hear. Henry Kissinger is far too important to make himself available for many mere ten-second evening news sound bites. He prefers the longer blocks of airtime regularly offered him by such shows as *This Week with David Brinkley* or *Nightline* (hosted by his friend Ted Koppel, and on which he appeared a record fourteen times between January 1985 and April 1988). But since 1982 Kissinger was on the ABC News payroll, according to a network spokeswoman, "to appear on breaking news stories" as well as "to suggest experts" to be called for on-air commentary and analysis. (Kissinger left ABC on September 13, 1989, when he accepted a seat on the board of CBS.)

Indeed, a pack of Kissinger cronies and business partners was granted a near monopoly as on-air network foreign-policy and national security experts. This means that during the turbulent Reagan period, which brought us the Central American crisis, the invasion of Grenada, the hype around Libya, and the emergence of Shi'ite Moslems as the new bogeymen, we got most of our network analysis from the very same men who brought us Vietnam. Discounting appearances by Kissinger himself, the group showed up 100 times during the 104 weeks of network newscasts in 1987 and 1988. They were peddled to U.S. viewers as "objective" political analysts, while all were, in fact, hard-line, cold-warrior Republicans (many of whom served directly with

Kissinger in the Nixon administration), ex-CIA agents (again mostly during Kissinger's tenure as secretary of state and/or national security adviser), partners in the multimillion-dollar consulting firm Kissinger and Associates, or resident scholars at the Washington, D.C.-based Center for Strategic and International Studies (CSIS)—at which Kissinger is one of four top "senior scholar-statesmen in residence."

THE INVISIBLE GAG

How consensus forms inside networks.

The findings of this study demonstrate who is allowed to shape television news, but they don't answer the question of why other informed, alternative voices are so uniformly excluded. Interviews with top network producers (who requested anonymity) offer some insight:

"It's not so much that you are told who to use or not to use," explains a producer who has worked at ABC and CBS. "There's just that Golden Rolodex that everyone goes to and everyone knows is safe. What I would call the 'brainwashing' is just too good to permit many violations. If you are doing a story about the health-care crisis, for example, you know you can go to the mildly critical expert who is going to say we need such and such additional funding. But you never go to the guy who you know is going to tell you what we really need is socialized medicine. Do that and . . . you'd mark yourself as someone to be kept an eye on."

"No one ever tells me don't use X," says a colleague. "It's just that most of your field producers don't even know who the dissidents, who the leftists, are. And if they do, then they have already made a decision that they are not 'credible,' not 'authoritative.' I have been able to get a few alternative voices on. When I'm overseas it is easier because the senior producers can't pull the bite even if they wanted to, because the feed is coming in at deadline from abroad and there's no way to patch the hole. When I've used radical sources domestically, it seems that my bosses are too politically naive to even figure out who it is I'm using. But that's the problem. Because the reporters and correspondents are just as naive, or ignorant, and are always going to go for the easy choices, the guys that everyone else uses."

Most of the field producers don't know who the dissidents or leftists are.

Explains another network producer: "Correspondents have to maintain a beat. You do that by maintaining an ideological stance that is more or less consistent, more or less acceptable to the people you are covering. Look at the three network Pentagon or national security correspondents. It's hardly a coincidence that [NBC's] Fred Francis is a known contra-lover, that [CBS's] David Martin's father was a veteran of the intelligence community, and [ABC's] John McWethy is so prodefense that he is known around ABC's halls as 'General McWethy.'

"There is an occasional stray script that will come in with a radical or even fresh perspective, and I have to say that it usually passes uncommented. Either the senior producer can't recognize that it is really different, or figures, what the hell, it's just a drop in the bucket. The downside," says this voice of experience behind the screen, "is that that sort of script is so damn rare you can count them on one hand over the course of a year." ♦

Questions for Discussion

1. In your opinion, if most experts called upon in network news are conservatives, does that make the news biased?
2. From your own observation of network news, do you find it to be biased in any political direction? Explain.

Media's Liberal Slant on the News

Brent H. Baker

The following article was published nearly a year before "All the Right Sources," but it almost seems like a direct response.

Brent Baker, executive director of the Media Research Center, which publishes a newsletter documenting liberal media bias, admits that Republicans and conservatives get jobs as commentators, but he makes a pretty convincing argument that the liberals get jobs as reporters, which gives them a lot more opportunity to slant the news.

Reading Difficulty Level: 3. Which, in all fairness, puts it on a level field with the reading that came before it.

Is it a liberal or anti-establishment bias?

For years, conservatives have argued that major American news organizations present the news with a liberal bias. Members of the media have rejected the contention, countering that the press simply reflects an anti-establishment bias. Who is correct? A look at how big media outlets—specifically ABC, CBS, and NBC; the three national news magazines; *The Washington Post;* and *The New York Times*—covered controversial issues over the past few years makes it clear that political reporting often reflects a tilt to the left. That does not mean every story slights the conservative position, but that, almost every time a report is unbalanced, it favors the position promoted by liberals.

Almost every time a report is unbalanced, it favors the position promoted by liberals.

Whether the issue is aiding the Contras, the results of economic policy, how George Bush conducted his presidential campaign, who is to blame for homelessness, or virtually any other hotly debated topic, one thing remains true—someone relying solely on the information dispensed by big media could not help but see conservative policies and actions as failures and look positively toward the liberal alternative viewpoint.

Someone relying solely on the information dispensed by big media could not help but see conservative policies and actions as failures.

There is no grand conspiracy at work here. The reason is simple enough. The views held by journalists naturally influence their reporting, and poll after poll has found that liberal positions hold the allegiance of most. The 1981 Lichter-Rothman survey of big media members determined 81% voted for George McGovern in 1972 and a large majority preferred Jimmy Carter over Gerald Ford four years later. A 1985 *Los Angeles Times* poll of reporters for large newspapers found three times as many consider themselves liberal as conservative. Less than 25% of them voted for Ronald Reagan in 1984.

On every issue, most reporters took the liberal side. Over 80% favored a woman's right to have an abortion, 66% opposed prayer in school, 78% wanted stricter gun control, 80% were against higher defense spending, and 75% rejected aid to the Contras. Another poll, by the Associated Press Managing Editors Association, revealed that barely 15% of journalists identified themselves as Republicans. The evidence has become so irrefutable that media pundits long ago gave up debating it. Instead, they fall back to another line of defense. However, as *New Republic* senior editor Fred Barnes wrote, in so doing, these "defenders of the press rely on precisely the sort of argument they would reject if made by others. Even if most journalists are liberal, then professionalism prevents this from influencing their stories. Now, what if a judicial nominee said he was a racist but that this wouldn't affect his views on civil rights cases." Who would believe that? Certainly, today's adversarial press would not.

Big media stars would not hesitate to question the objectivity of a newscast if all the producers and reporters once worked for the Heritage Foundation, a conservative Washington think-tank, and they would be right. Yet, people with equally strong convictions in the opposite direction already hold such key positions. Indeed, the Media Research Center [MRC] has compiled a list of over 110 reporters, editors, producers, and news division executives who have connections to liberal Democratic causes or politicians. In contrast, just 25—less than 25%—have any ties to conservatives or Republicans of any kind.

Top news executives at the three networks worked for well-known Democrats before obtaining media jobs.

These people are not just lowly assistants—far from it. Top news executives at the three networks worked for well-known Democrats before obtaining media jobs. David Burke, who became president of CBS News in 1988 after 11 years with ABC News, served as chief of staff to Sen. Edward Kennedy (D.-Mass.) from 1965 to 1971. The CBS News political editor since 1985, Dotty Lynch, was Gary Hart's pollster in 1984 and is a veteran of Sen. Kennedy's 1980 presidential attempt. Lynch's predecessor brought similar political preferences to his job. Wally Chalmers was running Kennedy's political action committee, the Fund for a Democratic Majority, when tapped by CBS just before the 1984 campaign.

The same pattern applies to the other networks. ABC's 1988 political coverage was run by vice president Jeff Gralnick, who served as press secretary to Sen. George McGovern in 1971. Barely a month after the 1984 election, NBC News hired Tim Russert, former chief of staff to Sen. Patrick Moynihan (D.-N.Y.) and counselor to New York's proudly liberal Gov. Mario Cuomo. Russert soon became the vice president overseeing the content of the *NBC Nightly News* and the *Today* show. He is now NBC's Washington bureau chief.

Most of those with Republican affiliations get behind-the-scenes public affairs jobs or become commentators, not reporters.

Most of those with Republican affiliations get behind-the-scenes public affairs jobs or become commentators, not reporters. ABC's George Will and CNN's Patrick Buchanan are good examples.

Numerous reporters dedicated themselves to promoting liberal policies before making a career change. ABC's Jeff Greenfield, frequently seen on *Nightline,* wrote speeches for Sen. Robert Kennedy. Rick Inderfurth, who covers national security issues for ABC News, gained his expertise by working for Senators McGovern and Hart in the mid-1970's. ABC's chief foreign correspondent, Pierre Salinger, was Pres. Kennedy's press secretary. In key behind-the-scenes positions, the same holds true. The producer of *Face the Nation,* the Sunday morning interview show on CBS, once toiled for Massachusetts Gov. Michael Dukakis. Deborah Johnson, executive producer of the CBS show *Nightwatch,* helped found the far-left magazine *Mother Jones* in 1975.

This preference for Democrats goes beyond the electronic media. *Time* magazine senior writer Walter Shapiro covered the 1988 campaign. His experience included writing speeches for candidate Jimmy Carter in 1976, and he was rewarded with a job under Labor Secretary Ray Marshall. *Newsweek* reporter Timothy Noah worked for a Democratic Congressional candidate before joining the magazine's Washington staff. Foreign affairs reporter Douglas Waller served as an aide to liberal Congressman Ed Markey (D.-Mass.) until joining *Newsweek* in 1988. At *U.S. News & World Report,* where former Reagan aide David Gergen served as editor until recently, senior editor James Killpatrick left in 1987 to handle press relations for Democrat Paul Simon's presidential campaign. Judith Miller, a *New York Times* editor, began her career as a reporter for *The Progressive* magazine.

Given the preponderance of liberals in newsrooms, it's no surprise their reporting shows little understanding of conservative views. Take the problem of homelessness. A story on the *CBS Evening News* is representative of how most journalists approach the topic. Susan Spencer reported that cuts in Federal housing subsidies were a key cause. She also considered that the minimum wage has not been increased "since 1981, while inflation has pushed up prices nearly 34%" as another reason. When the producer of the story was asked why the conservatives' explanation for the problem—that rent control artificially has reduced the supply of low-income housing in big cities—was not even mentioned in the supposedly balanced story, he responded: "I don't understand your point." In other words, he never even heard the argument before.

Given the preponderance of liberals in newsrooms, it's no surprise their reporting shows little understanding of conservative views.

Reliance on sources of information that match the reporter's preconceptions also frequently results in the same one-sided story. A Thanksgiving Day, 1988 report on CBS offers an excellent case study. Bob McNamara began his piece: "Seattle, the Pacific Northwest's most polished, prosperous city. With the rich bounty of its nearby waters, and its orchards, on the face of it these seem like the best of times. But here, as elsewhere, times could hardly be worse for thousands. Today, soup kitchens feed more people than ever, and sadly, more families, more children."

McNamara acknowledged 16,000,000 new jobs have been "created across the country in this decade, but there's a cruel hitch. A recent Senate committee report says that, of those new jobs, half of them pay wages below the poverty level for a family of four." McNamara failed to tell viewers one key fact—it was prepared by the Democratic staff of the Budget Committee. With a little research, he would have learned the same Census Bureau statistics the Democrats used show just the opposite after eliminating the Carter years from the average. Since 1982, 61% of these new jobs pay $20,800 a year or higher, twice the poverty level for a family of four.

McNamara's story represented much coverage on how America fared during eight years of Reagan's conservative economic policies. Far from serving as an uncritical conduit for Reagan to manipulate the public, national news outlets had a negative verdict on Reaganomics. "Are You Better Off?," *Time* asked. "For much of the middle class," it asserted, "the answer is no." Just like McNamara, *Time* accepted some very questionable statistics. The "middle class has been shrinking," the magazine argued, and "Reagan's tax cuts only worsened the skew." In fact, IRS figures that *Time* didn't mention show that the wealthy now pay a

Reliance on sources of information that match the reporter's preconceptions results in a one-sided story.

Reports which contradict the media's line conveniently are overlooked.

larger share of taxes collected and the working poor a smaller one. In addition, a 1988 Bureau of Labor Statistics study determined: "America's middle class has been shrinking since 1969, but mainly because more families have moved to the upper class." Reports which contradict the media's line conveniently are overlooked.

Since creating the term "Reaganomics," big media reporters have made it synonymous with negative developments. In 1987, the Media Research Center asked the Nexis news data retrieval system to locate the frequency of use of the term by *The Washington Post, The New York Times, Newsweek, Time,* UPI, and AP between 1981 and 1986. The findings were startling. As the 1981–82 recession deepened, reporters continually referred to "Reaganomics," using the term 1,957 times to blame the President's supply-side economic policies for stagnation and high unemployment. With the recovery in 1983–84, as Reagan's policies began taking effect, "Reaganomics" nearly dropped from the media's vocabulary. It was mentioned just 96 times by 1986. In fact, during the period examined, "Reaganomics" use directly followed the unemployment rate path.

Leaders and Dictators

In 1988, ABC weekend anchorman Sam Donaldson inadvertently revealed how the big media sees the world. Reviewing current events, he referred to "Soviet leader Gorbachev" and "Cuban leader Fidel Castro." He suddenly changed his tune and became far more descriptive when it came to Chile: "In Chile, a country ruled by military dictator Augusto Pinochet, demonstrators opposing his rule drew police tear gas and other riot control measures." Donaldson's double standard in labeling symbolized the troubling tendency of many reporters—looking critically at our nation's allies while overlooking the evils of our enemies.

The Media Research Center examined how ABC, CNN, CBS, and NBC covered six Sandinista statements promising compliance with peace accords vs. 10 instances when the regime violated peace agreements or publicly rejected Democratic reforms. Pledges for improvement were covered by at least three of the four networks every time, but actions which contradicted those pledges either barely were mentioned or completely ignored. Consequently, viewers saw more than five times as many stories portraying the Sandinistas as earnestly trying to develop a pluralistic society than instances when they reaffirmed their totalitarian nature.

For example, the *Miami Herald* reported Sandinista dictator Daniel Ortega publicly proclaiming that the Contras "should be thankful that we're not offering them the guillotine or the firing squad, which is what they deserve." The four TV networks did not consider the threat worth mentioning. When the Sandinistas claimed they would allow free speech and release all political prisoners, promises they subsequently failed to fulfill, all the networks covered the story.

Several years ago, Lucy Spiegel, a CBS News producer based in Managua, stated: "Personally, I think the Contras are worthless." That just might explain why Americans have seen far more TV reports detailing the human rights violations of the Contras while Sandinista violations rarely were raised.

CBS This Morning sent co-host Kathleen Sullivan to Cuba just before Christmas, 1988, but Castro's denial of basic human rights to his people did not interest her. Instead, viewers were treated to two days of glowing reports about life on the island. Sullivan referred to Cuba's "model health care program and lively arts scene." Her most incredible claim was that its young adults "all have benefited from Castro's Cuba." Can you imagine a network star uttering such a positive statement about a right-wing dictator while ignoring everything negative?

Some inevitably will argue these examples simply are carefully selected anecdotes that fail to prove a larger point. However, the coverage of two nearly identical events, the presidential conventions in 1988, provided findings that are more illuminating.

Media Research Center analysts watched over 100 hours of network coverage of the conventions. The study found that, far from displaying balance, TV correspondents labeled Republicans "conservative" more than four times as often as they noted the liberal views held by Democratic attendees the month before. The networks did not hesitate to raise repeatedly the Iran/Contra affair, the stalemate with Panama's Manuel Noriega, and the Republican "sleaze" factor, as well as presenting two prime-time nights focused almost exclusively on Dan Quayle's background. Lloyd Bentsen's PAC fund-raising scandal and the criminal investigations of Dukakis' state appointees were ignored.

TV correspondents labeled Republicans "conservative" more than four times as often as they noted the liberal views held by Democrats.

Indeed, from day one of the GOP convention, TV reporters echoed Democratic campaign themes and demanded that Republicans respond. NBC's Tom Brokaw, for example, asked Quayle one night: "You're opposed to abortion in any form. You have opposed the ERA and you're opposed to increasing the minimum wage, which is important to a lot of women out there. Aren't you going to have a hard time selling Dan Quayle to the women of this country?" In total, network reporters challenged Republicans with Democratic-issue questions on 128 occasions, two and one-half times more often than they posed Republican ones to Democrats.

Network reporters challenged Republicans with Democratic-issue questions two and one-half times more often than they posed Republican ones to Democrats.

Finally, the constant refrain of "Bush's gender gap problem" could be heard from liberal politicians as they argued he had little support from women. The networks picked up on the liberal agenda item and frequently raised the issue in campaign stories. Yet, when the facts quieted Bush's opponents, the media fell right in step, never conceding it was a party to an unfounded political myth.

CBS News reporter Bob Schieffer devoted a story to how women are "a big problem for George Bush because [they] don't seem to like him much." Schieffer cited a CBS News/*New York Times* poll which found "women favor Dukakis overwhelmingly, 53 to 35 percentage points, what some call a 'gender gulch.'" NBC's Lisa Myers was quick to explain why later that month. "In 1980, when he ran for president the first time, Bush didn't have problems with women," she asserted. "But then he became Reagan's vice president and changed positions on key women's issues." Now, he supports "an amendment banning abortion" and opposes the ERA.

With few in the newsroom who hold or even understand conservative views, reporters can't help but reflect the way they look at the world.

However, when the Bush gender gap started disappearing, so did the issue from TV screens. A September, 1988, CBS News poll determined Bush led among women 43 to 41%. Men preferred Bush by 53 to 37%, nearly the identical margin Dukakis held with women in June. How did the *CBS Evening News* handle the Dukakis gender gap among men? Lesley Stahl summarized the poll, but didn't consider the Dukakis problem worthy of mention, and NBC's Myers never retracted her earlier claim.

These are just a few examples of reporting that has made it impossible for the big media ever to squelch charges its reporting and selection of stories show a bias in favor of liberal politicians. With few in the newsroom who hold or even understand conservative views, reporters can't help but reflect the way they look at the world. As a result, the media won't be able to gain credibility as an impartial source of information until it makes a concerted effort to hire enough conservatives to bring balance to the newsroom and executive corridors. ♦

Questions for Discussion

1. In your opinion, if most news reporters are liberals, does that mean that their news reports are biased?
2. Do you agree that "someone relying solely on the information dispensed by big media could not help but see conservative policies and actions as failures and look positively toward the liberal alternative viewpoint?" (p. 405)

The Centrist Bias of the U.S. Media

Jeff Cohen

With one reading asserting that the media are biased toward conservatives, and another asserting that they are biased toward liberals, you might think that we've covered all bases. But Jeff Cohen, a writer for Extra!, *has yet another point of view.*

Extra! *is the in-house publication of an organization called FAIR, which stands for "Fairness and Accuracy in Reporting."*

Reading Difficulty Level: 1.

When mainstream journalists tell me that "our news doesn't reflect bias of the left or right," I ask them whether they are therefore admitting to reflecting bias of center. They react as if I've uttered an absurdity: "Bias of the center! What's that?"

It is a strange concept to many in the media. They can accept conservatism as an ideology with certain values, opinions, and beliefs. They can accept that progressivism carries with it values, opinions, and beliefs. But being in the center—being a centrist—is somehow not having an ideology at all. Somehow centrism is not an "ism" carrying with it values, beliefs, or opinions.

When we talk of the journalistic center or middle-of-the-road news media, we mean network TV news, *The New York Times* and *Washington Post* and similar mainstream dailies; AP and UPI; *Time*, *Newsweek*, etc.

From *Extra!* October/November 1989, the in-house publication of FAIR (Fairness and Accuracy in Reporting).

Neither left nor right, but biased just the same.

The journalistic center is not inert. It moves. It shifted slightly leftward in the mid-'70s in the wake of Watergate when reporters were allowed greater latitude for independent inquiry. In the '80s the journalistic center veered strongly rightward.

If, for simplicity's sake, we define the left as seeking substantial reform toward a more equitable distribution of wealth and power and the right as seeking to undo social reform and regulation and favoring a free marketplace that allows wide disparities in wealth and power, then we can define the political center as seeking to preserve the status quo, tinkering with the system only in small ways.

Unlike left-wing or right-wing publications, which are often on the attack, centrist propaganda emphasizes system-supporting news.

How do these three positions play out journalistically? Unlike left-wing or right-wing publications, which are often on the attack, centrist propaganda emphasizes system-supporting news. If scandals come to light, centrist propa-

Centrist propaganda focuses less on the scandal than on how well "the system works" in fixing it.

ganda often focuses less on the scandal than on how well "the system works" in fixing it!

When it comes to foreign policy, centrist propaganda sometimes questions this or that tactic, but it never doubts that the goal of policy is anything other than promoting democracy, peace, and human rights. Other countries may subvert, destabilize, or support terrorism. The United States just wages peace.

No matter what the evidence, centrist propaganda affirms that U.S. foreign policy is geared toward promoting democracy. Journalists are not unaware that the United States helped overthrow democratic governments—in Guatemala in '54, Brazil in '64, Chile in '73, for example—but these cases are considered ancient history and no longer relevant.

Some reporters act more like stenographers for those in power than journalists.

Mainstream journalists respond to such criticism by explaining that articles for the daily press are not history texts and cannot include everything. That's true, but centrist propaganda finds space for certain histories and not others. Many, if not most, of the reports on Hungary in the summer of 1989 traced human rights abuses to the Soviet suppression of the Hungarian uprising in 1956. By contrast, reports on Guatemala's current human rights situation rarely traced events to the U.S.-sponsored coup of 1954.

Perhaps the most graphic component of foreign policy coverage in centrist media is the inordinate number of (often unnamed) government sources: White House, State, Pentagon, U.S. Intelligence, etc. Some reporters act more like stenographers for those in power than journalists. In discussions of these reporters, the phrase "centrist propaganda" misses the mark. "State propaganda" is a more apt description. ♦

Question for Discussion

1. In your opinion, is there such a thing as "centrist bias"?

Suggested Readings

Those who are interested in forms of bias will be interested in the readings on stereotyping in the next chapter.

More On Liberal Bias

Eastland, Terry, "On the Record," *The American Spectator*, March 1990, p. 26 (2).

Farah, Joseph, "Inside the Fourth Estate," *The American Legion Magazine* Vol. 128, April 1990, p. 32 (3). The ideological gap between the liberal press and mainstream America.

Rusher, William A., "All the News That's Fit for Democrats," *National Review*, March 18, 1988. Also available in the third edition of *Mass Media Issues*, p. 254.

Rusher, William A., "Now It Can Be Told," *National Review* Vol. 41, January 27, 1989, p. 36 (5). Reminiscences of retiring publisher of *National Review*.

Wooster, Martin Morse, "Left-Wing Bananas," *Reason* Vol. 21, July, 1989, p. 44 (2). Left-wing magazines.

More On Conservative Bias

Herman, Edward S. and Gerry O'Sullivan, *The 'Terrorism' Industry; The Experts and Institutions that Shape Our View of Terror*. Reviewed by Allen Hunter in *The Progressive*, October 1990, p. 39 (3).

Herman, Edward S. and Noam Chomsky, "Propaganda Mill: The Media Churn Out the Official Line," *The Progressive* Vol. 52, June, 1988, p. 14 (4). Anti-communism.

Rosen, Jay, "Chatter from the Right," *The Progressive*, March, 1988. This reading, dealing with conservative talk shows on PBS, can also be found in the third edition of *Mass Media Issues*, p. 258 (4).

More On Other Forms of Bias

Hentoff, Nat, "A Pyrrhic Victory," *The Progressive* Vol. 54, May, 1990, p. 12 (2). Andy Rooney reinstated at CBS after his suspension for anti-gay remarks. Column.

Lawrence, John F., "Business News: The Terrible Truth," *Fortune* Vol. 117, April 25, 1988, p. 145 (4). (Daily press accounts of the economy show an antibusiness bias.)

Spikol, Art, "What's Black and White and Read All Over? There Are Times when Race Should Be Left Out of Things. But They're Rare, Says Our Columnist," *Writer's Digest*, October, 1989, p. 14 (3).

Stempel, Guido H. and John W. Windhauser, eds., *The Media in the 1984 and 1988 Presidential Campaigns* (Westport, Conn.: Greenwood Press, 1990.) A study of media bias in recent elections.

Willis, Jim, *The Shadow World: Life Between the News Media and Reality* (N.Y.: Praeger, 1991). Examines the factors that contribute to the journalist's often faulty perception of reality.

Stereotyping

The term "stereotype" comes from the Greek *stereos,* meaning firm, and *typos,* meaning model or type. A stereotype is an inflexible impression; its dictionary definition is, "a fixed notion about a person or group which is held by a number of people and allows for no individuality."

As we have pointed out earlier (specifically in Chapters 3, 8, 9, 10 and 12), the mass media help shape the world view of its audience members. As Gloria Steinem points out in the first reading in this chapter, when the media shape that world view in the form of a stereotype, it is potentially dangerous. More specifically, Steinem points out that the media's stereotypical view of women leads to abuse. In the final reading Robert Entman introduces the notion of "modern racism" and shows how local television news might make it worse.

Women in the Dark: Of Sex Goddesses, Abuse, and Dreams

Gloria Steinem

Gloria Steinem is the founder of Ms. *magazine and one of the leaders of contemporary feminism. She is also "a longtime movie addict" whose viewing over the years has led her to the observation that the movies' "sex goddess" image creates a particularly dangerous stereotype. Her look at the behind-the-scenes lives of some of our most famous sex symbols helps confirm her point of view.*

Reading Difficulty Level: 1. This one practically reads itself. "Atavistic" means having the characteristics of an earlier generation.

You are sitting in the magical darkness of a movie theater. Among the glamorous giants filling the screen are one special woman and one special man. You know they are attracted to each other by the tension, bantering, even hostility between them. You know they will end up together by her beauty and his authority, her vulnerability and his strength—in movie symbolism, even by their differences in height and weight.

Finally, there is the scene you knew would arrive; the whole audience has been waiting for it. He is about to overcome this tension by overcoming her.

At first she resists. He uses just enough strength to be a real man, but not quite enough to be a bad guy. She guards her virginity—or in a modern movie, the psychic virginity of her independence—with words, with the language of her body arching away, with her fists pushing against him.

Then he kisses her—and suddenly, everything changes. Her body softens, her fists unclench. The camera focuses on the ritual image: her hands sliding around his neck in total surrender.

As a little girl, I remember feeling betrayed. Why was the heroine giving in to a man who behaved like a bully?

As a little girl watching versions of this scene in Saturday matinees, I remember feeling betrayed. Why was the heroine giving in to a man who behaved like a bully? By the time I was a teenager, I had accepted this movie ritual as adult reality. When I got older and realized that even a little aggression was a sexual turnoff—that actually, trust and empathy were the real turn-ons—I still assumed that most other women must disagree; otherwise, what were all these dominant/submissive scenes doing on movie screens? Only when I was past 30 and feminism had arrived in my life did I finally stop believing movie dialogue and listen to what real women said. I discovered that most of them felt endangered by domination, as I did; that the few who found it sexual often had grown up with attention, love, sex, and violence so intertwined that they believed you couldn't get one without the others.

Since then, the pressures of rebellious women in front of the screen and creative women behind it have made changes. There are now Hollywood movies entirely about female friendships, from *The Turning Point* to *Beaches* and *Steel Magnolias;* female "buddy" movies like *Outrageous Fortune* that allow women some of the adventures once reserved for men (though only as comedies); and even a few mainstream exposés of gender politics: *The Color Purple, The Handmaid's Tale.*

But there is a backlash. Think of *Fatal Attraction, Presumed Innocent,* or much of *Working Girl,* with independent-women-we-love-to-hate. Or atavistic Cinderella stories—*The Goodbye Girl, Pretty Woman*—with heroines who need male rescue for money and acceptance (though they now teach men how to feel, instead of bringing only virginity). Most dangerous, there is the film tradition of woman-hatred. Its main-

---

From *Ms.,* January/February 1991. Reprinted by permission.

stream forms have become so violently sadistic that many movies are expurgated for television.

But a movie doesn't have to be violent to make a heroine go from resistance to surrender in the time it takes to say "male fantasy." It may be one of the most resonant themes in moviedom—and I think there is an unacknowledged reason why.

In the movies, women go from resistance to surrender in the time it takes to say "male fantasy."

There's always one more layer of truth. This one began to reveal itself while I listened to a friend describe a haunting memory from a college weekend in the 1960s. At a party, she had seen an older woman who looked drunk, out of place, but strangely familiar. A man at the party told her that this was Rita Hayworth. Whether in truth or bragging, he also said this once-great movie star had been kept upstairs in the fraternity house, having sex with almost anyone.

Rita Hayworth, the created sex goddess. (Photo by Bob Landry, *Life Magazine* © *Time Warner, Inc.)*

This story haunted me, too. It sent me out to buy *If This Was Happiness,* a new Hayworth biography by Barbara Leaming. Thanks to her exhaustive interviews of early friends and witnesses, and her access to Orson Welles, the second of Hayworth's five husbands, I sat up all night reading about the real woman behind those images that millions had worshiped in the dark.

Her name was Margarita Cansino, the daughter of Volga Hayworth, a onetime show girl, and an immigrant Spanish dancer named Eduardo Cansino. He had not wanted a daughter. "What," as he later complained to a reporter, "could I do with a girl?" After two boys were born, Margarita became the four-year-old servant who drew her father's bath, danced for money, and obeyed his commands. At six, when she was sent to school by her mother—against her father's wishes, since he opposed educating girls—Margarita had already become the insecure, shy, almost speechless girl that witnesses say she remained. When she was about 12, her father realized the uses of a daughter. "All of a sudden I wake up. Jesus! She has a figure! She ain't no baby anymore," as he explained to reporters. Made-up and costumed far beyond her years, she became a dancing partner he also presented as his wife in Tijuana nightclubs. In this period, if not before, incestuous sex was part of her duties. When drunk or angry, her father beat her—methodically, so the bruises wouldn't show above her costume.

This long-term sexual abuse was later described by Rita to Orson Welles, but even at the time, it was suspected by neighbors. It may also have been known to her mother, who apparently tried to stop it by sleeping in her daughter's room or accompanying them to Tijuana. But Eduardo was by all accounts a violent and controlling man, the dance act was the family's sole income, and Volga, too, sometimes escaped into drinking. When Eduardo lied Margarita's age up to 16 to keep her out of school, the family became even more isolated. Neighborhood kids remember seeing Margarita in only two ways: through the window practicing a dance over and over while her father shouted abuse, or sitting on the porch, not talking, refusing to join in, just staring into space.

How many ideals of female sexuality that we worshiped in the dark were actually images of female pain?

At 18, she "escaped" by eloping with a much older man whom Eduardo had asked to get her movie jobs—but this turned out to be only a change of masters. Her promoter-husband not only lived off her salary and supervised every dress and hairdo, but also promised and delivered her sexual services to men who might help with movie roles (and blackmailed her with this knowledge after she became a star and managed to escape him).

The persona promoted by Hollywood was the sexy, sultry, fiery Rita Hayworth, but off-camera, she was as different as she had been outside the onstage personality forced by her father. Obedient, eager to please, an obsessive worker whose most remarked-upon quality was sweetness, she was so quiet friends found it odd to hear words coming out of her mouth onscreen. Occasionally, with the aid of alcohol, she tapped the rage inside her. Alone with a close woman friend, she sometimes talked and relaxed. But mostly, she just dissociated from the world around her, as she had done sitting on the porch as a child. In roles like "Gilda," a nightclub temptress who drove men to distraction with sex, she assumed what Orson Welles called "a total impersonation."

In other words, both her real-life ravages and her sex-goddess roles might be recognized now as paradigms of sexual abuse: as the realistic damage it leaves behind, and as the victim-as-temptress fantasy that "justifies" abuse.

I began to wonder: How many ideals of female sexuality that we worshiped in the dark—in movie images and through the eyes of the real woman—were actually images of female pain? Here are random looks at the reality of five other "sex goddesses":

• Hedwig Kiesler, alias Hedy Lamarr, described Hollywood giant Cecil B. DeMille as believing that women "want to be taken, ruled,

(Photo by Bruce Cotler.)

and raped. That was his theory. In his pictures his women would usually reject a man, then get overpowered—and enjoy it." Like Hayworth, her sexual abuse came early—but more sporadically. Perhaps that gave her the strength to escape much earlier from marriage to a sadistic man who literally kept her under guard, to try to produce her own films, and even to disclose the backstage truth of *Ecstasy*, the first female orgasm on screen. It was produced by focusing on her face while the director repeatedly plunged a large pin into her bare buttocks.

• Dorothy Dandridge, the first "Negro" sex goddess in Hollywood, was left as a child in the care of a housekeeper who beat her often and cruelly, and inflicted a peculiar kind of sexual abuse: binding her developing breasts down with muslin cloths. Doomed by race to little work and by sex to roles that reinforced self-punishment, she died young; a casualty of drugs and alcohol.

• Norma Jeane Baker, alias Marilyn Monroe, was left in foster homes, raped in one of them, and thought herself invisible until 11, or when her body began to attract male attention. Like Hayworth, she was vulnerable all her life to father figures, used alcohol or chemicals to anesthetize rage and shyness, and was encouraged by Hollywood to play roles that perpetuated her deepest fear: that she was valueless except for sex.

Marilyn Monroe was encouraged by Hollywood to play roles that perpetuated her deepest fear: that she was valueless except for sex.

• Julia Jean Turner, alias Lana Turner, the daughter of a 16-year-old mother, also lived in a foster home, but talks little about her childhood. Nonetheless, she married one man who violently raped her own young daughter over such a long period that vaginal repair was necessary; lived with another man of such violence that her daughter stabbed and killed him in what became a famous Hollywood murder case; and was financially victimized by several of her seven husbands.

• Marilyn Pauline Novak, alias Kim Novak, was born to a father who wanted a son and tried to change everything about her, even her left-handedness. Like Hayworth, she was "created" by Harry Cohn, legendary exploiter of ac-

The sex goddess role has its resonance in the breadth and depth of sexual abuse.

tresses. Like Monroe, she suffered "dumb blond" roles and critical ridicule. In fact, her identification with Monroe caused her to flee Hollywood at the height of her own fame. "Look what can happen here," she told a friend after Monroe was found dead from pills and alcohol. "It could happen to me." She now lives quietly in California and is an animal rights activist.

I don't mean to say that these women were only victims. On the contrary, each tried to rebel. Hayworth resisted Harry Cohn's sexual advances and control; Lamarr become a pioneer movie producer; Dandridge tried for a more humane career in Europe; Monroe risked blacklisting by leaving Hollywood for New York; both Turner and her daughter Cheryl have survived to lead positive lives; and Novak had the courage to abandon money and glamour. If we had movies about those realities, we would have something of value.

But we who have been watching in the dark must realize that this sex goddess role has its resonance in the breadth and depth of sexual abuse.

It is as patriotic as the GIs who named a nuclear bomb "Gilda," put Hayworth's photo on it, and destroyed a South Pacific island for centuries to come. It is as humiliating as her feelings when she "almost went insane, she was so angry" about the bombing; and as commercial as Harry Cohn when he said she would be "unpatriotic" if she disowned it. It is as common as the nearly half of us reading these words who have experienced some sexual or other form of abuse and thus been turned into well-socialized women.

Until we boycott those movies, shout "bullshit" in the theater, and protest as seriously as against hate images that endanger other groups, the hand reaching around an aggressor's neck will be giving up, not giving in.

And it will be ours. ♦

Questions for Discussion

1. In your opinion, are movie stars usually happy people? What aspects of their lives would lead to happiness or unhappiness?
2. Do you agree that the "sex goddess" image is a dangerous one?

Modern Racism and the Images of Blacks in Local Television News

Robert M. Entman

It is extremely difficult to study racism in America today. Contemporary racism is a complex phenomenon, and those who hold racist ideas won't admit to them, largely because the media has made those ideas socially unacceptable.

Robert Entman is trying to understand today's racism, a quest that he has recently been sharing in a series of articles and books for the academic community. Old-fashioned racism included a belief that blacks were naturally inferior, or believing the correctness of segregation. The following paper introduces the concept of modern racism, which, according to Entman, has three components: First, a general feeling of hostility toward blacks; second, a resistance to their political demands, and third, the belief that racial discrimination no longer inhibits black achievement. Entman then analyzes how blacks are pictured on local news, to see if that might have some effect on modern racism. His data are based on only a one-week pilot study, but his results should inspire further research.

Robert Entman teaches Communication Studies, Journalism, and Political Science at Northwestern University.

Reading Difficulty Level: 10. This is written in the style and vocabulary of advanced scholarly writing. There's a certain amount of jargon—"affect" for "feelings," "polysemic" for "having multiple meanings"—and the syntax is a little dense. It reads slowly, but if you take the extra time it will make sense and, as is the objective of scholarly writing, inspire debate.

This paper probes one critical instance of the linkage between the practices of the mass media and the processes of cultural change: the relatively recent transformation of anti-black racism. Expressions of traditional racist sentiment have all but disappeared from the media and from public discourse generally. But social scientists have shown that racism has not evaporated (see Dovidio & Gaertner, 1986; Katz & Taylor, 1988a). Even as it has become so-

This paper probes the relatively recent transformation of anti-black racism.

This research was supported by grants from the Markle Foundation and from the Gannett Urban Journalism Center of Northwestern University. The author acknowledges helpful suggestions from David Protess and referees of CSMC.

Reprinted with permission from *Critical Studies in Mass Communication,* a publication of the Speech Communication Association, December, 1990.

One component of television programming, local news, may be contributing to the metamorphosis of white racism.

cially unacceptable to assert blacks' inherent inferiority or to endorse legal separation, a "modern" form of racism has arisen.[1] This is an attempt to explore how one component of television programming, local news, may be contributing to the metamorphosis of white racism; it is a prologue to, and justification for, more systematic research.

In the exploratory data reported here, 76% of all local TV stories about blacks fell into the categories of crime or politics. The treatment of blacks in these stories appears likely to unintentionally but systematically foster modern racism, which comprises three closely intertwined but analytically distinct sentiments.

The Components of Modern Racism

The first component of modern racism is anti-black affect—a general emotional hostility toward blacks. The hypothesis is that the emphasis and portrayal of crime in local TV news stimulates whites' animosity toward blacks.

The second element of modern racism is resistance to the political demands of blacks. Here, the paper hypothesizes that local TV's constructions of black political activities bolster such opposition.

[1]There is a somewhat arcane dispute among theorists over whether "symbolic" or "modern" racism is the proper label (cf. Sears, 1988, p. 55, note 1, to McConahay, 1986). "Modern" seems most appropriate to the theoretical concerns of this paper.

The third component of modern racism is a belief that racism is dead and that racial discrimination no longer inhibits black achievement. The study hypothesizes that this belief is reinforced by local television's use of black journalists and authority figures. Paradoxically, the images sustaining the modern racist notion that racism has ended may work at the same time to suppress old-fashioned racism.

The reasons for all these effects are hypothesized to lie in the commercial pressures the stations face and in an unintentional class bias that appears to suffuse the manufacture of news.

The next section offers background on the theory of modern racism, the part the media may play, and the exploratory data base. The section that follows takes up the three components of modern racism in turn, using qualitative content analysis to assess the possible contributions of local news to modern racism and to explore the simultaneous suppression of old-fashioned racism. The concluding section explores the implications.

Modern Racism and the Role of the Media

Modern racism is an updated and somewhat veiled form of anti-black sentiment. It is composed of a general and diffuse "anti-black affect" (Sears, 1988, p. 56), combined with disaffection over the continuing

(Photo by Bruce Cotler.)

claims of blacks on white resources and sympathies, rancor rooted in an attachment to traditional American, individualist values and in a conviction that racism has disappeared. Modern racists express "antagonism, resentment, and anger toward blacks' wishes, and a lack of sympathy with them" (Sears, 1988, p. 57). They believe that "the individual black's fate is not determined by treatment of blacks as a group, and that demands for help and special favors should not be granted to blacks as a group" (Sears, 1988, p. 57; cf. McConahay, 1986). After all, they believe, discrimination is largely a thing of the past, and blacks have the opportunity to compete in the marketplace like everyone else.

Modern racists believe that discrimination is largely a thing of the past.

Surveys now show only small minorities endorsing such traditional racist sentiments as "Black people are generally not as smart as whites" or "It is a bad idea for blacks and whites to marry one another" (see McConahay, 1986, p. 108). On the other hand, whites frequently endorse survey items intended to tap modern racism. Here are some examples (taken from the literature review in Sears, 1988, p. 57): "Blacks are getting too demanding in their push for equal rights" ("agree" is the modern racist answer); "It is easy to understand the anger of black people in America" ("disagree"); "Over the past few years, the government and news media have shown more respect to blacks than they deserve" ("agree"); and "Blacks have it better than they have ever had it before" ("agree"). Studies have shown both that such items comprise a psychometrically valid attitude scale (McConahay, 1986) and that scores on the scale predict policy attitudes and voting behavior at statistically significant levels (Sears, 1988).

The concept of modern racism has been attacked by some scholars.

The concept of modern racism has been attacked by some scholars. Some believe the real explanation for whites' hostility to blacks' striving is not *racial* prejudice but *group*-based conflict (Bobo, 1988); these observers think that white resentment arises from competition with black groups over scarce resources. Others argue that whites may oppose black politicians or government intervention in favor of blacks on conservative ideological grounds having nothing to do with racial animosity (Roth, 1990).[2] Both critiques have some merit, but the concept of modern racism appears well supported by the empirical methods of social psychology. The most convincing evidence is that scores on the modern racism scales predict behavior. Measures of individuals' attachment to group interests do not, and measures of old-fashioned racist views cannot (see especially Sears, 1988, and the many studies cited therein).

The Impact of Local Television News

Local television news promotes modern racism even as—and partially because—it delegitimizes old-fashioned racism.

The initial hypothesis of this study is that local television news promotes modern racism even as—and partially because—it delegitimizes old-fashioned racism. Local news operations in Chicago (and other major markets; see Entman, in press) appear responsive to black audiences and sensitive to the demands of overcoming traditional racism. They hire black reporters and anchors, and cover blacks' political activities assiduously. These actions appear rooted in economic pressures to attract black audiences and political pressures to please organized black interest groups. At least some of the images that result should help to challenge any white perceptions that blacks are innately inferior. At the same time, however, the responsiveness to black audiences no less than to white ones may contribute to the production of messages that stimulate or reinforce modern racism.

First, there is the issue of suppressing traditional racism. Along with the rest of the broadcast media, local TV news has been rendering the expression of old-fashioned racist sentiments socially unacceptable and thereby—to some indeterminate degree—actually reducing public adherence to the views. The suppression of old-fashioned racism would comprise the positive side of the "spiral of silence" advanced by Noelle-Neumann (1984), whereby a perception that the majority holds a certain opinion becomes self-fulfilling. In this process, those who hold contrary opinions fear disap-

[2]There has been some discussion of whether the term "racism" should be avoided because of just such arguments. More neutral descriptions such as "habitual disagreement with black policy positions" would miss part of the concept's essence and would evade the continuity with old-fashioned racism. See Katz and Taylor (1988b, p. 7).

(Photo by Bruce Cotler.)

proval and become reluctant to express what is perceived to be minority sentiment. The scarcity of public expressions of the idea feeds the impression that it is a minority stance and reinforces fear of expressing it.

While the model has been criticized, it seems possible that something akin to the spiral of silence has helped eliminate old-fashioned racist sentiments from public dialogue. As perhaps our primary "cultural forum" (Newcomb & Hirsch, 1984), the mass media would play a

The media play a pivotal role in spreading impressions that old-fashioned racism is now unacceptable.

pivotal role in spreading impressions that old-fashioned racism is now unacceptable.[3] On the level of overt messages, such an effect would arise from the absence of old-fashioned racist discourse in the news. Less obviously, the news could contribute to the lessening of old-fashioned racism by featuring positive images, especially of blacks performing well in important social roles such as TV reporter and anchorperson.

On the other hand, even though the United States has experienced a sharp drop in traditional racist opinion, many whites continue to oppose policies designed to ameliorate the effects of racism. In fact, the concept of modern racism emerged from social scientists' observing the contradiction between white Americans' endorsement of racial equality in the abstract and their often-intense opposition to concrete policies designed to produce more equality (see Katz & Taylor, 1988b; Sears, 1988). It appears likely that the news media's overt contribution to modern racism comes through the quoting of political leaders' and experts' attacks on affirmative action, the war on poverty, assertive black politicians, and other pro-black actors and policies. More subtly, it is argued here, the news media may be helping to encourage and legitimize modern racism by inadvertently reinforcing impressions of blacks as threatening, overly demanding, and undeserving. The media may be conveying a sense that modern racist sentiments (e.g., that government caters too much to blacks) are at least acceptable if not majority views among the white citizenry.

Clearly many white Americans support pro-black policies and candidates.[4] But the key finding of previous research is that many others who do *not* endorse traditional racist sentiments nonetheless score high on modern racism scales and consistently oppose pro-black policies and vote against black politicians.

[3]It is difficult to know to what extent traditional racism has actually disappeared and to what extent modern racism simply expresses the same sentiments in different form. The difficulty is caused in major part by the media's spiraling penetration of mass consciousness. It has become virtually impossible to use the instruments of survey research to measure racial prejudice directly; respondents who have minimal contact with current cultural products and norms know that certain answers are racist and that it is socially unacceptable to endorse (old-fashioned) racist views. Thus, survey instruments probably underestimate the proportion of the population that retains the belief in blacks' innate inferiority (cf. McConahay, 1986). But specialists in the area believe that there has been a real and substantial reduction in the proportion of whites accepting old-fashioned racist stereotypes (e.g., Bobo, 1988; Sears, 1988, p. 55).

[4]Other white Americans may support candidates who oppose pro-black policies because of those candidates' stands on a host of unrelated issues, from agriculture policy to inflation. The explanation of candidate choice is an enormously complicated task well beyond the scope of this paper, but the literature already cited (especially Sears, 1988) describes research showing the independent effect of modern racism on voting, controlling for other variables.

The Data

The data for this paper come from a single week of local news programming in Chicago, collected and analyzed to explore the connections between modern racism and television news in the concrete context of actual news messages. Thus these data are used to suggest future lines of inquiry, not to establish definitive propositions.[5]

This study included one hour per day of local news from each of the three network affiliates in Chicago: the half-hour local segment immediately preceding or following the network news in the early evening (6:00 P.M. for WMAQ and WLS, 5:30 P.M. for WBBM), and the half-hour segment broadcast at 10 P.M. , during the week of December 1–7, 1989. Chicago's VHF independent station, WGN, was excluded because the network affiliates obtain the overwhelming majority of the audience; informal observation indicated no systematic differences between WGN and the three bigger stations.

Two previous studies indicate strong similarities in local news emphases and formats across major urban markets. One (Entman, in press) included stations serving 13 of the nation's 25 largest markets; the other (Carroll, 1989) included stations serving 10 of the 30 largest markets. The consistency of local news across metropolitan areas suggests that the use of data only from Chicago is unlikely to cause serious distortions in the formation of hypotheses.

The data for this paper come from a single week of local news programming in Chicago.

It might also be argued that, as a profit-oriented hybrid of entertainment and journalism, local news does not merit the serious treatment normally accorded network news. But local news does deserve careful attention. One reason is that it far outdraws the networks in the Chicago market and probably many others, especially in the Central time zone, where the late local news starts at 10 rather than 11 P.M. and the network news comes on at 5:30 or 6:00 rather than 6:30 or 7:00 P.M. Indeed, the combined ratings for the three network affiliates' 10 P.M. news in a recent period was 42; when we add the VHF independent "superstation" WGN's 9 P.M. news, with a rating of 8, half the TV households in the Chicago area watch the late local news on the average night.[6] This compares with an average combined rating of 26 for the three network evening news shows (Nielsen, 1989). A second reason for looking at local news is that its racial

Local news far outdraws the networks in the Chicago market and probably many others.

[5]An equally important limitation is that the project omits the complex and ambiguous portrayals of blacks in local TV sports reporting and in network television entertainment, sports, and news programming. All of these areas merit their own research if we are to understand the full range of television's contributions to the images of blacks and the production of modern racism. On the racial content of television other than news, see, e.g., MacDonald (1983).

[6]Some households may watch both WGN at 9 and another station at 10, so that the actual percentage of households watching the late news may be slightly under 50%.

messages are anchored close to home and in all likelihood help to construct the audience's sense of community well-being and community threat in a way that the more distant and abstracted national news cannot.

The analysis included all news stories that depicted events caused by blacks or events that centrally involved blacks.

The analysis included all news stories that depicted events caused by blacks or events that centrally involved blacks. The criteria for this second category were that black persons appeared on the screen at least three times in medium or close-up shots and that black persons (other than reporters) spoke on camera at least twice.

Reinforcing Modern Racism

Table 1 lists the subjects of the news stories that centrally featured black persons. The key categories were crimes of violence explicitly reported as committed by blacks, which comprised 41% of all news in which blacks were prominantly featured; intraparty conflict (disputes over the sufficiency of black and white liberals in the Democratic party's official slate of candidates for local offices), which comprised 19%; and the entry of a black judge, Eugene Pincham, into the campaign for Cook County Board President, which comprised 15%. The first category illustrates the first hypothesized effect of local news—stimulating hostility and fear of blacks—and the second and third categories illustrate the second effect—reinforcing resentment of blacks' political demands.

It must be noted that the division into separate news categories and effects is for analytical clarity; the same news message can stimulate fear and resentment simultaneously, for example, and those emotions are likely to feed each other. Moreover, as with all media messages, these may be polysemic. Some whites, for example, may react sympathetically rather than fearfully to news of crime committed by blacks. A detailed understanding of audiences' interpretations awaits further research. The purpose here is to generate some plausible hypotheses on effects; to this end, the next section moves beyond the rather unrevealing percentage breakdown to a qualitative analysis of the coverage.

Component One: White Hostility and Black Crime News

For the week studied, violent crime committed by blacks was the largest category of local news.

For the week studied, violent crime committed by blacks was the largest category of local news. Of the eight instances in which blacks were the subjects of lead stories, six described violent crimes; the other two stories concerned the Democratic party's conflicts and the death of a black girl run over by a city bus. (One other lead story was about a black arrested for murder, but the race of the accused was not mentioned in that report.) Of course, the particular week studied could have been a

Table 1. Subjects of Stories Centrally Featuring Blacks on Three Local Chicago Newscasts, December 1–7, 1989.

Category	WBBM		WMAQ		WLS		Total	
	Seconds	% of Total	Seconds	% of Total	Seconds	% of Total	Seconds	%
Violent crime	536	39	727	39	782	44	2045	41
Intraparty conflict	123	9	656	35	173	10	952	19
Judge Pincham's candidacy	193	14	150	8	425	24	768	15
Nonviolent crime	58	4	0	0	0	0	58	1
Other	454	33	338	18	382	22	1174	24
Total	1364	99[a]	1871	100	1762	100	4997	100

[a]Rounding error.

period of unusually high violence. The point here, however, is not to determine the average proportion of local news devoted to violent crime committed by blacks but to explore how the images of crime may compound whites' hostility.

Several aspects of the crime reporting combined to suggest that blacks are more dangerous than whites. For example, the accused black criminals were usually illustrated by glowering mug shots or by footage of them being led around in handcuffs, their arms held by uniformed white policemen. None of the accused violent white criminals during the week studied were shown in mug shots or in physical custody.[7] The difference may be due to the fact that most of the whites were alleged organized crime figures of high economic status. They could afford bail money, good legal representation, and advice on handling the press.

Thus, the contrast in portrayals of black and white criminals reflects at least in part underlying differences in the social class of the perpetrators. Here is an instance of the inadvertent class bias of local TV news, a bias that may spur modern racism. Put simply, TV favors middle- or upper-class persons when they appear in the news, because those persons have the skills and resources to manipulate television's production practices. To counter this slant, journalists would have to understand the class bias and take steps to counteract it—suggesting that black lawbreakers put on business suits, for example, or asking police to allow them to walk freely for the news camera. But such

Accused black criminals were usually illustrated by glowering mug shots or by footage of them being led around in handcuffs.

[7]On the potential impact of such nonverbal and visual cues, see Graber (1990).

overt intervention in the construction of the subject's image would be impractical and would be viewed by editors as staging the news or editorializing. In the absence of such steps, crime coverage may compound whites' fear of blacks by showing black criminals more than white criminals surrounded with symbols of menace.

Crime coverage may compound whites' fear of blacks by showing black criminals surrounded with symbols of menace.

Within the category of crime, white victimization by blacks appeared to have especially high priority. During the week studied, the story of white victimization that obtained the most attention involved four white girls receiving razor cuts in a fight with two black girls on a Chicago bus, and the related charge by the victims that the black bus driver did nothing to help. Given the timing of the incident, each of the three stations had opportunities to cover it in five programs over three days; the affair was covered 11 of the possible 15 times. Three times it was the lead story, once the second story, and twice the third story. Four of the stories were over two minutes long, marking the event as unusually newsworthy. It is doubtful that this one fight had more serious physical or mental consequences for the participants than the other fights, assaults, rapes, and murders in the metropolitan area during the week. The racial tension that the story demonstrated and reinforced is probably what made it so newsworthy. It is unlikely that the incident would have received similar attention were all the participants white (or black).[8]

The whites' perspective on the event dominated the story. The black girls accused of the assault were never quoted directly. Their side was voiced through angry relatives talking to reporters (on only two of the stations). The white girls said the attack was unprovoked, the black relatives that the whites had instigated the fight with racial insults; but the whites' version was clearly favored through the order of presentation, the amount of time devoted to it, and the visuals. For example, the white girls were shown seated on a couch, presumably at an orderly home like that of middle-class viewers, calmly describing their ordeal, with numerous close-ups of their wounds. The alleged perpetrators' relatives spoke at the police station house, where the camera was hand-held and shaky, the lighting full of shadows, and the disordered scene hardly likely to promote credibility.

The contrast in presenting the whites' and blacks' cases may have been unavoidable, given normal station routines. As juveniles, the accused were inaccessible to journalists; since they were in custody, they could not be interviewed at home. In fact, the press generally slights the vantage of accused lawbreakers in favor of the prosecution

---

[8]Studies have shown that the majority of crime committed by blacks victimizes other blacks, and such crime goes largely unreported by the mainstream daily media (Protess, 1990).

(cf. Condit & Selzer, 1985). Television's class bias apparently assumes that the middle class, loyal to the forces of law and order, presumes accused perpetrators to be guilty, especially when the offenses are those normally associated with the lower classes (street crime).[9] All of this suggests that the stations did not deliberately derogate the defendants because of their race.

A secondary theme of the coverage on each station involved the whites complaining that the black bus driver failed to assist them. One station had him respond to the charges on camera, but he looked surly, sounded defensive, and came off badly in contrast with the articulate, aggrieved white girls, especially since this station (and the others) reported that he was suspended for his inaction by the Chicago Transit Authority (CTA). Barely mentioned was the driver's claim that he did call for help but found his radio inoperable. The driver said "That's not my job" when asked about his failure to assist the white girls. Two of the stations showed the black chief of the busdriver's union or some black fellow drivers defending the suspended man, thereby seeming to be more concerned about the job security and selfish interests of black drivers than the community interest in safe buses. The implicit message was that black drivers would not protect white passengers from violence because their racial loyalty overrode their human sympathy and their job obligations. Perhaps this is how the typical black bus driver feels; but the reporting did not probe the possibility that the driver did follow proper procedure, that drivers are not expected to intervene physically in fights, and that the CTA might have been hoping to deflect blame for the faulty radio by suspending the driver.

Local news grants a high priority to stories in which whites are victimized by blacks.

The high priority that local television grants white victimization by blacks, and crime generally—a priority that can stimulate modern racism—appears based in commercial imperatives. In large metropolitan areas, where the media market consists of dozens of political jurisdictions, local TV cannot focus too much on the politics and policy of any one jurisdiction, so it has to go with material of broader human interest. Hence its top four story categories are more emotionally evocative than informative: crime, fires, and accidents; human interest features; sports; and weather (Entman, 1989, pp. 110–113; cf. Carroll, 1989).

The Chicago stations made violent crime the most frequent subject of lead stories (44% of leads) during the week studied. The emphasis on crime explains why blacks who committed crimes were the ones most likely to be featured in the

[9]On law and order, and on the middle-class bias of the news in the United States and United Kingdom, see the studies collected in Cohen and Young (1981); on the "enduring values" of American journalism, including middle-class propriety, moderation, and order, see Gans (1979, pp. 51–52 and *passim;* cf. Hall *et al.*, 1978).

most prominent (lead) stories. This is a good example of the importance of commercial considerations in the production of news that may arouse the first component of modern racism, anti-black affect.

Component Two: White Resentment and Black Politics

Stations' efforts to attract and serve the black audience lead them to devote substantial time to black political activists and politicians.

Alleged criminals are not the only representations of black persons in the local news studied. Stations' efforts to attract and serve the black audience lead them to devote substantial time to black political activists and politicians (Entman, in press). But these black actors usually appeared pleading the interests of the black community as against the white power structure. Thus, news about blacks who acted politically conveyed the notion that they spoke and acted largely to advance special interests. Even though white leaders in Chicago typically come from recognizable ethnic power bases, they were more often presented as if they represented the entire community. The news equated black political action almost exclusively with special interest politics and white political action most frequently with public interest politics.

The news equated black political action almost exclusively with special interest politics.

The hypothesis is that exposure to this set of images, with "self-seeking" black leaders juxtaposed against "altruistic" white leaders, would tend to stimulate the second component of modern racism—resistance to and resentment of the organized political demands of blacks. It might also reinforce whites' general hostility to blacks.

It may be the case that most of the time black political leaders do speak up only for black interests; many theories of representation would endorse just such behavior. However, it seems highly unlikely that white political actors are as purely civic-minded as depicted in the implicit comparison constructed by the news. But the whites' halo does reflect genuine structural conditions. To protect white privileges, white politicians need only defend the status quo in general terms, or in terms of nonracial values such as meritocracy or low taxes. They do not need to use an overt rhetoric of white power; they need not mention power at all.

Many of the stories in Table 1 on "intraparty conflict," the largest category of stories after those on violent crime, consisted of black politicians and their "progressive" white allies complaining in angry or demanding tones about insufficient representation of blacks and progressives on the official Democratic slate. The coverage of the campaign of black Judge Eugene Pincham for president of the Cook County Board—the third largest category of stories in Table 1—is worthy of closer scrutiny.

Half of the Pincham stories quoted his 1987 remark to a black audience that said, essentially, that black persons who did not vote for Harold Washington for mayor "should be hung." This assertion, obviously hyperbolic and not a literal endorsement of execution, is a classic "gaffe"—a quote that damages the political standing of a politician while symbolizing a larger truth about him or her that journalists believe is otherwise hidden from the public. The suggestion was that Pincham was not only an ally of Washington but an extremist, a militant.

The coverage provided scant evidence on this matter, because none of the stations offered more than a few seconds of information on Pincham's record, qualifications, and policy proposals. They did offer brief sound bites in which Pincham said that he would emphasize eliminating government waste and keeping taxes down—hardly extremist goals. Much more time and emphasis were given to his quote about hanging. At best, the white audience would receive a confused and superficial message about Pincham's character, record, and policy stands; at worst, a negative impression of him as a racial militant. Ironically, though, Pincham himself might have welcomed the coverage—a militant image might have helped him build support among blacks, as will be discussed below.

Candidates are routinely given superficial treatment by journalists (cf. Entman, in press); broadcasters assume that policy substance bores audiences. Here again the typical practice, rooted in economic incentives, indirectly yielded news supportive of modern racism. Seizing on an emotional and symbolic event, employing the standard "campaign gaffe" script, the stations made it difficult for audiences to discern where this black politician stood and made it easy for them to stereotype him as a threatening militant.

Reporting on black political actors such as Pincham frequently showed them speaking to audiences. Sound bites usually depicted the black person talking loudly, often in what might be termed a "harangue" or "tirade" employing an emotional, rhetorical appeal rather than a calm, deliberative one. Such images may bolster the image of black political figures as more emotional and angry than white ones; the hypothesis would be that exposure to such depictions compounds the white audience's resistance to the demands of black leaders and possibly contributes to diffuse anti-black feelings as well.

Images of black political leaders show them as more emotional and angry than white ones.

The images may reflect, in part, a different style of interpersonal communication among blacks than among whites. Kochman (1981) suggests that black culture encourages the use of signs of emotion both more freely and more meaningfully. Also, the class composition of the black community in central cities differs from that of many white communities, so that black leaders must use different language codes to appeal to their audiences. Unaware of the differences in communicative styles, white audiences

Black leaders must use different language codes to appeal to their audiences.

(Photo by Bruce Cotler.)

might infer that whites have a fuller range of positive emotions than blacks, whose emotions in the news studied appear both more negative and less controlled. It is hardly the fault of television that blacks communicate differently from whites. But the resulting portrayals may reinforce feelings of estrangement and perhaps threat among whites, responses likely to augment modern racism. Kochman (1981) suggests as much in his portrayal of interpersonal communication between the races.

Portrayals of blacks may reinforce feelings of estrangement and perhaps threat among whites.

Television's frequent depictions of emotional speechifying do not simply reflect reality. Showing boisterous rhetoric makes commercial sense for stations; television abhors talking heads but is quite fond of shouting ones. Emotional conflicts over politics are presumed to interest audiences across local jurisdictions in a way that other political discourse and actions do not. This is one reason that local television often features the most fiery excerpts from speeches or shows footage of a citizen crying or shouting at a confrontational town meeting.

The emphasis on politics as emotional conflict means that black politicians tend to make the news when they are engaging in conflict. The local stations' news definitions give black leaders an incentive to act confrontationally if they want to get on the air, an incentive that may parallel their image-building needs in the black community. According to sociologist William Sampson (personal communication), to garner support in the black community, black leaders need to appear strong, demanding, and even angry in their dealings with the white power structure. Such performances may also attract black TV audiences, perhaps providing a vicarious feeling of power and participation. But those performances are unlikely to spur support among whites, support necessary for long-term political success in most communities.

Chicago's television stations are not responsible for the dynamics and incentives of black politics in the city. But because of local news practices, black political leaders who engage in angry rhetoric are more likely than others to get air time. This exploratory research suggests that, because of news organizations' very responsiveness to what they assume are audience interests—both the black interest in seeing tough black leaders and the white (and perhaps black) interest in dramatic and conflictual politics—the news is most likely to air the black leaders' emotional or angry sound bites.

Because of local news practices, black political leaders who engage in angry rhetoric are more likely than others to get air time.

In contrast to the high proportion of pictures and sounds of angry or demanding black voices, white political actors rarely shouted or harangued during the week studied. This lower average level of emotion may reflect the fact that those who hold power have less to complain about and need not shout to be heard by government. Incumbent officials also can control the news setting and the rules of engagement with journalists in a way that those outside or on the fringes of power cannot (Goldenberg, 1975). This dynamic could work in blacks' favor in cities that have black mayors. But here white leaders controlled the government and had opportunities to announce good news; black leaders were left more often to voice demands, along with the implicit call for higher budgets and taxes.

Black leaders were left more often to voice demands, along with the implicit call for higher budgets and taxes.

Component Three: The "Disappearance" of Racism and the Emergence of Black Authority

Other blacks appeared in local news occupying roles of respected authority.

Other blacks appeared in local news, usually occupying roles of respected authority. They included, most importantly, the many black anchorpersons and reporters, as well as black police officials in the stories themselves. The behavior and words of these authorities on screen were not linked in any way to their racial identities, and indeed denied black identity as it was constructed by the rest of the news. Such images could buttress perceptions that racism is no longer a problem for black persons and in this way contribute to the third component of modern racism.

The blacks who served as authoritative spokespersons did not talk in angry tones. They were unemotional and businesslike. They followed middle-class, white patterns of conversational communication (Kochman, 1981). Whether as journalists or as police officials describing a crime, they described the actions of poor and dangerous blacks without indicating any special feeling, symbolically showing that they were (through the perspective of the news they described) on the same side as whites. There was no difference between the reporting of black anchors and white anchors, which of course is what their job descriptions demanded. Voicing a black perspective would have meant defining the problems covered in the news—such as violent crime—in ways that might be endorsed by a majority of blacks.[10]

Black anchors may be particularly significant to the formation of whites' impressions. A separate study revealed that 11 of 13 stations in 13 of the nation's 25 largest markets employed at least one black in a co-anchor role (Entman, in press). For many white Chicagoans, the black anchors frequently employed by the Chicago stations may provide the most frequently encountered images of authoritative blacks.

It thus appears reasonable to hypothesize that the positive images of black authority in local news may unwittingly have two simultaneous effects: enhancing perceptions that racism is no longer a problem, thereby contributing to modern racism, while suppressing perceptions that blacks are incapable of working and associating successfully with whites, thus discouraging formation of old-fashioned racist sentiments. On one level, black anchors demonstrate that blacks are capable of behaving according to and reporting from the perspective of dominant white values. But the black anchors' very

---

[10]Blacks interpretations of crime's causes and cures are, on average, different from those of whites, and those differences could in theory construct a different narrative perspective on crime involving blacks. For example, poll evidence suggests that blacks are significantly more likely than whites to see discrimination as a major continuing problem (Sussman, 1988, p. 110).

presence may suggest that the system does allow blacks to become acceptable to—even earn more money than—most whites.[11] Showing attractive, articulate blacks in such a prestigious public role implies that blacks are not inherently inferior or socially undesirable—and that racism is no longer a serious impediment to black progress.[12]

Since major markets usually have a substantial proportion of black TV households, the white owners of local TV stations need to appeal both to majority white audiences and to that large black minority. The decisions that advance one goal may detract from the other. Since the anchors help personify the news and demonstrably draw viewers and maintain audience loyalty, a good compromise solution is to appeal to blacks by choosing black anchors.[13]

Black anchors may even attract some whites. The act of viewing local news with a black anchor (or *The Cosby Show;* cf. Steinman, 1990) can function for white viewers as symbolic affirmation that they are not racist. At the same time, local TV consistently features news that promotes anti-black affect in a veiled form by appearing to be "about" crime or political conflict rather than about black persons and their violations of community values. But of course the news is about both. Categorizing race-relevant issues as purely nonracial—such as claiming that the busing issue revolves only around the value of neighborhood schools, not race—is crucial to the perpetuation of modern racism. It allows those with modern racist feelings, who are sensitive to the social disapproval of racism, to disguise their anti-black affect to themselves, thus preserving their self-images as unprejudiced (see McConahay, 1986).

Showing attractive, articulate blacks in such a prestigious public role implies that racism is no longer a serious impediment to black progress.

Conclusion

Local news implicitly traces the symbolic boundaries of the community. The present exploration suggests that, in day-to-day news coverage, blacks are largely cast outside those boundaries. In the stories analyzed, crime reporting made blacks look particularly threatening, while coverage of politics exaggerated the degree to which black

The act of viewing local news with a black anchor (or, for that matter, The Cosby Show*) can function for white viewers as symbolic affirmation that they are not racist.*

[11]For evidence that blacks with college degrees earn much less than whites, and that the relative position of middle-class blacks actually deteriorated in the 1980s, see Harrison (1990).

[12]The dual-leveled signification of the black anchors might be paralleled by *The Cosby Show.* The Huxtable family, too, unavoidably and simultaneously endorses the propositions that blacks can be "just like us" middle-class white people and thus should evoke no fear, and that blacks can make it to the upper middle class and thus merit no special sympathy.

[13]Pressure from black organizations that are often active in big-city politics, and from FCC regulations (and indirectly, perhaps, Congress) that encourage affirmative action hiring, may also encourage employment of black anchors. White organizations cannot in a socially acceptable manner press for hiring whites so the only compelling community force operating on the matter of racial identity of anchors may come from blacks.

Crime reporting made blacks look particularly threatening, while coverage of politics exaggerated the degree to which black politicians practice special interest politics.

politicians (as compared with white ones) practice special interest politics. These images would feed the first two components of modern racism, anti-black affect and resistance to blacks' political demands. On the other hand, the positive dimension of the news, the presence of black anchors and other authority figures, may simultaneously engender an impression that racial discrimination is no longer a problem, bolstering the third component of modern racism, and an impression that blacks are not inferior and undesirable, working against old-fashioned racism.

The images and effects hypothesized here are not products of bad faith or malign intentions. Rather, they arise from TV journalists acting as they are trained to, given the limitations, pressures, and incentives confronting them in a highly competitive market. To change this situation, journalists would have to undertake explicit assessments of the possible impact of their stories and modify their reports to prevent undesirable effects. Operating under the strictures of "objectivity" and facing conflicting expectations and uncertainties, journalists are neither authorized nor eager to engage in such exercises. The implications of this research, then, is that local news is likely to continue the practices hypothesized here.

To be sure, images of blacks in the local news are complicated and replete with multiple potential meanings. And audiences bring to the news a variety of predispositions. Social scientists have no more than a rudimentary understanding of how audiences perceive and process media messages (see, e.g., Entman, 1989, chap. 4; Page, Shapiro, & Dempsey, 1987; see also Hartmann & Husband, 1974). Nonetheless, the exploratory study provides ample support for a hypothesis that local television's images of blacks feed racial anxiety and antagonism *at least* among that portion of the white population most predisposed to those feelings. Quantitative research on the impact of exposure to local TV news seems in order, as does extensive content analysis of large samples of local and network news. Such work would also illuminate the ways that television helps to alter and preserve dominant cultural values and structures of power. ♦

References

Bobo, L. (1988). Group conflict, prejudice, and the paradox of contemporary racial attitudes. In P. Katz & D.Taylor (Eds.), *Eliminating racism: Profiles in controversy* (pp. 85–114). New York: Plenum Press.

Carroll, R. (1989). Market size and TV news values. *Journalism Quarterly, 66* 49–56.

Cohen, S., and Young, J. (1981). *The manufacture of news: Social problems, deviance and the mass media* (rev. ed.). Beverly Hills: Sage.

Condit, C., and Selzer, J. A. (1985). The rhetoric of objectivity in the newspaper coverage of a murder trial. *Critical Studies in Mass Communication, 2,* 197–216.

Dovidio, J., and Gaertner, S. (Eds.). (1986). *Prejudice, discrimination, and racism: Theory and research.* New York: Academic Press.

Entman, R. (1989). *Democracy without citizens: Media and the decay of American politics.* New York: Oxford University Press.

Entman, R. (in press). Super Tuesday and the future of local television news. In P. Cook, D. Gomery, and L. Lichty (Eds.), *The Future of News.* Washington, DC: Woodrow Wilson Center Press.

Gans, H. (1979). *Deciding what's news.* New York: Pantheon Books.

Goldenberg, E. N. (1975). *Making the papers.* Lexington, MA: D.C. Heath.

Graber, D. (1990). Seeing is remembering: How visuals contribute to learning from television news. *Journal of Communication, 40*(3), 134–156.

Hall, S., Critcher, C., Jefferson, T., Clarke, J. and Roberts, B. (1978). *Policing the crisis: Mugging, the state, and law and order.* London: Macmillan.

Harrison, B. (1990, September 2). For blacks, a degree doesn't automatically mean higher incomes. *Los Angeles Times,* p. M4.

Hartmann, P., and Husband, C. (1974). *Racism and the mass media.* London: Davis-Poynter.

Katz, P. A., and Taylor, D. A. (Eds.). (1988a). *Eliminating racism.* New York: Plenum Press.

Katz, P. A., and Taylor, D. A. (1988b). Introduction. In P. A. Katz and D. A. Taylor (Eds.), *Eliminating racism* (p. 1–16). New York: Plenum Press.

Kochman, T. (1981). *Black and white styles in conflict.* Chicago: University of Chicago Press.

MacDonald, J. F. (1983). *Blacks and white TV.* Chicago: Nelson-Hall.

McConahay, J.B. (1986). Modern racism, ambivalence, and the modern racism scale. In J. Dovidio and S. Gaertner (Eds.), *Prejudice, discrimination, and racism: Theory and research* (pp. 91–125). New York Academic Press.

Newcomb, H., and Hirsch, P. M. (1984). Television as a cultural forum: Implications for research. In W. D. Rowland, Jr., and B. Watkins (Eds.), *Interpreting television: Current research perspectives* (pp. 58–73). Beverly Hills: Sage.

Nielsen, A. C. Co. (1989). *Nielsen station index* (Chicago metered market service for February 1989). New York: Nielsen Media Research.

Noelle-Neumann, E. (1984). *The spiral of silence: Public opinion—our social skin.* Chicago: University of Chicago Press.

Page, B., Shapiro, R., and Dempsey, G. (1987). What moves public opinion? *American Political Science Review, 81,* 23–45.

Protess, D. (1990, March). The news in black and white. *Chicago,* pp. 15–17.

Roth, B. M. (1990, Winter). Social psychology's "racism." *The Public Interest,* No. 98, 26–36.

Sears, D. O. (1988). Symbolic racism. In P. A. Katz and D. A. Taylor (Eds.), *Eliminating racism* (pp. 53–84). New York: Plenum Press.

Steinman, C. M. (1990, May 25). *Discourse of denial: White racism,* The Cosby Show, *and the case of Andy Rooney.* Paper presented at the Society for Cinema Studies, Washington, D.C.

Sussman, B. (1988). *What Americans really think.* New York: Pantheon Books.

Questions for Discussion

1. Do you agree with Entman's definition of modern racism? For example, is a feeling that racism no longer exists actually a form of racism?
2. Observe a few hours of your local news. Are blacks presented as they were in Entman's observation?

Suggested Readings

More On Gender Stereotyping

Cantor, Muriel G., "Feminism and the Media," *Society* Vol. 25, July-August 1988, p. 76 (6).

Haskell, Molly, "Peter Pantheism: Rite-of-Passage Movies—For Boys Only," *Vogue,* September 1988, p. 360 (1).

Haskell, Molly, "The Gods that Failed: Women Caught Between Family and Political Conviction," *Vogue,* July, 1988, p. 34 (1).

Kanner, Bernice, "Big Boys Don't Cry," *New York* Vol. 23, May 21, 1990, p. 20 (2). Men in advertising.

More On Racial Stereotyping

Cummings, Melbourne S., "The Changing Image of the Black Family on Television," *Journal of Popular Culture* Vol. 22, Fall, 1988, p. 75 (11).

Diamond, Edwin, "Black on White," *New York* Vol. 23, August 20, 1990, p. 38 (5). Race and crime in the African-American press.

Ehrenstein, David, "The Color of Laughter," *American Film* Vol. 13, September, 1988, p. 8 (4). Black entertainers and racism.

Kalter, Joanmarie, "Yes, There Are More Blacks on TV—But Mostly to Make Viewers Laugh," *TV Guide* Vol. 36, August 13, 1988, p. 26 (5).

Lichter, Robert S., Linda S. Lichter, Stanley Rothman, and Daniel Amundson, "Prime Time Prejudice: TV's Images of Blacks and Hispanics," *Public Opinion,* July / August 1987. This article can also be found in the third edition of *Mass Media Issues,* p. 273 (7).

Martindale, Carolyn, *The White Press and Black America* (Westport, Conn.: Greenwood Press, 1986). Examines the press coverage of African-Americans during the 1960s and 1970s.

Spikol, Art, "What's Black and White and Read All Over? There Are Times when Race Should Be Left Out of Things. But They're Rare," *Writer's Digest,* October, 1989, p. 14 (3).

Pornography and Obscenity

18

Years ago, when asked his views on pornography, Groucho Marx sniffed, "I'm against it. I don't even own a pornograph."

Groucho's comment reflected his contemporaries' feelings about pornography. At the time, pornography was not only a clear breach of morality, it was illegal. If you owned it or used it, you were a criminal. A variety of Supreme Court cases and the free speech movement in the campuses of the 1960s resulted in the liberalization of laws against pornography and obscenity. In recent years, however, new prosecutions have brought the pornography debate back to center stage.

This chapter contains two classic statements on the pros and cons of censoring pornography. They were both written in the early 1970s, before the age of AIDS and the success of the home VCR porno industry. Still, the underlying arguments are as valid today as they were when they were first written.

Pornography, Obscenity, and the Case for Censorship

Irving Kristol

Irving Kristol is a well-known conservative intellectual. A professor of Urban Values at New York University at the time the following article was written, he has served as editor of The Public Interest *magazine and as an advisor to President Reagan. In this essay, Kristol explains why he is in favor of the censorship of obscenity and pornography. In fact, he says, anyone who cares about the quality of life in America* has *to be for censorship, since a democracy cannot afford to be governed by "the more infantile and irrational parts" of its people.*

The case for censorship, Kristol contends, is the case against nihilism. Nihilism (literally, "belief in nothing") is the rejection of morality in the belief that there is no meaning in existence.

"What is at stake," Kristol tells us, "is civilization and humanity, nothing less."

Reading Difficulty Level: 10. But Worth It.

Being frustrated is disagreeable, but the real disasters in life begin when you get what you want.

In the United States and other democracies, censorship has to all intents and purposes ceased to exist.

Being frustrated is disagreeable, but the real disasters in life begin when you get what you want. For almost a century now, a great many intelligent, well-meaning, and articulate people—of a kind generally called liberal or intellectual, or both—have argued eloquently against any kind of censorship of art and/or entertainment. And within the past 10 years, the courts and the legislatures of most Western nations have found these arguments persuasive—so persuasive that hardly a man is now alive who clearly remembers what the answers to these arguments were. Today, in the United States and other democracies, censorship has to all intents and purposes ceased to exist.

Is there a sense of triumphant exhilaration in the land? Hardly. There is, on the contrary, a rapidly growing unease and disquiet. Somehow things have not worked out as they were supposed to, and many notable civil libertarians have gone on record as saying this was not what they meant at all. They wanted a world in which *Desire Under the Elms* could be produced, or *Ulysses* published, without interference by philistine busybodies holding public office. They have got that, of course; but they have also got a world in which homosexual rape takes place on the stage, in which the public flocks during lunch hours to witness varieties of professional fornication, in which Times Square has become little more than a hideous market for the sale and distribution of printed filth that panders to all known (and some fanciful) sexual perversions.

But disagreeable as this may be, does it really matter? Might not our unease and disquiet be merely a cultural hangover—a "hangup," as they say? What reason is there to think that anyone was even corrupted by a book?

This last question, oddly enough, is asked by the very same people who seem convinced that advertisements in magazines or displays of violence on television do indeed have the power to corrupt. It is also asked, incredibly enough and in all sincerity, by people—e.g., university professors and school

---

From *The New York Times Magazine,* March 28, 1971. Reprinted by permission of the author.

(Photo by Bruce Cotler.)

teachers—whose very lives provide all the answers one could want. After all, if you believe that no one was ever corrupted by a book, you have also to believe that no one was even improved by a book (or a play or a movie). You have to believe, in other words, that all art is morally trivial, and that, consequently, all education is morally irrelevant. No one, not even a university professor, really believes that.

To be sure, it is extremely difficult, as social scientists tell us, to trace the effects of any single book (or play or movie) on an individual reader or any class of readers. But we all know, and social scientists know it too, that the ways in which we use our minds and imaginations do shape our characters and help define us as persons. That those who certainly know this are nevertheless moved to deny it merely indicates how a dogmatic resistance to the idea of censorship can—like most dogmatism—result in a mindless insistence on the absurd.

The ways in which we use our minds and imaginations do shape our characters and help define us as persons.

I have used these harsh terms—"dogmatism" and "mindless"—advisedly. I might also have added "hypocritical." For the plain fact is that none of us is a complete civil libertarian. We all believe that there is some point at which the public authorities ought to step in to limit the "self-expression" of an individual or a group, even where this might be seriously intended as a form of artistic expression, and even where the artistic transaction is between consenting adults. A playwright or theatrical director might, in this crazy world of ours, find someone willing to commit suicide on the stage, as called for by the script. We would not allow that—any more than we would permit scenes of real physical torture on the stage, even if the victim were a willing masochist. And I know of no one, no matter how free in spirit, who argues that we ought to permit gladiatorial contests in Yankee Stadium, similar to those once performed in the Colosseum at Rome—even if only consenting adults were involved.

No society can be indifferent to the ways its citizens publicly entertain themselves.

The basic point that emerges is one that Professor Walter Berns has powerfully argued: no society can be utterly indifferent to the ways its citizens publicly entertain themselves.[1] Bearbaiting and cockfighting are prohibited only in part out of compassion for the suffering animals; the main reason they were abolished was because it was felt that they debased and brutalized the citizenry who flocked to witness such spectacles. And the question we face with regard to pornography and obscenity is whether, now that they have such strong legal protection from the Supreme Court, they can or will brutalize and debase our citizenry. We are, after all, not dealing with one passing incident—one book, or one play, or one movie. We are dealing with a general tendency that is suffusing our entire culture.

I say pornography and obscenity because, though they have different dictionary definitions and are frequently distinguishable as "artistic" genres, they are nevertheless in the end identical in effect. Pornography is not objectionable simply because it arouses sexual desire or lust or prurience in the mind of the reader or spectator; this is a silly Victorian notion. A great many nonpornographic works—including some parts of the Bible—excite sexual desire very successfully. What is distinctive about pornography is that, in the words of D. H. Lawrence, it attempts "to do dirt on [sex]. . . . [It is an] insult to a vital human relationship."

In other words, pornography differs from erotic art in that its whole purpose is to treat human beings obscenely, to deprive human beings of their specifically human dimension. That is what obscenity is all about. It is light years removed from any kind of carefree sensuality—there is no continuum between Fielding's *Tom Jones* and the Marquis de Sade's *Justine.* These works have quite opposite intentions. To quote Susan Sontag: "What pornographic literature does is precisely to drive a wedge between one's existence as a full human being and one's existence as a sexual being—while in ordinary life a healthy person is one who prevents such a gap from opening up." This definition occurs in an essay defending pornography—Miss Sontag is a candid as well as gifted critic—so the definition, which I accept, is neither tendentious nor censorious.

In the history of all literatures obscene words have always been the vocabulary of farce or vituperation.

Along these same lines, one can point out—as C. S. Lewis pointed out some years back—that it is no accident that in the history of all literatures obscene words—the so-called "four-letter words"—have always been the vocabulary of farce or vituperation. The reason is clear; they reduce men and women to some of their mere bodily functions—they reduce man to his

1. This is as good a place as any to express my profound indebtedness to Walter Bem's superb essay, "Pornography vs. Democracy," in the Winter 1971 issue of *The Public Interest.*

(Photo by Bruce Cotler.)

animal component, and such a reduction is an essential purpose of farce or vituperation.

Similarly, Lewis also suggested that it is not an accident that we have no offhand, colloquial, neutral terms—not in any Western European language at any rate—for our most private parts. The words we do use are either (a) nursery terms, (b) archaisms, (c) scientific terms, or (d) a term from the gutter (i.e., a demeaning term). Here I think the genius of language is telling us something important about man. It is telling us that man is an animal with a difference: he has a unique sense of privacy, and a unique capacity for shame when this privacy is violated. Our "private parts" are indeed private, and not merely because convention prescribes it. This particular convention is indigenous to the human race. In practically all primitive tribes, men and women cover their private parts; and in practically all primitive tribes, men and women do not copulate in public.

Man is an animal with a difference; he has a unique sense of privacy, and a unique capacity for shame when this privacy is violated.

We would not televise the agonized death of a well-known man because we would regard this as an obscene invasion of privacy.

It may well be that Western society, in the latter half of the twentieth century, is experiencing a drastic change in sexual mores and sexual relationships. We have had many such "sexual revolutions" in the past—and the bourgeois family and bourgeois ideas of sexual propriety were themselves established in the course of a revolution against eighteenth century "licentiousness"—and we shall doubtless have others in the future. It is, however, highly improbable (to put it mildly) that what we are witnessing is the Final Revolution which will make sexual relations utterly unproblematic, permit us to dispense with any kind of ordered relationships between the sexes, and allow us freely to redefine the human condition. And so long as humanity has not reached that utopia, obscenity will remain a problem.

One of the reasons it will remain a problem is that obscenity is not merely about sex, any more than science fiction is about science. Science fiction, as every student of the genre knows, is a peculiar vision of power: what it is really about is politics. And obscenity is a peculiar vision of humanity: what it is really about is ethics and metaphysics.

But when sex is public, the viewer does not see – cannot see – the sentiments and the ideals. He can only see the animal coupling.

Imagine a man—a well-known man, much in the public eye—in a hospital ward, dying an agonizing death. He is not in control of his bodily functions, so that his bladder and his bowels empty themselves of their own accord. His consciousness is overwhelmed and extinguished by pain, so that he cannot communicate with us nor we with him. Now, it would be, technically, the easiest thing in the world to put a television camera in his hospital room and let the whole world witness this spectacle. We don't do it—at least we don't do it as yet—because we regard this as an *obscene* invasion of privacy. And what would make the spectacle obscene is that we would be witnessing the extinguishing of humanity in a human animal.

Incidentally, in the past our humanitarian crusaders against capital punishment understood this point very well. The abolitionist literature goes into great physical detail about what happens to a man when he is hanged or electrocuted or gassed. And their argument was—and is, that what happens is shockingly obscene, and that no civilized society should be responsible for perpetrating such obscenities, particularly since in the nature of the case there must be spectators to ascertain that this horror was indeed being perpetrated in fulfillment of the law.

Sex—like death—is an activity that is both animal and human. There are human sentiments and human ideals involved in this animal activity. But when sex is public, the viewer does not see—cannot see—the sentiments and the ideals. He can only see the animal coupling. And that is why, when men and women make love, as we say, they prefer to be alone—because it is only when you are alone that you can make love, as distinct from merely copulating in an animal and casual way. And that, too, is why those who are voyeurs, if they are not irredeemably sick, also feel ashamed at what they are witnessing. When sex is a public spectacle, a human relationship has been debased into a mere animal connection.

It is also worth noting that this making of sex into an obscenity is not a mutual and equal transaction, but is rather an act of exploitation by one of the partners—the male partner. I do not wish to get into the complicated question as to what, if any, are the essential differences—as distinct from conventional and cultural differences—between male and female. I do not claim to know the answer to that. But I do know—and I take it as a sign which has meaning—that pornography is, and always has been, a man's work; that women rarely write pornography; and that women tend to be indifferent consumers of pornography.[2] My own guess, by way of explanation, is that a women's sexual experience is ordinarily more suffused with human emotion than is man's, that men are more easily satisfied with autoerotic activities, and that men can therefore more easily take a more "technocratic" view of sex and its pleasures. Perhaps this is not correct. But whatever the explanation, there can be no question that pornography is a form of "sexism," as the Women's Liberation Movement calls it, and that the instinct of Women's Lib has been unerring in perceiving that, when pornography is perpetrated, it is perpetrated against them, as part of a conspiracy to deprive them of their full humanity.

The making of sex into an obscenity is not a mutual and equal transaction, but is rather an act of exploitation.

But even if all this is granted, it might be said—and doubtless will be said—that I really ought not to be unduly concerned. Free competition in the cultural marketplace—it is argued by people who have never otherwise had a kind word to say for laissez-faire—will automatically dispose of the problem. The present fad for pornography and obscenity, it will be asserted, is just that, a fad. It will spend itself in the course of time; people will get bored with it, will be able to take it or leave it alone in a casual way, in a "mature way," and, in sum, I am being unnecessarily distressed about the whole business. The *New York Times*, in an editorial, concludes hopefully in this vein:

> In the end . . . the insensate pursuit of the urge to shock, carried from one excess to a more abysmal one, is bound to achieve its own antidote in total boredom. When there is no lower depth to descend to, ennui will erase the problem.

2. There are, of course, a few exceptions—but a kind that prove the rule. *L'Histoire d'O*, for instance, written by a woman, is unquestionably the most *melancholy* work of pornography ever written. And its theme is precisely the dehumanization accomplished by obscenity.

I would like to be able to go along with this line of reasoning, but I cannot. I think it is false, and for two reasons, the first psychological, the second political.

The basic psychological fact about pornography and obscenity is that it appeals to and provokes a kind of sexual regression.

The basic psychological fact about pornography and obscenity is that it appeals to and provokes a kind of sexual regression. The sexual pleasure one gets from pornography and obscenity is autoerotic and infantile; put bluntly, it is a masturbatory exercise of the imagination, when it is not masturbation pure and simple. Now, people who masturbate do not get bored with masturbation, just as sadists don't get bored with voyeurism.

In other words, infantile sexuality is not only a permanent temptation for the adolescent or even the adult—it can quite easily become a permanent, self-reinforcing neurosis. It is because of an awareness of this possibility of regression toward the infantile condition, a regression which is always open to us, that all the codes of sexual conduct ever devised by the human race take such a dim view of autoerotic activities and try to discourage autoerotic fantasies. Masturbation is indeed a perfectly natural autoerotic activity, as so many sexologists blandly assure us today. And it is precisely because it is so perfectly natural that it can be so dangerous to the mature or maturing person, if it is not controlled or sublimated in some way. That is the true meaning of Portnoy's complaint. Portnoy, you will recall, grows up to be a man who is incapable of having an adult sexual relationship with a woman; his sexuality remains fixed in an infantile mode, the prison of his autoerotic fantasies. Inevitably, Portnoy comes to think, in a perfectly *infantile* way, that it was all his mother's fault.

It is true that, in our time, some quite brilliant minds have come to the conclusion that a reversion to infantile sexuality is the ultimate mission and secret destiny of the human race. I am thinking in particular of Norman O. Brown, for whose writings I have the deepest respect. One of the reasons I respect them so deeply is that Mr. Brown is a serious thinker who is unafraid to face up to the radical consequences of his radical theories. Thus, Mr. Brown knows and says that for his kind of salvation to be achieved, humanity must annul the civilization it has created—not merely the civilization we have today, but all civilization—so as to be able to make the long descent backward into animal innocence.

What is at stake is civilization and humanity, nothing less.

What is at stake is civilization and humanity, nothing less. The idea that "everything is permitted," as Nietzsche put it, rests on the premise of nihilism and has nihilistic implications. I will not pretend that the case against nihilism and for civilization is an easy one to make. We are here confronting the most fundamental of philosophical questions, on the deepest levels. But that is precisely my point—that the matter of pornography and obscenity is not a trivial one, and that only superficial minds can take a bland and untroubled view of it.

In this connection I might also point out those who are primarily against censorship on liberal grounds tell us not to take pornography or obscenity seriously, while those who are for pornography and obscenity, on radical grounds, take it very seriously indeed. I believe the radicals—writers like Susan Sontag, Herbert Marcuse, Norman O. Brown, and even Jerry Rubin—are right, and the liberals are wrong. I also believe that those young radicals at Berkeley who provoked a major confrontation over the public use of obscene words, showed a brilliant political instinct. Once the faculty and administration had capitulated on this issue—saying: "Oh, for God's sake, let's be adult: what difference does it make anyway?"—once they said that, they were bound to lose on every other issue. And once Mark Rudd could publicly ascribe to the president of Columbia a notoriously obscene relationship to his mother, without provoking any kind of reaction, the S.D.S. had already won the day. The occupation of Columbia's buildings merely ratified their victory. Men who show themselves unwilling to defend civilization against nihilism are not going to be either resolute or effective in defending the university against anything.

I am already touching upon a political aspect of pornography when I suggest that it is inherently and purposefully subversive of civilization and its institutions. But there is another and more specifically political aspect, which has to do with the relationship of pornography and/or obscenity to democracy, and especially to the quality of public life on which democratic government ultimately rests.

Though the phrase, "the quality of life," trips easily from so many lips these days, it tends to be one of those clichés with many trivial meanings and no large, serious one. Sometimes it merely refers to such externals as the enjoyment of cleaner air, cleaner water, cleaner streets. At other times it refers to the merely private enjoyment of music, painting, or literature. Rarely does it have anything to do with the way the citizen in a democracy views himself—his obligations, his intentions, his ultimate self-definition.

Those young radicals at Berkeley who provoked a major confrontation over the public use of obscene words, showed a brilliant political instinct.

Instead, what I would call the "managerial" conception of democracy is the predominant opinion among political scientists, sociologists, and economists, and has, through the untiring efforts of these scholars, become the conventional journalistic opinion as well. The root idea behind this "managerial" conception is that democracy is a "political system" (as they say) which can be adequately defined in terms of—can be fully reduced to—its mechanical arrangements. Democracy is then seen as a set of rules and procedures, and nothing but a set of rules and procedures, whereby majority rule and minority rights are reconciled into a state of equilibrium. If everyone follows these rules and procedures, then a democracy is in working order. I think this is a fair description of the democratic idea that currently prevails in academia. One can also fairly say that it is now the liberal idea of democracy par excellence.

The desirability of self-government depends on the character of the people who govern.

I cannot help but feel that there is something ridiculous about being this kind of a democrat, and I must further confess to having a sneaking sympathy for those of our young radicals who also find it ridiculous. The absurdity is the absurdity of idolatry—of taking the symbolic for real, the means for the end. The purpose of democracy cannot possibly be the endless functioning of its own political machinery. The purpose of any political regime is to achieve some version of the good life and the good society. It is not at all difficult to imagine a perfectly functioning democracy which answers all questions except one—namely, why should anyone of intelligence and spirit care a fig for it?

There is, however, an older idea of democracy—one which was fairly common until about the beginning of this century—for which the conception of the quality of public life is absolutely crucial. This idea starts from the proposition that democracy is a form of self-government, and that if you want it to be a meritorious policy, you have to care about what kind of people govern it. Indeed, it puts the matter more strongly and declares that, if you want self-government, you are only entitled to it if that "self" is worthy of governing. There is no inherent right to self-government if it means that such government is vicious, mean, squalid, and debased. Only a dogmatist and a fanatic, an idolater of democratic machinery, could approve of self-government under such conditions.

And because the desirability of self-government depends on the character of the people who govern, the older idea of democracy was very solicitous of the condition of this character. It was solicitous of the individual self, and felt an obligation to educate it into what used to be called "republican virtue." And it was solicitous of that collective self which we call public opinion and which, in a democracy, governs us collectively. Perhaps in some respects it was nervously oversolicitous—that would not be surprising. But the main thing is that it cared, cared not merely about the machinery of democracy but about the quality of life that this machinery might generate.

And because it cared, this older idea of democracy had no problem in principle with pornography and/or obscenity. It censored them—and it did so with a perfect clarity of mind and a perfectly clear conscience. It was not about to permit people capriciously to corrupt themselves. Or, to put it more precisely: in this version of democracy, the people took some care not to let themselves be governed by the more infantile and irrational parts of themselves.

I have, it may be noticed, uttered that dreadful word, "censorship." And I am not about to back away from it. If you think pornography and/or obscenity is a serious problem, you have to be for censorship. I'll go even further and say that if you want to prevent pornography and/or obscenity from becoming a problem, you have to be for censorship. And lest there be any misunderstanding as to what I am saying, I'll put it as bluntly as possible; if you care for the quality of life in our American democracy, then you have to be for censorship.

But can a liberal be for censorship? Unless one assumes that being a liberal *must* mean being indifferent to the quality of American life, then the answer has to be yes, a liberal can be for censorship—but he ought to favor a liberal form of censorship.

Is that a contradiction in terms? I don't think so. We have no problem in contrasting *repressive* laws governing alcohol and drugs and tobacco with laws *regulating* (i.e., discouraging the sale of) alcohol and drugs and tobacco. Laws encouraging temperance are not the same thing as laws that have as their goal prohibition or abolition. We have not made the smoking of cigarettes a criminal offense. We have, however, and with good liberal conscience, prohibited cigarette advertising on television, and may yet, again with good liberal conscience, prohibit it in newspapers and magazines. The idea of restricting individual freedom, in a liberal way, is not at all unfamiliar to us.

I therefore see no reason why we should not be able to distinguish repressive censorship from liberal censorship of the written and spoken word. In Britain, until a few years ago, you could perform almost any play you wished—but certain plays, judged to be obscene, had to be performed in private theatrical clubs which were deemed to have a "serious" interest in theater. In the United States, all of us who grew up using public libraries are familiar with the circumstances under which certain books could be circulated only to adults, while still other books had to be read in the library reading room, under the librarian's skeptical eye. In both cases, a small minority that was willing to make a serious effort to see an obscene play or read an obscene book could do so. But the impact of obscenity was circumscribed and the quality of public life was only marginally affected.[3]

If you think pornography and/or obscenity is a serious problem, you have to be for censorship.

I am not saying it is easy in practice to sustain a distinction between liberal and repressive censorship,

3. It is fairly predictable that someone is going to object that this point of view is "elitist"—that, under a system of liberal censorship, the rich will have privileged access to pornography and obscenity. Yes, of course they will—just as, at present, the rich have privileged access to heroin if they want it. But one would have to be an egalitarian maniac to object to this state of affairs on the grounds of equality.

especially in the public realm of a democracy, where popular opinion is so vulnerable to demagoguery. Moreover, an acceptable system of liberal censorship is likely to be exceedingly difficult to devise in the United States today, because our educated classes, upon whose judgment a liberal censorship must rest, are so convinced that there is no such thing as a problem of obscenity, or even that there is no such thing as obscenity at all. But to counterbalance this, there is the further, fortunate truth that the tolerable margin for error is quite large, and single mistakes or single injustices are not all that important.

This possibility, of course, occasions much distress among artists and academics. It is a fact, one that cannot and should not be denied, that any system of censorship is bound, upon occasion, to treat unjustly a particular work of art—to find pornography where there is only gentle eroticism, to find obscenity where none really exists, or to find both where its existence ought to be tolerated because it serves a larger moral purpose. Though most works of art are not obscene, and though most obscenity has nothing to do with art, there are some few works of art that are, at least in part, pornographic and/or obscene. There are also some few works of art that are in the special category of the comic-ironic "bawdy" (Boccaccio, Rabelais). It is such works of art that are likely to suffer at the hands of the censor. That is the price one has to be prepared to pay for censorship—even liberal censorship.

Very few works of real literary merit were ever suppressed.

But just how high is this price? If you believe, as so many artists seem to believe today, that art is the only sacrosanct activity in our profane and vulgar world—that any man who designates himself an artist thereby acquires a sacred office—then obviously censorship is an intolerable form of sacrilege. But for those of us who do not subscribe to this religion of art, the costs of censorship do not seem so high at all.

If you look at the history of American or English literature, there is precious little damage you can point to as a consequence of the censorship that prevailed throughout most of that history. Very few works of literature—of real literary merit, I mean—ever were suppressed; and those that were, were not suppressed for long. Nor have I noticed, now that censorship of the written word has to all intents and purposes ceased in this country, that hitherto suppressed or repressed masterpieces are flooding the market. Yes, we can now read *Fanny Hill* and the Marquis de Sade. Or, to be more exact, we can now openly purchase them, since many people were able to read them even though they were publicly banned, which is as it should be under a liberal censorship. So how much have literature and the arts gained from the fact that we can all now buy them over the counter, that, indeed, we are all now encouraged to buy them over the counter? They have not gained much that I can see.

And one might also ask a question that is almost never raised: how much has literature lost from the fact that everything is now permitted? It has lost quite a bit, I should say. In a free market, Gresham's law can work for books or theater as efficiently as it does for coinage—driving out the good, establishing the debased. The cultural market in the United States today is being preempted by dirty books, dirty movies, dirty theater. A pornographic novel has a far better chance of being published today than a non-pornographic one, and quite a few pretty good novels are not being published at all simply because they are not pornographic, and are therefore less likely to sell. Our cultural condition has not improved as a result of the new freedom. American cultural life wasn't much to brag about 20 years ago; today one feels ashamed for it.

How much has literature lost from the fact that everything is now permitted?

Just one last point which I dare not leave untouched. If we start censoring pornography or obscenity, shall we not inevitably end up censoring political opinion? A lot of people seem to think this would be the case—which only shows the power of doctrinaire thinking over reality. We had censorship of pornography and obscenity for 150 years, until almost yesterday, and I am not aware that freedom of opinion in this country was in any way diminished as a consequence of this fact. Fortunately for those of us who are liberal, freedom is not indivisible. If it were, the case for liberalism would be indistinguishable from the case for anarchy; and they are two very different things.

But I must repeat and emphasize: what kind of laws we pass governing pornography and obscenity, what kind of censorship—or, since we are still a Federal nation—what kinds of censorship we institute in our various localities may indeed be difficult matters to cope with; nevertheless the real issue is one of principle. I myself subscribe to a liberal view of the enforcement problem: I think that pornography should be illegal and available to anyone who wants it so badly as to make a pretty strenuous effort to get it. We have lived with under-the-counter pornography for centuries now, in a fairly comfortable way. But the issue of principle, of whether it should be over or under the counter, has to be settled before we can reflect on the advantages and disadvantages of alternative modes of censorship. I think the settlement we are living under now, in which obscenity and democracy are regarded as equals, is wrong; I believe it is inherently unstable; I think it will, in the long run, be incompatible with any authentic concern for the quality of life in our democracy. ♦

Questions for Discussion

1. Are you for or against the censorship of pornography?
2. Do you believe that pornography has the psychological effects that Kristol claims, particularly in terms of shaping character?
3. Do you agree with Kristol that the purpose of democracy is to achieve some version of the good life and the good society? What, then, is the purpose of the media within society?

The Case Against Censorship

Hollis Alpert

In the next reading Hollis Alpert explains that he opposes pornography, but he would not make it illegal or attempt to censor it. While he admits that pornography is of interest only to "unimaginative clods," he does not regard it as a great evil.

Alpert is speaking not only from experience as a film critic, but as an expert witness who has been called to testify in many of the major pornography cases of his time. He worries mainly about two things: Artistic repression, since "yesterday's obscenity is not necessarily today's," and the impracticality of censorship, which would require a vast national enforcement effort reminiscent of George Orwell's 1984. *In short, he says, pornography is a very small problem when compared to the problem of censorship.*

Reading Difficulty Level: 5.

The idea of censorship, particularly when it is aimed against pornography, has its attractions.

The idea of censorship, particularly when it is aimed against pornography, has its attractions. What could be seemingly more wholesome than newsstands cleansed of those obnoxious little weekly sheets filled with gleeful celebrations of sexual acts, the more perverse the more gleeful? In what way would the community—any community—be harmed if stores purveying stacks of photographs, glossy magazines, and film strips devoted to illustrating what used to be known as private parts were closed down by police order? Or if cinema houses featuring acts of "love," natural and unnatural, were shuttered? Little would be lost, really.

From *Censorship: For and Against*, Harold H. Hart, Ed. (New York: Hart Publishing Co., 1971). Reprinted by permssion of the author.

Even so, I am against censorship.

Over the years, I have had occasion, for journalistic reasons, to examine the question of censorship. I have met and talked to censors; I have been called as an "expert" witness in court cases aimed at suppressing certain films. I have viewed a good part of the Kinsey Institute's collection of pornographic film material and talked to members of the staff. I have read a great many of the available works, legal, sociologic, and psychiatric, on the subject. Nothing I have encountered has changed the opinion stated above.

This is not to say that I, personally, have not been offended by some of what I have encountered. Pornography, according to the dictionary on my desk, is "writing, pictures, etc., intended to arouse sexual desire." It is nonsense to claim, as some do, that there is no such thing as pornography, and that the use of the word indicates something suspicious about the mental and emotional state of the accuser. (There *can* be something suspicious, of course.) Pornography, simply, does intend to arouse sexual desire, and it fails as pornography if it doesn't. The problem is, for the habitual fancier of the stuff, that it takes more and more to arouse; and as a result, the tendency is for pornography to go farther and farther beyond the pale. Unfortunately, there are limits; and eventually, pornography, even for the addict, becomes dull and stale. The problem for the non-addict is that it becomes increasingly offensive.

What I dislike most about pornography is not the fact of its existence, but the level of its taste which, for the most part, is abysmal. Pornography represents a market—literary, journalistic, and cinematic—for unimaginative clods, neurotics of many different persuasions, and the untalented everywhere. All such professional matters such as style, taste, craft, and artistry give way to the tasteless, the brainless, the mercenary, the scatological, the obscene. What is so annoying about obscenity, however it may be defined, is the mockery of human aspirations it essentially represents. I do not admire those who so proudly flaunt the banner of their sexual liberalism, for they mock what has meaning for me.

Therefore, I am not for pornography; I am merely against censoring it.

I am not for pornography; I am merely against censoring it.

I do not regard pornography as an evil, but some of it I regard as an abomination of sorts. I do not know if exposure to pornography harms either the young, the middle-aged, or the old, but this is not to say that it does not have its effects. It obviously increases the incidence (to use a Kinsey Institute term) of masturbation; but since we hear that masturbation is not harmful and that it is difficult to masturbate to excess, this would not seem to be necessarily a harmful effect.

I see very little reason to forbid pornography, except that I don't happen to like it.

I don't share the zeal of those who claim for pornography certain benefits for the repressed, the frustrated, the bewildered, and the confused; but I can see where, in certain cases, it might help overcome inhibitions, unwanted modesty, lack of ardor. Yet talking or a modicum of alcoholic drinking can achieve pretty much the same results. As an antidote for boredom and loneliness, pornography may well have some positive value. And by its very frankness, pornography may actually represent an improvement, educationally speaking, for the young who pick up their sexual knowledge on the street or even in some of those earnest sex education courses in schools.

But, again, its therapeutic value needs establishing far more than has been done up to now. In no country where the question has been studied has it yet been found that pornography increases crime. Where rape has been found to be on the rise, it is almost invariably due to social and economic conditions, not to the presence of pornography. While it probably does lead to more sexuality—conjugal and private—for those exposed and attracted to it, pornography does not seem to lead to much in the way of sexual abuse, and here I am speaking primarily of violent forms of sexuality.

Pornography does not seem to lead to much in the way of sexual abuse.

In prisons, however, where pornography clearly is not present, sexual abuse, particularly of the homosexual kind, has become a matter of shocking public knowledge.

So I see very little reason to forbid pornography, except that I don't happen to like it.

On the other hand, the mentality of those censors I have met, and of those who advocate censorship, has often filled me with foreboding. All too frequently they have a way of equating pornography with "Godless un-American Communists," and the like. They cite religious tracts, even the Bible (generally overlooking the Song of Solomon) as "scientific" reason for their opposition to pornography and for the straitjackets they would impose on publishing and film making. The zeal with which they have attempted to counterattack against the glut of smut is worrisome in itself, revealing, perhaps, of a secret attraction to what they publicly proclaim as "sinful." Beware he of the impassioned rhetoric. All too often his voice, his words, his tone, remind of the righteous Goebbels.

But it is hardly news that there exists a tremendous amount of cant and hypocrisy among those who assume that a battle against pornography is a battle for law and order. While researching material for "History of Sex in Cinema," a lengthy series published by *Playboy Magazine,* I found that the very pillars of our society—veterans' groups, patriotic organizations, policemen and firemen—were the principal supporters of the hoary American institution, the "stag party." During these evenings one or two hours of a collection of stag reels would be shown to an all-male audience, and where did the evening's entertainment come from? Often enough from the local police or fire chief—confiscated, of course.

While testifying for the release of *I Am Curious—Yellow* and other cinematic works confiscated by U.S. customs, I was interested to find that in conversation afterward with U.S. attorneys, a good many of them were not at all in agreement, personally, with the views they presented to the jurors. "Of course the film should be shown," said one young assistant district attorney, "it's really all a kind of infighting." Those twelve good men and true didn't exactly convince me either that the jury system was the best way to achieve a fair verdict.

In one case the attorneys for Customs didn't even bother to make a case for their point of view. They merely exhibited the film in question to the jurors, most of whom seldom left their television sets at night. They had no way of knowing precisely what was commonly shown in theaters across the country and around the world. The attorneys counted on only one thing: that they would be shocked by what they saw. They were, and they declared the film guilty. Of what? Of offensiveness to them, naturally.

And just as naturally, an appeals court overturned their verdict.

But of judges, too, I happen to be suspicious. One U.S. District judge, while upholding a Customs seizure of a film, presumably saw more of a sexually nefarious nature in it than I did; and the horrified language he used to describe those "unspeakable acts" was remarkably similar to what I once heard thundered from a pulpit. Too little separation of church and state, in other words.

Thus, I am inclined to think that pornography and what to do about it should be taken out of the legal sphere entirely. Lawyers and judges use terms like "indecent" without bothering to define "decency." Is killing a stranger in a strange land "decent"? Decent soldiers do it every day, are encouraged to do it, and are not termed indecent except when they rape one or more of the local women. "Does the film appeal to the prurient interest. . . ?" I have long given up attempting to discover what "prurient interest" means—not even the dictionary is of much help here. "The average member of the community." Who is he? And where is this community? Times Square? Scarsdale? Spanish Harlem? Birmingham, Alabama?

The zeal with which censors attack pornography might reveal a secret attraction to what they publicly proclaim as "sinful."

The legal battle continues to be fought over a terrain that is inadequately defined, and perhaps cannot be. It may not even exist any longer.

For look what we have: pornography shown in hundreds of theaters, openly; magazines of a crudity unimaginable just a few years ago; "revolutionary" newspapers filled with erotic junk.

In 1964, when my colleague (Arthur Knight) and I began to look into the erotic content of films, beginning with a clip of Fatima, who electrified Chicago's Columbian Ex-

The urge to create pornography has always existed and presumably always will.

position in 1893 with her "dance of the veils" and was subsequently immortalized on film in 1906, the stag film was very much underground, photographs showing male and female organs were still taboo, and movies were still obeying a set of restraints known as the Production Code.

Fatima, we discovered, was the first victim of movie censorship. Peep show patrons had been vouchsafed a glimpse of her belly as she undulated, and the authorities of that day quickly stenciled picket fences over the offending portion of her anatomy. It was not more than ten years before the question of movie censorship reached the august halls of Congress; we very nearly had a national censorship statute. And the agitation for such a statute has not died down to this day.

What agitated censors in 1906, 1916, 1926, and 1936, would strike us as silly and laughable today. A bit of revealed nudity, for instance, as in *Ecstasy*, brought out the Comstockery in thousands across the land. Remember how long it took for one of the literary masterpieces of our century, *Ulysses*, to be sold publicly? It was not hard to reach a conclusion that standards of morality have varied, not to say gyrated, from period to period. Yesterday's obscenity is not necessarily today's. Would that all pornography were as gracefully written as, say, *Fanny Hill*.

Technology has made pornography the realm of everyman.

But one thing has always existed and presumably always will: the urge to create pornography. And even more widespread is the curiosity it evokes and has evoked in untold millions. All efforts to suppress pornography have failed. If made illegal, it springs up illegally. If made legal, it springs up legally. Presumably, we will always have it. And in a measure never envisioned at a time when Victorian gentlemen took up their pens to relate their erotic experiences, real or imagined.

For technology has made pornography the realm of every man. When it was discovered that the home movie camera could be employed to record bedroom activities in private, processing plants, in self-protection, refused to develop such intimate and illegal (then) goings-on. But there was always that unscrupulous employee who knew how to turn a buck by channeling furtive prints into the furtive stag market. Thus, in the Kinsey Institute collection and many private ones, are 8 mm and 16 mm films made by amateurs and employing amateurs who were mortified to discover (when, on occasion, the police knocked on their doors) that their private activities were being viewed by thousands.

Surcease came in the form of the Polaroid camera. Stills could be taken and developed instantly without recourse to a lab, and one wonders how much effect this "development" had on the stock of the corporation. More realism came with the Polaroid color camera. One reason, perhaps, that Americans were so ready for public pornography was that they had become so adept at producing it privately.

Then came the home video outfit, an expensive toy, surely, but its uses at home immediately evident for those with the insatiable urge to view the sexual behavior of themselves and sometimes intimate friends and sometimes intimate strangers.

That is why I strongly suspect that the legal terrain has all but vanished. Within another few years, there may be only one way of quelling the production of pornography and the voyeuristic habits it entails. And that is to bring on "Big Brother," which would amount to electronic surveillance and eavesdropping in every suspected home, in corn fields and on boats, in barns, garages, and garrets.

And that is the main reason I am so strongly opposed to the censorship of pornography, for it would require, sooner or later, a vast national (even international) effort.

Must we live with it then?

Probably so. But should an actual community wish to control its availability, it does have a certain amount of legal leeway. The Supreme Court has already ruled that a community, a legally defined entity such as a township or a county, can "protect" its young by prosecuting those who purvey it to those under a certain age.

If sexual debasement has been ruled out of court, so to speak, as it has been by many, many "sexologists," psychiatrists, and so-called experts on the subject, surely the debasement of taste has not. And there are ways to make clear to the community why pornography usually represents a nadir level of taste. This judgment can be made on the theater owner who prefers to show "X" films over the less gamier kind because "it sells better." No reason not to let him know, through editorials and in community meetings, that his profit motive does not necessarily make him an admirable member of the community.

But censor him not, please, for the dangers in such action are too great.

The current flood of pornography may well be a symptom, but not with any certainty, of a moral decline. What has declined is the hold of religious faith, doctrine, and institutions over human impulses and desires. Even among the more devout, a demarcation now is being made between sexual and spiritual morality. With an increasing degree of scientific inquiry into the nature of human sexuality, sex has been taken out of the realm of the morally harmful when practiced, so the legal language tells us, among consenting adults. Pre-adult sex is on the rise, too, according to gynecologists.

One aspect of the generational gap is the difference between how young people and their elders view

One reason, perhaps, that Americans were so ready for public pornography was that they had become so adept at producing it privately.

The censorship of pornography would require, sooner or later, a vast national (even international) effort.

No code of censorship could possibly do justice to the liberalized attitudes toward sex that exist today.

the sex act. Among the older generation, there is still evidence of guilt and anxiety over sexual behavior that varies from what they assume to be the norm—and that norm being the sexual act practiced primarily for the purpose of procreation between females over 18 and males over 21. Taboos, though seldom spoken, still exist. The newer generation has tossed aside most of these taboos. Community standards—by which censorship has traditionally justified itself—vary widely and extremely and often within the same community. No code of censorship could possibly do justice to the liberalized attitudes toward sex that exist today.

The day may not be far off when the commonly accepted standards of today may totally reverse themselves. In fact, right now the most commonly approved sexual activity—marital copulation aimed at producing an offspring—is being viewed with alarm by many. For the population explosion, long due, is now imminent. The population projections for 10, 20, and 30 years from now are eerily frightening. The awful pity of it is that the most economically and educationally blighted groups reproduce the most and perpetuate the problems that create the most stress in this society and others. A new sexual ethic—already existing in many groupings—that substitutes pleasure and release of tensions as its primary goals certainly makes more practical sense if the human race is to survive with any degree of comfort. For there would now seem to be a real need to channel sexual instincts so that they do not result in a cancerous surplus of population.

Perhaps today's pornography can even be regarded as a primitive expression of society's as yet inchoate recognition that sex, divorced from its procreative aspect and even from romantic and sentimental notions of love, can have its positive values. And it can also be regarded as evidence of the widespread frustration that exists in the sexual area, for pornography gets its appeal from its fantasy portrayal of sex. Fantasies arise when instincts are frustrated. In pornography females of any age and racial or ethnic coloration are ever-willing. Males are ever-potent. Thus, whether in the printed word, in photographs, or moving film images, pornography presents to the reader or the viewer fantasy situations that have something to tell us about the human sexual condition.

The artist, viewing his fellows through his personal vision, has through the ages attempted to portray what he sees and to present his understanding of it. Censorship in his case has perpetrated heavy and sometimes reprehensible blunders. Such recognized literary artists as Joyce and Lawrence were for many years relegated to pirated editions that were sold from beneath the counter. What untold artistic riches still reside, barred from the gaze of civilized man, in the Vatican's rumored collection of erotic treasures?

The censor, when presented with this kind of evidence of artistic repression, usually has as his answer that a few geniuses may be deprived of their potential publics, but the many will benefit. But how? The censor, by hoping to bar all that he deems reprehensible, commits errors of taste at least equal to those committed by the most foul of pornographers. For each rules out a vast spectrum of gradations and distinctions.

Of the two dangers, restrictive censorship on the one hand and unrestrained pornography on the other, the latter would seem to be the lesser, by far. For the former can create real harm. The unscrupulous politician can take advantage of the emotional, hysterical, and neurotic attitudes toward pornography to incite the multitude toward approval of repressive measures that go far beyond the control of the printed word and the photographed image. Even with a report from a presidential commission that concluded that no societal or individual harm has resulted from the existence of pornography, highly placed officials still took the warpath against its dissemination. Since there seems to be no substantive base for the officials' stand, one must suspect other motives, the simplest one being, perhaps, that of corralling the votes of conservative elements of the population. Implicitly asking for censorship, they overlook the question of who should do the censoring. Whom shall we trust? Whom can we trust? How shall we agree on standards and criteria? Perhaps they don't really care.

I rather suspect that, left alone, the various media tend to regulate themselves. The largest mass medium, television, presents no pornography at all that I know of, unless it be that of violence which some would translate into fantasy sexual sadism and masochism. Thus disguised, much pornography finds its way into the most respectable channels.

Left alone, the various media tend to regulate themselves.

Movies are regulated by their markets, and major film companies now espouse four main grades of entertainment which tend to take into account existing types of theatrical exhibition and audiences.

Radio has only the disguised kind of pornography—actually, no more than mild erotic stimulation—that comes from certain kinds of music and suggestive lyrics.

Magazines run a vast gamut; but no one is prevented from reading *Commentary* or *Harper's* by the fact that girlie publications are sold at the same corner newsstand.

Actually, the human mind is so various in its interests that its concentration on pornography takes but a minute portion of its attention. It is at worst a flea that bites an elephant. It requires little effort to overlook it entirely. It does take enormous effort to try to do something about it; and in the long run, it is no more productive than flailing at windmills. ♦

Pornography is at worst a flea that bites an elephant.

Questions for Discussion

1. Alpert states that "left alone, the various media tend to regulate themselves." Do you agree or disagree?
2. In your opinion, what would Hollis Alpert say about Irving Kristol's essay? What would Kristol say about Alpert's?

Suggested Readings

If you haven't read them yet, you'll be interested in Julia Cameron's "Sex for Kicks," (page 186), Gloria Steinem's "Women in the Dark" (page 415), and George Will's "America's Slide Into the Sewer (page 218), as well as the following

On the Effects of Pornography

Corliss, Richard, "X Rated," *Time* Vol. 135, May 7, 1990, p. 92 (7). Foul language and explicit sex in popular culture.

Leo, John, "Polluting Our Popular Culture," *U.S. News & World Report* Vol. 109, July 2, 1990, p. 15 (1). 2 Live Crew: Column.

Linz, Daniel and Edward Donnerstein, "Sexual Violence in the Media," *World Health,* April–May 1990, p. 26 (2). Psychological effects.

Nobile, Philip, "The Making of a Monster," *Playboy* Vol. 36, July, 1989, p. 41 (5). About Ted Bundy, the mass murderer who, on the eve of his execution, claimed that pornography encouraged him to commit his sex killings.

Smith, Tom W., "The Sexual Revolution," *Public Opinion Quarterly* Vol. 54, Fall 1990, p. 415 (21). The polls—a report.

On the Censorship of Pornography

Cooper, Chris, "STOP Fights Obscenity, Not Speech," *Playboy,* December 1988, p. 57 (3). Response to the article on STOP (Stand Together Opposing Pornography) in Kansas City.

Gest, Ted, "The Drive to Make America Porn-Free: Tougher, Smarter Law Enforcers Are Winning Big over Smut Peddlers," *U.S. World News & World Report* Vol. 106, February 6, 1989, p. 26 (2).

Gold, Philip, "As TV Races to the Edge, Society Pulls in the Reins," *Insight* Vol. 5, May 8, 1989, p. 12 (3). Organized protest against sex, violence and offensive topics influences advertisers.

Hawkins, Gordon, and Franklin F. Zimring, *Pornography in a Free Society.* Reviewed in: *The Annals of the American Academy of Political and Social Science,* May, 1990, p. 191 (3), and in *Society* January–February 1990, p. 89 (3).

James, David, "Hardcore: Cultural Resistance in the Postmodern," *Film Quarterly* Vol. 42, Winter, 1988, p. 31 (9).

Moretti, Daniel S., *Obscenity and Pornography: the Law Under the First Amendment and State Constitutions* (New York: Oceana Publications, 1984).

O'Sullivan, John, "Philistines at the Gate," *National Review* Vol. 42, June 11, 1990, p. 6 (2). Controversy over National Endowment for the Arts funding of art with erotic content. Editorial.

"Smut is Snuffed in the Undirty Dozen," *U.S. News & World Report* Vol. 108, April 23, 1990, p. 16 (1). Places that fight pornography.

Swan, Susan and Frika Ritter, "Do We Need Laws Against Pornography?" *Chatelaine,* Vol. 63, April, 1990, p. 44 (2). Pro and Con debate.

Swomley, John M., "STOP Campaign Is Unethical," *Playboy* Vol. 35, December, 1988, p. 59 (3). Stand Together Opposing Pornography.

Virshup, Amy, "The Missionary's Position: Reverend Donald Wildmon of Tupelo, Mississippi, Aims to Bring God to the Airwaves: To Networks and Advertisers, He's the Devil," *Manhattan, Inc.* Vol. 6, July, 1989, p. 84 (8).

Winbush, Don, "Bringing Satan to Heel: Tired of Sex and Violence on the Air, the Rev. Donald E. Wildmon has Discovered that the Quickest, Most Effective Route to the Networks' Conscience Is Through Their Pocketbooks," *Time* Vol. 133, June 19, 1989, p. 54 (2).

Defining "Pornography" Is a Perennial Question

Anderson, Harry, "The Battle of Cincinnati: A Sexually Explicit Exhibition Divides the City," *Newsweek* Vol. 115, April 16, 1990, p. 27 (1). Robert Mapplethorpe exhibit at the Contemporary Arts Center.

Monsma, Stephen V., "Yelling 'Fire' in a Crowded Art Gallery: Are There No Limits to Artistic Freedom of Expression?", *Christianity Today* Vol. 34, October 22, 1990, p. 40 (2).

"What is Pornography?", *ARTnews* Vol. 88, October 1989, p. 138 (6). Question posed to various artists, writers, directors and politicians, and their responses.

Another Interesting Question Is, "How Should Feminists React to Pornography?" In Many of the Current Cases, There Were Feminists on Both Sides.

Assiter, Alison, *Pornography, Feminism and the Individual,* reviewed by Veronica Grgoocock, *New Stateman & Society,* January 12, 1990, p. 35 (2).

Dolan, Jill, "Desire Cloaked in a Trenchcoat," *The Drama Review* Vol. 33, Spring, 1989, p. 59 (9). Feminists and pornography.

Dority, Barbara, "Feminist Moralism, 'Pornography,' and Censorship," *The Humanist* Vol. 49, November–December 1989, p. 8 (3).

Dworkin, Andrea, *Pornography: Men Possessing Women.* Reviewed in *The New Republic,* February 19, 1990, p. 27 (5), and *Publishers Weekly,* Sept. 22, 1989, p. 50 (1).

Wilson, Elizabeth, "Against Feminist Fundamentalism," *New Statesman & Society,* June 23, 1989, p. 30 (4).

Wolfe, Alan, "Dirt and Democracy: Feminists, Liberals, and the War on Pornography," *The New Republic* Vol. 202, February 19, 1990, p. 27 (5).

Violence

19

There are many theories about the effects of media violence, and all of them are probably true to some degree. Take, for example, the *modeling* or *observational learning* hypothesis, which tells us that children and even some adults might copy the violence they observe in the media. When the movie "The Burning Bed," about a woman who kills her abusing husband, was first broadcast, hundreds of abused women called social agencies for help. But at least one man beat his wife senseless and another set his wife afire, all of which were attributed to modeled behavior.

Aggressive stimulation also explains why real-life violence sometimes follows violence in the media. This theory states that antisocial violence can be triggered by media portrayals, and that this effect is particularly true when the violence is realistic and justified, such as when a hero solves a problem by beating up a bully.

Desensitization is another effect; the theory says that when people are exposed to increasing amounts of violence, it takes more and more to shock them, and they become more accepting of violence in their lives.

Fear is also an effect. George Gerbner and other researchers at the University of Pennsylvania have found that people who watch a lot of television tend to fear the world more than light viewers.

A final theory is called *catharsis,* and this is the only one that suggests a beneficial roll for media violence. According to catharsis theory, children and unstable adults feel purged of aggressive frustrations by observing violence in the media, so they don't need to act out violently. Unfortunately, there aren't many research findings that back up the idea of catharsis.

The readings in this chapter examine not just violence in the media but also the larger question of violence in society at large. The first reading, Peter Plagens' "Violence in Our Culture," analyzes the level and effects of violence in the various ways we entertain ourselves. In the second reading Elayne Rapping explains why she believes society, and not the media, is to blame.

(Photo by Bruce Cotler.)

Violence in Our Culture

Peter Plagens

According to Peter Plagens, a writer for Newsweek, *violence is out of control in American entertainment. He gives many recent examples to back up his point of view.*

Reading Difficulty Level: 2.

If artists, as Ezra Pound said, are "the antennae of the race," they're picking up some plenty bad vibes these days. A few years ago, who would have imagined that one of this season's top-grossing films (no pun intended) would be about a psychopath who not only murders women but also skins them? Or that the actor who plays the film's helpful psychopath—his quirk is cannibalism, but he finally helps track down the nasty psychopath—would be introduced by Jay Leno on "The Tonight Show" to a studio audience whose female contingent oohed and aahed as if he were Mel Gibson? Or that meanwhile, over in the world of letters, a young novelist would describe in revolting detail, women (and, less notoriously, men, children and dogs) being tortured and butchered? Or that his novel, suppressed by its original publisher, boycotted by feminists and savaged by critics, would become a best seller? Or that the best mind in American musical theater would conceive a snappy show about the assassins of American presidents? Or that MTV would still be blaring last year's hit song about a teen incest victim pumping a bullet into her daddy's brain?

Sure, ultraviolent fare has always been out there—but up until now, it's always been *out there,* on the fringes of mass culture. Nowadays it's the station-wagon set, bumper to bumper at the local Cinema 1-2-3-4-5, that yearns to be titillated by the latest schlocky horror picture show. And the conglomerated, amalgamated media corporations obligingly churn out increasingly vicious movies, books and records. Mayhem has gone mainstream.

America's addiction to make-believe violence is like any other addiction: it takes more and more to accomplish less and less. Thirty-two people get offed in "RoboCop" (1987); the 1990 sequel serves up 81 corpses. The makers of "Die Hard 2" (1990) really outdo themselves: up from the original's 18 to a body count of 264 (this, of course, includes a plane crash that takes out more than 200 in one fell swoop). "Die Hard 2" makes "The Wild Bunch," a stomachchurner back in 1969, look, in retrospect, like "National Velvet." In his horrifying "Silence of the Lambs," director Jonathan Demme straddles the old and the new, taking a gruesome plot and filming it with Hitchcockian discretion and taste. "We wanted to exploit people's endless fascination with scary stories, and provide them with a tremendously powerful version of a scary story, but we didn't want to upset their lives," he explains.

America's addiction to make-believe violence is like any other addiction: it takes more to accomplish less and less.

But people *are* upset by the assault of brutal imagery on radio, TV, in the theaters, in best-selling books. It is not any one film or program that

From *Newsweek,* April 1, 1991.

It is not any one film or program that is singularly disturbing, it is the appalling accretion of violent entertainment.

is singularly disturbing, it is the appalling accretion of violent entertainment. It is the sense that things have gotten out of control. And there is legitimate alarm at what all this imaginary violence might be contributing to in an increasingly dangerous real life. According to a *Newsweek* Poll conducted by The Gallup Organization in mid-March, 40 percent think movie violence is a "very great" cause of the real kind and an additional 28 percent see it as a "considerable" factor (only 11 percent answered "very little").

American Martyr

Even as we express such heartfelt concerns, we are packing into the multiplexes, lapping up the fictive blood, renting $1.5 billion worth of "action" videos a year and eagerly awaiting the next Stephen King novel, "Like most Americans, I get off on make-believe violence to some appreciable degree," says King. "I was raised to think Audie Murphy and Sergeant York and Davy Crockett were great American heroes, that George Armstrong Custer was a great American martyr, and that Saddam Hussein needed to have his butt kicked. . . . In a violent world, where violence continues to be perceived as a solution, violent make-believe will continue to be a part of that world's imaginative diet."

"Maybe," says "GoodFellas" director Martin Scorsese, "we need the catharsis of bloodletting and decapitation like the ancient Romans needed it, as ritual but not real like the Roman circus." The Roman analogy is somewhat terrifying. What kind of people find it fun to drop a Vio-lence cassette into the tape deck? *(Break your knee caps, left then the right / Next your eyeballs, lose your sight.)* What kind of people cheer lustily when Bruce Willis pokes an icicle through an eye socket into a baddie's brain? Or, to elevate the level of discussion, what value is it to have as talented a writer as Paul Theroux write "Chicago Loop," about a man who ties up a woman and literally gnaws her to death: "He snapped at the ragged flesh like a mastiff."

To be fair, violent narratives go back a lot further than the Steadicam—or even the Marquis de Sade. But the amount of explicit carnage in both serious and popular fiction has exploded, and there's a similar trend in detective novels, whose villains have become increasingly psychotic and whose medical examiners must find it increasingly hard to act blasé. Victims in James Ellroy's "The Big Nowhere"—praised even in the culturally conservative Wall Street Journal—have their eyes poked out, genitals mutilated and (ho hum) their flesh chewed. And worst of all is detective *fact*. Rex Miller's "Chaingang" Bunkowski isn't as compelling a monster as the real-life serial killer Randy Kraft, subject of L.A. Times reporter Dennis McDougal's forthcoming "Angel of Darkness." Kraft tortured and murdered 67 people, snapping Polaroids throughout. Our fascination with such material is older than Lizzie Borden. What's new is the obsessively detailed description of all 40 whacks, with their attendant shrieks and splatters.

Movie violence these days is likewise clearer, louder, more anatomically precise and a lot sexier. When a gunslinger got shot in some black-and-white potboiler, all we saw was a white puff of smoke and a dab of fake blood. When Jamie Lee Curtis takes one in the arm in the protracted climax to Kathryn Bigelow's "Blue Steel" (1990), there's a slo-mo eruption of ersatz fabric, gristle and blood that ends up looking as pretty as a nature film's blooming desert rose. And the claret of Curtis's precious bodily fluid is nicely set off against the light blue of her uniform, which is melded subtly with the gray Wall Street facades. This movie isn't so much directed as it is designed.

Ammo Clips

In the past decade, a growing number of feature directors (Ridley Scott and Adrian Lyne, among them) got their training in TV advertising. They are masters of seduction. They can make a soda pop glisten and crackle so you can almost feel it on your tongue. Give them 30 seconds and they can make you feel the wind in your hair as a car takes a curve on the screen. This new breed of director has been bringing ad techniques to the larger screen. But where, on the small screen, one hears a pop can hiss, on the large screen one hears black matte ammo clips clackering like castanets. Or bones being cracked. "Today we have the technology to do sequences that are louder and bigger and more effective than before," says "Die Hard 2" director Renny Harlin. But it's not simply that the special effects are more sophisticated than before, it's the way in which—and the purpose to which—directors use them. In Harlin's film, Bruce Willis seems to be constantly rolling across the floor, blasting away at several neo-Nazi ninjas at once, making plate-glass partitions swell and break and sparkle like lovely surfers' waves. It's all so insidiously yummy that you lean forward to get closer to the action. Our ability to feel compassion is brutalized by excessive brutality, especially when it's given that Hollywood sheen.

Movie violence these days is clearer, louder, more anatomically precise and a lot sexier.

In all of pop culture (as in most of society) women are the victims of choice. "Consider this a divorce!" Arnold Schwarzenegger bellows just before he blows his wife away in "Total Recall." Audiences love it: she got hers! Just like Laura Palmer, "Twin Peaks's" homecoming queen, who was actually a *slut*, got hers. An awful lot of hostility against women is being played out in popular culture these days, and it's not pretty.

She begged me not to kill her, I gave her a rose.
Then slit her throat, watched her shake till her eyes closed
Had sex with the corpse before I left her
*And drew my name on the wall like Helter Skelter**

That's from the Geto Boys' recent "Mind of a Lunatic," a sort of "American Psycho" with a bass line. It sold about half a million copies. Maybe that was 500,000 too many.

Playwright Steve Tesich (whose currently running "The Speed of Darkness" has its own moments of stunning violence) notes, "I haven't seen a single anti-rape movie that doesn't promote rape. The very manner in which sexual scenes are shot causes rape to look like an activity that is energizing."

There are those who argue that none of this means much. That no one, except perhaps a lone sicko, listens to the Geto Boys and then jumps the next woman who passes by. That healthy American families don't rush out to buy Uzis just because Schwarzenegger seems so cool wielding one. But the psychological road between real life and make-believe doesn't run only one way. In this society, mass-produced and mass-consumed movies, books, records and TV programs are a considerable part of our real lives; they contribute greatly to making us behave the way we do. To argue otherwise is to consign the arts to a total passivity—always mere reflections, never real influences. The popular arts are certainly quick enough to claim allegedly *positive* effects of their noble-farmer movies, triumph-of-the spirit novels and anti-drug rock records; they ought to accept some blame for the negative ones.

The popular arts are certainly quick enough to claim allegedly positive effects: they ought to accept some blame for the negative ones.

Pop a Cassette

When it comes to the impact media violence has on children, well, moviemakers are quick to insist these flicks are not for kids. At the same time, they will market an unnecessarily violent film like the Arnold Schwarzenegger vehicle "Kindergarten Cop" as if it were meant for kindergartners (it isn't), and they hide behind the Motion Pictures Association of America's ratings system, as if an R rating means much anymore. When was the last time a kid was turned away from a theater for being underage? Any child can catch a movie on cable or pop a cassette into a VCR. Five years ago Purdue University researcher Glenn Sparks surveyed 5- to 7-year-old kids in suburban Cleveland. Twenty percent said they'd seen "Friday the 13th"; 48 percent had seen "Poltergeist"—in almost all cases they'd watched them on cable.

By the age of 18, the average American child will have seen 200,000 violent acts on television, including 40,000 murders, according to Thomas Radecki, re-

*Copyright 1989, N-the-Water Publishing, Inc.

search director for the National Coalition on Television Violence. (The average 2- to 11-year-old watches TV 25 hours a week.) University of Illinois psychologists Leonard Eron and L. Rowell Huesmann studied one set of children for more than 20 years. They found that kids who watched significant amounts of TV violence at the age of 8 were consistently more likely to commit violent crimes or engage in child or spouse abuse at 30. "We believe . . . that heavy exposure to televised violence is one of the causes of aggressive behavior, crime and violence in society," they wrote in 1984. "Television violence affects youngsters of all ages, of both genders, at all socioeconomic levels and all levels of intelligence. . . . It cannot be denied or explained away."

Seven years later, Huesmann remains convinced: "Serious aggression never occurs unless there is a convergence of large numbers of causes," he says, "but one of the very important factors we have identified is exposure to media violence. . . . If we don't do something, we are contributing to a society that will be more and more violent."

As disturbing and repellent as its subject was, Demme carefully considered what to show and not to show when transferring Thomas Harris's best-selling "The Silence of the Lambs" to the screen—a book so horrifyingly graphic that some Hollywood honchos deemed it unfilmable. It's the story of FBI trainee Clarice Starling (Jodie Foster), whose assignment is to crack the case of a serial killer who skins his female victims. She turns for guidance to a brilliant but violently psychopathic psychiatrist, Dr. Hannibal (the Cannibal) Lecter (Anthony Hopkins).

Kids who watched significant amounts of TV violence at the age of 8 were consistently more likely to commit violent crimes or engage in child or spouse abuse at 30.

Terrifying Ideas

Much of the movie's power comes from Demme's delicate, masterful use of suspense—planting terrifying ideas in our heads but leaving out a lot of potentially horrific images. "For a two-hour movie, there are very few minutes devoted to anything that would be described as a scene of violence or gore," the director says. "It makes you think about awful things and tries to stimulate the audience to use their imagination as much as possible."

The movie was extremely successful at the box-office. There are morgues full of recent films with more hurtling bodies, more blood, more slo-mo sundering of flesh and more preening self-satisfaction when, toward the end, good guys start dishing out punishment. But none are more successful in turning an extraordinary cast, literate screenplay and arty cinematography into an ode to the subtleties of violence. In one harrowing sequence, when Lecter does attack his keepers, Demme used a classic Hitchcockian trick: just as the Master of Suspense never showed the knife actually piercing Janet Leigh in the shower scene in "Psycho," we never see Hannibal so much as nibble somebody's ear. But for the aftermath of that sequence, Demme decided the scene of carnage was so tame—a long shot that pulled away from any detail—that the audience was cheated. "We were beginning to betray the book and more importantly we weren't giving the viewer the elements with which to react with appropriate horror to the idea of someone doing this to other people," he says. So in the editing room, Demme added one brief, graphic closeup of one victim. "We slam in there for just a split second," he explains, "so either you've looked away or you're going to get the relief of the pullback, but we're not going to rub the audience's face in it."

Because we are being so inundated with violent images, it is almost impossible to resist growing numb.

'Dirty Reality'

Brief as it is, Demme didn't flinch at showing "real" carnage—nor did he back off from an autopsy scene that shows glimpses of a partly skinned female corpse. More than two decades ago, in praising the landmark gore of "Bonnie and Clyde," critic Pauline Kael wrote, "The dirty reality of death—not suggestions but blood and holes—is necessary. . . . It is a kind of violence that says something to us; it is something that movies must be free to use."

It's an important point, the key to the somewhat elusive distinction between "good" violence and "bad" violence; what is art and what is gratuitous. Few movies are as raw or vicious as Martin Scorsese's extraordinary "GoodFellas." The blood and bullet holes in his true-life tale of modern gangsters have a brutal immediacy. "I know that violence personally," Scorsese says. "Growing up I had a sense that it could erupt at any moment, over nothing. It is really frightening." To critics who've charged he went overboard on the gore in a scene where a Mafia lieutenant is executed, he admits, "I never intended the scene to be so bloody," but says he felt it was necessary to "engrave on the minds" the real cost of the mob lifestyle. Forget engrave; Scorsese shatters. There is nothing seductive about the violence in "GoodFellas."

At the same time, because we are being so inundated with violent images—both artful and manipulative—it is almost impossible to resist growing numb. We risk becoming insensitive to the horror of suffering, and that is probably what worries social scientists most. "Sadly enough, that [numbing] is normal," says Edward Donnerstein, a professor at the University of California, Santa Barbara. "Think of the tape of the Los Angeles police beating Rodney King. Everyone was initially horrified, but now, when you've seen it several times, you've become desensitized. Your outrage is moral, intellectual, not visceral."

Last winter, following the massive box-office success of the comparatively benign "Ghost" and "Pretty Woman," the press was quick to predict the doom of violent biggies. "People were saying, 'You've got to make romantic comedies and lighter fare'," says Joe Roth, chairman of Twentieth Century Fox, studio to both the very violent "Predator 2" and the cozy comedy "Home Alone" (the third biggest hit of 1990, with that charming tyke still blow-torching the burglars). "But it was just a combination of studio execs who think it makes their job easier to follow trends, and journalists who have their own biases. They think they can wish [violent movies] away quickly. But there's no monolithic response against movies like these. 'Total Recall' grossed $117.5 million and 'Die Hard 2' grossed $112.7 million—those movies delivered. And now here comes 'New Jack City,' and it's a hit and it's hardly an upbeat, romantic little movie."

Roth ain't seen nothin' yet. "On the escalator of violence, no sooner has some movie established itself as the new standard, the pressure mounts in Hollywood to outdo it," says Todd Gitlin, professor of sociology at the University of California, Berkeley. The new standard for violence might be the $88 million "Terminator 2: Judgment Day." This bulging Schwarzenegger epic indicates not only where Hollywood will continue to put its serious money, but its ethical rationale as well. James Cameron, director of both "Terminator" films, explains: "If you're making films for mass-audience consumption, there is a fine line between action, which is good, and violence, which is bad. Now, basically action and violence are the same thing. The question is a matter of style, a matter of degree, a matter of the kind of moral stance taken by the film, the contextualization of the violence."

If you're making films for mass-audience consumption, there is a fine line between action, which is good, and violence, which is bad.

And what, you may well ask, is the moral context of the sequel to the film in which our Arnold strolled into a police station and mowed down 17 cops? "I think of 'T2' as a violent movie about peace," Cameron says with a laugh. "And I'm perfectly comfortable with these ambiguities. It's an action film about the value of human life." Such a have-it-both-ways attitude is not confined to Hollywood: Bret Ellis maintains that "American Psycho" is an anti-greed tract; Eazy-E, of the rap group famous for "F— the Police," joined a $2,500-a-pop GOP club for luncheon with President Bush, and the same public that complains about too much violence in its entertainment lines up to shell out for more. For the time being there's no light—just more fright—at the end of the tunnel. ♦

The same public that complains about too much violence in its entertainment lines up to shell out for more.

Question for Discussion

1. Is American entertainment too violent? If so, what is the solution?

The Uses of Violence

Elayne Rapping

Elayne Rapping, a communications professor at Adelphi University, believes that media are being hypocritical when they bemoan the level of violence in today's entertainment. She says that the media love violence, because the American people love violence.
Reading Difficulty Level: 8.

Are the media sincerely interested in killing their own fatted calf by doing away with their most lucrative commodity—sensationalism?

There was something suspicious about the recent *Newsweek* cover story glaringly headed "Violence Goes Mainstream" and subtitled, "Movies, Music, Books—Are There Any Limits Left?" Here's a clue: After stating with predictable alarm that media violence, previously to be found (according to *Newsweek*) "on the fringes of mass culture," has now reached "the station-wagon set, bumper to bumper at the local Cinema 1-2-3-4-5," the writers go on to assign blame. Who done it? "The amalgamated, conglomerated media corporations" which irresponsibly and greedily "churn out increasingly vicious movies, books, and records," of course. Who did you think?

The problem is that *Newsweek* itself is a central part of that conglomerated media world. My point is not the obvious one that public outrage over media violence is circular and hypocritical, although it is. To end the discussion there is to contribute to the confusion, to raise circularity to yet another level.

The real issue is motive. Why do the media constantly engage in this kind of *mea culpa* exercise? Are they sincerely interested in killing their own fatted calf by doing away with their most lucrative commodity—sensationalism? Not likely.

So what's really going on here? By projecting outrage and dismay, the media divert attention from the real issues—on the one hand, the relationship of media violence to actual social violence, and, on the other, the media's own involvement and investment in violence. Two assumptions pervade—and mystify—the public discourse on the "problem" of violence in the media. First is the question of quantity—the notion that the sheer number and intensity of violent representations is the key to how serious the problem is: the more violence, the worse for society. This brings us to the question of effects—the implication that media violence causes social violence and

Reprinted by permission from *The Progressive*, 409 East Main Street, Madison, WI 53703. From the August, 1991, issue.

that, by extension, more media violence causes more social violence.

These assumptions are not totally false. Common sense tells us there is some kind of relationship between what we see and what we believe and do. If that were not the case, art would have no power at all. But the fuzziness of the thinking about "causes" and "effects" leaves out intentions. It assumes, implicitly, a McLuhanesque kind of self-directing technology that somehow has an innate affinity for violence. "The camera loves violence," Brian de Palma has said, but it is de Palma himself who loves violence, just as it is always human beings, with personal agency and intent, who create and enable media violence.

Public discourse on media violence rarely conveys a sense of social, political, or economic context. It is as if people—like the subjects of the very laboratory experiments used to "prove" the media's responsibility for violence—were locked up in isolated little rooms with nothing but media experience to respond to. This is nonsense.

In fact, it is only the obscurantism of the "objective" social-science methodology used by communications scholars that induces us to forget the role of the real world in people's violent behavior and, more interestingly, in the content of the media. Does television think up this stuff with its little electronic brain and imagination? Was there no violence before media? We can't simply ignore the way media violence reflects and reinforces what is already out there.

The people who create media content aren't off in some ivory tower of creative spontaneity, operating without guidelines. They work for cultural organizations which, as Raymond Williams reminded us long ago, are "both in themselves and in their frequent interlock or integration with other institutions . . . part of the whole social and economic organization at its most pervasive."

Common sense tells us there is some kind of relationship between what we see and what we believe and do.

In other words, there are powerful corporations and governments which fund and regulate media and make the rules about what gets aired and what doesn't.

If media cause violence, who causes media? By ignoring themselves—as *Newsweek* does, for instance—the media self-analysis perpetuates an illogical but widely held theory: that we, as a society, abhor violence but somehow got ourselves mass media that love it and feed it to us to the point where we become "addicted." This, too, is nonsense.

We, as a society, love violence, sanction violence, thrive on violence as the very basis of our social stability, our ideological belief system. As Rap Brown used to say in the 1960s, "Violence is as American as cherry pie."

We, as a society, love violence, sanction violence, thrive on violence as the very basis of our social stability, our ideological belief system.

It should hardly be surprising, then, that our mass media and en-

It should hardly be surprising, then, that our mass media and entertainment systems glorify violence. It is our national pastime.

tertainment system glorify violence. It is our national pastime. It is the favorite tool of our leaders. It is, most recently, the source of our nation's finest hour, the great Nintendo war against the heathen Arab hordes. Does anyone worry that the media ecstasy over the destruction of Baghdad might induce television viewers to commit acts of violence? As a nation, we engaged in massive, atrocious acts of violence, and the media spurred us on. Why is this less troubling or less interesting than the case of a single murderer known to have liked to watch horror films?

If there is more media violence today, that is because there is more real and potential violence.

If there is more media violence today, that is because there is more real and potential violence. We have the technological means of annihilating ourselves and others in spectacular and gruesome ways, and this technology is increasingly available to broader segments of the population. This is understandably scary, and people are right to be fascinated by it. It is a crucial issue in our public life. It is a matter that needs to be understood, to be symbolically acted out in terms of public narratives which seem to explain and contain the terrifying subject.

The mass media provide this service, just as art always has. For the most part, the media present myths and symbolic narratives which distort and obscure the realities of social violence, taking agency and responsibility away from the social structure that actually benefits from it and projecting it onto other kinds of symbolic beings—monsters, demons, cabals of futuristic conspirators. But sometimes, in the hands of innovative artists, the dominant genres and narratives are subverted and larger social truths emerge about the real nature of violence in America—who really causes it and who benefits from it.

This is the context within which we should evaluate media products. Two recently publicized works of violent fiction, Jonathan Demme's film, *The Silence of the Lambs,* and Bret Easton Ellis's novel, *American Psycho,* have been singled out for their portrayals of some of the most vicious acts yet presented to media audiences. *American Psycho,* about a yuppie banker who goes around torturing and murdering various oppressed people for the fun of it, has been roundly attacked and even boycotted by feminists for its depictions of rape and torture of women. *The Silence of the Lambs,* on the other hand, which shows a young woman FBI agent single-handedly capturing a mass murderer and torturer of women, has been treated as a serious and intelligent work of art. Yet it seems to me that of the two works, *The Silence of the Lambs* is by far the more offensive and symbolically threatening to women.

Both of these works are horrifying in their mystification of the real sources of class and gender violence. Both are wonderful examples of the way mainstream media invariably hide the larger social and political forces that encourage and condone massive violence against women and the poor. Both metaphorically project the evil onto fictional madmen who come across as not really human, as beyond the limits of human nature and therefore not really part of the social community we inhabit.

Ellis's hero, for example, taunts a crippled homeless man with promises of money and then, in excruciating slow-motion detail, mutilates him. Metaphorically, of course, there is truth here about class relations and the violence done to the urban poor by the economic horrors of the 1980s. The yuppies did thrive as the poor increasingly suffered and even died. The problem is that Ellis's hero is a madman and a monster and what he does is projected as a physical, rather than political or economic, act of genocide.

Such fantasies use symbolic acts of violence to purge us of the horror of class injustice without ever displaying it in its true form. Poverty is a form of physical torture, but its form is complex and its perpetrators are vast and invisible. *American Psycho*'s simplistic scapegoat is metaphorically and emotionally useful but politically and intellectually mystifying.

The Silence of the Lambs does a similar thing. Violence against women, both economic and physical, is rampant and, again, the plot attributes it to a fictionalized monster so inhuman and grotesque as to attract no sense of identification from male audiences. What seems to save this film is the tough, attractive heroine, FBI agent Clarice Starling, played by Jodie Foster. She is, on the surface, the symbolic (feminist) counterpart to her creepy prey. Since she catches and kills the mass murderer she stalks, it seems that feminism triumphs and the sexist monster dies.

Except that he doesn't die. The real monster in this film is not the pathetic if terrifying transvestite killer but another mass murderer of women, the brilliant psychiatrist and cannibalistic killer Hannibal Lecter, played with suave and sexy charm by Anthony Hopkins. He is the expert Starling consults for help. He is the male presence who toys with her, intellectually and sexually, and who is always one step ahead of her, in control of their every encounter and her every move. There is never a moment in this film when Lecter's male gaze does not follow, intimidate, and penetrate Starling. She is his prey as much as the other monster is hers, and his sexual interest in her—played out as a flirtation of the most stereotypically sexist kind—is apparent.

Like the women-in-danger films of the 1970s, in which a madman stalked a teenage woman and mutilated her as the camera projected the action from his view point, *The Silence of the Lambs* conveys an eerie sense of sexual terror because the power relation between the two principals is so skewed toward the

Mainstream media invariably hide the larger social and political forces that encourage and condone massive violence against women and the poor.

male and because, in the end, he goes free, leaving Starling in a state of permanent anxiety because he may at any moment decide to come after her. The only reason he does not do so, he makes clear, is because he finds her cute.

This film and its hero (the cannibal) says volumes about the nature of violence against women and sexism in this society. It has little to do with the poor transvestite scapegoat who is purged. It is a glorification and reinforcement of the sexual and intellectual power relations of men and women. And it has nothing to say about political or economic realities. Violence again is a fictional ploy used to obscure political realities, to displace social evils onto physical crimes, and to replace generalized social violence with single super-human monsterdom.

We need to resist the censorship argument because it is so likely to backfire.

Violence is a fictional ploy used to obscure political realities, to displace social evils onto physical crimes and to replace generalized social violence with single superhuman monsterdom.

The point of these observations is not to call for censorship. After all, whose criteria, whose "readings" of these texts would we use? Jesse Helms's? We need to analyze them for what they reveal about social realities hidden beneath cultural myths. We need to educate ourselves in critical thinking. Popular art gives clues to social truths we ought to understand.

Even if we were to favor some form of censorship, the current thinking wouldn't help us much. Its equation of numbers and "badness" is obviously wrong. Meaning isn't interpreted by counting but by analyzing according to qualitative criteria. It isn't number of bodies (relatively few) that makes *The Silence of the Lambs* more disturbing than *American Psycho.* It is the elegant and attractive portrayal of misogyny as a terrifying, sexy game. The novel is ugly and its hero is vile. The film is entertaining and its hero/villain is a classic cinematic hunk.

But most importantly, we need to resist the censorship argument because it is so likely to backfire. No matter how much we deplore the sleaze and gore, we must keep a clear head about how they are used. Sleaze and gore are, after all, sometimes the most effective agents of consciousness-raising. It all depends on the nature of the work being considered. Films like *GoodFellas* or *River's Edge,* which depict wholly amoral, sociopathic acts of murder, are, in fact, attacks on the social realities supporting and encouraging violence.

A TV movie like *The Burning Bed,* which tells the story of Francine Hughes, the battered wife who set her husband's body on fire and was acquitted, was actually exemplary in its feminist depiction of the many social, cultural, and economic reasons for the epidemic of woman-battering. It revealed, in horrifying detail, the ideological and institutional factors that allowed Hughes—and so many other women—to suffer through years of torture without legal, social, or familiar support.

The day after the movie aired, to an audience of seventy-five million, many women left their abusive husbands for shelters they did not previously know existed. On the other hand, four women burned their husbands to death and one man set his wife on fire. How does one evaluate the "effects" of this very violent film? Did it cause five acts of violence or was its effect far more subtle and significant? Would we want it to be toned down or even censored?

Hardly. In fact, a comparison of *The Burning Bed* and *The Silence of the Lambs* reveals how art works, in its technique, to suggest meanings that are in no way related to the raw content of what the films present. Both films show vicious men torturing women. But camera angles, point of view, social detail, and context all serve to make the two films different in emotional effect. One creates a creepy fantasy of superhuman evil and lets sexism triumph dramatically; the other pulls the masks away from institutional complicity in domestic violence.

So where does this leave us? With luck a few steps ahead of the *Newsweek* Syndrome, the hypocritical and endless media ploy of screaming "Ain't it awful!" and "Let's ban it!" The problem, after all, is not media violence but real violence. We need to focus on the causes and the nature of that phenomenon.

The problem, after all, is not media violence but real violence. We need to focus on the causes and the nature of that phenomenon.

The media will be as violent as the world that creates them. Sometimes that's disturbing, but sometimes it is salutary. The media, like other public arenas, are a battleground—contested terrain in which ideological meanings are played out. As consumers, critics, and artists, we have to be in the game. But first we must know the rules. ♦

Question for Discussion

1. Do you agree that violence is an inherent part of American culture? Why or why not?

Suggested Readings

Those who are interested in the analysis of media violence might want to reread Gloria Steinem's "Women in the Dark," page 415, and/or Julia Cameron's "Sex for Kicks," page 186.

More On Violence in the Media

"Ads, Violence and Values," *Advertising Age* Vol. 61, April 2, 1990, p. 12 (1). Editorial dealing with the slaying of inner city teens over their Nike Air Jordan tennis shoes.

Baker, Susan, and Tipper Gore, "Some Reasons for 'Wilding': We're Sending a Message to Our Kids that Brutality is OK," *Newsweek* Vol. 113, May 29, 1989, p. 6 (2). Column.

Hoban, Phoebe, " 'Psycho' Drama," *New York,* December 17, 1990, pp. 32–37 (6). Simon and Schuster decided, at the last minute, that Bret Easton Ellis's slice-and-dice novel, *American Psycho,* was too loathsome to print. This is the inside story behind this decision and its ramifications.

Larner, Jeremy, "Violence for Fun and Profit," *Dissent* Vol. 36, Spring, 1989, p. 268 (3).

Linz, Daniel and Edward Donnerstein, "Sexual Violence in the Media," *World Health,* April–May 1990, p. 26 (2). Psychological effects.

Lopiparo, Jerome J., "Aggression on TV Could Be Helping Our Children," *Intellect,* April, 1977. This reading can also be found in the third edition of *Mass Media Issues,* p. 240.

Pattison, Robert, "The Mean Machine?", *The Nation* Vol. 247, August 13, 1988, p. 140 (3). Violence on television and violence in society.

Reschloss, Steven, "TV's Life of Crime," *Channels: The Business of Communications* Vol. 10, September 24, 1990, p. 12 (6). Violent Crime on television. (News).

Signorielli, Nancy, and George Gerbner, eds., *Violence and Terror in the Mass Media: An Annotated Bibliography* (Westport, Conn.: Greenwood Press, 1988). Comprehensive list of annotated citations, mostly from scholarly journals and books. Deals with terrorism and pornography as well as media violence. The editors are two of the most respected researchers of media violence.

Spock, Benjamin, "How On-Screen Violence Hurts Your Kids," *Redbook* Vol 170, November, 1987, p. 26 (2). A column by the famous baby doctor: what to do about mediated violence.

Yang, Ni and Daniel Linz, "Movie Ratings and the Content of Adult Videos: The Sex-Violence Ratio," *Journal of Communication* Vol. 40, Spring, 1990, p. 28 (15).

Privacy

20

Privacy is a broad issue. Legally, it involves everything from the unauthorized use of a name in an advertisement, to unlawful trespass in pursuit of a story. In this chapter, we first look at the way public figures give up their privacy. Then we look at the controversy over whether or not to report the name of a rape victim. Finally, we look at the practice of ''outing,'' the exposing of closet gays by some members of the gay community.

Whatever Happened to Privacy?

Julia Reed

In the following reading Julia Reed, an editor of Vogue, *analyzes the decline of private life for public figures.*

Reading Difficulty Level: 2.

An American has no sense of privacy. He does not know what it means. There is no such thing in the country.

George Bernard Shaw

Shaw may not have found much privacy in America in 1933, but millions of other people did. It was, after all, the same year FDR was sworn in as president, a man who managed to keep the fact that he could not even stand up by himself from the majority of his fellow Americans. Shaw was obviously onto something though—in the years since his pronouncement, privacy has indeed become the nation's most devalued commodity. The tip-off should have come in 1965 when LBJ proudly revealed his gall-

FDR managed to keep the fact that he could not even stand up by himself from the majority of his fellow Americans.

Donald Trump poses aboard his yacht. (Photo by Bruce Cotler.)

bladder scar to reporters—and TV cameramen—on the Bethesda Naval Hospital lawn. Today the entire nation presides over the removal of every presidential polyp, the dispensing of the first lady's every eyedrop. Shaw would have a lot to go on about.

In the beginning, publicity was managed—an art perfected by the early Hollywood moguls.

In the beginning, publicity was managed—an art perfected by the early Hollywood moguls to control public sentiment toward their stars, much as FDR's handlers controlled public sentiment toward their president. The news generated by the studios rarely intruded into the stars' private lives, because it was almost all fabricated. Joan Crawford was portrayed as Mommie Perfect; Rock Hudson's brief marriage was the smoke screen between the public and his private life. The press simply chose not to expose FDR's infirmity, just as JFK was portrayed as the quintessential family man. But the facades began to crack. Studio power began to ebb, and once invented, publicity could no longer be contained. With the all-seeing eye of television on them, reporters were forced to report all that could be seen. Finally, as the truth behind the smoke screens was revealed, the public felt cheated, then infused with the idea of the right to know. The grubbier, the more private the truth, the more real it seemed.

Now there are so many shovels to dish the dirt that we have become not just inured to it but addicted. The readership of *The National Enquirer* has risen to 20 million; last year the tabloid fetched $412.5 million at auction. In 1973 the nation gasped when Pat Loud told husband Bill their marriage was over on prime-time television; today we can tune in to *Divorce Court* and see the same thing. Alcoholics Anonymous has become a contradiction—the drying out of a star is the stuff of press conferences and TV movies. Last year novelist Allan Gurganus breezily discussed the late John Cheever's sexual desire for him, and why not? Cheever's own family made the author's love letters public.

Former hostage Terry Anderson recaptured some of his privacy following his release—but it took time. (Photo by Bruce Cotler.)

At his unsuccessful Senate confirmation hearings, John Tower's record was overlooked in favor of discussion of his more interesting private life. Never in our history has there been such a ravenous appetite for the intimate detail. When we run out of celebrities, we create new ones from increasingly unlikely sources. Chefs and agents, florists and leveraged-buy-out artists are among the darlings of the moment. Ladies once had their names in the paper the proverbial three times; now they hire high-powered publicists to launch their New York social careers with a gusto that would astonish even Undine Spragg. The gossip columnists who chronicle their exploits have become celebrities in their own right. Full disclosure is a term that no longer applies solely to politicians. We seem to require it of everybody who steps outside.

Full disclosure is a term that no longer applies solely to politicians. We seem to require it of everybody who steps outside.

Let me tell you about the very rich. They are different from you and me.

F. Scott Fitzgerald

Right. Once they were real quiet. They dressed down, stayed home, and never aired their laundry even if it was clean. J. P. Morgan so detested the limelight that he never attended a public meeting or made a single speech. In the eighteenth and nineteenth centuries privacy

In the eighteenth and nineteenth centuries privacy was almost exclusively a right of privilege.

was almost exclusively a right of privilege. While lower-class couples shared rooms with their children, the rich built houses with drawing rooms—to which they literally withdrew. "A lot of energy went into the line between what is public and what is private," says Robert Dalzell, a history professor at Williams College and author of *The Enterprising Elite.* "Now that line seems to have disappeared." Indeed. With the debut of *People,* Tom Wolfe marveled that the magazine "always showed you other people's living rooms." Now whole lives are put on display. When Donald Trump hired his wife, Ivana, to run the Plaza Hotel, he gleefully repeated the embarrassing fact that her salary was one dollar and all the dresses she could buy. During Malcolm Forbes's Moroccan birthday bash, even the guests' sleeping arrangements were released to the press. "People today are less secure in their position," says Dalzell. "If there are no generally agreed upon, long-established standards to define position, people must identify themselves as people of consequence. They invite the media in to portray them as people of prominence." Public relations guru John Scanlon agrees: "Victory in business is not enough. They get little satisfaction unless that victory is widely known."

Today, people must identify themselves as people of consequence. They invite the media in to portray them as people of prominence.

Never turn down an opportunity to have sex or go on TV.

Gore Vidal

It's not just the rich who are dying to expose themselves. Everybody wants to talk to Oprah and Geraldo and Phil. "It's that whole culture of narcissism thing," says Scanlon. "Everyone thinks his experience is at least as important as everyone else's." So we take to the tube in droves, complaining about our neighbors' dogs to Judge Wapner, about our spouses' not sleeping with us to Phil. Last year, for two days, Oprah Winfrey aired a tape of an intensely emotional marriage counseling workshop with real couples whose marriages were lost or saved before our eyes. Sally Field and Patrick Swayze are notorious for their Barbara Walters weeps. Walters thinks it's the camera: "When that gigantic eye is turned on them, they're almost afraid not to give something."

If any one event legitimized such behavior, it was PBS's 1973 broadcast of *An American Family,* documenting the lives of the seven Louds of Santa Barbara. During twelve hour-long episodes—edited down from three hundred hours of videotape recorded over seven months—millions of Americans were privy to the Louds' most private moments. Lance Loud marched out of the closet wearing blue lipstick and silk scarves, while his mother confronted her husband with his infidelity. By the end of the show the parents had split up, and American TV was changed forever. The Louds embraced the camera and

Latoya Jackson and Marla Maples meet the press. (Photo by Bruce Cotler.)

embodied Daniel Boorstin's definition of celebrity: they were famous just for being famous. It was an idea with a future—visibility has become an emblem of immortality, and everybody wants to live forever.

Visibility has become an emblem of immortality, and everybody wants to live forever.

In a world that is in no way stable, it is not clear any longer what standards are supposed to guide behavior.

Robert Dalzell

A society that no longer values privacy sooner or later becomes a society devoid of manners. Every American child who got kicked under the dining room table quickly learned that "some things just aren't discussed." But now things we asked innocently as children are asked purposefully by adults. Recently a reporter actually asked Barbara Bush how much she weighed, a figure, the first lady replied dryly, that even the president doesn't know. After Nancy Reagan had a mastectomy, public debates raged over a decision that had already been made—and acted on—by her and her doctor. Kitty Dukakis was hailed for admitting first her addiction to speed, then to alcohol, but when she drank rubbing alcohol the armchair doctors went at it again. Psychologists who had never met her speculated on why she might have done it in *The Boston Globe. People's* cover promised that "those close to her try to understand why she took a drink that could have killed her."

When the woman from the Eyewitness News team leans down to ask, "How did you feel when your sister got hit by a truck?" we no longer wince.

Among the most astounding revelations of the insider-trading scandal was that top executives who had not yet been proved guilty or even formally charged with a crime could be shackled in front of their colleagues and dragged out of their offices onto the street as the TV cameras rolled. They roll during private disasters as well as public. When the woman from the Eyewitness News team leans down to ask, "How did you feel when your sister got hit by a truck?" we no longer wince, we expect it. Kudos go to those who get the story first. No one is surprised that the sensational *Weekly World News* ran shots of Ted Bundy in the morgue, but last November even CNN's cameras brought us lingering postmortem shots of David Blundy, the heroic British journalist killed in El Salvador. On the screen, a cameraman's hand was shown lifting the sheet.

New Dukakis tragedy

KITTY DRANK RUBBING ALCOHOL

If I didn't someone else would.

Susan Cheever

On why she wrote a revealing memoir of her father, the novelist John Cheever

The current climate has given rise to the peculiar trend of going public as a defensive act. Susan Cheever says she wrote *Home Before Dark*, an acclaimed account of her father's life that includes discussions of his social pretensions, alcoholism, and his numerous affairs with men and women, as a sort of preemptive strike against the inevitable unauthorized biographers. Likewise, her brother edited their father's letters for publication. James Joyce's grandson recently announced that he burned the letters of his aunt, Joyce's daughter, because "I didn't want to have greedy little eyes and greedy little fingers going over them." Janna Malamud Smith has not yet decided what she will do with the letters of her own father, Bernard Malamud, but the choice is clear: destroy or reveal. "The fact is," says Malamud Smith, "if someone in your family has written good fiction, his privacy—and yours—has been traded away."

The current climate has given rise to the peculiar trend of going public as a defensive act.

Barbara Walters says she gets such publicity-shy guests as Robert Mitchum and Clint Eastwood on her specials for the same defensive reasons. "If they want to talk, TV is safer than newsprint. They set the tone. We don't talk to the manager they fired, the director they worked for." Roseanne Barr appeared after the *Enquirer* ferreted out the daughter she had given up for adoption. Eastwood came on after lurid tabloid accounts of his breakup with Sondra Locke. "In his own quiet way," says Walters, "he felt he could set it straight."

A tragic example of celebrity beat-the-clock is the story of Paul Michael Glaser, a film director and the star of TV's *Starsky and Hutch*, who was forced to make public his family's battle with AIDS after the *Enquirer* threatened to do it for him. Glaser's wife, Elizabeth, had become infected with AIDS after a blood transfusion. Her daughter, whom she nursed, died from the disease, and the couple's five-year-old son has tested positive. "We appealed to the *Enquirer*," says Paul Glaser. "We begged them not to run the story, but they said it was newsworthy." The Glasers' only choice was to beat the paper to the punch. They told their story to *The Los Angeles Times* and founded the Pediatric AIDs Foundation. Nonetheless, says Elizabeth, "this is very frightening, to imagine that people we don't know will find out the most private parts of our lives."

I never said, "I want to be alone." I only said, "I want to be left alone."

Greta Garbo

Wanting to be left alone invariably guarantees that someone will come after you. In 1955, William Faulkner was so distraught over a *Life* magazine profile he had objected to that he published a diatribe in *Harper's* ("On Privacy, the American Dream:

Wanting to be left alone invariably guarantees that someone will come after you.

What Happened to It") renouncing the entire American system. It is impressive, however, that he managed to hold the magazine off for eight years. Two years ago, J. D. Salinger had to file suit to block biographer Ian Hamilton's use of the author's letters—and in doing so was forced to expose more about himself than he had during the preceding twenty-three years. Novelist Thomas Pynchon has more successfully avoided the limelight—he has never given an interview and he hasn't been seen since 1963—but his mystique is such that a monthly newsletter containing reprints of his work and news of possible sightings circulates around the country. In the past decade writers like C. David Heymann and Kitty Kelley have earned millions publishing unauthorized biographies—Simon & Schuster will almost certainly earn a bigger return on its investment from Kelley's unauthorized biography of Nancy Reagan than it will from Ronald Reagan's own memoirs.

Nothing stops the paparazzi from getting a desired picture – except maybe a punch, and even then the rewards are handsome.

Nothing stops the paparazzi from getting a desired picture—except maybe a punch, and even then the rewards are handsome. When Cher's boyfriend Rob Camilletti knocked out a photographer who was staking out the star's house, fellow photographer Philip Ramey took pictures of the confrontation that have earned him tens of thousands. At Madonna's wedding helicopters from the tabloids whirred overhead, and at Michael J. Fox's Vermont nuptials, an *Enquirer* reporter tried to abduct Fox's fiancée's grandparents and offered money to an inn employee to carry a hidden camera. The couple fled a honeymoon in Anguilla after the *Enquirer* sent a team of six, but the *Star* caught them on Martha's Vineyard anyway.

Crucial to the public image of many current stars is the idea of aloneness, an exemplary shunning of the limelight, which must in itself be publicized.

Of course, some people employ Garbo's line as a strategy. Crucial to the public image of many current stars is the idea of aloneness, an exemplary shunning of the limelight, which must in itself be publicized. Though she occasionally runs from Ron Galella, Jackie Onassis obviously enjoys being a public figure; at the same time she earns admiration for having a private life. Sean Penn made a career of punching out photographers who hounded his then wife, Madonna. These days, he probably wishes there was still a photographer around for him to hit. It's easy to disdain the limelight when you know it will come after you.

You won't have Nixon to kick around anymore.

Richard Nixon

after the 1962 California gubernatorial election.

Unfortunately for Nixon, he was wrong. But his initial desire to drop out has been shared by many who have felt the real pain caused by the public digging into private lives. Socialite Ann Woodward killed herself after the publication of Truman

Capote's "La Côte Basque," a vengeful, gossipy short story that centered on Woodward's alleged murder of her husband. Howard Hughes became so reclusive and obsessed that upon his death it was said, "It's a shame Howard Hughes had to die to prove he was alive."

Barbara Walters thinks the invasion of privacy that automatically accompanies political life will discourage more and more people from entering it. Certainly the private lives of elected officials have never undergone closer scrutiny. When Bess Truman was first lady, she wouldn't even release to the press what she wore to White House teas; today every thread is accounted for (Was it a loan? Are the pearls real?). But Walters could be wrong. It could just be that more and more politicians will learn to put the proper "spin" on their private lives. Gary Hart invited the public to intrude on his private life, and it doomed his career. But George Bush made his private life work for him when almost nothing else would. He bared his emotions on the death of his daughter and won a debate. He invited the family to Kennebunkport and Roger Ailes made a video that may have put him over the top. By capitalizing on a very real strength, Bush was transformed from shrill and tense to warm and compassionate in the mind of the electorate. To refuse to be kicked around anymore defies the reality of political life. In an age when privacy is meaningless and private life is all, it seems pointless to capitalize on anything else. ♦

Politicians will learn to put the proper "spin" on their private lives.

In an age when privacy is meaningless and private life is all, it seems pointless to capitalize on anything else.

Question for Discussion

1. Do you agree with George Bernard Shaw that "An American has no sense of privacy"?

Rape: Report the Name

Michael Rouse

The issue of whether or not to publish the name of a rape victim strikes to the heart of the privacy issue. A rape is certainly news, but where does the public's right to know begin to negate the victim's right to privacy?

Two recent rape cases have kept this issue close to the forefront of the news. The first was the "Central Park Jogger" case (see George Will's article, page 218) and the second was the case of William Kennedy Smith.

Michael Rouse, who was the Managing Editor of the Durham (N.C.) Morning Herald at the time this article was written, believes that the victim's name should be published. Using an argument that is similar to Garry Wills's in Chapter 15, he explains why he believes publishing the name will help remove the stigma of being a rape victim.

Reading Difficulty Level: 3. Acceptance of the basic idea might be a problem here.

Those newspaper editors lacking the benefit of divine guidance usually call upon their own objective judgment when deciding such matters as the handling of crime stories. They consider how much information a reader wants and how much of it is important. What happened to whom? Did the police arrest anyone? The editors insist that their newspapers answer these questions.

That is what newspaper editors do usually—but not always. Not when rape is involved. It is here that many of us go out in search of divine guidance. We should not. We should treat rape much the same way we treat other crimes. (I do not claim divine guidance. Still, I cannot resist the opportunity to evangelize. It's the Southern in me.)

We should treat rape the way we treat other crimes.

Blasphemy, you may say. Rape is different. It is stigmatic. Like no other crime, it leaves its victim in shame. The stigma undergirds in some way nearly every argument for giving rape special handling in newspapers.

From the *ASNE Bulletin*, February, 1982. Reprinted by permission.

Bowing to it, many newspapers allow prosecuting witnesses in rape cases to bring their charges against a man anonymously. In some jurisdictions, where rape is a capital offense, they will not identify the chief accuser of a man who is on trial for his life. They are all-protective of the rights of the accused in every other instance. There is, rightly, no end to their suspicion of the police, the courts and other forces of the state which are against him. But if his charge happens to be rape, their faith in the system is absolute. It is so complete that they can lay aside for his case basic, objective news judgment. They do not consider that a man accused of rape can be innocent, that perhaps he is a victim, and not a perpetrator, that someone has made an honest mistake or for some reason is prosecuting him maliciously.

Newspapers should assume in rape cases, as in other crimes, that the accused is innocent. They do not convey that assumption when they identify him and grant a special privilege of anonymity to his accuser.

And, in the long run, they are not helping rape victims at all. Their practice tends to legitimize any stigma still attached to rape. Granted, we can't end an unjust stigma overnight simply by identifying rape victims. But the more we ignore the stigma, the more it will go on. We do not help matters by allowing it to control the policies of our press and other institutions.

Rape victims will be better off when rape is brought out of the closet.

Professor Gilbert Geis, a sociologist at the University of California in Irvine, conducted a study on media reporting of rape. By granting anonymity to prosecuting witnesses, he concluded, the media are "further imparting to the act of rape a particularly dirty, shameful nuance, rather than serving to portray it and its victims as no more than part of the criminal scene. . . . Anonymity is founded in the view that there is something degrading about being raped. . . . (Anonymity) suggests that the public will in some subtle manner conclude that the victim in a way contributed to her own fate. . . ."

In any case, the stigma once attached to rape has abated. That is evident, at least, in Durham, N.C., in the Arlington, Va., area and in Winfield Kan. In those communities people have arisen in heroic proportions against what they regarded as unfair treatment of rape victims. The objects of their wrath were the local newspapers. I do not agree that the newspapers treated the rape victims unfairly, but these protesters showed a realization that rape victims deserve sympathy, not censure. That attitude is more widespread than ever. Few people continue to believe that rape is degrading to a woman, that it makes her somehow a dirty person. Because of a stigma that isn't even there, most newspapers in covering rape allow critical, unfair exceptions to good reporting.

Rape victims will be better off when rape is brought out of the closet.

The Winfield case went to the (now defunct) National News Council on a complaint from two rape victims quoted by the *Winfield Daily Courier* in a report on a hearing. The *Courier* did not identify the prosecuting witnesses, but they complained that its description of their testimony was too explicit. The News Council found properly that the complaint was unwarranted.

The *Courier's* report included such testimony as "I . . . kept moving my pelvis so he couldn't penetrate," that the rapist "went ahead with what he was doing" when an alarm clock went off, that after intercourse with one victim the man "entered her rectum." That, frankly, is more than I would have said in my paper, but I am second-guessing. One must consider seriously what *Courier* Publisher Dave Seaton told the News Council. The council's report quoted him as saying that during the hurried moments in which he was considering the story before publication "two thoughts were strongly in mind.

One was his feeling that the paper had often been criticized for being too cautious and protective of the community. The other was a concern that the citizens of Winfield needed 'to know how severe rape cases are. . . . It seemed to me that there was a sound case to be made for having people face the harsh realities.' "

Rape to many of our readers is but an abstract concept.

Amen, brother. Rape to many of our readers is but an abstract concept. A good purpose is served by describing its horror, by putting it in perspective. The *Courier* put it in perspective.

John Rains, editorial page editor of the *Durham Morning Herald*, was a heavy contributor to an 18-part series of editorials in the *Herald* in 1978 when our paper was targeted for protests, pickets and boycott because of our policy on rape coverage. In the Winfield case, Rains wondered what would have happened if the hearing had been televised, a practice that might become widespread. Would the testimony have been bleeped out, as offensive words on talk-shows are sometimes censored? If TV coverage of trials ever becomes common, to what degree should the trials be censored? Who will do the censoring?

To what degree should newspapers censor court proceedings?

Hostility toward full reporting of rape knows no bounds among some readers and some public officials.

If you decide that your newspaper will censor less, you might be in for the fight of your life. Hostility toward full reporting of rape knows no bounds among some readers and some public officials.

At the *Northern Virginia Sun*, Publisher Herman J. Obermayer was faced with a resolution by the Falls Church City Council withdrawing any city advertisement from the *Sun* "so long as" it persisted in identifying prosecuting witnesses in rape cases at the point of trial. (The council members substituted "so long as" for "because of" in the motion so it would not appear that they were trying to coerce the free press!)

Also seeking to coerce the free press was the tax-supported Commission on Women in the Arlington area, which assisted in a drive to persuade readers to cancel their subscriptions to the *Sun*.

Like those in Winfield and Durham, these protestors believed divine guidance was on their side. They undoubtedly were not discouraged by editorials in some of the larger newspapers in the area which were critical of Obermayer's policy.

Although Falls Church continues to withhold legal ads from the *Sun*. which is more dependent upon such advertising than most dailies, Obermayer persists in his policy. "I do not see how you can have a type of crime in which the accused is denied the protection of the law, and I cannot sit by and accept the premise that there is a crime where an individual can go to prison for life without the witnesses being publicly identified," he told the National News Council.

The *Northern Virginia Sun* does not identify prosecuting witnesses in rape cases until the cases reach the trial stage. At the *Durham Sun*, the policy is to identify an adult prosecuting witness at the time a person is charged, not when the rape is merely reported. Our reasoning is that when a warrant is drawn, and not until then, the witness places a specific person in jeopardy. If she is 16 or under we do not identify her.

In 1978 police arrested a man on 11 rape charges after a series of attacks over several months. No names had been used when the rapes were reported but, in accordance with its policy, the *Herald* named the prosecuting witnesses when the man was charged. And while rape is not normally a front-page story, this arrest was.

The story ignited Durham's Rape Crisis Center, which organized the campaign to force us to change our policies. There were pickets, petitions, canceled subscriptions, a threatened boycott of our advertisers and, as at the *Winfield Courier* and the *Northern Virginia Sun*, an untold number of letters to the editor. We printed the letters for a while, then finally called a halt.

We met several times with our critics, including rape victims, to allow them to give us their views. Then we held a series of in-house meetings involving people from all departments of the newspaper to get other opinions. Finally, each newspaper established a committee from its own newsroom, chaired by the managing editor, for the final discussions and decision.

The policy that resulted was like our old one except for one change. Rape victims had said that after their names and addresses were published they were fearful that their attackers, or friends of the attackers, would return to punish them for prosecuting. We stopped publishing specific addresses of the witnesses, and now we use addresses that are less specific, such as Jane Smith of East Main Street. We felt that some address was needed for proper identification but that we could yield to some degree to relieve the fear of the victims. (That has caused us no problems, and we are considering extending the practice to other types of witnesses who become involved involuntarily in crimes.)

Rape victims had said that after their names and addresses were published they were fearful that their attackers, or friends of the attackers, would return to punish them for prosecuting.

Then we had our say in the 18-part series of editorials. The series was intended mainly to convey our reasoning. We wanted also to demonstrate that our policy was not adopted capriciously but with concern for everyone involved in a rape charge and with concern for our responsibility to report the news.

There has been no widespread campaign against the policy since then, but we continue to have problems with law-enforcement agencies. We usually end up getting the names from warrants, which are public records.

If you consider publishing the names, you will surely be asked whether you would want your own daughter's name in the paper if she were raped.

If you consider publishing the names, you will surely be asked whether you would want your own daughter's name in the paper if she were raped. But, of course, newspapers must base policy on professional judgment, not personal feelings. Otherwise you might reply, "Maybe not, but if my son were accused I certainly would want his accuser identified. Someone might come forth with important information about the case."

Of the arguments that we heard against our policy, the most common was the statement that publishing the names discouraged women from reporting rape and prosecuting rapists. If that is true it is an unfortunate but necessary trade-off. But it is not necessarily true.

Some women are reluctant for many reasons to report a rape—even to tell a close friend, much less describe it in detail to a stranger from the police department.

Once a person reports a rape, most of the people who are close to her probably will learn of it whether or not the newspaper prints her name. And of course the people close to her are the ones who matter to her.

As the stigma continues to subside, rape victims will be more inclined to call in the police. And facing the people close to them will be easier.

I am glad Professor Geis agrees with me. And I am particularly gratified if my paper's policy helps, even just a little, to lessen the stigma against innocent victims of rape. Still, I am a newsman, not a sociologist. And newspaper editors are supposed to report the news, accurately, fairly, and thoroughly. We are not supposed to recognize stigmas; we are not responsible for what simple-minded people might do with news once it is reported. ♦

Note: Results of Professor Geis' study are in the book *Deviance and the Mass Media*, edited by Charles Winick and published by Sage Publications.

Questions for Discussion

1. Do you agree or disagree with Rouse when he says, "Newspaper editors are not supposed to recognize stigmas; we are not responsible for what simple-minded people might do with news once it is reported"?
2. In your opinion, will reporting the rape victim's name help remove the stigma of being a rape victim?

Don't Victimize the Rape Victim Twice

Zena Beth McGlashan

Zena Beth McGlashan, a journalist, wrote the following article as an answer to Michael Rouse. It was published in the same journal as Rouse's article, two months later.

Reading Difficulty Level: 2.

Rape has indeed come out of the closet—as an issue which still needs thoughtful, frequent coverage. Rape victims, however, are still in that closet, edging their way toward the light.

Michael Rouse's self-labeled evangelical appeals to editors to adopt the policy of his paper—the *Durham* (N.C.) *Morning Herald*, which prints the names of victims as well as the accused when rape charges are filed—indicates Rouse to be a devotee of the "bullet theory" of communication. Because newspapers and other media have responded to the most recent wave of American feminism by running feature stories, first-person accounts (both anonymous and from women who have been willing to identify themselves) and news stories replete with rape statistics, Rouse would have us believe that only the "simple-minded" still attach some stigma to this crime and its victims.

From the *ASNE Bulletin*, April, 1982. Reprinted by permission.

A decade or so of public information doesn't re-mold society's biases. If change occurred on the tidy schedule which partially forms the basis for Rouse's argument, then women would have won the right to vote about 1858, ten years after the Seneca Falls Convention. History—and common wisdom such as that gained by being in the newspaper business for any length of time—tells us that society doesn't change its attitudes rapidly.

Rape victims are still in the closet, edging their way toward the light.

Important gains are being made in respect to women's willingness to report. According to the FBI Uniform Crime Reports, experts estimate that the more than 82,000 rapes reported to police in 1980 may represent only a small part of the number of rapes committed. However, that figure represents a 45 percent increase in reports from the 1976 total, which is encouraging to those dedicated to rape counseling and prevention. The FBI attributes this significant rise in reports to the growing number of rape crisis centers and an increased sensitivity by police in dealing with victims.

Chief among the reasons for not reporting rapes is the victims' fear of publicity.

The number of rapes reported is not mirrored in the number of arrests, which totaled 49 percent—up less than 1 percent from 1979 and 18 percent from 1976. Reluctance on the part of victims to sign arrest warrants—thus placing themselves in jeopardy—their inability to identify their assailants and police successes in carrying through on arrest warrants are among factors explaining the fact that slightly less than half the reported rapes resulted in arrests.

Federal guidelines for Uniform Crime Reports define forcible rape as a "women-only" crime. Apparently—and not surprisingly—government regulations may be caught in a "culture lag," evident in Rouse's and, to be fair, probably most people's thinking. We do tend to label rape as a crime inflicted solely on women.

However, men are also rape victims, as reflected in a recent *New York Times* story. Dr. Margaret McHugh, director of the child abuse team at Bellevue Hospital and an associate professor of pediatrics at New York University Medical Center, was quoted: "Sexual victimization of males is much more common than most people recognize, but we don't talk about it in our culture." Male rape, inflicted primarily by other men and not limited to children and adolescent boys, may be far more prevalent than we now realize, adding another layer to the sensitivity required of the press when helping the public learn about social problems. We may soon have to abandon our attitude toward male rape and sexual abuse as being a problem confined to prisons.

Rape counselors agree that chief among the reasons for not reporting rapes are the victims' fear of publicity, of attracting other potential rapists and of dreading the isolation that comes with the role of victim. Stigmatization still prevails. A well-educated friend of mine, when he learned about the rape of a woman we both knew, ruefully admitted to me later that his first thought was to "wonder what she had done to invite it."

Even for the strong victim, concern for others may have a chilling effect on whether she reports the crime. A student once told me that the reason she had not pressed charges against her attacker, whom she recognized, was not fear of confronting the man in court—"I'd really like to get that bastard"—but worry over what she anticipated would be her parents' traumatic reaction.

For most victims, going to court "is as much of a crisis as the act of rape," according to Ann Wolbert Burgess and Lynd Lytle Holmstrom, both of Boston College. In their book, *Rape: Crisis and Recovery,* they relate the court delays, the public setting and, in some instances, a continuing tendency to treat the victim "as if she were the offender" as stresses which victims must endure. Burgess, a professor of

Reporters catch up on the latest developments in the William Kennedy Smith rape trial in 1991. The victim's name and face were not shown, but she gave an interview on national TV as soon as the trial was over. Smith was acquitted. (Photo by Bruce Cotler.)

nursing, and Holmstrom, a sociology professor, also say that because the victim's character is examined as closely as that of the accused, then the victim must live with the "silent suspicion" that she was not raped after all, if the defendant is found not guilty. She may be considered by some to be psychotic, in search of attention. False accusation cases do happen. But these are overwhelmed by the number of cases in which the charge is firmly established, even if the accused's guilt is not proven well enough—for any of a number of legal reasons—for a jury decision to convict.

Counselors also agree that rape victims are far more liable to be threatened than are victims of other crimes. This undermines Rouse's

To recover psychologically, the victim needs to be able to control who knows about the rape.

condescending to print only general, not specific, victims' addresses with rape charges. Even in a metropolitan area, that policy may not provide a shred of protection. For example, when I lived in Los Angeles, mine was the only such name in the phone directory.

Rouse suggests that a victim's friends will know anyway. "Friends" is a broad term—like a rock dropped into a pond, the circle from its wake spreads farther and farther. If I were raped, I would not hide it from my family and close friends. But would I feel comfortable having all the people I know—from passing acquaintances at work to the man who okays my check at the supermarket—aware that I had been raped?

Margaret T. Gordon, chairwoman of the advisory committee to the National Health Institute's National Center for the Prevention and Control of Rape, says, "Prosecutors have made it clear that when newspapers print the names of rape victims, it discourages other victims from reporting rapes." This chilling effect of publicity relates to what Professor Gordon, director of the Center for Urban Affairs and Policy Research at Northwestern and a former news professional who also teaches courses at Northwestern's Medill School of Journalism, says is vital to the victim's psychological recovery: "She needs to be able to control who knows about the rape."

In one case, when a suburban newspaper printed the name of a victim without her consent or knowledge, the victim's son found out about his mother's rape when he was taunted by grade-school playmates, Gordon said. The newspaper editor was persuaded by an aroused community to abandon her policy which was based similarly to Rouse's—that the stigma will disappear more rapidly if the press provides equal treatment to the accused and the accuser.

Beverly Kees, executive director of the *Grand Forks* (N.D.) *Herald* and a former associate managing editor of the *Minneapolis Tribune*, says she has known women who have made the personal choice and talked to the press about their rapes. "I wish more women would," Kees said. But as for the newspapers making that choice for rape victims, "I don't think we've gotten to that point yet," because publication of a victim's name means that the "victim has become victimized twice."

Victims of rape are not traffic offenders. Johnny Carson, picked up for driving while intoxicated, can say on television: "I've learned my lesson; I sure won't do that again." Everyone understands. But what "lesson" is the rape victim supposed to learn from the publication of her identity? Is she supposed to come forward and say: "I've learned my lesson. I won't be raped again"?

For editors who may have found themselves swayed by Rouse's argument, reading Professor Gilbert Geis's article, which the Durham editor cites as support for his policy, may be helpful. The research, supported by funding from the National Center for the Prevention and Control of Rape, is a sociological review and interpretation of legal restrictions on rape coverage in United States and Great Britain. Geis, who has done extensive research about rape, does conclude, as Rouse reports, that giving equal treatment to the accused as well as the accuser may result in the "best redress of injustice," because society will be "fully informed about those processes and persons involved in and victims of injustice." Geis, however, also qualifies his conclusion by saying his opposition to anonymity is "perhaps but hopefully not, based on wishful thinking. . . ."

Concerning professional standards, one of my students here at the University of North Dakota insightfully observed that, just as we recognize both the law and the "spirit of the law," so should there be a "spirit of reporting" as well as the "law" of reporting. And a Durham resident told me, "If Mike Rouse wants to be fair, he could go the other way and choose not to reveal either name."

Rouse seems to want editors to believe that they're between a rock and a hard place: either choose "divine guidance" (heavenly beams directed to the newsroom?) or "objectivity." The editors I've been fortunate enough to work for have factored into their decisions such things as community standards and the "public good," as well as the difference between what the public "needs to know" and what isn't really necessary.

I learned a good deal from Walter Nelson, editor of the *Butte* (Mont.) *Standard,* 20 years ago. As an idealist fresh out of journalism school, I wondered why the local folks had not voted in favor of a governmental reform issue for which the paper had eloquently campaigned. Nelson, silver-haired and wise with decades of newspaper experience, smiled and told me: "One thing I've learned in this business is that people always do what they want to do."

Rouse's battle with the residents of Durham has not ended but has been fired up again by protests from the Duke University student body which sponsored a week-long rape education program. The policy of the Durham papers, both the *Herald* and the *Sun,* which leads directly to a decline in women's willingness to report rapes—much less go on to prosecute—is one which Rouse calls a "necessary tradeoff."

"If Mike Rouse wants to be fair, he could go the other way and choose not to reveal either name."

I would like to believe such lack of "censoring" does influence the rapid removal of any stigma rape has, adds to the education of the public and does not damage a victim seriously; that, in fact, it will be helpful toward having rape victims view their sexual violations as they would any other crime. But I keep returning to Walter Nelson's words about human nature. Editors, like their readers, are human. But they are also, I believe, generally more humane and careful with the power they wield to damage other human beings.

Society should be rid of its "hangups" about the criminal act of rape and its edgy attitudes toward rape victims, just as women should become stronger physically and in their attitudes toward themselves. In reality, we aren't there yet. And the weight of evidence indicates it's going to take a long time and much more counseling, education and judicious reporting about both victims' ordeals and rapists' motives before rape becomes a routine news event. By then—after many years of concentrated effort—perhaps we'll see substantial attitude change and, even more ideally, a significant decline in the incidence of the crime itself. ♦

Questions for Discussion

1. How should the identities of victim and accused be handled in a rape case?
2. Should victims and the accused be identified in the reports of *other* types of crimes?

Out Rage

Michael Matza

"Outing" is the act of exposing a homosexual against his or her will, an act usually done by the gay community. There are at least three reasons to "out" someone. One is to show that there are gays who are successful in all walks of life, and another is to punish gays who don't support gay causes. The third, interestingly, is similar to Michael Rouse's reason for wanting to publish the name of rape victims—i.e., to help remove the stigma. In the next reading Michael Matza, a reporter for the Philadelphia Enquirer, *tells about the current shape of outing.*

Reading Difficulty Level: 1. Although it's considerably higher if you're one of the people they name.

Their closets were invisible. So they hid in plain sight.

Rumors about their sexual preferences circulated privately. But rarely did they worry that such speculation would be printed in mainstream media, plastered across highway billboards or shouted from the Capitol steps.

Now, they worry.

Celebrities and politicians are seeing the doors to their inner sanctums forced open—and their alleged homosexuality blazoned—by militant, openly gay activists using a wildly controversial tactic called *outing*.

In one recent three month period, the targets included: two governors, one lieutenant governor, seven members of Congress, a recording industry mega-mogul, a renowned athlete, a school superintendent from a West Coast city, a married American fashion designer, two male actors who play "straight" love interests on television and in the movies, the female costar of a network series, the daughter of a female pop singer and four Philadelphia TV-news personalities.

An outing aimed at a major political figure may soon occur in a Southern state, where a man claiming to be the former lover of an incumbent congressman is preparing to run against him, activists say. The challenger is expected to out his former friend.

"There was an unwritten rule among gay people that you didn't 'out' someone," said Neil Miller, author of the recently published *In Search of Gay America: Women and Men in a Time of Change.*

Whose business is it who's gay? Some activists say it's important for the public to know.

With increasing frequency, that rule is being broken. Although outting is sometimes staged to "claim" reluctant role models, more often it is used to punish perceived hypocrites: people who, outers say, are secretly gay or bisexual but publicly critical of homosexuality.

"On its most basic level, an outing says the gentlemen's agreement we've honored thus far is no longer valid," said activist Michael Petrelis, 31, of Washington, who last month, along with fellow activist Carl Goodman, held a news conference on the Capitol steps to read out the names of 12 men and women in politics and music who, he said, are secretly gay.

Says one activist, "The gentleman's agreement we've honored thus far is no longer valid.

Pent-up rage about the AIDS health crisis, says author Miller, seems to have been one of the catalysts for outing. It reintroduced "radical, street-type action" to a liberation movement whose members clashed with police in Manhattan at the Stonewall Inn riots in 1969, but became "a conventional interest group" in the '70s and '80s.

In 1987 came the formation of the radical AIDS Coalition to Unleash Power (ACT-UP), a loose confederation of militant activists. Many of the nation's 50 ACT-UP chapters, including one in Philadelphia, take no official position on

---

From *The Philadelphia Inquirer,* June 28, 1990. Reprinted by permission.

outing. However, individual members, who may have lost friends and longtime companions to AIDS, tend to support it as the necessary rejection of business-as-usual in troubled times. "ACT-UP," said Miller, "gave license to people to act out—on a massive scale."

And act people have. On television: a gay author/activist recently outed a gubernatorial candidate in a Northeastern state during a talk-show discussion on outing. On billboards: activists altered Sen. Mark Hatfield's (R., Ore.) campaign road signs to read "closeted gay . . . living a lie . . . voting to oppress." At public events: Boston lesbians disrupted a female country singer's recent concert by shouting, "Why don't you just come out?"

Boston lesbians disrupted a female country singer's recent concert by shouting, "Why don't you just come out?"

For the supermarket tabloids, which have long made money from celebrity sex lives, outing has been something of a gossip mother lode. In recent months they have mined it mercilessly, with cover stories saying actors Richard Chamberlain and John Travolta are homosexual. Both of them have denied they are gay.

But the chief forum for outing, and the serious discussion of its pros and cons, has been the gay press. No publication has been more closely tied to the issue than *Outweek*, a New York magazine with a national circulation of 40,000, which in March published a detailed, posthumous outing of tycoon Malcolm Forbes. Columnist Michelangelo Signorile, 28, who wrote the Forbes article and is a staunch proponent of dragging public people out, peppers his weekly "Gossip Watch" with references to VIP's living allegedly closeted lives.

Signorile says he feels "an obligation" to tell his community about gays and lesbians in high places, but would never think of outing a gay schoolteacher, for example. "In the Malcolm Forbes thing, I was saying to kids, 'Don't let this happen to you,' where you can be one of the most powerful men in America and you have to live your life in the closet, paying people to have sex and not reveal it."

Outweek also pioneered the "peekaboo" list, which presents—entirely without editorial comment or proof—the names of public figures whom activists believe could be gay or bisexual.

Philadelphia's *Au Courant*, a gay tabloid with a weekly circulation of 10,000, published such a list—including the names of four local newscasters—on its May 14 cover.

"Anybody who knows me knows that saying I am a homosexual is the silliest thing they've ever heard," said one of the newsmen, who asked not to be identified.

M. Scott Mallinger, 20, assistant editor of *Au Courant* and author of the outing story that appeared on an inside page of the issue, said, "There shouldn't be such a stigma in having your name in a gay publication. If there is, naming names ought to be done more."

"There shouldn't be such a stigma in having your name in a gay publication. If there is, naming names ought to be done more."

Asked whether he had informed the newsmen they would be named, Mallinger said he had not. Nor was he particularly concerned with the consequences for them. He said it was "possible we caused [them] pain," but "also possible we've done a lot of good" and people won't be calling the next gay person derogatory names. "[Their] embarrassment is worth lives."

Au Courant editor Frank Broderick, 36, said that Travolta was on the *Au Courant* list because "a lot of people think gay men have to be effeminate," and "you don't think John Travolta and think effeminate." *The National Enquirer* published a story quoting a man claiming to be Travolta's former lover.

Conventional gay groups—including the National Gay and Lesbian Task Force, the Human Rights Campaign Fund and the Lambda Legal Defense and Education Fund—firmly oppose outing, calling it cannibalism, blackmail and psychological terrorism. The Philadelphia Lesbian and Gay Task Force takes no official position on outing, although its executive director, Rita Addessa, says, "No one can take the risk attendant to coming out for another person. [Outing] is larger than gay-bashing. It's discrimination. It's losing one's child, perhaps losing one's home."

"The lesbian and gay political movement is fundamentally about the individual's ability to define oneself," said Sue Hyde, director of the national task force's privacy project. "Outing violates people's right to be free from intrusion." As for outing as role-model "claiming," said Hyde: "I don't find people who have to be forced out to be . . . particularly good role models."

Petrelis, the activist who stood on the Capitol steps, said he wanted "the people on [his] list to say, 'Yes, I'm gay or lesbian, so what?' Or, failing that, to get them to say, 'I'm not gay or lesbian but I'll wear a pink triangle [a label for homosexuals used by the Nazis] in solidarity with the community."

As it happens, the people he named denied through a spokesman being homosexual, declined comment or could not be reached because an aide refused to ask. No major news organization published or broadcast their names.

The National Enquirer ***published a story quoting a man claiming to be Travolta's former lover.***

Petrelis plans to return to the Capitol to read a longer list on Oct. 11, the third annual "National Coming Out Day," an invention of National Gay Rights Advocates, of San Francisco.

Larry Gross, professor of communications at the Annenberg School of Communications at the University of Pennsylvania, and co-chair of the Philadelphia Lesbian and Gay Task Force, said, "The debate is not really whether it is right or wrong to expose someone's sexual orientation that they've kept hidden. The question is when is it appropriate? And under what circumstances?"

Even gays who express reservations about outing have less concern for the privacy of closeted politicians who have voted or spoken out against gay rights.

Even gays who express reservations about outing have less concern for the privacy of closeted politicians who have voted or spoken out against gay rights.

Citing what they believe is Hatfield's poor voting record since 1986 on legislation of concern to gays, ACT-UP members in Portland, Ore., have sniped at the senator since February 1989.

"The basic issue is not that he's a gay man," said ACT-UP spokeswoman Lori Kohler, 33, a lesbian medical student, "but that he's a gay man voting against other gays and lesbians. . . . It's not a titillating sex story; it's a political story."

Hatfield, who has been married since 1958 and who is entering his 24th year in the Senate, has long been the subject of rumor in his own state, and more recently has been the target of numerous ACT-UP demonstrations, or "zaps." In a letter to ACT-UP/Portland, addressed "to whom it may concern," Hatfield defended his voting record on appropriations for AIDS research and berated his attackers for spreading "false rumors." Press secretary Bill Calder, who did not return repeated calls for this story, has been quoted as saying that Hatfield "is not and never has been a homosexual."

A year ago, after Republicans circulated a memo saying that soon-to-be-elected House Speaker Tom Foley (D., Wash.) was "out of the liberal closet," openly gay Rep. Barney Frank (D., Mass.) struck back. Incensed by the innuendo, Frank stormed into the House Press Gallery and threatened to disclose the names of secretly gay Republicans if the rumors persisted. They stopped abruptly, and Frank never turned over his cards.

A spokesman for Foley has called the speculation about his boss "nothing but a bad rumor."

Not every outing is loud and antagonistic. An autograph signing by a famous athlete is a case in point. The sportsman, who is a spokesman for a line of athletic wear, attended a lunchtime promotion at Macy's in New York. Among the 60 people on hand that Friday to meet the star were 12 men from a gay group called Queer Nation.

When the activists got close enough to get autographs, said Bill Monaghan, an organizer of the zap, "they said things like, 'I think you'd be a really good gay role model were you to come out.' "

Monaghan, 40, a gay bookkeeper who came out when he was 20, said the zap was motivated by compassion, not rage. "It was," he said, "a visibility campaign to say there are gay men who support him if he is gay. . . . It was one on one. No splash, no screaming, no yelling. . . . Had we wanted to make it a media event, we could have."

According to Monaghan, the athlete "smiled" and "looked uncomfortable a bit." An attorney for the star said he was unavailable and had never mentioned the incident to her.

While activists argue that the movement needs the clout of elite homosexuals to help save lives, and that celebrities give up their privacy as the price of fame, Peter Haas, a gay entertainment-industry publicist formerly associated with a powerful national public relations agency and a critic of outing, says it's unfair to demand that "anybody who is other than heterosexual has an obligation to reveal that publicly. . . . Spokespersons for any cause can't be assigned."

Haas said he has heard stories about publicists' inventing heterosexual lives for closeted clients, and pairing them with seemingly heterosexual partners to create an illusion at awards ceremonies and movie premieres.

Signorile says such pairings are done all the time, and that gossip columnists who know better—and may be closeted themselves—show complicity when they perpetuate the myth that several prominent gays and lesbians are straight.

Signorile says these celebrities, because of their wealth, are virtually immune to the negative consequences of coming out, and by "passing" simply perpetuate stereotypes. "If people say, 'I don't want to know that so-and-so is gay, it ruins it for me,' I say to that, 'Too bad.' It puts a face to gay people."

He describes outing as an exercise in class loyalty, "a community calling its prominent members to accountability, whether they are doing bad things or just hiding the fact that they are gay. The Jewish community did the same thing. They helped each other hide. But if one was collaborating with the Nazis, they were exposed."

One publicist says it is unfair to demand that "anybody who is other than heterosexual has an obligation to reveal that publicly."

Closeted celebrities, Signorile complains, benefit from gay liberation "but don't give back the one thing they could give, which is public notoriety. They owe it to humanity as privileged people, especially at a time when there is this AIDS crisis."

The aggressive point man of outing hopes that naming names—lots of them—will "sensitize" heterosexuals.

"If I say someone is straight, I have not revealed anything private," said Signorile. "But if I say he is gay, there is the impression that I *have* . . . I'm kind of hoping that it gets to a saturated level. That people say, 'Richard Chamberlain, Malcolm Forbes—who *isn't* gay?' " ♦

A columnist points out, "If I say someone is straight, I have not revealed anything private . . ."

Questions for Discussion

1. Is outing an ethical act? Is it, in your opinion, an invasion of personal privacy?
2. Ethics aside, is outing a politically effective strategy?

Suggested Readings

Those interested in America's obsession with the private lives of her public figures will want to reread Peter Stromberg's article, "Elvis Alive," in Chapter 3.

More On the Privacy of Public Figures

Fenby, Jonathan, "Private Life and the Public Eye." *UNESCO Courier*, September, 1990, p. 20 (4). This is a special issue that focuses on "The Media: Ways to Freedom."

Gelman, David. " 'Outing': An Unexpected Assault on Sexual Privacy: Gay Activists Are Forcing Others Out of the Closet," *Newsweek* Vol. 115, April 30, 1990, p. 66 (1).

More On Privacy for Rape Victims

Elson, John, "Going Public with Rape: Should Victims Be Identified When the Crime Is Sexual Assault?" *Time* Vol. 155, April 9, 1990, p. 71 (1).

Kaplan, David A., "Should We Reveal Her Name? The Press Still Protects the Central Park Jogger," *Newsweek* Vol. 115. April 2, 1990, p. 46 (1).

Other Readings On the Issue of Privacy

Lipschultz, Jeremy Harris, "Mediasat and the Tort of Invasion of Privacy," *Journalism Quarterly* Vol. 65, Summer 1988, p. 507 (5). Research on the legal dimensions of privacy.

Minole, Grant B., "Liberalism, Privacy and Autonomy," *The Journal of Politics* Vol. 51, August 1989, p. 575 (24).

Norton, Clark, "Threats to Privacy: Is There No Confidentiality?" *Current*, January 1990, p. 14 (5).

"Slamming the Door At Their Feet," *The Economist* Vol. 314, March 31, 1990. p. 58 (1).

Index

E

F

G

H

O

P

R